RICHARD WRIGHT

RICHARD WRIGHT

EARLY WORKS

Lawd Today!
Uncle Tom's Children
Native Son

THE LIBRARY OF AMERICA

Volume arrangement, notes, and chronology copyright © 1991 by
Literary Classics of the United States, Inc., New York, N.Y.
All rights reserved.
No part of this book may be reproduced commercially
by offset-lithographic or equivalent copying devices without
the permission of the publisher.

Lawd Today! reprinted by arrangement with John Hawkins and Associates, Inc.
Uncle Tom's Children, *Native Son*, and "How 'Bigger' Was Born" reprinted
by arrangement with HarperCollins Publishers, Inc.

The paper used in this publication meets the
minimum requirements of the American National Standard for
Information Sciences—Permanence of Paper for Printed
Library Materials, ANSI z39.48—1984.

Distributed to the trade in the United States
and Canada by the Viking Press.

Library of Congress Catalog Number: 91-60540
For cataloging information, see end of Notes.
ISBN 0-940450-66-6

First Printing
The Library of America—55

Manufactured in the United States of America

Grateful acknowledgment is made to the National Endowment for the Humanities, the Ford Foundation, and the Andrew W. Mellon Foundation for their generous support of this series.

Contents

LAWD TODAY!

PART ONE: COMMONPLACE

. . . a vast Sargasso Sea—a prodigious welter of unconscious life, swept by groundswells of halfconscious
emotion . . .

Van Wyck Brooks' *America's Coming-of-Age*

LADIES AND GENTLEMEN, JACK BASSETT SPEAKING! STATION WGN, TRIBUNE SQUARE, CHICAGO. AT THE NEXT TONEBEAT THE TIME WILL BE EXACTLY EIGHT O'CLOCK, CENTRAL STANDARD TIME . . . TING! . . . COURTESY THE NEVERSTOP WATCH COMPANY, LADIES AND GENTLEMEN!

LOOK OUT OF YOUR WINDOW! WHAT DO YOU SEE FLAPPING SO PROUDLY AND SEDATELY AT EVERY COR-NER AND OVER EVERY BUILDING ENTRANCE? DOESN'T IT MAKE YOUR HEART SKIP A BEAT TO SEE OLD GLORY FLOATING THERE SO BEAUTIFULLY IN THE MORNING BREEZE?

MY DEAR FRIENDS, OUR FLAG IS FLYING HIGH TODAY IN HONOR OF ONE OF OUR GREATEST AMERICANS, A MAN WHO SAVED HIS COUNTRY AND BESTOWED THE BLESSINGS OF LIBERTY AND FREEDOM UPON MILLIONS OF HIS FELLOWMEN!

THIS IS FEBRUARY TWELFTH, ABRAHAM LINCOLN'S BIRTHDAY!

AT THIS TIME PROFESSOR WEATHERSPOON, HEAD OF THE DEPARTMENT OF HISTORY AT THE UNIVERSITY OF CHICAGO, WILL TELL YOU OF LINCOLN'S BACK-GROUND AND HIS GLORIOUS CAREER. PROFESSOR WEATHERSPOON! . . . UMMMMMMMPPH! . . . UUU-MMMMMMMPHMMM! . . . GOOD MORNING, EVERY-BODY! . . .

I.

No matter how hard he squinted his eyes and craned his neck, he could not see the top of the steps. But somebody was calling and he had to go up. He hollered, *Yeah, I'm coming right up, in just a minute!* And then he started. It was hard work, climbing steps like these. He panted and the calves of his legs ached. He stopped and looked to see if he could tell where the steps ended, but there were just steps and steps and steps. *Shucks, they needn't be in such a helluva hurry,* he thought as he stretched his legs and covered three and four steps at a time. Then, suddenly, the steps seemed funny, like a great big round barrel rolling or a long log spinning in water and he was on top treading for all he was worth and that voice was still calling. He stopped again, disgusted. *Hell, there just ain't no end to these steps! I'm just wasting time! Ain't moving a peg! And that old sonofabitch up there sounds just like my boss, too!*

Jake stirred and burrowed his head deeper into a pillow. He sighed, swallowed, pulled his knees toward the pit of his stomach, and turned his face from the sun glare.

The steps blazed and shivered in a mist of bright gold, as if about to vanish. Then they grew real and solid. He was still running, thinking *That guy's still calling. What in hell can he be wanting?* He hollered again, *Keep your shirt on, for Chrissakes! I'm coming!* He was flying up steps now, mounting whole blocks of steps, miles and miles of steps, but even at that the end was not in sight. *What to hell? There's a joke here somewhere! Damn tooting!* He stopped, sighed, wiped sweat from his forehead, and looked to see how many steps he had covered. He was right where he had started! He shook his head, mumbling to himself, *Jeeesus, all that running for nothing . . . Yeah, there's a trick in this.* But that guy, that guy who had a voice just like his boss, was still calling.

Jake turned and lay on his stomach. His head rested in the crook of his right elbow. His left arm clung close to his side, dingy palm upcurled. He smacked his lips softly, as though over a dainty and dissolving morsel.

The steps stretched endlessly up. He was taking them five

at a time now, not even pausing for breath. A deep sweet gladness suffused his limbs. He would get there soon if he kept this up. All steps ended somewhere. He yelled, *I'm coming! I'm coming!* Then the voice boomed so loud in his ears he stopped and tried to make out what it was saying.

Jake struggled out of sleep and propped himself upon an elbow. A pair of piggish eyes blinked at sunlight. Low growls escaped his halfparted lips and his hands fumbled comically for the runaway sheet. He swallowed several times and his Adam's apple jumped up and down from his chin to his collarbone, like a toy monkey on a string. His eyes smarted, watering. He saw the bed and the dresser and the carpet and the walls melting and shifting and merging into a blur. His loins felt heavy and exhausted. He closed his eyes and his mind groped, thinking, *What was I dreaming?* He remembered being on the very brink of something, on the verge of a deep joy. *Now what was I dreaming?* He tried to think, but a wide gap yawned in his mind. And that guy was still calling.

. . . GARRISON, FORERUNNER OF LINCOLN, WAS A MAN WHOSE SOUL WAS AFLAME WITH A HOLY CAUSE. GOING AGAINST THE ADVICE OF HIS FRIENDS AND THE WARNINGS OF HIS ENEMIES, HE DECLARED HIMSELF OUTSPOKENLY AGAINST SLAVERY AND OPPRESSION . . .

Gawddamn! That old radio woke me up! A vague sense of rows and rows of steps came again. *Now what was I dreaming?* It seemed very, very important that he should remember. He screwed up his eyes, but the dream steps were drowned in a vast blackness, like a slow movie fadeout. He had been going somewhere in a great big hurry; he had been thirsting, longing for something. But each time he had got almost to it, each time it was almost his, somebody had called.

. . . I AM IN EARNEST—I WILL NOT EQUIVOCATE—I WILL NOT EXCUSE—I WILL NOT RETREAT A SINGLE INCH—AND I WILL BE HEARD . . .

Jake's mouth twitched. He flung one black leg from under the sheet and groaned. The air of the room was close. Heat was melting tiny cakes of grease in his nappy hair. He raised his hand and scratched at a thin stream of slickness oozing down the ebony nape of his neck. His face wrinkled, he opened his mouth and bawled:

"Lil!"

"Hunh?"

"Shut that door!"

"Hunh?"

"Shut that Gawddamn door, I said!"

He heard the door slam. *That bitch! How come she leave that door open and wake me up?* He settled down again and the mood of his dream came back. He imagined his loins straining against a warm, nude body. He breathed softly as the muscles of his diaphragm grew taut. A hot, melting ball glowed in his solar plexus. His head drooped and his lips touched the starched pillowcase. He doubled his legs, bringing his knees again to the pit of his stomach. He felt the warm body pressing close to him, covering him, heating his blood. *Milkman! Milkman!* He jumped. *Gawddamn!* It was no use; he could not sleep anymore. Through a sixinch opening in the window came the harsh throb of an auto motor. He sat up, his eyes meeting a glare of sunshine pouring slantwise through voile curtains. *Gawd, is it morning already?* He wagged his head and tried to swallow a nasty taste. He made a wry face and tried again. *Arrrrk! Naw.* He simply could not swallow it. He eased down again, his head striking a sharp edge. He fumbled with his hand and brought before his eyes a small, yellow booklet. UNITY, he read. A MAGAZINE DEVOTED TO CHRISTIAN HEALING. He saw the picture of a haloed, bearded man draped in white folds; the man's hand was resting upon the blond curls of a blueeyed girl. Beneath the picture ran a caption: EVERY HOUR OF THE DAY AND NIGHT JESUS FLOWS ALL THROUGH ME. *What makes Lil keep all this trash in bed?* He hurled the book across the room, hearing the leaves flutter with a dry sound.

He stood up, dazed somewhat from sleep. He licked his lips and rubbed his eyes with the backs of his hands. His mouth gaped, revealing two rows of gleaming gold. It gaped wide. Wider. Wider still. Then it closed slowly, emitting a hippopotamic grunt, *Yyaaarph!* His eyes watered sympathetically as he stood rigid with his head tilted backward. *Jeeesus, I feel rotten.* He drew a long breath; something itched deep in his nose. Then it came:

"Ker . . . ker . . . kerchoossneeeeze!"

He bent double. When he straightened he wiped his nose and eyes on the sleeves of his redgold pyjamas, and groaned:

"Aw, hell . . ."

He was thirsty and his mouth tasted salty. He licked his lips and swallowed again to get rid of that disgusting taste. Adding to his sluggish confusion was a sickening hunger. His stomach felt like a vacuum with a black rat gnawing around inside of it. He got a cigarette from his pack and struck a match. His fingers trembled so the flame flickered out. *My nerves is just all shot,* he thought. When the cigarette was lit he screwed up his eyes and scratched himself, slowly, along the ribs, deep in the groin, around the navel, and between the thighs. He wanted a little more sleep, just a little more. But he knew it was useless. *How come Lil leave that door open? How come she turn that radio on so early?* He flushed hot with anger, but the smell of boiling coffee and sizzling bacon cooled him. He sighed, looking aimlessly around the room, at the curtains, at the sunshine, at the blooming red flowers in the carpet. His attention centered on his scheme rack, a little honeycomblike wooden case before which were piled hundreds and hundreds of tiny white cards. *Lawd, I ain't fooled with that scheme in almost a month now. And I got to go up and pass a test on it in about two weeks.* Merely to think of it made his head feel heavy. He had to learn that scheme, learn where each card went, and when it went where it went, and on what train. *Let's see now. Six o'clock sweat. Chicago and Evans. 15. Number 2. Except on Sundays. That's for Paris, Illinois. Then at ninethirty comes Chicago and Evans. 9. Number 2. Let's see now. That's except Saturdays. Then comes ten fortyfive. Yeah, that's Danville and Cairo. 131. Number 1. That goes by way of* . . . He frowned, screwing up his eyes and biting his lips. *Where do that Danville and Carbondale go?* He could not remember. And he had nine hundred little white cards like that to commit to memory. Well, he would try to study a little after breakfast. After he had eaten a good meal his mind would be fresh and keen.

As in a dream he ambled to the bathroom, his fat black feet spreading like cobraheads upon the carpet. He turned the cold water faucet in the washbowl and looked around for a glass. *That bitch! How come she can't never do nothing right? You can never find a thing you want when she's around!* Stooping, he cupped his fingers under the stream and gulped huge swallows of water overflowing the brim of his palms. *Yeah, I feel lots better now.* He stood up, fronting the mirror. The reflection showed a face round as a full moon and dark as a starless midnight. In an oily expanse of blackness were set two cunning eyes under which hung flabby pouches. A broad nose squatted fat and soft, its two holes gaping militantly frontward like the barrels of a shotgun. Lips were full, moist, and drooped loosely, trembling when he walked. A soft roll of fat seeped out of his neck, buttressing his chin. Shaggy sideburns frizzled each temple.

He ran his fingers through his hair, scratching an itchy scalp. He brought them away sticky and greasy. Thrusting out his jaw, he touched bristles on his chin. He needed a haircut and a shave. Badly. *Shucks, how come you got to waste a hour getting your hair cut? How come you got to shave every day?* He took down his mug and shaving brush and turned on the hot water. Wisps of vapor warmed his chest and face. *Christ, that feels good!* The smell of coffee and sizzling bacon became stronger. Slowly, he was waking up; even his mind began to work a little.

He cocked his head, poising his whitely lathered brush an inch from his chin. He heard Lil talking to somebody in the kitchen. He bent lower, listening. *What in hell can she find to talk about all the time? I certainly would like to know. And bawling her out don't seem to do a bit of good, neither. Yeah, she's going to keep on with her foolishness till I teach her a damn good lesson one of these days. And furthermore, it ain't right for a decent woman to stand talking commonlike that way to strangers. And she knows that!* Jake sat the mug down, hurried to the bathroom door, and listened with his ear to the keyhole. *Still talking! And laughing, too! What to hell? What she think this is, a picnic?* He slammed down the brush and pushed through the door.

He entered the kitchen just as Lil threw back her head,

laughing. Her shoulders were shaking. But when she saw Jake she sobered. The milkman hastily picked up his rack.

"Good morning," said the milkman.

Jake did not answer. He came and stood in the middle of the floor, his legs wide apart.

"You up already, Jake?" Lil asked in a strained voice. Jake shook his head, his mouth twisting into a crooked smile.

"Naw, I'm still asleep."

Lil fumbled for a dishtowel and began to polish an already glittering spot on the stove. The milkman groped for the doorknob.

"Well, I reckon I'll be getting along," he said.

"Be sure and bring me an extra pint of cream tomorrow," said Lil.

"O.K.," said the milkman, and was gone.

Jake slouched heavily on to a chair and frowned at the floor. Lil went to the icebox and got a carton of eggs. She bit her lip and kept her shoulders stiff, as though expecting a blow.

"Lil?" His voice held a familiar, an ominous portent.

She lowered her head an inch and placed a skillet on the stove. As she lit the gas her face was placid, as though she had not heard. Sometimes that forestalled him, pretending like that.

"Lil!" Anger was creeping into his voice.

"I hears you, Jake." She spoke placatingly.

"Act like it then!"

She broke an egg into the skillet. Jake's toes gripped the linoleum as though even they were angry with her.

"Woman, I'm still talking to you!"

She sprinkled salt over the egg.

"What's wrong with you?"

"Nothing."

"Don't you hear me talking?"

"Yeah, I hears you, Jake."

"Why in hell don't you act like it?"

She broke a second egg. A part of the white caught on the edge of the skillet and hardened slowly. Jake rose from his chair.

"Is you deaf?"

"Naw, I ain't deaf. I hears you real plain."

"I just wanted to know," he said. "On account of if you was, I can fix you so you can hear real good from now on."

His face was six inches from hers.

"What in hell can you see in a milkman's mug to make you want to keep talking to him all day—that's what I want to know!"

Lil cleared her throat, bent lower over the skillet, and fiddled the eggs with a longhandled fork.

"Now, listen, woman, I'm talking to you!"

"Nothing," she answered. "I don't see nothing."

"How come you keep talking to him?"

Business of turning the first egg over. Jake gripped her shoulder, pulling her from the stove.

"Ain't you going to talk to me?"

"Please, Jake, for Chrissake, let's don't start all that again!"

"Start what? What in hell you mean? Is you crazy! You's the one what's starting! Ain't I told you about that milkman before, a dozen times if one?"

Tenderly, Lil flipped the second egg over with a wide paddle. Jake gripped her arm, digging long nails into her flesh.

"I'm talking to you, bitch!"

"Yes, Jake."

"Ain't I told you about that milkman before?"

"Yes, Jake."

"You know what you fixing for yourself if you keep on?"

"Yes, Jake."

"How come you keep talking to him?"

Lil turned and faced him meekly. Her shoulders slumped as if she were placing all evidence before him for an impartial judgement, as if she were throwing herself upon his mercy, his ultimate sense of fairness.

"What you want me to do, Jake? Act like I'm wild? Can't I say good morning to folks when they say good morning to me? Honest to Gawd, I said no more to that milkman than I do to Mrs. Thomas . . ."

"I ain't no fool! I heard you talking to that milkman ten minutes on end! I reckon he can't hear good, hunh? I reckon it takes ten minutes to tell him to bring you a bottle of cream, hunh? Woman, don't you try to play me cheap!"

"I ain't playing you cheap."

"You turned that radio on so I wouldn't hear what you was telling him!"

"Lawd, Jake . . ."

"Now just say you didn't!"

She gaped at him.

"I ain't blind! I can see what's going on before my eyes! You can't put a damn thing over on me, and ain't no use you trying. And I reckon that sweet laugh you gave him was part of the order, too, hunh?" He swayed his body forward, his face leering.

Lil sighed.

"I sure wish you wasn't so foolish, Jake . . ."

He shoved her from the stove again.

"Don't you call me a fool!"

"I didn't call you a fool!"

"Watch out how you talk to me!"

"I wish you could look at things sort of straight."

"I can look straight enough to see what you doing!"

Lil turned on him. As she spoke her whole body shook as though she had lost control of her nerves. She seemed impelled by an imperious, inner need.

"Just 'cause you so loose you think everybody's loose! If you was half as fair with me as I is with you, we wouldn't never fuss. But it's just like a person who's cheating to think another one is . . ." She stopped abruptly, choking. "And you know . . . You know . . . You know I ain't in no condition to dddo wwwhat yyyou thinking . . . You . . ." The muscles in her throat grew tight with resentment and she could not go on.

"Aw, cut the sob stuff! It don't work with me! You ain't as sick as you always trying to make out! You can always do everything you want to do but *that*!"

"You ought to be 'shamed!"

"Aw, I'm on to you! You just done made up your mind that you ain't going to be no good to me, that's all. But don't you think you putting that much over on me!" He measured a distance of half of an inch on his thumb and forefinger. "I know what you up to! You just one more no good woman, that's all!"

"If I is, you the cause of it! You the cause of it! You the cause of it!" she repeated monotonously.

"Shut up!"

"You the cause . . ."

"I said shut up!"

The words died in her throat.

"You ain't no good and you ain't never been no good! You been that way ever since I married you! And don't think it's just lately I noticed it, neither! Even before you started going to that Gawddamn doctor you was no good!"

Lil clutched convulsively at her apron. Her fork tinkled to the floor. She picked it up and faced him again, her eyes swollen now with tears. She panted her words, her eyes wide.

"Naw, I ain't no good! And I thank my Gawd in Heaven I'll never be no good to you no more! And I hopes to Christ I'll never be! I ain't no good and I thank Gawd now! I'm sick! Yeah, I'm sick! And you the cause of it. So when you think of wanting any of me just remember you the cause of it! You tricked me! You knows you did! You knowed I didn't know what was happening to me when you fooled me into going to that old quack doctor . . . Now you black and evil enough to try to take it all out on me . . . Maybe I'll never be well again . . . I wished I had gone on and had that baby than bbbe aaall mmmessed up this way . . ."

Her knees sagged. She was crying hard now. Jake watched her closely with eyes that glittered.

"You ain't no good and you ain't never been no good!"

She turned her face to the window to cheat him of the satisfaction of her tears. Eggs were burning and the kitchen was filling with smoke.

"Tend to your cooking, you slut! I reckon you think I ought to be happy standing here watching my money burning up on a skillet!"

"I can't do nothing when yyyou kkkeep on bbobothering me!"

"Shut up and cook!"

She dried her eyes, and, coughing because of the smoke, dumped the charred eggs into a garbage pail, and washed the skillet.

"You can do everything you want to do but tend to your own business!" he told her with deep gravity.

He was quiet because he had won; she was quiet because she had lost. But neither was quit of the other. He knew that she would not take the last word. And she felt that he was not yet satisfied with what he had done. Silently, both searched for words that would wound. Seconds passed. Lil found such words first.

"Jake," she began quietly, "you better make a payment to the doctor. I had to go see him yestiddy and the bill was almost five hundred dollars. He ain't been paid a thing in almost a month now, and it's getting long past due."

He turned away, waving a scornful palm.

"Tell him I ain't got no money."

"You get paid day after tomorrow."

"That's none of your Gawddamn business!"

"Well, you just as well pay him now. He says I got to have a operation, and the bill'll be twice as big."

"Got to have *what*?"

"A operation."

"Operation?"

"I got to be operated on in a month."

"When he tell you that?"

"Yestiddy, when I saw him."

"Operated on for what?"

"He says I got a tumor."

"Tumor?"

"Yeah, a tumor!"

Jake looked at her as though he had never seen her before.

"What in hell you doing going getting a tumor?"

"I done run off too many times fooling with you! That's how come I got it!"

"That's a Gawddamn lie!"

"Well, the doctor says so!"

"That's just your little red wagon, then!"

"He says it'll cost five hundred dollars, and that's just *your* little red wagon!"

"Yeah," Jake spoke through clenched teeth. "I can just see myself giving that damn quack five hundred dollars for you to get rid of a tumor. What you think I is, the United States'

Mint? And you got the nerve to tell me I'm the cause of it! How about all the other niggers you been running around with?"

"There ain't been nobody but you!"

"Tell that quack he can get my money when hell freezes over!"

"If you don't pay 'im he can get your job!"

Jake's eyes went red. She had touched his sore spot—his government job. Her complaint on him at the Post Office would throw him out of work. Twice before she had complained, and one more time would just about put an end to him.

"You mighty damn eager to pay that quack. You ain't no good to me but you's a plenty damn good to him. You been going to that sonofabitch a long time, almost seven years. I can't make out what in hell he's doing to keep treating you all this time . . ."

"Whatever he's doing's all your fault and you got to pay for it!"

"I done ask you for the last time to shut up!"

He stiffened. His jaws clamped viselike. He wanted to slap her, slap her a blow that would make her hold her mouth forever. But he could not do that without being egged on more. He had reached that point where deep in him he longed for her to goad him just a little more, just a bit more. He wanted ever so badly to slap her, but he wanted to feel impelled. He trembled. His eyes wandered nervously about the kitchen, seeking for a clue, for a point of departure. Suddenly, he felt the emptiness of his stomach and remembered his hunger.

"Quit your Gawddamn jawing and put something to eat on my table!"

Lil looked at him quietly.

"You ain't washed. You ain't ready to eat yet."

Something tightened in him. All the hate of his marriage welled up. Lil seemed to have gone far beyond the power of his words to cut and wound.

"If you don't like the way I'm running this show, why in hell don't you get out?"

Lil poured cream into a pitcher.

"I'm staying 'cause this is my home, and you going to support me! Don't think you going to get out of it, neither, not long as you working . . ."

Nails bit into palms. If he could only think of something to say to her that would make her so mad she would get up and leave, something so hot and hard that she would never want to forgive him, never want to see him again—something that would get rid of her once and for always.

"I can't see how come any slut wants to be hanging around a man who don't want her, I just can't see . . ."

"I knows you can't see, but I'm staying! I knows you don't want me, but you going to support me!"

He rammed his hands into the pockets of his pyjamas, and leaned against the window casing.

"And suppose I don't support you?"

"Then I'll go down to that Post Office and tell 'em!"

"The day you go down to that Post Office and snitch on me again, that's the day you going to be sorry!"

"And the day you stop paying these bills that's the day you going to be sorry!"

He came to her side.

"I done took about enough off of you!"

"You ain't through taking yet!"

"Shut up, you lowbellied slut!"

"If I'm a slut now I was one when you married me!"

"I didn't want you in the first place!"

"You had a funny way of showing it!"

"If you hadn't lied and said you was big, I wouldn't've never married you, neither."

"You went around with your tongue lapping out to get me," said Lil, placing knives and forks upon the table.

"Don't cross talk me, woman!"

"You did!"

"Listen, pack your duds and get going! I don't want you!"

"Make me!"

"I don't want you, hear me!"

"And I don't want you, neither! All I want from you is support, and I'm going to get it or get your job!"

He leaned over her, his eyes fastened on her bare neck, his hands hanging limply at his sides.

"You can't talk this way to me!"

"Then don't talk to me!"

A hot sense of elation bubbled in him. He felt the muscles of his back stiffening. Just a few more words from her, just a few more, and, by God, he would slap her into the middle of next Christmas. His right hand itched. His voice dropped to a low growl.

"I'm asking you for the last time to shut up!"

Lil knew she was risking danger, but she could not resist.

"Make me!"

She dodged, but too late. Jake's open palm caught her square on her cheek, sounding like a pistol shot. She spun around from the force of the blow, falling weakly against the wall, screaming.

"Don't you hit me no more! Don't you hit me no more!"

He was at her side, his raised palm open and threatening.

"I said shut up!"

She ducked and let out a sharp scream. He jerked her from the wall. She stumbled into the middle of the floor, barricading her face behind arms and elbows.

"I ask you to shut up!"

As she screamed again, he brushed her arms aside and slapped her a quick onetwo with the front and back of his palm on both sides of her face. She sank to her knees, her bosom too full to utter a sound.

"Ain't you going to shut up!"

He stood over her, his legs wide apart, his hands dug deep into his pockets, looking at her heaving bosom.

"Get up!"

"I'm going to fix you," she sobbed. "So help me Gawd, I'm going to fix you . . ."

"I said get up!"

He kicked her in her side with his foot.

"This is the last time you going to do this to me!"

"I told you to get up! You act like you want some more!"

He bent over to slap again. Quickly she dragged along the floor out of his reach, and pulled to her feet, turning her face from him.

"You want some more?"

"Naw, Jake . . ."

He caught her left wrist in his right hand.

"Tell me what you going to do about it?"

"Jake, please . . ."

"Tell me what you going to do about it?" he asked again, twisting her arm slowly up her back.

"Turn me loose!"

He gave her arm a sixinch twist. Pain made her suck her breath in sharply. She fell to her knees.

"You breaking my arm!"

"Tell me what you going to do about it?"

"Nothing," she breathed. "Nothing."

He shoved her from him.

"Put something to eat on my table before I give you some more!"

Sniffing and blinded by tears, she fumbled for the handle of the coffee pot.

II.

HE LUMBERED back to the bathroom, massaging his tingling palms and mumbling to himself. He had slapped Lil so hard his fingers felt cold. But deep in him he knew he had not done what he wanted; he had not solved anything. *This bitch is ruining me,* he thought as he stared at the white lather drying on his shaving brush. She was taking every ounce of joy out of his life. She had piled up a big doctor's bill, a bill so big that it seemed he could never pay it. Then she had gone like a fool and burned up his eggs, eggs that cost cold, hard cash. *And on top of that she goes and gets herself a Gawddamn tumor!* He slammed the brush into the bowl and turned on the hot water. Each week his bills were mounting; each week he was falling further behind. He gritted his teeth. *That bitch!*

About him sunshine poured through green curtains, splashed the white bathtub, glinted on the metal faucets and shivered in little ghostly patches on the tile floor. He softened his brush and looked miles deep into the white tiles, thinking *If Lil goes and haves that operation it'll put me almost a thousand dollars in debt to that doctor. And that ain't counting all the other bills I owe, neither. And if I don't pay 'em they'll kick me off my job . . .* A wave of self-pity swept through him. *What to hell? What in the world can a man do? I'm just like a slave . . .* He owed so many debts he did not know which debt to pay first. And a thousand dollar doctor bill would just about fix him for good. If he went to a loan bank and borrowed a thousand dollars, how long would it take him to pay it back? *Let's see now,* he thought, moving his lips silently. *If I pay back two and a half on each payday, that'll make five dollars a month. Let's see now. Five dollars a month? Twelve months in a year. Five times twelve is . . . Is . . . Let's see now. Five times two is ten. Write your naught and carry your one. Five times one is five, and one to carry makes six. Yeah, sixty dollars. Sixty dollars a year.* Now how many years would it take him to pay that off? In his imagination he pictured the numeral one and annexed three naughts. He then drew two long white lines and placed the figure sixty to the left. *Now let's see. Six into ten goes how many times? That's right! One! And six from ten leaves four. All right, go on and bring down the naught, making it forty. And six into forty goes . . . Let's see now.* He screwed up his eyes as he had done long years ago when standing at the blackboard in grammar school. *Six into forty goes . . . Four times six is twenty-four. And five times six is thirty. And six times six is thirtysix. Yeah, six times. And there's just a little left over. But that don't matter much. The main thing is that it'll take sixteen years . . . Sixteen years! Good Gawd!* Then there were other bills: the furniture bill and the rent bill and the gas bill and the light bill and the bill at the Boston Store and the insurance bill and the milk bill. His eyes grew misty with tears, tears of hatred for Lil and tears of pity for himself. *My life is just all shot to hell. I wouldn't be in all this mess if it wasn't for her. She ain't no good no way I can figger it!*

He was broke. There was but one way out; he would have to go to somebody, like Jones, maybe, and borrow enough to tide him over till the fifteenth of the month. But even if he borrowed he would not pay the doctor today. *I'll be Gawd-damned if I pay that quack today! Naw, naw, not today!* He had already promised Al and Bob and Slim he would stand the treats tonight. He could not get out of that so easily. It was his turn, and what kind of a sport would he be if he held them up? *They'll call me cheap. Aw, to hell with that quack! He'll just have to wait, that's all! Ain't no sense in a man working himself to death just to pay a quack doctor bill. And if Lil gets smart and tries any of them sly tricks of hers . . .* He swallowed.

He whipped the brush around in the mug, thinking *And what to hell! She oughtn't be so damned worried, nohow. Ain't she always reading Unity books? Ain't she always talking about how she trusts Gawd? Yeah, she ought to ask Gawd to get rid of that tumor for her.* His face softened. Out of the soil of his anger an idea bloomed. *The very next time she tells me about that damned tumor I'll tell her to let Unity take care of it. Let them bastards send up a silent prayer! Give her a dose of her own sweet medicine!* He smiled, his wounded vanity soothed.

His temper subsided and he turned to the mirror. *Can't I put off shaving 'til tomorrow? My face don't look so bad, do it?* He touched the stiff bristles, reflectively. *Naw, I can't go round all day with my face looking like this.* He caught more hot water and lathered his brush. The bristles rustled with a dry sound as he mopped his chin. Whitened, he opened the medicine cabinet and searched the shelves. *Where's my razor?* The last time he had used it he had left it in here, right behind the iodine. He pushed back cold cream jars and bluegreen bath salts. No razor. *That bitch!*

"Lil!"

"Hunh?"

"Where in Gawd's name you hide my razor?"

"Razor?"

"Yeah, razor! Is your ears stopped up?"

Lil came to the bathroom door with a salt shaker in one hand and a dishtowel in the other. Her eyes avoided him.

"Come on in here, woman, and find my razor! Can't you see I'm *waiting*!"

"Just a minute . . ."

"Where you put my razor?"

"I seen it somewhere . . ."

"*Put*, you mean. How come you hide it, anyhow?"

"I didn't hide . . ."

"Why can't you leave my things where they belong?"

Lil jammed the salt shaker into her apron pocket and went into the bedroom. Jake ambled after, scowling.

"How come you looking in here?"

"I'm trying to remember where I put it . . ."

"Remember?" he growled. "Remember? Yeah, like you remember burning eggs under your nose."

"Jake, give me a second . . ."

"Give you hell! Get my razor!"

Absentmindedly, she banged drawers, pulled up a dresser scarf, and glanced under a pillow. Jake came to her side.

"What you looking under that pillow for?"

"Honest to Jesus, Jake, I'm trying to think . . ."

He grabbed her arm.

"Who was here yestiddy after I was gone?"

Her shoulders slumped. Jake placed one hand firmly about her throat.

"You want me to open your mouth to see if you got a tongue?"

"Naw, Jake."

"What in hell make you want to hide my razor?"

She tried to answer, but he tightened his fingers.

"Can't you talk, you dumb bitch!"

"Jake, nnnobody wwwas hhhere . . ."

"You lying!"

"I cccross my hhheart and sssswear . . ."

He pushed her to the wall.

"Find my razor before I choke you into a black spasm!"

Meekly, she searched. Finally, both to her surprise and Jake's, she found the razor under a shallow dish upon the dresser. He snatched it from her.

"Jake, don't you remember you left it in here yestiddy?"

He remembered, but the mere act of remembering made him angrier.

"Did I ask you anything?"

"Naw, but you . . ."

"Then hold your old big mouth till I speak to you!"

Lifting the razor to the light, he examined it. Unchipped. He squinted his eyes, but he could not even see a tiny hair. If he could only find just one little nick! But not one! He could scarcely keep the irritation out of his voice.

"Get back in the kitchen and keep your hands off of my things, hear me? If you don't I'm going to fix you good one of these mornings!"

He stropped the razor, shaved, nicked himself, cursed, and jabbed the wound with a styptic pencil. He inspected the tiny scratch minutely, wondering if it would disfigure his face in any way. *Yeah, that bitch! She's always making me nervous. I wouldn't've cut myself if it hadn't been for her damn dumbness!*

But when he was in the tub his anger ebbed. The warm water laved his loins. He stretched out, closed his eyes, and let his body soak. He kicked his legs, revelling in the feel of suds. On drifting wisps of vapor his mind winged away. Deep in the tile walls he saw the dim outlines of a soft, brown body. His eyelids drooped. The water lapped at his diaphragm and his flesh swooned in oozy eddies. A sweet lump rose in his stomach and traveled upwards, filling his throat. He lifted the washrag and squeezed it slowly, making the water trickle against his skin. His lips sagged and he sighed. The woman's body hovered nearer, growing in solidity. Uneasily, in spite of himself, he stirred; the delicious feeling petered out. He shook his head and studied the shiny soap bubbles, thinking, *Jeeesus*. He sang:

> *"I woke up too soon*
> *The spell was broken*
> *I woke up too soon*
> *Ending a dream*
> *You were so beautiful*
> *So wonderful*
> *And so divine*
> *There was such tenderness in your caress*
> *You were almost mine . . ."*

As he soaped his armpits and groin:

> *"You took away my soldiers when you took away your love*
> *You said it was a plaything I wasn't worthy of*
> *You packed away my soldiers on a shelf way up above*
> *And I'm just little boy blue . . .*
> *You took away my candy when you took away your kiss*
> *I never thought to lose a thing would make me feel like this*
> *But now I know you took away the thing I'll always miss*
> *And I'm just little boy blue . . ."*

He dried himself, pulled on his BVD's, socks, and washed his hands in a stream of sunshine. He felt good, but the bathtub mood still lingered.

> *"Got me doing things, things I never thought I'd do-oo-oo*
> *Got me doing things, some are silly, some are new-oo-oo*
> *Got me saying things, things I never said before-o-o*
> *Got me saying things like you're the one I adore-o-o . . ."*

He next tackled the big job of the morning. His hair had to be combed, combed flat so that not a ripple, not a crinkle, not a crease must show. Going to the mirror, he surveyed the unruly strands with the apprehensive air of a veteran fieldmarshall inspecting the fortifications and wire entanglements of an alien army. He wore his hair in the style of Negro bangs. His nappy forelocks reared fanwise in a wooly black flare which had to be bullied into a billiard ball smoothness.

Years of dealing with this foe had taught him many devices

of strategy. The first barrage was with water, and plenty of it. Going to the washbowl, he dampened his hair till rivulets streamed down his neck. Then, seizing his comb like a colt .45, he tried to force an opening through enemy lines. The battle waxed furious. The comb suffered heavy losses, and fell back slowly. One by one teeth snapped until they littered bathmat and washbowl. Mangled and broken things they lay there, brave soldiers fallen in action, many of them clutched in the death grip of enemy hairs. After three minutes of attack the strands abandoned their trenches and retreated disorderly.

Jake now brought forth the most powerful weapon at his command. This deadly contraption was a pink jar of hair pomade labeled, LAY 'EM LOW. Its chief ingredient was a stout beeswax, a substance as fatal to insurgent kinks as was mustard gas in Flanders. He rammed his forefinger deep into the jar and pulled forth on a nail a dab of yellow stickiness the size of a walnut. He smeared it vigorously between his palms, and delivered a sudden broadside. Not a man fell. Only with the impact of a second assault did a few waver or weaken. Tightening his lips and spreading his fingers, he launched drive upon drive till the brave fellows broke at the knees. Then he pinned them tight, pummelled them into a foul and gluey morass.

He was breathing hard. He resorted to the comb again. A hot skirmish on the left and right flanks had each warweary strand clinging to his scalp like troops in shellholes under bombardment. The enemy was conquered! Jake peered into the mirror. His head was a solid mass of black slickness. He smiled, thinking with satisfaction *If a fly'd light on that he'd slip up and break his neck . . .*

He went into the bedroom and looked through the pockets of his trousers for a stocking cap. This ingenious implement of exploitation, this standing army which a conquering nation leaves to guard a conquered one, is made from the top of a woman's stocking. It is elastic, about four inches long, tied securely at the top, and when stretched tightly over the cranium resembles the gleaming skin of a huge onion. He was in a hurry, for, failing to get his hair under this peace treaty immediately, it would soon flounce back into a thousand triumphant kinks. He searched in vain. After a few minutes he stood in the middle of the room, emptyhanded, angryeyed.

"Lil!"

No answer.

"Liiiil!"

No answer.

"Woman, you hear me calling!"

Still no answer. His voice swelled throughout the flat like the roar of a lion.

"Liiiiiiiiiiiiiiiiiiil!"

"Just a minute, Jake."

She came leisurely to the door.

"Where was you?"

"On the back porch."

"You don't belong there."

"I . . ."

"How come you didn't answer when I called?"

"I didn't hear you . . ."

"Running your old fat mouth like always, hunh?"

She hung her head.

"Who was you talking to this time?"

"Mrs. Thomas."

"What in hell can you find to talk about all the time?"

She swallowed and sighed.

"Tell me what you want, Jake. I'm cooking breakfast."

"Well, just you wait awhile now. If you got time enough to gab with that Thomas bitch then you got time enough to wait till I tell you what I want." He continued to smooth his hair down with the palms of his hands.

Lil closed her eyes and leaned weakly against the bedpost.

"Where's my stocking cap?"

"Stocking cap?"

"Yeah, stocking cap! Stocking cap! Stocking cap! Can't you never understand nothing?"

"I don't know, Jake. I ain't had it. I don't need no cap like that nohow." Complacently she patted her own smooth and kinkless hair.

"What you trying to signify?"

He advanced a step.

"I ain't trying to signify nothing," she said quickly.

"Well don't, if you knows what's good for you! I done told you I wants a stocking cap!"

"But I ain't got nothing but my new stockings. You done ruined all my stockings already, tearing 'em up for caps. And how you lose so many caps, anyhow?"

"What's that got to do with it? I said I wants a cap!"

"But I ain't *got* none, Jake!"

"*Get* one, then!"

"I told you I ain't got nothing but my *new* stockings!"

"Ain't you going to get me a cap?"

"I ain't . . ."

"I'll get one!"

He brushed her aside and headed for her dresser.

"Jake, please! Not my *new* stockings!"

"GET ME A STOCKING CAP!"

She scurried for the clothes closet.

He stood waiting, thinking, *She better not fool with me no more today . . .*

She returned with an old hose.

"Here, Jake. You better take good care of this, 'cause if you lose it I ain't got no more."

"Thought you said you didn't have none?"

She averted her eyes and left the room. Tugging, he pulled the cap down over his hair. An hour of pressure would dry the water and grease. His hair would remain in place all day. Going to the mirror, he struck a pose and smiled. Again he sang:

> *"I think of you with every breath I take*
> *And every breath becomes a sigh*
> *Not a sigh of despair*
> *But a sigh that I care for you . . ."*

III.

JAKE STOOD before the ten suits hanging in his closet and tried to make up his mind. His fingers strayed from one to the other, feeling the texture of the goods. He did not want to wear the black, nor the blue, nor the brown. They were all right, but he just did not want to wear them. He was not in the mood. He shook his head at a grey tweed. It was much too light in color and weight for winter wear. And so was the tan. He passed over three more because they were double-breasted. *Shucks, everybody's wearing doublebreasted suits these days.* His choice finally narrowed down to a light green one-button sack and a winereddish ensemble with pleated trousers. He liked the winereddish one because it was so roomy and made him look fifteen or twenty pounds heavier, like a bigtime football player. *But shucks, I done wore that old suit so much lately.* He fingered the green; he pictured himself swinging along the street in the sunshine. He imagined eyes following him. *Yeah, I'll wear that green.* After he had slid into the trousers, he stood looking down at the keen creases, smiling with critical approval.

"Sharp as a tack," he said.

And because he was wearing the green suit, he decided on lowcut, brown suede shoes with high Cuban heels and toes that tapered to a point. He tied the shoestrings in a neat, tight bow. Spotlessly white spats capped the bargain. Next, he put on a softcollared lavender shirt which contrasted pleasingly with his broad, red, elastic suspenders. Then he tried a black tie, a green tie, a brown tie, and a red tie. In the end he selected a wide yellow one studded with tiny blue halfmoons. He added a delicate finishing touch by inserting a huge imitation ruby that burned like a smear of fresh blood. Squaring his shoulders, he buttoned coat and vest and adjusted with sensitive fingers the purple embroidered orange handkerchief that peeped out of his breast pocket. He sprayed each of his coat lapels with violetscented perfume, then pivoted on his heels in the middle of the rug and brought himself to a sudden halt in front of the dresser mirror.

"Like a Maltese kitten," he said.

27

Well, I reckon I'll go in and eat some now, eat a nice, big, hot breakfast. Then I'll study my scheme some. Yeah, I got to study that scheme. I can't keep on putting it off and putting it off all the time. Then I'll walk out awhile. Hunt up some of the old gang, maybe . . .

Breakfast was laid on the kitchen table. He sat down opposite Lil, who was reading a copy of *Unity*, with her face cupped mournfully in her hands. Jake stared at her, and then at the turnedback page that faced him. Across the top of it he saw a wide spread of yellow, Egyptian wings, under which ran a slogan: A PAGE OF SUNSHINE FOR EVERYDAY. Her interest in the book irked him. *Every time she pokes her head into them damn books I can't hardly talk to her.* He groped for something to say, something that would rouse her out of her smug complacency. *By Gawd, she sets there just like I didn't slap her a few seconds ago!* He picked up the sugarbowl.

"Well?"

Lil lifted her eyes momentarily.

"Hunh?"

"Ain't you eating?"

"Naw."

"What's griping you?"

"Nothing."

"How come you ain't eating?"

"I just ain't hungry."

"Well, I *is*! And you ain't hurting me a damn bit if you don't *never* eat!"

He sweetened his coffee and sucked a long sip.

"Where my paper?"

Lil fetched the morning's paper from the porch. Rearing back in the chair, he opened it and read the headline aloud.

ROOSEVELT STRIKES AT MONEY CHANGERS
WILL DRIVE THEM FROM THE TEMPLE, HE SAYS

"Hunh," Jake grunted as he laid the paper aside and took up a slice of toast. "That's what *he* says! And what he says is just so much hot air. Nobody'll ever tell these rich American men what to do. Naw, siree! Not so long as Gawd's sun shines. Cold, hard cash runs this country, always did and always will. You can put that in your hat and bet your bottom dollar on it. And what to hell! Who is these old Democrats, anyhow? I'll tell you what they is! They's crazy troublemakers! They ain't got no money. And what in hell can a man do without money? Tell me that! Nothing! And empty words don't mean a damn thing, neither. Say, who's going to tell old man Morgan and old man Rockefeller and old man Ford what to do? Who? WHO?" Jake stabbed the air with his fork. "Why them men owns and runs the country! And furthermore, these old Democrats is always starting wars. Old Wilson started one, and now they want to put another Democrat in office to start another one. Everybody knows these old Democrats is hotheaded, so why put 'em in office? People's crazy! Crazy with the heat! They don't know white from black! Shucks, old Hoover was doing all right, only nobody couldn't see it, that's all . . . I'm going to stick with the Republicans. Old Abe Lincoln is the ship and all else is the sea . . . Now, who said that? . . ."

He frowned, screwing up his eyes. He crammed a piece of toast in his mouth, chewed, and flushed it down with a gulp of coffee. Lil went to the sink and took a tall, dark bottle from a shelf. Jake watched her pour a tablespoon level full.

"What's that you drinking?"

"Medicine," she answered.

"What kind is it?"

"Mrs. Lydia E. Pinkham's Vegetable Compound."

"What you taking it for?"

"My nerves."

"Aw, that stuff ain't doing you no good. You just throwing my money away . . ."

"I'm sick, Jake."

"You always sick."

She swallowed the medicine.

"I got to take something," she sighed.

Jake jerked his lips, took a mouthful of egg and bacon, and turned to the paper again. *I'm going to stop her from throwing my money away one of these days . . .*

GERMANY DEMANDS ARMS EQUALITY
VOWS TO BOLT LEAGUE IF DENIED

"See! There she goes! What did I tell you? They's loose

again! I always did say they should've wiped them monkeys
off the map while they was at it. Them sonsofbitches is sure
one slick and trickery lot—I'm here to tell you. I remembers
way back during the War when old Reverend Harmond—
he's dead now, poor fellow—said that them guys was closer
to savages than anybody. And, by Gawd, he sure knowed
what he was talking about, too! Yeah, you better watch them
German Devils; they's a ornery and lousy lot as sure as you
born. You know one thing? They say them German guys got
some kind of a poison gas over there that's so strong and
powerful that all they got to do is just skeet some of it in the
air and when you smell it you'll curlup and die like a chinch!
Just think of that! You know, they say them German soljers
took them little Beljum babies—little, innocent, newborn
babies, mind you, now—raped 'em and stuck 'em with bayo-
nets to telegram posts. How can people do things like that?
And shucks, if they happen to come across a French woman,
no matter how old she was, that was just too bad. Every soljer
in the German army would pile her, and when they got
through there wasn't nothing left. Just think now: One soljer
after another getting on one poor little woman, and she just
laying there and can't do nothing. And ain't no policemen
around to bother you . . ." Jake paused, wagged his head,
and gazed deep into the checkered tablecloth. "A soljer gets a
chance to do a lot of things . . ."

He poised a piece of egg on the tip of his fork and squinted
at another headline.

G-MEN SPREAD NET FOR GANGSTERS

"Now what's wrong with them Government? What they
want to bother them poor guys for? They ain't doing nothing
but robbing a few banks. Aw, I know what's wrong with 'em.
They's just jealous because they's not splitting their dough
with them, that's all. They don't want them gangsters to
make so much money. Why, them gangsters is sports, *real*
sports . . . The papers say they ain't never snitched on none
of their pals. I was reading just the other day where one of
them guys was laying in the hospital dying and the cops was
trying to get him to tell who shot 'im and he wouldn't talk,
wouldn't say a word. He just looked up at 'em and smiled! By

Gawd, it takes guts to die like that. And all the time they's alive they walk around knowing that at any time somebody might shoot 'em down. Jeeesus, it takes nerve to be a gangster! But they have a plenty of fun. Always got a flock of gals hanging on their arms. Dress swell in sporty clothes. Drive them long, sleek automobiles. And got money to throw away . . . They don't live long, but I bet they sure have a hell of a sweet time while they do live. Better time than a lot of us who work hard every day for a measly living."

He broke a piece of toast and spread it with strawberry jam. As he chewed he watched Lil's eyes following the printed lines of her *Unity*. *That woman's going to read herself blind!* Again he searched for something to say that would rouse her to a sharp sense of his presence.

"I think anybody that don't like gangsters is crazy!" he spoke loudly.

"Hunh?"

"The government is out after gangsters," said Jake, tapping the paper with his knife.

"Gangsters?"

"Yeah, gangsters, deaf woman!"

Lil stared. Jake laid down his knife, cocked his head, and looked at her with infinite compassion.

"Woman, what makes you so dumb? Don't you never try using your brains sometimes? Don't you never think of nothing that's serious?"

"I don't know, Jake."

"How come you don't know?"

"I wasn't listening to you reading."

"You could learn something if you didn't keep that empty head of yours stuck into them Gawddamn *Unity* books all the time."

Lil's eyes widened.

"Jake, this is Gawd's word!"

"Gawd's hooey! It's a gyp game, that's all!"

"You blaspheming Gawd!"

"So what?"

"Don't you know that Gawd can slap you dead right where you is?"

"Aw, woman, don't be dumb!" he said, glaring as though

she had threatened him. "This is the last time you're going to read that stuff in my house, get me? Don't send no more of my money off for that damn trash, you hear?"

Lil swallowed. Jake turned disdainfully to the paper.

HITLER CALLS ON WORLD TO SMASH JEWS

"Now, that's something for everybody to think about. It shows that people's waking up. That's what's wrong with this country, too many Jews, Dagos, Hunkies, and Mexicans. We colored people would be much better off if they had kept them rascals out. Naw, the American white man went to sleep; he didn't have sense enough to let us black people have a break. He had to let them Jews and all in. Now they got the country sewed up; every store you see is run by a Jew, and the foreigners. And they don't think about nobody but themselves. They ought to send 'em all back where they come from. That's what I say."

Jake paused and drained his cup.

"You want some more coffee?"

"Yeah, fill it up."

He stirred his cup and read again.

EINSTEIN SAYS SPACE BENDS

"Humph! Now this is what I call crazy! Yes, siree, just plumb crazy! This guy takes the prize. What in hell do he know about space bending? How in hell can he see space bending when he can't even *see* space? I'm asking you? You know one thing, these old newspapers sure tries hard to fool folks. See, now, a dumb guy would fall for all this kind of stuff. See how folks get their minds made up for 'em? You got to watch sharp and do your own thinking in this old world if you don't want to be fooled. Now, if you ask me, this guy Einstein's just fooling everybody, just saying things to get his name in the papers. Shucks, I could do that. And suppose space do bend, what to hell then? . . . I bet my soul he's a Jew."

Jake turned the page.

COMMUNISTS RIOT IN STREETS OF NEW YORK

"Gawddamn! Wonder how come the police let them guys

go on like that? Now them guys, them Commoonists and Bolshehicks, is the craziest guys going! They don't know what they want. They done come 'way over here and wants to tell us how to run *our* country when their *own* country ain't run right. Can you beat that for the nerve of a brass monkey? I'm asking you? Why don't they stay in their own country if they don't like the good old USA? That's what I want to know! And they go around fooling folks, telling 'em they going to divide up everything. And some folks ain't got no better sense than to believe it, neither. Just weakminded, that's all! Now look here, if I got two suits and another guy ain't got none, they want to take one of mine and let *him* have it! A fool can see that that's wrong! And how are they going to do all this? With bombs and dynamite! What can be wrong with some folks' brains? I wonder! And over in Roosia where they in power folks is starving to death. And now they want to get us in the same fix. What's wrong with folks when they act like that? If they get in power and tell you to do something and you don't do it, then they lines you up against a wall and shoots you down! That's no lie, I was reading it just the other day in the *Tribune* . . ."

"But, Jake!"

"Hunh?"

"Folks is starving over here, too."

"Aw, you talk like a fool!"

"The papers said so."

"Nobody but lazy folks can starve in this country!"

"But they can't get no work."

"They don't want no work!"

"And they burned a colored man alive the other day."

"Who?"

"The white people in this country."

"Shut up! You don't know what you talking about!"

"Well, they *did*!"

"How you know?"

"It was in the papers."

"Aw, that was down South, anyhow."

"But the South's a part of this country."

Jake stopped chewing and glared at her.

"Woman, is you a *Red*?"

Lil blinked. Jake turned back to the paper.

HOODLUMS ABDUCT MILLIONAIRE'S SON

"Well, what you know about that? You see, it just goes to show that rich folks has their troubles just the same as us. After all, it ain't no difference. I'm telling you, Old Man Trouble don't mind nobody. You'd think them folks with all their millions and millions of dollars would be safe and sound from everything. But they ain't, not by a long shot. When you get right down at the bottom of things and start thinking real hard about 'em you begin to see that that's the funny thing about life. When you boil it all low you'll see that everybody gets a equal break in the end . . ." He looked out of the window, dreamily. "Well, I guess all of us got to get a certain amount of worry in this old world, not matter what. Look like things just works that way, somehow or other. The good Lawd's done got it all figgered out in His own good fashion. It's got to be that way so there can be some justice in this world, I reckon . . ." His voice trailed off uncertainly.

He drained his cup of coffee, lit a cigarette, leaned his elbows on the table, and sighed. The coffee warmed his blood; he could feel his heart pumping pleasantly. Each time he inhaled the huge breaths of smoke it seemed as though he were going to fall asleep. His head lolled; a lazy thought crawled slowly through his brain. *Lawd, how good it feels after you done eat a good meal.* His eyelids drooped. *Wouldn't it be good now if I could go back to bed and sleep some? Yeah, but that would start Lil's old big mouth again. And I don't want to hear her no more today.* Not that he cared two straws about what Lil would say, but he just did not feel like arguing on a full stomach. It would be much better to go out somewhere, get some fresh air, and loaf around till worktime. Maybe he would walk over to the poolhall and hear what the old gang was saying. Or maybe he would drop over to Bob's place and play a game or two of bridge. *And I got to get a haircut.* No, he must not forget to get his hair cut; he could not be around the sweet girls tonight with hair bristling like cockle burrs on his neck. *Yeah, I'll walk out awhile.* He sighed, his legs feeling deliciously heavy.

"Jake," Lil called humbly from across the table.

He held still, pretending he had not heard. *That bitch is going to ask me for something*. He knew it; he could feel it in his bones.

"Jake," she called again, this time a little louder.

"Hunh?"

"What you want me to fix for dinner?"

"Nothing."

"I got to fix something. So tell me what you want."

"I said *nothing*."

"Ain't you going to be home for dinner?"

"Naw."

"But I ain't got no money, Jake."

"I told you I wasn't going to be home for dinner."

"I got to have some money. I got to eat, even if you ain't here."

"I ain't got no money!"

"But everything's out! I got to get something."

"What in hell do you do with so much money?"

"I spends it right here in the house for something to eat."

"I give you *two* dollars the other day."

"But that's all gone!"

"Aw, you just throw money away."

"I made two dollars last for three days!"

"Go to the store and ask the man to let you have something on credit."

"The bill up there's so *big*."

"Ask 'im anyhow!"

"He told me to ask you when you going to pay 'im."

"Tell 'im I'll pay 'im soon."

"We owe so much I'm 'shamed to go there."

"Woman, if you 'shamed to go and ask a man for something to eat, you just stay hungry, see?"

"Jake, please, leave me some money."

"Go to another store and get some groceries."

"I can't!"

"How come? You lame?"

"We owe 'em all bills. They won't let me have nothing."

"Listen, for the last time, I ain't got no money! NOW QUIT TALKING TO ME!"

Jake waddled into the livingroom and slouched across a soft

chair; his legs dangled over the sides and his head nestled in the hollow of a pillow. *Gawd, I feel lazy . . . And that ain't no lie . . . A good cup of coffee sure makes you feel good.* It made his body languid and made his mind work rapidly. *Jeeesus, if I could only feel this way all the time . . .*

Dreamily, he looked out of the window. The day was dazzlingly bright. That portion of the sky he could see was marvelously blue. Tons of golden sunshine splashed the streets and houses. How queer the drab bricks looked when lit by the light of the sun! The upstretching branches of the trees seemed to be pleading for spring rain. How oddly beautiful it was to be February! A lost spring day set like a jewel amongst the dreary winter ones! *Yeah, it's almost warm enough to go without a winter coat.*

He yawned and scratched his thigh, thinking *I ought to go in and study my scheme some now. Right now would be a good time to put in some hard work.* But he did not move. His body relaxed; he could feel his toes tingling pleasantly. He gazed drowsily at the keen creases in his trousers, thinking *I don't feel like studying now. Maybe I'll wait till morning. That'll be better . . .*

A sweet looseness seeped into Jake's bones. He closed his eyes and his blood sogged slowly through his veins like warm milk. He could feel a faint tinge of the sun's warmth even through the windowpane. He pushed his fingers down into his trousers, between his belt and the flat of his stomach. His lips became moist and sagged. His groin felt hot; an uneasy feeling, elusive and light as a feather, played over the surface of his stomach. The muscles of his thighs stretched taut and his mind became hazy. Out of a mist loomed the face of a woman, of *the* woman. The face was brown, winsome, and delicately ovalshaped. Eyelids drooped with languorous passion. Wet lips hovered closer and closer. He could almost see the velvety sheen of her skin. His head swam; his skin glowed as though it were near a soft flame. He doubled his legs as a fugitive feeling of delight burned in his diaphragm. He stirred restlessly, and his shoulders twitched as though he were a child nestling deeper into a mother's bosom. A tiny trickle of saliva drooled out of the corner of his mouth; a look of suspense came into his face . . .

"Jaaake!"

He jerked, frowned, and wiped his mouth with the back of his hand.

"Hell," he breathed.

He closed his eyes and curled himself again, seeking to recapture the lost mood.

"Jaaaaaaake!"

His face contorted savagely.

"What in *hell* you want?"

"You looked in the mailbox yet?"

"Hell, naw! And quit bothering me!"

Again he lowered his head, trying to resuscitate the mood. He was very still, very quiet, but, alas, the mood would not come. *Gawddamit to hell! A man just can't get no rest or peace around Lil.*

He screwed up his eyes, stretched his arms above his head, and yawned.

"Aaaaaaaaahhheellll," he whispered in a breath that seemed to escape involuntarily.

He put on a light grey top coat with huge buttons of liquid pearl and a black hat with a tiny red feather peeping timidly in the back. Grabbing his mahoganyhandled cane, he went slowly down the steps, his mind lost in a warm fog.

IV.

W HEN IN THE VESTIBULE he twirled the dial on the mailbox. A bundle of multicolored circulars and advertisement throwaways spilled into his hands. He went to the light at the glass door and read the first.

BELIEVE IT OR NOT
a mountain of golden dollars waits for you
$$$$$$ A SURE HIT $$$$$$ A BULL'S EYE BARGAIN
$$$$$$ ACT NOW $$$$$$
RISK NOTHING——PAY AFTER YOU WIN
NOTICE—To all number players who are keeping house or can furnish references: Come to see me at once! Bring the year, month, day, and hour of your birth! And I will give you a running gig that will fall immediately. YOU PAY ONLY AFTER YOU WIN! Be sure and bring your last three drawings, and if you have difficulty hitting spiritual gigs I will give you *free* advice as to what to do.
YOU CAN'T LOSE
THE MYSTERIOUS THREESTAR MEDIUM
4545 Vincennes Avenue
Chicago

"Huuuumm . . . There might be something to this. I'll show it to Lil when I get back; she's always having dreams. But, shucks, she don't keep after nothing what she starts, and you got to keep after these old numbers if you want to win something."

He read another:

ASTONISHING$$$$$$ASTOUNDING$$$$$$
UNBELIEVABLE$$$$$$BUT TRUE
LADIES AND GENTLEMEN: LEND ME YOUR EARS!!
I MAKE NUMBERS COME OUT IN ASHES—
I MAKE THE UNSEEN WORLD VISIBLE!
The Second Coming Incense is the most mysterious incense the world has ever known! See for yourself! After the piece has burned you will find numbers in the ashes!

38

THEY COME STRAIGHT FROM THE SPIRIT WORLD!
Send 50¢ in stamps for a full size trial box,
or $1.00 for a full supply.
YOU CAN'T LOSE!
THE EASTERN CELESTIAL MAGIC COMPANY
3667 South State Street, Chicago

"I ain't never heard of nothing like this before; maybe there's something in it if it comes straight from the spirit world."

Still another:

VIM AND VIGOR AND VITALITY
FOR ALL MEN AND WOMEN

Does your back ache? Does your head ache? Are your nerves on edge? Do you feel tired and exhausted all the time? Do you have to get out of bed at night? IF SO, THERE'S HELP FOR YOU AT LAST!

Weak manhood causes a decided change in affections. And this, being not understood, causes mistrust and unhappy homes. LISTEN: YOU SHOULD NOT BE OLD AT SIXTY! If you are suffering from weak manhood or weak womanhood you should take DOCTOR WILLIAM LOUIS SPEEDY'S POWERFUL IMPOTENCY CASTIGATOR FOR MALES AND FEMALES TODAY! It will make a new person or we will give you your money back under our *Golden Seal Moneyback Guarantee*! Just take one bottle and then watch the change that will come over your mate! A full size bottle for only $2.50. Six full size bottles for $12.00.

Send today and avoid worry.
THE DEMOCRATIC PATENT MEDICINE STORE
500 Clay Street
Parson, Pa.
(Read the Testimonial below)

Dear Sir:

I began suffering from weak manhood when I was twenty years old. I worried for years. I spent hundreds of dollars on doctors and glandular treatments, but I got no satisfactory results. I gave up, then I heard of DOCTOR WILLIAM LOUIS SPEEDY'S POWERFUL IMPOTENCY CASTI-GATOR FOR MALES AND FEMALES. I decided to try it. When I had taken two bottles I underwent a wonderful change, and after taking six bottles I have had no more trouble. It would be hard to find a more popular man than I. I am now sixty years old. You may print this letter if you wish.

Yours humbly,
(Signed) Gabriel Collins
Pastor of the Sunrise Baptist Church

"Shucks, I don't need nothing like this, yet," smiled Jake. And still another:

READ THIS TESTIMONIAL
TO WHOM IT MAY CONCERN:

A year ago, before my twelfth baby was born, I was terribly sick. My feet and legs were swollen to twice their normal size. I had weak, nervous fits and hot flashes. I was so rundown that I once flowed for two months. I was, oh, so irregular and almost died each time with cramps. I had dizzy spells and blind spells. I was despondent and had given up all hope. But every cloud has a silver lining and the darkest hour is just before dawn. And so one morning I found—like a Holy Message from the Great God on High—your card in my mailbox recommending VIRGIN MARY'S NEVERFAIL HERB AND ROOT TONIC FOR NERVOUS AND RUNDOWN WOMEN. I told my husband and doctor about it, and they laughed at me. But since everything else had failed I decided to try it. I was flat on my back when I began taking it. On the second bottle I felt stronger, and was able to set up. Then the great thing happened. My twelfth bottle put me on my feet. I would solemnly swear to these experiences before the UNITED STATES SUPREME COURT. I still use VIRGIN MARY'S NEVERFAIL HERB AND ROOT TONIC FOR NERVOUS AND RUN-DOWN WOMEN, and now weigh 203 pounds and still gaining, bless the Lord! You may use this letter if you think it will help others to be saved.

I am yours to sing your praises,
(Signed) Mrs. Cora Saunders
Atlanta,
Ga.

ALL WOMEN ORDER YOUR BOTTLE
WITHOUT DELAY TODAY!
ONLY $2.00
VIRGIN MARY'S NEVERFAIL
HERB AND ROOT TONIC
FOR NERVOUS AND RUNDOWN WOMEN, INC.
534 Fountain Street,
Coldwater, Miss.

"I'm sure going to show this to Lil. This thing might save me some money," Jake mumbled with a quiet sense of elation. He read the last one:

HE STOPPED HIS WHISKEY DRINKING
by
James' Only Wife

I
I'm the happiest little woman
In all this little town;
And my merry laugh and singing
Takes the place of sigh and frown,
For JAMES HAS QUIT HIS DRINKING
And is like himself once more,
And the world is just a paradise
With such happiness in store!

II
One day I read some verses—
Molly's Miracle, the name,
And I said, "That's James exactly,
And I'll send and get the same."
So I sent for SUREFIRE TREATMENT
(As sly as sly could be)
And I put it in James' supper
And I put it in his tea.

III
And it didn't taste a little bit:
Had no odor, so, you see—
It was the smoothest kind of sailing

For little Doctor Me.
And I watched and prayed and waited,
  (And cried some, too, I guess)
And I didn't have the greatest faith,
  I'm ashamed now to confess.

IV

And James never thought a minute
  He was being cured of drink,
And soon he's well as any one.
  It makes me cry to think!
Just makes me cry for gladness,
  I'm so proud to be his wife —
Since he is cured of drinking,
  And leads a nice, new life.

V

"Since James he quit adrinking!"
  I can't say it times enough!
And hates and loathes a liquor
  As he would a poison stuff.
And when I say my prayers at night
  As thankful as can be —
I pray for James the most of all —
  Then for SUREFIRE TREATMENT!

HOME TREATMENT FOR ALL DRUNKARDS

Odorless and tasteless when used as directed. Any lady can give it secretly at home in tea, coffee, or food.

COSTS YOU NOTHING TO MAKE A TRIAL

If you have a husband, wife, brother, sister, sweetheart, father, mother, or friend who is a victim of liquor, send your name and address on the coupon below. It has helped thousands and should be just the very thing you want. You may be thankful as long as you live that you did it.

THE SUREFIRE TREATMENT COMPANY, INC.

654 Elm Street,
Jackson,
Mississippi.

Very thoughtfully he tore this into tiny pieces and let it filter through his fingers to the tile floor. His lips puckered.

Lil's just crazy enough to want to try this on me if she found it. And there ain't no mail at all. That's right . . . This is a holiday. He sorted out the circulars which appealed to him and put them into his pocket. He swung through the door and strolled along the street, drawing from a cigarette. Autos hummed by on rubber tires and their honkhonk seemed real music to him. The air was warm and felt good to his skin. He threw his cigarette away, whistled the refrain from a popular blues song, and jingled the silver coins in his pocket. His mind was as calm as a lookingglass. A plump, brownskinned girl passed; unconsciously he pulled his hat to a rakish angle and jingled his silver louder. He looked up at the wide sweep of blue sky and felt how good it was merely to be alive. As he passed a newsstand his eyes caught for a fleeting moment a black and white picture of a nude, halfcharred body of a Negro swinging from the end of a rope. At the top of the picture ran a caption:

DEATH TO LYNCHERS

Jake grunted and whistled louder. He turned a corner and came upon a black boy and a black girl playing upon a pair of tall, wooden steps leading up to an old threestory house.

"I'll beat you up!" one yelled.

"I bet you can't!" the other answered.

Jake watched them scamper up to the top landing. The steps reminded him of something, but he could not tell what it was. He frowned, thinking, *Doggone it, seems like I done forgot something.* He stopped in the middle of the sidewalk and watched the children again. What he was trying to re-member hovered on the tip of his tongue; it seemed that in a moment he would speak it. But he could not. He strolled on and lit another cigarette. When he reached the end of the block, when he was no longer trying to remember, it came to him, surged up: the steps, his running, the voice, his whole dream . . . *Yeah, I want to play my dream. I knowed I was forgetting something. I believe I'll go to the Black Gold Policy Wheel . . .* . He hurried down the block, turned a corner, and knocked softly at a narrow door.

"Who's that?"

"Jake!"

"O.K."

The door swung in.

"What you know, Skinner?"

"Don't know. What you know?"

"Don't know. How's the numbers?"

"Oh, some folks catching and some folks ain't."

The room was crowded, smoky, and there was a low-pitched drone of conversation broken at intervals by shouts. A lifesized pastel of a dark, blackbearded man hung on a rear wall, captioned:

KING SOLOMON

He got a handful of varicolored policy slips from a small table and examined them. They were named *Black Gold*, *Red Devil*, *East & West*, *Interstate*, *Lucky Strike*, *Harlem*, *Bronx*, *Tia Juana*, *Old State*, *Chicago*, and so on. Jake's lips moved silently, recounting what numbers had pulled recently in all the wheels. *Sickrow . . . Gee, if I knowed about old Lil's operation I could've caught something. Murderrow . . . Razorrow . . . Bloodrow . . . Moneyrow . . . Looks like these old numbers is falling for somebody. I'm going to see if they'll fall for me.*

He had been playing policy off and on for five years, but had never broken even. He was still behind. How much? He did not know. He played such small sums that he never missed them greatly, and did not bother to keep an account. But he was on the losing side. One time he had caught as high as twenty dollars, and he had played back forty dollars trying to catch twenty more. He would play consistently for about a week and lose consistently, then he would swear off and call the whole thing a fool's game. But a vivid dream would be the signal for his answering again the call of the numbers.

Policy is an elaborate kind of lottery. It is played with 78 numbers, running from 1 to 78, 24 of which are chosen at each drawing to be printed on varicolored slips of paper. Some wheels have one drawing per day, some two, and some as high as three. The 24 numbers on each policy slip are divided into groups of 12 each, and each group of 12 in turn comprises the "leg" of a "book". The player's ability to dream, guess, figure, or otherwise arrive at what three numbers will "fall" in the "leg" of a "book" means that he will win a "gig". A "gig" pays 100 to 1, that is, a dollar for a cent. And who would not take a chance like that?

Of course, Jake had heard that these numbers were capable of being arranged and rearranged to upwards of 70,000 different combinations, and he knew he would never be able to guess or figure out an average rate of recurrence. And he was much too shrewd to trust such a small thing as numbers to fortune tellers, spiritualists, and the like; these people were consulted only in case of a deep, lifeanddeath crisis. He reasoned correctly that if they could tell him what numbers would "fall", they would play the numbers themselves and get rich. He had a much better and surer scheme; he arrived, or tried to arrive, at the right "gig" through the medium of the dream. He had implicit faith in his dreams; did they not come from some source which no man knew? And for the "key" to his dreams he consulted *King Solomon's Wheel of Life and Death Dream Book*. There was only one hitch to this: a dream sometimes had so many possible interpretations, it referred to so many different combinations of numbers, that it was impossible to "cover" the dream. Hence, even the dream lost sometimes. But when a dream was especially vivid, like the one he had had last night, there were great odds that he would win. He could "feel" it.

The increasing noise and clatter of the place told him that soon the morning's drawing would be pulled. With his hands in his pockets and a cigarette slanting across his chin, he stood in the middle of the room and listened to the numbers being called.

"16, 18, 22 . . ."

"45, 68, 50 . . ."

A fat, brownskinned woman came to him, holding a pad of paper and a pencil.

"What you saying, Jake?"

"Aw, I ain't saying nothing."

"You playing this morning?"

"Maybe. I don't know."

"What you see last night?"

"Aw, Mabel, I saw a hell of a lot. I couldn't half sleep for dreaming, all night long."

"That sounds like money, man."

"I dreamed about steps."

"Steps?"

"Yeah."

"Gee, that sounds good!" said Mabel, turning, holding her paper and pencil ready. "Say, Martha!" she called to an old black woman sitting with a thick book in her hands behind a rickety table. "Say, Martha, what's the Steprow?"

Without looking up, the old woman repeated, "Steprow?", and began to turn the pages of *King Solomon's Wheel of Life and Death Dream Book* with a wet thumb. Then she called:

"Steprow: 6, 17, 26 . . ."

And as the numerical interpretations of Jake's dream were called, Mabel jotted them on to her pad.

"How much you want to play on it?" she asked.

"Make it fourbits," said Jake.

"Aw, come on. Play more than that," said Mabel.

"Make it sixbits then," said Jake, knowing that the more he played the higher her commission would be.

"That's swell," she said. "And what else you dream?"

"Let me see now . . . You see, I thought I was running up some steps."

"Give me that Runningrow, Martha?" Mabel called.

The old wrinkled thumb turned the dirty leaves.

"Runningrow: 11, 15, 67 . . ."

"You want to play this, too?"

Jake hesitated.

"Listen, Jake," said Mabel, coming close to him. "You just as well play 'em both. Suppose the Runningrow comes out and you done only played the Steprow? You see, you'll be out of luck."

"All right," said Jake. "Give me twobits on that."

"Make it fourbits, Jake."

"All right. Fourbits then."

"And what else you dream?"

"I ain't got no more money," said Jake.

"Now, listen here, Jake, you better play your whole dream if you want to catch something. That's the big trouble with people playing policy; they won't cover a dream. You can never tell what's the really important thing in a dream, so you has to play safe and cover it all to be sure. Now, what else you dream?"

"Well, I thought I was running up some steps and somebody was calling me. You know, I thought it was my boss man on the job."

"That Boss Manrow's lucky. A man just caught it yestiddy." Mabel turned. "Say, Martha, give me that Boss Manrow!"

"Boss Manrow?"

The leaves rustled.

"Boss Manrow: 17, 21, 37 . . ."

"Come on, Jake, and play it. You'll have your whole dream covered, then."

"Give me sixbits on that one, too. And that's all I'm going to play today. I ain't got but fifty cents to get to work and back."

"Honey, if all your numbers come you'll have two hundred dollars," said Mabel.

"Jeeesus," said Jake.

Mabel left him and wandered about the room, looking for other customers. Jake leaned against a wall and listened to the voices calling numbers. *Lawd, if I catch two hundred dollars I won't have to borrow nothing from Jones.*

"Jim, what you dream last night?"

"Man, I dream about snakes."

"Say, Martha, give me that Snakerow!"

"Snakerow? Snakerow: 16, 32, 64 . . ."

"Give me a dime on it. I want to try to catch something to pay my rent."

"Say, Honey, what you dream?"

"Lawd, child, I dreamed about a dead man!"

"A *dead* man?"

"Yes, siree! He was laidout right in my room."

"That Deadrow always pulls. You want a gig?"

"I ain't got but three cents."

"Anything with the name of Uncle Sam on it is good around here."

"O.K."

"Say, Martha, what's the Deadrow?"

"Deadrow? Deadrow: 9, 19, 29 . . ."

"You know one thing? I dreamed I saw a ghost last night."

"Ghostrow? Ghostrow: 20, 25, 30 . . ."

"What you dream?"

"Shucks, I dreamed I was pregnant."

"*Pregnant?*"

"Nothing different!"

Jake laughed and looked at the crowd surrounding the woman, eager to get her number in order to play her dream.

"I ain't never seen that Pregnantrow fail!"

"What's that, Martha?"

"Pregnantrow? Pregnantrow: 11, 22, 50 . . ."

"You better play it!"

"Books are closed! Books are closed!" a heavy voice called.

Jake turned and saw a fat, black man with a cigar in his mouth standing in the door leading to the Wheel.

"Books are closed!" echoed round and round the room.

Activity stopped. The Wheel was brought into the center of the floor; it consisted of a small wooden stand upon which rested a huge lard can. The can held 78 pieces of rubber hose cut to oneinch lengths. In each of these pieces of hose was a curled strip of oil cloth on which numbers had been stamped. A "checker" with a green eyeshade inspected the pieces of hose to see that all was fair. Two hundred pairs of eyes watched eagerly. Finally, it was ascertained to the satisfaction of all present that the 78 numbers were in the 78 pieces of hose.

"All right! Let her go!" the fat, black man called.

"Who wants to pull?"

"I do!"

"Let me pull!"

"Let a lady pull!"

"Naw, let a man pull!"

Jake pushed forward.

"Say, I ain't never pulled!" he called.

"Here's a man what ain't never pulled!"

"Yeah, let 'im pull! He'll be lucky!"

"Come you, if you want to pull!"

The crowd surged around Jake.

"Pull my number, partner!"

"Lawd, I hope you pulls something for me!"

Jake was blindfolded with a strip of black silk. The 78 pieces of hose were put into the lard can and shaken vigorously, then the top was eased off slowly so that the numbers would not be disturbed.

"All right, Mister, you can pull now."

Jake reached gropingly into the can. He was trembling. *Jeesus, if I can only pull my numbers!* Slowly and tenderly, he lifted twelve numbers, one after the other, lifted them as though he were lifting nuggets of gold. As he brought forth each piece of hose a "checker" took it and punched out the small bit of oil cloth and called the number.

"Lawd, have mercy! That's the first number of my gig!"

"Mister, please pull something for me!"

"All my numbers but *one*!"

"Lawd, let me catch something, let me catch something . . ."

A man in an inky apron hovered over a rickety machine and set each number into type as it was called. When the first "leg" was completed, the 12 pieces of hose with the bits of oil cloth reinserted were put back into the can with the rest of the numbers and shaken again. Then Jake pulled out 12 more numbers for the second "leg". Two seconds after the drawing stopped the machine clattered and a whirlwind of varicolored slips of paper began to pile up. Jake snatched the cloth from his eyes and grabbed one.

BLACK GOLD

192	AM	182
78		64
75		39
47		13
45		65
38		10
51		26
41		55
26		38
13		17
18		28
73		23
8		73

Sweat stood on his forehead as he compared his numbers with the numbers on the slip. *Let see now . . . Boss Manrow: 17, 21, 37 . . . Let see . . . Hunh! Only one number! 17 . . . Let's see about my Runningrow. 11, 15, 67 . . . Nothing fell . . . Gawd . . . Let me see my Steprow now. Lawd, I ought to catch something somewhere . . . Hot dog! Here's 17 . . . And here's my 26, over in the other leg . . . And ain't no 6 at all . . . Ain't that a bitch?* His lips hung loose and he stared vacantly at the floor. *Gawddamn these sonofabitching numbers!* He crushed the paper into a tight wad and threw it into a corner. *If I hadn't played them numbers I would've had two dollars anyhow, now I'm almost dead broke . . .* He stumbled out into the sunshine.

He walked slowly, head down, tugging at his collar; he felt hot and uncomfortable about the neck. It seemed as though everything was going wrong this morning. *First, it's Lil and her big mouth. Then it's these Gawddamn numbers! I'll never be fool enough to play them things again!* He crossed a street and turned north. *Yeah, maybe if I'd played all the numbers I could get on my dream, I would've won something.* Yes, he would try that next time. He would break that policy wheel yet. Just wait. He would win five hundred dollars, or maybe five thousand, or maybe five hundred thousand . . . He'd win so much the owner would be pleading with him to borrow some of it back so he could pay off his customers. Just wait.

He paused at a corner. *Wonder what Lil's doing now?* His muscles stiffened and there flashed through his mind a vivid picture of Lil talking to the milkman. *Yeah, that guy might've waited till he thought I was gone and slipped back up there. Maybe they's carrying on now? By Gawd!* His face hardened. *Yeah, any woman what won't have nothing to do with her own husband's sure messing with some other man.* He saw Lil as he had seen her that morning when he had come into the kitchen; he saw her head thrown back, her eyes closed with laughter, her shoulders shaking. He whirled and walked rapidly down an alley, heading toward home. No woman was going to cheat on him! Not if he could help it! He reached his alley and hurried down to his back gate. There was no milk wagon in sight. *Maybe he ain't there? But you can never tell. If he's there he's got sense enough not to leave his wagon setting out in the back of my house where I can see it. The wagon might be around the corner somewhere. And he might be up there right now . . .* He pulled up the back steps, taking them four at a time, his breath coming heavily. Gaining the landing, he crept softly to the glass panel of his kitchen door and peeped in. He relaxed. There was Lil, sitting almost as he had left her. She was still at the breakfast table. Her back was to the door and her face was buried in her arms. Jake smiled. A copy of *Unity* was spread with the pages open at her elbow; from where he was standing he could read the large type on the title page:

JESUS SILENTLY HELPS . . .

He eased back down the steps. *She's all right. But she better not try any tricks on me.* When he reached the street he walked idly, feeling a haunting and hungering sense of incompleteness.

V.

JAKE LOITERED in front of a movie house, looking at lurid posters. In the center of the sidewalk was a huge yellow billboard with purplebordered placards. A wide strip of green canvas with white letters read:

THE DEATH HAWK
For Three Days Only—See It Now
Tuesday—Wednesday—Thursday
—starring—
JACK BLACKSTONE   and   GLORIA GOLDENROD
GREATEST OF ALL FLYING PICTURES . . .
ACTION . . . SUSPENSE . . .
THRILLS AND STOLEN LOVE

He stepped closer.

The first poster showed

a bluehelmeted aviator in a bloodred monoplane darting shooting speeding zooming careening out of a bank of snow-white clouds in hot pursuit of two green monoplanes and just above the cockpit of the red plane the hero's head could be seen and his eyes were blazing deathly hate and his lips were skinned back over his teeth in a horrible avenging grin and the faces of the two aviators in the fleeing planes were desperate despairing hopeless and at the side of the hero sat a golden-haired blueeyed girl operating a machinegun spewing fire and death and the girl's hair was blown straight back in the wind and her eyes were widened in fear and

the next poster showed

the hero creeping into a darkened garage on feet of feathers upon a small ratlike creature who had a huge hammer and a gleaming chisel in his hands all raised and he was about to puncture the gas tank of an auto in which the goldenhaired girl was seated but behind the hero unsuspected unseen un-heard crept a blackbearded giant whose snarling teeth were stained no doubt by whiskey or tobacco juice and who had a

huge monkeywrench upraised and ready to swish crash smash
heave it down upon the curly head of the innocent hero and

the next poster showed

a group of gangsters who looked like mexicans or japs or reds
or huns or just some kind of desperate foreigners and these
men were stationed high upon the edge of a sheer cliff overlooking the sea and a rocky coast far below and two of them
had the hero's bound tied trussed body upon their shoulders
and were about to dash it far below to the rocks and the
hero's body was tense taut alert straining against the ropes
that held him and instead of looking with horror at the rocks
far below which meant death he was gazing with love into the
eyes of the goldenhaired blueeyed girl who lay on the ground
gagged tied bound trussed and above the girl stood a darkly
handsome stranger in a tall silk hat and a winged collar and a
frocked coat and in his delicate snowwhite hands which had
never worked hard and honestly for a living was a tiny pearl-
handled revolver and his slitty black eyes were fastened hard
upon the girl's exposed thigh and his red lips were smirking
and

the next poster showed

the darkly handsome stranger seated in the dimlit booth of a
chinese restaurant with all those funny kind of writings all
round the wall you know the kind of writing that looks like a
bunch of snakes all trying to bite one another and the goldenhaired girl was seated opposite the darkly handsome stranger
and she was dabbing her large beautiful sleepy dreamy pale
blue eyes with a tiny white handkerchief and the darkly handsome stranger was looking at her with infinite satisfaction as
he twirled his waxed mustache and immediately behind the
girl's chair partly hidden by thick black curtains unsuspected
unseen unheard stood an evileyed slanteyed yellowfaced
spoolchinned bonycheeked tightlipped chinkchink chinaman
and in his long skinny yellow fingers fingers that had nails
that could slit a man's jugular vein and in these fingers was a
black vial with the word knockout drops marked plainly and
the chinaman was slowly dropping black drops into the girl's
glass unsuspected unseen unheard and

the next poster showed

the brunette hero having recovered from his death dash into the sea in the process of delivering a fast hard straight sweet true uppercut to the darkly handsome stranger's chin and

the next poster showed

three planes high over mountains and two of the planes were green and one was red and the red plane was sailing free and easy into the clouds with machinegun smoking and the two green planes were enveloped in smoke and flames and were headed earthward in dizzy tailspins and

the last poster showed

the hero and the goldenhaired blueeyed girl seated comfort- ably in their bloodred monoplane which was zooming like an eagle into a rosy afterglow and the hero's hands were resting lightly upon the controls but the girl's arms were about him and their lips were meeting in a blissful kiss . . .

Jake wagged his head and sighed. If the show had been open he would have gone in, but it did not open until one o'clock and he had to go to work. *That must be a damn good picture. I'd like to see it before it leaves this place. Being a aviator sure must be fun, 'specially when you on top of another plane and can send it spinning down like that . . .* As he turned away his eyes lingered on the poster where the girl was tied so that her thigh was exposed.

VI.

IF IT AIN'T old Jake Jackson, the bigleaguer!"
Jake felt a hard clap on his right shoulder.

"Well, if it ain't old Streamline!" said Jake, shaking hands with a small, yellow, bareheaded man whose coalblack hair was brushed close to his head.

"Lawd, Jake, I ain't seen you since we was in the minor league."

"Yeah, it's been a long time," said Jake.

"How you hitting these days?"

"Oh, soso. I ain't complaining. How's it with you?"

"Can't even see the ball, boy! Tough titty!"

"What's the matter?"

"They just throwing that ball too fast for me, Jake."

"I reckon it's tough for everybody," said Jake.

"Tough ain't no word for it. Man, sometimes I can't even get to the plate."

"Yeah?"

"Look like the game's about over for me if I don't get some work soon . . ."

"It's really tough."

"I can't hit. All I can do is bunt and run it out . . ."

"Aw, it's a bitch," said Jake, pursing his lips and looking off.

They were silent for a moment. Jake looked at Streamline's shabby clothes. *He's raggety's a dime mop . . .* He felt a little sorry for Streamline, but not too sorry. Streamline's slick black hair always irked him, made him envious and uneasy. That was why he was called Streamline, on account of that slick, straight, black hair of his. *And that old stuck up sonofa-bitch struts around bareheaded just to show off his slick wool. He thinks he's better than anybody else just 'cause he's yellow . . .*

"You still playing ball for Uncle Sam, Jake?"

"Yeah," Jake answered dryly. "I'm still going."

"You lucky if you still on somebody's team."

"Well, I don't know about that," said Jake, regaining his sense of superiority and feeling that he could allow something. "When you boil it all down, it's just the same with everybody. Even with my good job I ain't got nothing."

"But when you got a job you on firstbase," said Streamline.

"Oh, it beats a blank," Jake conceded ruefully, lighting a cigarette.

Streamline shifted restlessly from one foot to the other, watching Jake out of the corner of his eyes.

"Say, Jake, couldn't you be a pinchhitter for a poor guy that's down and out? I hate to ask you, but I ain't eat today . . ."

"Honest to Gawd, Streamline, I ain't got nothing but carfare to work and back. I just got through paying the milkman . . ."

"That's all right," said Streamline hastily. "It's a damn tough game."

"If I had it, I'd let you have it. You know I would . . ."

"Sure, sure . . . You always played ball."

They were silent again. Jake gazed down to the corner where the traffic lights flashed from green to red, and back to green again. He spat carefully into the gutter.

"Swell day."

"Yeah, it'll be time for baseball pretty soon."

"You get tired of staying cooped up in the house all the time."

"Say, wasn't that too bad about old Mussellinni going over into Ethiopia and knocking old Haile Salassie for a homerun?"

"Wasn't it, though?" answered Jake.

"And Jeeesus, old Joe Louis losing to Schmeling."

"Boy, that made me sick," said Jake.

"You know," said Streamline seriously, "it looks like we black folks is just about to be shutout. We done got two outs on us in the ninth inning. Old Haile Salassie and Joe Louis *both* done struck out!"

"Seems that way," said Jake, wagging his head.

"Well, I'm moving on and see if I can't steal a base on somebody," said Streamline, laughing uneasily.

"See you later."

"So long."

VII.

IN THE MIDDLE of the block Jake saw coming toward him a young black girl whose little firm breasts shook with each step she took. He stared hard and unblinkingly at the gentle sway of her buttocks until she turned a corner. Another woman passed and he could see the prints of her breasts even through the spring coat she wore. He looked at the store-fronts to see where he was. *Doc's place is along here somewhere. Yeah, there it is, down the street a bit.* He walked toward a barberpole that revolved in the sunshine like a bright stick of peppermint candy. Above the pole swung a sign.

DOC HIGGINS' TONSORIAL PALACE

He pressed his face against the glass and looked inside. The shop was crowded with a mass of waving arms and flashing teeth and twisted black faces. *What in the world's going on in there?* He pushed into the doorway, sniffing odors of hair lo-tion and lather. A whirlwind argument was raging; everybody was screaming at once, contending for the right to speak by trying to drown out the other's voice. He edged in as far as he could and then tiptoed to get a look. In the center of the crowd five black faces were yelling at one another. He caught a glimpse of Doc Higgins, his small, fat mouth opening and shutting rapidly, his head bobbing back and forth as though his neck were made of rubber. At the end of each sentence Doc's head would jerk violently backward, making his white goatee and white hair tremble. His voice was far heavier than all the rest, and he finally took the floor by sheer lungpower, pounding his chubby fist into his fat palm. *Yeah, this is good! Old Doc's setting on somebody!*

"Nigger, is you a plumb fool?" screamed Doc.

"Wait, let me tell you something, Doc," pleaded Duke, a skinny, black man with a sharp face.

"You can't tell me nothing," shouted Doc Higgins.

"Listen to me a minute, will you, Doc!"

"Listen to you for what?"

"I want to tell you something . . ."

"How come I got to listen to a little snot like you?"

"If you'll just listen I'll tell you a lot you ought to know!"

"Like hell you will!"

The crowd surged, pushing one another.

"Let 'im talk, Doc!"

"Give 'im a chance, Doc!"

"What's the matter, you scared, Doc?"

Doc whirled, his eyes blazing.

"I ain't scared of nothing that's born of woman!"

"Let me talk, then," asked Duke.

Doc took a swift step backwards and swept Duke with his eyes from his head to his feet.

"What you know about life?"

"All due respect to your white hair, I knows a lot more than you."

"Listen, boy," said Doc, mildly and compassionately, "I was kicking and scratching in this old world before you were kneehigh to a grasshopper . . ."

"Aw, Doc, let Duke talk!"

"He's scared," said Duke.

"Naw, I ain't scared. I just ain't going to let no dirty little sneaking Commoonist come in here and tell me what to do with my money! Get out and make your own money, like I did!"

Everybody shouted and Jake edged closer. The argument had him keyed to a high pitch. He was itching to get into it. He could handle guys like Duke. *Just let me get at 'im!* Each time Doc spoke he followed the movements of Doc's lips with his own and nodded approval.

"Where can a man get a job?" Duke screamed.

"You don't want no job!" Doc bawled.

"That's a lie and you know it!"

"Aw, Duke, I know your kind inside and out!"

"Answer his question, Doc. He asked you where can a man get a job!"

"I ain't suppose to tell 'im," said Doc.

"We ain't the only ones who's out of work," said Duke.

"So what?"

"Times ain't like they was when you was young, Doc."

"So what?"

"How can a man get a job when there ain't none?"

"Make your own job like I did!"

"Doc, you can't see facts! You blind!"

"Aw, you niggers full of crap!"

Doc whirled around and bumped into Jake.

" 'Lo, Jake." He grabbed Jake's shoulder and turned again to Duke. "Here's a sensible young man with a good, steady job. Here's somebody your own age. Ask 'im something. Say, Jake, tell this loudmouthed Know Nothing something!"

Jake smiled and looked down at the keen creases in his trousers. Duke eyed him sullenly.

"How many before me, Doc?" asked Jake, ignoring him.

"You next."

When Jake pulled off his coat and vest his government badge glittered on his suspenders. Doc pointed to it.

"See that, Duke?"

"Yeah. What about it?"

"This man's with Uncle Sam, win, lose, or draw."

"He's losing," said Duke.

"Like hell I is!" snapped Jake. "What you think you going to do, overthrow the government?"

"If we have to, yes."

Jake laughed, without smiling, mirthlessly.

"Nigger, you'd last as long trying to overthrow the government as a fart in a wind storm!"

Doc grabbed the back of the barberchair and let out a high, whinnying laugh.

"I ain't alone," said Duke stubbornly. "There's millions like me. Maybe not in this country yet, but over in Russia . . ."

"There he goes!" said Jake. "If you talk to a crackbrain two minutes he'll start slobbering about Roosia! Why can't you *red* niggers get some sense in your heads? Don't you know them Reds is just using you? When they get tired of you they throw you away like a dirty sock! Look at the Doc here! He's a race man! A precinct captain. A business man. A property owner. He's got pull with all the big politicians down in the Loop. And here you, raggety and dirty, going around talking about overthrowing the government. Doc's setting pretty; why don't you play the game? What you bellyaching about?"

"Gawddamn right I'm setting pretty," mumbled Doc, stropping his razor. "And I'm going to stay that way."

"You guys just wait and see," said Duke. "A few of you guys got something, but most of the black people in this country ain't got nothing. All them sharecroppers . . ."

"To hell with them!" said Jake. "Let 'em look out after themselves!"

"But they ain't got nothing to eat," insisted Duke.

"Is you hungry?" asked Jake, taking a dime out of his pocket.

"Naw," said Duke.

"Well, what you squawking about?"

"There's thousands of people starving . . ."

"Is we the cause of that?" asked Doc.

"Naw, but it don't make no difference . . ."

"Listen Duke," said Doc, slipping his arm around Duke's shoulders. "Let me tell you a story. Once upon a time there was a little frog. Somebody threw that frog into a churn of milk. Now that frog kicked and kicked and kicked and tried to get out. After awhile he saw little pieces of yellow butter coming, like little pieces of gold, see? Well, the frog kept kicking and kicking and all that butter came together into one great big yellow ball. Then, you know what that frog did? He jumped on top of that ball of butter and hopped right out of the churn . . ." Doc paused and pulled from his pocket a thick roll of green bills. "You see this?"

"Yeah," mumbled Duke.

"You know what this is?"

"It's money . . ."

"Naw, fool! It's butter!"

Jake bent to the floor and slapped his thigh. Doc held the roll of bills for awhile under Duke's nose, then rammed it back into his pocket, and let out a long laugh. The crowd began to file slowly out, making wry faces at one another.

"Go get some butter, you chumps!" yelled Jake.

"You guys just wait," threatened Duke.

"You talk like a fool," said Doc.

"Two fools," said Jake.

Duke filed out with the rest and slammed the door.

"Did you ever see such a nutty bastard?" asked Doc, tucking the white cloth around Jake's neck.

"Doc," said Jake. "Niggers is just like a bunch of crawfish

in a bucket. When one of 'em gets smart and tries to climb out of the bucket, the others'll grab hold of 'im and pull 'im back . . ."

"Ain't it the truth? What can you do with such a fool?"

"He'll wake up some day," said Jake.

They were silent a moment. Doc combed Jake's hair, preparatory to cutting it.

"Well, what you know, Jake?"

"I'm having trouble with that bitch of mine."

"Yeah, what seems to be the matter?"

"Aw, she's sick again."

"What's the trouble this time?"

"She's gone and got herself a tumor."

"A tumor?"

"Yeah."

"Gee, man, that's serious," said Doc, shaking his head sympathetically.

"Now she's got to be operated on."

"Damn, that's tough."

"It's going to cost me five hundred bucks."

Doc took a huge chew of tobacco and spat a long brown stream into a spittoon.

"She's sticking you up aplenty . . ."

"But that ain't half of it."

"What's happened?"

"Aw, I had to slap her a few times this morning."

"That's bad. She might report you."

"Yeah, that's just what I'm scared of."

"You know the government's pretty hard on you now for things like that."

"That's what I want to talk with you about."

"O.K. Shoot."

"You know I've been up before that Board twice."

"Yeah, and they ain't standing for no foolishness now. They know times is bad and they can always get men to work."

"You still got some pull with the Post Master, ain't you?"

"Well, in a way."

"I want you to put in a good word for me, Doc."

"Well, Jake, I'm telling you. So much has been going on lately, it's sort of hard to get at them guys unless."

"Unless what?"

"Well, you have to make them guys want to talk to you. You see, I have to go through four or five men now to get to the Post Master. And them guys want money."

"What do you think it'll cost?"

"It'll cost you a hundred dollars, Jake."

"Jeeesus, Doc!"

"Aw, I know it's tough, Jake. But that's the way the land lays these days . . ."

"But, Doc, I got to pay out five hundred for that operation."

They were silent. Doc was now cutting Jake's hair with the clippers. *Buzzzzzzzzz* . . . The big clock on the wall went *ticktock . . . ticktock . . . ticktock . . .* Jake lit a cigarette and spat a shred of tobacco. Doc laid his hand on Jake's shoulder.

"Well, Jake, I'll tell you. Since it's you, and since you're a friend of mine, I'll do the job for seventyfive."

"You can't do no better?"

"Not a cent."

"Well, how soon can you get to the Post Master?"

"When can you give me something?"

"Payday."

"How much?"

"Maybe I can squeeze out a fivedollar payment . . ."

"O.K. Since it's you, Jake, I'll do it."

"That's swell, Doc. Gee, that sure takes a big load off my chest. If she done been down I'll 'phone you, and tell 'em, Doc, that that woman of mine is just nuts, see? Tell 'em I'm doing all I can."

"Just leave it to me. I'll fix it up."

The clippers went *buzzzzzzzzzzz* . . . Jake took a last draw from his cigarette and flicked it into the spittoon.

"You know, Jake, some niggers is sure funny."

"What's that?"

"I was just thinking about Duke."

"Aw," said Jake, waving his hand. "Them kind of niggers is crazy!"

"But what we going to do with 'em?"

"Say, don't you worry. If they tie up with them Reds and

start anything, the white folks'll take care of 'em good and plenty."

"You know one thing?"

"What's that?"

"Niggers talk too much."

"Nothing hurts a duck but his bill."

"If they kept their damn mouths shut and tried to get hold of something, some money, or property, then they'd get somewhere."

"Sure. Now, what would I do in my case if it wasn't for men like you who's done something and can help me?"

"That's right."

"Aw, them niggers ought to be taken out and shot."

"Shooting's too good for 'em."

They were silent again. Doc was now trimming Jake's hair with the shears. *Clip . . . Clip . . . Clip . . . Clip . . .* Doc spat the long brown stream into the spittoon.

"Swell weather we're having."

"You bet."

"Feel's like spring's done come."

"Yeah; and it feels good, too."

"Make's a man feel young again."

"That ain't no lie."

Jake looked out of the window at the traffic moving by. He began to hum a tune and swing his feet gently. Then, for some inexplicable reason, he stopped humming and began to whistle softly. With a look of boredom, he stopped whistling and watched the reflection of Doc in the mirror. He followed the shining glint of the shears as they rose and fell. Sighing, he looked out of the window again. Like a scrap of paper blown by wind, his attention wandered. He looked at the ceiling. At the floor. Then at the flyspecked electric globe that burned above his head. His eyes finally rested on a faded calendar. For the want of something better to do he spelled out the words slowly in a low breath:

GUARANTEED INSURANCE

He frowned. Sighed. Crossed his legs. Lit another cigarette. Drummed his fingers on the arm of the chair.

"Say, Jake?"

"Yeah?"

"You see in the papers where old lady Lucy Rosenball donated a million dollars to the colored folks for a college down south?"

"Yeah, I was reading about that. That was swell."

"Wasn't it, though?"

"That means the colored people's making progress."

"You bet."

"You know, she sure is a nice old lady."

"Yeah. The paper said she's done donated about five million to build a hospital for stray cats and dogs."

"Now you know she must got a kind heart."

"Yeah, some white folks is good, that way."

"You know, I always said that we colored folks ought to stick with the rich white folks . . ."

"That's the only way we'll ever get anywhere."

"Ain't that what old Booker Washington said? Cooperate and get along?"

"That's right."

"That's what Duke ought to think about instead of running around here talking about overthrowing the government . . ."

"Aw, he's crazy!"

"Wonder what in the world can be wrong with some folks' brains?"

"Just dumb, that's all. Just plain dumb."

As the shears clipped about Jake's neck he sighed, and lazily shifted his weight from one buttock to the other. The continual clipping made him drowsy.

"Just a minute," said Doc. "I want to turn on the radio."

"O.K."

The radio poured forth a volume of martial music; the music stopped and a man spoke:

. . . THE MYSTIC CHORDS OF MEMORY, STRETCHING FROM EVERY BATTLEFIELD AND PATRIOT GRAVE TO EVERY LIVING HEART AND HEARTHSTONE ALL OVER THIS BROAD LAND, WILL YET SWELL THE CHORUS OF THE UNION WHEN AGAIN TOUCHED, AS THEY SURELY WILL BE, BY THE BETTER ANGELS OF OUR NATURE . . .

"What's that?" asked Doc.

"What?"

"That on the radio. A speech or something?"

"Aw, naw. Just something about the Civil War," said Jake, yawning.

"Civil War?"

"Yeah. This is old Abe Lincoln's Birthday, you know."

"Oh."

. . . LET US FORGET OURSELVES AND JOIN HANDS, LIKE BROTHERS, TO SAVE THE REPUBLIC. IF WE SUCCEED, THERE WILL BE GLORY ENOUGH FOR ALL . . .

Jake listened awhile and was soon sleeping again. He tilted forward.

"Hold up!"

"Hunh?"

"Set up straight, man."

Jake straightened, shook his head and sucked back loose saliva. The shears went *clip . . . clip . . . clip . . . clip . . .* The clipping and the radio made Jake doze again. Doc spat his long brown stream.

"Say, Jake?"

"Yeah?"

"That Civil War sure was some war, wasn't it?"

"You bet your sweet life it was," said Jake, belching.

"And a lot of guys was killed in that war, too."

"War's a bad thing."

"Oh, yeah. War's bad all right."

"And old Abe Lincoln sure was a smart man."

"A *great* man."

"He was what I call a man of Gawd," said Doc in a deep, bass voice.

"He couldn't've done what he done if he didn't have Gawd with 'im," said Jake.

"You got to take Gawd with you."

"Yeah, because you can't do nothing without 'im."

"You know, that makes me think of a good old Christian woman I used to know," began Doc. "She was a widow with nine children on her hands. And man, you know one thing, that woman raised all nine of them children and not a one of them was ever in a jail."

"Gawd sure must have been with her," said Jake, wagging his head in admiration.

"You *know* He was!"

"He's the only one what can guide you through such tough days as that."

"The only one."

"You know, I heard about a soljer that went through the war wearing a Bible right next to his heart. He went all through the war and come out without a *scratch*."

"See what *faith* can do!"

"Folks in the old days use to work miracles."

"Jesus walked on water, you know."

"It's all in how much faith you got."

"Yeah, faith's the main thing."

"Faith can move mountains."

Doc's mouth became full of spit and he could not talk. The shears went *clip . . . clip . . . clip . . . clip . . .* Jake's head tilted.

"Hold up Jake."

"Oh, Lawd! Man, I'm sleepy's hell!"

. . . PRESIDENT LINCOLN ISSUED A CALL FOR VOLUN- TEERS. THE RESPONSE WAS OVERWHELMING IN ITS GEN- EROSITY AND INTENSITY. THE MINERS, THE FARMERS, AND WORKERS OF ALL TRADES DROPPED THEIR TOOLS AND SWARMED INTO THE RANKS OF THE UNION ARMIES . . .

"O.K."

"You through?"

"Yeah."

Jake got down and stretched.

"What's the damages, Doc?"

"Four bits."

Jake paid, giving fifteen cents for a tip.

"Thanks. Come in soon."

"O.K. And don't forget what I told you about my wife."

"Oh, naw. I'll telephone right down when you get in touch with me."

Jake put on his hat and coat.

"See you later, Old Timer."
"So long, Big Shot."
As he went through the door the radio sang:

> . . . JOHN BROWN'S BODY LIES AMOULDERING
> IN THE GRAVE,
> HIS SOUL GOES MARCHING ON . . .

VIII.

JAKE STOOD on the corner of 47th Street and Forestville
Avenue. Sunshine was spread everywhere and the intense
light hurt his eyes. His arms and legs felt heavy and slightly
numb, as though they were watersoaked. He licked his lips,
mumbling, *Gawd, but I'm sleepy.* If he could only sleep right
now, if he could only close his eyes and rest his head upon
something soft. There was in the air a faint, sweet smell, a
tantalizing presage of spring. A slow restlessness made him
wriggle his toes in his shoes. He had a longing to see green
grass, to go into the park and stretch out flat on his back with
his face to the sky. He fumbled in his vestpocket for a match,
split it with a thumbnail, and dug at a cavity in a back tooth.
He took out his watch; it was nine o'clock. He had a full
three hours before worktime. He leaned against a steel telephone post and let the match dangle loosely from his lips. He
wanted to go somewhere, but he could not think of a suitable
place. Above all, he did not want to go home; he was in no
mood to argue with Lil now. *But that bitch better watch her
step.* He looked at the pavement; something cold seemed to
come over him. *Yeah, I been too easy with her. I got to crack
down; I been letting her have her way too long.* Two thin spirals
of smoke eddied from his nostrils into sunshine. He squinted
his eyes, feeling lazy and restless and a little sad. He wanted
something, and that something hungered in him, deeply. He
went into a drugstore, bought a package of cigarettes, and
walked west on 47th Street to his favorite poolroom, the *Side-
Pocket Billiard Nook*; but he did not go in. The noise emanat-
ing from the halfopened doorway told him that he was not in
a mood for the antics of the old gang. But where could he
go? He wondered if his pal, Bob, were up. *Dammit, that's the
big trouble with Bob; he always sleeps so late.* Well, he had to kill
some time; he turned on to South Parkway and went south,
swinging his body importantly. About him traffic roared and
horns honked. People came and went; each seemed to have a
definite destination. Their hurry made him hurry. He turned
to his right and walked up 48th Street. He was going to
Bob's, but, really, he did not want to go to Bob's. He wanted

to go somewhere else; he thought of a certain apartment and a certain woman. He looked at his watch again; it was five minutes past nine. *Yeah, that's the big trouble with working part of the day and part of the night. When you're off there ain't no place to go.* He paused at 48th Street and Michigan Avenue, in front of the George Cleveland Hall Branch of the Chicago Public Library. People were going in and out. Across the door a sign read:

LIBRARY CLOSED—LEGAL HOLIDAY
Only Reference Rooms Opened

He studied the building with curiosity. *That's right. I ain't never looked around in one of them joints.* The rows upon rows of dullcolored books struck him as being peculiarly odd. They seemed somehow funny, something like a game, or like the little dolls in a shooting gallery. He tiptoed and saw many people bent over desks. *I wonder what they charge you to go in there?* He had long planned to visit one of these places, but it had always happened that he could never get around to it. *I'd just like to go in and look around, like I done that time me and Lil went to the Field Museum.* But not today. *Naw, naw, not today.* He would go some other time when he had lots of time; that would be better. Some Saturday afternoon when he was off and did not have anything else to do. *Yeah, it would be a damn good idea to come here for a picnic someday, bring a nice big lunch and stay around all day. Then I can tell old Bob and Al and Slim all about the big books I seen and they'll be jealous as hell . . .*

He walked toward 47th Street again, and near the end of the block he saw a black boy sitting in a window reading a book. He shook his head. *Too much reading's bad.* It was all right to read the newspapers, and things like that; but reading a lot of books with fine print in them and no pictures would drive you crazy. Especially young people. His mind went back to his boyhood; he remembered a schoolmate of his who had become queer from trying to memorize the Bible. *Yeah, too much reading's bad. It addles your brains, and if you addle your brains you'll sure have bookworms in the brain.* His poor old grandmother had told him that when he was a child, and he had never forgotten it, and had never had bookworms. But it was all right if you were studying for the pulpit. *Oh, yeah;*

that's different. Gawd's angels'll watch over you then and keep you from going crazy. And anyhow, making folks crazy was God's way with those who wanted to know too much. Many are called and few are chosen. He had never been chosen.

When he reached Bob's place he stood on the sidewalk, smoking, and could not make up his mind. Well, he might as well. He had nothing else to do. He went into the vestibule, rang the bell, and in answer to a buzzer, climbed to the third apartment. Bob, a man as black as himself, stood holding the door.

"Think about the Devil and he comes!"

"Who you calling a Devil?"

"You, you rascal!"

"How you today, Bob?"

"Soso. How's yourself?"

"Aw, pretty good. What you know?"

"Nothing. Same old 6's and 7's. What you know?"

"Nothing, man. I was just passing and thought I'd drop in."

"I'm glad you come. I was just setting here wishing somebody'd come along."

"If Al and Slim'd come over we could have a good game of bridge."

"Yeah, Lawd. Set down."

"O.K."

"Smoke?"

"Naw, got some."

They lit cigarettes and puffed awhile silently.

"How's the weather out?"

"Swell. Feels like spring."

"I sure wish summer'd hurry up and come on."

"Yeah, give me summer any day."

"Me too, boy."

"But we got a lot of cold weather coming yet."

"Oh, no doubt of that."

"March'll bring a lot of cold blizzards."

"And April a lot of sleet and rain."

"Yeah, we got a lot of cold weather coming yet."

"Oh, yeah."

Bob coughed up something into his mouth and swallowed it.

"Say, what we doing tonight?" he asked.

"How about this new place I was telling you about?"

"Where is it?"

"Over on Calumet."

"Who runs it?"

"Aw, some dame named Rose. They got gambling, women . . ."

"That suits me."

"But I'm broke."

"Same here."

"Say, if I can get a loan from old Jones today, will you sign for me?"

"Sure."

"I tried to catch some policy this morning, but didn't have no luck."

"Aw, them numbers ain't no good."

Jake leaned back in his chair and yawned.

"I ssssure dddonnnnnn't feeeel like wwwworking to-day . . ."

"Me neither."

"Feels sort of lowdown."

"Gee, I hate to have that feeling come down on me."

"That old lazy, blue feeling . . ."

"If I had some dough we could go to that flat we was at last Tuesday."

"Jeeeesus!"

They looked at each other and grinned.

"Say?" asked Jake.

"Hunh?"

"Got anything on your hip?"

"Sure, want a little nip?"

"Yeah, I'm in the dumps."

"O.K."

Bob left for the interior of the flat and came back with a small glass and an ambercolored flask.

"Help yourself."

"Naw, you pour it."

Bob poured the glass full.

"Ain't you drinking?" asked Jake.

"Naw, I'm on the wagon."

"Aw, man, come on. Ain't no fun this way."

"Naw, I tell you."

"What's the matter?"

"Aw . . ."

Bob halfturned and waved his hand disgustedly.

"What's eating you?"

"It's down on me again, Jake."

"You let a little thing like that keep you from drinking?"

"It's running, Jake. The doctor said . . ."

"Aw, hell!"

Jake tossed the whiskey down his throat, then sat looking at Bob with a pitying smile.

"Listen, Bob, that ain't no worse'n a bad cold. That doctor don't know what he's talking about. I had it. A man ain't a man unless he's done had it. Come on and drink."

"Naw, the last time I got drunk I nearly died."

"You ain't no good."

"Humph!" grunted Bob. "Man, you don't *know*. This thing's a bitch! I been around here feeling like I wanted to go out every hour and pull up trees by their roots!"

"Who you catch it from?"

"I wish I could find the bitch!"

"Gee, nigger, you in a helluva fix. Your wife riding you for alimony, and you got a dose."

"It's hell," said Bob, sitting down and stretching out his legs.

"Well," said Jake. "You ain't no worse off'n me."

"How's that?"

Jake told Bob of Lil, of how Doc had promised to help him, and of how much he owed.

"Hell, you lucky and don't know it," said Bob.

"You nuts!"

"Listen, long as that old wife stays single, I got to pay that twenty bucks a week alimony for her and them kids. On top of that I got my own expenses. And on top of that, I got this damn dose. Some times I think I'm going nuts, no kidding . . . It's hell when you have to set in your room, knowing even if you went out you can't do nothing. You know, I never knowed what a woman meant till this thing got so bad on me. I just set here and feel like running and jumping straight through that stone wall."

"You ain't no good," said Jake, taking another drink. "Ain't you really going to take just one . . . One won't hurt you."

"Not so you can notice it."

"The trouble with you is, you was too easy on your wife," Jake said meditatively. "You ought to seen me bearing down on old Lil this morning."

"Yeah, I wish I had beat her now," said Bob. "She lied to the judge and told 'im I beat her anyhow."

"See? Either you trick them or they'll trick you."

"I reckon you right. I know if I had it to go through with again I'd sure do different. And just think . . ." Bob stood up, his lips flexing. "Just think that old bitch told the judge I was running around with other women, and what was *she* doing?"

"They all that way, Bob."

"She made me pay the court costs and I believe my soul there was something between her and that lawyer. One of these days I'm going to get good and mad and throw up everything. Sometimes I feel like quitting my job just to get even with her."

"Yeah, but ain't no use of cutting off your nose to spite your face."

Bob smote his fist in his palm, sighed, and sat down again.

"Uuuuunmp! This is good stuff," said Jake, licking his lips. "Hell, Bob, take a little, just a little."

"I tell you I ain't drinking. I can't forget last time. Honest to Gawd, I felt like taking that Tribune Tower and turning it bottomside upwards a hundred times a day."

They were silent. Steam hissed in the radiator. Jake belched and nestled his head deep into a corner of the sofa. He was pleasantly vacuous; he could hear the faint noises in the street below and now and then the dull rumble of the faraway "L". He crossed his legs, uncrossed them, sat up straight for about five seconds, leaned over a second, then sat up straight again.

"Gawd, I wish Al and Slim would come on."

"Me too."

"We could have a game then."

"Don't time pass slow?"

"Don't it?"

"Just drags."

"Makes you nervous."

" 'Specially when you ain't got nothing to do."

"I never did like to just *set*."

"Me neither."

"Yeah, it gets on your nerves."

Jake took another drink.

"Say, ain't it too bad about Slim?"

"Jake, he's a sick man."

"You reckon . . ."

"He's getting worst."

"That guy ought to go west for his T.B."

"If he stays around here he's making a date with the under-taker."

"The Post Office ain't no place for a man with consumption."

"You telling me?"

"He was so weak the other day he had to check out and go home."

"Was that the reason why he left?"

"Sure. He was about to drop."

"Yeah, his eyes is always feverish."

"He keeps a fever around a hundred all the time."

"Jeeesus!"

"You know, it goes all through me just to hear that guy cough."

"Yeah, seems like his insides is coming up."

"And he drinks too damn much."

"Maybe he wants to keep from worrying."

"Maybe so."

"Hell, he ain't got but a few more years. He just as well get something out of life. You don't live but once."

"Shucks, Bob, you got it easy, compared with him."

"Yeah, I reckon I'm lucky after all."

"Ain't it funny about folks what's got T.B. They a hound for women . . ."

"Yeah, looks like Slim just can't get enough."

"Lawd, that guy sure loves his meat."

"He's a hound dog from way back yonder."

"Looks like T.B. just drives 'em to it."

"Yeah, old Slim just can't help himself."

"He's a good old fellow, though."

"They don't make 'em any better'n Slim."

"Yeah, he's a brick."

"Ain't it funny how two guys like Slim and Al can be so different?"

"Ain't it, though? Al's a mess! That nigger thinks he's a bigshot."

"He's a sarjant in the National Guard now."

"For *real*?"

"Sure. He got a drag with the Colonel."

"He's always bragging about what a great soljer he is."

"But he's the toughest nigger I ever seen."

"He don't never get tired."

"He ain't got sense enough to get tired."

"And can eat! Lawd!"

"Al says he's going to get what he can out of this world 'cause he don't live but once."

"Maybe he's right."

"Maybe so."

"Lawd, but I ain't never seen a nigger stingy's he is."

"He says he saving his money to be a bigtime politician."

"That nigger tried to make a political speech during the elections. He got up in a church and forgot what he was going to say. Did the people laugh? . . ."

"He says he's going to open up a beer tavern next year."

"He's always going to *do* something."

"You know one thing, we here laughing at old Al, but that nigger is just dumb enough to turn out to be something sure enough."

"Yeah, you never can tell."

"A lot of folks who ain't nothing turn out to be something, sometimes."

The door bell rang.

"That maybe Al or Slim now," said Bob, rising and going into the hall.

"How you, mugs!" a deep, bass voice boomed from down the stairs.

"It's Al," Bob hollered to Jake.

"Tell 'im to come on up!" said Jake.

Al, fat, black, filled the doorway with a yellow chinchilla coat. He was puffing, pursing his lips and walling his eyes.

"Lawd, to come up them steps of yours just about kills a man!"

"Aw, come on," said Jake. "You can stand it. You a soljer, ain't you?"

"When you drag two hundred and fifty pounds up three floors, you done done something, if you ask me." He threw his coat and hat over on the sofa, then turned and looked searchingly at Jake and Bob. "What's wrong with you two guys? You look like a couple of sick hens."

"Nothing wrong with me," said Jake.

"Like hell there ain't," said Al gruffly, "I was just by Doc's getting a shave and he told me."

"Well, ain't that enough to be droopy about?" asked Jake.

"And what's wrong with you?" asked Al, turning to Bob.

"Same old thing."

"What's eating you guys? Snap out of it! Don't let that stuff worry you!"

"Al, you the funniest guy!" said Jake. "Don't you never worry?"

"Worry for what?"

"About things?"

"Hell, naw!"

"Not even about that yellow gal who left you?"

"I can get another one just like the other one," said Al. "They all feel alike in the dark."

"You just like a piece of iron," mumbled Bob.

"How you do it, Al?" asked Jake.

"Join the National Guard and find out," said Al.

"I want to ask you something, Al."

"Shoot."

"What you eat for breakfast this morning?"

Al pushed back his coat and hat on the sofa and stretched out, his face turned ceilingward. He puffed a few moments; trying to get his breath.

"Let's see now . . . I ate half a loaf of bread, all toasted golden brown and buttered. I reckon, I ain't sure now, but I reckon I ate about ten scrambled eggs; it might've been more. And a pound of bacon dripping with good old grease. And a pot of coffee. And some plum preserves. I had a apple on my way here, and I'm hungry now."

"Good Gawd!"

"Nigger, how come you eat that way?"

" 'Cause I like to."

"No wonder you don't never worry."

"I'm going to be eating when I die," said Al.

"Have a drink," said Bob. "You, too, Jake."

They poured drinks.

"Bob ain't drinking," said Jake to Al. "He's running."

"You bad as a little baby," said Al.

"Now if Slim would come we could have that game," said Jake.

"Yeah, I feel like bridge this morning," said Al.

"It wouldn't be bad," said Bob, rising. "I'll be back in a moment."

Al and Jake laughed.

"Don't turn over the house, now!"

"I'm going home," said Jake jokingly. "You might come running out of that bathroom and want to choke us to death."

"You guys wait till you get a dose, then you'll see it ain't nothing to laugh about."

"Aw, you just ain't no good."

When Bob was gone, Al and Jake emptied the flask.

"You know," said Al, licking his lips, "a guy in New York done sent a man here to open a church down on Michigan. The guy says he's Gawd."

"Gawd?" asked Jake, straightening.

"Yeah; he calls hisself Father Divine."

"What's wrong with 'im?"

"I don't know. All I know is, he sent a disciple here and folks is over there praying to 'im."

"Jeeesus Christ," said Jake. "Do they sure enough believe 'im?"

"They must to, they pray to 'im."

"What he tell 'em to fool 'em that way?"

"He tells 'em to drop everything and follow him."

Bob came back, bringing another bottle of whiskey.

"Here, help yourself . . . Say, who's that say they Gawd?"

"A guy in New York."

"A nigger?"

"Sure, he's black as the Ace of Spades."

"And what the white folks say about it?"

"Lots of 'em believing 'im. They say he's got ten thousand folks following 'im."

"You say *white* folks?"

"Sure, it was in the papers."

Bob let out a long, loud laugh.

"Don't laugh, nigger," said Al. "How you know? He might really be Gawd."

"Is you done gone nuts, too?" asked Bob.

"Well, how you know he *ain't* Gawd?" asked Al.

"You know, Gawd did say He was coming again," said Jake.

"And this might be Him," said Al.

"If He is coming, He ain't coming back in no nigger skin," said Bob.

"How come He ain't? He was born in a manger the last time."

"You can't tell what Gawd'll do," said Jake.

"They say there's a lot of proof that he is Gawd," said Al.

"What proof?"

"Well, for one thing the Bible says that Gawd's Church is going to be built on a rock that the very gates of hell can't go against . . ."

"Yeah . . ."

"Well, this Father Divine's done built his church on Manhattan Island. Ain't that a rock?"

They were silent, thinking.

"Yeah, folks say it's a rock . . ."

"It's a rock all right, but . . ."

"And he heals folks," said Al.

"Well," said Jake. "I ain't saying he is Gawd, and I ain't saying he ain't Gawd."

"Yeah," said Al, warming to his subject. "All the folks hates us black people, so Gawd might have done made up His mind to show 'em that everybody's equal in His sight. So He might come down in a black skin, see? He come as a Jew the last time, and how come He won't come as a nigger now? You see, He'd fool all the white folks then."

"Boy!" said Bob, "If that guy *was* Gawd, wouldn't the white folks just die!"

They laughed. The door bell rang.

"I bet that's Slim!"

Slim, tall, brown, thinfaced, came through the door, coughing a little jerky cough. His eyes were bright and hard and he seemed in high spirits. He moved across the room quickly and threw his coat and hat on the sofa.

"What you niggers doing?" he asked.

"Waiting for you so we could play a game of bridge," said Jake.

Slim looked at Al.

"You want to take 'em on this morning?"

"*Them* lambs? Hell, yeah!" said Al.

"Wait a minute. I'll get a table and some cards and we'll see *who's* lambs!" said Bob.

"Calling us *lambs*," sneered Jake, after Bob had gone.

"You can't play no bridge," said Al.

"We beat you last Tuesday," said Slim.

"And didn't we beat you last Saturday?"

"Aw, we done beat you guys more times than a man can remember."

"Listen at that nigger lie!" said Al.

Bob came back, set up the card table, and arranged the chairs. They sat. Bob took the deck and commenced shuffling.

"Look at this nigger, will you?" asked Al, turning to Slim.

"What?" asked Bob, innocently.

"Now, ain't this a *dog*!"

"Nigger, what you talking about?" asked Bob.

"Is you just going to *take* the deal?" asked Al.

"You full of stuff!" said Bob, continuing to shuffle the cards.

"Stuff my ass! Let's cut for this deal!"

Bob paused.

"What you trying to signify?"

"Signify hell!" exclaimed Al, clamping his hand over the deck. "Ain't we going to cut for this deal?"

"Take your hands off the cards!" said Jake to Al. "You want me to sock you in your fat puss!"

Al stood up, took a step backward, placed his hands on his hips, and glared.

"Now, ain't this a bitch!" he said.

"I'll sock you so hard your ancestors'll feel it," said Jake.

"And I'll be the last man you'll ever sock!" said Al, leaning forward.

Slim stood up and banged his black fist on the table.

"We's going to cut for this deal, or there ain't going to be no deal!" he said. "What you niggers think we is, anyhow? Think we's just going to *give* you the deal? This ain't no charity station . . ."

"Aw, dry up!" said Bob, throwing the deck on the table. "We can all cut . . ."

"Damn right!" said Al.

Bob cut an ace.

"I thought it was going to be my deal," he said.

"Aw, nigger, shut up and deal the cards!" said Al.

"I was doing that," said Bob coolly.

Jake lost patience and pushed his chair back, yelling:

"You niggers keep your shirts on!"

"Here she comes!" said Bob dealing.

They were silent, examining and sorting their hands. Finally, Al looked up, tapped the table with his cards, and said to Bob:

"Wake up and say what you going to do!"

Bob frowned and slouched deeper into his chair. He was trying to decide between a Notrump and a Club bid. But he was afraid to bid the Notrump until he found out how the Clubs were distributed.

"Well," he drawled, his voice low and serious, "I reckon I'll bid a little Club."

Al glared challengingly.

"I'm taking you out with a Diamond!" he bawled.

Jake leaned over and whispered into Al's ear:

"One Heart, Sweetheart."

Slim hesitated and stared into Al's face as though trying to read a message there.

"I'm passing," he said.

There was silence. Jake could hear his watch ticking in his vestpocket. He felt a sense of fullness, of wellbeing; it was the first he had felt that day. He held his cards in his right hand, close together, so that he could see at a glance all the denominations he had. His eyes enveloped Bob's face with a steady, benevolent gaze.

"You got the right spirit," said Bob, turning to Slim. "I'm bidding two Notrumps!"

"Passing," said Al. "You can have it."

"Three Notrumps," Jake whispered again into Al's ear.

"Aw, nigger, cut it out!" said Al, pushing Jake back.

Slim looked at his hand. He had a terrible bust. But he had four Diamond cards and Al had bid Diamonds. He also had four Club cards, even though Bob had bid Clubs. Spades had not been mentioned. Slim's lips moved several times before he spoke.

"I'm ddddoubling yyou," he stammered.

"Is you crazy?" asked Bob. "Well, I'm *re*doubling."

"Pass."

"Pass."

"Pass."

"Let's go, Al," said Jake.

Al led with the five of Diamonds. Jake spread his hand. Bob pulled the seven of Diamonds from the Dummy. Slim crossed it with the ten. Bob thought fast; he blinked his eyes. He had been doubled and he had redoubled. He had better lay low this time; he was going to lose the King or the Queen any-way. He ducked the trick, playing the six of Diamonds. Jake swallowed, his stomach contracting.

"Thank you, boss," said Slim, stacking the cards.

Slim led back with the Jack of Diamonds. Bob frowned. The room became so silent that they could hear the rumble of the "L" as though it were many blocks closer than it really was. Bob was nervous and tense; he did not want to be shut out of the Diamonds. The thought that he had been doubled and that he had in turn redoubled haunted him.

"Here's the King," he sighed, laying down the King of Diamonds.

"I wouldn't touch it," said Al, playing the Deuce.

Bob pulled the four of Diamonds from the Dummy, taking the trick. He had to see what he could get out of his Hearts and see about it quickly. He took two Heart tricks with the Ace and King, but lost the Queen. Al and Slim were bossing Diamonds. Slim led with the Trey, and sweat beaded on Bob's forehead. Reluctantly, he threw his poor Queen under the axe of Al's Ace. Al then turned the eight and nine of Diamonds, downing Bob's bid of three Notrumps by one. Jake and Bob sat still, gazing emptily at the backs of the cards.

"You's one down, *re*doubled!" boomed Slim, marking down the score.

"Easy's taking candy from a baby!" laughed Al.

"Smoother'n velvet!" laughed Slim, rearing back in his seat and blowing smoke to the ceiling.

"Like rolling off a log!" sang Al, shuffling the cards.

"Like sliding down a greasy pole!"

"Like snapping your fingers!"

"Like spitting!"

"Like falling in love with a high yellow!"

Al and Slim leaned back in their chairs and roared with laughter.

"Come on, you niggers," railed Jake. "Cut out the monkey business and play cards!"

"And don't make so Gawddamn much noise," said Bob.

"Oh, so that's it! You niggers getting just a little bit mad, hunh?" asked Al.

"They just can't take it," said Slim.

"Wait and do your gassing when the game's over," said Bob.

"And the one what laughs last is the one what laughs best," said Jake.

"Not 'less you got something to laugh about," said Al, pityingly.

"How about the way we beat you guys last Tuesday?" asked Bob.

"Oh, they forget all about such *little* things as that," said Jake.

Al and Slim rose and shook each other's hand solemnly.

"Boy, we got 'em going back to ancient history," said Al.

"We going to make 'em go back to the Garden of Eden before we gets through with 'em," said Slim.

Jake and Bob took their defeat with stoical smiles. The cards were cut, and Al dealt.

```
                    ♠  K-7
                    ♡  K-4-3-2
                    ◇  Q-9-6
                    ♣  J-9-5-3

 ♠  Q-J-10-5-2    ┌─────────────────┐    ♠  9-8-6-3
 ♡  10-9-5        │      Slim       │    ♡  J-6
 ◇  7-5-3-2       │ Jake       Bob  │    ◇  K-8-4
 ♣  7             │       Al        │    ♣  K-6-4-2
                  └─────────────────┘
                    ♠  A-4
                    ♡  A-Q-8-7
                    ◇  A-J-10
                    ♣  A-Q-10-8
```

"Let's go," said Slim.

"One Notrump," said Al.

"I ain't got a Gawddamn thing," whined Jake, squirming in his chair.

"Don't confess to me!" said Slim haughtily, "I ain't no priest!"

"But you can't play when you ain't got nothing," said Jake.

"What you want us to do about it?" asked Slim.

"I bet Al didn't half shuffle them cards," mumbled Bob.

"Don't get smart, nigger," said Al. "You done had your deal."

"Play cards!" Jake bawled disgustedly. "I'm passing."

"Same here," said Slim.

Bob tapped his consent. Jake led with the Queen of Spades.

Slim spread his hand and Al pulled the King from it. Bob tossed in the eight of Spades, and Al put the four, taking the trick. Al paused and studied his hand and the Dummy. He wondered if he could trap the missing Diamond and Club Kings. He tried the Club, pulling the Jack from the Dummy. Bob nonchalantly tossed in the Deuce.

"Is you kidding?" asked Al, playing the eight spot from his hand. Reluctantly Jake surrendered the seven.

Al smiled and leaned toward Bob; he flexed his fingers in Bob's face as though he were a dentist about to pull a tooth.

"Just set real still and don't cry," he said. "This'll be very painless."

Slim also leaned to Jake and said:

"I hope those few lines found you well."

"Nigger, play cards!" snorted Bob.

"You guys ain't got no sense," said Jake.

Al pulled the Trey of Clubs from the Dummy; Bob still held out, giving up only the fourspot. Al crossed it with the ten. Jake discarded the Deuce of Spades.

"I'm going to murder that old King of yours," said Al, neatly stacking the trick. "Just you wait and see. Linger along, but die he must!"

Again, Al led from the Dummy, bringing out the five of Clubs. With an air of innocent unconcern Bob slid out the sixspot. Al covered it with the Queen, taking the fourth trick after Jake had sleepily discarded the Deuce of Diamonds. Al hunched his shoulders and puffed his jaws, stifling laughter.

"Come on, little baby, it ain't going to hurt none," he said, touching Bob under the chin with his finger. "Papa's doing this for your own good."

Al then banged down the Ace of Clubs with a crash that all but upset the table. Jake curled his lips and discarded the five of Spades. Al drew the ninespot from the Dummy, and turned to watch Bob. Bob turned his head and threw in the King.

"It didn't hurt much, did it, Honey?"

Al led the Queen of Hearts from his hand, taking Jake's nine, and pulling the King from the Dummy. Bob gave up the six, giving Al his seventh trick. Mercilessly, Al finessed the Diamonds through Bob in the same way he had finessed the Clubs, trapping the King.

"Boys," announced Al, rearing back and looking blissfully at the ceiling, "I believe my soul it's a Grand Slam!"

Al turned all thirteen tricks and let out a whoop.

"Let's don't play no more," said Slim, with mock concern.

"How come?" asked Jake.

"We ain't got no competition."

"Like hell," said Bob.

"But what's the use of playing you chumps? We *know* we can beat you."

Slim rose hurriedly and grabbed his hat and coat.

"I got to send a telegram," he said.

They looked at him.

"To who?"

"For what?"

"I'm going to get in touch with old Ely Culbertson and ask 'im don't he want another partner."

Al grabbed Slim and they danced around the room. Jake sat fingering the deck with a sick smile.

"If you going to play, come on and set down," said Bob, rising. "I'll be back in a minute."

"Look what we made 'im do!" yelled Al.

"Don't drink the iodine," said Slim, coughing slightly.

Al and Slim sat again. Bob came back with his hands trembling and his eyes looking a little bloodshot. Al cut the deck and Jake began to deal.

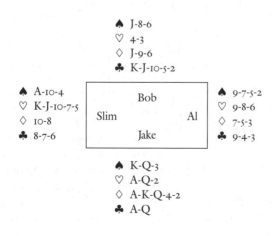

Jake smiled when he took up his first card, and when he had his whole hand before him a golden grin spread from ear to ear.

"What you saying?" asked Slim impatiently.

"Just a little Diamond," said Jake modestly, closing his eyes.

"One Heart," said Slim.

Bob looked at Jake, puzzled.

"Two clubs," he said.

"Passing," said Al.

"Three diamonds," said Jake.

"Passing."

"Four Clubs," said Bob.

Al tapped.

"Four Notrumps!" boomed Jake.

"Passing," whispered Slim.

"Five Hearts," said Bob.

"Passing," said Al. "What you guys doing? Having a contest all between yourselves?"

"Five Notrumps," said Jake.

Slim tapped.

"Six Clubs," said Bob, punching Al in the ribs.

Al threw his cards on the table and said:

"I'm passing from now on."

"Six Notrumps," said Jake.

Slim looked at his hand, and said:

"I'm doubling you on general principles!"

Bob tapped.

"Same here," said Al.

"*Re*doubled on the same general principles," said Jake.

Slim and Bob and Al tapped their consent to pass. Locked in the grip of conflicting impulses, Slim sat still and mute; then hesitantly, with his hand trembling, he led with the Jack of Hearts. Bob spread his hand. Al shook his head when he saw it. Jake pulled the Trey of Hearts from the Dummy. Al gave up the six, and Jake took the trick with the Queen. He brought back the Trey of Spades, to which Slim yielded the fourspot. Jake pulled the Jack of Spades from the Dummy. Al played the deuce. Jake frowned, wondering who had the Ace. He counted his sure tricks; he had five Club tricks, five Diamond tricks and one Heart trick. *O, Gawd, if I can only make this a redoubled Grand Slam I'll pay 'em all back!* He grew so excited he began to sweat. Only the King of Hearts and the Ace of Spades were out against him. Somebody had held out the Ace of Spades, Al or Slim, he did not know whom. He decided to save his Heart trick till the last, hoping to catch the King. This was the best bet since the Ace of Spades was out against him. He laid down five Club tricks, taking one from his hand and four from the Dummy. The Dummy was still in. He led the Diamond from the Dummy, turning one from the Dummy and four from his hand. Very slowly he eased the Ace of Diamonds out of his hand into Slim's face, saying:

"Come on, little baby, papa's waiting for you!"

Bob flopped deep into his chair and yelled, upsetting the table. Jake turned to him and asked with mock humbleness:

"Didn't somebody tell me a little while ago that we was playing against *champeens*?"

Bob sobered, looked thoughtful, and said:

"Seems like I did hear something like that, come to think of it. But, Holy Cats, that was too doggone easy to be against *Champeens.*"

"You know," said Jake, putting his arms around Bob's shoulders, "I think they's gone and got mixedup as to who they *is. We* is the mens they *thought* they was . . ."

Bob laughed uproariously. It was a very peculiar laugh, beginning noiselessly, a sharp expulsion of breath coming from the diaphragm; an expulsion that travelled slowly upwards, holding those who heard it in suspense, and finally cracking in a loud guffaw which terminated in something resembling a pig's squeal. Jake, galvanized by Bob's laughter, grabbed the sides of the upturned table and rolled off the chair on to the floor, his face contorted in a spasm of merriment. Each time he could regain his breath he would moan:

"Lawd . . . Lawd . . ."

Jake and Bob laughed so long that Al and Slim began laughing. And when Jake and Bob saw that they had made their opponents laugh at their *own* defeat, they laughed harder. Presently, they stopped laughing at the joke Jake had made, and began laughing because they were all laughing. And they laughed because they had laughed. They paused for breath, and then they laughed at how they had laughed; and because they had laughed at how they had laughed, they laughed and laughed and laughed. Suddenly Slim's laugh turned into a violent cough. He stood up, bent over with his hands touching the floor, and his long thin body heaved and rocked. Jake, Al, and Bob stood about him, silent, anxious.

"Here," said Bob, offering the flask. "Drink something."

When Slim tried to swallow he coughed and whiskey splashed his vest and trousers. Finally, he forced some of it down his throat. His face was wet with sweat. They led him to the sofa; he leaned back, closed his eyes, and breathed heavily. Steam sang in the radiator and from far off came the rumble of the "L".

IX.

Now that Slim had stopped coughing, Jake relaxed and felt better. Slim's spells always bothered him; each time he saw Slim like that he had a feeling that he was being warned of something. He pushed himself far back in his seat, thinking, *He's all right. He's been coughing like that a long time now.* Al was sitting on the far end of the sofa, next to Slim, knotting his fingers. Jake looked around, feeling empty, missing something.

"Where Bob?"

Al grunted wearily:

"Same old place."

Jake made a pretense of laughing, but it got no further than a mere shaking of shoulders. He was relieved to see Bob coming through the door, head down, fastening his beltbuckle. It was as though someone had whispered, *It's O.K. The house ain't on fire.* He leaned back and closed his eyes. *I'm getting nervous as hell.* And he knew that as long as he sat this way his nervousness would increase. He glanced around, restless, on edge. Slim was much better; he was wiping his face with a damp handkerchief. *What to hell? Slim's all right.* Jake's mind fished about, trying to get hold of an idea to cover his feeling of uneasy emptiness. He noticed that Al was wearing a new shirt, a light green one with delicate white pencil stripes running vertically. Al's fat face rested in smug repose, and Jake wanted to disturb it, possess it, make some of the strength of that repose his own.

"So you got a new shirt, hunh, Al?" asked Jake quietly, tentatively, sucking his teeth and throwing his leg over the arm of the chair.

Al modestly stroked the collar of his shirt with his fingers.

"Yeah, I picked it up yesterday."

"Where you steal it from?"

"Steal it? Nigger, you can't steal shirts like this!"

"You didn't buy it!"

"How come I didn't? Ain't I got money?" said Al. He was sitting upright, his round black face flushed with mock indignation.

"What did you ever buy?" asked Jake.

Al rose, rammed his hands deep into his pockets, and stood in front of Jake.

"You go into Marshall Field's and *steal* a shirt! It takes kale to wear clothes like this!"

"Marshall Field's?"

"Yeah. *Marshall Field's!*"

"The closest you ever got to Marshall Field's was the showwindow," said Jake.

"That's a Gawddamn lie!" said Al.

Slim and Bob listened silently, hoping for a bout of the dozens between the two.

"Whoever heard of a nigger going into Marshall Field's and buying a *green* shirt?" asked Jake, as though to himself.

"Aw, nigger, quit signifying! Go buy *you* a shirt!"

"I don't need no shirts. I got a plenty!"

"This nigger setting here wearing this purple rag around his throat talking about he's got a plenty shirts. *Some*body wake 'im up!"

Slim and Bob laughed.

"I can change *five* shirts to your *one*," boasted Jake.

"The onliest way you can do that is to pull off the one you has on *now* and put it on *five* times," said Al.

Slim and Bob laughed again.

"Listen, nigger," said Jake. "I was wearing shirts when you was going around naked in Miss'sippi!"

Slim and Bob opened their mouths wide and slumped deep into their seats.

"Hunh, hunh," said Al. "That was the time when you was wearing your hair wrapped with white strings, wasn't it?"

"*White* strings? Aw, Jake . . . Hehehe!" Bob could not finish for the idea tickled him so.

"Yeah," said Jake. "When I was wearing them white strings on my hair old Colonel James was sucking at your ma's tits, wasn't he?"

"Jeeesus," moaned Slim, pressing his handkerchief hard against his mouth to keep from coughing. "I told a piece of iron that once and it turned *redhot*. Now, what would a poor *meat* man do?"

Al glowered and fingered his cigarette nervously.

"Nigger," Al said slowly, so that the full force of his words would not be missed, "when old Colonel James was sucking at my ma's tits I saw your little baby brother across the street watching with slobber in his mouth . . ."

Slim and Bob rolled on the sofa and held their stomachs. Jake stiffened, crossed his legs, and gazed out of the window.

"Yeah," he said slowly, "I remembers when my little baby brother was watching with slobber in his mouth, your old grandma was out in the privy crying 'cause she couldn't find a corncob . . ."

Slim and Bob groaned and stomped their feet.

"Yeah," said Al, retaliating with narrowed eyes. "When my old grandma was crying for that corncob, your old aunt Lucy was round back of the barn with old Colonel James' old man, and she was saying something like this: 'Yyyyou kknow . . . Mmmister Cccolonel . . . I jjjust ddon't llike to ssssell . . . my ssstuff . . . I jjjust lloves to gggive . . . iiit away . . .' "

Slim and Bob embraced each other and howled.

"Yeah," said Jake. "I remembers when old aunt Lucy got through she looked around and saw your old aunt Mary there watching with her finger stuck in her puss. And old aunt Lucy said, 'Mary, go home and wash your bloomers!' "

Slim and Bob beat the floor with their fists.

Al curled his lips and shot back:

"Hunh, hunh, yeah! And when my old Aunt Mary was washing out her bloomers the hot smell of them soapsuds rose up and went out over the lonesome graveyard and your old greatgreatgreat grandma turned over in her grave and said: 'Lawd, I sure thank Thee for the smell of them pork chops You's cooking up in Heaven . . .' "

Slim grabbed Bob and they screamed.

"Yeah," drawled Jake, determined not to be outdone, "When my old greatgreatgreat grandma was smelling them pork chops, your poor old greatgreatgreat*great* grandma was a Zulu queen in Africa. She was setting at the table and she said to the waiter: 'Say waiter, be sure and fetch me some of them missionary chitterlings . . .' "

"Mmmmm . . . miss . . . missionary chitterlings?" asked Slim, stretching flat on the floor and panting as one about to die.

"Yeah," said Al. "When my greatgreatgreatgreat grandma who was a Zulu queen got through eating them missionary chitterlings, she wanted to build a sewerditch to take away her crap, so she went out and saw your poor old greatgreat-greatgreat*great* grandma sleeping under a coconut tree with her old mouth wide open. She didn't need to build no sewer-ditch . . ."

"Jeeesus!" yelled Slim, closing his eyes and holding his stomach. "I'm *dying*!"

Jake screwed up his eyes, bit his lips, and tried hard to think of a return. But, for the life of him, he could not. Al's last image was too much; it left him blank. Then they all laughed so that they felt weak in the joints of their bones.

X.

"WHAT TIME you got there, Bob?" asked Jake.

"Quarter to eleven."

"We better start now. We don't want to be late."

"Yeah, we better go."

They rose, put on hats, coats, and got their canes. Just as they were about to go out of the door, Bob stepped to the mirror and straightened his tie.

"Nigger, what you looking at?" asked Al.

"Ain't that a good looking dog?" asked Bob, pointing to his reflection.

Al grabbed Bob by the shoulder and swung him around.

"It's a wonder this didn't crack that glass!"

"What you beefing about? You talk like you's a John Gilbert or something . . ."

Al came close and whispered:

"I never will be as ugly as you is . . ."

Jake and Slim laughed. Bob threw his arm about Al's neck and bent his head to the light.

"Look!" he called to the others. "Did you ever see anybody with kinky *eyebrows*?"

Jake and Slim clapped their hands and dropped to the floor.

"But, look!" called Al, catching Bob by the chin. "Did you ever see anybody with kinky *mustaches*?"

Jake and Slim sniffled and wiped away loose saliva with the backs of their hands.

"When a man's got kinky *eyebrows* he just can't *get* no uglier," said Bob.

"Gawd sure must of had the bellyache when he gave you that kinky mustache," said Al.

Bob thought quickly, wondering what he could say to answer. But Al beat him.

"Say, nigger, I bet you the hair on your chest is kinky?"

Jake and Slim grabbed their knees and moaned.

"That's a Gawddamn lie!" said Bob, hurriedly buttoning his coat.

"I'll bet you it *is* kinky," said Al, emboldened by Bob's evasiveness.

"That's a lie!" said Bob, turning away.

Al advanced and pulled off his diamond ring.

"Say, I'll bet you this against nothing that it *is* kinky!"

Jake and Slim rolled over chairs and beat their palms against their thighs.

"Come on, show us," said Al.

"Aw, nigger, go on," said Bob.

Al came close and tried to open Bob's coat.

"Come on, let's see!"

"Get away, nigger!"

"I'm going to open your shirt, so help me Gawd!" said Al, tugging.

Bob backed away.

"Listen here, nigger, if you don't get away from me I'll sock you straight in your fat puss!"

"Lawd, today!" whispered Al, prancing off triumphantly.

"Well, even if I is got kinky hair on my chest, it just goes to show I'm a man, see?"

"Yyyyyyyyeah," said Al, tiptoeing close and cooing into Bob's ear. "You's a man, but you's a uuuuuuugyly man . . ."

Jake and Slim kicked the walls of the room with the toes of their shoes.

XI.

T HEY FILED down the steps and went out. A deluge of sunshine bathed the streets and houses. The air was warm and clear. Traffic had thickened and there was a blare of auto horns. Women went in and out of stores with shopping bags filled with groceries. Boys and girls, free from school for the holiday, spun tops and played hopscotch upon the pavements in ragged sweaters. Often Jake and Al and Slim and Bob had to walk around them to keep from breaking up their games.

"Look!"

"What?"

"Where?"

"Over there? What's that going on over there?"

"Come on, let's go and see!"

A hefty, short, jetblack man was standing on the lowered rear gate of a truck haranguing passersby. He spluttered out of one corner of his mouth, his chest heaving laboriously as though he were shortwinded. Each time he raised his arm for emphasis his checkered suit flapped and fluttered in the air like a flag. A red tie with a horseshoe stickpin nestled between the wings of a soiled collar, and each jerk of his neck set up a shower of white and blue sparks. His lips were plump and loose, and his little red eyes were all but drowned in the oily fat of his cheeks. A round potbelly rose and bulged over a wide belt like an inflated balloon, giving the notion that at any moment he was likely to explode, and vanish.

"Come closer, folks, come closer! Don't block the sidewalk! Step right up 'n' don't be scared!"

"Come on, let's see what he's saying."

"Yeah, move in closer."

The man placed upon a rickety card table a square box made of meshed wire. Then, before the crowd could realize what was happening, he pulled out a huge rattle snake and wrapped its brown, scaly body around his neck.

"Uuuhhhh!"

The crowd marveled and fell back.

"Come closer, folks, come closer! Nothing kin bother yuh

as long as Ah'm's here! Ah's got all the Powers of Evil in mah control! Come closer, folks, come closer! Ah's got a great message fer yuh!"

The snake lifted its head warily and darted its blueblack tongue. In a few minutes the crowd doubled. The man smiled and stroked the snake's head with stumpy fingers. When satisfied with the size of his audience, he spoke:

"LAdees 'n' Gen'meeeeeens: Ah'm's the SNAKE MAN! Ah wuz BO'N 'bout FORTEEEEY YEars erGO on the banks of the FAMous NILE in the great COUNtreeeeey of AFRIker, yo' COUNtreeeeeey 'n' mah COUNtreeeey—in tha' LAN' where, in the YEars gone by, yo' FATHER 'n' mah FATHER ruled suPREME! In mah FATHER'S day the PRINCES 'n' CROWNED heads of YOURpe came t' his feets astin' fer ADVICE, astin' t' be tol' things they couldn't TELL themselves, astin' t' have things DONE they couldn't do themselves. The CROWNED heads of YOURpe respected mah FATHER—he wuz the WISE man of the NILE! Mah FRIENDS, Ah'm's mah FATHER'S son, not only in FLESH, but in SPERIT! FER TWENTEEEEEEEY YEars Ah set at mah FATHER'S feets 'n' soppedup the WISDOM of his GREAT MIN'! T'DAY, Ah'm's here t' give YUH the beneFIT of mah FATHER'S GREAT WISDOM! Ah'm's here t' TELL yuh the SECRET of GOOD 'n' the SECRET of EVIL! Ah'm's here t' TELL yuh the SECRET of LIFE 'n' the SECRET of DEATH! . . . Be still, Patsy, be still! . . ."

He paused and stroked the rattler's scaly body.

"Say, he's from Africa!"

"Yeah, he knows a lot of secrets!"

"He sure must know something to charm that snake that way!"

"You telling me?"

". . . But 'fo' Ah goes inter that, mah FRIENDS, Ah wanna give yuh some INDIcation of mah SINGULar POWERS! Yuh see HERE in mah han's is TWO steel rings MADE in the FAR OFF COUNtreeeeey of JApan. Mah FRIENDS, these rings is made of SOLID STEEL, 'n' if there's anybody in this DISTINGUISHED AUDIENce, be he MALE or FEMALE, who thinks he kin BEN' or BREAK these rings he has a chance t' try 'n' win FIVE DOLLARS in COL' CASH! ANYbody wanna try? Who? *Who?* WHO? DON'T BE SCARED, FOLKS! STEP right up 'n' try! Now, WHO wanna try? WHO? Yuh, Mister? Yes, suh! Here yuh is! TRY wid all yo' MIGHT 'n' STRENGTH! PULL HARD, Mister, PULL HARD! Why, whut's the MATTER, Mister? Can't yuh BEN' or BREAK these LITTLE rings? NAW? Sho 'nough? Haa! Haa! Give 'em here! Waal, who else wanna try?"

"I bet I could break them Gawddamn rings!"

"I bet I could, too!"

"Let's try!"

"Say, let me at them rings, Mister!"

"Let me see if I can break 'em!"

" . . . Awright, suh! Here yuh is! Yuh kin TRY! 'N' 'member, if yuh BEN' or BREAK 'em, yuh wins FIVE DOLLARS in COL' CASH! . . ."

Jake strained with all his might against the steel rings, but could not bend nor break them.

"Whut these rings made out of?" he asked, puzzled.

"Let me try!"

"I want a hand at 'em!"

"Don't give 'em back till I get at 'em!"

They grunted, squirmed, puffed, bent double; but the little steel rings remained perfectly round, slender, shiny. Smiling sheepishly, they handed them back.

". . . Yuh couldn't BEN' or BREAK 'em, mah FRIENDS? Naw? Tha's jus' too BAD! Yuh missed FIVE DOLLARS in COL' CASH! Waal, WHO else wanna TRY? WHO else? Who? *Who?* WHO? NOBODY? Waal, waal, mah FRIENDS, lemme show yuh something! Lemme show yuh jus' WHUT kin be done wid these rings! SEE! LOOK HARD! LOOK CLOSE! THE CLOSER YUH LOOK THE LESS YUH SEE! The han' is FASTERN'N the EYE! PRESTO! PRESTO! SEE! The rings is locked in each other . . ."

"Jeeeesus! Yuh see that?"

"I'm looking right at 'im!"

"That guy's a wizard!"

"You telling me?"

". . . Now, mah FRIENDS, yuh wanna know jus' how Ah did it? Naw! Naw! Ah can't tell yuh tha', mah FRIENDS! Tha's not fer yuh t' know, mah FRIENDS! Tha's some of mah FATHER'S POWER, mah good, GREAT OL' FA-THER who advised 'n' guided the CROWNED HEADS of YOURpe! Now, mah FRIENDS, let's git down t' bis'ness. Ah'm's here t'day t' give yuh a MESSAGE OF HOPE! Be still, Patsy, be still! . . . Mah FRIENDS, yuh see this GLASS? Waal, it's jus' a ORD'NARY drinkin' glass, the kind yuh 'n' me drinks WATER out of! Ah'm's gonna fill this GLASS wid CLEAN PURE WATER, RAIN WATER, which is the only PURE WATER THERE IS! RAIN WATER'S the WATER Gawd Awmighty put here fer his chillun t' drink, the WATER HE cleaned 'n' purified HISSE'F! See there! See how clear 'tis? GAWD'S water, mah FRIENDS, GAWD'S water! IT'S CLEAN 'N' PURE 'N' SPARKLIN', LIKE YUH 'N' ME WUZ WHEN WE WUZ BO'N INTER THIS DARK WORLD! Awright, so fer, so good! Now, whut hap-pens? YUH MENS KNOWS! Yuh bergin t' treat tha' ol' body, tha' PRECIOUS ol' body, CARELESS 'n' ROUGH, didn't YUH? Don't la'gh, men, don't la'gh! Ah'm's talkin' t' yuh straight from the SHOULDER! This is a MATTER of LIFE 'N' DEATH! Yuh bergin t' ketch col's, didn't YUH? Don't la'gh, men, don't la'gh! Yuh went 'n' got married, didn't YUH? Men, Ah'm's astin' yuh *not* t' la'gh! 'Cause yuh 'n' me knows a woman do take a CERTAIN strength from a man, don't she? Mah FRIENDS, lemme show yuh jus' whut happened t' yo' bodies durin' all these YEars! Be still, Patsy, be still! . . ."

"Get up closer!"

"That guy's smart!"

"Yeah, he knows what he's talking about!"

". . . Yuh see this GLASS of PURE WATER? Waal, Ah'm gonna po' jus' a little bit of this ACID inter it! Jus' a *little* bit, see? SEE! WATCH how DARK the water TURNS! SEE! LOOK how BLACK it's gittin'! Mah FRIENDS, tha's whut happened t' yo' bodies! . . ."

"Geeeeeee! It turned black!"

"I wonder what was that he put in it?"

"He said it was *acid*!"

"Yeah, it must of been *acid* of some kind!"

". . . Yo' bodies is DEFILED! Ah knows jus' how yuh FEELS when yuh gits outta bed in the MO'NIN'S! Yuh gits up TIRED, don't yuh? There's a nasty taste in yo MOUTH, ain't it? Yes, mah FRIENDS, Ah knows! Them ol' LIMBS feels like they don't wanna MOVE, don't they? Mah FRIENDS, Ah knows! . . ."

"That guy talks like he's telling the truth."

"Yeah, I believe he knows what he's talking about, all right."

"You know, sometimes I feels that way myself when I gets up in the mornings."

". . . Now, mah FRIENDS, there's a CURE fer all this! IF IT WUZN'T SO AH WOULDN'T TELL YUH! Gawd in all His MIGHT 'n' GLORY'S done fixed this CURE fer US! Does yuh think HE woulda let all this happen widout puttin' a CURE here? Tell me, does yuh THINK tha'? O YE OF LITTLE FAITH! Does yuh THINK HE thinks LESS of yuh'n He do the BEES'S of the FIEL'S? Tell me, does yuh? HIS EYE IS ON THE SPARROW 'N' AH KNOWS HE'S WATCHIN' ME! Ain't yuh got no *faith*? FAITH'S THE SUBSTANCE OF THINGS YUH HOPE FER 'N' THE EVIDENCE OF THINGS YUH CAN'T SEE! Mah FRIENDS, tha's true, 'n' 'fo' one *jot* or *tittle* of GAWD'S PRECIOUS WORD fails the HEAVEN 'n' the EARTH shall pass erway! So it wuz written, mah FRIENDS, so it wuz written! Be still Patsy, be still! . . . LIS'EN, ain't yuh never seed a little DOG nosin' erbout in the GRASS 'n' WEEDS huntin' fer SOMETHING? Sho, yuh did. Mah FRIENDS, tha' little DOG wuz lookin' fer something GAWD planted there fer HIS sake! HE WUZ LOOKIN' FER THA' HERB WHUT GAWD PUT THERE T' CURE EVER' LIVIN' THING IN THIS WORLD OF HIS'N! Mah FRIENDS, mah FATHER showed me tha' herb when Ah wuz a boy 'n' tol' me how t' fix it! AH'S GOT THA' HERB WID ME T'DAY! Looka here! Lemme show yuh a han'ful. SEE! Ain't the leaves *hard* 'n' *little*? . . ."

"Can you see 'em?"

"Yeah, I can see 'em."

"What they look like?"

"Oh, they's just some little curlup green leaves."

". . . There ain't no herb in all the world tha' looks like THIS, mah FRIENDS! Now, lemme show yuh the power of this herb. Lemme show yuh how it *works*! SEE! Ah'm's puttin' jus' a little in this here glass of BLACK water 'n' yuh jus' stan' RIGHT where yuh is 'n' watch GAWD'S AWMIGHTY'S HAN' at work! WATCH GAWD'S HAN' MOVE 'FO' YO' EYES! LOOK! LOOK CLOSE! See how the water CLEARS! It ain't never FAILED, mah FRIENDS, it ain't *never* FAILED! THIS WATER IS NOW JUS' AS CLEAR 'N' PURE AS IT WUZ THE DAY IT COME FROM THE HAN' OF GAWD! Lis'en, mah FRIENDS, Ah'm's tellin' yuh GAWD'S truth! WHUT THESE LITTLE HERBS DID FER THIS WATER THEY KIN DO FER YUH! THEY'LL DO THIS FER YUH IF YUH'LL ONLY LET 'EM, 'N' THA'S THE GOSPEL TRUTH! . . ."

"Hooooooooly Jeeesus! He turned that water *white* again!"

"Now, ain't that something!"

"He's got the real stuff!"

"That guy's a wizard!"

". . . LADeeees 'n' Gen'meeeeens, mah UNIVERSAL HERB CUREALL MEDICINE CURES NERVOUS-NESS 'N' PNEUMONIA, MEASLES 'N' MENINGITIS, CORNS 'N' CANCERS, CONSUMPTION 'N' WHOOP-IN' COUGH, RINGWORM 'N' RHEUMATISM, CAR-BUNCLES 'N' LUMBAGO, 'N' ALL THE DIVERS AIL-MENTS OF THE HUMAN BODY! It prevents as well as cures, so if yuh ain't got nothin' t' matter wid yuh right now, git a bottle anyhow, jus' t' make sho . . . They's only one dollar per bottle, LADeeees 'n' Gen'meeeeeens! Who wants one? Awright, Mister. Jus' one dollar! Thank yuh! Awright, now, who wants ernother one? Tha's fine! Jus' one dollar! Thank yuh! Now, who wants ernother one? Here yuh is, lady! Take mah word fer it! Yuh'll never be sorry yuh bought it! Awright, jus' one dollar a bottle! Who wants ernother one? Be still, Patsy, be still! . . ."

"Yuh got any money?"

"Man, I ain't got penny *one*!"

"Me neither."

"I just got carfare to work."

"But I wants one of them bottles."

"Me too."

". . . Now, mah FRIENDS, if yuh ain't got a dollar wid yuh right now, jus' step up here 'n' leave me yo' name 'n' address, 'n' Ah'll see tha' yuh gits a bottle of mah UNIVERSAL HERB CUREALL MEDICINE delivered right t' yo' home BRIGHT 'n' EARLY in the mo'nin'! . . ."

After they had left their names and addresses, they walked in the direction of the "L" station.

"You know, I'd like to study and learn something like that," said Jake.

"Yeah, I ain't never seen nobody do the things he done."

"Me neither."

"A man must make a lot of money in a business like that."

"He's a magician," said Jake.

"You know, that stuff might help this dose I got," said Bob.

"And maybe it'll keep me from coughing so much," said Slim.

"I'm going to make Lil take some of that," said Jake. "It might save her from that operation."

"A stitch in time saves nine," said Al.

XII.

I'M HUNGRY."

"You ain't by yourself."

"Let's get a sandwich and a maltedmilk."

"I'm broke," said Jake. "Just got carfare to work and back."

"Come on. I'll stake you," said Bob.

At 47th Street and South Parkway they entered a Walgreen drug store, took seats on stools at a white porcelain counter, pushed their hats far back on their heads, and waited to be served. Presently, a plump, mulatto girl dressed in a white and blue uniform brought four small glasses of ice water.

"What you gen'mens have?"

"What we going to eat?" asked Jake.

"Oh, I reckon I'll take one of the club sandwiches and a maltedmilk," said Bob, scratching his head.

"Same here," said Al. "Only make mine two sandwiches."

"Ditto," said Slim.

"Five sammies 'n' fo' malts!" the girl yelled aside out of the corner of her mouth.

"Five sammies 'n' fo' malts!" a bass voice echoed from behind a screen.

The girl swung around so that the flesh on her oversized buttocks trembled.

"Now, ain't that something!"

"The stuff's here!"

"Not bad!"

"She's at the post!"

"She's off!"

"She's a winner!"

"By five lengths!"

"Without a call!"

"That's a Packard Chassis," said Jake. "And I'll bet my bottom dollar it can run."

"You's wrong! That's a Rolls Royce chassis, the kind I likes to drive," said Slim.

"She's built for service, all right," said Bob.

A black hand pushed from behind the screen four tall silverlooking cans and a plate of toast. The girl put the cans under electricwhippers; there was a buzzing as the icecream, chocolate, milk, and malt were mixed.

"Make it snappy, Sweetstuff!" called Jake. "We's working men and we's got a clock to punch."

"Oh, yeah?" asked the girl, bringing the maltedmilks.

"Yeeeeeah," said Jake.

"Working mens is sure hard to find these days," said the girl.

"We knows it," said Bob.

"In fact, I just can't seem to find one," said the girl, lifting her eyebrows.

"You telling us?" asked Bob.

They laughed and the girl's face fell and her lips pouted. Seeing they would not flirt, she went to the rear of the store and turned on the radio.

. . . IN THE LATTER PART OF 1862 MEADE AND LEE SPARRED AND FEINTED CAUTIOUSLY FOR AN OPENING TO DEAL A TELLING BLOW . . .

"Say, that radio's talking about the Civil War!"

"This is old Lincoln's birthday, you know."

"Yeah."

"War's a terrible thing."

"Somebody said war was hell."

"I think a guy named Herman said that."

"Yeah," said Slim. "I heard my boy talking about him the other night."

"Say," whispered Jake through a mouthful of sandwich. "That chicken ain't bad."

"Who?"

"That dame, *there*," said Jake, jerking his head.

"Aw . . ." said Al. "A gold digger, that's all."

"Yeah," agreed Slim. "She's got 'gimme' all over her face."

"A halfwhite broad like that is hard as hell to manage," said Al.

"Them highyellows is stuckup and think they's better anybody else," said Slim.

"Yeah," said Bob. "They thinks they's the whole cheese just 'cause they looks like white women."

"You guys nuts," snorted Jake. "They ain't so bad if you knows how to handle 'em."

"Oh, yeeeeeah?"

"I could make her walk a chalkline."

"You made the last yellow one you had do that, didn't you?" asked Slim.

"Oh, I didn't want that old toughmeat," said Jake.

They laughed.

"Well, how about the one you had last year?" asked Jake, scowling.

Slim took a huge bite of sandwich, ignoring him.

"Say, I'm *talking* to you!"

"Who? Me?"

"Ain't this a *bitch!*" asked Jake, laying down his sandwich and turning to the others for support.

"What *is* you talking about!" demanded Slim.

"I'm talking about that yellow gal who gutted your pocketbook last year," said Jake.

"*What* yellow gal?"

"You mean to say you don't remember when you went around here drooping like a sick chicken?"

"Hell naw!"

"You got a damn good memory, that's all I got to say!" said Jake.

They laughed; Slim sipped his maltedmilk as though he had not heard.

The girl came back and leaned against the counter so that the bulge in her stomach showed. She appeared to be about eighteen or nineteen, and had a clear, yellow skin. Holding her marooncolored eyes wide and innocent, she lightly caressed her brasstinted hair, tucking in a loose strand here and a stray curl there, pretending she was not aware of the men but only of the traffic flowing past the glass window. Her lips were full, wide, and bloodred; she wet them frequently and slowly with the tip of her tongue. She yawned, raising her elbows high above her head, exposing hairy armpits. Her fat fingers loosened and the towel she held dropped to the floor. As she bent to pick it up her dress rose and showed a naked stretch of thigh. Jake hunched Bob.

"Aw, cheap," Bob mumbled.

They finished and lit cigarettes.

"What's the damages, Gingerbread?"

"Dollar eighty?"

"Here's mine."

"And mine."

"Aww . . ." said Bob, pushing their money back. "This one's on me. Keep the change, Sweetmeat."

"Thanks!" said the girl, exposing six gold teeth.

As they went out the radio sang:

. . . AND THE WHOLE NIGHT THROUGH LINCOLN PACED WITH HIS HANDS KNOTTED BEHIND HIS BACK, MUMBLING MOURNFULLY: WHY DON'T THEY COME? WHY DON'T THEY COME? . . .

They hurried in the direction of the "L" station.

"What's that?" asked Al.

"Sounds like music."

"Sounds like a brass band."

"A radio, maybe," said Bob as they came to a corner and paused for a red light.

"I sure wish I had dated that dame up," said Jake ruefully.

"*What* dame?"

"That dame in the drugstore."

"Jeesus! You still thinking about her?"

"She wasn't so bad," said Jake.

"Man, I hears a band playing somewhere."

"One of them calliopes, maybe," said Slim.

"Did you see her stommick when she leaned against that counter?" asked Jake.

"Whose stommick?"

"That mama in the drugstore."

"Aw, nuts to you!" said Bob. "Let's walk up. I got to get to a bathroom . . ."

"Nigger, hush!" said Slim, bending over with laughter. "You'll start me to coughing."

"She wasn't so bad," said Jake again.

They crossed a street, turned a corner, and came in sight of a parade some two or three blocks away. It was led by a band whose musical instruments gleamed blindingly in sunshine.

"Gee! Let's look at this!"

"Come on!"

On a high banner made of green satin and trimmed with purple frills were words in tall letters of red:

ONWARD TO AFRICA

Young brownskinned high school girls with dirty stockings and rundown heels stood on curbstones, clapping their hands. Scrawny waifs scurried in and out of the crowd, yelling encouragement to the musicians. Clerks in hotdog stands, drugstores, grocerystores, and drygoods stores craned their necks over counters to get a glimpse. Jake and his pals paused in the open door of a garage to watch. From their rear came the sound of a radio:

. . . WE ARE COMING, FATHER ABRAHAM, THREE HUNDRED THOUSAND MORE, FROM MISSISSIPPI'S WINDING STREAM, AND FROM NEW ENGLAND'S SHORE . . .

Behind the banner came the band, playing *Onward Christian Soldiers*. Immediately in front marched a young girl twirling a long, brass baton; she was biglimbed, fleshy; she had thick red lips and deep, dark eyes. Her shoulders, draped in a black cape, were thrown back, exposing a bosom full enough to spill. She walked with short, mincing steps, her spine arched inward, her eyes halfclosed. She smiled a continuous smile, as though supremely satisfied. Her uniform fitted her snugly, and her body jerked in answer to every twist of the music. She twirled the gleaming brass baton so fast that it was almost invisible; she spun it in one hand and then the other; she spun it under one foot and then the other; she spun it over her head and then behind her back; then she strutted with it resting lightly upon her shoulders as though she were carrying a precious burden. Suddenly, she stopped, cut a few steps from the Charleston, Balled the Jack, crooned snatches from a popular blues song, and tipped off softly in perfect time to the music, her face severely militant, her baton held high, her buttocks trembling delicately. The men in the crowd went wild, smiting their thighs and striking one another in the back with the palms of their hands.

"Laaaaaaaawd, today!"

"Now, ain't that something!"

"The hottest stuff in town!"

"This is homecooking!"

"Strut your stuff, woman!"

"Don't give 'em nothing, gal; keep everything!"

"Look at that salty dog!"

Following the girl an enormous grey horse pranced and struck sparks from the pavement. Sitting astride the horse's back was a fat, black man whose flesh shook like fresh jelly upon his bones. A tall, silk hat, gleaming like a newlyblackened stovepipe, sat askantly upon his wooly head. His suit was skyblue, his shoes the color of oxblood, his spats light grey with mother of pearl buttons. He wore white kid gloves and held his hands stiffly in front of him, grasping the reins selfconsciously, as though he were expecting his picture to be snapped at any moment. Around his ample shoulders flapped a red, green, and black sash upon which was pinned a huge, golden, fivepointed star. The horse trampled at a side gait, and the man bowed condescendingly to the left and to the right.

"Who's that guy?" Jake asked involuntarily.

"That's the Supreme Undisputed Exalted Commander of the Allied Imperial African War Councils unto the Fourth and Last Generations," said a tall, black stranger.

"Jeeesus!" breathed Jake, his lips parting with awe.

Then came two flags: the American flag and the African flag. The African flag was composed of three wide stripes of red, green, and black. In the center was the fivepointed black star. Next came a group of men wearing black uniforms decorated with clusters of gold braid. They marched in close formation, eight abreast, their left feet hitting the pavement in unison to the beats of the music. These were the supreme generals of a mythical African republic, and the medals of unfought wars and unwon victories clinked against their uniforms with every rattle of the drums. Their shoulders were straight, their faces up, and their eyes gazed into the far distance, as though piercing concrete and steel, as though entranced by some strange mirage upon the horizon. A yellow silk banner trimmed in blue told the public that this was the

SUPREME IMPERIAL WAR COUNCIL

Next came a group also wearing black uniforms, but with
not so much gold braid. These were ordinary generals, and
they marched with the glittering blades of unsheathed swords
held rigidly at arm's length. Their eyes were also fastened
upon the distance, but not the far distance; it was a more
immediate distance, a distance in accord with their rank. A
floating banner of scarlet told the public that this was the

ASSISTANT SUPREME IMPERIAL WAR COUNCIL

Next followed a group which a white banner described as
the *First Motor Corps*. They were dressed simply in black uniforms, and had just a tiny sprig of gold braid on each shoulder. The gaze of their eyes did not reach beyond the bosoms
and buttocks of the women on the sidewalks. Then came the
Black Cross Nurses dressed in black and white uniforms,
marching quickly with tight lips and proud faces. Their eyes
seemed to say: "Lissen, you old white folks, we kin take care
uv de wounded black soljers, but ain't none of yo' wounded
white soljers gwine to git any 'tenshun here."

There were no privates in the parade.

"That's hot, ain't it?"

"You telling me?"

"Lawd, that band can *really* play!"

A black woman with three teeth missing came through the
crowd passing out leaflets. Jake took one. Al, Slim, and Bob
looked over his shoulders as he read.

P R E A M B L E

The International Negro Uplift Association and the
African Communities Council is a noble, friendly,
kindly, brotherly, helpful, decent, respectable, law abiding, progressive, humanitarian, charitable, educational,
instructive, constructive, institutional, benevolent, religious, fraternal, expansive, growing, and rising society;
and is founded by persons desiring to the utmost to
work for the general uplift of the Negro people of the
world. And the members pledge themselves upon the
solemn faith of their black forebears to do all in their
power to conserve the rights of all Mankind, believing
always in the Brotherhood of Man, the Sisterhood of

Woman, and the Fatherhood of God. The motto of the organization is, *One God! One Aim! One Destiny!* Therefore, let Justice and Mercy be done to all Mankind, realizing that if the Strong oppresses the weak, war, floods, strife, pestilence, plague, revolution, earthquakes, cyclones, and tornadoes will forever mark the path of Man; but, with Love, Faith, and Charity towards all the reign of Peace and Plenty will be heralded into the world, and the generations of men shall be called Blessed.

"Boy, that sounds like the Constitootion!"

"They sure got a lot of brains to write something like that!"

"Yeah, they's smart."

"Come on, man! We going to be late."

"You know what I don't like about them folks?" asked Jake.

"What?"

"They wants us to go back to Africa."

"I don't like that, neither."

"They's sure nuts on that point."

"And if we went back to Africa, what would we do?"

"You'll have to ask them that."

"Aw . . . They nuts as hell," said Jake, with an impatient wave of the hand.

They passed a beauty parlor and the scent of burning hair stung their nostrils. From a doorway a black woman stepped to the sidewalk and came briskly forward. Her hair was shining jet, and was brushed straight back, plastered to her head. The contrast between the overdose of white powder and the natural color of her skin was so sharp that she looked like two people instead of one; it was as if her ghost were walking in front of her.

"She's ready!"

"She's mellow!"

"She's pig meat!"

"Naw, she's gnat's liver!"

"Laaaaawd, today!"

Turning quickly into the "L" station, they mounted steel steps, laid their dimes upon the till, went through the revolving

gate, and stood upon the platform, waiting for the train.
They could still hear the dying strains of the band even above
the roar of the traffic. They did not talk; they were feeling the
surges of memory the music had roused in their minds. They
did not agree with the parade, but they did agree with the
music. There came upon them the memories of those Sunday
mornings in the South when they had attended church.

"You know," said Jake, out of the depths of a confused
mood, "maybe them folks is right, who knows?"

"Maybe so."

"Wait a minute," said Bob. "I'll be right back!"

"You can't!" said Slim. "Here comes the train now."

Bob stood still and looked hard at the dirty planks of the
platform.

"This thing is killing me," he mumbled.

They laughed and Slim started coughing. The train roared
up and they took seats facing one another. Bob sat tense, his
knees close together. Slim heaved into his handkerchief. Al
fished in his pockets for a match to pick his teeth, and failing
to find one, closed his eyes, leaned back, and sighed. Jake bent
forward and looked at his dim reflection in the windowpane. When Slim's coughing subsided, he sat hunched and
drummed his fingers nervously on the windowsill. Bob
crossed his legs with a slow, tender motion and pulled his hat
far down over his eyes.

"This 'L' is sure running slow," he sighed.

"Take it easy," said Jake.

"It won't kill you," said Al.

The "L" clacked rhythmically over steel rails and the buildings flying past grew taller. They blinked their eyes each time
sunlight flickered in and out of the coach. Obliquely across
the aisle a white woman propped her feet upon a vacant seat,
exposing the curved ascent of white thighs. Jake nudged Bob
with his elbow.

"Look," he whispered.

"Hunh?"

"Look!"

"What?"

"Jeeesus, you blind!"

Bob looked.

"Laaaaawd," he breathed.

Stealthily, Bob kicked Slim.

"Slim!"

"Yeah?"

"Look, *fool!*"

Slim looked and his mouth dropped open. He hunched Al.

"Al, look at the woman!"

"Where?"

"Over there, nigger!"

Al looked.

"Wheeeeeeeeeeeee!" he whistled softly.

They moved in their seats as though on pins, looking alternately at the woman and out of the window. Finally, Jake rolled his eyes heavenward and sang in an undertone:

"Oh, Lawd, can I ever, can I ever? . . ."

Bob screwed up his eyes, shook his head, and answered ruefully:

"Naw, nigger, you can never, you can never . . ."

Slim sat bolt upright, smiled, and countered hopefully:

"But wherever there's life there's hope . . ."

Al dropped his head, frowned, and finished mournfully:

"And wherever there's trees there's rope . . ."

Jake grabbed his sides, threw back his head, and let out a long laugh. Slim tried to laugh, but began heaving into his handkerchief. Bob sat with a mixed expression of pain and ecstasy. Al gripped his knees and howled. They kept so much noise that passengers turned and stared, wondering what on earth was the matter with those four black men.

Part Two: Squirrel Cage

. . . Now, when you study these long, rigid rows of desiccated men and women, you feel that you are in the presence of some form of life that has hardened but not grown, and over which the world has passed . . .

—Waldo Frank's *Our America*

. . . IT WAS THE MOST DIFFICULT PERIOD OF LINCOLN'S LIFE. GENERAL LEE LAUNCHED A FURIOUS AND BITTER OFFENSIVE AGAINST THE UNION LINES, INFLICTING MURDEROUS DAMAGE; DURING SEVEN GORY DAYS THIRTYSIX THOUSAND MEN GAVE UP THEIR LIVES. THEN BUELL AND BRAGG LOCKED HORNS IN A DESPERATE SCRAMBLE ON TENNESSEE SOIL IN WHICH EIGHT THOUSAND MEN WERE SLAIN. WITH SOME FIFTY THOUSAND MEN U. S. GRANT CLUTCHED AT VICKSBURG AND FAILED, LEAVING THOUSANDS DEAD UPON THE FIELD. THE REBEL'S DEADLY AND INSISTENT HAMMERBLOWS AT THE UNION LINES HAD SET THE WAR DEPARTMENT IN WASHINGTON IN A PANIC . . .

I.

WHEN THE TRAIN stopped at the Congress Street "L" Station, they hurried off the platform, through the swinging gates, down the narrow stairs, and swung westward along Jackson Boulevard. Noon crowds jammed the sidewalks. It was getting cold; from Lake Michigan a stiff wind blew, rustling the flags draped over doorways. The Loop sky was murky with smoke and the sun hung like a dim red ball above the tops of skyscrapers. With the hard heels of their shoes clicking on the pavement, the four men walked silently and looked in the showwindows at the new spring styles.

The clang of traffic, the array of color, and the riot of flickering lights infected Jake with a nervous and rebellious eagerness. He did not want to leave all this life in the streets; he had a feeling that he was missing something, but what it was he did not know. His teeth seemed gritty and he held them on edge in a tight clamp. He moved with a sort of slinking, swaying motion, something like a sick cat, with the handle of his cane hooked over his forearm and his hands thrust deep into his coat pockets. When he became aware of his tense anxiety, he knew he had been worrying about Lil. Had she been here already? Was this the showdown? Would Doc Higgins do as he had promised? Would he be called up before the Board of Review today? *If Doc can't fix things and Lil's done been here I'm in one helluva mess!* Yes, if Doc could not help him he would have to get busy and prepare a good lie to tell the Board of Review. He tried to remember what lies he had told in the past, but could not. He would have to prepare something new and strong this time. And looming ahead of him were eight long black hours of work. He was already tired and a little sleepy.

They paused for the red light at State Street, and when the green flashed, hurried across, down to Dearborn Street, then to the employees' entrance of the Chicago Post Office. It was a huge, dark grey building, almost the color of the sky, occupying a square block. Just to look at it depressed Jake. A sudden sense of all the weary hours he had spent within those blackened walls filled him with foreboding. As he mounted the steps he wondered if he would have to go on this way year after year 'til he died. Was this *all*? Deep in him was a dumb yearning for something else; somewhere or other was something or other for him. But where? How? All he could see right now was an endless stretch of black postal days; and all he could feel was the agony of standing on his feet till they ached and sweated, of breathing dust till he spat black, of jerking his body when a voice yelled.

"Lawd, I'd give my right ball to be off today," he sighed.

"It ain't you, it's me," said Bob.

"Every day in this joint's a nail in my coffin," said Slim.

"When you planning on going west for that cough of yours?"

"They won't give me a transfer."

"But what you going to do?"

"What to hell can I do?"

"Look like it's getting colder," said Jake as they fell into the line that was forming in the doorway.

"Yeah," sighed Al.

They got their badges and held them in the palms of their hands as the line inched forward. Jake looked at the skinny red neck of a white man and felt somebody breathing hot on the back of his own neck. He swallowed and blinked his eyes, hating all this. He fingered the silver coins in his pocket and their soft clink made him remember that he was almost broke.

"Say, youall?" he called. "Will you sign for me today? I got to get a loan from old Jones."

"I can't sign," said Al. "I owe two hundred in there already."

"How about you, Bob?"

"I'll sign."

"And you, Slim?"

"Yeah, I'll sign."

"That means we'll have a blowout tonight," said Jake gleefully. "It's on me!"

"Swell!"

They finally passed the armed guard who was inspecting the badges and saying monotonously: "O.K." A wave of dust struck their eyes and nostrils as they waded through an ocean of gloom and letterracks. A penetrating drone hovered persistently, filling their bodies with a faint, nervous tremor. Here and there, like dull, glowering eyes, were dingy lights partly hidden by green shades. The clatter of cancelling machines rose like the rumble of an underground volcano. Turning to the left, they went down a short flight of stairs and into the Post Office swingroom. It was a large, barnlike place crowded with small tables. Bob hurried off to the right, in the direction of the men's washroom. Al, Slim, and Jake pushed their way to the checkingcounter where they got numbered slips of paper in exchange for their hats, coats, and canes. From the stairway white clerks and black clerks with spent, washedout faces were coming off duty, pouring into the canteen, shouting, laughing. Jake wished that his eight hours were already put in; he wished that he were among those about to go home, to shows, to taverns, or to some lively flat where a party would be held. He stood with a wry smile on his face and answered greetings.

"What you saying, Jake?"

"Ain't saying."

"How goes it, Jake?"

"Slow, Jim. How's the mail up there?"

"She's light right now, but they's expecting it to be heavy's a dog."

He heard the clerks shouting at one another.

"Aw, Sid, don't go home! Let's play some bridge!"

"O.K. Get you a partner!"

"Say, Horace, you going home?"

"Let's eat first!"

"Lawd, am I tired?"

The white clerks got their hats and coats and hurried up the stairs. Many of them carried books under their arms; most of them were young students who regarded their jobs in the Post Office as something temporary to tide them through the University. Jake scowled as he watched their tense, eager faces. *Them white boys always in a hurry to get somewhere. And soon's they get out of school they's going to be bigshots. But a nigger just stays a nigger.* He turned and looked toward the tables; many of the Negro clerks had remained to play bridge.

"White folks sure is funny," Jake said to Slim.

"How's that?"

"They don't never set down and take things easy."

"Hell, naw," said Al. "They figgering on how to get up in the world."

"They rush about like bees."

"Yeah, but ain't no use of a black man rushing."

"Naw, 'cause we ain't going nowhere."

"When a black man gets a job in the Post Office he's done reached the top."

"We just as well take it easy and have some fun, 'cause the white folks got us hogtied."

Tables began to rattle from the thud of cards being whacked down. Hoarse shouts cut through the smoky air. Though there were no written rules of segregation, it was generally assumed that Negroes would occupy one end of the canteen and whites the other. However, if a mixture was found nothing was said. But Jake always felt that he wanted to sit with his own race because he did not know the whites so well. He definitely preferred the company of his own color; they understood him and he understood them.

"You reckon old Jones is in his office?" Jake asked.

"Hard to tell. This is a holiday, you know."

"Gee, I almost forgot that! What time you got?"

"It's fifteen after twelve."

"Come on. We got time to pull the deal," said Jake.

"Let's wait for Bob."

When Bob came they raced up the stairs, and a minute later stood in a stuffy office facing a fisheyed white man who sat behind a battered desk.

"Hello, Jake!"

"How you, Mister Jones?"

"Fair. Howdy, boys!"

Bob, Al, and Slim murmured greetings and crowded close.

"Well, what's on your mind?"

Jake hesitated, hung his head, smiled, scratched his chin, his lip, and drawled:

"I'm broke."

"You're always broke, Jake."

"But I'm in trouble this time."

"What seems to be the matter?"

"Well, you see, my wife's got to be operated on."

"That's too bad. And you're looking for dough, eh?"

"That's the truth! My wife's going to the hospital and I got to have a hundred dollars."

"How can you pay back a hundred dollars?" asked Jones, tilting in his swivel chair.

Jake blinked.

"I'm working everyday. I'll pay you back like I been paying all the time."

"Yes, but . . ."

"I done borrowed money from you before and paid it back, ain't I?"

"Yes, you have, but . . ."

"But *what*?"

"Well," said Jones, sighing and toying with a black inkwell on his desk. "I'd advise you to have a talk with Swanson or somebody on the Board of Review. I've word from upstairs not to issue any loans to clerks whose jobs are uncertain."

"Un . . . Un*cer*tain? How? Mister Jones, I still got my job. How come you say that?"

"You'd better see the Board," said Jones, sitting the inkwell down firmly. "If you come out all right with them, then come back and see me."

Jake stood before the desk, head down, the tips of his fingers resting nervously on a green blotter. He was conscious of a vague numbness creeping down his shoulders. Was this Lil's trick? *Is she done been here already?*

"Is she done been here already, Mister Jones? My wife?"

"You'd better see the Board, Jake," said Jones, thumbing through a pile of papers.

When outside the door Jake spat and growled:

"Gawddamn her guts! She's done it!"

"But didn't Doc say he was going to fix it?"

"She beat us to it."

"You better go and see that Board and talk like hell," said Al.

"Look here, Bob," said Jake. "I want you to do something. What time you got?"

"It's eighteen after twelve. We checkin at twelvethirty."

"Listen! While I'm at the Board, go down and 'phone Doc for me, see?"

"Sure!"

"Tell 'im I'm in for it! Tell 'im Lil's done been here and done her dirty work! Ask 'im can't he do *some*thing! Ask 'im to 'phone old Swanson right *now*."

"O.K.," said Bob, running for the stairs.

"What you going to tell the Board?" asked Slim.

Jake did not answer; he dragged his left foot slowly across the steel and spat again:

"Gawddamn that bitch's soul!"

"Anything I can do, Jake?" asked Al.

"You know I'm with you," said Slim.

"Aw, it's all right," Jake drawled, squinting out over rows and rows of letterracks. "You guys go on. I'll see you later."

They left him standing in the middle of the steel floor, just opposite the stairway. He wanted to give Bob time to get in touch with Doc Higgins before he went upstairs; he walked slowly over to a wall and leaned against it. That sense of uneasiness which had haunted him all day descended now with abrupt finality, and became real. This was it. He could not dodge any longer. The best thing to do was to go up and face that Board and have done with it. *They can't kill me,* he thought desperately. *All they can do is just fire me.* But he knew that he did not want them to do even that; he knew that by taking such an attitude he was trying to fool himself, trying to muster up a false courage. But in order to keep them from firing him, what could he tell? He moved toward the foot of the stairs, seeing Lil's face hovering before him. Involuntarily the muscles of his arms flexed with a desire to reach out and clutch her throat. He would settle with her. Just wait until he was off from work, just wait until tonight. *What I'm going to do to her won't be funny!* It was hard climbing the stairs with clerks jostling him and shouting at one another, over and around him. Their indifference seemed somehow an insult; he wanted to tell these clerks about this terrible thing Lil had done, he wanted them to know what a pickle of a fix she had gotten him into. *It's all my own fault,* he thought regretfully. *I should've tricked her before she tricked me* . . . When he reached the third floor he remembered Bob's threat to throw up everything, to quit his job to get even with his wife. Yes, he ought to do that. He ought to walk out of here right now and never be seen or heard of again. Then Lil would be stranded and sorry. *She'd see what a fool she's been.* But if he did that what was he to do afterwards? Where could he find work? He was broke and there were a thousand men, black and white, waiting to take his job. *If I had only saved some money during these long years I would drop Lil and this lousy job flat. I'd leave this place before you could spit!* He walked around a narrow, circular balcony and stopped before a door, trembling. *Doc sure ought to could do something.* His impulses were deadlocked and his underwear stuck to his skin with hot sweat. He swallowed three times before he could bring his hand to touch the doorknob. *Aw, hell,* he thought again, screwing up his courage as he pushed the door in, *they sure can't kill me.* A white stenographer paused with her fingers suspended over the keys of her typewriter, and asked:

"Whom do you want to see?"

"Mister Swanson, Ma'm."

"The name?"

"Jackson, Jake Jackson."

"Just a moment."

She pushed a button and spoke softly into a transmitter. Presently a white man appeared in the rear door of the office.

"Oh, hello, Jake!"

"How you, Mister Swanson?"

"You want to see me?"

"Yes, sir. I want to see the Board."

"Oh, yeah!" said Swanson, nodding. "We were just about to send for you. Come on in."

Jake walked into a small office and took a seat on the edge of a chair. The office contained three desks, at two of which sat white men, and at the third a Negro. *There's that Gawddamn nigger Howard,* Jake thought bitterly. *He would have to be here.* Howard sat with a green fountain pen poised in his long black fingers.

"So you're in to see us again, hunh, Jackson?" asked Howard.

"Yeah, but what for?" asked Jake, shifting his feet around.

"Don't *you* know?" Howard asked.

"Naw."

"Well, what did you come in here for?" asked Swanson. "We weren't going to send for you for another hour yet."

"Oh, yes, sir! I . . . I was trying to get a loan from Mister Jones. He told me to come in here."

"What do you want with a loan?"

"Well, my wife's sick."

"And Jones wouldn't let you have it?"

"Naw, sir. He said to come and talk with the Board."

"You make $2,100 a year, don't you, Jake?"

"Yes, sir."

"What do you do with your money?"

"Why, I spends it to live."

There was a short silence.

"We want to have a serious talk with you, Jackson," said Howard.

The two white men wagged their heads and smiled. Howard beat a soft tattoo on the desk with his fountain pen. Jake sat awkwardly, looking from one to the other, trying to feign innocent bewilderment. *Yeah, it takes a black sonofabitch to rub it into his own people!*

"Draw your chair up closer, Jake," asked Swanson.

"Yes, sir."

Jake looked again at Howard and wished that that Negro was anywhere right now but here. *How can I talk to these white folks with that nigger setting watching me? If I try to beg 'em to go easy on me, he'll think I'm a Uncle Tom . . .* A sense of shame spread over him. *He's setting there at that desk just like he's a white man. Hell, he's the one who's a Uncle Tom!* He saw Swanson light a cigar and lean back in his chair. The room was quiet save for the faint hiss of steam in the radiator and the soft clacking of the stenographer's typewriter in the outer office. An itchy feeling, like a tiny trickle of hot water, oozed down the center of his back. He knew he should have been talking, but he did not know what to say. He did not know how much Lil had told. He carried his hand nervously across his forehead and licked his lips.

"Jake, do you know of any reason why you should be in the Postal Service?" asked Swanson.

He flinched in spite of himself; he had been expecting something, but nothing this cold, this final.

"Yes, ssssir . . . I do my work, don't I?"

"We're asking *you*," said Swanson.

"I want to make a living for my family," Jake spluttered.

"So do a million other men," said Swanson.

He knew he had been put on the defensive, and he decided desperately to turn the tables.

"How come you talk to me like this, Mister Swanson? There ain't been no complaint against me, is there?"

The tip of Swanson's cigar glowed red; he took it out of his mouth and turned to the other white man, an elderly, grey-haired one.

"You want to tell him, Anderson?"

Anderson in turn looked at Howard.

"You want to tell 'im, Howard?"

Howard looked at Jake and laughed.

"Well, look like it's my dirty work," he said, laying the fountain pen aside. "Listen, Jackson, have you been doing anything that would make you unfit for the Postal Service?"

"Naw! What you mean?"

"Your wife was in this morning."

"You mean she come *here*?"

"She did."

"How come she do that?"

"You can't guess?"

"I swear to Gawd I can't!"

"She lodged a complaint against you."

"Lawd, have mercy!" Jake exclaimed. "I know what you guys talking about now! Shucks, that ain't *nothing*! Youall got me dead wrong . . ." He paused, ignoring Howard, and turned to Swanson. "Mister Swanson, she don't know what she's doing! She's sick and nervous! She's been acting queer like that for a long time now. She's got to be operated on. I was just in to see Mister Jones in the Credit Union, trying to get some money to have her sent to the hospital . . ."

"What do you mean? Your wife acting queer?"

"She just don't know what she's doing!"

"Why don't you have her observed?" asked Anderson.

"What's that?"

"Why don't you have her watched to see what's wrong with her?"

"Shucks, I see her every day. I know what's wrong with her."

"I mean, if she's that bad, why don't you send her to the psychopathic?"

"To Mister who?"

"To the crazyhouse," said Howard, twisting down the corners of his mouth.

"I never thought of that," said Jake, blinking.

"Jake, this is the third time you've been before us in the last six months," said Swanson.

"I just couldn't help them other times, Mister Swanson."

"You were before us for drinking on the job once."

"But I ain't never been drunk on the job no more."

"And then you were in for debt dodging."

"It was my wife! She makes them debts! She . . ."

"We're not interested in who makes them," said Howard. "They're yours. You should handle your affairs so they won't come into this office. This isn't a nursery."

"Yes, sir. I knows that . . . Now, if you just let me handle my wife this time . . ."

"Haven't you *already* handled her?" asked Anderson.

"How you mean?"

"Your wife says you beat her."

"Naw, sir! That's a lie and Gawd knows it!" Jake ran to the desk, the muscles of his face jerking. "I swear before Almighty Gawd I ain't never touched that woman! She's just out of her head! I wouldn't hit a sick woman . . ." He became strangled, coughed, swallowed. "Mister Swanson, I'll tell you what's wrong, I'll tell you the *whole* story! That woman ain't got cat sense! She keeps me head over heels in debt. She treats me like I'm a buzzard! She wants a fur coat and a piano and I can't get 'em for her. You gentlemens knows how much money I make, and how on earth can I buy things like that for her? She threatened me and said she was coming down here and say I beat her if I didn't buy 'em. Now she's done done it . . ." He looked at the floor, overcome with the villainy of it. "How could she live if I wasn't taking care of her? Mister Swanson, youall can't hold me responsible for a crackbrained woman! She told youall them lies for pure evil black spite . . ."

"Her arms were black and blue with bruises," said Anderson.

"I slept with her last night and I ain't seen no bruises," said Jake.

"Where did she get 'em from?" asked Howard.

"She must have done it herself, 'cause Gawd Almighty knows I didn't do it."

"How on earth could she do that?"

"I don't know. All I know is, *I* didn't do it!"

"She says you kicked her in her side with your foot."

"Kicked her!" Jake stepped back with amazement. "Kicked her? Do I look like a man what would kick a *sick* woman?"

"We're not concerned with how you look," said Swanson.

"Mister Swanson, please, you got to listen to me! As Gawd in Heaven's my judge, I done done all I can for that woman. I done done as much as any man *could* do! For seven years that woman's been sick on my hands, and for seven years I done paid them doctor bills. I owe five hundred dollars right now . . . I ain't the kind of a man what would kick a sick woman! Youall knows I wouldn't do nothing like that . . ."

"I'm sorry, Jake," sighed Swanson. "It's reached the point where we can't believe you any longer."

Jake glanced at Howard, swallowed his shame, and plunged desperately.

"Mister Swanson, I'm a black man. You can see my skin. I loves my race. I'm proud to be black. I wouldn't do nothing on earth to drag my race down. I ain't the kind of a man what would beat his wife and stand here before you white gentlemens . . ."

"How long was your wife acting queer?"

"Well, for about three months, anyway."

"What did she do to make you think she was acting queer?"

"She did everything. She throwed my money away. She ran around with other men. That's how come she's sick now, running with other men. That's how come she got a tumor . . . Mister Swanson, listen, I bet I know how come she got them bruises! She got 'em from that guy she's fooling with! He beat her . . . He . . ."

"That's enough, Jake," said Swanson, swinging around and

pulling out a drawer. "Here's a form for your resignation. Fill it out and have it back to us by the fifteenth of the month. Your pay ends on this period."

"Mister Swanson, for Gawd's sake!"

"That'll be all!"

Jake stood stonily, his right hand raised, his mouth open.

"Youall just *can't* throw a man off his job like this!"

"You're throwing yourself off, Jackson," said Howard.

"You can give me just one more chance, Mister Swanson."

"You've had three chances."

"Youall don't know what I done been through with . . ."

"We're not concerned with that."

Jake's eyes burned and the room blurred; when he spoke his voice quavered.

"I done worked hard all these long years for the government. I ain't bothered nobody. I'm just a poor, hardworking black man. I ain't got nothing and Gawd knows I ain't never going to have nothing. I was a good worker. Youall knows I was. My life ain't been no bed of ease. I done had it hard all my days and I ain't complained. Now youall can have just a little mercy on me. Just a *little* . . . Please, youall, give me one more chance . . . Just *one* more . . ."

"You're not doing yourself any good by carrying on that way," said Howard, shaking his head.

The telephone rang. *Lawd, I hope that's Doc!* Swanson lifted the receiver. Jake eased back to his seat and wiped sweat from his face.

"Hello!"

" . . . "

"Yeah, this is he."

" . . . "

"Who? Doc Higgins? Yeeeah . . ."

" . . . "

"Well, I don't know. It's pretty bad."

" . . . "

"This is the third time in six months."

" . . . "

"No."

" . . . "

"Did the Post Master say that?"

"..."

Swanson sighed and looked at Jake.

"How much? Oh, all right . . ."

"..."

"Now listen to me: If I do, it's the very last time, you hear?"

Jake knew it was Doc. *If he can only get me out of this!* He looked at Howard. *Gawddamn nigger licking white folks' boots!* The receiver clicked. Swanson faced Jake.

"How long have you been working here, Jake?"

"Going on nine years, now."

"Why can't you do better than you're doing?"

"I'll do better, Mister Swanson."

"I don't want you to come into this office no more than you want to come in here."

"Yes, sir. I know."

"Hereafter, you keep your business *out* of here!"

"Yes, sir. My wife ain't *never* coming in here no more!"

"This is the last time you're coming before us, you hear? Next time you won't even be given a hearing. We're getting tired of this!"

"Yyyyyou mmmmean I get another chance?"

"Yes, but you don't deserve it . . ."

"Thank you, sir! Thank you!"

"All right! Get to work!"

As he went through the door Howard's pitying smile caught his eye and lingered in his mind, rankling, bitter. When he was at the bottom of the steps he stopped and stared, stared through the brick and steel walls of the Post Office, stared all the way to the South Side of the city where Lil was. *I'm going to break that bitch's neck if it's the last thing I ever do! I'm going to stomp her guts out as sure as my name's Jake Jackson . . .*

II.

"Hᴏᴡ ʏᴏᴜ come out, Jake?"
Bob tugged at his sleeve.

"Wasn't nothing to it," Jake answered, grinning. "How can they work the United States mails without *me*?"

"Doc fix it?"

"Sure! He 'phoned in when I was getting my walking-papers."

"You sure one lucky dog. I thought you was a goner."

"And was I sweating? But wait till I get my hands on that bitch!"

"Say, I wouldn't bother her for awhile . . ."

"The only reason I don't is 'cause I can't find her."

"Oh, yeah. Doc told me to tell you it'd cost you a hundred and fifty."

"Hundred and fifty? My Gawd! Aw, well . . . I guess it was worth it. If he hadn't've done something I would've had no job."

"Come on! There's Al and Slim!"

They hurried to the Mailing Division.

"What happened?"

"You beat the rap?"

"Smooth as butter," said Jake, waving his palm with nervous bravado, still hot and wet with sweat. "They can't keep a good man down."

They got their timecards from the racks and punched in. A voice was bawling:

"LINE UP FOR DETAIL!"

As they fell into line and moved toward the Detail Station, they could hear the detail clerk barking out numbers.

"Jake Jackson," called Jake when he was opposite the desk.

"Ten on table nine!"

"Robert Madison," called Bob.

"Eleven on table nine!"

"Albert Johnson," called Al.

"Twelve on table nine!"

"Nathan Williams," called Slim.

"Thirteen on table nine!"

With heads bent, they shuffled across the steel floor in the direction of the tables.

A post office table is a heavy, oblong, wooden contrivance resembling generally a diningroom table, only much larger and sturdier. It is supported by six to eight wooden posts and stands about three feet from the floor, coming in height up to the average man's belt. Its surface, usually about eighty feet square, is formed into a shallow trough by a fiveinch bordering of wood; its bottom is covered with a thin sheeting of smooth steel. Upon these tables sacks of mail are dumped indiscriminately as they come in from the mailtrucks. It is the duty of clerks assigned here to sort this mail according to size, weight, and class. Long business letters are called "lumber", and are sorted, faced leftward with the stamp turned downward into small wooden or steel trays. Ordinary correspondence letters are called "small", and are stacked likewise, but to one end of the trays and to themselves. When these trays are filled they are carried to the cancelling machines where the letters are postmarked. Special delivery and airmail letters are put to one side in a corner of the table to be collected by a clerk whose sole duty is to see that they are dispatched immediately to their proper sections for speedy service. All second, third, and fourth class mail is thrown into labeled gurneys. For eight long hours a clerk's hands must be moving ceaselessly, to and fro, stacking the mail. At intervals a foreman makes rounds of inspection to see that all is going well. Under him works a legion of catfooted spies and stoolpigeons who snoop eternally. Along the walls are slits through which detectives peep and peer.

Jake, Al, Bob, and Slim stood at table nine rolling their sleeves and adjusting their trays.

"Another day another dollar."

"A million days a million dollars."

"Reckon we'll ever make it?" asked Al.

"Don't know, boy, don't know," said Slim, shaking his head.

"We'll have to save more'n a dollar a day to make a million," said Bob.

"And we'll have to live a thousand years," said Jake.

"It's a bitch," said Al.

"It's more'n a bitch," said Slim with a deep sigh.

"The work ain't hard and the boss ain't mean," sang Al.

"Just like lard from New Orleans," sang Bob.

They laughed.

"That song's a lie," said Jake.

"You telling me?"

"Old Uncle Sam's sure mean to his black boys," said Al.

"He's got us under his thumb and we can't rise no higher'n he wants us to," said Slim.

"You ever hear of a uncle treating his nephews like Uncle Sam treats us?" asked Bob.

"Hell, naw!"

"It ain't in the books!"

"It's 'cause we's *black* nephews."

"You know how come he treats us this way?" asked Jake.

"How come?"

"Uncle Sam's sister was raped by a nigger . . ."

They laughed again.

"Jake, you crazy!"

"Well, she must've been raped," said Jake. "I can't figger out no other reason why the white folks hate us so."

He lifted a full sack of mail from a truck, tossed it to the table, dragged it toward him, dumped it, and flung the empty bag over his shoulder into a canvas gurney. He rubbed his hands together and looked at the mail. He did not want to touch it. Then he began to sort, letter by letter. The cold mail chilled his fingers. Already his throat was getting dry from dust; he wished he had remembered to buy a plug of tobacco. He heard Slim's cough bubbling in his throat incessantly like water bubbling in a fountain. Bob stood about a foot away from the table, half bent over, afraid to let the bordering of wood touch his middle anywhere. In order to take as much weight off his feet as possible, Jake leaned heavily against the table as he worked. His feet began to sweat and the calves of his legs numbed slowly. As time passed all the noises gradually fused into one general din and imperceptibly dulled his senses. A strong light directly above his head worried his eyes and he looked at it about every five minutes, frowning. The eight long hours loomed ahead like a series of black pits, and he tried not to think of them. He could not find a suitable position for his body; he rested his weight on one side for a few moments and then the other. He crossed his feet, uncrossed them, stood awhile with one foot on top of the other, then straightened, sighing. The edge of an envelope caught irritatingly under the tip of a thumbnail and he threw it aside with such violence that Slim asked with concern:

"What's the matter?"

"Nothing," he breathed.

When his first tray was filled he carried it to a scale.

"What's the weight?" a clerk called.

"Nineteen pounds," Jake answered.

"O.K."

The weight of his tray was jotted into a huge black ledger. He piled the mail on a long counter in front of a row of cancelling machines and came back to the table. He looked at Al, whose black face rested in an expression of calm vacuity. Al's fat hands moved one over the other, stacking the mail. He was talking to a white clerk who stood at his side; his voice droned, heavy, musical, satisfied. Jake wished he had been near Al so he could have talked with him; there was something in Al which always made him feel sure of himself. And Al was a soldier, a member of the Illinois National Guard. For over a year now Al had been worrying him to join. *Maybe it wouldn't be a bad idea to get into that thing.* Al was a swell fellow, easy to get along with. *It'd be hot if I could get into his company . . .*

As the first two hours dragged by he began to feel a vast emptiness, a sort of black, resigned peace; he felt like a man who had clung to the vertical surface of a wall so long by his fingernails, hanging by his own weight, that he had grown used to it. Conscious thought drifted away and he became aware of the dark part of his blood and nerves, whispering, suggesting, counselling. His body waxed warm and the images of his mind swirled into a huge grey blot. He grew pleasurably conscious of where the table pressed against his loins, and he leaned against it harder. His genitals began to swell; his eyes did not move from the mail; his lips became moist and hung loose; he was a little dizzy; he straightened suddenly, uttering a curse to himself with a soft expulsion of breath, *Gawddamn . . .*

"Say, Jake?"

"Hunh?"

"I was talking to old Slaughter of the N.A.A.C.P.* this morning. He told me them guys in Washington's planning to send a commission down here to investigate how we colored clerks work."

"To investigate *us*?"

"That's what he said."

"How come they want to do that?"

"Well, somebody in Congress done said we ain't working like the white clerks."

"That's a Gawddamn lie!"

"They just doing that 'cause there's more black clerks working in the Mailing Division than whites."

"Slaughter was saying that the white clerks around here's done got up some kind of organization to run us and the Jews out."

"Well, the white folks didn't want this job when times was good."

"No white man wanted to work nights and breathe all this dust."

"And now 'cause the Depression's on, they want to kick us out."

"Look like the white folks don't want us to have *nothing*!"

"Ain't there some kind of union running on this job?"

"Yeah, but it ain't no damn good."

"Unions ain't nothing but a gyp game."

"And most unions don't want no black members nohow."

"This is the way I feel about it. I don't want to belong to nothing the white folks don't want me to belong to. I ain't going to lick their boots."

"If white folks could make us buy the air we breathe they would."

"They always cooking up something to make trouble."

"Wonder how they think we's going to live?"

"They ain't thinking about that."

"This is about the best job a black man can get and they don't even want us here."

*National Association for the Advancement of Colored People

"It's sure hell when you think about it."

"And thinking don't help none."

"Naw, you'll go nuts then."

"I wonder what'll ever happen to black folks!"

"Gawd only knows."

"The white man's Gawd in this land."

"If he says you live, you live."

"And if he says you die, you die."

"Let's checkout to the can," called Bob.

Al laughed.

"Is it breaking you down, Bob?"

"Honest to Gawd, sometimes I feel like shooting my brains out and having it over with."

"It's a great life if you don't weaken," said Slim.

"It'll get better," said Al, clapping Bob's shoulder. "Live in hope."

"Let's go," said Jake.

They filed to the detail desk and gave their names and tablenumbers to a clerk who jotted them down into a huge black ledger, opposite which was inserted the time of day. They had fifteen minutes in which to empty their bowels and bladders and checkin again.

"Come on," said Bob, leading the way past windows and tables piled high with mail.

"Gee, it's cloudy out."

"Look like it wants to snow."

"Yeah, it's getting cold again."

The lavatory was full of clerks, black and white. A hot stench of urine and tobacco smoke choked the air. There was a soft murmur of conversation, like a continuous groan. Some clerks sat on stools with the covers down; they had pulled off their shoes and were squeezing sweaty stockingedfeet in their hands to ease the pain of standing all day. Others leaned against the walls with halfclosed eyes. At the left end of the lavatory, high up in the side of the wall, were the inevitable slits for spying. Other than the entrance door, there was no ventilation, and over the quiet flow of talk rose the never-ending drone of an acre of machines.

Almost ripping his belt loose, Bob made for a commode and flopped down.

"Look, old Bob's got to set down to leak," said Jake.

"Man, you bad's a woman," laughed Al.

"Aw, qqquit rrrazzing 'im," coughed Slim.

Jake watched Bob close his eyes, bite his lips, lean his head back against a wall, and knot his fingers in pain between his legs.

"You know one thing?" said Slim.

"What?"

"That nigger's sick."

"You telling me?"

Jake averted his head, cleared his throat with a deep belly-grunt, and spat a black gob of dustfilled phlegm into a urine commode. He glanced furtively out of the corners of his eyes to see who was smoking; a few were, stealthily. He rushed out his pack of cigarettes, lit one by bending low and cupping his hands, sucked three long draws, snuffed it, and put the butt into his vestpocket. He held the smoke in his lungs as long as he could, hearing the whispering rustle of tissuepaper and the constant gurgle of water. Then he let it eddy slowly through his nostrils. It felt good. He would finish the butt next time. To be caught smoking meant a hundred demerits.

"What place is this where we going tonight?" asked Slim.

"To a joint run by a dame named Rose."

"Where abouts?"

"Over on Calumet."

"Hot spot?"

"That's what I hear."

"Any good meat going to be there?"

"What you think I'm taking you for?"

"I feel like tearing up something tonight."

"Lawd, you sure tore up the last mama you had."

"Boy, that dame said she didn't *never* want to see me no more!"

"You ought to go easy on 'em, Slim."

"Can't help myself, man. The only thing I like better than meat is more meat."

Jake laughed.

Al edged close, buttoning his pants and holding a crumpled newspaper under his arm.

"I see where that Python Killer got the chair," he said.

"Yeah? Let's see."

"Aw, they ain't going to burn her. They'll pardon her just before her time's up."

Al spread the paper and a knot of clerks gathered.

"Jeeesus, she's a hotlooking mama!"

"Now, just look at her! Setting up there smoking that cigarette with her legs crossed!"

"What's she setting on?"

"She's setting on the edge of the bathtub!"

"They say she cut a guy's throat and let the blood run down the drain."

"She killed six men. She drugged 'em and then smothered 'em to death with pillows when they was sleeping."

"But from the looks of that baby I wouldn't mind taking a chance on being smothered at night."

"Boy, if she tried to smother me I'd *show* her some smothering!"

"Maybe that was what was wrong with her men. They couldn't *smother* right."

They laughed.

"Yeah, but she was a hardhearted old bitch. She dug holes in her basement and buried the men she killed."

"How in hell could a woman looking that good do things like that?"

"You never can tell. Some of these babies look like sugar but they's poison inside."

"That woman was a bloodsucker."

"Look at the picture of that snake that guy drawed in. Got that snake wrapped around a man's neck."

"That's to show you she was just like a snake . . ."

" . . . a Python."

"And look, here's her face all marked and plotted out."

"What it say?"

"Her eyes is close together, meaning she's mean."

"And her bottom lip pokes out, meaning she's deceitful. She fooled folks."

"And that thick neck? What it say about it?"

"That means," read Al: " 'Uncontrollable passions, masculine feelings.' "

"Gawd, she must've been tough."

"She was tough. She bumped off six men."

"The papers say she got a kink in her brain."

"How that happen?"

"Maybe she fell when she was a baby . . ."

" . . . and bumped her head?"

"You reckon if they smoothed that kink out she'd get all right?"

"How in hell can they do that? They'd have to open up her skull."

"Aw, them papers don't know what they's talking about. Folks is just born to kill, and if they's born to kill, they'll kill, that's all!"

"Yeah, you have to do what Gawd's done planned for you to do."

"What's going to happen to you is going to happen."

"And nothing you can do ain't going to help none."

"That reminds me of that Tiger Woman . . ."

"And the Cat Killer . . ."

"And the Canary Girl, the one who had the sweet voice and killed all her babies . . ."

"And them thrill guys, Loeb and Leopold . . ."

"Aw, it's some strange folks in the world . . ."

Somebody pulled a chain and water tumbled and droned.

"Let's go," Bob whispered, leaning against a wall, his eyes bloodshot, slowly fastening his belt, his breath coming fast.

"How you feel?" asked Jake.

"I'll be all right in a second, but I hope I don't never have to come in here no more as long as I live . . ."

"Aw, buck up," said Al, catching Bob's arm. "Ain't nothing as bad's it seems."

Having been out fifteen minutes, they checked in again.

"Jake Jackson."

"Sixtynine on the small!"

"Robert Madison."

"Seventy on the small!"

"Albert Johnson."

"Seventyone on the small!"

"Nathan Williams."

"Seventytwo on the small!"

Bentbacked and with their eyes on the dirty steel, they

shuffled in the direction of the small letterracks. There were six rows, each row some forty feet long with letterracks on both sides of the row. Each took his place in front of a case. Above their eyes swung an electric bulb with a green shade which deflected a circle of light over the fronts of honeycomblike pigeonholes. To all four sides were suspended catwalks in which were slits for spying. Midway between their loins and knees was a wooden ledge about twelve inches wide upon which rested their trays of mail. Mingling with the drone of voices and the clatter of machines was the constant sound of rusty steel grating upon rusty steel. Each pigeonhole was labeled: Texas, Mississippi, Indiana, New York, Rhode Island, California, Michigan, Illinois, Florida . . . This was known as the Primary Separation, that is, the first separation which the mail underwent when it was brought into the Post Office. Above their heads was a maze of moving belts carrying sorted mail to state sections, and each time a steel tray struck a roller a loud clank was heard. To their rear was a battery of cancelling machines which threw off an odor of hot ink. Every six or seven feet was a rusty spittoon surrounded with sawdust. No mail had as yet come from the cancelling machines and Jake stood with his knee resting upon the ledge.

"MAIL FOR PRIMARY SEPARATION!" a voice bawled.

As one man the line of clerks turned to the right and filed to the end of the aisle. Each picked up a tray of mail and set it upon a scale; its weight was jotted down into a big black ledger.

"Your number?" a clerk asked Jake.

"Sixtynine on the small," Jake answered.

The weight of each man's mail and the time of day were jotted down opposite the number, and this number referred to his name; hence at any moment it could be told how much work each clerk had done, and what rate of speed. When back at his case, Jake propped his knee again upon the ledge, caught his left hand full of letters, licked his right thumb, and threw letters into the pigeonholes: Rhode Island—Delaware—Idaho—Maine—Tennessee—Michigan . . . He paused, cleared his throat, spat, adjusted the green shade on his light, and threw again. He had thrown this separation for so many years that it had become automatic with him. Slim was on his right, wheezing. Bob was to his left, shifting from foot to foot, biting his lips, frowning. Somewhere he heard Al's deep voice droning, laughing, quietly joyous. *That nigger don't never worry.* Sleep hung heavy in his blood and his legs were getting stiff. He remembered the scene in the office when he had stood before the Board. A new hatred against the Negro, Howard, rose up in him. *He just had to put his two cents in! Just to showoff! I'm sure glad old Doc got me out of that jam, if for nothing but to show that black nigger that he ain't the only chicken on the roost. Let 'im wash his face with it, by Gawd!* He remembered still another scene when Howard had hurt his feelings. He had been before the Board and Howard had used the word "Negro" in front of Swanson. *He could've called me colored at least.* It was all right for one Negro to call another Negro "nigger"; but when in front of white folks one ought to be careful. *And that word ain't the same when a white man uses it. There's something he puts in it that ain't right.* And he resented a great many other things like that. When he went to the movies he always wanted to see Negroes, if there were any in the play, shown against the background of urban conditions, not rural ones. Anything which smacked of farms, chaingangs, lynchings, hunger, or the South in general was repugnant to him. These things had so hurt him once that he wanted to forget them forever; to see them again merely served to bring back the deep pain for which he knew no salve.

"CLEAN OUT!"

As he dropped his handful of mail he heard a hundred other hands dropping theirs. He turned to the right again and followed the line of white men and black men who weaved in and out of the long rows of letterracks. Some sentimental thought always made him carry a Northern state rather than a Southern one. He never wanted to carry Mississippi, his home state. *That's one state I'm damn glad to be* from. He held his left arm stiff and straight, pointing floorward, about a foot from his body with the open palm of his hand extended upward. From each Illinois hole he took a handful of mail and stacked it in his left hand until it reached his chin, walking slowly from case to case. When he could take no more, he went to the traystation where he dumped the mail into a large tray, set the metal notch which would guide it to its section, and placed it upon a moving belt. The tray bumped off into the hazy air, clanking over the belt, carrying the mail to state sections where it would be sent to the ends of the world. Jake turned on his heel like a robot and started another cleanout.

"FILL IN!"

He was at his case again, throwing mail.

"I'm going to Jones at swingtime to see if he'll let me have that money," said Jake to Slim. "You want to come with me?"

"Sure."

"You, Bob?"

"O.K."

Another set of clerks were checking in at the Detail Station. Trucksful of dirty, wet mail bags stood in the aisles, waiting to be unloaded and sorted.

"It must be raining or snowing," said Slim.

"It's snowing," said Bob, bending and looking out of a window.

"Here come the cunts!" called Al.

A group of about fifteen Negro women were checking in at the Detail Station. Most of them were beyond thirty, having come into the Post Office during the days of the World War when the postal service was undermanned. They were round-shouldered and dumpylooking, and as they passed in the direction of their detail, white clerks and black clerks turned their heads to look at them.

"Them pale faces sure look at them women like they was bitches," said Jake.

"They got it coming to 'em," said Bob.

"Yeah, let a nigger woman make fifty dollars a week and she begins to think she's too good for her own race," said Jake.

"Aw, forget them cunts," said Al.

"I ain't worrying about 'em," said Jake. "But it just makes my blood boil to see a nigger woman grinning at a white man like them cunts do. And these white men around here don't give a good Gawddamn about us. We'll just be clerks as long as we stay here, but they's got a chance to rise as high as a man can go . . ."

"You right about that," said Slim.

"The race ought to stick together," said Bob.

"You know," said Jake, "the time they caught that nigger woman and that white clerk screwing in the office I was 'shamed to look a white man in the face around here. I felt they was laughing at me."

"I felt the same way myself."

"They look at us like we's dogs anyhow, and when our women ain't got no better sense'n to act like dogs, that makes 'em feel they's treating us right."

"I'd like to horsewhip every black cunt who so much as *looks* at a white man," said Jake.

"You ain't by yourself."

"That reminds me," began Jake. "I . . ."

"INSPECTION!"

A sudden voice boomed into Jake's ear and made him start. He turned and looked into the red face of a white man. It was the section inspector. Jake sighed, laid down his mail, and stepped aside. The inspector went through the case, examining each hole. Two New York letters were found in the Missouri hole; one Michigan letter was found in the city (Chicago) hole; and four letters bound for Pennsylvania were found in the New Mexico hole. The inspector finished and tapped the eight misthrown letters gently against the letter-rack. He looked at Jake a whole minute before he spoke.

"What's the matter, Jackson?"

"Nothing," Jake drawled, trying to smile.

"You think this is something to laugh about, hunh?"

"Naw, sir. I know it ain't . . ."

"You bet your boots it's not! Now, what's wrong?"

"Ain't nothing wrong."

"You sick?"

"Naw, sir."

"Sleepy?"

"Naw, sir."

"How do you account for these eight misthrown letters?"

"I don't see how in the world it happened," said Jake. "I was working pretty careful . . ."

"Yeah," sneered the inspector. "You were working carefully, all right! You've been running your mouth like a blue-streak for half an hour! Why don't you quit playing around and do your work!"

Jake's neck grew hot. The inspector had spoken in a loud, harsh voice.

"I'm doing my work," Jake whined, trying to placate the man. "I went to the can a few minutes ago. Somebody must've been working on my case . . ."

"You lying! You just came here! I saw you! You haven't been anywhere since you've been on this case," said the inspector, taking out his note book. "I'm going to give you a writeup."

"Do it and quit yelling at me!" Jake snapped.

"Don't give me none of your lip!"

"Don't give me none of *yours!*"

"Who do you think you're talking to!"

"You didn't have to yell at me!"

"I'll talk to you like I damn please!"

"Naw, you wouldn't if you wasn't in here!"

"You *threatening* me!"

"Give me my writeup and quit talking to me!"

"I'm not taking orders from you!"

Jake stepped back and flung his arms wide.

"Why don't you pick on somebody else?"

"Why don't you stop fooling around?"

"I ain't fooling around," said Jake stubbornly.

"Don't this look like it?" asked the inspector, shaking the letters in his face.

Jake trembled. He was conscious that two hundred men had stopped work and were watching him. He knew he was already in bad, and it would not do him any good to face that Board again. He swallowed and made an attempt to get back to his case, but the inspector stepped in front of him, blocking the way.

"Wait a minute! You think you're going to delay the United States mail and get off this easy?"

Jake looked at him with a dogged, fixedunder stare. He felt his muscles flexing. He was trying to keep from getting mad.

"Look what you've done!" the inspector railed. "Not a man in the whole section can work because of your big lip! You think you're going to get away with *that*?"

"You started it," Jake growled.

"*I* threw those letters wrong, *did* I?" the inspector screamed.

Something hot engulfed Jake and his head swam. He felt as he had felt that morning when Lil had talked back to him. He heard his voice speaking loudly.

"How come you don't pick on some of them white clerks? How come you always hopping on us colored boys! Gawd-dammit, I'm sick of this if ain't nobody else is . . ."

"Aw, come on, Jake!" said Al, grabbing his arm.

"Leave me alone!" Jake bawled.

"It's all right!" said Slim.

"Hush, Jake!" said Bob.

They held him.

"I'm recommending you for two hundred demerits," said the inspector. "You're going to hear from this."

Jake broke from his friends and walked with his head down to the end of the aisle and stood, glowering. *Gawddamn that white bastard's soul!* He did not return to his case until after the inspector had finished, closed his note book, shoved it into his hippocket, and walked swaggeringly away.

They worked for awhile in silence.

"Seems like the white folks just wants to ride a nigger to death," Jake mumbled.

Slim coughed, bending over, holding on to the ledge for support.

"Yeah," he said, between wheezes. "But there ain't nothing a man can do about it."

"You just have to swallow it and like it," said Bob.

"I wanted to push his puss in," said Jake.

"It wasn't you, it was me," said Al.

"And he didn't look at a single case but mine," said Jake.

"Shhsh . . ."

Out of the corner of his eye Jake saw the inspector standing at the end of the aisle, watching. He bent his head lower and threw his mail faster. *You sonofabitch! It ain't always going to be this way!* His mind went abruptly blank. He could not keep on with that thought, because he did not know where that thought led. He did not know of any other way things could be, if not *this* way. Yet he longed for them *not* to be this way.

He felt that something vast and implacable was crushing him; and he felt angry with himself because he had to stand it. He had an impulse to whirl and sweep his arm in a wide swift arc and brush away everything. But there was nothing he could solve by doing that; he would only get into more trouble. And the feeling that he could do nothing doubled back upon him, fanning the ashes of other dead feelings of not being able to do anything, and he was consumed in a fever of bitterness.

"Here comes some white cunt," whispered Bob.

To his left Jake saw a party of six young white girls coming down the aisle. They were being led by Swanson who stopped now and then to explain the mechanism of the mail to them.

"Ladies, this is the Primary Separation . . ."

Jake pushed letter after letter into the pigeonholes, feeling the eyes of the white inspector on him from the end of the aisle, and feeling the eyes of the white women on him from behind. There swept through him a sense of outrage, deep, hot, wild. He was conscious of the sticky sweatstains in the armpits of his shirt, and he felt the edges of his wet BVDs cutting into his loins.

". . . from here the mail is sent to state sections, where . . ."

The voice was moving on. He heard murmurs of laughter, light, silvery. Through lowered eyes he glimpsed the flash of a fleshcolored ankle. *They's looking at us like we was monkeys in a zoo!* A phrase he had heard an old Negro preacher say down South in his youth welled up in his consciousness, ringing in his ears like a bell. *Lawd, if I had my way I'd tear this building down!* If only there was something he could do to pay the white folks back for all they had ever done! Even if he lost his own life in doing so! But what could he do? He felt the loneliness of his black skin. *Yeah, some foreign country ought to whip this Gawddamn country! Some black country ought to do it!* He remembered the parade he had seen that morning when he was on his way to work. *Yeah, maybe they's right. Who knows?* He saw millions of black soldiers marching in black armies; he saw a black battleship flying a black flag; he himself was standing on the deck of that black battleship surrounded by black generals; he heard a voice commanding: "FIRE!"

Booooooooom! A black shell screamed through black smoke and he saw the white head of the Statue of Liberty topple, explode, and tumble into the Atlantic Ocean . . . *Gawddamn right!*

He sighed, blinking, pushing a letter for Mississippi through the twelveinch guns of the black battleship. He was sleepy. And thirsty. He went to the fountain and got a drink; then he held his wrists under the icecold stream of water to chill his blood in order to keep awake. When back at his case he continued building dreams of a black empire. He had reached that point in his imagined epic where black troops were about to conquer the whole world when a metallic gong boomed throughout the Mailing Division, and a voice yelled:

"TWELVETHIRTY CLERKS CHECKOUT FOR LUNCH!"

There immediately followed the dying moan of many dynamos and the irregular clacking of wheels slackening speed. Jake sighed and turned on his heel with almost a prayer in his heart. *Thank Gawd for that . . .*

III.

"OH, SO YOU'RE back again, hunh, Jake?" asked fisheyed Jones.

"Yes, sir."

Jones toyed reflectively with the inkwell.

"Still looking for dough?"

"I'm still working. It'll be safe with me."

Jones opened the inkwell and peered cautiously inside.

"How bad you want this dough, Jake?"

"I'm on my hind legs," said Jake, grinning.

"How much you want?"

"One hundred iron men."

Jones compressed his lips and pushed the inkwell to a far spot on the desk where he seemed to see it with a new objectivity.

"That's a lot of dough, Jake."

"But a hundred's what I want."

"Yeah, but that's a lot of dough."

"Now, look here, Mister Jones, you knows me. Your dough's safe with me. If I don't pay you back you can get a judgement against me."

"Oh, I know that, all right. I believe you'll pay."

"Well, can I get a hundred?"

"I'll sign for 'im," said Slim.

"And I'll sign," said Bob.

Jones lit his cigar, spat a shred of tobacco, and pushed the inkwell farther away.

"It'll cost you twenty dollars, Jake," he said, looking up directly. "I'll have to charge you high because we've let so much money out this week."

Jake hesitated. *Twenty bucks is a lot of dough to pay for a hundred. But I got to get something from somewhere . . .*

"Well, I reckon that's O.K."

"How long you want it?"

"I'll start paying you back this payday."

"That's the way to talk!"

Jones filled his fountain pen from the inkwell and commenced writing out the form.

"Make it snappy," said Jake. "We ain't got but a halfhour to eat in."

"It won't take but a minute."

Jake winked and Bob gave him an answering wink. When the form was all filled out, Slim and Bob attached their names.

"Here you are," said Jones, counting out the bills.

"Yes, sir."

"You going to strut your stuff tonight, Jake?" asked Jones.

"I ain't going to do nothing different."

"How about your wife?"

"Oh, yes, sir . . . I'll have enough left for her. Yes, sir!"

Jones leaned back, chuckled, rolled his cigar from one corner of his mouth to the other, and drummed his long white fingers caressingly upon the tarnished top of the inkwell.

They made a wild dash for the canteen. It was crowded, hot, smoky. They stood in long queues and stamped their feet as the smell of food whetted their hunger. Jake bought cabbage and hamhocks. Bob, sauerkraut and frankfurters. Slim, baked beans and sweet potatoes. Al, pork roast, white potatoes, and ten slices of white bread. Each got a pint milk bottle full of coffee and sweetened it from a huge public sugarbowl with a spoon chained securely to the end of a counter. When their trays were filled they placed them on the edges of a table, leaving the center clear so there would be room to play bridge. Bob pulled from his hippocket a frayed deck of cards; Jake grabbed it and dealt. They arranged their hands, chewing, holding whole slices of bread in their mouths to save the time of lifting a slice for each bite. After they had bid, Slim mumbled through a mouthful of beans:

"Awright, let her go!"

"Here she comes!" sang Al, leading with an ace.

Jake was elated. Now and then he stretched his neck and forced down a halfchewed wad of cabbage. The one hundred dollars nestled compactly in his hippocket. Only one thing blocked the road to complete freedom; he had four more hours to work. But after that . . . He flipped down his card to each trick and wagged his head from side to side in tune to an imaginary jazz melody.

"Lawd, I'm going to paint the town red!" he sang.

"I'm going to be the tail on your kite!" sang Al.

"And I'm going to be the shadow on the ground," sang Slim.

"What you going to do, Bob?" Jake asked.

Bob smiled sickly, dealing the second hand. They laughed.

"I'll string along," said Bob. "But I ain't promising I'll do nothing."

"Aw, just looking at a dame won't hurt you none," said Al.

"It's thinking about 'em what hurts," said Bob.

"Keep your mind where your treasure is," sang Al.

They laughed again. At the end of the fourth hand Bob rose and said:

"We got five minutes. I'll meet you guys upstairs."

"Take it easy, Bob," said Slim, doubling up with a fit of coughing.

The huge quantity of hot food they had bolted made them drowsy and constricted about the heart. They filed heavily back to the Mailing Division.

"Jake Jackson."

"Machine twenty."

"Robert Madison."

"Machine twentyone."

"Albert Johnson."

"Machine twentytwo."

"Nathan Williams."

"Machine twentythree."

Belching and sucking their teeth, they trudged slowly to the cancelling machines and threw the levers; a loud metallic clatter rose and the floor shook beneath their feet. To their right was a long ledge piled high with uncancelled mail. In a little swinging shelf under the edge of each machine was a tiny drawer with metalcut numbers and letters showing the time of day; these numbers and letters had to be inserted in the machine every halfhour. Jake adjusted the time on his machine, grabbed a handful of "small" mail and let it run through the narrow slit whose bottom was a moving belt. The mail fluttered out the other end, stacking itself automatically, cancelled. When enough had been run through to fill the container, a carrier carted it off in steel trays. Jake's carrier was a tall, black West Indian Negro, and Jake did not like

West Indian Negroes, and especially the tall, black West Indian Negro who was carrying mail off his machine. He was a tightlipped and thinlipped fellow who walked about with his head up and his back straight; he never talked much and he held his eyes at an angle that made it seem to Jake he was looking down upon him from some great height. Jake had heard this Negro boast that he had not been born under the Stars and Stripes, but under the Union Jack; that his foreparents had never been slaves, and that he had always been a free man. *And he don't even want to talk like us,* thought Jake bitterly, ramming handful after handful of mail into the machine. *He's got to put a twist on every word. Why in hell they let them bastards come into this country's a mystery to me.* And his dislike for West Indian Negroes made him think of Filipinos. *Them little cute bastards!* He spat into a spittoon. He did not like the straight, slick, black hair of the Filipinos, nor their small mouths, nor their straight noses, nor the smell of the perfume they used. *And they think they's too good to marry a black woman. They got to marry white. Hell, they's colored just like we is!* And he remembered that one of the Filipinos was studying art at the Chicago Art Institute; he had seen him showing his water colors to white clerks on the job. *Who in hell wants to mess around with stuff like that but a sissy?* And Jake also remembered that last year one of the Filipinos' wives had given Slim a date, and after Slim had seen her once he had to dodge for a week to get the woman off his track. *That just goes to show that them sissies ain't no good. All they fit for is to make some dame ripe for a good man.* He smiled, shooting handsful of mail through the machine. The last image of the white woman tracking Slim down appeased him, and he grew oblivious of the West Indian Negro who carried mail off his machine.

He looked at the clock; only fortyfive minutes had elapsed since lunch. *Gawd, how slow the time passes!*

"LISTEN FOR NEW DETAIL!"

Jake held himself ready to hear the hurriedly barked words that were coming. A foreman walked from machine to machine with a pad of paper and pencil poised.

"Jake Jackson," Jake mumbled when the foreman was opposite him.

"Fat stock, handstamp!"

"Albert Johnson."

"Fat stock, handstamp!"

"Robert Madison."

"Fat stock, handstamp!"

"Nathan Williams."

"Fat stock, handstamp!"

They flicked levers; the machines clattered slowly to silence. The bottoms of their feet tingled when the floor was still. In single file they dragged across the steel again and took places at little individual tables which were piled high with uncancelled mail too thick to be handled by machine. It was called "fat stock". On each table, opposite the elbow, was a black dauber which had inserted in its bottom steel discs to make imprints of post marks. Round black inkpads scented the air with a sharp, fresh smell, like that of raw meat. Jake made sure that his dauber had the correct time of day, and pulling pieces of mail toward him with his left hand, he began stamping with the dauber, hitting the inkpad and then the stamps on the letters. *Boombomp, boombomp, boombomp, boombomp* . . . Four licks a second, two hundredforty licks a minute. He paused and wiped his inksmeared thumb on a wad of greasy cotton. He hated handstamping; there was no way to loaf or talk here. Either he stamped steadily or a foreman bawled. A conflict rose in him. Should he continue handstamping or checkout to the lavatory and rest? He decided to stay; he did not want to risk another quarrel with the foremen; he was in enough trouble already. Then suddenly peace came; he felt tired no longer; his left hand drew the letters toward him and his right hand struck them with the dauber. *Boombomp, boombomp, boombomp, boombomp* . . . His mind and body had fallen into the rhythm of the thing.

In the faces and attitudes of the clerks the strain of the workday had begun to tell. Limbs moved with increasing listlessness. Slight puffs appeared beneath eyes that looked out with beaten, hangdog expressions. Crowns of heads were covered with thin layers of dark grey dust. Lips grew stiff and dry from thirst. The spittoons became filled with black mucus. Nervously exhausted from years of racking labor, some worked with spasmodic jerkings of arms and shoulders. Now and then they looked at the clock and sighed from a numbing weariness of spirit. Sometimes images would flit aimlessly into their minds and then aimlessly out again, like stray cats slinking across deserted streets at midnight. Often they were on the verge of speaking, but the sheer triviality of what they wanted to say weighted their tongues into silence. And then, too, talking, no matter of what brand, took a certain amount of energy, energy they were reluctant to spare when hand-stamping. During the slow seep of hours their fatigued nerves magnified the sensations of their bodies. They felt their hearts pumping laboriously. Each tingle of the skin was something to be investigated and wondered at. They scratched their scalps, their thighs, their groins, screwing up their eyes in perplexity.

"We's about to catch up with this stuff," said Slim with a sticky throat.

Jake saw that the trough holding the fat stock was nearly empty. When the last piece had been stamped, they stood at the tables and relaxed.

"Lawd, I'm tired!"

"Look like my flesh ain't got no feeling."

"Seem like these last four hours ain't never going to end."

"Ain't it funny how when you was a kid you could play all day and never get tired?"

"Yeah, and now just two hours is enough to poop you out!"

"You know one thing?"

"What?"

"I wouldn't get so damn tired if I knowed where some of this mail was going."

"Some people asking for money to get home, maybe."

"And somebody telling somebody that somebody else is dead, maybe."

"Yeah, maybe a lot of great things in these letters."

"It's hard to just move your hands all day and not see what you doing."

"Like a squirrel turning in a cage."

"This kind of work'll drive a guy nuts."

"I'm thinking he's nuts when he takes a job like this."

"But you got to eat."

"That ain't no lie."

"Sometimes I feel like being just a hobo."

"And never think about nothing."

"If you don't never work you'll come out in the end just about as good as you would if you did work."

"Seems that way."

A foreman rushed up, bawling:

"All through?"

No one answered. The foreman looked into the empty trough and whirled with notebook and pencil poised.

"All right, let's go!"

"Jake Jackson," Jake drawled, tired and slow.

"Fill in on third and fourth class!"

"Robert Madison."

"Third and fourth class!"

"Albert Johnson."

"Third and fourth class!"

"Nathan Williams."

"Third and fourth class!"

They were now out of the division where the first class mail was handled, and away from the rush. They could take it a little easier and talk. They stacked circulars into canvas gurneys, making neat rows. Mail from Sears & Roebuck, Montgomery Ward, Marshall Field . . .

"Say, Jake?" said Al.

"Yeah?"

"I want to ask you something."

"Shoot."

"You know I been in the National Guard for five years now."

"Yeah, I know."

"How come you won't make up your mind and join us?"

"Aw, I don't know, Al . . ."

"You ought to, Jake. It's a great life. You just the type of guy we need."

"Aw, I been too busy to think about it," drawled Jake.

"You missing a lot if you don't come in with us. The only thing next to the National Guard is the United States Army, you know."

"Yeah?"

"It ain't in every state we colored folks can join the National Guard."

"Aw, I reckon I'm kind of soft," said Jake, smiling.

"One good drill a week'd do you fine. Put some pep into you."

"Oh, I reckon it would."

"And there's that twoweek vacation every year with pay. Jake, boy, you don't know what a swell time we have down at Camp Grant. It's a great bunch of fellows. Swimming, boxing, racing . . . And don't tell nobody, but a little firewater and a dame or two. And Jake, all the officers is colored, just like we is. Say, you'd like it! You'd be wild about it! And listen, how would you like to have a night off every week away from all this damn dust?"

"Sounds good!"

"Nigger, you'd be a better man if you joined up with us," said Al, punching Jake playfully in the ribs.

Jake turned and looked honestly and seriously at Al.

"Tell me, what's this thing for?"

"Ain't nothing to it, Jake. Look, when the Reds start something, we put 'em down, see? If some guys think they can strike and tieup things, we stop 'em, see? If riots break out, we's right on hand, see? Boy, you should have heard the speech the Governor handed us last week. It was a pip! And Jeeesus, you get *paid* for it! And here's something that's right down your alley; when you get into any trouble in the Post Office, they ain't as hard on you as they is when you ain't a soljer . . ."

"Sure enough?"

"Absolutely, man. You wouldn't've had to pay all that dough out to Doc if you was in the National Guard," said Al. "Our Colonel could've done you some good for nothing."

"Say, that ain't bad at all," said Jake.

"There ain't nothing like it," pronounced Al, chewing a piece of gum. "Come on down with me next week and join. I'll see that you's put in my company . . ."

"Well, I'll think about it," Jake drawled.

"How come you got to *think* about it? Come on down."

"Naw, not next week."

"Lawd, you sure is one more lazy nigger," said Al, pulling down the corners of his mouth.

"Shucks!" said Slim. "If my lungs was all right I'd join."

"I couldn't pass that shortarm inspection," said Bob.

They laughed.

"Jake's just *lazy*," said Al again, with emphasis.

"I ain't no lazy than you is," retorted Jake.

"The army'll make a man out of you," said Al.

"Hell, I'm a man already," said Jake.

"That's just what *you* think! A soljer knows how to whip a woman's jelly."

"You talk like I don't know how to whip a woman's jelly!"

"You got to prove it to me," said Al.

"I can whip it till the butter comes," said Jake.

They laughed again.

"But not like a soljer," said Al.

"Aw, nigger," said Jake, "whose butter you ever whip to make you brag so?"

"I done whipped more jelly than you, I bet."

"That's a lie!"

"You wouldn't be in all the mess you in now with that dame of yours if you was in the army and knowed how to handle a woman."

"How's that?"

"A soljer never lets a woman get the best of 'im. He knows how to handle 'em."

"I know how to handle 'em," said Jake.

"You *didn't*!"

Jake scratched his head and frowned.

"Aw, I just got a little mixedup with old Lil," he drawled. "Something slipped . . . I had it all figgered out, and then something went wrong and she had to go and get sick!"

"How's that?" asked Slim.

"What happened?" asked Bob.

"Well, you see," said Jake, "I tricked her into having that first operation. She was just a little dummy when I married her, just seventeen. She would've believed that water wasn't wet if I had told her so. I could have pissed up her back and made her think it was raining. Well, one morning she comes to me all sad and serious, and says she's going to have a baby. At first I tried to get her to go to a quack to get some medicine so she'd pass the damn thing, but she was scared stiff. She had heard of gals dying from them kind of operations

and I couldn't get her to move a peg. Then I gets busy and
hatches up a smart scheme. I goes to my quack and makes a
deal with him; I told him to tell her she just couldn't have a
baby, that her hips was too little, that she'd die, or just anything as long as she wouldn't have it. Who in hell wants a lot
of sticky babies? He put the job over and she was shaking like
a leaf; she was between the Devil and the deep blue sea.
While the quack was working on her from one end, I was
working on her from the other; in no time we had her so she
didn't know if she was going or coming. I told her that it
would kill her to have that baby, and she went flying down to
the quack, begging 'im to pull that damn thing out of her,
and do it quick. It cost me five hundred iron men . . . Boy,
them quacks'll gut you if you let 'em. Quacks and mouth-
pieces get all a postal clerk's money. Abortions and divorces
. . . But Lawd! When she found out what I done! You see,
she didn't take the operation so well and had to go to a hospital. They told her the truth about everything. And what did
they do that for? Was she *mad*? She cussed me as long as she
could see me! And her health ain't been worth a good Gawddamn since. But the bad part of it is, she won't take my word
for nothing now, won't believe a thing I say . . ."

"Aw," said Al, waving his palm scornfully. "You tried to
trick her, all right; but you let her get the best of you even at
that . . ."

"Hell, I couldn't help it if she got sick, could I?"

"Let me tell you how to handle a woman," said Al.

"Come on," said Slim. "Let's hear it."

"This is the way the army teaches you: This is floating-
power, fourwheel brakes action. You see, she was about ten
years older'n me, and was a hashslinger in a 36th Street eat-
shop. She had a damn good job and was pulling down fifteen
bucks a week. Now, she wasn't so awfully goodlooking, but
she had a shape that was out of the books, and that's the
truth, so help me! She was husky and built like a horse; she
was a match for any buck. No toothpick guy could keep that
baby satisfied, I'm telling you. And man, if she really loved a
guy she'd give 'im the kind of love that would make a wildcat
squall. And she wasn't halfway about it, neither. If she was
gone on a guy she'd take 'im in and keep 'im up, buy his

clothes and cigarettes. She said she wanted all her men to be wellrested, and if you could've seen how she eaglerocked them big hams of hers when she walked, you would've knowed just what she meant. Boy, that mama could've loved a whole army of men and had plenty of love to spare.

"Well, this is how it all happened. It was easy's pie. In fact, she's the one what did all the running, 'cause I didn't want her at first. Every time I went to the joint to eat supper she'd invite me to her place. I went up a few times and she piled my plate so high with greens, fat meat, egg cornbread I couldn't eat it all. I knowed she was trying to snare me, but I knowed that a lot of other guys had done had her, and I wasn't so hot on taking secondhanded goods, see?

"Then all of a sudden my shift in the stockyards shut down. It was in the dead of the winter and wasn't nothing going on, so I picks up this dame like a hundredcarat diamond.

"Boy, did she swipe home some good eats from that eat-shop! It makes my mouth water enough to spit just to think about it. She would come in at night all loaded down like a twolegged express company and start pulling grub out of her bosom and bloomers, and before you knowed it the table'd just be covered with hams, cakes, pies, pigtails, hog's head, chitterlings, pork chops, steaks, roasts, chickens, greens . . . Lawd, today!

"But she was a funny woman; maybe if it hadn't been for all them damn freakish ways of hers I would've been with her yet. At first I just couldn't make out what made her act so screwy. Today she'd act like a lamb, and tomorrow she'd be a regular redhot hyena.

"Well, this is the way she'd act. She'd come in and unload all the grub she'd done swiped, and then start cussing. And did that baby know some cuss words? When she opened up the air'd jump around your head. And she'd start about just any old thing, so no matter what you did you could never tell just where she'd break out. Maybe I'd forgot to put my dirty shirt in the old clothes bag, and she'd ask me: 'Is you a pig?' And right away I'd tell her: 'Naw, darling. I'll move it right now.' But that wouldn't satisfy that baby none. One word would lead to another and before you knowed it we was in the biggest kind of fuss.

"One night while we was fussing she said: 'And what does you do? I works hard all day and you just sets on your can, doing nothing!' 'Well, baby,' I says, 'I'm willing to work, you know.' 'Like hell you is!' she yells. 'I don't want no tired mens sleeping with me in the bed at night!'

"Man, the whole mess had me so I didn't know my head from my feets. One night after supper when we was fussing I says to her: 'Listen, baby, let's call it quits.' Boy, she broke down and cried like a fool. 'I loves you better'n any man I ever had!' she tells me. 'Don't leave me, Daddy Darling, please . . .' Well, I stayed, but the very next night she started all over again.

"One night when there was about a foot of snow piled up on the ground, we had a howling big fuss. Even if I didn't have nowhere to go, I was getting good and sick of her by this time, and I stood up for my rights. 'Listen here, you catty bitch!' I says, 'either you close your trap or I'll smack you to a low gravy!' Boy, her hair stood up on end! She dropped the smoothing iron she was ironing with and tore at me like a Bengal tiger and started clawing my face like all hell. 'How's that for a catty bitch?' she asks me.

"Now get this straight. I ain't no man what goes around fighting women, see? But what happened that night just couldn't be helped. I figgered I had done taken about enough off her already. So right then and there I gives her two ringing, sounding slaps that sends her reeling into a corner, squalling bloody murder. She stays on her knees awhile with her face in her hands, moaning. Then all of a sudden she comes at me again. This time I means business; I grabs both of her hands in my left hand and slaps her till she slobbers. She opens up her mouth, clouds up her eyes, and begins to rain tears like all outdoors, begging and pleading with me: 'Don't hit me no more, Daddy Darling, please . . .'

"The funny thing about it all was she got soft and chummy with me after that. For about a week everything was peaches and roses. Then she started again. I beat her again. You see, I had done found her soft spot. Man, that woman just craved for men to beat her. When she'd come in at night all washed-out from standing on her feets all day and feeling in the dumps from bending over a redhot stove, there wasn't nothing in all the world better'n being beat black and blue till she forgot all about her tiredness and could cuddleup in my arms for a little love . . .

"I left her about three months after that. Slipped off and didn't leave no word. I was tired and sick of her, fedup. And anyhow, I had done started losing weight from too damn much exercise . . ."

Jake, Slim, and Bob bent over the table with laughter.

"Wooooooow!" Jake spluttered. "You sure had her number!"

"It's all in knowing how," said Al. "They learn you that in the National Guard."

"Nigger, you crazy!"

"No kidding, now. Come on down and join up with us, Jake."

"Well . . ."

"You'll like it."

"Not this week, anyhow."

"Then next week?"

"Wwwell . . . Er . . . Aw, yeah, I'll sign up next week."

"Man, let me shake your hand," said Al, grabbing Jake. Jake straightened his face in hard, serious lines and spoke with deep gravity:

"It ain't a bad idea to have a gun in your hand when trouble breaks out."

A loud laugh made them turn around. A white clerk stood, watching and listening. Jake, Al, Slim, and Bob stared at him without smiling.

"Gee, that was some hot story," said the white clerk. "Let's hear another one."

Wordlessly, they turned away. A minute passed. They heard the footsteps of the white clerk dying away on the steel floor.

"Can you beat that?" asked Slim.

"That sonofabitch!" spat Al.

"They never want to have nothing to do with us, but when we's talking about women they's always sticking their damn noses in," said Bob.

"Yeah, a white bastard's always thinking we never talk about nothing but cunt," said Jake.

They were silent, resentful, hurt.

IV.

DIRECTLY BEHIND THEM a window framed a square portion of the evening's flying snow. The wind, rising and dying, howled like a lost dog in a vast wilderness. They stacked batches of mail carefully on the table, pressed them together firmly, and carried them slowly to gurneys. When they grew tired like this, when most of their workaday preoccupations had been drowned in exhaustion, their basic moods would blend and fuse. They had worked in this manner for so many years that they took one another for granted; their common feelings were a common knowledge. And when they talked it was more like thinking aloud than speaking for purposes of communication. Clusters of emotion, dim accretions of instinct and tradition rose to the surface of their consciousness like dead bodies floating swollen upon a night sea.

"Lawd, I'm tired . . ."

". . . and sleepy . . ."

". . . I could curlup and snooze till the cows come home."

"Ain't it funny how dopey you feel after you done downed a big meal?"

"It puts you on the bum."

"Makes your legs feel like lead."

"I can't hardly hold my eyes open."

"That's 'cause we ate too much . . ."

". . . and can't get no fresh air."

"Sleep's a queer thing."

"It's next to being dead."

"It just comes down on you all at once . . ."

". . . and then you got to sleep."

"A man can't do without sleep."

"You spend a third of your life sleeping."

"You know, I never thought of that."

"But going to sleep's the funny thing."

"Lawd, I like going to sleep."

"It's like slipping off into nothing."

"You ever remember going to sleep?"

"Naw."

"You get in the bed sleepy and tired . . ."

". . . and the first thing you know it's morning . . ."

". . . and all the time you's sleeping your heart keeps right on beating . . ."

". . . and you living and ain't thinking about living at all."

"Sort of scares you when you think about it."

"Yeah, it makes you shaky when you think how little stands between you and death."

"Death's an awful thing!"

"No matter how hard you try to figger it out . . ."

". . . it's something you just can't get use' to . . ."

". . . and a man'll go nuts just wondering about it."

"Look like you ought to have more'n *one* chance at dying . . ."

". . . like them cats that got nine lives."

"Yeah."

"Wouldn't seem so bad, then."

"Naw."

"But you can never have a chance like that."

"Never!"

"I can't see head or tail in the whole damn thing!"

"It's just there and you think and think and think . . ."

". . . and cold chills run up and down your spine."

"But you know, when I sleep I like to dream."

"Me too."

"What makes dreams?"

"Stumps me."

"Some folks say dreams is warnings and if you watch 'em you can tell what's going to happen."

"Yeah, that's what the guys in the Bible did . . ."

". . . old Noah . . ."

". . . and Jacob . . ."

". . . and David."

"But some dreams can scare you."

"Yeah, Lawd!"

"Ever dream you was falling . . ."

". . . and wake up and find yourself sweating?"

"Lots of times."

"I dreamed about steps last night."

"Gee, I had a funny dream. I thought I was trying to put out a building that was on fire."

"I dreamed about a river, a big, slow moving, deep river. There was a boat running down the middle of it all piled high with cotton."

"I dreamed I was out in the woods hunting, just shooting a gun. *Blooom! Blooom! Blooom!*"

"But I don't like to dream about dead folks!"

"Hell, naw!"

"Say, you ever see a ghost?"

"Plenty times!"

"Shucks, I saw one walk right into a brick wall once, and then I couldn't see 'im."

"Jeeesus!"

"What you do?"

"Hell, I run!"

"I saw something that beats that. We lived in a house once where a door slammed all night long, opening and shutting. They say a whore was murdered in there."

"Aw, that ain't nothing. We lived in a house once where we heard somebody walking around our bed every night, *bomp! bomp! bomp! bomp!*"

"What youall do?"

"We moved out of there real quick!"

"Aw, I done seen something ain't none of youall never seen. I was walking along a road down South one night and saw a man with no head on . . ."

"With no *head* on?"

"With *no* head on."

"Ain't this a bitch!"

"Wasn't you scared?"

"I couldn't move."

"Where he go?"

"Well, I turned around to look and he was gone . . ."

"Gone?"

"Gone, man."

"Shucks, I *never* want to see nothing like that!"

"You know, I once heard a guy say your body changes every seven years."

"Yeah?"

"How's that?"

"I don't know. You just change all over and you's still the same guy."

"Look like you ought to change into somebody else."

". . . don't it?"

"There's sure a lot of queer things going on in the world."

"Life's a funny thing."

"Say, take a look at this!"

"What?"

"Here's a piece of mail sent out by a guy what calls himself Saint Paul . . ."

"Read it!"

"Here, you read it, Al!"

"Look! Two trains, all loaded with people. One train's heading for Heaven and the other's heading for Hell . . ."

"Who's that over there?"

"That's the Devil with a pitchfork . . ."

"And what's that?"

"That's his tail curling round and round."

"Lawd, today!"

"And who's that other guy?"

"That's Jesus . . ."

"And what's that he's got?"

"He's holding a snowwhite lamb in his arms."

"And look at all them white angels . . ."

". . . and the people . . ."

". . . millions of 'em!"

"Read the thing!"

WHICH RAILROAD WILL YOU TAKE???????????????

, , , , , , , , , , , , , , , , , , ,

THE EVERLASTING DAMNATION
RAILWAY CORPORATION

✳ ✳ ✳ ✳ ✳ ✳ ✳ ✳ ✳ ✳ ✳

The Quickest and Shortest Route to the Hottest Depths
of
H E L L

# # # # # # # # # # #

MUCH TIME AND MANY MILES SAVED BY
THIS ROUTE AND YOU WILL ENJOY TER-
RIFICALLY EVIL SCENERY EVERY TORTUOUS
MILE OF THE   *W A Y*

. . . .

THIS TRAIN STOPS AT THE FOLLOWING
POINTS WEST:

South through Dismal Swamp; Southwest through
Murderer's Gap; Allnight Stopover at Hangman's
Gorge; East through Doubt Thoroughfare; North
through Skeptical Valley; and passing through the fol-
lowing cities: Fire and Brimstone Metropolis, Pleasure
Harbor, Saint Haughty, Atheistville, Infidel City, Fort
Worldly, Sinburg, New Trespassing, Evilsford, Dis-
honor Island, Sciencedale, Temptation Mound, Radical
Hill, Prideston, Liarsport, and Whiskey Terminal.

ф ф ф ф ф ф ф ф ф ф ф ф

REACHING THE GREAT VALLEY OF THE
SHADOW OF ETERNAL DEATH AT BLACK
MIDNIGHT AND PLUNGING ITS PASSENGERS
INTO THE BOTTOMLESS PITS OF EVERLAST-
ING WOE!!!!!!!

- - - - - - - - - - -

M A I N   D E P O T:
Corner Unbelief and Disobedience Streets

ALL HOURS OF THE DAY AND NIGHT SPE-
CIAL TRAINS ARE RUNNING FROM:

Thomas Paine Avenue, Dime Novel Park, Theatre Lane,
Dopedel, Blasphemers' Hall, Smokers' Furnace, Mastur-
bation Alley, Prostitution Boulevard, Dancehall Station,
Highball Lagoon, Adultery Depot, Greed Mountain,
Gambling Pause, Ingersoll Canyon, Evolution Grounds,
and Communist Junction.

* *

LIGHTNING SPECIALS FROM SUICIDE AVENUE
AT ALL HOURS!!

* *

EXTRA TRAINS AND SPECIAL COACHES ON
SUNDAYS AND HOLIDAYS!

ALL ABOARD!

F A R E: T H Y S O U L
PRINCE LUCIFER, *President*.

"Turn it over . . ."

". . . and see what it says on the other side."

"This stuff makes your flesh creep."

"You reckon anybody ever do *all* them things?"

"Look at all that fire . . ."

". . . and smoke . . ."

". . . and them little black imps!"

"Hell's a terrible place!"

"It must be awful to burn and burn . . ."

". . . forever and ever . . ."

". . . and not ever burn up!"

"Boy, the guy what drawed that picture sure knowed what
he was doing."

"Come on, Al, read the other side!"

WHICH RAILROAD WILL YOU TAKE???????????????
, , , , , , , , , , , , , , , , , , ,

THE SALVATION AND REDEMPTION RAILWAY
COMPANY, INC.!!!
* *
RUNNING DAILY FROM THE BLACK VALE OF
SINFUL TEARS TO THE GLORY GATES OF THE
GREAT BEYOND!!

V I A

Resurrection Mound, Christian Hill, Baptism Vale,
Conversion Junction, Contrite Soul Terminal, Mount
Calvary, Rugged Cross, Rock of Ages, River of Life,
New Jerusalem, Paradise Garden, Everlasting Happi-
ness, Daily Prayer, Sacrifice Harbor, Temperanceville,
Honesty Line, and Repentance Lane.

T H R O U G H

THE VALLEY OF THE SHADOW OF DEATH BY
BROAD DAYLIGHT!

φ φ φ φ φ φ φ φ φ φ φ φ φ

STOPPING AT THE FOLLOWING POINTS:

Meditation Valley, Crucifixion Canyon, Faith Bend,
Hope Lagoon, Charity Station, Holy Vineyards, Tem-
ple of Joy, River of Milk and Honey, Gates of Saint
Peter, Peaceport, Prosperityburg, Blissdom, Sanctuary
Town, Penticostal Depot, Grace Boulevard, Glory Park,
Angel City, and Fort Love.

STRAIGHT TO THE GRAND CENTRAL DEPOT
OF THE UNIVERSE IN THE CITY OF GOD
WITHOUT A CHANGE OF CARS!!!!!!!!!!!!!!!!!!!!!!

TRAINS AT ALL HOURS OF YOUR LIFE!!!!!

MAIN DEPOT:
Corner Faith and Repentance Streets
ALL CARS ARE FIRST CLASS ——— NO HALF
FARES!!!!!
(No Excursion Tickets! No Round Trip Tickets!
No Passes! And No Stopovers!)
ℬℬℬℬℬℬℬℬℬℬℬℬℬℬℬℬℬℬℬℬℬℬℬℬℬℬℬℬℬℬℬℬℬ
THESE TRAINS ARE NEVER LATE AND LEAVE
RIGHT UP TO THE VERY

HOUR OF DEATH

ALL ABOARD!

Jesus Christ, *President*

"You know one thing? Folks is sure getting smart these
days."

"They's getting weaker and wiser."

"They's done figgered out every *single* thing."

"They's done mapped out things so plain that even a fool
couldn't go wrong if he wanted to."

"Some folks say that shows that the end of time ain't far
off."

"Yeah, Gawd might get tired of folks wanting to know too much and end everything."

"But Gawd sure must've been with the guy to make 'im write a thing like that."

"He must've showed 'im a vision."

"Man, Gawd's work's a mystery!"

"I reckon that old song's right what says you'll understand it better bye and bye."

"You just can't figger out Gawd's plans . . ."

". . . and there ain't no use trying."

"Gawd works in a funny way . . ."

". . . His wonders to perform."

"You know, my ma use' to say that all the time."

"Ain't it funny how somebody can map out the *whole* life of the *whole* world—like Gawd did . . ."

". . . and make all them trees and flowers and birds . . ."

". . . and make people and put the breath of life in 'em . . ."

". . . and set it all to running and spinning . . ."

". . . like some kind of machine . . ."

". . . and know everything what's going to happen before it happens?"

"You just can't help wondering how it all got started . . ."

". . . and how come it was all started . . ."

". . . and why is everything so big . . ."

". . . so big you's lost in it . . ."

". . . that moon . . ."

". . . them clouds . . ."

". . . and that sun . . ."

". . . a big ball of fire . . ."

". . . and all them miles and miles of empty sky . . ."

". . . and them stars!"

"It makes your head swim!"

"Scares you just to think about it."

"Jeeesus, all this must of been made for *some*thing."

"Yeah, it couldn't've all been made for *no*thing."

"Funny how some fools can stand up and say there *ain't* no Gawd."

"Ain't it though?"

"They ought to know *some*body must've started all this."

"It couldn't start by it*self*."

"Nobody but a *fool* couldn't see that."

"That's right."

"That's right, all right."

"But Gawd lets some folks in on a lot of secrets. Like old Edison . . ."

"He was a wizard!"

"They called 'im a genius."

"He invented the 'lectric light . . ."

". . . and made the lightning work just like a man plows a horse."

"White folks *al*ways inventing something."

"They's smart."

"The white folks do everything so easy . . ."

". . . working together like a army . . ."

". . . marching to war!"

"Sometimes when I think about it I almost hate myself."

"Yeah, sometimes I wish I was anything but a nigger."

"We don't stick together."

"If three niggers is trying to do something, one of 'em's going to trip the others up . . ."

". . . sell 'em out . . ."

". . . to the white folks . . ."

". . . like a Judas!"

> *"Niggers is evil*
> *White folks too*
> *So glad I'm a Chinaman*
> *I don't know what to do . . ."*

"Yeah, the white folks always work and plot together . . ."

". . . that's why they runs the world."

"The papers say old Edison and Ford was big friends."

"They was what you call successful men."

"You know, I was reading in the papers the other day how all great men started out poor . . ."

". . . some of them even lived in log cabins . . ."

". . . and most of 'em was Christians, too . . ."

". . . like old Benjamin Franklin . . ."

". . . and old Abe Lincoln . . ."

". . . and old Rockefeller."

"They got to be successful by following the Golden Rule."

"Yeah, they did to other men what they wanted them men to do to them . . ."

". . . and Gawd rewarded 'em."

"You'll get your reward if you do right."

"Gawd sees to that. He's done figgered out all kind of ways to reward folks."

"And He can punish you, too."

"Oh, yeah."

"I heard tell of lightning killing a little girl 'cause she said she didn't believe in Gawd."

"And I heard tell of a man who went blind 'cause he laughed at a blind man."

"When I was a boy my grandma told me about a man who killed a hunchback. He went to sleep and the next morning he woke up with a hunch in *his* back."

"Gawd'll sure settle with you if you don't do right, now."

"Yeah, He evens up everything."

"Sometimes Gawd waits 'til you's on your deathbed and then He makes you pay."

"Yeah; a real black guy lived in our town down South and he was evil as sin. When he come to die it took 'im a week. He just laid there on his deathbed and screamed and howled. He couldn't eat or sleep. He said a fat hog was standing by his bed with a letter for 'im in his feets . . . You know, the hog had the letter in his hooves . . ."

"Have mercy, Lawd!"

"Gawd was punishing that man!"

"You telling me?"

"But Gawd can reward you, too."

"Yeah, remember that guy Wrigley what made millions of dollars just selling chewinggum?"

"And that English guy what made a lot of money selling tea? What was his name?"

"Lipton, wasn't it?"

"That's him."

"And when he got to be a old man he spent his last days trying to win a silvercup by racing boats . . ."

"He did?"

"Yeah, it was in the papers."

"Shucks, we use' to play that when we was kids."

"Lawd, that must be a good way to live!"

"Nothing to think about but sport . . ."

"Just live . . ."

". . . from day to day . . ."

". . . and have pleasure . . ."

". . . eating . . ."

". . . sleeping . . ."

". . . women . . ."

". . . everything you want . . ."

". . . and nothing to worry about."

"Yeah, like them bigtime baseball players."

"You know, some of them big league players make *fifty thousand* dollars a year."

"Lawd, what would I do with fifty thousand dollars?"

"That's more money than a man can think about."

"A sporting life's a easy life . . ."

". . . a sweet life."

"Talking about sports . . . I see where the Cubs is busting up their team, throwing away all the bum players."

"Yeah, we ought to have some hot baseball in the National League next year."

"Old Wrigley's trying to buy up a pennantwinning outfit."

"Aw, I don't like them Cubs. Give me the Sox any day."

"Aw, the Cubs is all right."

"How can they be all right when the Sox beat 'em every year in the city series?"

"That don't mean nothing. The Cubs done won the pennant in the National League more times than the Sox done won it in the American."

"But that don't prove a thing! That just goes to show that the American League's tougher than the National!"

"Like hell it do! Some of the best pitchers in the world's in the National League!"

"Pitching ain't *every*thing! *Hitting's* what counts! And the American League's got the hitters!"

"But look at how many games the Cubs done *won*! When you count 'em all up, you'll see they done won *more'n* the Sox!"

"But against *who*?"

"The National League!"

"Aw, *any*body can lick them hicks!"

"You got a grudge against the Cubs, that's all!"

"Gawddamn right! They don't want no colored folks out at Wrigley Field. The white folks throwed a pop bottle at me one day."

"But that ain't no reason to be against the Cubs."

"Why the hell ain't it? I'm against *any*body what's against *me*!"

"Aw, them white folks don't know you alive!"

"Don't care if they don't. I don't like them Cubs!"

"What to hell! How come we can't stand up for our own race? We got some baseball players that's just as good as they got. Who wants to go around whooping it up for the white folks all the time when we got our own stuff?"

"Well, that *is* right. We got old Joe Louis and there ain't never been nobody like him."

"Lawd, it sure made me feel good all the way down in my guts when old Joe socked Baer."

"I said to myself, let them white folks *chew* that."

"When that radio said that Joe'd done won, I jumped up and flew out into the street. I didn't know *where* I was going!"

"Man, I felt like leaping a mile high in the air and just screaming!"

"Just think now . . . He marries a gal, goes into the ring the same day, and knocks a guy coocoo!"

"You know how come old Joe Louis done that?"

"Naw."

"Why?"

"Well, old Joe got in that ring that night with his hair all slicked back and old Baer didn't have no better sense'n to ruffle it. Old Joe just cocked his left and knocked his block off . . ."

"Hohohoho!"

"Hahahaha!"

"Nigger, you crazy!"

"But old Joe oughtn't've married that dame."

"Hell, naw!"

"That woman'll make 'im weak."

"Damn right."

"You know a woman ruined old Samson."

"Oh, Joe's young yet . . ."

". . . maybe he'll get use' to it."

"Lawd, I hope so."

"And I'll *never* believe as long as I live that old Joe lost to Schmeling fair."

"Aw, he was doped."

"He could've whipped old Schmeling with one hand if he hadn't been doped."

"The white folks tricked 'im."

"They giving Joe the same old screwing they gave Jack Johnson."

"The white folks just ain't going to let no black man get to the top."

"Naw; just when you think you's nearly there they's done tripped you up."

"You see, they think if they let *one* black man rise that high, then *all* the rest of the black folks'll want to rise."

"Yeah, the white folks'll treat *one* black man all right, but when it's more'n one they gets hard."

"They's scared . . ."

". . . and mean."

"Aw, boy, they's watching us."

"Shucks, I believe my soul old Joe can lick *any*body!"

"Yeah, but he ain't as good as old Jack Johnson."

"The hell he ain't!"

"He couldn't've *touched* old Jack with a glove!"

"And Jack couldn't've touched *him* neither!"

"Jack was the greatest *defensive* fighter that ever was!"

"And Joe's the greatest *hitter* that ever was!"

"But how can you knock a man out when you can't *hit* 'im?"

"But Joe's a *counter*puncher! Soon's Jack'd try to hit 'im, Joe'd *kill* 'im!"

"Look, see? This is the way old Joe stands, with his left hand high . . ."

"And this is the way old Jack stands, ready for 'im . . ."

"All right, now . . . You lead . . ."

"All right."

"See!"

"Hell, wait a minute!"

"Old Joe would've done socked 'im *right* on the chin!"

"Nigger, you crazy! Jack would've *ducked* that!"

"Aw, you don't know nothing!"

"I wonder who would've won if them two could've got together? I mean old Joe like he is now and old Jack when he was in his prime . . ."

"That's hard to tell."

"Lawd, but it would've been a *fight*, though!"

"You telling me?"

"Boy, I want to see just *one* fight like that before I die!"

"I bet you Joe'll never be champion."

"How come?"

" 'Cause the white folks is scared it'll stir up riots all over the country."

"Yeah, I like to hear 'em tell about how folks acted when old Jack beat old Jim Jeffries . . ."

"You know, they say down South the day Jack Johnson beat Jim Jeffries a nigger walked into a white cafe and asked the white bartender: " 'Say, white man, give me a cup of coffee strong and black as Jack Johnson and a beef steak all beat up bleeding and red like Jim Jeffries.' "

"Woooooooow!"

"What happened?"

"They mobbed that bastard!"

"Jeeesus Christ!"

"Well, I heard a story that said old Jack was driving down Michigan Boulevard in Chicago in his highpowered Packard and a cop arrested 'im for speeding. When they brought him before the judge the judge said: 'Fifty dollars!' Well, old Jack just reached down in his jeans and hauled out a hundreddollar bill and said: 'Keep it all, Judge! I'm going back at the same rate of speed!' "

"Lawd, today!"

"A man's on top when he can do a thing like that!"

"Old Jack was a dog!"

"Aw, folks'd fight about Jack."

"Yeah, that's the trouble, they did too much fighting."

"Them race riots they had just about drove 'im out of the ring."

"A riot's a terrible thing."

"I came to Chicago just two weeks before that big riot they had."

"The white folks was killing up niggers like flies."

"The hell they was! The newspapers said we got the worst of it, but we *didn't*."

"There was *five* white folks killed for every *black* man."

"You see, the white folks try to make us believe we got the worst of it so's we'll be scared . . ."

"Yeah, they doing everything to beat us down."

"I remember when that riot started . . ."

". . . right down on 31st Street . . ."

". . . on the lake beach . . ."

". . . one summer day . . ."

". . . and the white folks stoned a little black boy and drowned 'im 'cause he was swimming in the wrong part of the lake."

"Now, ain't that a bitch! Swimming in the *wrong* part of the *lake* . . ."

". . . and the lake is *miles* big."

"That's as bad as killing a man for breathing."

"I wonder is there anything a white man won't do?"

"They make us live in one corner of the city . . ."

". . . like we was some kind of wild animals . . ."

". . . then they make us pay anything they want to for rent . . ."

". . . 'cause we can't live nowhere but where they tell us!"

"I remember when they use' to run us out of our homes with bombs."

"Even when you's dead, they tell you where to go."

"Lawd, today! Jim Crow *graveyards*!"

"Ain't *that* a bitch!"

"Who in hell can a *dead* black man hurt?"

"Maybe a black spirit'll rape a white spirit."

"Aw, nigger, hush!"

"Hohohoho!"

"Hahahaha!"

"You know, down South when a black man goes into a white store to buy a cigar he has to say: 'Mister, please give me one of them *Mister* John Ruskin cigars . . .' Hahaha!"

"They make you drink your milk with *bluing* in it . . . He-hehe!"

"They don't allow no *white* hen to lay no *black* eggs, or *black* hens to lay *white* eggs . . . Hohoho!"

"They make the colored folks dye the sheets on their beds *black*! Hahaha!"

"They kill a *black* cow if she gives white milk . . . He-hehe!"

"Nigger, hush! Hahaha!"

"Well, it might sound like a joke, but Gawd knows it almost the truth!"

"It wasn't no joke when all them folks was dying in the streets in that riot."

"I seen a black guy take a white man and club his brains out in that riot."

"I heard a man say he saw a black guy slash a white street-car conductor from ear to ear."

"It's bad luck for a black man anywhere."

"There's somebody always after you, making you do things you don't want to do."

"You know, the first time I ever set down beside a white man in a streetcar up North, I was expecting for 'im to get up and shoot me."

"Yeah, I remember the first time I set down beside a white woman in a streetcar up North. I was setting there trembling and she didn't even look around."

"You feel funny as hell when you come North from the South."

"I use' to walk around all day feeling like I done forgot something."

"Yeah, every time I'd see a white man I'd feel like getting off the sidewalk to let 'im pass, like we had to do in the South."

"It took me a long time to get use' to feeling what freedom was like."

"Ain't it funny how some few folks is rich and just millions is poor?"

"And them few rich folks owns the whole world . . ."

". . . and runs it like they please . . ."

". . . and the rest ain't got nothing?"

"Well, you know Gawd said the poor'll be with you always . . ."

". . . and He was right, too."

"Some folks just ain't got no brains, that's all. If you divided up all the money in the world right now we'd be just where we is tomorrow."

"But don't you think all the white folks is smart. Some of 'em's crazy! I saw in the papers the other day where some old white woman over in Paris said a rose is a rose is a rose is a rose . . . She wrote it in a book and when they asked her what it was she wouldn't tell . . ."

"Wouldn't tell?"

"Wouldn't tell, man."

"Jeeesus, that sounds like old Cab Calloway."

"Aw, hell, he ain't never said nothing that crazy."

"But man, the smartest white guy I ever seen was Big Bill Thompson."

"That guy wasn't scared of *no*body!"

"Yeah, that old *Chicago Tribune* sure hated 'im 'cause he give the colored folks so much."

"I heard old Big Bill say once that he'd do more for the colored folks if the other white folks'd let 'im."

"Yeah, they was hard on 'im 'cause he was our friend."

"Say, didn't he build a big school for us?"

"I don't know."

"He did something for us 'cause everybody says he did."

"Yeah, but I can't remember what he did."

"Me neither."

"He was a great man . . ."

". . . something like old Teddy Roosevelt who carried a big stick and talked soft . . ."

". . . and this other Roosevelt's just like 'im."

"But that old Wilson was a tricky bastard!"

"He tried to mess this country up . . ."

". . . by getting us in all that war."

"Yeah, when they find out the truth about that guy I'll bet you he was a Red!"

"He wanted all the nations to get together . . ."

". . . and that's just what the *Tribune* says the Reds want."

"They say a Red's international."

"What's international?"

"Damn if I know."

"Some folks say Roosevelt's a Red."

"But he ain't international."

"How you know?"

"Well, nobody knows just what these white folks is up to."

"But, boy! That guy over in Roosia! That Leenine . . ."

". . . he was a dog!"

"He scared the piss out of them rich white folks!"

"And they scared *yet*!"

"Boy, he tricked 'em!"

"You ever see his picture?"

"Yeah; all that beard . . ."

". . . and them eyes . . ."

". . . and that mouth all screwed up . . ."

". . . like he could bite nails . . ."

". . . and that chin turned up in the air."

"Lawd, that man must've been weaned on vinegar!"

"And them eyebrows of his'n . . ."

". . . going straight up . . ."

". . . like a Chink's."

"I'll bet you when they find out about 'im they'll find he had some Chink blood in 'im."

"Maybe that was why he was so sly and could fool 'em all."

"He must've had something!"

"And his old pal . . ."

"What was his name?"

"Tricksky, wasn't it?"

"Something like that. But was he hardboiled? With that hair all flying . . ."

". . . and them eyes that looked like they could see through you."

"I saw in the paper where they run 'im out of Roosia. He was too hot for them Reds even."

"I heard a Jew boy say that guy wanted a revolution that went on always . . ."

"*Al*ways?"

"*Always*, man!"

"What kind of revolution's that?"

"Damn if I know."

"Gawddamn, I'm scared of them kind of folks."

"Yeah, everybody's scared of them guys."

"The Reds sure scared them white folks down South when they put up that fight for the Scottsboro boys."

"The American white man is a natural born coward."

"You know one thing, if somebody ever started in on these white folks in honest, you could run 'em square into the ocean."

"They ain't never come up against nothing hard yet."

"And the first time they do they's going to mess all over themselves."

"A white man wouldn't fight you fair for nothing."

"He gangs you."

"And once they get you down they don't have no mercy."

"Look like it's fun to them to see people suffer."

"That's 'cause they ain't happy . . ."

". . . and they take it all out on you."

"That's the reason why we had to get out of the South . . ."

". . . and stop slaving for them white folks from 'kin 'til can't' . . ."

". . . from sunup to sundown . . ."

". . . rain or shine . . ."

". . . picking cotton 'til your back feels like it's going to break in two . . ."

". . . and that sun so hot you can't even sweat . . ."

". . . and hoeing 'til your hands blister . . ."

". . . and plowing . . ."

". . . shucking corn . . ."

". . . killing hogs . . ."

". . . cooking molasses . . ."

". . . hauling logs . . ."

". . . laying them railroad ties . . ."

". . . swinging that hammer . . ."

". . . to drive them hard, hard steel spikes!"

"Gawd, when you think of all the work we black folks done done . . ."

". . . and ain't got a damn thing to show for it all . . ."

". . . but bent backs and weak minds . . ."

". . . you feel like going outdoors and looking up at the sun and cussing Gawd!"

"A naughts a naught
A figger's a figger
All for the white man
None for the nigger . . ."

"It's the truth!"

"Gawd knows it is!"

"There ain't nothing worse'n a Southern white man but two Southern white men . . ."

". . . and the only thing worse'n two Southern white men is two Southern rattle snakes!"

"But some of the white folks in the South's pretty good."

"Yeah, the rich ones."

"That's 'cause they got money to live on and don't have to worry."

"But the poor white man's death to a poor black man."

"They grudge you the ground you stand on."

"They's the ones what lynch and burn us."

"Crackers!"

"Rednecks!"

"Hillbillies!"

"And don't they look awful . . ."

". . . with them old bleachedout blue eyes . . ."

". . . sunk way back in their heads . . ."

". . . and that old dead stringy hair . . ."

". . . falling down over their faces . . ."

". . . like a dirty mop . . ."

". . . and them old thin mouths all drawed in . . ."

". . . and when they talk they whine through their noses . . ."

". . . like starved cats!"

"And Lawd, they lazy's the day is long . . ."

". . . laying around in the sun . . ."

". . . like tiredout hounddogs . . ."

". . . licking their sores . . ."

". . . and about ready to die!"

"And *mean?*"

"I ain't never seen folks what could laugh at suffering like they can."

"When other folks is happy, they suffer . . ."

". . . and when other folks is suffering, they's happy!"

"I think Gawd must've made them folks wrongsideout-ward."

> *"Don't like liver*
> *Don't like hash*
> *Rather be a nigger*
> *Than poor white trash . . ."*

"Lawd, when I was down South I use' to dream about Chicago!"

"Chicago seemed like the Promised land!"

> *"Heaven is up*
> *South is down*
> *Lawd, Lawd*
> *I'm Northward Bound . . ."*

"I remember the day I left the train was so full of black folks coming North I had to stand up all the way to Chicago."

"A white guy who was looking for men to work in the stockyards asked me if I wanted to come, and I walked off, just walked off and caught the train."

"When folks told me about the North I couldn't believe it was true."

"Yeah, a lot of the old folks said it was just a lie to trick us up North so's the white folks up here could put us in slavery."

"I remember little boys walking around singing: *'Lawd, I'd ruther be a lamppost in Chicago than the President of Miss-'sippi . . .'*"

"And there was another song: *'I'm going to shake the dust of the South off my feet forever . . .'*"

"Them was the days when we lived in hope."

"Yeah, but there was some goodtimes in the South . . ."

". . . when the white folks wasn't nowhere around . . ."

". . . and the guys all gathered around in the backyard with guitars . . ."

". . . playing and singing . . ."

". . . and that evening sun going down . . ."

". . . red like blood . . ."

". . . and that old lazy river flowing South . . ."

". . . and the womenfolks standing around sort of sad-like . . ."

". . . waiting for you to say something . . ."

". . . and you feel like you want to

> *Shake it to the East*
> *Shake it to the West*
> *Shake it to the one*
> *You love the best . . .*"

". . . and you got a aching in your bones . . ."

". . . like you got to do what you want to do or die!"

"Yeah, Gawd! That feeling that makes you want to howl and moan . . ."

". . . like a wildcat in a swamp!"

"Lawd, today!"

"This life and another one!"

"There was some good days in the South . . ."

"Yeah, in the summer . . ."

". . . when you didn't have nothing to do but lay in the sun and live."

"I use' to get out of the bed feeling tired, didn't want to do *nothing*!"

"Look like the South just makes a man feel like a million-aire!"

"I use' to go swimming in the creek . . ."

"Fishing's what I love! Seems like I can smell them catfish frying right now!"

"And in the summer when the Magnolia trees is in blossom . . ."

". . . you can smell 'em for half a mile!"

"And them sunflowers . . ."

". . . and honeysuckles."

"You know, we use' to break them honeysuckles off the stem and suck the sweetness out of 'em."

"And them plums . . ."

". . . so ripe they was busting open!"

"And sugarcane . . ."

". . . and blackberries . . ."

". . . juicy and sweet!"

"And in the summer at night the sky's so full of stars you think they going to fall . . ."

". . . and the air soft and warm . . ."

". . . smelling like water."

"And them long rains in the winter . . ."

". . . rain sometimes for a week . . ."

". . . and you set inside and roast corn and sweet potatoes!"

"Boy, the South's good . . ."

". . . and bad!"

"It's Heaven . . ."

". . . and Hell . . ."

". . . all rolled into one!"

"The only difference between the North and the South is, them guys down there'll kill you, and these up here'll let you starve to death."

"Well, I'd rather die slow than to die fast!"

"Jews, Catholics, and niggers . . ."

". . . the South's sure hard on 'em!"

"But shucks, I don't mind how bad they treat them Jews. They run 'em out of the old countries and they come over here and treat us just like the folks over there treated them."

"Yeah, when a white man's hard on a Jew it's 'cause he's got it coming to 'im."

"And them Catholics . . . Them's the sly guys!"

"Yeah, all that plotting with the Pope."

"I reckon the white folks is right when they's against them."

"But why in hell they so hard on us?"

"We don't do nothing."

"And we been in this country long's any of 'em."

"They say they lynch us to keep their women pure . . ."

"Hell, I don't believe that!"

"You know, a friend of mine told me a story once. He was going down South with two Northern white men, driving the car for 'em. They got down in Miss'sippi and was riding along a country road when they spied three white gals, flagging 'em . . . Well, the white guy told the black guy to stop the car. He did. The white gals got in and all of 'em started drinking. After awhile they felt like doing it, and so they went into the woods. Now this black guy was scared. The white men carried their gals off and started pumping away. But this black guy just stood up. The gal asked 'im what was the matter. He wouldn't even talk. He just stood there with his mouth open, thinking about all the black men the white folks done killed and burned. And this gal was laying there squirming and panting, hot as fire. She got so mad she pulled off her shoe and beat 'im over the head with it, run 'im back to the car . . . That shows you there ain't no trouble with black men bothering white women. Hell, they scared . . ."

"I know I was scared."

"Shucks, I wouldn't hardly look at one when I was down South."

"If a white woman had smiled at me I would've started running."

"I saw 'em hang a man once."

"Yeah?"

"He was a young guy who'd done killed a white man . . ."

"Was he scared?"

"Naw, he just stood still with his eyes on the sky and didn't say a mumbling word . . ."

"Lawd!"

"The old sheriff just pulled the handle and the trapdoor dropped and the man shot down and that rope got tight . . . It was almost dark and he just hung there, jerking a little with his head to one side. Pretty soon he was dead."

"Gee, I ain't never seen no hanging."

"Me neither."

"Well, don't see none, 'cause you won't be able to sleep for a week."

"The white folks just done made up in their minds they ain't going to let no black man rise!"

"But the Bible says Ethiopia's going to stretch forth her hand some day."

"Look like old Mussellinni's done stopped that."

"Aw, that don't mean nothing. You can't tell what plan Gawd's got up his sleeve."

"Naw, you can't. Gawd wouldn't let nothing like that happen without doing *some*thing about it."

"He's going to fix 'em some day."

"It'll be like the preacher say: A Great GettingUp Morning!"

"Shucks, the preachers say we black folks was a great race once."

"Sure, them was the times when we was in Africa."

"Black folks ruled the world then."

"You see, every race gets its chance. The black folks, then the yellow folks, then them Greeks, and on down the line . . . The white folks is holding the fort now."

"But them white folks done covered up our records so's we won't know how great we is."

"They say there was a great black man in Roosia."

"Who?"

"His name was Pumpkin, wasn't it?"

"What he do?"

"He wrote books."

"That make 'im great?"

"Oh, yeah. I heard of 'im. I heard a preacher say he got killed fighting with a white man . . ."

"Now, that sounds something like it."

"They say old Solomon was a black man."

"He was the wisest man in the world."

"Some folks say Peter was black."

"You ever see them pictures with black angels on 'em?"

"Sure."

"We got one at home."

"A colored guy done wrote a book proving that *Jesus* was black!"

"He might've been. If he was, these white folks'd keep it from us so's we can't have no pride in ourselves."

"Aw, them white bastards is slick!"

"But things can't go on like this always."

"You know, I wish there was a man somewhere who knowed how to lead and who could lead . . ."

"A guy who wouldn't steal . . ."

". . . and lie . . ."

". . . and grab your woman when your back is turned."

". . . and who would know how to speak out all these things so folks'd understand 'em . . ."

". . . and who wouldn't be scared!"

"There'll be a man like that some day . . ."

". . . and things start to change then."

"You know, honest, for something like that I wouldn't mind maybe fighting and dying."

"Yeah, when you feel that a lot of folks feel like you feel."

"I reckon that's what the preacher calls faith."

"It's something you hate like hell to talk about, but you's always wishing somebody else felt that way, too."

"A lot of times I been wanting to do things I just wouldn't do."

"And I bet a lot of other folks feel the same way."

"Now . . . Wait a minute . . . Now, you see, if *all* the folks felt like that, why in hell don't they *do* something?"

"Do what?"

"What we's talking about . . ."

"Aw, hell! Some guy's got something *you* want, and you got something *he* wants, and when you start to do something you bump into each other . . ."

"Yeah, like you see trains crashing up in the movies."

"But, shucks, if we all was in the same train going in the same direction . . ."

"Aw, man, ain't no sense in talking about things like this."

"Yeah, the more you talk about 'em the more you can't feel 'em."

"You know, the white folks who built this country must've felt something like that."

"Yeah, but they don't feel like that now. One half of 'em's mad at the other."

"Say you remember that colored guy who use' t' preach over the radio?"

"That guy who said everybody's got to come under one command?"

"Yeah."

"Maybe that's what he was talking about."

"Maybe it was."

"But it'd take a strong guy to make all these folks come under one command."

"You telling me?"

"Like old Hitler . . ."

". . . and Mussellinni."

"Nigger, Wops, Frogs, Dagos, Chinks, Japs, Kikes . . . Lawd, it's a mess!"

> *"Red, white, and blue*
> *Your Pa's a lousy Jew*
> *Your Ma's a dirty Dago*
> *And what in hell is you? . . ."*

"Well, I reckon the best thing for a guy to do is get together with a woman."

"State Street Mama!"

> *"My name is Jim Taylor*
> *My John is a whaler*
> *And my balls weigh ninetynine pound*
> *If you know any ladies*
> *Who want any babies*
> *Just tell 'em Jim Taylor's in town . . ."*

"Hahaha!"

"Hohoho!"

"Say, you remember the first meat you ever had?"

"Gee, it makes me laugh to think about it!"

"Who was the first meat you ever had, Al?"

"Aw, I don't know."

"Naw, I don't want to tell that."

"You scared?"

"Naw."

"Tell us . . ."

"Aw, she was my cousin . . . Hahaha!"

"Hohoho!"

"Who was your first meat, Jake."

"Well, my ma sent me out in the country to visit my uncle and he wasn't home. His wife asked me to stay all night . . ."

"What happened?"

"Hell, you *know* what happened!"

"I bet you was like a wild bull!"

"Aw, naw, now! *She* started at me!"

"I *bet* she didn't!"

"And the next morning I run all the way home!"

"You, Slim? Come on . . ."

"It was a preacher's wife. He was away preaching a funeral . . ."

"Ain't this a bitch?"

"How old was you?"

"Just thirteen . . ."

"Come on, now. You, Bob . . ."

"All I got to say is, a young boy ain't got no conscience . . . Hahaha!"

"You never forget that first time."

"A woman always wants you."

"Yeah, if you ain't got nothing else you can always get a woman."

"But some women's so damn much trouble."

"They always want so much."

"Just a handful of gimme . . ."

". . . and a lifeful of sorrow!"

"You can't do with 'em and you can't do without 'em!"

"Gee, that reminds me!"

"What?"

"Ain't I showed you them pictures?"

"What pictures?"

"You ain't showed us nothing."

"Them pictures I bought from the Chink?"

"Naw!"

"Boy, this is the hottest stuff in town!"

"Let's see 'em!"

"Look and weep, niggers!"

"Read what it say!"

"Hold it up so I can see!"

"Wait a minute and let Jake read it!"

> *"I love you once*
> *I love you twice*
> *I love you next*
> *To Jesus Christ . . ."*

"Open 'em up!"

"Yeah, let's see 'em!"

"Take your time, nigger!"

"Good Gawd Almighty!"

"Let me see 'em!"

"Quit pulling!"

"Don't tear 'em, nigger!"

"Hold the thing up!"

"Boy, look how he's got her!"

"Look how he's holding her!"

"He's riding her like a stallion!"

"He's riding her like a bicycle!"

"And she look like she likes it!"

"Sure she likes it!"

"Look at her eyes!"

"And her stommick!"

"She's biting her lips!"

"Come on, man! Let's see the next one!"

"Wheeeeeeeeee!"

"Do, re, mi, fa, sol, la, ti, do!"

"If he ain't got a grip on her!"

"Hold 'em up and let me see 'em!"

"Look like she's about to scream!"

"Look at them tits!"

"Lawd, today!"

"Good Gordin Gin!"

"Get off my foot!"

"You act like you gone crazy."

"That's a different woman from what was in the others!"

"Yeah, but it's the same man."

"And she looks like a real young girl."

"Look like she's gone to sleep."

"You'd look that way too if you had in you what she's got in her."

"Turn it over. Let's see the next one."

"Hunh! Now, ain't that something!"

"How can folks do things like that?"

"Doggone it, that's going too far for me!"

"Folks'll do *any*thing."

"They must pay folks a lot of money to take their pictures that way."

"Nigger, put them pictures in your pocket."

"Where you get 'em from?"

"I bought 'em from a Chink."

"How much?"

"Five bucks."

"He got any more?"

"I don't know. You'll have to see 'im."

"You know, them pictures must've been made in France."

"The Chink said they was made in France. That's how come they cost so much."

"They say French folks is immoral."

"Yeah, that's where all the freakish stuff comes from."

"A French woman'll do *any*thing!"

"You ought to hear some of them soljers talk that went to France."

"Gee, I'd like to go to France."

"Me too."

"Me too."

"Me too."

"Man, you know one thing? A woman's *funny!*"

"Oh, they funny, all right."

"Ain't it queer how a man just keeps thinking about 'em?"

"Just can't seem to get 'em off your mind."

"There's something about 'em that just draws you, no matter what."

"And you can't help yourself."

"And that feeling a woman gives you!"

"Jeeesus!"

"Boy, it's a terrible thing!"

"It's like fire!"

"Like ice!"

"Like a 'lectric shock!"

"It knocks you out!"

"It gets you all over . . ."

". . . in your head . . ."

". . . and legs . . ."

". . . and thighs . . ."

". . . like somebody pouring warm water over you!"

"It lifts you up and then lets you down . . ."

". . . and you want to go to sleep . . ."

". . . but in a little while you want to go again."

"It's a funny feeling."

"It's the greatest feeling in the world."
"Yeah, but a man couldn't stand that feeling for long."
"Naw, he just couldn't bear it."
"It'd kill 'im."

PART THREE: RATS' ALLEY

. . . But at my back in a cold blast I hear
The rattle of the bones, and chuckle spread from ear to ear.
                                    —T. S. Eliot's *Wasteland*

. . . A SHOT, A SCREAM, A CLOUD OF SMOKE—ALL IN A SPLIT SECOND OF TIME. THE BULLET ENTERED THE LEFT SIDE OF PRESIDENT LINCOLN'S HEAD, PASSED THROUGH THE BRAIN, AND STOPPED JUST SHORT OF THE LEFT EYE. HE WAS RUSHED TO A ROOM OPPOSITE FORD'S THEATRE, AND THERE HE LINGERED AMONG TENDER FRIENDS UNTIL MORNING. AT TWENTY-TWO MINUTES PAST SEVEN O'CLOCK HE DIED. AS HE BREATHED HIS LAST SECRETARY STANTON SAID:

"Now, he belongs to the ages . . ."

I.

WHEN THEY were least expecting it, when their minds had strayed on a daydreaming pilgrimage, the gong for quittingtime boomed throughout the Mailing Division.

"TWELVETHIRTY CLERKS CHECKOUT!"

As though they were dead men come suddenly to life, they dropped the mail and ran to the timecard racks; then, holding to bannisters, they galloped down the winding steel stairs three steps at a time and pushed their way into the smelly washroom.

"Make it snappy!" called Jake, rubbing white lather about his neck.

"Cccome on, fffor Cchrissake!" coughed Slim. "I wwwant to wwwash!"

"Move over!" said Al.

"Youall wait for me!" Bob yelled, running for the commodes.

As they received their hats, coats, and canes their faces assumed expressions of healthy interest. Legs and arms which had moved listlessly swung with buoyant energy; voices which had been low monotones rose in relieved shouts.

"Let's go!" called Jake, jamming his arms awkwardly into his coat.

"Coming!"

They filed out upon the front steps and stood huddled amid swirling snowflakes with their coatcollars turned up. Heavy spouts of vapor rolled from their lips and lingered a moment in the cold air, then vanished. About them the muffled thunder of traffic crashed in a falling shroud of white. The headlights of autos swerved around corners and glared momentarily.

"Well where do we go from here?" asked Al.

"How about some cigars?" asked Jake.

"Sure thing."

A few minutes later they were standing in a doorway, puffing cigars and looking at the passing traffic with a superb detachment. They were almost satisfied now, but not quite. Each felt that something was lacking, and that lack hungered over and above ordinary hunger; they could feel it in their stomachs, in their legs, even in the tips of their fingers. Jake rolled his cigar from one corner of his mouth to the other.

"Say, how about some likker?"

"Now you talking!"

With a halfpint flask sagging in each of his coatpockets, Jake stood again in a doorway.

"It's near eleven bells," said Al.

"Let's get going."

"I want to buy a paper first," said Slim. "Here, boy!"

"Wheeeeee!" Al whistled through his teeth for a roving taxi.

Brakes screamed; a car swerved to the curb; a door swung open, and the four of them piled in.

"Fortyfive fiftyeight Calumet!" Jake called.

"O.K."

As the car lumbered southward over snowcovered streets, Jake nestled into a corner and felt the flasks pressing against his sides.

"How about a little nip?"

Jake, Al, and Slim drank.

"Aw, come on, Bob. One shot won't hurt you."

"Naw."

"Aw, man, take a drink."

Bob sat tensely on the edge of the seat. His lips moved several times, but he said nothing. Jake pushed the bottle into his hands; he held it, his lips parted in fascination and indecision.

"Don't be a wet blanket!"

Bob tilted the flask and drank.

"It sure can't kill me," he said, blowing to cool the fiery burn.

"You don't live but once," said Al.

Slim pulled out the newspaper and squinted at the headline.

"What's the news?" asked Jake, closing his eyes.

"They say Japan's done grabbed *all* Manchooria."

"Yeah?"

"And they say a hundred million Chinks in China's done gone Red."

"Now them Chinks is funny folks," said Bob.

"Yeah, they eat with sticks."

"They eat rats, too."

"And rotten eggs."

"A Chink'll do *any*thing."

"They say they killing up more Jews in Germany," read Slim.

"*Some*body always killing them Jews!"

"You know, I saw in the papers where they plotting to rule the whole world."

"Yeah, they got all the gold hid away now."

"Them rookies is *slick*."

"And they done lynched another nigger down South," said Slim.

"Yeah?" asked Jake, turning slightly.

"They burnt 'im alive," said Slim.

"Well, Gawddammit, they ought to lynch 'em if they ain't got no better senses to stay down there."

"I wouldn't live in a place like that," said Al.

"That's how come I left," said Bob.

"They say old Roosia's done gone and got a army of eighteen million men," said Slim.

"Aw, them Reds can't fight," said Al.

"And here's the picture of a guy what can play the violin with his toes," said Slim.

"With his *toes*?"

"Let's see it!"

"Gee, that's going some!"

"Say, I seen a guy shoot pool blindfolded once."

"I seen a guy play a guitar standing on his *head*."

"Some folks can do almost anything."

"It's a natural born gift."

Slim threw the paper aside and they rode awhile in silence. Jake thought of the one hundred dollars on his hip and sang:

"*Yellow taxis, yellow money, yellow women . . .*"

They chuckled and puffed languidly. Now and then they took the black weeds out of their mouths and eyed the glowing tips.

"Damn good smoke."

"You bet."

"Draws well."

"Yeah."

The taxi swung to a snowbanked curb.

"Well, here we is, boys!" Jake announced. The snow had slackened a bit. As Jake paid the bill Slim led the way into the vestibule.

"Looks like a swell joint."

"Hope they got some redhot mamas up there."

"Don't worry about that."

In answer to Slim's three pressures of the bell the door buzzed. Midway up the steps they could hear the sound of muffled music and the rhythm of pounding feet. At the top of the landing they were met by a buxom, brownskinned woman.

"Hello, Rose!" called Jake.

"Glory be! If it ain't my four Aggravating Papas!" said Rose, flinging her arms wide.

"And you don't know how aggravating," said Jake as he caught her around the waist.

"Look like you's ready for business tonight," said Rose.

"You'll be surprised," said Slim, slapping her fleshy buttocks.

Rose shook her finger at them playfully.

"Come on, now! Be a good boy for mama! . . . I'm mighty proud you brought your pals along, Jake. We can have some good times here . . . Now, youall just come right in and take off your coats and hats and hang 'em in the closet and make yourselves at home. What you don't see, ask for it. And when you gets hungry step back in the diningroom and eat some of the best chitterlings you ever tasted. Ain't no need for youall to be a bit bashful around here. Just throw your troubles away . . ."

They pushed into a big room jammed with dancers. Shouts, laughter, and snatches of song swung through the smoky air. A threepiece jazz band—a cornet, a drum, and a piano—made raucous music in a corner. There were gamblers, pimps, petty thieves, dope peddlers, smallfry politicians, grafters, racketeers of various shades, athletes, high school and college students in search of "life", and hordes of sexeager youngsters. The women were white, ivory, yellow, light brown, medium brown, solid brown, dark brown, near black, and black. They wore red, yellow, brown, blue, purple, and black gowns with V shapes reaching down almost to their waists. Their bosoms were high and bulging, and they danced with an obvious exaggeration of motion.

With the stump of his cigar clamped in his teeth, Jake stood just inside the door and looked over the crowd. He watched the women's bodies swing and a warm glow spread from his stomach to his chest. A deep sense of ease and freedom pervaded him; he stood with his legs wide apart and with his thumbs hooked in the armholes of his vest. *This don't look like a bad crowd.* He knew some of them from other times. There was Blue Juice, a pimp who boasted that he controlled more women than any single Negro on the South Side. There was Ben Kitty, known far and wide for his skill at billiards. And there was a tall, slender, brownskinned man called One Barrel; it was reputed that he was so stingy he breathed only out of one barrel of his nose. *Naw, this ain't bad at all.* Jake smiled and listened to voices call to and fro.

"Have a sip, Daddy!"

"Come on and let's get lowdown!"

"I don't care! I don't care!"

"Whip that piano, Bopeep!"

"Aw, dance that thing!"

"Lawd! Lawd!"

Bob tugged at Jake's sleeve.

"Say, Jake?"

"Yeah?"

"Slip me something. I'm going to shoot some craps in the backroom."

"Sure," said Jake, laughing and slipping a fivedollar bill into Bob's hand. "You just out of luck, Bob."

"Call me when youall's ready to eat."

"O.K."

Slim grabbed a stocky, mulatto girl with Slavic features and started dancing. Al was talking to a thin black girl.

"Say, partner?"

Jake turned and faced a short, skinny, black man with bloodshot eyes.

"Want some weeds?"

"Naw."

"Only twobits."

"Naw."

"Aw, come on."

"Naw, I tell you!"

Jake walked off. He did not want to smoke any Marihuana cigarettes. *Likker's good enough for me.* He saw some of the younger men and women huddled in corners sucking hungrily at cigarettes. They inhaled deeply, held the smoke in their lungs as long as they could, and beat their chests to absorb the essence of the smoke. *That's a sissy's way to get high.*

Jake lolled, his eyes roving somberly. He was trying to pick out a woman. Finally, he went to a yellow one who was walking alone to and fro in front of a window at the far end of the room. She was of medium height with broad hips and she welcomed him with a wide, wet smile. He walked her to the center of the floor and they swung into a dance.

"Where you been all my life?" he asked, tightening his arm.

"Where you been all *my* life?" she countered, nestling close.

Back and across the room they swayed like trees bending to strong winds. Feet went thrumpthrump, thrumpthrump, thrumpthrump . . .

"Shake that thing!" somebody yelled.

"What's your name?" Jake asked his girl.

"Blanche, Sweet Papa. What might be yours?"

"Just Jake," he said, swinging her through a narrow opening between the dancers.

"You works in the Post Office, Sweet?"

"Sure thing, Baby."

"Look like you and me's going to hit it off O.K.," she said, throwing the naked part of her arm about his neck.

"I knows we is," he said.

"Sweet Papa," she breathed into his ear.

"How long you been in this joint?" he asked.

"About a week."

"Like it?"

"I don't mind."

"How's tricks."

"Slow."

"Don't look like a babe like you ought to have no trouble."

"Honey, these niggers ain't got no money."

"I got money."

"You look like it."

"Been in Chi long?"

"About a week, I told you."

"Oh, so you started right in here."

"Yeah, but I'm looking for a steady daddy."

"String along with me, Babe."

She laughed. They stood still in a tight knot of dancers and moved only their hips and knees. Jake looked at the yellow sweep of her bosom. *She ain't bad.* The music sank to a low keep, sobbing the *St. Louis Blues*; he felt Blanche rolling her stomach to him, softly. Their eyes met and his lips parted.

"Say?" he asked.

"What's the matter, Papa?"

"Who learned you that?"

"You'd be surprised."

Jake laughed and whirled her over the floor. *Naw, she ain't bad at all.*

"I'm hungry."

"Plenty of grub in the back."

"What you say, let's eat?"

"Just's you say, Papa."

Jake gathered his party and led them through two rear rooms and into a little curtained nook. Rose hovered above them.

"I had this table all saved just 'specially for youall," she said. "I thought youall'd want it sort of privatelike."

"You knows your stuff, Rose," said Jake.

"Nothing different," she answered.

"This is a mellow joint," said Al.

"How come you ain't got a gal?" Rose asked Bob.

"Oh, I'm laying off for awhile," Bob mumbled.

"He's teething," said Jake.

They laughed. Bob rolled his eyes, took out his flask, and swallowed a deep drink. Rose placed her hand tenderly on the back of his neck.

"Listen," she said. "When you gets well come and see me and I'll fix it so's you won't never have to teethe no more."

"I'll be around," said Bob.

"Now, youall get ready to eat a heap tonight," coaxed Rose, polishing the top of the table with her dishtowel.

"What you got that's good?" asked Jake.

"Well, I got some chitterlings, turnip greens cooked with smoked ribs, Spanish rice, slaw, spaghetti, egg cornbread, pigtails, barbecue, beer, and whiskey," sang Rose.

Al sucked back loose saliva.

"Hush your mouth!"

"Folks, order anything you want!" said Jake, with a sweeping wave of his hand.

"I wants some chitterlings," said Blanche.

"I wants some of that barbecue," said Slim's girl.

"Make it four chitterlings and four barbecues and beer and slaw all around," bawled Jake. "The stuff's on me tonight!"

"Coming up!" sang Rose.

"Have some cigarettes," said Jake.

They lit up and blew smoke into one another's face. The men appraised the girls' lips, throats, shoulders, and bosoms. The girls sighed and looked wistfully at their plates.

"It's been a long time since we's been around with any Post Office dudes," sighed Blanche.

"Well, you got a good chance to make up for lost time tonight," said Jake.

There was a short silence during which each man edged his chair closer to the table.

The girls' eyes assumed lights of coy innocence and the men's jaws assumed lines of aggressiveness.

"Youall sure ought to see our rooms upstairs," suggested Blanche.

"Yeah?"

"We got the cutest beds . . ."

"You know who we is?" asked Slim.

"Who?"

"We's the official bedinspectors," he said.

They laughed. The lights were lowered just enough to give the room a dreamlike air. The naked flesh of the women's arms gleamed satinly under the soft sheens of the floorlamp. Rose brought two long platters of steaming food.

"Go to it, folks! This ain't no dicty joint and you can eat till you bust!"

Rose went from glass to glass and poured foaming beer.

"I'm going to turn on the radio so's youall can have some music," she said as she left. "And if you want anything, just call."

"O.K."

A crashing chord of martial music rose and died away; a voice spoke.

. . . AT ANTIETAM McCLELLAN AND LEE CLASHED IN A SANGUINARY STRUGGLE IN WHICH THE BLOOD OF TWENTY-TWO THOUSAND MEN STAINED THE SOIL . . .

"What in hell is *that*?"

"Aw," drawled Bob, nodding sleepily. "That's that Civil War . . ."

"Slide the salt down this way!"

"Give me that cornbread!"

"Hand me that sauce!"

"Llllet mmmme ssse . . . Let me see that ssssslaw," coughed Slim.

The hot, greasy food was washed down by huge draughts of cold beer.

"More beer here, Rose!" Jake bawled.

"Coming, Mister Post Office Man!" she sang, sidling up to get the empty bottles.

They ate, ramming knives deep into their mouths.

"Pheeeeeeeeeeew!" exclaimed Al's girl. "I ain't going to eat no more. I'm scared of getting too fat."

"Too *fat*?"

"Yeah."

Al raised his eyes and looked intently at her fleshy bosom.

"Don't let a little thing like that worry you none, Sweetheart," he said eagerly through a mouthful of chitterlings whose grease oozed from the corners of his lips. "The fatter the berry the sweeter the juice!"

"Why, you naaaaaaasty maaaaaan!" she said, widening her eyes in mock shame.

The girls dropped their knives and forks and covered their mouths with their hands to smother giggles. Jake, Al, and Bob, and Slim leaned back in chairs, opened their mouths as

wide as their jaws would permit, clapped their hands protect-
ingly over their swollen stomachs, and gave vent to a roar of
merriment that drowned out the radio. When their guffaws
had simmered down to mere sniffles, Jake asked Al:

"How you know about how much juice in a fat berry?"

"Oh, I know, all right," said Al, wiping the crumbs and
grease from his lips with the back of his hand.

"Talk like you done had some business with fat berries,"
said Blanche.

"I ain't missed it," said Al.

They laughed again.

"If that's the case, you gals better eat a heap," said Slim.

"Oh, I reckon we got juice enough," said Blanche.

"You *sure?*" asked Jake.

"We *ought* to know," said Blanche.

"Who told you?" asked Jake.

"Ain't nobody never kicked on us none," said Blanche.

"That's fair enough," said Al, waving his fork. "If ain't nobody else kicked, then we can't kick."

"If our customers ain't satisfied, they tell us. If they is they
tell others," said Blanche.

The four men bent low over their plates as their mouths
flew open again. The girls clapped them heartily on their
backs to increase their ribaldry.

. . . NOW SHERMAN'S TROOPS WERE SWEEPING A BELT
MANY MILES WIDE WITH THE ZEST OF MEN OUT FOR A
HOLIDAY. THEY WERE ROBBING IT OF EVERY EDIBLE
THING. THEY BURNT MILLS. THEY TORE UP RAILROADS
AND PILED THE RAILS IN BLAZING HEAPS AND TWISTED
THEM WHILE STILL HOT AROUND THE TRUNKS OF FOREST
TREES . . .

"How's we doing!"

"Hey, hey!"

"Youall's O.K.," said Slim.

"You got my vote," said Al.

"Say, Rose! More chitterlings and barbecue here!" called
Jake.

When they had sopped their plates and drained the last of
the beer, they leaned back in their chairs, sighing and sup-

pressing belches. The beer and hot food made them sleepy. Blanche yawned.

"Shucks, I feel like a snake what's done swallowed a chicken," she mumbled.

The men tried to smile, but could not; they were full and listless.

"Let's dance, folks," said Jake in a dead tone.

"O.K. with me," sighed Al.

No one moved. The music in the front room was now going so loud that they heard it even through the partitions. Feet went thrumpthrump, thrumpthrump, thrumpthrump . . . The house seemed to rock in a vast darkness. The monotonous rhythm was like a thousand fingers tapping the taut skin of a kettle drum in the midst of a deep forest. At intervals the muffled cry of the cornet rose up and died away like the midnight wail of a lovesick tomcat. The piano moaned like a woman in labor.

"Aw, I want to dance," said Al's girl.

"Me too," said Slim's girl.

"O.K.," said Al.

No one moved. Jake yawned and belched.

"Rose!" he called.

"Coming!"

"How about some likker!"

"Sure thing!"

It was not until they had had four rounds of whiskey that they felt like moving.

"This stuff's really good," said Jake.

. . . WITH MALICE TOWARD NONE, WITH CHARITY FOR ALL, WITH FIRMNESS IN THE RIGHT AS GOD GIVES US TO SEE THE RIGHT, LET US FINISH THE WORK WE ARE IN . . .

"Come on! Let's finish the bottle!"

"Yeah, let's drink!"

Bob swayed forward, slobbering.

"Yeeeeeah, what to hell!"

II.

WHEN THE BOTTLE was empty, Jake reached for his pocketbook, placed it upon the table, and exposed to view a thick wad of green bills. Blanche peeped into it and exclaimed:

"Lawd, man! You sure wellheeled!"

He smiled at her.

"What's the matter, Honey?" He turned to Rose. "What I owe you, Sweetmeat?"

"Just twelvefifty," she said diffidently.

Jake gave her three fivedollar bills.

"Keep the change, Toots!"

"That's what I love about a sport!" sang Rose.

He led his party back to the front room. Stimulated by alcohol, they glided on to the floor in answer to the call of the music. Their limp bodies swayed bonelessly to every tug of the rhythm. The air was heavy and damp. They tightened their arms as the music grew personal, selfish, sexual. Their eyes became vague and dreamy. Stomach rubbed stomach. Sweat beaded on black temples. Nostrils gleamed. Thick lips grew wet and sagged, trembling when bodies were swung. Now and then a slight moan was heard; it was as though someone had become so charged with emotion that he could contain it no longer. The pounding piano, the incessant shuffling of feet, and the sobbing cornet invoked a spirit of emotional surrender so intense that its driving force manifested itself in the hard, drawn lines of their faces. Feet went thrumpthrump, thrumpthrump, thrumpthrump . . . Rose pushed her way into the center of the room and yelled:

"Is everybody happy?"

"In Heaven with my feets hanging out!"

"We's got the world in a jug . . ."

". . . and the stopper in our hands!"

Rose filled her lungs and yelled again:

"I SAY, IS EVERYBODY HAPPY?"

"Yeah, Lawd!"

"WELL, GIVE 'EM SOME MUSIC AND LET 'EM DANCE THE TIME DOWN!"

The band beat out *Tiger Rag*. As Jake danced his head was tilted backward. The expression upon his face was peculiar, paradoxical; it was relaxed and flabby, yet somehow eager and watchful. There was in it a sort of childish trustfulness. The music caroled its promise of an unattainable satisfaction and lured him to a land whose boundaries receded with each step he took. When the music slowed he felt tired, but when it went faster, he went faster. Each time it reached a high pitch of intensity he verged on the limits of physical feeling, as though beyond this was nothing but sleep, death; but when it sank, quavering, sighing, disillusioned, his muscles slackened, hungering for more. The room became so crowded he could hardly move. Bopeep played *Is It True What They Say About Dixie?*, and he slid over the floor, shifting from foot to foot. With each twist of his shoulders he felt the yielding softness of Blanche's body; he placed the open palm of his right hand in the center of her back and pressed her closer to him; he straightened till he felt her touching him at almost every point; then he pranced and swayed in one spot in a tight knot of dancers, his lips hanging loose. Blanche's breath came warm on the side of his neck and he heard her whisper:

"That's murder, Papa."

"I want to be electrocuted," he said.

"Oh, play it, Mister Piano Man, play it!" a young, black girl yelled, breaking suddenly from her partner and dancing alone in the center of the room, flinging her legs and arms in all directions. The rest paused, formed a circle about her and began to clap their hands, each clap falling midway between the beats of the music and creating a sharp and imperious syncopation. The girl's eyes rolled wildly; her head bobbed back and forth and she flung her limbs heavily as though she were drugged with warm wine. She advanced with the palms of her hands holding hard to her thighs and retreated with the tips of her fingers pressed deep into the soft flesh of her stomach. The dance became slower and slower till nothing moved but the muscles in her hips. Finally she gaped her mouth like a fish out of water and sank to her knees, moaning:

"Lawd . . . Lawd . . ."

"Do it, gal!"

"Show 'em you ain't scared!"

"Come on, Papa," Blanche urged. "Let's get in close where we can see."

"O.K., Baby."

He caught her around the waist and rammed his way into the crowd. All about him he felt the pressure of eager bodies. Blanche lunged suddenly and her arms clung to his neck for support. He held her on her feet.

"What's the matter?"

Blanche turned and sneered:

"Watch where you going, nigger!"

Jake whirled, ready for fight. A tall, black man bowed and grinned.

" 'Scuse me," he said meekly.

"How come you can't look where you walking?" Jake growled, starting forward.

Blanche pulled him back.

"Aw, Daddy, forget 'im. He ain't nobody."

Jake's jaws clamped tight and his eyes followed the man till he disappeared through a rear door. He felt good tonight; he felt like hitting somebody. *What he doing trying to run over me?*

Another girl had come into the center of the ring and was dancing to the tune of *Sister Kate*. Her hair flew about her head, sometimes screening her face. Her thin body whirled like a spinningtop; her dress rose and floated at the level of her hips, revealing the smooth, cool brown of her legs.

"Dance that thing, gal!" croaked a man who was so drunk he looked crosseyed.

Another girl came in. Bopeep played *Handy Man*. With her feet still, she swayed her hips and crooned:

> *"He hauls my ashes*
> *He strokes my fiddle*
> *Threads my needle*
> *Creams my wheat*
> *Lawd, he's a damn good man to have around . . ."*

"Do it, Sadie, do it!"

Jake felt giddy; he clapped his hands, closed his eyes, threw back his head, and yelled:

"DO IT A LONG OLD TIME!"

A stout, black woman waddled into the center of the ring and called to Bopeep:

"Play my piece!"

She sang in a cracked, nasal alto, uttering one line while she walled her eyes to the left, and uttering another line while she walled her eyes to the right.

> "*Two old maids in a foldingbed*
> *One turned to the other, and said:*
> *'Yes, we have no bananas, Delight,*
> *We have no bananas tonight'* . . ."

Jake bent double with laughter.

> "*Two old maids in a foldingbed*
> *One turned to the other and said:*
> *'Darling, you are growing old;*
> *There're silver threads among your gold'* . . ."

Jake hugged Blanche and screamed. When the song ended she danced. Her flaccid buttocks and bosom shivered like fluid. Her eyes were closed, her face lifted ceilingward, her lips tightly compressed. She seemed absorbed in an intense feeling burning in her stomach and she clawed her fingers hungrily in the air.

"Pick them cherries, gal! Pick 'em!"

Abruptly, the dance changed; her legs leaped into the air; her body ran riot with a goal of its own. The muscles of her stomach rose and fell insatiably. The music whirled faster and she whirled faster. She seemed to have lost all conscious control, seemed possessed by the impelling excitement of her nervous system. The climax came when she clasped her knees together in a steellike clamp and wrapped her arms tightly about her heaving bosom. She trembled from head to feet, her face distorted in orgiastic agony.

A thin black woman grabbed her boy friend and bit his ear till blood came.

"Lawd, today!"

Jake pulled Blanche into a corner. His eyes burned red and he bit his lips.

"Say, how about it?" he asked tensely, huskily.

"About what?"

"What you going to charge?"

He held her arm in a nervous grip.

"Quit! You hurting my arm!"

"Aw, come on."

She disengaged herself and cooed:

"What you talking about, Honey?"

"I want you. Ain't that plain? Now, what you going to charge me?"

Blanche smiled and walked off as though she had not heard. He followed, like a little dog.

"Aw, come on!"

"Not much," she said, looking off.

"But *how* much?"

"I'll charge you what it's worth."

"What's it worth?"

"Well . . ."

"Well, *what*?"

She walked off again. Jake tagged her sleeve. She turned and looked at him intently.

"How much you got, Big Boy?"

"What's that got to do with it?"

She rounded her lips and spoke coolly:

"Ten dollars."

"Jeeesus," said Jake. "What you think I is?"

"Take it or leave it, Big Boy. If you don't want to do business, I'm moving on . . ."

"Wait a minute."

He frowned, dropped his cigarette, crushed it with his heel, and blew out a lungful of smoke. *Ten bucks is a lot of money. But, shucks . . .*

"Where can we go?"

"Upstairs."

"O.K.," he said. "What about my pals, two more?"

"Stay here. I'll see if I can't make it ten apiece."

Impatiently, he waited in a corner with his hands jammed into his pockets. He saw Blanche talking with Blue Juice at the far end of the room. Blue Juice was looking at him, and the shadow of a doubt flitted across his roused senses. He lit another cigarette, still watching Blanche. *What . . . What she talking to him . . .* He looked away. A relaxation was settling in his nerves. *I'm going to buy some more likker,* he thought as he clinked the coins in his pocket. Blanche came back smiling.

"It's O.K.," she said.

"Come on," said Jake. "Let's see Rose. I want some likker."

When in the back room he took the bottle from Rose and reached for his pocketbook. It was not in his hippocket. He felt the others, then sat the bottle down and went through each pocket, his lips hanging open.

"Where's my money?" he mumbled.

"Is you done lost something, Sugar?" Blanche asked.

"I can't find my money."

He searched his pockets again, took a step backward, and looked from Blanche to Rose.

"Somebody done got my money," he said incredulously.

"Maybe you dropped it somewhere," suggested Rose.

Jake headed for the rear room where they had eaten. Rose and Blanche followed, looking at each other. He jerked back the chairs, looked under the table. It was not there. He stood silently and stared at the floor.

"Is you done lost it, Honey?" asked Blanche, tearful with distress.

Jake looked at her and his mind cleared slowly. *I done been tricked!* But by whom? How? Then he remembered the tall, black Negro who had bumped into him. He remembered Blanche clinging to his neck, diverting his attention from the man.

"Did that black nigger what bumped into me take my money?"

"What you talking about, Sweetheart?"

"You know what I'm talking about!"

"I swear I don't!"

"That nigger what bumped into me when we was watching 'em dancing!"

"What nigger?" pleaded Blanche.

"That sonofabitch!"

Jake whirled and elbowed his way through the crowd. Rose and Blanche trailed. He stood in the center of the front room and stared at the dancers. The man was nowhere around. He turned to Blanche.

"Where's that nigger?" he growled.

"You mean the man I cussed at?"

"You know Gawddamn well what I mean!"

"Honey, that man been gone from here."

"Where he gone?"

"How I know?"

"What kind of a looking man was he?" asked Rose, tenderly placing her hand on his sleeve. Jake opened his mouth to answer, but no words came. He felt like a fool. He wanted to grab something and smash it. Grab just anything and smash it to death. He knew it was useless to try to get his money now, and knowing filled him with rage. *These lowlife bastards! I ain't going to let 'em play me cheap and get away with it! Ain't no man alive going to play me for a sucker!* The room grew misty and he looked at Blanche, at her yellow throat, at her red lips, at her wide, dark eyes.

"I don't want no trouble," he drawled.

"Oh, Lawd!" moaned Rose, wringing her hands. "Mister Jake, we ain't got your money."

Jake felt people crowding around him and he gave a hard shove with his elbow.

"Don't crowd me now," he said huskily. " 'Cause I might hurt somebody."

They backed away and left him standing in an empty circle. He could not take his eyes off Blanche's yellow face. His muscles were flexing slowly.

"I'm asking you for the last time to tell me who got my money," he said.

"That man's gone, Honey," whined Blanche.

He grabbed her arm.

"Where he go!"

"Turn me loose! You crazy!"

Jake raised his palm.

"You know who got my money!"

"Don't you hit me!" she screamed.

Jake grabbed for her and felt a hard hand on his shoulder. He was spun around.

"Don't you touch that woman!"

He looked into the black face of Blue Juice.

"Hunh?" Jake asked.

"I don't chew my tobacco but once," spat Blue Juice.

He saw Ben Kitty and One Barrel standing ready for him, their legs wide apart, their hands thrust deep into their pockets. His neck flushed hot as fire. He had been robbed and these men were here to see that he did not bother Blanche who had helped to rob him. He swallowed and something seemed to turn upsidedown in his stomach. *They got my money. These bastards!*

"Where's the nigger that bumped into me?"

"Go find 'im!" said Blue Juice.

"I'd like to make you tell where he is!" Jake said to Blanche.

"Do it," said Blue Juice. "Do it and get your gutstring cut loose."

Jake saw Bob, Al, and Slim edge into the crowd.

"What's the matter, Jake."

"Somebody bothering you?"

"Say, what's this?"

"These bastards done rolled me," said Jake, emboldened by the presence of his friends.

"You calling me a bastard?" asked Blue Juice, stepping close.

The crowd closed in and Jake felt himself being pushed against a wall. The music had stopped and he could hear his blood beating against his temples. His breath came fast and short.

"The nigger who took my dough's a bastard!" he said stubbornly.

"Did I take your dough?" asked Blue Juice.

Jake did not answer.

"Just say I did and I'll make you think you's a cat trying to cover up mess on a tin roof!"

"Who got your money, Jake?" asked Al.

"This woman here knows who got it," said Jake.

"She don't know," said Blue Juice.

"What you taking up for her for?" asked Jake.

" 'Cause I'm man enough to," said Blue Juice.

"It ain't no skin off your nose if I make that bitch tell!"

"Don't you call her a bitch!"

"I *did*!" said Jake with hot pride.

He saw the blow coming and tried to duck, but tried too late. It caught him low on the neck; a pain shot through his chest; the room tilted and he fell flat on his face. He heard screams, heard Al and Slim calling. He scrambled to his feet and reached for Blue Juice. Something hit him at the base of the skull and the world went red, then grey. He was on the floor, in a world of grey pain, hearing screams and pounding feet. His whole life flowed hotly into his eyes, his stomach, his hands. *I'll kill 'im! I'll kill 'im!* He rolled over and tried to get up; he was still on his knees when something cold touched his temple, like cold metal it was, and it touched lightly, like a feather. He felt himself pitching forward, felt his fingers clawing weakly at the ridges in the wooden floor, and then suddenly the world went black . . .

III.

JAKE JAKE JAKE His head sagged from side to side. *jake jake jake* He heard someone calling. *Hunh? Hunh?* He was trying to answer, trying to see where he was, wondering what made everything so awfully cold. A hard pain throbbed in his temples and at the base of his skull. A white and black world wavered before his eyes, then slowly righted itself, grew real, solid, freezing. His strength came gradually and his feet slipped on ice as he tried to stand.

"Jake! Jake!"

"Yeeeeah," he drawled.

"How you feel? You O.K.?"

"Yeah."

He raised his eyes and saw Slim bending over and coughing out great white plumes of vapor. Bob was lurching near a fence, moaning. He understood now. They were in an alley. The snow had stopped and the sky had cleared to a hazy blue. An icy wind ached his face and burned the tips of his ears. He wanted to sink into the ground and sleep forever.

"Come on," said Al. "Let's go somewhere and get warm."

They struggled to the street and stumbled into a beer tavern. Jake flopped limply into a chair, propped his elbows on a table, held his head in his hands, and closed his eyes. *Gawddamn everything!*

"If I had a gun I'd go back up there and blow that whore's brains out," he groaned.

"Aw, forget her. Them guys'd kill you," said Al.

"That's a nest of rattlesnakes," said Slim.

"Every nigger in that joint had a gun or a knife or a blackjack."

"I kept feeling that whore was tricking me," Jake mumbled.

Bob lay with his head cradled in his arms.

"Wake up, Bob!" said Al.

"What's the matter with 'im?" asked Jake.

"He's almost out. His dose and that whiskey just about fixed 'im."

Jake sorted out some coins.

"Here, get a halfpint" he said, giving the money to Al.

The three of them drank. They tried to awaken Bob, but he would not move.

"Somebody'll have to lug 'im home," sighed Jake.

"Slim and me'll take 'im," said Al. "We live his way."

"Lawd, but what happened? The last thing I remember I was trying to get a piece of that Blue Juice."

"They ganged you."

"Them guys is in a syndicate."

"We had to battle like wildcats to get you out of there alive."

"Old Ben Kitty was on you like white on rice."

"The whole mob of 'em was trying to do you in."

"It was old One Barrel what socked you behind the head, then I grabbed 'im."

"And old Blue Juice hit you in the temple with brass knuckles."

"Yeah," said Jake. "I thought the whole building had done fell on me. They hurt youall?"

"Naw, they backed up a little when they saw we'd fight."

"But boy, if it hadn't been for Rose pleading and screaming they was planning on using guns."

"And that Blanche dame did a quick fadeout."

"I saw her with a knife a foot long."

"That bitch!" said Jake.

"Where in Gawd's name you find that place?" asked Slim.

"Some bird down at the *Nook* told me to go there."

"He sure sent you into a mess of trouble."

"Some guy wanted to call the Law and Rose almost scratched his eyes out."

"I'm sure glad didn't no Law come."

"Yeah, they'd've been hard on us at the job about getting in jail."

"It would've been the end of me," sighed Jake.

Al clenched his fist and let it fall disgustedly upon the table.

"Just when we had them dames all lined up, this had to happen!"

"Jeeesus, look at me!" Jake demanded, almost indignantly. "Every red cent of that hundred dollars is gone. I'm right where I started!"

"Aw, hell! Ain't no use in thinking about it."

"Naw, you'll go nuts then."

They drank again.

"My head feels big's a barrel."

"What time you got?"

"Threethirty."

"Jeeesus!"

"Is it that late?"

"Yep."

"Let's get going."

"Yeah, we got to work tomorrow."

But they did not move. Above their heads an old clock ticked away the time. Jake blew his nose, pulled the stopper out of the bottle, drank and passed it around.

"Come on, let's get some sleep."

Al and Slim lifted Bob. Jake walked alone, rocking a little and pushing his flask into his hippocket. He caught his breath as he went through the door; the wind was keen and painful.

"It's cold!"

"It must be below zero!"

As they huddled in the doorway, Bob lurched toward the ground. Al caught him.

"Try to stand up, Bob! You ain't no baby!"

They lit cigarettes behind turnedup coatcollars.

"I sure would've been in a tough spot if it hadn't been for youall," sighed Jake.

"We got to watch out sharp next time."

"Yeah, we got to be careful."

Jake yawned.

"I'm sleepy."

"Me too."

"Let's get out of this cold."

They stepped gingerly to the sidewalk.

"Well," sighed Al. "I'll do you like the farmer did the potato."

"How's that?" Jake asked, twisting his lips into a wan smile.

"Plant you now and dig you later."

Slim laughed without opening his mouth.

"Aw, we had a good time, anyway."

"Oh, yeah."

"Sure."

Slim shifted restlessly from foot to foot and looked around.

"Say, how about another drink?" he asked abruptly.

"Sure," said Jake.

They drank again and licked their lips. Bob began to whimper.

"It's coming down on 'im again," said Al.

Bob broke from Al and crawled on his hands and knees in the snow. When Al tried to lift him, he fought him off and beat his fists against the air.

"He's wet," said Al.

"Pick 'im up," said Jake. "Don't let 'im wallow in that snow."

Bob bent his head to his knees and screamed; his scream was as sharp as the cold wind. When his breath was gone he lifted his face with teeth clenched and bared.

"Come on, Bob," said Slim, tugging at his shoulder.

"Nigger, you'll freeze to death like that," admonished Al.

"Here," said Jake. "Make 'im drink."

"Hold 'im up! He can't stand!"

"Here, Bob, drink! It'll make you feel better!"

"Hell, he won't drink."

"But, shucks, we got to make 'im drink. How you going to lug 'im home with him moaning and screaming like that?"

Al and Slim lifted Bob and Jake forced whiskey down his throat.

"Drink, man! You'll catch pneumonia fooling around like this."

The whiskey drooled down Bob's lips and chin.

"Take 'im home," said Jake.

Al and Slim moved forward heavily, supporting Bob between them.

"Well, so long."

"So long."

Jake heard Slim's whacking cough, heard Al's heavy voice pleading with Bob, heard their footsteps crunching in the snow, dying away. He watched them bend against the icy wind as they turned a corner.

He was alone in the deserted street with a deep sense of desolation. He could hardly hold his eyes open. His head throbbed and a loud ringing filled his ears. He pulled his hat low over his face, felt the flask in his hippocket, patted it, and sneezed. *Hell*, he sighed and wiped his nose with the back of his hand. Whiskey burned like a ball of fire in his solar plexus and braced him against the wind. Each step he took called for concentration and effort. He coughed and a string of phlegm swung from his lips. He bent over and shook; it still swung. He caught the string between his fingers and flung it to the snow. He stumbled blindly as the full force of the alcohol swept over him. Holding to a lamppost, he took out his money and counted it, piece by piece. He had exactly eighty-five cents. *One hundred dollars gone in one night! And I got to pay Doc. Gawddamn that whore!* He straightened, smiled, and yelled to the top of his voice:

"BUT WHEN I WAS FLYING I WAS A FLYING FOOL!"

He tried to put his money back into his pocket and dropped the nickels and dimes into the soft snow. He scratched with his fingers, but could not find a penny. He spat and lurched on. *Shucks, there's more money where that come from.* His mind cleared a bit and he found himself standing on a dark corner. A streetcar clanked by. He looked up, startled. Then he simpered and waved his hand at the car's disappearing taillight. A cold, swift wind lifted his hat and carried it into darkness. He clutched wildly. Stumbled.

"That sonofaBITCH!"

He was a block from home now. Just as he was about to step into the street a black limousine shot past and set his coat and tie awry. He wagged his head. *Got to be careful. Can't get run over. Naw, naw, not by a long shot.* He took another drink and things began to whirl. Streetlamps swelled to the size of full moons, rising and falling when he lowered and lifted his eyes. The snowcovered pavement developed tall hillocks and deep valleys. Hard lines curved sinuously and curves assumed the rigidity of angles. Another streetcar flew by, its screech gritting painfully into his raw nerves. He stopped and shouted:

"WHEN YOU GET TO WHERE YOU GOING TELL 'EM ABOUT ME!"

After what seemed hours of confusion he found himself

hugging tightly at a steel telephone pole, opposite his home. A dim light burned in his window. *Yeah, she's up there! I'm going up and pay her off tonight! By Gawd, I'll teach her who's boss, who wears the pants . . .* When in the vestibule it took him five minutes to find his keys and open the door. He paused several times on the stairs and shook his head to clear away the mists. He listened in front of his flat, but could not hear a sound. The key finally found the hole and he pushed the door in softly. He stood a moment, as though frozen, looking, not breathing. On the edge of a circle of light cast by the floorlamp Lil knelt at the side of the bed, her face lying on the quilt, turned toward him. She was asleep. *Ain't this a bitch! Gone to sleep on her knees, praying . . . So help me Gawd, I'm going to give her something to pray for!* He slipped off his coat and hat and dropped them to the floor. The room was like a dim, warm dream, and his head seemed far away from his body, whirling. He stuck a cigarette in the corner of his mouth and lit it, then brought out the halffilled flask, still watching Lil sleeping on her knees. He drained the bottle and waited. His flesh began to tingle; a hot flame spread out from his stomach and engulfed him. The room swayed. His lips flexed and he hurled the empty bottle with a swift motion square into the dresser mirror. There was a crash and splintering glass showered the floor. Lil awoke with a violent start and straightened in fright. She screamed and backed into a corner while still on her knees. Jake lurched toward her.

"That wake you up?"

"Jake!"

"Yeeeeah, this is Jake. Ain't you glad to see me?"

"You drunk," she breathed.

"How you think I'd be?"

"Please, Jake! You drunk, go to bed!"

"Like hell I will! I'm going to learn you something to-night!"

She was sitting on her knees with her legs doubled under her. He looked at the brown sweep of her calves, brown that dissolved and merged with the warm air of the room.

"Get up!"

"Hush," she whispered. "Folks can hear you."

"GAWDDAMMIT, I WANT 'EM TO HEAR!"

She started to cry.

"You thought you was going to make me lose my job, didn't you? Well, you didn't! I still got it and I'm going to keep it even if I have to split your head wide open!" He was standing over her, his face wet with sweat, his eyes red. "Next time you snitch on me I'm going to send you to the crazy-house, you hear? The white folks said you was crazy, and you is! You hear me, YOU CRAZY!"

"You'll wake everybody up, Jake. You drunk . . ."

"GAWDDAMN RIGHT I'M DRUNK! I want the world to know I'm drunk! I don't care what they think! They don't feed me! And I want 'em to know you's a lousy, crazy bitch!"

"Gawd have mercy on you, Jake."

"I don't want nobody to have no mercy on me!"

"You don't never stay home and when you do come in you come in drunk."

"What I want to stay home for? To look at *you*? Like hell!"

"While you out having a good time with your money, I'm here sick and hungry."

"That's your hard luck!"

"You got your friends to drink and talk with and I ain't got nothing."

"You don't need nothing."

"Jake, don't you never think of nobody but yourself?"

"Gawd made me like I is, and I'm going to stay that way!"

"You making my life full of misery."

"Look at me! I'm laughing, ain't I?"

"You kill everything you touch."

"If you don't shut your big mouth I *will* kill you!"

He caught the wall to steady himself. His cigarette fell from his lips and hot sparks showered his hands. A hammer of pain beat at the base of his skull. Fumes of darkness circled around him; he was straining with all his might to keep from falling. He kept telling himself, *I got to show her. I got to show this bitch something!* He grabbed the window shade and gave it a twist that sent it to the top of the ceiling, flapping. *I'll show her!* He turned to the dresser and reached three times for a toy glass elephant; finally he caught it in his fist. The room whirled and Lil's brown legs whirled with it, crowding his eyes. He threw

the elephant into the windowpane; glass splintered and icy
wind rushed in.

"Jake! Jake!"

He threw a bowl. A brush. A glass puppy. He reached for
something else; the room tilted and he pulled off the dresser
scarf, emptying the things on the floor with a loud clatter.
There was a heavy deafness in his ears and he had to shout in
order to hear himself.

"LET 'EM HEAR! LET 'EM HEAR!"

He tried to get to her and stumbled over a chair. She rose,
crouching, her mouth open, her eyes wide. With numbed fingers he clutched a handful of her gown on each shoulder and
jerked.

"Don't beat me! Don't beat me, Jake!"

He grabbed for her throat and she gave a lunge; he went
backwards and pulled her with him. She got up and started
for the door. While still on his knees he caught the hem of
her gown and held her. He stumbled to his feet and rammed
her against a wall.

"You hit me, didn't you?"

"Naw, Jake!"

He ripped her gown half open. She sucked her breath in
sharply, lunged again and threw him against the bed. When
she struggled for the door this time he caught her wrist and
swung her around.

"I'm going to see how sick you is!"

She tried to wrench herself free.

"Where you think you going?"

"Naw, naw," she spoke in a breath softer than a whisper
with her eyes fixed in horror upon his face. He attempted to
drag her to the middle of the floor and she sank to her knees.
He tried to lift her and she bit his hand. Blood leaped to his
head and he knocked her into the floorlamp, sending it
sprawling. The room darkened save for the cold light of the
sky.

"You bitch!" he breathed in a voice half curse and half sob.

He bent and slapped her across her eyes and she screamed.
He bent to slap her again but she eluded him and crawled
over the bed. Her cheeks were bleeding. He looked at her, his
breath coming slowly and heavily through his open mouth,

drying his lips. The room was freezing cold; in the semidark-
ness he saw her breath turning white as it struck the icy wind.
I'm going to fix you! When he went toward her she stooped
quickly and came up with a jagged edge of windowpane
clutched in her fist. Her voice was high, hysterical, in one
breath, on a dead level.

"Naw . . . Naw . . ."

His jaw sagged. He swallowed, wanting another drink.

"Put that glass down!"

He lunged for her arm and missed.

"JAKE!"

When he grabbed for her again she brought the piece of
glass down across his head. A hot anger made him hold his
breath.

"I'm going to kill you!"

She backed to the wall, holding the piece of glass above her
head. He leapt, trying to grasp her wrists; she struck him
again. He staggered, growled, and tried to catch her hand.
When she hit him this time he flopped weakly on the bed; he
felt something warm oozing down his left cheek. A black
whirlpool was sucking him under. He looked dully at the
busted window, at the shards of glass glinting fitfully on the
floor. He dabbed at his scalp with the edge of a sheet and
fumbled at his shirt with sticky fingers, leaving red prints. He
rubbed his eyes and face clumsily with cold fists and a convul-
sion of nervous misery made him sigh out a plaintive whimper. His face twitched. He belched. He shuddered from the
chill that was seeping into the marrow of his bones as darkness roared in his brain.

Lil dropped the piece of glass; its edges were stained from
cuts in her hand. She stood over Jake a moment and watched
his drunken sleep. Then she pulled down the shade, wrapped
herself in a coat and sank to the floor. She pressed a wad of
her gown hard into the cuts in her palm to stem the flow of
blood and rested her head on her knees.

"Lawd, I wish I was dead," she sobbed softly.

Outside an icy wind swept around the corner of the building, whining and moaning like an idiot in a deep black pit.

UNCLE TOM'S CHILDREN

Contents

The post Civil War household word among Negroes — "He's an Uncle Tom!" —which denoted reluctant toleration for the cringing type who knew his place before white folk, has been supplanted by a new word from another generation which says: —"Uncle Tom is dead!"

The Ethics of Living Jim Crow

AN AUTOBIOGRAPHICAL SKETCH

I

M Y FIRST LESSON in how to live as a Negro came when I was quite small. We were living in Arkansas. Our house stood behind the railroad tracks. Its skimpy yard was paved with black cinders. Nothing green ever grew in that yard. The only touch of green we could see was far away, beyond the tracks, over where the white folks lived. But cinders were good enough for me and I never missed the green growing things. And anyhow, cinders were fine weapons. You could always have a nice hot war with huge black cinders. All you had to do was crouch behind the brick pillars of a house with your hands full of gritty ammunition. And the first woolly black head you saw pop out from behind another row of pillars was your target. You tried your very best to knock it off. It was great fun.

I never fully realized the appalling disadvantages of a cinder environment till one day the gang to which I belonged found itself engaged in a war with the white boys who lived beyond the tracks. As usual we laid down our cinder barrage, thinking that this would wipe the white boys out. But they replied with a steady bombardment of broken bottles. We doubled our cinder barrage, but they hid behind trees, hedges, and the sloping embankments of their lawns. Having no such fortifications, we retreated to the brick pillars of our homes. During the retreat a broken milk bottle caught me behind the ear, opening a deep gash which bled profusely. The sight of blood pouring over my face completely demoralized our ranks. My fellow-combatants left me standing paralyzed in the center of the yard, and scurried for their homes. A kind neighbor saw me and rushed me to a doctor, who took three stitches in my neck.

I sat brooding on my front steps, nursing my wound and waiting for my mother to come from work. I felt that a grave injustice had been done me. It was all right to throw cinders.

The greatest harm a cinder could do was leave a bruise. But broken bottles were dangerous; they left you cut, bleeding, and helpless.

When night fell, my mother came from the white folks' kitchen. I raced down the street to meet her. I could just feel in my bones that she would understand. I knew she would tell me exactly what to do next time. I grabbed her hand and babbled out the whole story. She examined my wound, then slapped me.

"How come yuh didn't hide?" she asked me. "How come yuh awways fightin'?"

I was outraged, and bawled. Between sobs I told her that I didn't have any trees or hedges to hide behind. There wasn't a thing I could have used as a trench. And you couldn't throw very far when you were hiding behind the brick pillars of a house. She grabbed a barrel stave, dragged me home, stripped me naked, and beat me till I had a fever of one hundred and two. She would smack my rump with the stave, and, while the skin was still smarting, impart to me gems of Jim Crow wisdom. I was never to throw cinders any more. I was never to fight any more wars. I was never, never, under any conditions, to fight *white* folks again. And they were absolutely right in clouting me with the broken milk bottle. Didn't I know she was working hard every day in the hot kitchens of the white folks to make money to take care of me? When was I ever going to learn to be a good boy? She couldn't be bothered with my fights. She finished by telling me that I ought to be thankful to God as long as I lived that they didn't kill me.

All that night I was delirious and could not sleep. Each time I closed my eyes I saw monstrous white faces suspended from the ceiling, leering at me.

From that time on, the charm of my cinder yard was gone. The green trees, the trimmed hedges, the cropped lawns grew very meaningful, became a symbol. Even today when I think of white folks, the hard, sharp outlines of white houses surrounded by trees, lawns, and hedges are present somewhere in the background of my mind. Through the years they grew into an overreaching symbol of fear.

It was a long time before I came in close contact with white folks again. We moved from Arkansas to Mississippi. Here we had the good fortune not to live behind the railroad tracks, or close to white neighborhoods. We lived in the very heart of the local Black Belt. There were black churches and black preachers; there were black schools and black teachers; black groceries and black clerks. In fact, everything was so solidly black that for a long time I did not even think of white folks, save in remote and vague terms. But this could not last forever. As one grows older one eats more. One's clothing costs more. When I finished grammar school I had to go to work. My mother could no longer feed and clothe me on her cooking job.

There is but one place where a black boy who knows no trade can get a job, and that's where the houses and faces are white, where the trees, lawns, and hedges are green. My first job was with an optical company in Jackson, Mississippi. The morning I applied I stood straight and neat before the boss, answering all his questions with sharp yessirs and nosirs. I was very careful to pronounce my *sirs* distinctly, in order that he might know that I was polite, that I knew where I was, and that I knew he was a *white* man. I wanted that job badly.

He looked me over as though he were examining a prize poodle. He questioned me closely about my schooling, being particularly insistent about how much mathematics I had had. He seemed very pleased when I told him I had had two years of algebra.

"Boy, how would you like to try to learn something around here?" he asked me.

"I'd like it fine, sir," I said, happy. I had visions of "working my way up." Even Negroes have those visions.

"All right," he said. "Come on."

I followed him to the small factory.

"Pease," he said to a white man of about thirty-five, "this is Richard. He's going to work for us."

Pease looked at me and nodded.

I was then taken to a white boy of about seventeen.

"Morrie, this is Richard, who's going to work for us."

"Whut yuh sayin' there, boy!" Morrie boomed at me.

"Fine!" I answered.

The boss instructed these two to help me, teach me, give me jobs to do, and let me learn what I could in my spare time.

My wages were five dollars a week.

I worked hard, trying to please. For the first month I got along O.K. Both Pease and Morrie seemed to like me. But one thing was missing. And I kept thinking about it. I was not learning anything and nobody was volunteering to help me. Thinking they had forgotten that I was to learn something about the mechanics of grinding lenses, I asked Morrie one day to tell me about the work. He grew red.

"Whut yuh tryin' t' do, nigger, git smart?" he asked.

"Naw; I ain' tryin' t' git smart," I said.

"Well, don't, if yuh know whut's good for yuh!"

I was puzzled. Maybe he just doesn't want to help me, I thought. I went to Pease.

"Say, are you crazy, you black bastard?" Pease asked me, his gray eyes growing hard.

I spoke out, reminding him that the boss had said I was to be given a chance to learn something.

"Nigger, you think you're *white*, don't you?"

"Naw, sir!"

"Well, you're acting mighty like it!"

"But, Mr. Pease, the boss said . . ."

Pease shook his fist in my face.

"This is a *white* man's work around here, and you better watch yourself!"

From then on they changed toward me. They said good-morning no more. When I was just a bit slow in performing some duty, I was called a lazy black son-of-a-bitch.

Once I thought of reporting all this to the boss. But the mere idea of what would happen to me if Pease and Morrie should learn that I had "snitched" stopped me. And after all, the boss was a white man, too. What was the use?

The climax came at noon one summer day. Pease called me to his work-bench. To get to him I had to go between two narrow benches and stand with my back against a wall.

"Yes, sir," I said.

"Richard, I want to ask you something," Pease began pleasantly, not looking up from his work.

"Yes, sir," I said again.

Morrie came over, blocking the narrow passage between the benches. He folded his arms, staring at me solemnly.

I looked from one to the other, sensing that something was coming.

"Yes, sir," I said for the third time.

Pease looked up and spoke very slowly.

"Richard, *Mr.* Morrie here tells me you called me *Pease.*"

I stiffened. A void seemed to open up in me. I knew this was the show-down.

He meant that I had failed to call him *Mr.* Pease. I looked at Morrie. He was gripping a steel bar in his hands. I opened my mouth to speak, to protest, to assure Pease that I had never called him simply *Pease*, and that I had never had any intentions of doing so, when Morrie grabbed me by the collar, ramming my head against the wall.

"Now, be careful, nigger!" snarled Morrie, baring his teeth. "*I* heard yuh call 'im *Pease!* 'N' if yuh say yuh didn't, yuh're callin' me a *lie*, see?" He waved the steel bar threateningly.

If I had said: No, sir, Mr. Pease, I never called you *Pease*, I would have been automatically calling Morrie a liar. And if I had said: Yes, sir, Mr. Pease, I called you *Pease*, I would have been pleading guilty to having uttered the worst insult that a Negro can utter to a southern white man. I stood hesitating, trying to frame a neutral reply.

"Richard, I asked you a question!" said Pease. Anger was creeping into his voice.

"I don't remember calling you *Pease*, Mr. Pease," I said cautiously. "And if I did, I sure didn't mean . . ."

"You black son-of-a-bitch! You called me *Pease*, then!" he spat, slapping me till I bent sideways over a bench. Morrie was on top of me, demanding:

"Didn't yuh call 'im *Pease?* If yuh say yuh didn't, I'll rip yo' gut string loose with this bar, yuh black granny dodger! Yuh can't call a white man a lie 'n' git erway with it, you black son-of-a-bitch!"

I wilted. I begged them not to bother me. I knew what they wanted. They wanted me to leave.

"I'll leave," I promised. "I'll leave right *now.*"

They gave me a minute to get out of the factory. I was warned not to show up again, or tell the boss.

I went.

When I told the folks at home what had happened, they

called me a fool. They told me that I must never again attempt to exceed my boundaries. When you are working for white folks, they said, you got to "stay in your place" if you want to keep working.

II

My Jim Crow education continued on my next job, which was portering in a clothing store. One morning, while polishing brass out front, the boss and his twenty-year-old son got out of their car and half dragged and half kicked a Negro woman into the store. A policeman standing at the corner looked on, twirling his nightstick. I watched out of the corner of my eye, never slackening the strokes of my chamois upon the brass. After a few minutes, I heard shrill screams coming from the rear of the store. Later the woman stumbled out, bleeding, crying, and holding her stomach. When she reached the end of the block, the policeman grabbed her and accused her of being drunk. Silently, I watched him throw her into a patrol wagon.

When I went to the rear of the store, the boss and his son were washing their hands at the sink. They were chuckling. The floor was bloody and strewn with wisps of hair and clothing. No doubt I must have appeared pretty shocked, for the boss slapped me reassuringly on the back.

"Boy, that's what we do to niggers when they don't want to pay their bills," he said, laughing.

His son looked at me and grinned.

"Here, hava cigarette," he said.

Not knowing what to do, I took it. He lit his and held the match for me. This was a gesture of kindness, indicating that even if they had beaten the poor old woman, they would not beat me if I knew enough to keep my mouth shut.

"Yes, sir," I said, and asked no questions.

After they had gone, I sat on the edge of a packing box and stared at the bloody floor till the cigarette went out.

That day at noon, while eating in a hamburger joint, I told my fellow Negro porters what had happened. No one seemed surprised. One fellow, after swallowing a huge bite, turned to me and asked:

"Huh! Is tha' all they did t' her?"

"Yeah. Wasn't tha' enough?" I asked.

"Shucks! Man, she's a lucky bitch!" he said, burying his lips deep into a juicy hamburger. "Hell, it's a wonder they didn't lay her when they got through."

III

I was learning fast, but not quite fast enough. One day, while I was delivering packages in the suburbs, my bicycle tire was punctured. I walked along the hot, dusty road, sweating and leading my bicycle by the handle-bars.

A car slowed at my side.

"What's the matter, boy?" a white man called.

I told him my bicycle was broken and I was walking back to town.

"That's too bad," he said. "Hop on the running board."

He stopped the car. I clutched hard at my bicycle with one hand and clung to the side of the car with the other.

"All set?"

"Yes, sir," I answered. The car started.

It was full of young white men. They were drinking. I watched the flask pass from mouth to mouth.

"Wanna drink, boy?" one asked.

I laughed as the wind whipped my face. Instinctively obeying the freshly planted precepts of my mother, I said:

"Oh, no!"

The words were hardly out of my mouth before I felt something hard and cold smash me between the eyes. It was an empty whisky bottle. I saw stars, and fell backwards from the speeding car into the dust of the road, my feet becoming entangled in the steel spokes of my bicycle. The white men piled out and stood over me.

"Nigger, ain' yuh learned no better sense'n tha' yet?" asked the man who hit me. "Ain' yuh learned t' say *sir* t' a white man yet?"

Dazed, I pulled to my feet. My elbows and legs were bleeding. Fists doubled, the white man advanced, kicking my bicycle out of the way.

"Aw, leave the bastard alone. He's got enough," said one.

They stood looking at me. I rubbed my shins, trying to stop the flow of blood. No doubt they felt a sort of contemptuous pity, for one asked:

"Yuh wanna ride t' town now, nigger? Yuh reckon yuh know enough t' ride now?"

"I wanna walk," I said, simply.

Maybe it sounded funny. They laughed.

"Well, walk, yuh black son-of-a-bitch!"

When they left they comforted me with:

"Nigger, yuh sho better be damn glad it wuz us yuh talked t' tha' way. Yuh're a lucky bastard, 'cause if yuh'd said tha' t' somebody else, yuh might've been a dead nigger now."

IV

Negroes who have lived South know the dread of being caught alone upon the streets in white neighborhoods after the sun has set. In such a simple situation as this the plight of the Negro in America is graphically symbolized. While white strangers may be in these neighborhoods trying to get home, they can pass unmolested. But the color of a Negro's skin makes him easily recognizable, makes him suspect, converts him into a defenseless target.

Late one Saturday night I made some deliveries in a white neighborhood. I was pedaling my bicycle back to the store as fast as I could, when a police car, swerving toward me, jammed me into the curbing.

"Get down and put up your hands!" the policemen ordered.

I did. They climbed out of the car, guns drawn, faces set, and advanced slowly.

"Keep still!" they ordered.

I reached my hands higher. They searched my pockets and packages. They seemed dissatisfied when they could find nothing incriminating. Finally, one of them said:

"Boy, tell your boss not to send you out in white neighborhoods after sundown."

As usual, I said:

"Yes, sir."

V

My next job was as hall-boy in a hotel. Here my Jim Crow education broadened and deepened. When the bell-boys were busy, I was often called to assist them. As many of the rooms in the hotel were occupied by prostitutes, I was constantly called to carry them liquor and cigarettes. These women were nude most of the time. They did not bother about clothing, even for bell-boys. When you went into their rooms, you were supposed to take their nakedness for granted, as though it startled you no more than a blue vase or a red rug. Your presence awoke in them no sense of shame, for you were not regarded as human. If they were alone, you could steal side-long glimpses at them. But if they were receiving men, not a flicker of your eyelids could show. I remember one incident vividly. A new woman, a huge, snowy-skinned blonde, took a room on my floor. I was sent to wait upon her. She was in bed with a thick-set man; both were nude and uncovered. She said she wanted some liquor and slid out of bed and waddled across the floor to get her money from a dresser drawer. I watched her.

"Nigger, what in hell you looking at?" the white man asked me, raising himself upon his elbows.

"Nothing," I answered, looking miles deep into the blank wall of the room.

"Keep your eyes where they belong, if you want to be healthy!" he said.

"Yes, sir."

VI

One of the bell-boys I knew in this hotel was keeping steady company with one of the Negro maids. Out of a clear sky the police descended upon his home and arrested him, accusing him of bastardy. The poor boy swore he had had no intimate relations with the girl. Nevertheless, they forced him to marry her. When the child arrived, it was found to be much lighter in complexion than either of the two supposedly legal parents. The white men around the hotel made a great joke of it. They spread the rumor that some white cow must have scared the poor girl while she was carrying the baby. If you were in their presence when this explanation was offered, you were supposed to laugh.

VII

One of the bell-boys was caught in bed with a white prostitute. He was castrated and run out of town. Immediately after this all the bell-boys and hall-boys were called together and warned. We were given to understand that the boy who had been castrated was a "mighty, mighty lucky bastard." We were impressed with the fact that next time the management of the hotel would not be responsible for the lives of "trouble-makin' niggers." We were silent.

VIII

One night, just as I was about to go home, I met one of the Negro maids. She lived in my direction, and we fell in to walk part of the way home together. As we passed the white night-watchman, he slapped the maid on her buttock. I turned around, amazed. The watchman looked at me with a long, hard, fixed-under stare. Suddenly he pulled his gun and asked:

"Nigger, don't yuh like it?"

I hesitated.

"I asked yuh don't yuh like it?" he asked again, stepping forward.

"Yes, sir," I mumbled.

"Talk like it, then!"

"Oh, yes, sir!" I said with as much heartiness as I could muster.

Outside, I walked ahead of the girl, ashamed to face her. She caught up with me and said:

"Don't be a fool! Yuh couldn't help it!"

This watchman boasted of having killed two Negroes in self-defense.

Yet, in spite of all this, the life of the hotel ran with an amazing smoothness. It would have been impossible for a stranger to detect anything. The maids, the hall-boys, and the bell-boys were all smiles. They had to be.

IX

I had learned my Jim Crow lessons so thoroughly that I kept the hotel job till I left Jackson for Memphis. It so happened that while in Memphis I applied for a job at a branch of the optical company. I was hired. And for some reason, as long as I worked there, they never brought my past against me.

Here my Jim Crow education assumed quite a different form. It was no longer brutally cruel, but subtly cruel. Here I learned to lie, to steal, to dissemble. I learned to play that dual role which every Negro must play if he wants to eat and live.

For example, it was almost impossible to get a book to read. It was assumed that after a Negro had imbibed what scanty schooling the state furnished he had no further need for books. I was always borrowing books from men on the job. One day I mustered enough courage to ask one of the men to let me get books from the library in his name. Surprisingly, he consented. I cannot help but think that he consented because he was a Roman Catholic and felt a vague sympathy for Negroes, being himself an object of hatred. Armed with a library card, I obtained books in the following manner: I would write a note to the librarian, saying: "Please let this nigger boy have the following books." I would then sign it with the white man's name.

When I went to the library, I would stand at the desk, hat in hand, looking as unbookish as possible. When I received the books desired I would take them home. If the books listed in the note happened to be out, I would sneak into the lobby and forge a new one. I never took any chances guessing with the white librarian about what the fictitious white man would want to read. No doubt if any of the white patrons had suspected that some of the volumes they enjoyed had been in the home of a Negro, they would not have tolerated it for an instant.

The factory force of the optical company in Memphis was much larger than that in Jackson, and more urbanized. At least they liked to talk, and would engage the Negro help in conversation whenever possible. By this means I found that many subjects were taboo from the white man's point of view. Among the topics they did not like to discuss with Negroes were the following: American white women; the Ku Klux Klan; France, and how Negro soldiers fared while there; French women; Jack Johnson; the entire northern part of the United States; the Civil War; Abraham Lincoln; U. S. Grant; General Sherman; Catholics; the Pope; Jews; the Republican Party; slavery; social equality; Communism; Socialism; the 13th and 14th Amendments to the Constitution; or any topic calling for positive knowledge or manly self-assertion on the part of the Negro. The most accepted topics were sex and religion.

There were many times when I had to exercise a great deal of ingenuity to keep out of trouble. It is a southern custom that all men must take off their hats when they enter an elevator. And especially did this apply to us blacks with rigid force. One day I stepped into an elevator with my arms full of packages. I was forced to ride with my hat on. Two white men stared at me coldly. Then one of them very kindly lifted my hat and placed it upon my armful of packages. Now the most accepted response for a Negro to make under such circumstances is to look at the white man out of the corner of his eye and grin. To have said: "Thank you!" would have made the white man *think* that you *thought* you were receiving from him a personal service. For such an act I have seen Negroes take a blow in the mouth. Finding the first alternative distasteful, and the second dangerous, I hit upon an acceptable course of action which fell safely between these two poles. I immediately—no sooner than my hat was lifted—pretended that my packages were about to spill, and appeared deeply distressed with keeping them in my arms. In this fashion I evaded having to acknowledge his service, and, in spite of adverse circumstances, salvaged a slender shred of personal pride.

How do Negroes feel about the way they have to live?

How do they discuss it when alone among themselves? I think this question can be answered in a single sentence. A friend of mine who ran an elevator once told me:

"Lawd, man! Ef it wuzn't fer them polices 'n' them ol' lynch-mobs, there wouldn't be nothin' but uproar down here!"

Is it true what they say about Dixie?
Does the sun really shine all the time?
Do sweet magnolias blossom at everybody's door?
Do folks keep eating 'possum, till they can't eat no more?
Is it true what they say about Swanee?
Is a dream by that stream so sublime?
Do they laugh, do they love, like they say in ev'ry song? . . .
If it's true, that's where I belong.

—Popular Song.

I

Big Boy Leaves Home

I

---

*Y*O MAMA *don wear no drawers* . . .
Clearly, the voice rose out of the woods, and died away. Like an echo another voice caught it up:
Ah seena when she pulled em off . . .
Another, shrill, cracking, adolescent:
N she washed 'em in alcohol . . .
Then a quartet of voices, blending in harmony, floated high above the tree tops:
N she hung 'em out in the hall . . .
Laughing easily, four black boys came out of the woods into cleared pasture. They walked lollingly in bare feet, beating tangled vines and bushes with long sticks.
"Ah wished Ah knowed some mo lines t tha song."
"Me too."
"Yeah, when yuh gits t where she hangs em out in the hall yuh has t stop."
"Shucks, whut goes wid *hall*?"
"*Call.*"
"*Fall.*"
"*Wall.*"
"*Quall.*"
They threw themselves on the grass, laughing.
"Big Boy?"
"Huh?"
"Yuh know one thing?"
"Whut?"
"Yuh sho is crazy!"
"Crazy?"
"Yeah, yuh crazys a bed-bug!"
"Crazy bout whut?"
"Man, whoever hearda *quall*?"
"Yuh said yuh wanted something t go wid *hall*, didnt yuh?"

"Yeah, but whuts a *quall*?"

"Nigger, a *qualls* a *quall*."

They laughed easily, catching and pulling long green blades of grass with their toes.

"Waal, ef a *qualls* a *quall*, whut IS a *quall*?"

"Oh, Ah know."

"Whut?"

"Tha ol song goes something like this:

> *Yo mama don wear no drawers,*
> *Ah seena when she pulled em off,*
> *N she washed em in alcohol,*
> *N she hung em out in the hall,*
> *N then she put em back on her QUALL!*"

They laughed again. Their shoulders were flat to the earth, their knees propped up, and their faces square to the sun.

"Big Boy, yuhs CRAZY!"

"Don ax me nothin else."

"Nigger, yuhs CRAZY!"

They fell silent, smiling, drooping the lids of their eyes softly against the sunlight.

"Man, don the groun feel warm?"

"Jus lika bed."

"Jeeesus, Ah could stay here ferever."

"Me too."

"Ah kin feel tha ol sun goin all thu me."

"Feels like mah bones is warm."

In the distance a train whistled mournfully.

"There goes number fo!"

"Hittin on all six!"

"Highballin it down the line!"

"Boun fer up Noth, Lawd, boun fer up Noth!"

They began to chant, pounding bare heels in the grass.

> *Dis train boun fo Glory*
> *Dis train, Oh Hallelujah*
> *Dis train boun fo Glory*
> *Dis train, Oh Hallelujah*
> *Dis train boun fo Glory*
> *Ef yuh ride no need fer fret er worry*

Dis train, Oh Hallelujah
Dis train . . .

Dis train don carry no gambler
Dis train, Oh Hallelujah
Dis train don carry no gambler
Dis train, Oh Hallelujah
Dis train don carry no gambler
No fo day creeper er midnight rambler
Dis train, Oh Hallelujah
Dis train . . .

When the song ended they burst out laughing, thinking of a train bound for Glory.

"Gee, thas a good ol song!"

"Huuuuummmmmmmmmmman . . ."

"Whut?"

"Geeee whiiiiiiz . . ."

"Whut?"

"Somebody don let win! Das whut!"

Buck, Bobo and Lester jumped up. Big Boy stayed on the ground, feigning sleep.

"Jeeesus, tha sho stinks!"

"Big Boy!"

Big Boy feigned to snore.

"Big Boy!"

Big Boy stirred as though in sleep.

"Big Boy!"

"Hunh?"

"Yuh rotten inside!"

"Rotten?"

"Lawd, cant yuh smell it?"

"Smell whut?"

"Nigger, yuh mus gotta bad col!"

"Smell whut?"

"NIGGER, YUH BROKE WIN!"

Big Boy laughed and fell back on the grass, closing his eyes.

"The hen whut cackles is the hen whut laid the egg."

"We ain no hens."

"Yuh cackled, didnt yuh?"

The three moved off with noses turned up.

"C mon!"

"Where yuh-all goin?"

"T the creek fer a swim."

"Yeah, les swim."

"Naw buddy naw!" said Big Boy, slapping the air with a scornful palm.

"Aw, c mon! Don be a heel!"

"N git *lynched*? Hell naw!"

"He ain gonna see us."

"How yuh know?"

"Cause he ain."

"Yuh-all go on. Ahma stay right here," said Big Boy.

"Hell, let im stay! C mon, les go," said Buck.

The three walked off, swishing at grass and bushes with sticks. Big Boy looked lazily at their backs.

"Hey!"

Walking on, they glanced over their shoulders.

"Hey, niggers!"

"C mon!"

Big Boy grunted, picked up his stick, pulled to his feet, and stumbled off.

"Wait!"

"C mon!"

He ran, caught up with them, leaped upon their backs, bearing them to the ground.

"Quit, Big Boy!"

"Gawddam, nigger!"

"Git t hell offa me!"

Big Boy sprawled in the grass beside them, laughing and pounding his heels in the ground.

"Nigger, whut yuh think we is, hosses?"

"How come yuh awways hoppin on us?"

"Lissen, wes gonna double-team on yuh one of these days n beat yo ol ass good."

Big Boy smiled.

"Sho nough?"

"Yeah, don yuh like it?"

"We gonna beat yuh sos yuh cant walk!"

"N dare yuh t do nothin erbout it!"

Big Boy bared his teeth.

"C mon! Try it now!"

The three circled around him.

"Say, Buck, yuh grab his feets!"

"N yuh git his head, Lester!"

"N Bobo, yuh git berhin n grab his arms!"

Keeping more than arm's length, they circled round and round Big Boy.

"C mon!" said Big Boy, feinting at one and then the other.

Round and round they circled, but could not seem to get any closer. Big Boy stopped and braced his hands on his hips.

"Is all three of yuh-all scareda me?"

"Les git im some other time," said Bobo, grinning.

"Yeah, we kin ketch yuh when yuh ain thinkin," said Lester.

"We kin trick yuh," said Buck.

They laughed and walked together.

Big Boy belched.

"Ahm hongry," he said.

"Me too."

"Ah wished Ah hada big hot pota belly-busters!"

"Cooked wid some good ol salty ribs . . ."

"N some good ol egg cornbread . . ."

"N some buttermilk . . ."

"N some hot peach cobbler swimmin in juice . . ."

"Nigger, hush!"

They began to chant, emphasizing the rhythm by cutting at grass with sticks.

> *Bye n bye*
> *Ah wanna piece of pie*
> *Pies too sweet*
> *Ah wanna piece of meat*
> *Meats too red*
> *Ah wanna piece of bread*
> *Breads too brown*
> *Ah wanna go t town*
> *Towns too far*
> *Ah wanna ketch a car*
> *Cars too fas*
> *Ah fall n break mah ass*
> *Ahll understan it better bye n bye . . .*

They climbed over a barbed-wire fence and entered a stretch of thick woods. Big Boy was whistling softly, his eyes half-closed.

"LES GIT IM!"

Buck, Lester, and Bobo whirled, grabbed Big Boy about the neck, arms, and legs, bearing him to the ground. He grunted and kicked wildly as he went back into weeds.

"Hol im tight!"

"Git his arms! Git his arms!"

"Set on his legs so he cant kick!"

Big Boy puffed heavily, trying to get loose.

"WE GOT YUH NOW, GAWDDAMMIT, WE GOT YUH NOW!"

"Thas a Gawddam lie!" said Big Boy. He kicked, twisted, and clutched for a hold on one and then the other.

"Say, yuh-all hep me hol his arms!" said Bobo.

"Aw, we got this bastard now!" said Lester.

"Thas a Gawddam lie!" said Big Boy again.

"Say, yuh-all hep me hol his arms!" called Bobo.

Big Boy managed to encircle the neck of Bobo with his left arm. He tightened his elbow scissors-like and hissed through his teeth:

"Yuh got me, ain yuh?"

"Hol im!"

"Les beat this bastard's ass!"

"Say, hep me hol his *arms*! Hes got aholda mah *neck*!" cried Bobo.

Big Boy squeezed Bobo's neck and twisted his head to the ground.

"Yuh got me, ain yuh?"

"Quit, Big Boy, yuh chokin me; yuh hurtin mah neck!" cried Bobo.

"Turn me loose!" said Big Boy.

"Ah ain got yuh! Its the others whut got yuh!" pleaded Bobo.

"Tell them others t git t hell offa me or Ahma break yo neck," said Big Boy.

"Ssssay, yyyuh-all gggit ooooffa Bbig Boy. Hhhes got me," gurgled Bobo.

"Cant yuh hol im?"

"Nnaw, hhes ggot mmah nneck . . ."

Big Boy squeezed tighter.

"N Ahma break it too less yuh tell em t git t hell offa me!"

"Ttturn mmmeee lllloose," panted Bobo, tears gushing.

"Cant yuh hol im, Bobo?" asked Buck.

"Nnaw, yuh-all tturn im lloose; hhhes got mah nnneck . . ."

"Grab his neck, Bobo . . ."

"Ah cant; yugurgur . . ."

To save Bobo, Lester and Buck got up and ran to a safe distance. Big Boy released Bobo, who staggered to his feet, slobbering and trying to stretch a crick out of his neck.

"Shucks, nigger, yuh almos broke mah neck," whimpered Bobo.

"Ahm gonna break yo ass nex time," said Big Boy.

"Ef Bobo coulda hel yuh we woulda had yuh," yelled Lester.

"Ah wuznt gonna let im do that," said Big Boy.

They walked together again, swishing sticks.

"Yuh see," began Big Boy, "when a ganga guys jump on yuh, all yuh gotta do is jus put the heat on one of them n make im tell the others t let up, see?"

"Gee, thas a good idee!"

"Yeah, thas a good idee!"

"But yuh almos broke mah neck, man," said Bobo.

"Ahma smart nigger," said Big Boy, thrusting out his chest.

II

They came to the swimming hole.

"Ah ain goin in," said Bobo.

"Done got scared?" asked Big Boy.

"Naw, Ah ain scared . . ."

"How come yuh ain goin in?"

"Yuh know ol man Harvey don erllow no niggers t swim in this hole."

"N jus las year he took a shot at Bob fer swimmin in here," said Lester.

"Shucks, ol man Harvey ain studyin bout us niggers," said Big Boy.

"Hes at home thinkin about his jelly-roll," said Buck.

They laughed.

"Buck, yo mins lowern a snakes belly," said Lester.

"Ol man Harveys too doggone ol t think erbout jelly-roll," said Big Boy.

"Hes dried up; all the saps done lef im," said Bobo.

"C mon, les go!" said Big Boy.

Bobo pointed.

"See tha sign over yonder?"

"Yeah."

"Whut it say?"

"NO TRESPASSIN," read Lester.

"Know whut tha mean?"

"Mean ain no dogs n niggers erllowed," said Buck.

"Waal, wes here now," said Big Boy. "Ef he ketched us even like this thered be trouble, so we just as waal go on in . . ."

"Ahm wid the nex one!"

"Ahll go ef anybody else goes!"

Big Boy looked carefully in all directions. Seeing nobody, he began jerking off his overalls.

"LAS ONE INS A OL DEAD DOG!"

"THAS YO MA!"

"THAS YO PA!"

"THAS BOTH YO MA N YO PA!"

They jerked off their clothes and threw them in a pile under a tree. Thirty seconds later they stood, black and naked, on the edge of the hole under a sloping embankment. Gingerly Big Boy touched the water with his foot.

"Man, this waters col," he said.

"Ahm gonna put mah cloes back on," said Bobo, withdrawing his foot.

Big Boy grabbed him about the waist.

"Like hell yuh is!"

"Git outta the way, nigger!" Bobo yelled.

"Throw im in!" said Lester.

"Duck im!"

Bobo crouched, spread his legs, and braced himself against Big Boy's body. Locked in each other's arms, they tussled on the edge of the hole, neither able to throw the other.

"C mon, les me n yuh push em in."

"O.K."

Laughing, Lester and Buck gave the two locked bodies a running push. Big Boy and Bobo splashed, sending up silver spray in the sunlight. When Big Boy's head came up he yelled:

"Yuh bastard!"

"Tha wuz yo ma yuh pushed!" said Bobo, shaking his head to clear the water from his eyes.

They did a surface dive, came up and struck out across the creek. The muddy water foamed. They swam back, waded into shallow water, breathing heavily and blinking eyes.

"C mon in!"

"Man, the waters fine!"

Lester and Buck hesitated.

"Les wet em," Big Boy whispered to Bobo.

Before Lester and Buck could back away, they were dripping wet from handsful of scooped water.

"Hey, quit!"

"Gawddam, nigger! Tha waters col!"

"C mon in!" called Big Boy.

"We jus as waal go on in now," said Buck.

"Look n see ef anybodys comin."

Kneeling, they squinted among the trees.

"Ain nobody."

"C mon, les go."

They waded in slowly, pausing each few steps to catch their breath. A desperate water battle began. Closing eyes and backing away, they shunted water into one another's faces with the flat palms of hands.

"Hey, cut it out!"

"Yeah, Ahm bout drownin!"

They came together in water up to their navels, blowing and blinking. Big Boy ducked, upsetting Bobo.

"Look out, nigger!"

"Don holler so loud!"

"Yeah, they kin hear yo ol big mouth a mile erway."

"This waters too col fer me."

"Thas cause it rained yistiddy."

They swam across and back again.

"Ah wish we hada bigger place t swim in."

"The white folks got plenty swimmin pools n we ain got none."

"Ah useta swim in the ol Missippi when we lived in Vicksburg."

Big Boy put his head under the water and blew his breath. A sound came like that of a hippopotamus.

"C mon, les be hippos."

Each went to a corner of the creek and put his mouth just below the surface and blew like a hippopotamus. Tiring, they came and sat under the embankment.

"Look like Ah gotta chill."

"Me too."

"Les stay here n dry off."

"Jeeesus, Ahm col!"

They kept still in the sun, suppressing shivers. After some of the water had dried off their bodies they began to talk through clattering teeth.

"Whut would yuh do ef ol man Harveyd come erlong right now?"

"Run like hell!"

"Man, Ahd run so fas hed thinka black streaka lightnin shot pass im."

"But spose he hada gun?"

"Aw, nigger, shut up!"

They were silent. They ran their hands over wet, trembling legs, brushing water away. Then their eyes watched the sun sparkling on the restless creek.

Far away a train whistled.

"There goes number seven!"

"Headin fer up Noth!"

"Blazin it down the line!"

"Lawd, Ahm goin Noth some day."

"Me too, man."

"They say colored folks up Noth is got ekual rights."

They grew pensive. A black winged butterfly hovered at the water's edge. A bee droned. From somewhere came the sweet scent of honeysuckles. Dimly they could hear sparrows twittering in the woods. They rolled from side to side, letting sunshine dry their skins and warm their blood. They plucked blades of grass and chewed them.

"Oh!"

They looked up, their lips parting.

"Oh!"

A white woman, poised on the edge of the opposite embankment, stood directly in front of them, her hat in her hand and her hair lit by the sun.

"Its a woman!" whispered Big Boy in an underbreath. "A *white* woman!"

They stared, their hands instinctively covering their groins. Then they scrambled to their feet. The white woman backed slowly out of sight. They stood for a moment, looking at one another.

"Les git outta here!" Big Boy whispered.

"Wait till she goes erway."

"Les run, theyll ketch us here naked like this!"

"Mabbe theres a man wid her."

"C mon, les git our cloes," said Big Boy.

They waited a moment longer, listening.

"Whut t hell! Ahma git mah cloes," said Big Boy.

Grabbing at short tufts of grass, he climbed the embankment.

"Don run out there now!"

"C mon back, fool!"

Bobo hesitated. He looked at Big Boy, and then at Buck and Lester.

"Ahm goin wid Big Boy n git mah cloes," he said.

"Don run out there naked like tha, fool!" said Buck. "Yuh don know whos out there!"

Big Boy was climbing over the edge of the embankment.

"C mon," he whispered.

Bobo climbed after. Twenty-five feet away the woman stood. She had one hand over her mouth. Hanging by fingers, Buck and Lester peeped over the edge.

"C mon back; that womans scared," said Lester.

Big Boy stopped, puzzled. He looked at the woman. He looked at the bundle of clothes. Then he looked at Buck and Lester.

"C mon, les git our cloes!"

He made a step.

"Jim!" the woman screamed.

Big Boy stopped and looked around. His hands hung loosely at his sides. The woman, her eyes wide, her hand over her mouth, backed away to the tree where their clothes lay in a heap.

"Big Boy, come back n wait till shes gone!"

Bobo ran to Big Boy's side.

"Les go home! Theyll ketch us here," he urged.

Big Boy's throat felt tight.

"Lady, we wanna git our cloes," he said.

Buck and Lester climbed the embankment and stood indecisively. Big Boy ran toward the tree.

"Jim!" the woman screamed. "Jim! Jim!"

Black and naked, Big Boy stopped three feet from her.

"We wanna git our cloes," he said again, his words coming mechanically.

He made a motion.

"You go away! You go away! I tell you, you go away!"

Big Boy stopped again, afraid. Bobo ran and snatched the clothes. Buck and Lester tried to grab theirs out of his hands.

"You go away! You go away! You go away!" the woman screamed.

"Les go!" said Bobo, running toward the woods.

CRACK!

Lester grunted, stiffened, and pitched forward. His forehead struck a toe of the woman's shoes.

Bobo stopped, clutching the clothes. Buck whirled. Big Boy stared at Lester, his lips moving.

"Hes gotta gun; hes gotta gun!" yelled Buck, running wildly.

CRACK!

Buck stopped at the edge of the embankment, his head jerked backward, his body arched stiffly to one side; he toppled headlong, sending up a shower of bright spray to the sunlight. The creek bubbled.

Big Boy and Bobo backed away, their eyes fastened fearfully on a white man who was running toward them. He had a rifle and wore an army officer's uniform. He ran to the woman's side and grabbed her hand.

"You hurt, Bertha, you hurt?"

She stared at him and did not answer.

The man turned quickly. His face was red. He raised the rifle and pointed it at Bobo. Bobo ran back, holding the clothes in front of his chest.

"Don shoot me, Mistah, don shoot me . . ."

Big Boy lunged for the rifle, grabbing the barrel.

"You black sonofabitch!"

Big Boy clung desperately.

"Let go, you black bastard!"

The barrel pointed skyward.

CRACK!

The white man, taller and heavier, flung Big Boy to the ground. Bobo dropped the clothes, ran up, and jumped onto the white man's back.

"You black sonsofbitches!"

The white man released the rifle, jerked Bobo to the ground, and began to batter the naked boy with his fists. Then Big Boy swung, striking the man in the mouth with the barrel. His teeth caved in, and he fell, dazed. Bobo was on his feet.

"C mon, Big Boy, les go!"

Breathing hard, the white man got up and faced Big Boy. His lips were trembling, his neck and chin wet with blood. He spoke quietly.

"Give me that gun, boy!"

Big Boy leveled the rifle and backed away.

The white man advanced.

"Boy, I say give me that gun!"

Bobo had the clothes in his arms.

"Run, Big Boy, run!"

The man came at Big Boy.

"Ahll kill yuh; Ahll kill yuh!" said Big Boy.

His fingers fumbled for the trigger.

The man stopped, blinked, spat blood. His eyes were bewildered. His face whitened. Suddenly, he lunged for the rifle, his hands outstretched.

CRACK!

He fell forward on his face.

"Jim!"

Big Boy and Bobo turned in surprise to look at the woman.

"Jim!" she screamed again, and fell weakly at the foot of the tree.

Big Boy dropped the rifle, his eyes wide. He looked around. Bobo was crying and clutching the clothes.

"Big Boy, Big Boy . . ."

Big Boy looked at the rifle, started to pick it up, but didn't. He seemed at a loss. He looked at Lester, then at the white man; his eyes followed a thin stream of blood that seeped to the ground.

"Yuh done killed im," mumbled Bobo.

"Les go home!"

Naked, they turned and ran toward the woods. When they reached the barbed-wire fence they stopped.

"Les git our cloes on," said Big Boy.

They slipped quickly into overalls. Bobo held Lester's and Buck's clothes.

"Whut we gonna do wid these?"

Big Boy stared. His hands twitched.

"Leave em."

They climbed the fence and ran through the woods. Vines and leaves switched their faces. Once Bobo tripped and fell.

"C mon!" said Big Boy.

Bobo started crying, blood streaming from his scratches.

"Ahm scared!"

"C mon! Don cry! We wanna git home fo they ketches us!"

"Ahm scared!" said Bobo again, his eyes full of tears.

Big Boy grabbed his hand and dragged him along.

"C mon!"

III

They stopped when they got to the end of the woods. They could see the open road leading home, home to ma and pa. But they hung back, afraid. The thick shadows cast from the trees were friendly and sheltering. But the wide glare of sun stretching out over the fields was pitiless. They crouched behind an old log.

"We gotta git home," said Big Boy.

"Theys gonna lynch us," said Bobo, half-questioningly.

Big Boy did not answer.

"Theys gonna lynch us," said Bobo again.

Big Boy shuddered.

"Hush!" he said. He did not want to think of it. He could not think of it; there was but one thought, and he clung to that one blindly. He had to get home, home to ma and pa.

Their heads jerked up. Their ears had caught the rhythmic jingle of a wagon. They fell to the ground and clung flat to the side of a log. Over the crest of the hill came the top of a hat. A white face. Then shoulders in a blue shirt. A wagon drawn by two horses pulled into full view.

Big Boy and Bobo held their breath, waiting. Their eyes followed the wagon till it was lost in dust around a bend of the road.

"We gotta git home," said Big Boy.

"Ahm scared," said Bobo.

"C mon! Les keep t the fields."

They ran till they came to the cornfields. Then they went slower, for last year's corn stubbles bruised their feet.

They came in sight of a brickyard.

"Wait a minute," gasped Big Boy.

They stopped.

"Ahm goin on t mah home n yuh better go on t yos."

Bobo's eyes grew round.

"Ahm scared!"

"Yuh better go on!"

"Lemme go wid yuh; theyll ketch me . . ."

"Ef yuh kin git home mabbe yo folks kin hep yuh t git erway."

Big Boy started off. Bobo grabbed him.

"Lemme go wid yuh!"

Big Boy shook free.

"Ef yuh stay here theys gonna lynch yuh!" he yelled, running.

After he had gone about twenty-five yards he turned and looked; Bobo was flying through the woods like the wind.

Big Boy slowed when he came to the railroad. He wondered if he ought to go through the streets or down the track. He decided on the tracks. He could dodge a train better than a mob.

He trotted along the ties, looking ahead and back. His cheek itched, and he felt it. His hand came away smeared with blood. He wiped it nervously on his overalls.

When he came to his back fence he heaved himself over. He landed among a flock of startled chickens. A bantam rooster tried to spur him. He slipped and fell in front of the kitchen steps, grunting heavily. The ground was slick with greasy dishwater.

Panting, he stumbled through the doorway.

"Lawd, Big Boy, whuts wrong wid yuh?"

His mother stood gaping in the middle of the floor. Big Boy flopped wordlessly onto a stool, almost toppling over. Pots simmered on the stove. The kitchen smelled of food cooking.

"Whuts the matter, Big Boy?"

Mutely, he looked at her. Then he burst into tears. She came and felt the scratches on his face.

"Whut happened t yuh, Big Boy? Somebody been botherin yuh?"

"They after me, Ma! They after me . . ."

"Who!"

"Ah . . . Ah . . . We . . ."

"Big Boy, whuts wrong wid yuh?"

"He killed Lester n Buck," he muttered simply.

"Killed!"

"Yessum."

"Lester n Buck!"

"Yessum, Ma!"

"How killed?"

"He shot em, Ma!"

"Lawd Gawd in Heaven, have mercy on us all! This is mo trouble, mo trouble," she moaned, wringing her hands.

"N Ah killed im, Ma . . ."

She stared, trying to understand.

"Whut happened, Big Boy?"

"We tried t git our cloes from the tree . . ."

"Whut tree?"

"We wuz swimmin, Ma. N the white woman . . ."

"*White* woman? . . ."

"Yessum. She wuz at the swimmin hole . . ."

"Lawd have mercy! Ah knowed yuh boys wuz gonna keep on till yuh got into somethin like this!"

She ran into the hall.

"Lucy!"

"Mam?"

"C mere!"

"Mam?"

"C mere, Ah say!"

"Whutcha wan, Ma? Ahm sewin."

"Chile, will yuh c mere like Ah ast yuh?"

Lucy came to the door holding an unfinished apron in her hands. When she saw Big Boy's face she looked wildly at her mother.

"Whuts the matter?"

"Wheres Pa?"

"Hes out front, Ah reckon."

"Git im, quick!"

"Whuts the matter, Ma?"

"Go git yo Pa, Ah say!"

Lucy ran out. The mother sank into a chair, holding a dish rag. Suddenly, she sat up.

"Big Boy, Ah thought yuh wuz at school?"

Big Boy looked at the floor.

"How come yuh didnt go t school?"

"We went t the woods."

She sighed.

"Ah done done all Ah kin fer yuh, Big Boy. Only Gawd kin hep yuh now."

"Ma, don let em git me; don let em git me . . ."

His father came into the doorway. He stared at Big Boy, then at his wife.

"Whuts Big Boy inter now?" he asked sternly.

"Saul, Big Boys done gone n got inter trouble wid the white folks."

The old man's mouth dropped, and he looked from one to the other.

"Saul, we gotta git im erway from here."

"Open yo mouth n talk! Whut yuh been doin?" The old man gripped Big Boy's shoulders and peered at the scratches on his face.

"Me n Lester n Buck n Bobo wuz out on ol man Harveys place swimmin . . ."

"Saul, its a *white* woman!"

Big Boy winced. The old man compressed his lips and stared at his wife. Lucy gaped at her brother as though she had never seen him before.

"Whut happened? Cant yuh-all talk?" the old man thundered, with a certain helplessness in his voice.

"We wuz swimmin," Big Boy began, "n then a white woman comes up t the hole. We got up right erway t git our cloes sos we could git erway, n she started screamin. Our cloes wuz right by the tree where she wuz standin, n when we started t git em she jus screamed. We tol her we wanted our cloes . . . Yuh see, Pa, she wuz standin right *by* our cloes; n when we went t git em she jus screamed . . . Bobo got the cloes, n then he shot Lester . . ."

"*Who* shot Lester?"

"The white man."

"Whut white man?"

"Ah dunno, Pa. He wuz a soljer, n he had a rifle."

"A soljer?"

"Yessuh."

"A *soljer*?"

"Yessuh, Pa. A soljer."

The old man frowned.

"N then whut yuh-all do?"

"Waal, Buck said, 'Hes gotta gun!' N we started runnin. N then he shot Buck, n he fell in the swimmin hole. We didn't see im no mo . . . He wuz close on us then. He looked at the white woman n then he started to shoot Bobo. Ah grabbed the gun, n we started fightin. Bobo jumped on his back. He started beatin Bobo. Then Ah hit im wid the gun. Then he started at me n Ah shot im. Then we run . . ."

"Who seen?"

"Nobody."

"Wheres Bobo?"

"He went home."

"Anybody run after yuh-all?"

"Nawsuh."

"Yuh see anybody?"

"Nawsuh. Nobody but a white man. But he didnt see us."

"How long fo yuh-all lef the swimmin hole?"

"Little while ergo."

The old man nervously brushed his hand across his eyes and walked to the door. His lips moved, but no words came.

"Saul, whut we gonna do?"

"Lucy," began the old man, "go t Brother Sanders n tell im Ah said c mere; n go t Brother Jenkins n tell im Ah said c mere; n go t Elder Peters n tell im Ah said c mere. N don say nothin t nobody but whut Ah tol yuh. N when yuh git thu come straight back. Now go!"

Lucy dropped her apron across the back of a chair and ran down the steps. The mother bent over, crying and praying. The old man walked slowly over to Big Boy.

"Big Boy?"

Big Boy swallowed.

"Ahm talkin t yuh!"

"Yessuh."

"How come yuh didnt go t school this mawnin?"

"We went t the woods."

"Didnt yo ma send yuh t school?"

"Yessuh."

"How come yuh didnt go?"

"We went t the woods."

"Don yuh know thas wrong?"

"Yessuh."

"How come yuh go?"

Big Boy looked at his fingers, knotted them, and squirmed in his seat.

"AHM TALKIN T YUH!"

His wife straightened up and said reprovingly:

"Saul!"

The old man desisted, yanking nervously at the shoulder straps of his overalls.

"How long wuz the woman there?"

"Not long."

"Wuz she young?"

"Yessuh. Lika gal."

"Did yuh-all say anythin t her?"

"Nawsuh. We jus said we wanted our cloes."

"N whut she say?"

"Nothin, Pa. She jus backed erway t the tree n screamed."

The old man stared, his lips trying to form a question.

"Big Boy, did yuh-all bother her?"

"Nawsuh, Pa. We didn't *touch* her."

"How long fo the white man come up?"

"Right erway."

"Whut he say?"

"Nothin. He jus cussed us."

Abruptly the old man left the kitchen.

"Ma, cant Ah go fo they ketches me?"

"Sauls doin whut he kin."

"Ma, Ma, Ah don wan em t ketch me . . ."

"Sauls doin whut he kin. Nobody but the good Lawd kin hep us now."

The old man came back with a shotgun and leaned it in a corner. Fascinatedly, Big Boy looked at it.

There was a knock at the front door.

"Liza, see whos there."

She went. They were silent, listening. They could hear her talking.

"Whos there?"

"Me."

"Who?"

"Me, Brother Sanders."

"C mon in. Sauls waitin fer yuh."

Sanders paused in the doorway, smiling.

"Yuh sent fer me, Brother Morrison?"

"Brother Sanders, wes in deep trouble here."

Sanders came all the way into the kitchen.

"Yeah?"

"Big Boy done gone n killed a white man."

Sanders stopped short, then came forward, his face thrust out, his mouth open. His lips moved several times before he could speak.

"A *white* man?"

"They gonna kill me; they gonna kill me!" Big Boy cried, running to the old man.

"Saul, cant we git im erway somewhere?"

"Here now, take it easy; take it easy," said Sanders, holding Big Boy's wrists.

"They gonna kill me; they gonna lynch me!"

Big Boy slipped to the floor. They lifted him to a stool. His mother held him closely, pressing his head to her bosom.

"Whut we gonna do?" asked Sanders.

"Ah done sent fer Brother Jenkins n Elder Peters."

Sanders leaned his shoulders against the wall. Then, as the full meaning of it all came to him, he exclaimed:

"Theys gonna git a mob! . . ." His voice broke off and his eyes fell on the shotgun.

Feet came pounding on the steps. They turned toward the door. Lucy ran in crying. Jenkins followed. The old man met him in the middle of the room, taking his hand.

"Wes in bad trouble here, Brother Jenkins. Big Boy's done gone n killed a white man. Yuh-alls gotta hep me . . ."

Jenkins looked hard at Big Boy.

"Elder Peters says hes comin," said Lucy.

"When all this happen?" asked Jenkins.

"Near bout a hour ergo, now," said the old man.

"Whut we gonna do?" asked Jenkins.

"Ah wanna wait till Elder Peters come," said the old man helplessly.

"But we gotta work fas ef we gonna do anythin," said Sanders. "Well git in trouble jus standin here like this."

Big Boy pulled away from his mother.

"Pa, lemme go now! Lemme go now!"

"Be still, Big Boy!"

"Where kin yuh go?"

"Ah could ketch a freight!"

"Thas *sho* death!" said Jenkins. "Theyll be watchin em all!"

"Kin yuh-all hep me wid some money?" the old man asked.

They shook their heads.

"Saul, whut kin we do? Big Boy cant stay here."

There was another knock at the door.

The old man backed stealthily to the shotgun.

"Lucy go!"

Lucy looked at him, hesitating.

"Ah better go," said Jenkins.

It was Elder Peters. He came in hurriedly.

"Good evenin, everbody!"

"How yuh, Elder?"

"Good evenin."

"How yuh today?"

Peters looked around the crowded kitchen.

"Whuts the matter?"

"Elder, wes in deep trouble," began the old man. "Big Boy n some mo boys . . ."

" . . . Lester n Buck n Bobo . . ."

" . . . wuz over on ol man Harveys place swimmin . . ."

"N he don like us niggers *none*," said Peters emphatically. He widened his legs and put his thumbs in the armholes of his vest.

" . . . n some white woman . . ."

"Yeah?" said Peters, coming closer.

" . . . comes erlong n the boys tries t git their cloes where they done lef em under a tree. Waal, she started screamin n all, see? Reckon she thought the boys wuz after her. Then a white man in a soljers suit shoots two of em . . ."

" . . . Lester n Buck . . ."

"Huummm," said Peters. "Tha wuz ol man Harveys son."

"Harveys son?"

"Yuh mean the one tha wuz in the Army?"

"Yuh mean Jim?"

"Yeah," said Peters. "The papers said he wuz here fer a vacation from his regiment. N tha woman the boys saw wuz jus erbout his wife . . ."

They stared at Peters. Now that they knew what white person had been killed, their fears became definite.

"N whut else happened?"

"Big Boy shot the man . . ."

"Harveys *son*?"

"He had t, Elder. He wuz gonna shoot im ef he didnt . . ."

"Lawd!" said Peters. He looked around and put his hat back on.

"How long ergo wuz this?"

"Mighty near an hour, now, Ah reckon."

"Do the white folks know yit?"

"Don know, Elder."

"Yuh-all better git this boy outta here right now," said Peters. "Cause ef yuh don theres gonna be a lynchin . . ."

"Where kin Ah go, Elder?" Big Boy ran up to him.

They crowded around Peters. He stood with his legs wide apart, looking up at the ceiling.

"Mabbe we kin hide im in the church till he kin git erway," said Jenkins.

Peters' lips flexed.

"Naw, Brother, thall never do! Theyll git im there sho. N anyhow, ef they ketch im there itll ruin us all. We gotta git the boy outta town . . ."

Sanders went up to the old man.

"Lissen," he said in a whisper. "Mah son, Will, the one whut drives fer the Magnolia Express Comny, is taking a truck o goods t Chicawgo in the mawnin. If we kin hide Big Boy somewhere till then, we kin put im on the truck . . ."

"Pa, please, lemme go wid Will when he goes in the mawnin," Big Boy begged.

The old man stared at Sanders.

"Yuh reckon thas safe?"

"Its the only thing yuh *kin* do," said Peters.

"But where we gonna hide im till then?"

"Whut time yo boy leavin out in the mawnin?"

"At six."

They were quiet, thinking. The water kettle on the stove sang.

"Pa, Ah knows where Will passes erlong wid the truck out on Bullards Road. Ah kin hide in one of them ol kilns . . ."

"Where?"

"In one of them kilns we built . . ."

"But theyll git yuh there," wailed the mother.

"But there ain no place else fer im t go."

"Theres some holes big ernough fer me t git in n stay till Will comes erlong," said Big Boy. "Please, Pa, lemme go fo they ketches me . . ."

"Let im go!"

"Please, Pa . . ."

The old man breathed heavily.

"Lucy, git his things!"

"Saul, theyll git im out there!" wailed the mother, grabbing Big Boy.

Peters pulled her away.

"Sister Morrison, ef yuh don let im go n git erway from here hes gonna be caught shos theres a Gawd in Heaven!"

Lucy came running with Big Boy's shoes and pulled them on his feet. The old man thrust a battered hat on his head. The mother went to the stove and dumped the skillet of corn pone into her apron. She wrapped it, and unbuttoning Big Boy's overalls, pushed it into his bosom.

"Heres somethin fer yuh t eat; n pray, Big Boy, cause thas all anybody kin do now . . ."

Big Boy pulled to the door, his mother clinging to him.

"Let im go, Sister Morrison!"

"Run fas, Big Boy!"

Big Boy raced across the yard, scattering the chickens. He paused at the fence and hollered back:

"Tell Bobo where Ahm hidin n tell im t c mon!"

IV

He made for the railroad, running straight toward the sunset. He held his left hand tightly over his heart, holding the hot pone of corn bread there. At times he stumbled over the ties, for his shoes were tight and hurt his feet. His throat burned from thirst; he had had no water since noon.

He veered off the track and trotted over the crest of a hill, following Bullard's Road. His feet slipped and slid in the dust. He kept his eyes straight ahead, fearing every clump of shrubbery, every tree. He wished it were night. If he could only get to the kilns without meeting anyone. Suddenly a thought came to him like a blow. He recalled hearing the old folks tell tales of blood-hounds, and fear made him run slower. None of them had thought of that. Spose blood-houns wuz put on his trail? Lawd! Spose a whole pack of em, foamin n howlin, tore im t pieces? He went limp and his feet dragged. Yeah, thas whut they wuz gonna send after im, blood-houns! N then thered be no way fer im t dodge! Why hadnt Pa let im take tha shotgun? He stopped. He oughta go back n git tha shotgun. And then when the mob came he would take some with him.

In the distance he heard the approach of a train. It jarred him back to a sharp sense of danger. He ran again, his big shoes sopping up and down in the dust. He was tired and his lungs were bursting from running. He wet his lips, wanting water. As he turned from the road across a plowed field he heard the train roaring at his heels. He ran faster, gripped in terror.

He was nearly there now. He could see the black clay on the sloping hillside. Once inside a kiln he would be safe. For a little while, at least. He thought of the shotgun again. If he only had something! Someone to talk to . . . Thas right! Bobo! Bobod be wid im. Hed almost fergot Bobo. Bobod bringa gun; he knowed he would. N tergether they could kill the whole mob. Then in the mawning theyd git inter Will's truck n go far erway, t Chicawgo . . .

He slowed to a walk, looking back and ahead. A light wind skipped over the grass. A beetle lit on his cheek and he brushed it off. Behind the dark pines hung a red sun. Two bats flapped against that sun. He shivered, for he was growing cold; the sweat on his body was drying.

He stopped at the foot of the hill, trying to choose between two patches of black kilns high above him. He went to the left, for there lay the ones he, Bobo, Lester, and Buck had dug only last week. He looked around again; the landscape was bare. He climbed the embankment and stood before a row of black pits sinking four and five feet deep into the earth. He went to the largest and peered in. He stiffened when his ears caught the sound of a whir. He ran back a few steps and poised on his toes. Six foot of snake slid out of the pit and went into coil. Big Boy looked around wildly for a stick. He ran down the slope, peering into the grass. He stumbled over a tree limb. He picked it up and tested it by striking it against the ground.

Warily, he crept back up the slope, his stick poised. When about seven feet from the snake he stopped and waved the stick. The coil grew tighter, the whir sounded louder, and a flat head reared to strike. He went to the right, and the flat head followed him, the blue-black tongue darting forth; he went to the left, and the flat head followed him there too.

He stopped, teeth clenched. He had to kill this snake. Jus had t kill im! This wuz the safest pit on the hillside. He waved the stick again, looking at the snake before, thinking of a mob behind. The flat head reared higher. With stick over shoulder, he jumped in, swinging. The stick sang through the air, catching the snake on the side of the head, sweeping him out of coil. There was a brown writhing mass. Then Big Boy was upon him, pounding blows home, one on top of the other.

He fought viciously, his eyes red, his teeth bared in a snarl. He beat till the snake lay still; then he stomped it with his heel, grinding its head into the dirt.

He stopped, limp, wet. The corners of his lips were white with spittle. He spat and shuddered.

Cautiously, he went to the hole and peered. He longed for a match. He imagined whole nests of them in there waiting. He put the stick into the hole and waved it around. Stooping, he peered again. It mus be awright. He looked over the hillside, his eyes coming back to the dead snake. Then he got to his knees and backed slowly into the hole.

When inside he felt there must be snakes all about him, ready to strike. It seemed he could see and feel them there, waiting tensely in coil. In the dark he imagined long white fangs ready to sink into his neck, his side, his legs. He wanted to come out, but kept still. Shucks, he told himself, ef there wuz any snakes in here they sho woulda done bit me by now. Some of his fear left, and he relaxed.

With elbows on ground and chin on palms, he settled. The clay was cold to his knees and thighs, but his bosom was kept warm by the hot pone of corn bread. His thirst returned and he longed for a drink. He was hungry, too. But he did not want to eat the corn pone. Naw, not now. Mabbe after erwhile, after Bobod came. Then theyd both eat the corn pone.

The view from his hole was fringed by the long tufts of grass. He could see all the way to Bullard's Road, and even beyond. The wind was blowing, and in the east the first touch of dusk was rising. Every now and then a bird floated past, a spot of wheeling black printed against the sky. Big Boy sighed, shifted his weight, and chewed at a blade of grass. A wasp droned. He heard number nine, far away and mournful.

The train made him remember how they had dug these kilns on long hot summer days, how they had made boilers out of big tin cans, filled them with water, fixed stoppers for steam, cemented them in holes with wet clay, and built fires under them. He recalled how they had danced and yelled when a stopper blew out of a boiler, letting out a big spout of steam and a shrill whistle. There were times when they had the whole hillside blazing and smoking. Yeah, yuh see, Big Boy wuz Casey Jones n wuz speedin it down the gleamin rails

of the Southern Pacific. Bobo had number two on the Santa
Fe. Buck wuz on the Illinoy Central. Lester the Nickel Plate.
Lawd, how they shelved the wood in! The boiling water
would almost jar the cans loose from the clay. More and more
pine-knots and dry leaves would be piled under the cans.
Flames would grow so tall they would have to shield their
eyes. Sweat would pour off their faces. Then, suddenly, a peg
would shoot high into the air, and

Pssseeeezzzzzzzzzzzzzzzzzzzzzz . . .

Big Boy sighed and stretched out his arm, quenching the
flames and scattering the smoke. Why didnt Bobo c mon? He
looked over the fields; there was nothing but dying sunlight.
His mind drifted back to the kilns. He remembered the day
when Buck, jealous of his winning, had tried to smash his
kiln. Yeah, that ol sonofabitch! Naw, Lawd! He didnt go t say
tha! Whut wuz he thinkin erbout? Cussin the dead! Yeah, po
ol Buck wuz dead now. N Lester too. Yeah, it wuz awright fer
Buck t smash his kiln. Sho. N he wished he hadnt socked ol
Buck so hard tha day. He wuz sorry fer Buck now. N he sho
wished he hadnt cussed po ol Bucks ma, neither. Tha wuz
sinful! Mabbe Gawd would git im fer tha? But he didnt go t
do it! Po Buck! Po Lester! Hed never treat anybody like tha
ergin, never . . .

Dusk was slowly deepening. Somewhere, he could not tell
exactly where, a cricket took up a fitful song. The air was
growing soft and heavy. He looked over the fields, longing
for Bobo . . .

He shifted his body to ease the cold damp of the ground,
and thought back over the day. Yeah, hed been dam right
erbout not wantin t go swimmin. N ef hed followed his right
min hed neverve gone n got inter all this trouble. At first hed
said naw. But shucks, somehow hed just went on wid the res.
Yeah, he shoulda went on t school tha mawnin, like Ma told
im t do. But, hell, who wouldnt git tireda awways drivin a
guy t school! Tha wuz the big trouble, awways drivin a guy t
school. He wouldnt be in all this trouble now ef it wuznt fer
that Gawddam school! Impatiently, he took the grass out of
his mouth and threw it away, demolishing the little red school
house . . .

Yeah, ef they had all kept still n quiet when tha ol white

woman showed-up, mabbe shedve went on off. But yuh never kin tell erbout these white folks. Mabbe she wouldntve went. Mabbe tha white man woulda killed all of em! All *fo* of em! Yeah, yuh never kin tell erbout white folks. Then, ergin, mabbe tha white woman woulda went on off n laffed. Yeah, mabbe tha white man woulda said: *Yuh nigger bastards git t hell outta here! Yuh know Gawddam well yuh don berlong here!* N then they woulda grabbed their cloes n run like all hell . . . He blinked the white man away. Where wuz Bobo? Why didn't he hurry up n c mon?

He jerked another blade and chewed. Yeah, ef pa had only let im have tha shotgun! He could stan off a whole mob wid a shotgun. He looked at the ground as he turned a shotgun over in his hands. Then he leveled it at an advancing white man. *Boooom!* The man curled up. Another came. He reloaded quickly, and let him have what the other had got. He too curled up. Then another came. He got the same medicine. Then the whole mob swirled around him, and he blazed away, getting as many as he could. They closed in; but, by Gawd, he had done his part, hadnt he? N the newspapersd say: NIGGER KILLS DOZEN OF MOB BEFO LYNCHED! Er mabbe theyd say: TRAPPED NIGGER SLAYS TWENTY BEFO KILLED! He smiled a little. Tha wouldnt be so bad, would it? Blinking the newspaper away, he looked over the fields. Where wuz Bobo? Why didnt he hurry up n c mon?

He shifted, trying to get a crick out of his legs. Shucks, he wuz gittin tireda this. N it wuz almos dark now. Yeah, there wuz a little bittie star way over yonder in the eas. Mabbe tha white man wuznt dead? Mabbe they wuznt even lookin fer im? Mabbe he could go back home now? Naw, better wait erwhile. Thad be bes. But, Lawd, ef he only had some water! He could hardly swallow, his throat was so dry. Gawddam them white folks! Thas all they wuz good fer, t run a nigger down lika rabbit! Yeah, they git yuh in a corner n then they let yuh have it. A thousan of em! He shivered, for the cold of the clay was chilling his bones. Lawd, spose they foun im here in this hole? N wid nobody t hep im? . . . But ain no use in thinkin erbout tha; wait till trouble come fo yuh start fightin it. But ef tha mob came one by one hed wipe em all out.

Clean up the whole bunch. He caught one by the neck and choked him long and hard, choked him till his tongue and eyes popped out. Then he jumped upon his chest and stomped him like he had stomped that snake. When he had finished with one, another came. He choked him too. Choked till he sank slowly to the ground, gasping . . .

"Hoalo!"

Big Boy snatched his fingers from the white man's neck and looked over the fields. He saw nobody. Had someone spied him? He was sure that somebody had hollered. His heart pounded. But, shucks, nobody couldnt see im here in this hole . . . But mabbe theyd seen im when he wuz comin n had laid low n wuz now closin in on im! Praps they wuz signalin fer the others? Yeah, they wuz creepin up on im! Mabbe he oughta git up n run . . . Oh! Mabbe tha wuz Bobo! Yeah, Bobo! He oughta clim out n see ef Bobo wuz lookin fer im . . . He stiffened.

"Hoalo!"

"Hoalo!"

"Wheres yuh?"

"Over here on Bullards Road!"

"C mon over!"

"Awright!"

He heard footsteps. Then voices came again, low and far away this time.

"Seen anybody?"

"Naw. Yuh?"

"Naw."

"Yuh reckon they got erway?"

"Ah dunno. Its hard t tell."

"Gawddam them sonofabitchin niggers!"

"We oughta kill ever black bastard in this country!"

"Waal, Jim got two of em, anyhow."

"But Bertha said there wuz *fo*!"

"Where in hell they hidin?"

"She said one of em wuz named Big Boy, or somethin like tha."

"We went t his shack lookin fer im."

"Yeah?"

"But we didnt fin im."

"These niggers stick tergether; they don never tell on each other."

"We looked all thu the shack n couldnt fin hide ner hair of im. Then we drove the ol woman n man out n set the shack on fire . . ."

"Jeesus! Ah wished Ah coulda been there!"

"Yuh shoulda heard the ol nigger woman howl . . ."

"Hoalo!"

"C mon over!"

Big Boy eased to the edge and peeped. He saw a white man with a gun slung over his shoulder running down the slope. Wuz they gonna search the hill? Lawd, there wuz no way fer im t git erway now; he wuz caught! He shoulda knowed theyd git im here. N he didnt hava thing, notta thing t fight wid. Yeah, soon as the blood-houns came theyd fin im. Lawd, have mercy! Theyd lynch im right here on the hill . . . Theyd git im n tie im t a stake n burn im erlive! Lawd! Nobody but the good Lawd could hep im now, nobody . . .

He heard more feet running. He nestled deeper. His chest ached. Nobody but the good Lawd could hep now. They wuz crowdin all round im n when they hada big crowd theyd close in on im. Then itd be over . . . The good Lawd would have t hep im, cause nobody could hep im now, nobody . . .

And then he went numb when he remembered Bobo. Spose Bobod come now? Hed be caught sho! Both of em would be caught! They'd make Bobo tell where he wuz! Bobo oughta not try to come now. Somebody oughta tell im . . . But there wuz nobody; there wuz no way . . .

He eased slowly back to the opening. There was a large group of men. More were coming. Many had guns. Some had coils of rope slung over shoulders.

"Ah tell yuh they still here, somewhere . . ."

"But we looked all over!"

"What t hell! Wouldnt do t let em git erway!"

"Naw. Ef they git erway notta woman in this town would be safe."

"Say, whuts tha yuh got?"

"Er pillar."

"Fer whut?"

"Feathers, fool!"

"Chris! Thisll be hot ef we kin ketch them niggers!"

"Ol Anderson said he wuz gonna bringa barrela tar!"

"Ah got some gasoline in mah car ef yuh need it."

Big Boy had no feelings now. He was waiting. He did not wonder if they were coming after him. He just waited. He did not wonder about Bobo. He rested his cheek against the cold clay, waiting.

A dog barked. He stiffened. It barked again. He balled himself into a knot at the bottom of the hole, waiting. Then he heard the patter of dog feet.

"Look!"

"Whuts he got?"

"Its a snake!"

"Yeah, the dogs foun a snake!"

"Gee, its a big one!"

"Shucks, Ah wish he could fin one of them sonofabitchin niggers!"

The voices sank to low murmurs. Then he heard number twelve, its bell tolling and whistle crying as it slid along the rails. He flattened himself against the clay. Someone was singing:

"We'll hang ever nigger t a sour apple tree . . ."

When the song ended there was hard laughter. From the other side of the hill he heard the dog barking furiously. He listened. There was more than one dog now. There were many and they were barking their throats out.

"Hush, Ah hear them dogs!"

"When theys barkin like tha theys foun somethin!"

"Here they come over the hill!"

"WE GOT IM! WE GOT IM!"

There came a roar. Tha mus be Bobo; tha mus be Bobo . . . In spite of his fear, Big Boy looked. The road, and half of the hillside across the road, were covered with men. A few were at the top of the hill, stenciled against the sky. He could see dark forms moving up the slopes. They were yelling.

"By Gawd, we got im!"

"C mon!"

"Where is he?"

"Theyre bringing im over the hill!"

"Ah got a rope fer im!"

"Say, somebody go n git the others!"

"Where is he? Cant we see im, Mister?"

"They say Berthas comin, too."

"Jack! Jack! Don leave me! Ah wanna see im!"

"Theyre bringin im over the hill, sweetheart!"

"AH WANNA BE THE FIRS T PUT A ROPE ON THA BLACK BASTARDS NECK!"

"Les start the fire!"

"Heat the tar!"

"Ah got some chains t chain im."

"Bring im over this way!"

"Chris, Ah wished Ah hada drink . . ."

Big Boy saw men moving over the hill. Among them was a long dark spot. Tha mus be Bobo; tha mus be Bobo theys carryin . . . They'll git im here. He oughta git up n run. He clamped his teeth and ran his hand across his forehead, bringing it away wet. He tried to swallow, but could not; his throat was dry.

They had started the song again:

"We'll hang ever nigger t a sour apple tree . . ."

There were women singing now. Their voices made the song round and full. Song waves rolled over the top of pine trees. The sky sagged low, heavy with clouds. Wind was rising. Sometimes cricket cries cut surprisingly across the mob song. A dog had gone to the utmost top of the hill. At each lull of the song his howl floated full into the night.

Big Boy shrank when he saw the first tall flame light the hillside. Would they see im here? Then he remembered you could not see into the dark if you were standing in the light. As flames leaped higher he saw two men rolling a barrel up the slope.

"Say, gimme a han here, will yuh?"

"Awright, heave!"

"C mon! Straight up! Git t the other end!"

"Ah got the feathers here in this pillar!"

"BRING SOME MO WOOD!"

Big Boy could see the barrel surrounded by flames. The mob fell back, forming a dark circle. Theyd fin im here! He had a wild impulse to climb out and fly across the hills. But his legs would not move. He stared hard, trying to find Bobo. His eyes played over a long dark spot near the fire. Fanned by wind, flames leaped higher. He jumped. That dark spot had moved. Lawd, thas Bobo; thas Bobo . . .

He smelt the scent of tar, faint at first, then stronger. The wind brought it full into his face, then blew it away. His eyes burned and he rubbed them with his knuckles. He sneezed.

"LES GIT SOURVINEERS!"

He saw the mob close in around the fire. Their faces were hard and sharp in the light of the flames. More men and women were coming over the hill. The long dark spot was smudged out.

"Everbody git back!"

"Look! Hes gotta finger!"

"C MON! GIT THE GALS BACK FROM THE FIRE!"

"Hes got one of his ears, see?"

"Whuts the matter!"

"A woman fell out! Fainted, Ah reckon . . ."

The stench of tar permeated the hillside. The sky was black and the wind was blowing hard.

"HURRY UP N BURN THE NIGGER FO IT RAINS!"

Big Boy saw the mob fall back, leaving a small knot of men about the fire. Then, for the first time, he had a full glimpse of Bobo. A black body flashed in the light. Bobo was struggling, twisting; they were binding his arms and legs.

When he saw them tilt the barrel he stiffened. A scream quivered. He knew the tar was on Bobo. The mob fell back. He saw a tar-drenched body glistening and turning.

"THE BASTARDS GOT IT!"

There was a sudden quiet. Then he shrank violently as the wind carried, like a flurry of snow, a widening spiral of white feathers into the night. The flames leaped tall as the trees. The scream came again. Big Boy trembled and looked. The mob was running down the slopes, leaving the fire clear. Then he saw a writhing white mass cradled in yellow flame, and heard screams, one on top of the other, each shriller and shorter than the last. The mob was quiet now, standing still, looking up the slopes at the writhing white mass gradually growing black, growing black in a cradle of yellow flame.

"PO ON MO GAS!"

"Gimme a lif, will yuh!"

Two men were struggling, carrying between them a heavy can. They set it down, tilted it, leaving it so that the gas would trickle down to the hollowed earth around the fire.

Big Boy slid back into the hole, his face buried in clay. He had no feelings now, no fears. He was numb, empty, as though all blood had been drawn from him. Then his muscles flexed taut when he heard a faint patter. A tiny stream of cold water seeped to his knees, making him push back to a drier spot. He looked up; rain was beating in the grass.

"Its rainin!"

"C mon, les git t town!"

" . . . don worry, when the fire git thu wid im hell be gone . . ."

"Wait, Charles! Don leave me; its slippery here . . ."

"Ahll take some of yuh ladies back in mah car . . ."

Big Boy heard the dogs barking again, this time closer. Running feet pounded past. Cold water chilled his ankles. He could hear raindrops steadily hissing.

Now a dog was barking at the mouth of the hole, barking furiously, sensing a presence there. He balled himself into a knot and clung to the bottom, his knees and shins buried in water. The bark came louder. He heard paws scraping and felt the hot scent of dog breath on his face. Green eyes glowed and drew nearer as the barking, muffled by the closeness of the hole, beat upon his eardrums. Backing till his shoulders pressed against the clay, he held his breath. He pushed out his hands, his fingers stiff. The dog yawped louder, advancing, his bark rising sharp and thin. Big Boy rose to his knees, his hands before him. Then he flattened out still more against the bottom, breathing lungsful of hot dog scent, breathing it slowly, hard, but evenly. The dog came closer, bringing hotter dog scent. Big Boy could go back no more. His knees were slipping and slopping in the water. He braced himself, ready. Then, he never exactly knew how—he never knew whether he had lunged or the dog had lunged—they were together, rolling in the water. The green eyes were beneath him, between his legs. Dognails bit into his arms. His knees slipped backward and he landed full on the dog; the dog's breath left in a heavy gasp. Instinctively, he fumbled for the throat as he felt the dog twisting between his knees. The dog snarled, long and low, as though gathering strength. Big Boy's hands traveled swiftly over the dog's back, groping for the throat. He felt dognails again and saw green eyes, but his fingers had found the throat. He choked, feeling his fingers sink; he choked, throwing back his head and stiffening his arms. He felt the dog's body heave, felt dognails digging into his loins. With strength flowing from fear, he closed his fingers, pushing his full weight on the dog's throat. The dog heaved again, and lay still . . . Big Boy heard the sound of his own breathing filling the hole, and heard shouts and footsteps above him going past.

For a long, long time he held the dog, held it long after the last footstep had died out, long after the rain had stopped.

V

Morning found him still on his knees in a puddle of rainwater, staring at the stiff body of a dog. As the air brightened he came to himself slowly. He held still for a long time, as though waking from a dream, as though trying to remember.

The chug of a truck came over the hill. He tried to crawl to the opening. His knees were stiff and a thousand needle-like pains shot from the bottom of his feet to the calves of his legs. Giddiness made his eyes blur. He pulled up and looked. Through brackish light he saw Will's truck standing some twenty-five yards away, the engine running. Will stood on the runningboard, looking over the slopes of the hill.

Big Boy scuffled out, falling weakly in the wet grass. He tried to call to Will, but his dry throat would make no sound. He tried again.

"Will!"

Will heard, answering:

"Big Boy, c mon!"

He tried to run, and fell. Will came, meeting him in the tall grass.

"C mon," Will said, catching his arm.

They struggled to the truck.

"Hurry up!" said Will, pushing him onto the running-board.

Will pushed back a square trapdoor which swung above the back of the driver's seat. Big Boy pulled through, landing with a thud on the bottom. On hands and knees he looked around in the semi-darkness.

"Wheres Bobo?"

Big Boy stared.

"Wheres Bobo?"

"They got im."

"When?"

"Las night."

"The mob?"

Big Boy pointed in the direction of a charred sapling on the slope of the opposite hill. Will looked. The trapdoor fell. The engine purred, the gears whined, and the truck lurched forward over the muddy road, sending Big Boy on his side.

For a while he lay as he had fallen, on his side, too weak to move. As he felt the truck swing around a curve he straightened up and rested his back against a stack of wooden boxes. Slowly, he began to make out objects in the darkness. Through two long cracks fell thin blades of daylight. The floor was of smooth steel, and cold to his thighs. Splinters and bits of sawdust danced with the rumble of the truck. Each time they swung around a curve he was pulled over the floor; he grabbed at corners of boxes to steady himself. Once he heard the crow of a rooster. It made him think of home, of ma and pa. He thought he remembered hearing somewhere that the house had burned, but could not remember where . . . It all seemed unreal now.

He was tired. He dozed, swaying with the lurch. Then he jumped awake. The truck was running smoothly, on gravel. Far away he heard two short blasts from the Buckeye Lumber Mill. Unconsciously, the thought sang through his mind: Its six erclock . . .

The trapdoor swung in. Will spoke through a corner of his mouth.

"How yuh comin?"

"Awright."

"How they git Bobo?"

"He wuz comin over the hill."

"Whut they do?"

"They burnt im . . . Will, Ah wan some water; mah throats like fire . . ."

"Well git some when we pass a fillin station."

Big Boy leaned back and dozed. He jerked awake when the truck stopped. He heard Will get out. He wanted to peep through the trapdoor, but was afraid. For a moment, the wild fear he had known in the hole came back. Spose theyd search n fin im? He quieted when he heard Will's footstep on the runningboard. The trapdoor pushed in. Will's hat came through, dripping.

"Take it, quick!"

Big Boy grabbed, spilling water into his face. The truck lurched. He drank. Hard cold lumps of brick rolled into his hot stomach. A dull pain made him bend over. His intestines seemed to be drawing into a tight knot. After a bit it eased, and he sat up, breathing softly.

The truck swerved. He blinked his eyes. The blades of day-light had turned brightly golden. The sun had risen.

The truck sped over the asphalt miles, sped northward, jolt-ing him, shaking out of his bosom the crumbs of corn bread, making them dance with the splinters and sawdust in the golden blades of sunshine.

He turned on his side and slept.

II

Down by the Riverside

I

ACH STEP he took made the old house creak as though
the earth beneath the foundations were soggy. He wondered how long the logs which supported the house could
stand against the water. But what really worried him were
the steps; they might wash away at any moment, and then
they would be trapped. He had spent all that morning trying
to make them secure with frayed rope, but he did not have
much faith. He walked to the window and the half-rotten
planks sagged under his feet. He had never realized they were
that shaky. He pulled back a tattered curtain, wishing the dull
ache would leave his head. Ah been feverish all day. Feels like
Ah got the flu. Through a dingy pane he saw yellow water
swirling around a corner of the barn. A steady drone filled his
ears. In the morning the water was a deep brown. In the
afternoon it was a clayey yellow. And at night it was black,
like a restless tide of liquid tar. It was about six feet deep and
still rising; it had risen two feet that day. He squinted at a
tiny ridge of foam where the yellow current struck a side of
the barn and veered sharply. For three days he had been
watching that tiny ridge of foam. When it shortened he had
hopes of seeing the ground soon; but when it lengthened he
knew that the current was flowing strong again. All the seeds
for spring planting were wet now. They gonna rot, he
thought with despair. The morning before he had seen his
only cow, Sally, lowing, wagging her head, rolling her eyes,
and pushing through three feet of water for the hills. It was
then that Sister Jeff had said that a man who would not follow a cow was a fool. Well, he had not figured it that way.
This was his home. But now he would have to leave, for the
water was rising and there was no telling when or where it
would stop.

Two days ago he had told Bob to take the old mule to
Bowman's plantation and sell it, or swap it for a boat, any

277

kind of a boat. N Bob ain back here yit. Ef it ain one thing its ernother. When it rains it pos. But, Lawd, ef only tha old levee don break. Ef only tha ol levee don break . . .

He turned away from the window, rubbing his forehead. A good dose of quinine would kill that fever. But he had no quinine. Lawd, have mercy!

And worst of all there was Lulu flat on her back these four days, sick with a child she could not deliver. His lips parted in silent agony. It just did not seem fair that one man should be hit so hard and on so many sides at once. He shifted the weight of his body from his right foot to his left, listening for sounds from the front room, wondering how Lulu was. Ef she don have tha baby soon Ahma have t git her outta here, some way . . .

He leaned against a damp wall. Whut in the worls keepin Bob so long? Well, in a way all of this was his own fault. He had had a chance to get away and he had acted like a fool and had not taken it. He had figured that the water would soon go down. He had thought if he stayed he would be the first to get back to the fields and start spring plowing. But now even the mule was gone. Yes, he should have cleared-out when the Government offered him the boat. Now he had no money for a boat, and Bob had said that he could not even get near that Red Cross.

He took a gourd from the wall and dipped some muddy water out of a bucket. It tasted thick and bitter and he could not swallow it. He hung the gourd back and spat the water into a corner. He cocked his head, listening. It seemed he had heard the sound of a shot. There it was again. Something happenin in town, he thought. Over the yellow water he heard another shot, thin, dry, far away. Mus be trouble, mus be trouble somewhere. He had heard that the white folks were threatening to conscript all Negroes they could lay their hands on to pile sand- and cement-bags on the levee. And they were talking about bringing in soldiers, too. They were afraid of stores and homes being looted. Yes, it was hard to tell just what was happening in town. Shucks, in times like these theyll shoota nigger down jus lika dog n think nothin of it. Tha shootin might mean anything. But likely as not its jus some po black man gone . . .

He faced the window again, thinking, Ahma git mah pistol outta tha dresser drawer when Ah go inter Lulus room. He rolled the tattered curtain up as far as it would go; a brackish light seeped into the kitchen. He looked out; his house was about twelve feet above the water. And water was everywhere. Yellow water. Swirling water. Droning water. For four long days and nights it had been there, flowing past. For a moment he had the illusion that that water had always been there, and would always be there. Yes, it seemed that the water had always been there and this was just the first time he had noticed it. Mabbe somebody jus *dropped* them houses n trees down inter tha watah . . . He felt giddy and a nervous shudder went through him. He rubbed his eyes. Lawd, Ah got fever. His head ached and felt heavy; he wanted sleep and rest.

The view opposite his window was clear for half a mile. Most of the houses had already washed away. Nearby a few trees stood, casting black shadows into the yellow water. The sky was grey with the threat of rain. Suddenly every muscle in his body stretched taut as a low rumble of thunder rose and died away. He shook his head. Nothin could be worsen rain right now. A heavy rainll carry tha ol levee erway sho as hell . . .

"Brother Mann!"

He turned and saw Sister Jeff standing in the hall door.

"How Lulu?" he asked.

The old woman shook her head.

"She poly."

"Yuh reckon shell have it soon?"

"Cant say, Brother Mann. Mabbe she will n mabbe she wont. She havin the time of her life."

"Cant we do nothin fer her?"

"Naw. We jus have t wait, thas all. Lawd, Ahm scared shell never have tha baby widout a doctah. Her hips is jus too little."

"There ain no way t git a doctah now."

"But yuh gotta do something, Brother Mann."

"Ah don know whut t do," he sighed. "Where Peewee?"

"He sleep, in Lulus room."

She came close to him and looked hard into his face.

"Brother Mann, there ain nothin t eat in the house. Yuh gotta do something."

He turned from her, back to the window.

"Ah sent Bob wid the mule t try t git a boat," he said.

She sighed. He swallowed with effort, hearing the whisper of her soft shoes die away down the hall. No boat. No money. No doctah. Nothin t eat. N Bob ain back here yit. Lulu could not last much longer this way. If Bob came with a boat he would pile Lulu in and row her over to that Red Cross Hospital, no matter *what*. The white folks would take her in. They would *have* to take her in. They would not let a woman die just because she was black; they would not let a baby kill a woman. They would *not*. He grew rigid, looking out of the window, straining to listen. He thought he had heard another shot. But the only sound was the drone of swirling water. The water was darkening. In the open stretches it was a muddy yellow; but near the houses and trees it was growing black. Its gittin night, he thought. Then came the sound of shots, thin, dry, distant. Wun . . . Tuh . . . Three . . .

"Brother Mann! Its Bob!"

He hurried to the front door, walking heavily on the heels of his big shoes. He saw Bob standing far down on the long steps near the water, bending over and fumbling with a coil of rope. Behind him a white rowboat trembled in the current.

"How yuh come out, Bob?"

Bob looked up and flashed a white grin.

"See?" he said, pointing to the white boat.

Mann's whole body glowed. Thank Gawd, we gotta boat! Now we kin git erway . . .

"Who yuh git it from?"

Bob did not answer. He drew the rope tight and came up the steps.

"Ahm one tired soul," Bob said.

They went into the hall. Mann watched Bob pull out a pocket handkerchief and mop his black face. Peewee came in, rubbing his eyes and looking at Bob.

"Yuh git a boat, Uncle Bob?"

"Keep quiet, Peewee," said Mann.

Sister Jeff and Grannie came and stood behind Peewee. They looked from Bob to Mann. Bob tucked his handkerchief away, taking his time to do it, laughing a little.

"Lawd, Ahm one tired soul," he said again.

"Who bought the mule?" asked Mann.

"Ol man Bowman bought the mule, but he didnt wanna pay me much." Bob paused and pulled out a crumpled wad of one-dollar bills. "He gimme fifteen dollahs . . ."

"Is tha *all* he give yuh?"

"Ever penny, so hep me Gawd! N tha ol stingy white ape didnt wanna gimme tha, neither. Lawd, ol man Bowman hada pila dough on im big ernuff t choka cow! Ah swear t Gawd Ah never wanted t rob a man so much in all mah life . . ."

"Don yuh go thinkin sin, Bob!" said Grannie. "Wes got ernuff trouble here now widout yuh thinkin sin!"

Bob looked at her.

"Its a boat!" cried Peewee, running from the front door.

Mann stood fingering the bills.

"But how yuh git tha boat, Bob?" he asked.

"Is it our boat?" Peewee asked.

"Hush, Peewee!" Grannie said.

"Don worry! Yuhll git a chance t ride in tha boat, Pee-wee," said Bob. He laughed and caught Peewee up in his arms. He looked around, then dropped into a chair. "When Ah lef Bowmans place Ah caughta ride downtown in a motorboat wid Brother Hall. Ah went everwheres, lookin high n low fer a boat. Some wanted forty dollahs. Some fifty. Ah met one man whut wanted a hundred. Ah couldnt buy a boat nowheres, so Ah ups n steals a boat when nobody wuz lookin . . ."

"Yuh *stole* the boat?" asked Mann.

"There wouldnt be no boat out there now ef Ah hadnt."

"Son, yuh a fool t go stealin them white folks boats in times like these," said Grannie.

Bob slapped his thigh and laughed.

"Awright, Ma. Ahll take the boat back. Hows tha? Wan me t take it back?"

Grannie turned away.

"Ah ain gonna ride in it," she said.

"Awright. Stay here n drown in the watah," said Bob.

Mann sighed.

"Bob, Ah sho wished yuh hadnt stole it."

"Aw," said Bob with an impatient wave of his hand. "Whut yuh so scared fer? Ain nobody gonna see yuh wid it. All yuh gotta do is git in n make fer the hills n make fer em quick. Ef Ah hadnt stole tha boat yuh all woulda had t stay here till the watah washed yuh erway . . ." He pushed Peewee off his knee and looked up seriously. "How Lulu?"

"She poly," said Sister Jeff.

Grannie came forward.

"Whutcha gonna do, Mann? Yuh gonna take Lulu in the boat Bob done stole? Yuh know them white folks is gonna be lookin fer tha boat. Sistah James boy got killed in a flood jus like this . . ."

"She cant stay here in the fix she in," said Mann.

"Is Ah goin, Pa?" asked Peewee.

"Shut up fo Ah slaps yuh!" said Grannie.

"Whutcha gonna do, Brother Mann?" asked Sister Jeff.

Mann hesitated.

"Wrap her up," he said. "Ahma row her over t the Red Cross Hospital . . ."

Bob stood up.

"Red Cross Hospital? Ah thought yuh said yuh wuz gonna make fer the hills?"

"We gotta git Lulu t a doctah," said Mann.

"Yuh mean t take her in the boat Ah *stole*?"

"There ain nothin else t do."

Bob scratched his head.

"Mann, Ahm mighty scared yuhll git in trouble takin tha boat thu town. Ah stole tha boat from the Pos Office. Its ol man Heartfiels, n yuh know how he hates niggers. Everbody knows his boat when they see it; its white n yuh couldnt git erway wid it. N lissen, theres trouble a-startin in town, too. Tha levees still over-flowin in the Noth, n theys spectin the one by the cement plant t go any minute. They done put ever nigger they could fin on the levee by the railroad, pilin san n cement bags. They drivin em like slaves. Ah heard they done killed two-three awready whut tried t run erway. N ef anything happened t yuh, yuh just couldnt git erway, cause two mo bridges done washed erway this mawnin n ain no trains runnin. Things awful bad there in town. A lotta them white folks done took down wid typhoid, n tha Red Cross is vaxinatin everbody, black n white. Everwhere Ah looked wuznt nothin but white men wid guns. They wuz a-waiting fer the soljers when Ah lef, n yuh know whut tha means . . ."

Bob's voice died away and they could hear Lulu groaning in the front room.

"Is yuh gonna take her, Brother Mann?" asked Sister Jeff.

"There ain nothin else t do," said Mann. "Ahll try t take tha boat back t the white folks aftah Ah git Lulu t the hospital. But Ah sho wish yuh hadnt stole tha boat, Bob. But we gotta use it now. Ah don like t rile them white folks . . ."

"Ah ain goin in tha boat!" said Grannie. "Ah ain goin outta here t meet mah death today!"

"Stay here n drown, then!" said Mann. "Ahm takin Lulu t the hospital!"

Grannie cried and went into the front room. Sister Jeff followed.

"Pa, is Ah goin?" asked Peewee.

"Yeah. Git yo cloes. N tell Grannie t git hers ef she don wanna stay here, cause Ahm gittin ready t leave!"

Bob was restless. He pursed his lips and looked at the floor.

"Yuh gotta hard job, rowin tha boat from here t the hospital. Yuhll be rowin ergin the current ever inch, n wid a boat full itll be the Devil t pay. The watahs twelve foot deep n flowin strong n tricky."

"There ain nothin else t do," sighed Mann.

"Yuh bettah take something wid yuh. Tha ain nobodys plaything there in town."

"Ahma take mah gun," said Mann. "But Ahm sho sorry yuh had t steal them white folks boat . . ."

Like a far away echo a voice floated over the water.

"Brother Mann! Yuh there, Brother Mann!"

"Thas Elder Murray," said Bob.

Mann opened the door. It was pitch black outside. A tall man was standing in a rowboat, his hand holding onto a rope by the steps.

"Tha yuh, Brother Mann?"

"How yuh, Elder?"

"Yuh all ain gone yit?"

"We jus fixin t go. Won't yuh come up?"

"Jus fer a minute."

Murray came up the steps and stood in the doorway, rubbing his hands.

"How Sistah Lulu?"

"We aimin t take her t the Red Cross . . ."

"Yuh mean t say she ain had tha baby *yit*?"

"She too little t have it widout a doctah, Elder."

"Lawd, have mercy! Kin Ah see her?"

Mann led the way into Lulu's room where a smoking pine-knot made shadows blink on the walls. Bob, Peewee, Sister Jeff, Grannie, Murray and Mann stood about the bed. Lulu lay on top of the bed-covers, wrapped in a heavy quilt. Her hair was disordered and her face was wet. Her breath came fast.

"How yuh feelin, Sistah Lulu?" asked Murray.

Lulu looked at him weakly. She was a small woman with large shining eyes. Her arms were stretched out at her sides and her hands clutched the quilt.

"How yuh feelin?" asked Murray again.

"She awful weak," said Grannie.

Murray turned to Mann.

"Lissen, yuh bettah be mighty careful takin tha boat thu town. Them white folks is makin trouble n that currents strong."

Mann turned from the bed to the dresser, eased his pistol out of the top drawer and slipped it into his pocket.

"Pa, whuts that?" asked Peewee.

"Hush!" said Mann.

"Brothers n Sistahs, les all kneel n pray," said Murray.

They all got to their knees. Lulu groaned. For a split second a blue sheet of lightning lit up the room, then a hard clap of thunder seemed to rock the earth. No one spoke until the last rumble had rolled away.

"Lawd Gawd Awmighty in Heaven, wes a-bowin befo Yuh once ergin, humble in Yo sight, a-pleadin fer fergiveness n mercy! Hear us today, Lawd! Hear us today ef Yuh ain never heard us befo! We needs Yuh now t hep us n guide us! N hep these po folks, Lawd! Deys Yo chillun! Yuh made em n Yuh made em in Yo own image! Open up their hearts n hep em t have faith in Yo word! N hep this po woman, Lawd! Ease her labor, fer Yuh said, Lawd, she has t bring foth her chillun in pain . . ."

Mann closed his eyes and rested his hands on his hips. That slow dull ache had come back to his head. He wished with all his heart that Elder Murray would hurry up and get through with the prayer, for he wanted to be in that boat. He would not feel safe until he was in that boat. It was too bad Bob had to steal it. But there was no help for that now. The quicker wes in tha boat the bettah, he thought. Ef them white folks come by here n take it back well all be jus where we wuz befo. Yeah, Ahma take tha boat back t the white folks aftah Ah git Lulu t the hospital. Oh, yeah! Mabbe the Elderll take *mah* boat n lemme have *his* since hes on his way t the hills? Lawd, yeah! Thall be a good way t dodge them white folks! Ahma ast im . . .

" . . . Lawd, Yuh said call on Yo name n Yuhd answer! Yuh said seek n fin! Today wes callin on Yuh n wes seekin Yuh, Lawd! Yuh said blieve in the blooda Yo son Jesus, n today wes blievin n waitin fer Yuh t hep us! N soften the hard hearts of them white folks there in town, Lawd! Purify their hearts! Fer Yuh said, Lawd, only clean hearts kin come t Yuh fer mercy . . ."

Mann rubbed his eyes and cleared his throat. Naw, he thought, ain no use astin the Elder t take mah boat. Hell wanna know why n then Ahll have t tell im Bob stole it. N the Elder ain gonna hep nobody he thinks ain doin right. Mabbe ef Ah tol ol man Heartfiel jus why Bob stole his boat mabbe he wont hol it ergin me? Yeah, he oughta be glad ef Ah brings im his boat back. N yeah, mabbe the Elder kin take Sistah Jeff n Bob t the hills in his boat? Thad hep a lots . . .

" . . . n save our souls for Jesus sake! Ahmen!"

Murray stood up and began to sing. The others chimed in softly.

Ahm gonna lay down mah sword n shiel
Down by the riverside

Down by the riverside
Down by the riverside
Ahm gonna lay down mah sword n shiel
Down by the riverside
Ah ain gonna study war no mo . . .

Ah ain gonna study war no mo
Ah ain gonna study war no mo
Ah ain gonna study war no mo
Ah ain gonna study war no mo
Ah ain gonna study war no mo
Ah ain gonna study war no mo . . .

Murray wiped his mouth with the back of his hand and fumbled with his hat.

"Waal, Brothers n Sistahs. Ahm gittin on t the hills. Mah folks is there awready. Ah gotta boatloada stuff outside, but theres room fer two-three mo ef anybody wanna go."

"Kin yuh take Sistah Jeff n Bob erlong?" asked Mann.

"Sho!"

Grannie was crying; she pulled on her coat and went into the hall. Bob came from the kitchen with a bundle. Mann lifted Lulu in his arms. Murray held the door for him. Peewee followed, holding a ragged teddy bear. Sister Jeff put out the pine-knot. They all paused in the front doorway.

"Bob, yuh bettah go down n steady tha boat," said Mann.

"Lemme go wid yuh!" said Peewee.

"Yuh c mere!" said Grannie, grabbing his arm.

Bob pulled the boat close to the steps. Mann went down sideways, slowly.

"Take it easy, Brother Mann!" called Murray.

Mann stepped into the boat and rested Lulu in the back seat. Bob held her by the shoulders.

"C mon, yuh all!" Mann called to Grannie and Peewee.

They came, stepping gingerly. Murray helped them down.

"Ahll see yuh all at the hills!" he said.

Bob and Sister Jeff got into Murray's boat. Murray was first to shove off.

"Ahm gone, folks! Good-bye n Gawd bless yuh!"

"Good-bye!"

Mann grasped the oars, wet the handles to prevent creaking, dipped, pulled, and the boat glided outward, over the
darkening flood.

II

To all sides of Mann the flood rustled, gurgled, droned,
glistening blackly like an ocean of bubbling oil. Above his
head the sky was streaked with faint grey light. The air was
warm, humid, blowing in fitful gusts. All around he was
ringed in by walls of solid darkness. He knew that houses and
trees were hidden by those walls and he knew he had to be
careful. As he rowed he could feel the force of the current
tugging at his left. With each sweep of the oars he weighed
the bulk of the boat in his back, his neck, his shoulders. And
fear flowed under everything. Lawd, ef only tha ol levee don
break! An oak tree loomed ghostily, its leaves whispering. He
remembered it had stood at the fork of a road. His mind
weaved about the clue of the tree a quick image of cornfield
in sunshine. He would have to turn here at a sharp angle and
make for the railroad. With one oar resting, he turned by
paddling with the other. The boat struck the current full, and
spun. He bent to with the oars, straining, sweeping hard,
feeling that now he must fight. He would have to keep the
boat moving at a steady pace if he wanted to row in a straight
line. And the strokes of the oars would have to be timed, not
a second apart. He bent to, lifting the oars; he leaned back,
dipping them; then he pulled with tight fingers, feeling the
glide of the boat over the water in darkness. Lawd, ef only tha
ol levee don break!

He began to look for the cotton-seed mill that stood to the
left of the railroad. He peered, longing to see black stack-
pipes. They were along here somewhere. Mabbe Ah done
passed it? He turned to the right, bending low, looking. Then
he twisted about and squinted his eyes. He stopped the boat;
the oars dangled. He felt a sudden swerve that tilted him.

"Peewee, keep still!" Grannie whispered.

Lulu groaned. Mann felt wild panic. Quickly he retraced in
his mind the route over which he thought he had come, and
wondered what could be on the ground, what landmarks the

water hid. He looked again, to the right, to the left, and over his shoulder. Then he looked straight upward. Two tall, black stack-pipes loomed seemingly a foot from his eyes. Ah wuznt lookin high ernuff, he thought. Westward would be houses. And straight down would be Pikes' Road. That would be the shortest way.

"Pa, is we there?" asked Peewee.

"Hush!"

He rowed from the stack-pipes, rowed with the houses in his mind, yearning for something to come out of the darkness to match an inner vision. Every six or seven strokes he twisted around to look. The current became stiff and the darkness thickened. For awhile he had the feeling that the boat was not moving. He set his heels, bent to as far as he could go, and made his sweeps with the oars as long as his arms could reach. His back was getting tired. His fingers burned; he paused a second and dipped them into the cold black water. That helped some. But there was only darkness ahead of him each time he turned to look for the houses on Pikes' Road. He wondered if he were on the *wrong* side of the mill! Mabbe Ahm headin the wrong way? He could not tell. And with each yard forward the current grew stiffer. He thought of the levee. Suddenly the boat swerved and spun. He caught his breath and plied the oars, losing all sense of direction. Is tha ol levee done broke? He heard Grannie cry: "Mann!" The boat leaped: his head hit something: stars danced in the darkness: the boat crashed with a bang: he clung to the oars, one was loose: but the other was jammed and would not move. The boat was still save for a hollow banging against a wall he could not see. He dropped the oars and groped his hands ahead in the darkness. Wood. Ridged wood. Is these them houses? He sensed that he was drifting backwards and clutched with his fingers, wincing from the sharp entry of splinters. Then he grabbed something round, cold, smooth, wet . . . It was wood. He clung tightly and stopped the boat. He could feel the tugging and trembling of the current vibrating through his body as his heart gave soft, steady throbs. He breathed hard, trying to build in his mind something familiar around the cold, wet, smooth pieces of wood. A series of pictures flashed through his mind, but none fitted. He groped higher, thinking with his fingers. Then suddenly he saw the whole street: sunshine, wagons and buggies tied to a water trough. This is old man Toms sto. And these were the railings that went around the front porch he was holding in his hands. Pikes' Road was around the house, in front of him. He thought a moment before picking up the oars, wondering if he could make it in that wild current.

"Whuts the mattah, Mann?" Grannie asked.

"Its awright," he said.

He wanted to reassure them, but he did not know what to say. Instead he grabbed the oars and placed one of them against an invisible wall. He set himself, flexed his body, and gave a shove that sent the boat spinning into the middle of the current. He righted it, striving to keep away from the houses, seeking for the street. He strained his eyes till they ached; but all he could see were dark bulks threatening on either side. Yet, that was enough to steer him clear of them. And he rowed, giving his strength to the right oar and then to the left, trying to keep in the middle.

"Look, Pa!"

"Whut?"

"Hush, Peewee!" said Grannie.

"Theres lights, see?"

"Where?"

"See? Right there, over yonder!"

Mann looked, his chin over his shoulder. There were two squares of dim, yellow light. For a moment Mann was puzzled. He plied the oars and steadied the boat. Those lights seemed *too* high up. He could not associate them. But they were on Pikes' Road and they seemed about a hundred yards away. Wondah whut kin tha be? Maybe he could get some help there. He rowed again, his back to the lights; but their soft, yellow glow was in his mind. They helped him, those lights. For awhile he rowed without effort. Where there were lights there were people, and where there were people there was help. Wondah whose house is tha? Is they white folks? Fear dimmed the lights for a moment; but he rowed on and they glowed again, their soft sheen helping him to sweep the oars.

"Pa, cant we go there?"

"Hush, Peewee!"

The closer the lights came the lower they were. His mind groped frantically in the past, sought for other times on Pikes' Road and for other nights to tell him who lived where those yellow lights gleamed. But the lights remained alone, and the past would tell him nothing. Mabbe they kin phone t town n git a boat t come n git Lulu? Mabbe she kin res some there. The lights were close now. Square yellow lights framed in darkness. They were windows. He steered for the lights, feeling hunger, fatigue, thirst. The dull ache came back to his head: the oars were heavy, almost too heavy to hold: the boat glided beneath the windows: he looked up, sighing.

"Is this the hospital, Pa?" asked Peewee.

"We goin in there, Mann?" asked Grannie.

"Ahma call," said Mann.

He cupped his hands to his mouth.

"Hello!"

He waited and looked at the windows; he heard the droning water swallow his voice.

"Hello!" he hollered again.

A window went up with a rasping noise. A white face came into the light. Lawd! Its a white man . . .

"Whos there?"

"Mann!"

"Who?"

"Mann! Mah wifes sick! Shes in birth! Ahm takin her t the hospital! Yuh gotta phone in there?"

"Wait a minute!"

The window was empty. There was silence; he waited, his face turned upward. He plied the oars and steadied the boat in the swift current. Again a white face came through. A pencil of light shot out into the darkness; a spot of yellow caught the boat. He blinked, blinded.

"Yuh gotta phone there, Mistah?" he called again, dodging the glare of the flash-light.

Silence.

"Mah wifes sick! Yuh gotta phone!"

A voice came, cold, angry.

"Nigger, where you steal that boat?"

The window became filled with white faces. Mann saw a white woman with red hair. He fumbled for the oars in fear. He blinked his eyes as the light jumped to and fro over his face.

"Where you steal that boat, nigger! Thats *my* boat!"

Then Mann heard softer voices.

"Thats our boat, Father! Its *white!*"

"Thats our boat, Henry! Thats *our* boat . . ."

"Dont you hear me, nigger! Bring that boat back here!"

There were two pistol shots. Grannie screamed. Mann swept the oars blindly; the boat spun. Lawd, thas Heartfiel! N hes gotta gun! Mann felt the water rocking him away.

"Nigger, dont you take that boat! Ill kill you!"

He heard two more shots: loudly the boat banged against wood: he was thrown flat on his back. He jerked up and tried to keep the yellow windows in sight. For a moment he thought the windows were dark, but only the flash-light had gone out. He held his breath and felt the boat skidding along a wall, shaking with the current. Then it was still: it seemed it had become wedged between two walls: he touched a solid bulk and tried to shove away: the boat lurched: a shower of cold water sprayed him: the boat became wedged again: he looked for the windows: a third square of light burst out: he watched a white man with a hard, red face come out onto a narrow second-story porch and stand framed in a light-flooded doorway. The man was wearing a white shirt and was playing the yellow flare over the black water. In his right hand a gun gleamed. The man walked slowly down an outside stairway and stopped, crouching, at the water's edge. A throaty voice bawled:

"Nigger, bring that boat here! You *nigger!*"

Mann held still, frozen. He stared at the gun in the white man's hand. A cold lump forced its way up out of his stomach into his throat. He saw the disc of yellow sweep over the side of a house. The white man stooped, aimed and shot. He thinks Ahm over there! Lawd! Mann's mouth hung open and his lips dried as he breathed.

"You sonofabitch! Bring my boat here!"

"Mann!" Grannie whispered.

Mann fumbled in his pocket for his gun and held it ready.

His hand trembled. He watched the yellow disc jump fitfully over the black water some fifty feet from him. It zig-zagged, pausing for instants only, searching every inch of the water. As it crept closer Mann raised his gun. The flare flickered to and fro. His throat tightened and he aimed. Then the flare hovered some five feet from him. He fired, twice. The white man fell backwards on the steps and slipped with an abrupt splash into the water. The flash-light went with him, its one eye swooping downward, leaving a sudden darkness. There was a scream. Mann dropped the gun into the bottom of the boat, grabbed the oars, threw his weight desperately, shoved out from the wall and paddled against the current.

"Henry! Henry!"

Mann rowed: he heard Grannie crying: he felt weak from fear: he had a choking impulse to stop: he felt he was lost because he had shot a white man: he felt there was no use in his rowing any longer: but the current fought the boat and he fought back with the oars.

"Henry! Henry!"

It was a woman's voice, pleading; then a younger voice, shrill, adolescent, insistent.

"The nigger killed im! The nigger killed father!"

Mann rowed on into the darkness, over the black water. He could not see the lights now; he was on the other side of the building. But the screams came clearly.

"Stop, nigger! *Stop!* You killed my father! You bastard! You nigger!"

"Henry! Henry!"

Mann heard Grannie and Peewee crying. But their weeping came to him from a long way off, as though it were as far away as the voices that were screaming. It was difficult for him to get his breath as he bent on the left oar, then the right, keeping the boat in the middle of the bulks of darkness. Then all at once he was limp, nerveless; he felt that getting the boat to the hospital now meant nothing. Two voices twined themselves in his ears: Stop, nigger! Stop, nigger! Henry! Henry! They echoed and re-echoed even after he was long out of earshot.

Then suddenly the rowing became a little easier. He was in the clear again, away from the houses. He did not worry about directions now, for he knew exactly where he was. Only one half mile across Barrett's Pasture, and he would strike streets and maybe lights. He rowed on, hearing Grannie's crying and seeing Heartfield coming down the narrow steps with the flash-light and the gun. *But he shot at me fo Ah shot im . . .* Another thought made him drop the oars. *Spose Heartfiels folks phone to town n tel em Ah shot im?* He looked around hopelessly in the darkness. *Lawd, Ah don wanna ride mah folks right inter death!* The boat drifted sideways, shaking with the tug of the current.

"Lulu," Grannie was whispering.

"How Lulu?" Mann asked.

"She sleep, Ah reckon," sighed Grannie.

Naw, Ahm goin on, no mattah whut! He could not turn back now for the hills, not with Lulu in this boat. Not with Lulu in the fix she was in. He gritted his teeth, caught the oars, and rowed. High over his head a plane zoomed; he looked up and saw a triangle of red and green lights winging through the darkness. His fingers were hot and loose, as though all the feeling in his hands had turned into fire. But his body was cool; a listless wind was drying the sweat on him.

"There the lights o town, Mann!" Grannie spoke.

He twisted about. Sure enough, there they were. Shining, barely shining. Dim specks of yellow buried in a mass of blackness. *Lawd only knows whut wes ridin inter . . .* If he could only get Lulu to the hospital, if he could only get Grannie and Peewee safely out of this water, then he would take a chance on getting away. He knew that that was what they would want him to do. He swept the oars, remembering hearing tales of whole black families being killed because some relative had done something wrong.

A quick, blue fork of lightning lit up the waste of desolate and tumbling waters. Then thunder exploded, loud and long, like the sound of a mountain falling. It began to rain. A sudden, sharp rain. Water trickled down the back of his neck. He felt Grannie moving; she was covering Lulu with her coat. He rowed faster, peering into the rain, wanting to reach safety before the boat caught too much water. Another fifty yards or so and he would be among the houses. *Yeah, ef they ast me erbout Heartfiel Ahma tell em the truth . . .* But he knew he did not want to do that. He knew that that would not help him. But what else was there for him to do? Yes, he would have to tell the truth and trust God. Nobody but God could see him through this. Bob shouldna stole this boat . . . But here Ah am in it now . . . He sighed, rowing. N this rain! Tha ol levee might go wid this rain . . . Lawd, have mercy! He lowered his chin and determined not to think. He would have to trust God and keep on and go through with it, that was all. His feet and clothes were wet. The current stiffened and brought the boat almost to a standstill. Yeah, he thought, theres Rose Street. He headed the boat between two rows of houses.

"Halt! Who goes there?"

He pulled the oars. A glare of light shot from a second-story porch and made him blink. Two white soldiers in khaki uniforms leaned over the bannisters. Their faces were like square blocks of red and he could see the dull glint of steel on the tips of their rifles. Well, he would know now. Mabbe they done foun out erbout Heartfiel?

"Where you going, nigger?"

"Ahm takin mah wife t the hospital, suh. Shes in birth, suh!"

"What?"

"Mah wifes in birth, suh! Ahm takin her t the Red Cross!"

"Pull up to the steps!"

"Yessuh!"

He turned the boat and paddled toward steps that led down to the water. The two soldiers loomed over him.

"Whats your name?"

"Mann, suh."

"You got a pass?"

"Nawsuh."

"Don't you know youre violating curfew?"

"Nawsuh."

"What was all that shooting back there a little while ago?"

"Ah don know, suh."

"Didnt you hear it?"

"Nawsuh."

"Frisk im, Mac," said one of the soldiers.

"O.K. Stand up, nigger!"

One of the soldiers patted Mann's hips. *Lawd, Ah hope they don see tha gun in the boat . . .*

"Hes awright."

"What you say your name was?"

"Mann, suh."

"Where you from?"

"The South En, suh."

"I mean where you bring that boat from?"

"The South En, suh."

"You *rowed* here?"

"Yessuh."

"In *that* boat?"

"Yessuh."

The soldiers looked at each other.

"You aint lying, are you, nigger?"

"Oh, nawsuh," said Mann.

"What wrong with your woman?"

"She's in birth, suh."

One of the soldiers laughed.

"Well, Ill be Goddamned! Nigger, you take the prize! I always heard that a niggerd do anything, but I never thought anybody was fool enough to row a boat against that current . . ."

"But Mistah, mah wifes sick! She been sick fo days!"

"O.K. Stay here. Ill phone for a boat to take you in."

"Yessuh."

One of the soldiers ran up the steps and the other hooked Mann's boat to a rope.

"Nigger, you dont know how lucky you are," he said. "Six men were drowned today trying to make it to town in rowboats. And here you come, rowing *three* people . . ."

The soldier who had gone to telephone came back.

"Mistah, please!" said Mann. "Kin Ah take mah wife in there, outta the rain?"

The soldier shook his head.

"Im sorry, boy. Orders is that nobody but soldiers can be in these houses. Youll have to wait for the boat. Its just around the corner; it wont be long. But I dont see how in hell you rowed that boat between those houses without drowning! It mustve been tough, hunh?"

"Yessuh."

Mann saw a motorboat swing around a curve, its head-light sweeping a wide arc, its motor yammering. It glided up swiftly in a churn of foam. It was manned by two soldiers whose slickers gleamed with rain.

"Whats the rush?"

"Boy," said one of the soldiers, "I got a nigger here who beat everybody. He rowed in from the South End, against the current. Can you beat that?"

The soldiers in the boat looked at Mann.

"Says you!" said one, with a scornful wave of his white palm.

"Im telling the truth!" said the soldier. "Didn't you, boy?"

"Yessuh."

"Well, what you want us to do about it? Give im a medal?"

"Naw; his bitch is sick. Having a picaninny. Shoot em over to the Red Cross Hospital."

The soldiers in the boat looked at Mann again.

"They crowded out over there, boy . . ."

"Lawd, have mercy!" Grannie cried, holding Lulu's head on her lap.

"Mistah, please! Mah wife cant las much longer like this," said Mann.

"Awright! Hitch your boat, nigger, and lets ride!"

Mann grabbed the rope that was thrown at him and looped it to a hook on the end of his boat. He was standing when one of the soldiers yelled:

"Watch yourself, nigger!"

The motor roared and the boat shot forward; he fell back against Grannie, Lulu and Peewee. He straightened just as they made the turn. His boat leaned, scooping water, wetting him; then it righted itself. The rest of the drive was straight ahead, into darkness. He had hardly wiped the water out of his eyes before they slowed to a stop. His fingers groped nervously in the bottom of the boat for the gun; he found it and slipped it into his pocket.

"Awright, nigger, unload!"

He stood up and fronted a row of wide steps.

"Is this the hospital, suh?"

"Yeah; straight up!"

He lifted Lulu and stepped out. Grannie followed, leading Peewee by the hand. When he reached the top of the steps the door was opened by another white soldier.

"Where you going?"

"Ah got mah wife, suh. She sick . . ."

"Straight on to the back, till you see the sign."

"Yessuh."

He walked down a dim-lit hall. Grannie and Peewee shuffled behind. He smelled the warm scent of ether and disinfectant and it made him dizzy. Finally, he saw the sign:

FOR COLORED

He pushed open a door with his shoulder and stood blinking in a blaze of bright lights. A white nurse came.

"What you want?"

"Please, Mam . . . Mah wife . . . She sick!"

The nurse threw back the quilt and felt Lulu's pulse. She looked searchingly at Mann, then turned quickly, calling:

"Doctor Burrows!"

A white doctor came. He looked at Lulu's face. Her eyes were closed and her mouth was open.

"Bring her here, to the table," said the doctor.

Mann stretched Lulu out. Her face, her hair, and her clothes were soaking wet. Her left arm fell from the table and hung limp. The doctor bent over and pushed back the lids of her eyes.

"This your woman?"

"Yessuh."

"How long was she in birth?"

"Bout fo days, suh."

"Why didnt you bring her sooner?"

"Ah didnt hava boat n the watah had me trapped, suh."

The doctor lifted his eyes, rubbed his chin, and looked at Mann quizzically.

"Well, boy, shes dead."

"Suh?"

Grannie screamed and grabbed Peewee. The doctor straightened and laid the stethoscope on a white, marble-topped table. Lightning flicked through the room and thunder rolled rumblingly away, leaving a silence filled with the drone of hard, driving rain.

"*Suh!*" said Mann.

III

"Well, boy, its all over," said the doctor. "Maybe if you could have gotten her here a little sooner we could have saved her. The baby, anyway. But its all over now, and the best thing for you to do is get your folks to the hills."

Mann stared at the thin, black face; at the wet clothes; at the arm hanging still and limp. His lips moved, but he could not speak. Two more white nurses and another white doctor came and stood. Grannie ran to the table.

"Lulu!"

"Its awright, Aunty," said the doctor, pulling her away.

Grannie sank to the floor, her head on her knees.

"Lawd . . ."

Mann stood like stone now. Lulu dead? He seemed not to see the white doctors and nurses gathering around, looking at him. He sighed and the lids of his eyes drooped half-way down over the pupils.

"Poor nigger," said a white nurse.

Blankly, Mann stared at her. He wet his lips and swallowed. Something pressed against his knee and he looked down. Peewee was clinging to him, his little black face tense with fear. He caught Peewee by the hand, went over to the wall and stood above Grannie, hesitating. His fingers touched her shoulders.

"Awright," said the doctor. "Roll her out."

Mann turned and saw two white nurses rolling Lulu through a door. His throat tightened. Grannie struggled up and tried to follow the body. Mann pulled her back and she dropped to the floor again, crying.

"Its awright, Grannie," said Mann.

"You got a boat, boy?" asked the doctor.

"Yessuh," said Mann.

"Youre lucky. You ought to start out right now for the hills, before that current gets stronger."

"Yessuh."

Again Mann looked at Grannie and twice his hands moved toward her and stopped. It seemed that he wanted ever so much to say something, to do something, but he did not know what.

"C mon, Grannie," he said.

She did not move. A white nurse giggled, nervously. Mann stood squeezing his blistered palms, taking out of the intense pain a sort of consolation, a sort of forgetfulness. A clock began to tick. He could hear Grannie's breath catching softly in her throat; he could hear the doctors and nurses breathing; and beyond the walls of the room was the beat of sweeping rain. Somewhere a bell tolled, faint and far off.

Crash!

Everybody jumped. One of the nurses gave a short scream.

"Whats that?"

"Aw, just a chair fell over. Thats all . . ."

"Oh!"

The doctors looked at the nurses and the nurses looked at the doctors. Then all of them laughed, uneasily. There was another silence. The doctor spoke.

"Is that your mother there, boy?"

"Yessuh. Mah ma-in-law."

"Youll have to get her out of here."

"C mon, Grannie," he said again.

She did not move. He stooped and picked her up.

"C mon, Peewee."

He went through the door and down the hall with Peewee pulling at the tail of his coat.

"Hey, you!"

He stopped. A white soldier came up.

"Where you going?"

"Ahm gittin mah boat t take mah family t the hills . . ."

"Your boat was commandeered. Come over here and wait awhile."

"Comman . . ."

"We were short of boats and the boys had to take yours. But Ill get a motorboat to take you and your family to the hills. Wait right here a minute . . ."

"Yessuh."

He waited with Grannie in his arms. Lawd, they got me

now! They knowed that was Heartfiel's boat! Mabbe they fixin t take me erway? What would they do to a black man who had killed a white man in a flood? He did not know. But whatever it was must be something far more terrible than at other times. He shifted his weight from foot to foot. He was more tired than he could ever remember having been. He saw Lulu lying on the table; he heard the doctor say: Well, boy, shes dead. His eyes burned. Lawd, Ah don care whut they do t me! Ah don care . . .

"Pa, where ma?"

"She gone, Peewee."

"Ain she comin wid us?"

"Naw, Peewee."

"How come, Pa?"

"She gonna stay wid Gawd now, Peewee."

"Awways?"

"Awways, Peewee."

Peewee cried.

"Hush, Peewee! Be a good boy, now! Don cry! Ahm here! N Grannies here . . ."

The white soldier came back with the colonel.

"Is this the nigger?"

"Thats him."

"Was that your rowboat outside?"

Mann hesitated.

"Yessuh, Capm."

"A white boat?"

"Yessuh."

"Are you sure it was yours?"

Mann swallowed and hesitated again.

"Yessuh."

"What was it worth?"

"Ah don know, Capm."

"What did you pay for it?"

"Bout f-fifty dollahs, Ah reckon."

"Here, sign this," said the colonel, extending a piece of paper and a pencil. "We can give you thirty-five dollars as soon as things are straightened out. We had to take your boat. We were short of boats. But Ive phoned for a motorboat to take you and your family to the hills. Youll be safer in that anyway."

"Yessuh."

He sat Grannie on the floor and sighed.

"Is that your mother there?"

"Yessuh. Mah ma-in-law."

"Whats wrong with her?"

"She jus ol, Capm. Her gal jus died n she takes it hard."

"When did she die?"

"Jus now, suh."

"Oh, I see . . . But whats wrong with you? Are you sick?"

"Nawsuh."

"Well, you dont have to go to the hills. Your folksll go on to the hills and you can stay here and help on the levee . . ."

"Capm, please! Ahm tired!"

"This is martial law," said the colonel, turning to the white soldier. "Put this woman and boy into a boat and ship them to the hills. Give this nigger some boots and a raincoat and ship him to the levee!"

The soldier saluted.

"Yessir, Colonel!"

"CAPM, PLEASE! HAVE MERCY ON ME, CAPM!"

The colonel turned on his heels and walked away.

"AHM TIRED! LEMME GO WID MAH FOLKS, PLEASE!"

The soldier glared at Mann.

"Aw, c mon, nigger! What in hells wrong with you? All the rest of the niggers are out there, how come you dont want to go?"

Mann watched the soldier go to the door, open it and look out into the rain.

"Mann!" Grannie whispered.

He leaned to her, his hands on his knees.

"Yuh go on t the levee! Mabbe them Heartfiel folks is out t the hills by now. Git over t where our folks is n mabbe yuh kin git erway . . ."

"C mon!" called the soldier. "Heres your boat!"

"*Here*, Grannie," whispered Mann. He slipped the fifteen dollars he had gotten from Bob into her hands.

"Naw," she said. "*Yuh* keep it!"

"Naw, *take* it!" said Mann. He pushed the money into the pocket of her coat.

"C MON, NIGGER! THIS BOAT CANT WAIT ALL NIGHT FOR YOU!"

He picked Grannie up again and carried her down the steps. Peewee followed, crying. It was raining hard. After he had helped them into the boat he stood on the steps. Lawd, Ah wished Ah could go!

"All set?"

"All set!"

The motor droned and the boat shot out over the water, its spotlight cutting ahead into the rain.

"Good-bye!" Peewee called.

"Good-bye!" Mann was not sure that Peewee had heard and he called again. "Good-bye!"

"C mon, boy! Lets get your boots and raincoat. Youre going to the levee."

"Yessuh."

He followed the soldier into the office.

"Jack, get some hip-boots and a raincoat for this nigger and call for a boat to take him to the levee," the soldier spoke to another soldier sitting behind a desk.

"O.K. Heres some boots. And heres a raincoat."

The first soldier went out. Mann hoisted the boots high on his legs and put on the raincoat.

"Tired, nigger?" asked the soldier.

"Yessuh."

"Well, youve got a hard night ahead of you, and thats no lie."

"Yessuh."

Mann sat down, rested his head against a wall, and closed his eyes. Lawd . . . He heard the soldier talking over the telephone.

"Yeah. Yeah."

"   . . ."

"The Red Cross Hospital."

"   . . ."

"The niggers here now, waiting."

"   . . ."

"O.K."

Mann heard the receiver click.

"The boatll be along any minute," said the soldier. "And

while youre resting, unpack those boxes and lay the stuff on the floor."

"Yessuh."

Mann stood up and shook his head. A sharp pain stabbed at the front of his eyes and would not leave. He went to the back of the room where a pile of wooden boxes was stacked and got a crowbar. He pried open the top of a box and began to pull out raincoats and rubber boots. He worked mechanically, slowly, leaning against boxes, smelling fresh rubber and stale tobacco smoke. He felt the pistol in his pocket and remembered Heartfield. Ah got t git outta here some way. Go where they cant fin me. Lawd, take care Grannie! Take care Peewee, Lawd! Take care Bob! N hep me, Lawd. He thought of Lulu lying stretched out on the marble table with her arm hanging limp. He dropped the bundle of raincoats he was holding and bent over, sobbing.

"Whats the matter, nigger?"

"Ahm tired, Capm! Gawd knows Ahm tired!"

He slipped to the floor.

"What you crying about?"

"Capm, mah wifes dead! *Dead!*"

"Shucks, nigger! You ought to be glad youre not dead in a flood like this," said the soldier.

Mann stared at the blurred boots and raincoats. Naw, Lawd! Ah cant break down now! Theyll know somethings wrong ef Ah keep acting like this . . . Ah cant cry bout Lulu now . . . He wiped tears from his eyes with his fingers.

"Kin Ah have some watah, Capm?"

"Theres no water anywhere. You hungry?"

He was not hungry, but he wanted to reassure the soldier.

"Yessuh."

"Heres a sandwich you can have."

"Thank yuh, suh."

He took the sandwich and bit it. The dry bread balled in his mouth. He chewed and tried to wet it. Ef only that ol soljerd quit lookin at me . . . He swallowed and the hard lump went down slowly, choking him.

"Thatll make you feel better," said the soldier.

"Yessuh."

The door swung in.

"Awright, boy! Heres your boat! Lets go!"

"Yessuh."

He put the sandwich in his pocket and followed the soldier to the steps.

"Is this the nigger?"

"Yeah!"

"O.K. Pile in, boy!"

He got in; the boat turned; rain whipped his face. He bent low, holding onto the sides of the boat as it sped through water. He closed his eyes and again saw Heartfield come out on the narrow porch and down the steps. He heard again the two shots of his gun. But he shot at me fo Ah shot im! Then again he saw Lulu lying on the table with her arm hanging limp. Then he heard Peewee calling. Goodbye! Hate welled up in him; he saw the two soldiers in the front seat. Their heads were bent low. They might fin out any minute now . . . His gun nestled close to his thigh. Spose Ah shot em n took the boat? Naw! Naw! It would be better to wait till he got to the levee. He would know somebody there. And they would help him. He knew they would. N them white folks might be too busy botherin wid tha levee t think erbout jus one po black man . . . Mabbe Ah kin slip thu . . .

The boat slowed. Ahead loomed the dark stack-pipe of the cement plant. Above his head a hundred spot-lights etched a wide fan of yellow against the rain. As the boat swerved through a gate entrance and pulled to a platform, he saw lights and soldiers, heard voices calling. Black men stood on the edges of the platforms and loaded bags of sand and cement into boats. Long lines of boats were running to and fro between the levee and the cement plant. He felt giddy; the boat rocked. Soldiers yelled commands. An officer stepped forward and bawled:

"You get im!"

"Yeah!"

"O.K.! We got another one here! C mon, boy, hop in!"

A black boy moved forward.

"Mistah, kin Ah hava drinka watah?" asked the boy.

"Hell, naw! Theres no water anywhere! Get in the boat!"

"Yessuh."

Mann moved over to make room. He felt better already. He was with his people now. Maybe he could get away yet. He heard the officer talking to the soldiers.

"Hows things?"

"Pretty bad!"

"Hows it going?"

"Still overflowing from the North!"

"You think itll hold?"

"Im scared it wont!"

"Any cracks yet?"

"Shes cracking in two places!"

One of the soldiers whistled.

"Awright, let her go!"

"O.K.!"

The boat started out, churning water.

"Yuh gotta cigarette, Mistah?"

Mann turned and looked at the boy sitting at his side.

"Naw; Ah don smoke."

"Shucks, Ah sho wish theyd lemme handle one of these boats," said the boy.

As they neared the levee Mann could see long, black lines of men weaving snake-fashion about the levee-top. In front of him he could feel the river as though it were a live, cold hand touching his face. The levee was a ridge of dry land between two stretches of black water. The men on the levee-top moved slowly, like dim shadows. They were carrying heavy bags on their shoulders and when they reached a certain point the bags were dumped down. Then they turned around, slowly, with bent backs, going to get more bags. Yellow lanterns swung jerkily, blinking out and then coming back on when someone passed in front of them. At the water's edge men unloaded boats; behind them stood soldiers with rifles. Mann held still, looking; the boat stopped and waited for its turn to dock at the levee.

Suddenly a wild commotion broke out. A siren screamed. On the levee-top the long lines of men merged into one whirling black mass. Shouts rose in a mighty roar. There came a vague, sonorous drone, like the far away buzzing in a sea-shell. Each second it grew louder. Lawd! thought Mann. That levees gone! He saw boats filling with men. There was a thunder-like clatter as their motors started up. The soldiers in the front seat were yelling at each other.

"You better turn around, Jim!"

The boat turned and started back.

"Wait for that boat and see whats happened!"

They slowed and a boat caught up with them.

"Whats happened?"

"The levees gone!"

"Step on it, Jim!"

Mann held his breath; behind him were shouts, and over the shouts was the siren's scream, and under the siren's scream was the loud roar of loosened waters.

IV

The boat shot back. The siren shrieked at needle-pitch, high, thin, shrill, quivering in his ears; and yellow flares turned restlessly in the sky. The boat slowed for the platform. There was a loud clamor and men rushed about. An officer bawled:

"Line up the boats for rescue work!"

"Its risin! Cant yuh *see* it risin?" The boy at Mann's side was nudging him. Mann looked at the water; a series of slow, heaving swells was rocking the boat. He remembered that the water had been some inches below the level of the platform when he had first come; now it was rising above it. As the men worked their boots splashed in the water.

"Who can handle a boat?" the officer asked.

"Ah kin, Mistah!" yelled the boy.

"Get a partner and come on!"

The boy turned to Mann.

"Yuh wanna go?"

Mann hesitated.

"Yeah. Ahll go."

"C mon!"

He climbed out and followed the boy to the end of the platform.

"Where are we sending em, General?" the officer asked.

"Shoot the first twenty to the Red Cross Hospital!"

"O.K.!" said the officer. "Whos the driver here?"

"Ahm the driver!" said the boy.

"Can you really handle a boat?"

"Yessuh!"

"Is he all right?" asked the general.

"Ah works fer Mistah Bridges," said the boy.

"We dont want too many niggers handling these boats," said the general.

"We havent enough drivers," said the officer.

"All right; let him go! Whos next?"

"Yours is the Red Cross Hospital, boy! Get there as fast as you can and get as many people out as you can and take em to the hills, see?"

"Yessuh!"

"You know the way?"

"Yessuh!"

"Whats your name?"

"Brinkley, suh!"

"All right! Get going!"

They ran to a boat and scrambled in. Brinkley fussed over the motor a minute, then raced it.

"All set!"

"O.K.!"

The boat swung out of the wide gate entrance; they were the first to go. They went fast, against the current, fronting the rain. They were back among the houses before Mann realized it. As they neared the hospital Mann wondered about the boy at his side. Would he help him to get away? Could he trust him enough to tell? If he could only stay in the boat until they carried the first load to the hills, he could slip off. He tried to see Brinkley's face, but the rain and darkness would not let him. Behind him the siren still screamed and it seemed that a thousand bells were tolling. Then the boat stopped short; Mann looked around, tense, puzzled.

"This ain the hospital," he said.

"Yeah, tis," said Brinkley.

Then he understood. He had been watching for the steps up which he had carried Lulu. But the water had already covered the steps and was making for the first floor. He looked up. The same white soldier who had let him in before was standing guard.

"C mon in!"

They went in. The hospital was in an uproar. Down the hall a line of soldiers pushed the crowds back, using their rifles long-wise. The colonel came running out; he carried an axe in his hand.

"How many boats are coming?"

"Bout twenty, suh," said Brinkley.

"Are they on the way?"

"Yessuh."

"Theyll have to hurry. That water is rising at the rate of five feet an hour!"

The colonel turned to Mann.

"Come here, boy!"

"Yessuh!"

Mann followed the colonel up a flight of stairs. They stopped in a hall.

"Listen," began the colonel. "I want you . . ."

The lights went out, plunging them in darkness.

"Goddamn!"

Mann could hear the colonel breathing in heavy gasps. Then a circle of yellow light played over a wall. The colonel was standing in front of him with a flash-light.

"Get two of those tables from back there and pile one on top of the other, right here," said the colonel, indicating a spot just left of the stairway.

"Yessuh!"

When the tables were up the colonel gave Mann the axe.

"Get up there and knock a hole through that ceiling!"

"Yessuh!"

He scampered up and fumbled for a hold on the rickety tables. When he was on top the colonel set the beam of the flash-light on the ceiling.

"Work fast, boy! Youve got to cut a hole through there so we can take people out if that water beats the boats!"

"Yessuh!"

He whacked upward; with each blow the axe stuck in the wood; he set his feet wide apart on the tables and jerked downward to pull it out. He forgot everything but that he must cut a hole through this ceiling to save people. Even the memory of Lulu and Heartfield was gone from him. Then the lights came back just as suddenly as they had gone. He knew that that meant that the electric plant at the South End was threatened by water. As he swung the axe he felt sweat breaking out all over his body. He heard the colonel below him, fidgeting. The lights dimmed and flared again.

"Keep tha light on me, Capm!"

"Awright; but hurry!"

He had six planks out of the ceiling now. He used his hands and broke them off; his fingers caught splinters. He heard someone running up the steps. He looked down; a soldier was talking to the colonel.

"Its above the steps, Colonel! Its traveling for the first floor!"

"Any boats here yet?"

"Just three, sir!"

"Order everybody to this floor, and keep them quiet even if you have to shoot!"

"Yessir!"

Mann heard the soldier running down the steps.

"C mon, boy! Get that hole bigger than that! Youve got to cut a hole through that roof yet!"

"Yessuh!"

When the hole was big enough he pushed the axe through and pulled himself into the loft. It was dark and he could hear the rain pounding. Suddenly the siren stopped. He had been hearing it all along and had grown used to it; but now that he could hear it no longer the silence it left in his mind was terrifying.

"Ah need some light up here, Capm!"

"Keep cutting! Ill get somebody to bring the flash-light up!"

The roof was easier to cut than the ceiling. He heard someone climbing up behind him. It was a white soldier with a flash-light.

"Where you want it, boy?"

"Right here, suh!"

Quickly he tore a wide hole: he felt a rush of air: rain came into his face: droning water filled his ears: he climbed onto the roof and looked below. Opposite the hospital a bunch of motorboats danced in the current. He stiffened. There was a loud cracking noise, as of timber breaking. He stretched flat on the roof and clung to the wet shingles. Moving into one of the paths of yellow light was a small house, turning like a spool in the wild waters. Unblinkingly he watched it whirl out of sight. *Mabbe Ah'll never git outta here . . .* More boats were roaring up, rocking. Then he stared at the water rising; he could *see* it rising. Across from him the roofs of one-story houses were barely visible.

"Here, give a lift!"

Mann caught hold of a white hand and helped to pull a soldier through. He heard the colonel hollering.

"All set?"

"Yessuh!"

"Send the boats to the side of the hospital! We are taking em from the roof!"

Boats roared and came slowly to the wall of the hospital.

"Awright! Coming through!"

On all fours Mann helped a white woman struggle through. She was wrapped in sheets and blankets. The soldier whipped the rope around the woman's body, high under her arms. She whimpered. *Lawd, Lulu down there some-where,* Mann thought. *Dead! She gonna be lef here in the flood . . .*

"C mon, nigger, n give me a hand!"

"Yessuh!"

Mann caught hold of the woman and they took her to the edge of the roof. She screamed and pulled back.

"Let her go!"

They shoved her over and eased her down with the rope. She screamed again and hung limp. They took another, tied the rope, and eased her over. One woman's face was bleeding; she had scratched herself climbing through the hole. Mann could hear the soldier's breath coming in short gasps as he worked. When six had been let down a motor roared. A boat, loaded to capacity, crawled slowly away. The water was full of floating things now. Objects swirled past, were sucked out of sight. The second boat was filled. The third. Then the fourth. The fifth. Sixth. When the women and children were gone they began to ease the men over. The work went easier and faster with the men. Mann heard them cursing grimly. Now and then he remembered Lulu and Heartfield and he felt dizzy; but he would urge himself and it would pass.

"How many more, Colonel?" asked a soldier.

"About twelve! You got enough boats?"

"Just enough!"

Mann knew they had gotten them all out safely when he saw the colonel climb through. Brinkley came through last.

"Heres one more boat, without a driver!" a soldier called.

"Thas mah boat!" said Brinkley.

"Then you go next!" said the colonel.

Mann looped one end of the rope around a chimney and tied it. Brinkley caught hold and slid down, monkey-like. The colonel crawled over to Mann and caught his shoulder.

"You did well! I wont forget you! If you get out of this, come and see me, hear?"

"Yessuh!"

"Here, take this!"

Mann felt a piece of wet paper in his fingers. He tried to read it, but it was too dark.

"Thats the address of a woman with two children who called in for help," said the colonel. "If you and that boy think you can save em, then do what you can. If you cant, then try to make it to the hills . . ."

"Yessuh!"

The colonel went down. Mann was alone. For a moment a sense of what he would have to face if he was saved from the flood came to him. Would it not be better to stay here alone like this and go down into the flood with Lulu? Would not that be better than having to answer for killing a white man?

"Yuh comin?" Brinkley called.

Mann fumbled over the roof for the axe, found it, and stuck it in his belt. He put the piece of paper in his pocket, caught hold of the rope, and crawled to the edge. Rain peppered his face as he braced his feet against the walls of the house. He held still for a second and tried to see the boat.

"C mon!"

He slumped into the seat; the boat lurched. He sighed and shed a tension which had gripped him for hours. The boat was sailing against the current.

"Heres somebody callin fer hep," said Mann, holding the piece of paper in front of Brinkley.

"Take the flash-light! Switch it on n lemme see ef Ah kin read it!"

Mann held the flash-light.

"Its Pikes Road!" said Brinkley. "Its the Pos Office! Its Miz Heartfiel . . ."

Mann stared at Brinkley, open-mouthed; the flash-light dropped into the bottom of the boat. His fingers trembled and the wind blew the piece of paper away.

"Heartfiel?"

"Ahma try t make it!" said Brinkley.

The boat slowed, turned; they shot in the opposite direction, with the current. Mann watched the head-light cut a path through the rain. Heartfiel?

V

"Watch it!"

Mann threw his hands before his eyes as though to ward off a blow. Brinkley jerked the boat to the right and shut off the motor. The current swept them backwards. In front the head-light lit a yellow circle of wet wood, showing the side of a house. The house was floating down the middle of the street. The motor raced, the boat turned and sailed down the street, going back over the route they had come. Behind them the house followed, revolving slowly, looming large. They stopped at a telegraph pole and Mann stood up and held the boat steady by clinging to a strand of cable wire that stretched above his head in the dark. All about him the torrent tumbled, droned, surged. Then the spot of light caught the house full; it seemed like a living thing, spinning slowly with a long, indrawn, sucking noise; its doors, its windows, its porch turning to the light and then going into the darkness. It passed. Brinkley swung the boat around and they went back down the street, cautiously this time, keeping in the middle of the current. Something struck. They looked. A chair veered, spinning, and was sucked away. An uprooted tree loomed. They dodged it. They heard noises, but could not tell the direction from which they came. When they reached Barrett's Pasture they went slower. The rain had slackened and they could see better.

"Reckon we kin make it?" asked Brinkley.

"Ah don know," whispered Mann.

They swung a curve and headed for Pikes' Road. Mann thought of Heartfield. He saw the woman with red hair standing in the lighted window. He heard her scream, Thats our boat, Henry! Thats our boat! The boat slowed, swerving for Pikes' Road. Mann had the feeling that he was in a dream. Spose Ah tol the boy? The boat rushed on into the darkness. Ef we take tha woman t the hills Ahm caught! Ahead he saw a box bob up out of water and shoot under again. But mabbe they didn't see me good? He could not be sure of that. The light had been on him a long time while he was under that window. And they knew his name; he had called it out to them, twice. He ought to tell Brinkley. Ahm black like he is. He oughta be willin t hep me fo he would them . . . He tried to look into Brinkley's face; the boy was bent forward, straining his eyes, searching the surface of the black water. Lawd, Ah *got* t tell im! The boat lurched and dodged something. Its mah life ergin theirs! The boat slid on over the water. Mann swallowed; then he felt that there would not be any use in his telling; he had waited too long. Even if he spoke now Brinkley would not turn back; they had come too far. Wild-eyed, he gazed around in the watery darkness, hearing the white boy yell, You nigger! You bastard! Naw, Lawd! *Ah got t tell im!* He leaned forward to speak and touched Brinkley's arm. The boat veered again, dodging an object that spun away. Mann held tense, waiting, looking; the boat slid on over the black water. Then he sighed and wished with all his life that he had thrown that piece of paper away.

"Yuh know the place?" asked Brinkley.

"Ah reckon so," whispered Mann.

Mann looked at the houses, feeling that he did not want to look, but looking anyway. All he could see of the one-story houses were their roofs. There were wide gaps between them; some had washed away. But most of the two-story houses were still standing. Mann craned his neck, looking for Mrs. Heartfield's house, yet dreading to see it.

"Its erlong here somewhere," said Brinkley.

Brinkley turned the boat sideways and let the spot-light play over the fronts of the two-story houses. Mann wanted to tell him to turn around, to go back, to make for the hills. But he looked, his throat tight; he looked, gripping the sides of the boat; he looked for Mrs. Heartfield's house, seeing her hair framed in the lighted window.

"There it is!" yelled Brinkley.

At first Mann did not believe it was Mrs. Heartfield's house. It was dark. And he had been watching for two squares of yellow light, two lighted windows. And now, there it was, all dark. Mabbe they ain there? A hot wish rose in his blood, a wish that they were gone. Just gone anywhere, as long as they were not there to see him. He wished that their white bodies were at the bottom of the black waters. They were now ten feet from the house; the boat slowed.

"Mabbe they ain there," whispered Mann.

"We bettah call," said Brinkley.

Brinkley cupped his hand to his mouth and hollered:

"Miz Heartfiel!"

They waited, listening, looking at the dark, shut windows. Brinkley must have thought that his voice had not carried, for he hollered again:

"Miz Heartfiel!"

"They ain there," whispered Mann.

"Look! Somebody's there! See?" breathed Brinkley. "Look!"

The window was opening; Brinkley centered the spot of light on it; a red head came through. Mann sat with parted lips, looking. He leaned over the side of the boat and waited for Mrs. Heartfield to call, Henry! Henry!

"Miz Heartfiel!" Brinkley called again.

"Can you get us? Can you get us?" she was calling.

"We comin! Wait a . . ."

A deafening noise cut out his voice. It was long, vibrant, like the sound of trees falling in storm. A tide of water swept the boat backwards. Mann heard Mrs. Heartfield scream. He could not see the house now; the spot-light lit a path of swirling black water. Brinkley raced the motor and jerked the boat around, playing the light again on the window. It was empty. There was another scream, but it was muffled.

"The watahs got em!" said Brinkley.

Again the boat headed into the middle of the current. The light was on the empty window. The house was moving down the street. Mann held his breath, feeling himself suspended over a black void. The house reached the center of the street and turned violently. It floated away from them, amid a sucking rush of water and the sound of splitting timber. It floundered; it shook in a trembling grip; then it whirled sharply to the left and crashed, jamming itself between two smaller houses. Mann heard the motor race; he was gliding slowly over the water, going toward the house.

"Yuh reckon yuh kin make it? Reckon we kin save em?" asked Brinkley.

Mann did not answer. Again they were ten feet from the house. The current speeding between the cracks emitted a thunderous roar. The outside walls tilted at an angle of thirty degrees. Brinkley carried the boat directly under the window and held it steady by clinging to a piece of jutting timber. Mann sat frozen, staring: in his mind he saw Mrs. Heartfield: something tickled his throat: he saw her red hair: he saw her white face: then he heard Brinkley speaking:

"Ahll hol the boat! Try t git in the windah!"

As though he were outside of himself watching himself, Mann felt himself stand up. He saw his hands reaching for the window ledge.

"Kin yuh make it? Here . . . Take the flash-light!"

Mann put the flash-light in his pocket and reached again. He could not make it. He tip-toed, standing on the top of the boat, hearing the rush of water below. His legs trembled; he stretched his arms higher.

"Kin yuh make it?"

"Naw . . ."

He rested a moment, looking at the window, wondering how he could reach it. Then he took the axe from his belt and thrust it into the window; he twisted the handle sideways and jerked. The blade caught. He leaned his weight against it. It held. He pulled up into the window and sat poised for a moment on his toes. He eased his feet to the floor. He stood a second in the droning darkness and something traveled over the entire surface of his body; it was cold, like the touch of wet feathers. He brought out the flash-light and focused it on the floor. He tried to call out Mrs. Heartfield's name, but could not. He swept the light: he saw a broken chair: a crumpled rug: strewn clothing: a smashed dresser: a tumbled bed: then a circle of red hair and a white face. Mrs. Heartfield sat against a wall, her arms about her two children. Her eyes were closed. Her little girl's head lay on her lap. Her little boy sat at her side on the floor, blinking in the light.

"Take my mother!" he whimpered.

The voice startled Mann; he stiffened. It was the same voice that had yelled, You nigger! You bastard! The same wild fear he had known when he was in the boat rowing against the current caught him. He wanted to run from the room and tell Brinkley that he could find no one; he wanted to leave them here for the black waters to swallow.

"Take my mother! Take my mother!"

Mann saw the boy's fingers fumbling; a match flared. The boy's eyes grew big. His jaw moved up and down. The flame flickered out.

"Its the nigger! Its the nigger!" the boy screamed.

Mann gripped the axe. He crouched, staring at the boy, holding the axe stiffly in his right fist. Something hard began to press against the back of his head and he saw it all in a flash while staring at the white boy and hearing him scream, "Its the nigger!" Yes, now, if he could swing that axe they would never tell on him and the black waters of the flood would cover them forever and he could tell Brinkley he had not been able to find them and the whites would never know he had killed a white man . . . His body grew taut with indecision. Yes, now, he would swing that axe and they would never tell and he had his gun and if Brinkley found out he would point the gun at Brinkley's head. He saw himself in the boat with Brinkley; he saw himself pointing the gun at Brinkley's head; he saw himself in the boat going away; he saw himself in the boat, alone, going away . . . His muscles flexed and the axe was over his head and he heard the white boy screaming, "Its the nigger! Its the nigger!" Then he felt himself being lifted violently up and swung around as though by gravity of the earth itself and flung face downward into black space. A loud commotion filled his ears: his body rolled over and over and he saw the flash-light for an instant, its one eye whirling: then he lay flat, stunned: he turned over, pulled to his knees, dazed, surprised, shocked. He crawled to the flash-light and picked it up with numbed fingers. A voice whispered over and over in his ears, Ah gotta git outta here . . . He sensed he was at an incline. He swayed to his feet and held onto a wall. He heard the sound of rushing water. He swept the spot of yellow. Mrs. Heartfield was lying face downward in a V-trough to his right, where the floor joined the wall at a slant. The boy was crawling in the dark, whimpering "Mother! Mother!" Mann saw the axe, but seemed not to realize that he had been about to use it. He knew what had happened now; the house had tilted, had tilted in the rushing black water. He saw himself as he had stood a moment before, saw himself standing with the axe raised high over Mrs. Heartfield and her two children . . .

"Yuh fin em? Say, yuh fin em?"

Mann flinched, jerking his head around, trembling. Brinkley was calling. A chill went over Mann. He turned the spot on the window and saw a black face and beyond the face a path of light shooting out over the water. *Naw . . . Naw . . .* He could not kill now; he could not kill if someone were looking. He stood as though turned to steel. Then he sighed, heavily, as though giving up his last breath, as though giving up the world.

Brinkley was clinging to the window, still calling:

"C mon! Bring em out! The boats at the windah! C mon, Ah kin hep t take em out!"

Like a sleepwalker, Mann moved over to the white boy and grabbed his arm. The boy shrank and screamed:

"Leave me alone, you nigger!"

Mann stood over him, his shoulders slumped, his lips moving.

"Git in the boat," he mumbled.

The boy stared; then he seemed to understand.

"Get my mother . . ."

Like a little child, Mann obeyed and dragged Mrs. Heartfield to the window. He saw white hands helping.

"Get my sister!"

He brought the little girl next. Then the boy went. Mann climbed through last.

He was again in the boat, beside Brinkley. Mrs. Heartfield and her two children were in the back. The little girl was crying, sleepily. The boat rocked. Mann looked at the house; it was slanting down to the water; the window through which he had just crawled was about a foot from the level of the rushing current. The motor raced, but the roar came to him from a long ways off, from out of a deep silence, from out of a time long gone by. The boat slid over the water and he was in it; but it was a far away boat, and it was someone else sitting in that boat; not he. He saw the light plunging ahead into the darkness and felt the lurch of the boat as it plowed through water. But none of it really touched him; he was beyond it all now; it simply passed in front of his eyes like silent, moving shadows; like dim figures in a sick dream. He felt nothing; he sat, looking and seeing nothing.

"Yuh hardly made it," said Brinkley.

He looked at Brinkley as though surprised to see someone at his side.

"Ah thought yuh wuz gone when tha ol house went over," said Brinkley.

The boat was in the clear now, speeding against the current. It had stopped raining.

"Its gittin daylight," said Brinkley.

The darkness was thinning to a light haze.

"Mother? Mother . . ."

"Hush!" whispered Mrs. Heartfield.

Yes, Mann knew they were behind him. He felt them all over his body, and especially like something hard and cold weighing on top of his head; weighing so heavily that it seemed to blot out everything but one hard, tight thought: They got me now . . .

"Theres the hills!" said Brinkley.

Green slopes lay before him in the blurred dawn. The boat sped on and he saw jagged outlines of tents. Smoke drifted upward. Soldiers moved. Out of the depths of his tired body a prayer rose up in him, a silent prayer. Lawd, save me now! Save me now . . .

VI

It was broad daylight. The boat had stopped. The motor had stopped. And when Mann could no longer feel the lurch or hear the drone he grew hysterically tense.

"Waal, wes here," said Brinkley.

With fear Mann saw the soldiers running down the slopes. He felt the people in the seat behind him, felt their eyes on his back, his head. He knew that the white boy back there was hating him to death for having killed his father. He knew the white boy was waiting to scream, "You nigger! You bastard!" The soldiers closed in. Mann grabbed the side of the boat; Brinkley was climbing out.

"C mon," said Brinkley.

Mann stood up, swaying a little. They got me now, he thought. He stumbled on dry land. He took a step and a twig snapped. He looked around and tried to fight off a feeling of unreality. Mrs. Heartfield was crying.

"Here, take this blanket, Mrs. Heartfield," said one of the soldiers.

Mann walked right past them, waiting as he walked to hear the word that would make him stop. The landscape lay before his eyes with a surprising and fateful solidity. It was like a picture which might break. He walked on in blind faith. He reached level ground and went on past white people who stared sullenly. He wanted to look around, but could not turn his head. His body seemed encased in a tight vise, in a narrow black coffin that moved with him as he moved. He wondered if the white boy was telling the soldiers now. He was glad when he reached the tents. At least the tents would keep them from seeing him.

"Hey, you! Halt, there!"

He caught his breath, turning slowly. A white soldier walked toward him with a rifle. Lawd, this is it . . .

"Awright, you can take off that stuff now!"

"Suh?"

"You can take off that stuff, I say!"

"Suh? Suh?"

"Take off those boots and that raincoat, Goddammit!"

"Yessuh."

He pulled off the raincoat. He was trembling. He pushed the boots as far down his legs as they would go; then he stooped on his right knee while he pulled off the left boot, and on his left knee while he pulled off the right.

"Throw em over there in that tent!"

"Yessuh."

He walked on again, feeling the soldier's eyes on his back. Ahead, across a grassy square, were black people, his people. He quickened his pace. Mabbe Ah kin fin Bob. Er Elder Murray . . . Lawd, Ah wondah whuts become of Peewee? N Grannie? He thought of Lulu and his eyes blurred. He elbowed into a crowd of black men gathered around a kitchen tent. He sighed and a weight seemed to go from him. He looked into black faces, looked for hope. He had to get away from here before that white boy had the soldiers running him to the ground. He thought of the white boats he had seen tied down at the water's edge. Lawd, ef Ah kin git inter one of em . . .

"Yuh had some cawfee?"

A small black woman stood in front of him holding a tin cup. He smelt steam curling up from it.

"Yuh had yo cawfee yit?" the woman asked again. "There ain nothin here but cawfee."

"Nom."

"Here."

He took the extended cup and stood watching the steam curl. The woman turned to walk away.

"Mam, yuh seen a man by the name of Bob Cobb?"

"Lawd knows, Mistah. We don know whos here n who ain. Why don yuh ast over t the Red Cross Station? Thas where everybodys signin in at."

No, he could not go to the Red Cross. They would catch him there surely. He walked a few steps, sipping the coffee, watching for white faces over the brim of his cup. Then suddenly he felt confused, as though all that had happened a few hours ago was but a dream. He had no need to be afraid now, had he? Just to imagine that it was all a dream made him feel better. Lawd. Ahm sho tired! He finished the cup and looked over to the tent. Heat was expanding in his stomach. He looked around again. There were no white faces. Black men

stood, eating, talking, Ahma ast some of em t hep me . . .
He went over and extended his cup for another helping. The
black woman stared, her eyes looking beyond him, wide with
fear. He heard her give a short, stifled scream. Then he was
jerked violently from behind; he heard the soft clink of tin as
the cup bounded from his fingers. The back of his head hit
the mud.

"Is this the nigger?"

"Yeah; thats the one! Thats the nigger!"

He was on his back and he looked up into the faces of four
white soldiers. Muzzles of rifles pointed at his chest. The
white boy was standing, pointing into his face.

"Thats the nigger that killed father!"

They caught his arms and yanked him to his feet. Hunched,
he looked up out of the corners of his eyes, his hands shield-
ing his head.

"Get your hands up, nigger!"

He straightened.

"Move on!"

He walked slowly, vaguely, his hands high in the air. Two
of the soldiers were in front of him, leading the way. He felt a
hard prod on his backbone.

"Walk up, nigger, and dont turn rabbit!"

They led him among the tents. He marched, staring
straight, hearing his shoes and the soldiers' shoes sucking in
the mud. And he heard the quick steps of the white boy keeping pace. The black faces he passed were blurred and merged
one into the other. And he heard tense talk, whispers. For a
split second he was there among those blunt and hazy black
faces looking silently and fearfully at the white folks take some
poor black man away. Why don they hep me? Yet he knew
that they would not and could not help him, even as he in
times past had not helped other black men being taken by the
white folks to their death . . . Then he was back among the
soldiers again, feeling the sharp prod of the muzzle on his
backbone. He was led across the grassy square that separated
the white tents from the black. There were only white faces
now. He could hardly breathe.

"Look! They caughta coon!"

"C mon, they gotta nigger!"

He was between the soldiers, being pushed along, stumbling. Each step he took he felt his pistol jostling gently against his thigh. A thought circled round and round in his mind, circled so tightly he could hardly think it! They goin t kill me . . . They goin t kill me . . .

"This way!"

He turned. Behind him were voices; he knew a crowd was gathering. He saw Mrs. Heartfield looking at him; he saw her red hair. The soldiers stopped him in front of her. He looked at the ground.

"Is this the nigger, Mrs. Heartfield?"

"Yes, hes the one."

More white faces gathered around. The crowd blurred and wavered before his eyes. There was a rising mutter of talk. Then he could not move; they were pressing in.

"What did he do?"

"Did he bother a white woman?"

"She says he did something!"

He heard the soldiers protesting.

"Get back now and behave! Get back!"

The crowd closed in tightly; the soldiers stood next to him, between him and the yelling faces. He grabbed a soldier, clinging, surging with the crowd. They were screaming in his ears.

"Lynch im!"

"Kill the black bastard!"

The soldiers struggled.

"Get back! You cant do that!"

"Let us have im!"

He was lifted off his feet in a tight circle of livid faces. A blow came to his mouth. The crowd loosened a bit and he fell to all fours. He felt a dull pain in his thigh and he knew he had been kicked. Out of the corners of his eyes he saw a moving tangle of feet and legs.

"Kill the sonofabitch!"

"GET BACK! GET BACK OR WE WILL SHOOT!"

They were away from him now. Blood dripped from his mouth.

"The general says bring him in his tent!"

He was snatched up and pushed into a tent. Two soldiers

held his arms. A red face behind a table looked at him. He saw Mrs. Heartfield, her boy, her little girl. He heard a clamor of voices.

"Keep those people back from this tent!"

"Yessir!"

It grew quiet. He felt faint and grabbed his knees to keep from falling. The soldiers were shaking him. He felt warm blood splashing on his hands.

"Cant you talk, you black bastard! Cant you talk!"

"Yessuh."

"Whats your name?"

"Mann, suh."

"Whats the charge against this nigger?"

"Looting and murder, General."

"Whom did he kill?"

"Heartfield, the Post Master, sir."

"*Heart*field?"

"Yessir."

"He stole our boat and killed father!" said the boy.

"Do you confess that, nigger?"

"Capm, he shot at me fo Ah shot im! He shot at me . . ."

"He stole our boat!" yelled the boy. "He stole our boat and killed father when he told him to bring it back!"

"Are you sure this is the man?"

"Hes the one, General! His name is Mann and I saw him under our window!"

"When was this?"

"Last night, at the Post Office."

"Who saw this?"

"I did," said Mrs. Heartfield.

"I saw im!" said the boy.

"Ah didnt steal that boat, Capm! Ah swear fo Gawd, Ah didnt!"

"You did! You stole our boat and killed father and left us in the flood . . ."

The boy ran at Mann. The soldiers pulled him back.

"Ralph, come here!" called Mrs. Heartfield.

"Keep still, sonny," said a soldier. "We can handle this!"

"Did you have that boat, nigger?" asked the general.

"Yessuh, but . . ."

"Where did you get it?"

He did not answer.

"What did you do with the boat?"

"The man at the hospital took it. But Ah didnt steal it, Capm . . ."

"Get Colonel Davis!" the general ordered.

"Yessir!"

"Nigger, do you know the meaning of this?"

Mann opened his mouth, but no words came.

"Do you know this means your life?"

"Ah didnt mean t kill im! Ah wuz takin mah wife t the hospital . . ."

"What did you do with the gun?"

Again he did not answer. He had a wild impulse to pull it out and shoot, blindly; to shoot and be killed while shooting. But before he could act a voice stopped him.

"Search im!"

They found the gun and laid it on the table. There was an excited buzz of conversation. He saw white hands pick up the gun and break it. Four cartridges spilled out.

"He shot daddy twice! He shot im twice!" said the boy.

"Did he *bother* you, Mrs. Heartfield?"

"No; not *that* way."

"The little girl?"

"No; but he came back to the house and got us out. Ralph says he had an axe . . ."

"When was *this*?"

"Early this morning."

"What did you go back there for, nigger?"

He did not answer.

"Did he *bother* you *then*, Mrs. Heartfield?"

"He was going to kill us!" said the boy. "He was holding the axe over us and then the house went over in the flood . . ."

There was another buzz of conversation.

"Heres Colonel Davis, General!"

"You know this nigger, Colonel?"

Mann looked at the ground. A soldier knocked his head up.

"He was at the hospital."

"What did he do there?"

"He helped us on the roof."

"Did he have a boat?"

"Yes; but we took it and sent him to the levee. Here, he signed for it . . ."

"What kind of a boat was it?"

"A white rowboat."

"That was *our* boat!" said the boy.

The piece of paper Mann had signed in the hospital was shoved under his eyes.

"Did you sign this, nigger?"

He swallowed and did not answer.

A pen scratched on paper.

"Take im out!"

"White folks, have mercy! Ah didnt mean t kill im! Ah swear fo Awmighty Gawd, Ah didnt . . . He shot at me! Ah wuz takin mah wife t the hospital . . ."

"Take im out!"

He fell to the ground, crying.

"Ah didnt mean t kill im! Ah didnt . . ."

"When shall it be, General?"

"Take im out *now*! Whos next?"

They dragged him from the tent. He rolled in the mud. A soldier kicked him.

"Git up and walk, nigger! You aint dead yet!"

He walked blindly with bent back, his mouth dripping blood, his arms dangling loose. There were four of them and he was walking in between. Tears clogged his eyes. Down the slope to his right was a wobbly sea of brown water stretching away to a trembling sky. And there were boats, white boats, free boats, leaping and jumping like fish. There were boats and they were going to kill him. The sun was shining, pouring showers of yellow into his eyes. Two soldiers floated in front of him, and he heard two walking in back. He was between, walking, and the sun dropped spangles of yellow into his eyes. They goin t kill me! They goin . . . His knees buckled and he went forward on his face. For a moment he seemed not to breathe. Then with each heave of his chest he cried:

"Gawd, don let em kill me! Stop em from killin black folks!"

"Get up and walk, nigger!"

"Ah didnt mean t do it! Ah swear fo Gawd, Ah didnt!"

They jerked him up; he slipped limply to the mud again.

"What we going to do with this black bastard?"

"We will have to carry 'im."

"Ill be Goddamn if *I* carry 'im."

One of them grabbed Mann's right arm and twisted it up the center of his back.

"Gawd!" he screamed. "Gawd, have mercy!"

"You reckon you can walk now, nigger?"

He pulled up and stumbled off, rigid with pain. They were among trees now, going up a slope. Through tears he saw the hazy tents of the soldiers' camp. Lawd, have mercy! Once there and he would be dead. There and then the end. Gawd Awmighty . . .

"Gotta cigarette, Charley?"

"Yeah."

A tiny flame glowed through spangles of yellow sunshine. A smoking match flicked past his eyes and hit waves of green, wet grass. His fear subsided into a cold numbness. Yes, now! Yes, through the trees! Right thu them trees! Gawd! They were going to kill him. Yes, now, he would die! He would die before he would let them kill him. Ahll die fo they kill me! Ahll *die* . . . He ran straight to the right, through the trees, in the direction of the water. He heard a shout.

"You sonofabitch!"

He ran among the trees, over the wet ground, listening as he ran for the crack of rifles. His shoes slipped over waves of green grass. Then came a shot. He heard it hit somewhere. Another sang by his head. He felt he was not running fast enough; he held his breath and ran, ran. He left the hazy trees and ran in the open over waves of green. He veered, hearing rifles cracking. His right knee folded; he fell, rolling over. He scrambled up, limping. His eyes caught a whirling glimpse of brown water and shouting white boats. Then he was hit again, in the shoulder. He was on all fours, crawling to the edge of the slope. Bullets hit his side, his back, his head. He fell, his face buried in the wet, blurred green. He heard the sound of pounding feet growing fainter and felt something hot bubbling in his throat; he coughed and then suddenly he could feel and hear no more.

The soldiers stood above him.

"You shouldntve run, nigger!" said one of the soldiers. "You shouldntve run, Goddammit! You shouldntve run . . ."

One of the soldiers stooped and pushed the butt of his rifle under the body and lifted it over. It rolled heavily down the wet slope and stopped about a foot from the water's edge; one black palm sprawled limply outward and upward, trailing in the brown current . . .

III

Long Black Song

I

Go t sleep, baby
Papas gone t town
Go t sleep, baby
The suns goin down
Go t sleep, baby
Yo candys in the sack
Go t sleep, baby
Papas comin back . . .

OVER AND OVER she crooned, and at each lull of her voice she rocked the wooden cradle with a bare black foot. But the baby squalled louder, its wail drowning out the song. She stopped and stood over the cradle, wondering what was bothering it, if its stomach hurt. She felt the diaper; it was dry. She lifted it up and patted its back. Still it cried, longer and louder. She put it back into the cradle and dangled a string of red beads before its eyes. The little black fingers clawed them away. She bent over, frowning, murmuring: "Whut's the mattah, chile? Yuh wan some watah?" She held a dripping gourd to the black lips, but the baby turned its head and kicked its legs. She stood a moment, perplexed. Whuts wrong wid tha chile? She ain never carried on like this this tima day. She picked it up and went to the open door. "See the sun, baby?" she asked, pointing to a big ball of red dying between the branches of trees. The baby pulled back and strained its round black arms and legs against her stomach and shoulders. She knew it was tired; she could tell by the halting way it opened its mouth to draw in air. She sat on a wooden stool, unbuttoned the front of her dress, brought the baby closer and offered it a black teat. "Don baby wan suppah?" It pulled away and went limp, crying softly, piteously, as though it would never stop. Then it pushed its fingers against her breasts and wailed. Lawd, chile, whut yuh wan? Yo ma cant hep yuh less she knows whut yuh wan. Tears

329

gushed; four white teeth flashed in red gums; the little chest
heaved up and down and round black fingers stretched floorward. Lawd, chile, whuts wrong wid yuh? She stooped
slowly, allowing her body to be guided by the downward tug.
As soon as the little fingers touched the floor the wail quieted
into a broken sniffle. She turned the baby loose and watched
it crawl toward a corner. She followed and saw the little
fingers reach for the tail-end of an old eight-day clock. "Yuh
wan tha ol clock?" She dragged the clock into the center of
the floor. The baby crawled after it, calling, "Ahh!" Then it
raised its hands and beat on top of the clock Bink! Bink!
Bink! "Naw, yuhll hurt yo hans!" She held the baby and
looked around. It cried and struggled. "Wait, baby!" She
fetched a small stick from the top of a rickety dresser. "Here,"
she said, closing the little fingers about it. "Beat wid this,
see?" She heard each blow landing squarely on top of the
clock Bang! Bang! Bang! And with each bang the baby smiled
and said, "Ahh!" Mabbe thall keep yuh quiet erwhile. Mabbe
Ah kin git some res now. She stood in the doorway. Lawd,
tha chiles a pain! She mus be teethin. Er something . . .

She wiped sweat from her forehead with the bottom of her
dress and looked out over the green fields rolling up the hill-
sides. She sighed, fighting a feeling of loneliness. Lawd, its
sho hard t pass the days wid Silas gone. Been mos a week
now since he took the wagon outta here. Hope ain nothin
wrong. He mus be buyin a heapa stuff there in Colwatah t be
stayin all this time. Yes; maybe Silas would remember and
bring that five-yard piece of red calico she wanted. Oh, Lawd!
Ah *hope* he don fergit it!

She saw green fields wrapped in the thickening gloam. It
was as if they had left the earth, those fields, and were floating
slowly skyward. The afterglow lingered, red, dying, somehow
tenderly sad. And far away, in front of her, earth and sky met
in a soft swoon of shadow. A cricket chirped, sharp and
lonely; and it seemed she could hear it chirping long after it
had stopped. Silas oughta c mon soon. Ahm tireda staying
here by mahsef.

Loneliness ached in her. She swallowed, hearing Bang!
Bang! Bang! Tom been gone t war mos a year now. N tha ol
wars over n we ain heard nothin yit. Lawd, don let Tom be

dead! She frowned into the gloom and wondered about that awful war so far away. They said it was over now. Yeah, Gawd had t stop em fo they killed everbody. She felt that merely to go so far away from home was a kind of death in itself. Just to go that far away was to be killed. Nothing good could come from men going miles across the seas to fight. N how come they wanna kill each other? How come they wanna make blood? Killing was not what men ought to do. Shucks! she thought.

She sighed, thinking of Tom, hearing Bang! Bang! Bang! She saw Tom, saw his big black smiling face; her eyes went dreamily blank, drinking in the red afterglow. Yes, God; it could have been Tom instead of Silas who was having her now. Yes; it could have been Tom she was loving. She smiled and asked herself, Lawd, Ah wondah how would it been wid Tom? Against the plush sky she saw a white bright day and a green cornfield and she saw Tom walking in his overalls and she was with Tom and he had his arm about her waist. She remembered how weak she had felt feeling his fingers sinking into the flesh of her hips. Her knees had trembled and she had had a hard time trying to stand up and not just sink right there to the ground. Yes; that was what Tom had wanted her to do. But she had held Tom up and he had held her up; they had held each other up to keep from slipping to the ground there in the green cornfield. Lawd! Her breath went and she passed her tongue over her lips. But that was not as exciting as that winter evening when the grey skies were sleeping and she and Tom were coming home from church down dark Lover's Lane. She felt the tips of her teats tingling and touching the front of her dress as she remembered how he had crushed her against him and hurt her. She had closed her eyes and was smelling the acrid scent of dry October leaves and had gone weak in his arms and had felt she could not breathe any more and had torn away and run, run home. And that sweet ache which had frightened her then was stealing back to her loins now with the silence and the cricket calls and the red afterglow and Bang! Bang! Bang! Lawd, Ah wondah how would it been wid Tom?

She stepped out on the porch and leaned against the wall of the house. Sky sang a red song. Fields whispered a green prayer. And song and prayer were dying in silence and shadow. Never in all her life had she been so much alone as she was now. Days were never so long as these days; and nights were never so empty as these nights. She jerked her head impatiently, hearing Bang! Bang! Bang! Shucks! she thought. When Silas had gone something had ebbed so slowly that at first she had not noticed it. Now she felt all of it as though the feeling had no bottom. She tried to think just how it had happened. Yes; there had been all her life the long hope of white bright days and the deep desire of dark black nights and then Silas had gone. Bang! Bang! Bang! There had been laughter and eating and singing and the long gladness of green cornfields in summer. There had been cooking and sewing and sweeping and the deep dream of sleeping grey skies in winter. Always it had been like that and she had been happy. But no more. The happiness of those days and nights, of those green cornfields and grey skies had started to go from her when Tom had gone to war. His leaving had left an empty black hole in her heart, a black hole that Silas had come in and filled. But not quite. Silas had not quite filled that hole. No; days and nights were not as they were before.

She lifted her chin, listening. She had heard something, a dull throb like she had heard that day Silas had called her outdoors to look at the airplane. Her eyes swept the sky. But there was no plane. Mabbe its behin the house? She stepped into the yard and looked upward through paling light. There were only a few big wet stars trembling in the east. Then she heard the throb again. She turned, looking up and down the road. The throb grew louder, droning; and she heard Bang! Bang! Bang! There! A car! Wondah whuts a car doin comin out here? A black car was winding over a dusty road, coming toward her. Mabbe some white mans bringing Silas home wida loada goods? But, Lawd, Ah *hope* its no trouble! The car stopped in front of the house and a white man got out. Wondah whut he wans? She looked at the car, but could not see Silas. The white man was young; he wore a straw hat and had no coat. He walked toward her with a huge black package under his arm.

"Well, howre yuh today, Aunty?"

"Ahm well. How yuh?"

"Oh, so-so. Its sure hot today, hunh?"

She brushed her hand across her forehead and sighed.

"Yeah; it is kinda warm."

"You busy?"

"Naw, Ah ain doin nothin."

"Ive got something to show you. Can I sit here, on your porch?"

"Ah reckon so. But, Mistah, Ah ain got no money."

"Havent you sold your cotton yet?"

"Silas gone t town wid it now."

"Whens he coming back?"

"Ah don know. Ahm waitin fer im."

She saw the white man take out a handkerchief and mop his face. Bang! Bang! Bang! He turned his head and looked through the open doorway, into the front room.

"Whats all that going on in there?"

She laughed.

"Aw, thas jus Ruth."

"Whats she doing?"

"She beatin tha ol clock."

"Beating a *clock*?"

She laughed again.

"She wouldnt go t sleep so Ah give her tha ol clock t play wid."

The white man got up and went to the front door; he stood a moment looking at the black baby hammering on the clock. Bang! Bang! Bang!

"But why let her tear your clock up?"

"It ain no good."

"You could have it fixed."

"We ain got no money t be fixin no clocks."

"Havent you got a clock?"

"Naw."

"But how do you keep time?"

"We git erlong widout time."

"But how do you know when to get up in the morning?"

"We jus git up, thas all."

"But how do you know what time it is when you get up?"

"We git up wid the sun."

"And at night, how do you tell when its night?"

"It gits dark when the sun goes down."

"Havent you ever had a clock?"

She laughed and turned her face toward the silent fields.

"Mistah, we don need no clock."

"Well, this beats everything! I dont see how in the world anybody can live without time."

"We jus don need no time, Mistah."

The white man laughed and shook his head; she laughed and looked at him. The white man was funny. Jus lika lil boy. Astin how do Ah know when t git up in the mawnin! She laughed again and mused on the baby, hearing Bang! Bang! Bang! She could hear the white man breathing at her side; she felt his eyes on her face. She looked at him; she saw he was looking at her breasts. Hes jus lika lil boy. Acks like he cant understan *nothin*!

"But you need a clock," the white man insisted. "Thats what Im out here for. Im selling clocks and graphophones. The clocks are made right into the graphophones, a nice sort of combination, hunh? You can have music and time all at once. Ill show you . . ."

"Mistah, we don need no clock!"

"You dont have to buy it. It wont cost you anything just to look."

He unpacked the big black box. She saw the strands of his auburn hair glinting in the afterglow. His back bulged against his white shirt as he stooped. He pulled out a square brown graphophone. She bent forward, looking. Lawd, but its pretty! She saw the face of a clock under the horn of the graphophone. The gilt on the corners sparkled. The color in the wood glowed softly. It reminded her of the light she saw sometimes in the baby's eyes. Slowly she slid a finger over a beveled edge; she wanted to take the box into her arms and kiss it.

"Its eight o'clock," he said.

"Yeah?"

"It only costs fifty dollars. And you dont have to pay for it all at once. Just five dollars down and five dollars a month."

She smiled. The white man was just like a little boy. Jus lika chile. She saw him grinding the handle of the box.

"Just listen to this," he said.

There was a sharp, scratching noise; then she moved nervously, her body caught in the ringing coils of music.

When the trumpet of the Lord shall sound . . .

She rose on circling waves of white bright days and dark black nights.

. . . and time shall be no more . . .

Higher and higher she mounted.

And the morning breaks . . .

Earth fell far behind, forgotten.

. . . eternal, bright and fair . . .

Echo after echo sounded.

When the saved of the earth shall gather . . .

Her blood surged like the long gladness of summer.

. . . over on the other shore . . .

Her blood ebbed like the deep dream of sleep in winter.

And when the roll is called up yonder . . .

She gave up, holding her breath.

I'll be there . . .

A lump filled her throat. She leaned her back against a post, trembling, feeling the rise and fall of days and nights, of summer and winter; surging, ebbing, leaping about her, beyond her, far out over the fields to where earth and sky lay folded in darkness. She wanted to lie down and sleep, or else leap up and shout. When the music stopped she felt herself coming back, being let down slowly. She sighed. It was dark now. She looked into the doorway. The baby was sleeping on the floor. Ah gotta git up n put tha chile t bed, she thought.

"Wasnt that pretty?"

"It wuz pretty, awright."

"When do you think your husbands coming back?"

"Ah don know, Mistah."

She went into the room and put the baby into the cradle.

She stood again in the doorway and looked at the shadowy box that had lifted her up and carried her away. Crickets called. The dark sky had swallowed up the earth, and more stars were hanging, clustered, burning. She heard the white man sigh. His face was lost in shadow. She saw him rub his palms over his forehead. Hes jus lika lil boy.

"Id like to see your husband tonight," he said. "Ive got to be in Lilydale at six o'clock in the morning and I wont be back through here soon. I got to pick up my buddy over there and we're heading North."

She smiled into the darkness. He was just like a little boy. A little boy selling clocks.

"Yuh sell them things alla time?" she asked.

"Just for the summer," he said. "I go to school in winter. If I can make enough money out of this Ill go to Chicago to school this fall . . ."

"Whut yuh gonna be?"

"*Be?* What do you mean?"

"Whut yuh goin t school fer?"

"Im studying science."

"Whuts tha?"

"Oh, er . . ." He looked at her. "Its about why things are as they are."

"Why things is as they *is?*"

"Well, its something like that."

"How come yuh wanna study tha?"

"Oh, you wouldnt understand."

She sighed.

"Naw, Ah guess Ah wouldnt."

"Well, I reckon Ill be getting along," said the white man. "Can I have a drink of water?"

"Sho. But we ain got nothin but well-watah, n yuhll have t come n git."

"Thats all right."

She slid off the porch and walked over the ground with bare feet. She heard the shoes of the white man behind her, falling to the earth in soft whispers. It was black dark now. She led him to the well, groped her way, caught the bucket and let it down with a rope; she heard a splash and the bucket grew heavy. She drew it up, pulling against its weight, throwing one hand over the other, feeling the cool wet of the rope on her palms.

"Ah don git watah outta here much," she said, a little out of breath. "Silas gits the watah mos of the time. This buckets too heavy fer me."

"Oh, wait! Ill help!"

His shoulder touched hers. In the darkness she felt his warm hands fumbling for the rope.

"Where is it?"

"Here."

She extended the rope through the darkness. His fingers touched her breasts.

"Oh!"

She said it in spite of herself. He would think she was thinking about that. And he was a white man. She was sorry she had said that.

"Wheres the gourd?" he asked. "Gee, its dark!"

She stepped back and tried to see him.

"Here."

"I cant see!" he said, laughing.

Again she felt his fingers on the tips of her breasts. She backed away, saying nothing this time. She thrust the gourd out from her. Warm fingers met her cold hands. He had the gourd. She heard him drink; it was the faint, soft music of water going down a dry throat, the music of water in a silent night. He sighed and drank again.

"I was thirsty," he said. "I hadnt had any water since noon."

She knew he was standing in front of her; she could not see him, but she felt him. She heard the gourd rest against the wall of the well. She turned, then felt his hands full on her breasts. She struggled back.

"Naw, Mistah!"

"Im not going to hurt you!"

White arms were about her, tightly. She was still. But hes a *white* man. A *white* man. She felt his breath coming hot on her neck and where his hands held her breasts the flesh seemed to knot. She was rigid, poised; she swayed backward, then forward. She caught his shoulders and pushed.

"Naw, naw . . . Mistah, Ah cant do that!"

She jerked away. He caught her hand.

"Please . . ."

"Lemme go!"

She tried to pull her hand out of his and felt his fingers tighten. She pulled harder, and for a moment they were balanced, one against the other. Then he was at her side again, his arms about her.

"I wont hurt you! I wont hurt you . . ."

She leaned backward and tried to dodge his face. Her breasts were full against him; she gasped, feeling the full length of his body. She held her head far to one side; she knew he was seeking her mouth. His hands were on her breasts again. A wave of warm blood swept into her stomach and loins. She felt his lips touching her throat and where he kissed it burned.

"Naw, naw . . ."

Her eyes were full of the wet stars and they blurred, silver and blue. Her knees were loose and she heard her own breathing; she was trying to keep from falling. But hes a *white* man! A *white* man! Naw! Naw! And still she would not let him have her lips; she kept her face away. Her breasts hurt where they were crushed against him and each time she caught her breath she held it and while she held it it seemed that if she would let it go it would kill her. Her knees were pressed hard against his and she clutched the upper parts of his arms, trying to hold on. Her loins ached. She felt her body sliding.

"Gawd . . ."

He helped her up. She could not see the stars now; her eyes were full of the feeling that surged over her body each time she caught her breath. He held her close, breathing into her ear; she straightened, rigidly, feeling that she had to straighten or die. And then her lips felt his and she held her breath and dreaded ever to breathe again for fear of the feeling that would sweep down over her limbs. She held tightly, hearing a mounting tide of blood beating against her throat and temples. Then she gripped him, tore her face away, emptied her lungs in one long despairing gasp and went limp. She felt his hand; she was still, taut, feeling his hand, then his fingers. The muscles in her legs flexed and she bit her lips and pushed her toes deep into the wet dust by the side of the well and tried to wait and tried to wait until she could wait no longer. She whirled away from him and a streak of silver and blue swept across her blood. The wet ground cooled her palms and knee-caps. She stumbled up and ran, blindly, her toes flicking warm, dry dust. Her numbed fingers grabbed at a rusty nail in the post at the porch and she pushed ahead of hands that held her breasts. Her fingers found the door-facing; she moved into the darkened room, her hands before her. She touched the cradle and turned till her knees hit the bed. She went over, face down, her fingers trembling in the crumpled folds of his shirt. She moved and moved again and again, trying to keep ahead of the warm flood of blood that sought to catch her. A liquid metal covered her and she rode on the curve of white bright days and dark black nights and the surge of the long gladness of summer and the ebb of the deep dream of sleep in winter till a high red wave of hotness drowned her in a deluge of silver and blue that boiled her blood and blistered her flesh *bangbangbang* . . .

II

"Yuh bettah go," she said.

She felt him standing by the side of the bed, in the dark. She heard him clear his throat. His belt-buckle tinkled.

"Im leaving that clock and graphophone," he said.

She said nothing. In her mind she saw the box glowing softly, like the light in the baby's eyes. She stretched out her legs and relaxed.

"You can have it for forty instead of fifty. Ill be by early in the morning to see if your husbands in."

She said nothing. She felt the hot skin of her body growing steadily cooler.

"Do you think hell pay ten on it? Hell only owe thirty then."

She pushed her toes deep into the quilt, feeling a night wind blowing through the door. Her palms rested lightly on top of her breasts.

"Do you think hell pay ten on it?"

"Hunh?"

"Hell pay ten, wont he?"

"Ah don know," she whispered.

She heard his shoe hit against a wall; footsteps echoed on the wooden porch. She started nervously when she heard the roar of his car; she followed the throb of the motor till she heard it when she could hear it no more, followed it till she heard it roaring faintly in her ears in the dark and silent room. Her hands moved on her breasts and she was conscious of herself, all over; she felt the weight of her body resting heavily on shucks. She felt the presence of fields lying out there covered with night. She turned over slowly and lay on her stomach, her hands tucked under her. From somewhere came a creaking noise. She sat upright, feeling fear. The wind sighed. Crickets called. She lay down again, hearing shucks rustle. Her eyes looked straight up in the darkness and her blood sogged. She had lain a long time, full of a vast peace, when a far away tinkle made her feel the bed again. The tinkle came through the night; she listened, knowing that soon she would hear the rattle of Silas' wagon. Even then she tried to fight off the sound of Silas' coming, even then she wanted to feel the peace of night filling her again; but the tinkle grew louder and she heard the jangle of a wagon and the quick trot of horses. Thas Silas! She gave up and waited. She heard horses neighing. Out of the window bare feet whispered in the dust, then crossed the porch, echoing in soft booms. She closed her eyes and saw Silas come into the room in his dirty overalls as she had seen him come in a thousand times before.

"Yuh sleep, Sarah?"

She did not answer. Feet walked across the floor and a match scratched. She opened her eyes and saw Silas standing over her with a lighted lamp. His hat was pushed far back on his head and he was laughing.

"Ah reckon yuh thought Ah wuznt never comin back, hunh? Cant yuh wake up? See, Ah got that red cloth yuh wanted . . ." He laughed again and threw the red cloth on the mantel.

"Yuh hongry?" she asked.

"Naw, Ah kin make out till mawnin." Shucks rustled as he sat on the edge of the bed. "Ah got two hundred n fifty fer mah cotton."

"Two hundred n fifty?"

"Nothin different! N guess whut Ah done?"

"Whut?"

"Ah bought ten mo acres o lan. Got em from ol man Burgess. Paid im a hundred n fifty dollahs down. Ahll pay the res next year ef things go erlong awright. Ahma have t git a man t hep me nex spring . . ."

"Yuh mean hire somebody?"

"Sho, hire somebody! Whut yuh think? Ain tha the way the white folks do? Ef yuhs gonna git anywheres yuhs gotta do just like they do." He paused. "Whut yuh been doin since Ah been gone?"

"Nothin. Cookin, cleanin, n . . ."

"How Ruth?"

"She awright." She lifted her head. "Silas, yuh git any lettahs?"

"Naw. But Ah heard Tom wuz in town."

"In *town?*"

She sat straight up.

"Yeah, thas whut the folks wuz sayin at the sto."

"Back from the war?"

"Ah ast erroun t see ef Ah could fin im. But Ah couldnt."

"Lawd, Ah wish hed c mon home."

"Them white folks sho's glad the wars over. But things wuz kinda bad there in town. Everwhere Ah looked wuznt nothin but black n white soljers. N them white folks beat up a black soljer yistiddy. He wuz jus in from France. Wuz still wearin his soljers suit. They claimed he sassed a white woman . . ."

"Who wuz he?"

"Ah don know. Never saw im befo."

"Yuh see An Peel?"

"Naw."

"Silas!" she said reprovingly.

"Aw, Sarah, Ah jus couldnt git out there."

"Whut else yuh bring sides the cloth?"

"Ah got yuh some high-top shoes." He turned and looked at her in the dim light of the lamp. "Woman, ain yuh glad Ah bought yuh some shoes n cloth?" He laughed and lifted his feet to the bed. "Lawd, Sarah, yuhs sho sleepy, ain yuh?"

"Bettah put tha lamp out, Silas . . ."

"Aw . . ." He swung out of the bed and stood still for a moment. She watched him, then turned her face to the wall.

"Whuts that by the windah?" he asked.

She saw him bending over and touching the graphophone with his fingers.

"Thasa graphophone."

"Where yuh git it from?"

"A man lef it here."

"When he bring it?"

"Today."

"But how come he t leave it?"

"He says hell be out here in the mawnin t see ef yuh wans t buy it."

He was on his knees, feeling the wood and looking at the gilt on the edges of the box. He stood up and looked at her.

"Yuh ain never said yuh wanted one of these things."

She said nothing.

"Where wuz the man from?"

"Ah don know."

"He white?"

"Yeah."

He put the lamp back on the mantel. As he lifted the globe to blow out the flame, his hand paused.

"Whos hats this?"

She raised herself and looked. A straw hat lay bottom upwards on the edge of the mantel. Silas picked it up and looked back to the bed, to Sarah.

"Ah guess its the white mans. He must a lef it . . ."

"Whut he doin *in our room?*"

"He wuz talkin t me bout tha graphophone."

She watched him go to the window and stoop again to the box. He picked it up, fumbled with the price-tag and took the box to the light.

"Whut this thing cos?"

"Forty dollahs."

"But its marked fifty here."

"Oh, Ah means he said fifty . . ."

He took a step toward the bed.

"Yuh lyin t me!"

"Silas!"

He heaved the box out of the front door; there was a smashing, tinkling noise as it bounded off the front porch and hit the ground.

"Whut in hell yuh lie t me fer?"

"Yuh broke the box!"

"Ahma break yo Gawddam neck ef yuh don stop lyin t me!"

"Silas, Ah ain lied t yuh!"

"Shut up, Gawddammit! Yuh did!"

He was standing by the bed with the lamp trembling in his hand. She stood on the other side, between the bed and the wall.

"How come yuh tell me tha thing cos *forty* dollahs when it cos *fifty*?"

"Thas whut he tol me."

"How come he take *ten* dollahs off fer yuh?"

"He ain took nothin off fer me, Silas!"

"Yuh lyin t me! N yuh lied t me bout Tom, too!"

She stood with her back to the wall, her lips parted, looking at him silently, steadily. Their eyes held for a moment. Silas looked down, as though he were about to believe her. Then he stiffened.

"Whos this?" he asked, picking up a short yellow pencil from the crumpled quilt.

She said nothing. He started toward her.

"Yuh wan me t take mah raw-hide whip n make yuh talk?"

"Naw, naw, Silas! Yuh wrong! He wuz figgerin wid tha pencil!"

He was silent a moment, his eyes searching her face.

"Gawddam yo black soul t hell, don yuh try lyin t me! Ef yuh start layin wid white men Ahll hoss-whip yuh t a incha yo life. Shos theres a Gawd in Heaven Ah will! From sunup t sundown Ah works mah guts out t pay them white trash bastards whut Ah owe em, n then Ah comes n fins they been in mah house! Ah cant go into their houses, n yuh know Gawddam well Ah cant! They don have no mercy on no black folks; wes just like dirt under their feet! Fer ten years Ah slaves lika dog t git mah farm free, givin ever penny Ah kin t em, n then Ah comes n fins they been in mah house . . ." He was speechless with outrage. "Ef yuh wans t eat at mah table yuhs gonna keep them white trash bastards out, yuh hear? Tha white ape kin come n git tha damn box n Ah ain gonna pay im a cent! He had no bisness leavin it here, n yuh had no bisness lettin im! Ahma tell tha sonofabitch something when he comes out here in the mawnin, so hep me Gawd! Now git back in tha bed!"

She slipped beneath the quilt and lay still, her face turned to the wall. Her heart thumped slowly and heavily. She heard him walk across the floor in his bare feet. She heard the bottom of the lamp as it rested on the mantel. She stiffened when the room darkened. Feet whispered across the floor again. The shucks rustled from Silas' weight as he sat on the edge of the bed. She was still, breathing softly. Silas was mumbling. She felt sorry for him. In the darkness it seemed that she could see the hurt look on his black face. The crow of a rooster came from far away, came so faintly that it seemed she had not heard it. The bed sank and the shucks cried out in dry whispers; she knew Silas had stretched out. She heard him sigh. Then she jumped because he jumped. She could feel the tenseness of his body; she knew he was sitting bolt upright. She felt his hands fumbling jerkily under the quilt. Then the bed heaved amid a wild shout of shucks and Silas' feet hit the floor with a loud boom. She snatched herself to her elbows, straining her eyes in the dark, wondering what was wrong now. Silas was moving about, cursing under his breath.

"Don wake Ruth up!" she whispered.

"Ef yuh say one mo word t me Ahma slap yuh inter a black spasm!"

She grabbed her dress, got up and stood by the bed, the tips of her fingers touching the wall behind her. A match flared in yellow flame; Silas' face was caught in a circle of light. He was looking downward, staring intently at a white wad of cloth balled in his hand. His black cheeks were hard, set; his lips were tightly pursed. She looked closer; she saw that the white cloth was a man's handkerchief. Silas' fingers loosened; she heard the handkerchief hit the floor softly, damply. The match went out.

"Yuh little bitch!"

Her knees gave. Fear oozed from her throat to her stomach.

She moved in the dark toward the door, struggling with the dress, jamming it over her head. She heard the thick skin of Silas' feet swish across the wooden planks.

"Ah got mah raw-hide whip n Ahm takin yuh t the barn!"

She ran on tiptoe to the porch and paused, thinking of the baby. She shrank as something whined through air. A red streak of pain cut across the small of her back and burned its way into her body, deeply.

"Silas!" she screamed.

She grabbed for the post and fell in dust. She screamed again and crawled out of reach.

"Git t the barn, Gawddammit!"

She scrambled up and ran through the dark, hearing the baby cry. Behind her leather thongs hummed and feet whispered swiftly over the dusty ground.

"Cmere, yuh bitch! Cmere, Ah say!"

She ran to the road and stopped. She wanted to go back and get the baby, but she dared not. Not as long as Silas had that whip. She stiffened, feeling that he was near.

"Yuh jus as well c mon back n git yo beatin!"

She ran again, slowing now and then to listen. If she only knew where he was she would slip back into the house and get the baby and walk all the way to Aunt Peel's.

"Yuh ain comin back in mah house till Ah beat yuh!"

She was sorry for the anger she knew he had out there in the field. She had a bewildering impulse to go to him and ask him not to be angry; she wanted to tell him that there was nothing to be angry about; that what she had done did not matter; that she was sorry; that after all she was his wife and still loved him. But there was no way she could do that now; if she went to him he would whip her as she had seen him whip a horse.

"Sarah! Sarah!"

His voice came from far away. Ahm goin git Ruth. Back through dust she sped, going on her toes, holding her breath.

"Saaaarah!"

From far off his voice floated over the fields. She ran into the house and caught the baby in her arms. Again she sped through dust on her toes. She did not stop till she was so far away that his voice sounded like a faint echo falling from the

sky. She looked up; the stars were paling a little. Mus be gittin near mawnin. She walked now, letting her feet sink softly
into the cool dust. The baby was sleeping; she could feel the
little chest swelling against her arm. She looked up again; the
sky was solid black. Its gittin near mawnin. Ahma take Ruth t
An Peels. N mabbe Ahll fin Tom . . . But she could not walk
all that distance in the dark. Not now. Her legs were tired.
For a moment a memory of surge and ebb rose in her blood;
she felt her legs straining, upward. She sighed. Yes, she would
go to the sloping hillside back of the garden and wait until
morning. Then she would slip away. She stopped, listening.
She heard a faint, rattling noise. She imagined Silas' kicking
or throwing the smashed graphophone. Hes mad! Hes sho
mad! Aw, Lawd! . . . She stopped stock still, squeezing the
baby till it whimpered. What would happen when that white
man came out in the morning? She had forgotten him. She
would have to head him off and tell him. Yeah, cause Silas jus
mad ernuff t kill! Lawd, hes mad ernuff t kill!

III

She circled the house widely, climbing a slope, groping her
way, holding the baby high in her arms. After awhile she
stopped and wondered where on the slope she was. She remembered there was an elm tree near the edge; if she could
find it she would know. She groped farther, feeling with her
feet. Ahm gittin los! And she did not want to fall with the
baby. Ahma stop here, she thought. When morning came she
would see the car of the white man from this hill and she
would run down the road and tell him to go back; and then
there would be no killing. Dimly she saw in her mind a
picture of men killing and being killed. White men killed the
black and black men killed the white. White men killed
the black men because they could, and the black men killed
the white men to keep from being killed. And killing was
blood. Lawd, Ah wish Tom wuz here. She shuddered, sat on
the ground and watched the sky for signs of morning. Mabbe
Ah oughta walk on down the road? Naw . . . Her legs were
tired. Again she felt her body straining. Then she saw Silas
holding the white man's handkerchief. She heard it hit the

floor, softly, damply. She was sorry for what she had done.
Silas was as good to her as any black man could be to a black
woman. Most of the black women worked in the fields as
croppers. But Silas had given her her own home, and that was
more than many others had done for their women. Yes, she
knew how Silas felt. Always he had said he was as good as any
white man. He had worked hard and saved his money and
bought a farm so he could grow his own crops like white
men. Silas hates white folks! Lawd, he sho hates em!

The baby whimpered. She unbuttoned her dress and
nursed her in the dark. She looked toward the east. There! A
tinge of grey hovered. It wont be long now. She could see
ghostly outlines of trees. Soon she would see the elm, and
by the elm she would sit till it was light enough to see the
road.

The baby slept. Far off a rooster crowed. Sky deepened.
She rose and walked slowly down a narrow, curving path and
came to the elm tree. Standing on the edge of a slope, she saw
a dark smudge in a sea of shifting shadows. That was her
home. Wondah how come Silas didnt light the lamp? She
shifted the baby from her right hip to her left, sighed, struggled against sleep. She sat on the ground again, caught the
baby close and leaned against the trunk of a tree. Her eye-lids
drooped and it seemed that a hard cold hand caught hold of
her right leg—or was it her left leg? she did not know
which—and began to drag her over a rough litter of shucks
and when she strained to see who it was that was pulling her
no one was in sight but far ahead was darkness and it seemed
that out of the darkness some force came and pulled her like a
magnet and she went sliding along over a rough bed of
screeching shucks and it seemed that a wild fear made her
want to scream but when she opened her mouth to scream
she could not scream and she felt she was coming to a wide
black hole and again she made ready to scream and then it
was too late for she was already over the wide black hole falling falling falling . . .

She awakened with a start and blinked her eyes in the sunshine. She found she was clutching the baby so hard that it
had begun to cry. She got to her feet, trembling from fright
of the dream, remembering Silas and the white man and Silas'

running her out of the house and the white man's coming.
Silas was standing in the front yard; she caught her breath.
Yes, she had to go and head that white man off! Naw! She
could not do that, not with Silas standing there with that
whip in his hand. If she tried to climb any of those slopes he
would see her surely. And Silas would never forgive her for
something like that. If it were anybody but a white man it
would be different.

Then, while standing there on the edge of the slope looking
wonderingly at Silas striking the whip against his overall-
leg—and then, while standing there looking—she froze.
There came from the hills a distant throb. Lawd! The baby
whimpered. She loosened her arms. The throb grew louder,
droning. Hes comin fas! She wanted to run to Silas and beg
him not to bother the white man. But he had that whip in his
hand. She should not have done what she had done last night.
This was all her fault. Lawd, ef anything happens t im its mah
blame . . . Her eyes watched a black car speed over the crest
of a hill. She should have been out there on the road instead
of sleeping here by the tree. But it was too late now. Silas was
standing in the yard; she saw him turn with a nervous jerk
and sit on the edge of the porch. He was holding the whip
stiffly. The car came to a stop. A door swung open. A white
man got out. Thas im! She saw another white man in the
front seat of the car. N thats his buddy . . . The white man
who had gotten out walked over the ground, going to Silas.
They faced each other, the white man standing up and Silas
sitting down; like two toy men they faced each other. She saw
Silas point the whip to the smashed graphophone. The white
man looked down and took a quick step backward. The white
man's shoulders were bent and he shook his head from left to
right. Then Silas got up and they faced each other again; like
two dolls, a white doll and a black doll, they faced each other
in the valley below. The white man pointed his finger into
Silas' face. Then Silas' right arm went up; the whip flashed.
The white man turned, bending, flinging his hands to shield
his head. Silas' arm rose and fell, rose and fell. She saw the
white man crawling in dust, trying to get out of reach. She
screamed when she saw the other white man get out of
the car and run to Silas. Then all three were on the ground,

rolling in dust, grappling for the whip. She clutched the baby and ran. Lawd! Then she stopped, her mouth hanging open. Silas had broken loose and was running toward the house. She knew he was going for his gun.

"Silas!"

Running, she stumbled and fell. The baby rolled in the dust and bawled. She grabbed it up and ran again. The white men were scrambling for their car. She reached level ground, running. Hell be killed! Then again she stopped. Silas was on the front porch, aiming a rifle. One of the white men was climbing into the car. The other was standing, waving his arms, shouting at Silas. She tried to scream, but choked; and she could not scream till she heard a shot ring out.

"Silas!"

One of the white men was on the ground. The other was in the car. Silas was aiming again. The car started, running in a cloud of dust. She fell to her knees and hugged the baby close. She heard another shot, but the car was roaring over the top of the southern hill. Fear was gone now. Down the slope she ran. Silas was standing on the porch, holding his gun and looking at the fleeing car. Then she saw him go to the white man lying in dust and stoop over him. He caught one of the man's legs and dragged the body into the middle of the road. Then he turned and came slowly back to the house. She ran, holding the baby, and fell at his feet.

"Siiilas!"

IV

"Git up, Sarah!"

His voice was hard and cold. She lifted her eyes and saw blurred black feet. She wiped tears away with dusty fingers and pulled up. Something took speech from her and she stood with bowed shoulders. Silas was standing still, mute; the look on his face condemned her. It was as though he had gone far off and had stayed a long time and had come back changed even while she was standing there in the sunshine before him. She wanted to say something, to give herself. She cried.

"Git the chile up, Sarah!"

She lifted the baby and stood waiting for him to speak, to tell her something to change all this. But he said nothing. He walked toward the house. She followed. As she attempted to go in, he blocked the way. She jumped to one side as he threw the red cloth outdoors to the ground. The new shoes came next. Then Silas heaved the baby's cradle. It hit the porch and a rocker splintered; the cradle swayed for a second, then fell to the ground, lifting a cloud of brown dust against the sun. All of her clothes and the baby's clothes were thrown out.

"Silas!"

She cried, seeing blurred objects sailing through the air and hearing them hit softly in the dust.

"Git yo things n go!"

"Silas."

"Ain no use yuh sayin *nothin* now!"

"But theyll kill yuh!"

"There ain nothin Ah kin do. N there ain nothin yuh kin do. Yuh done done too Gawddam much awready. Git yo things n go!"

"Theyll kill yuh, Silas!"

He pushed her off the porch.

"GIT YO THINGS N GO T AN PEELS!"

"Les *both* go, Silas!"

"Ahm stayin here till they come back!"

She grabbed his arm and he slapped her hand away. She dropped to the edge of the porch and sat looking at the ground.

"Go way," she said quietly. "Go way fo they comes. Ah didnt mean no harm . . ."

"Go way fer whut?"

"Theyll *kill* yuh . . ."

"It don make no difference." He looked out over the sun-filled fields. "Fer ten years Ah slaved mah life out t git mah farm free . . ." His voice broke off. His lips moved as though a thousand words were spilling silently out of his mouth, as though he did not have breath enough to give them sound. He looked to the sky, and then back to the dust. "Now, its all gone. *Gone* . . . Ef Ah run erway, Ah ain got nothin. Ef Ah stay n fight, Ah ain got nothin. It don make no difference which way Ah go. Gawd! Gawd, Ah wish alla them white folks wuz dead! *Dead*, Ah tell yuh! Ah wish Gawd would kill em *all*!"

She watched him run a few steps and stop. His throat swelled. He lifted his hands to his face; his fingers trembled. Then he bent to the ground and cried. She touched his shoulders.

"Silas!"

He stood up. She saw he was staring at the white man's body lying in the dust in the middle of the road. She watched him walk over to it. He began to talk to no one in particular; he simply stood over the dead white man and talked out of his life, out of a deep and final sense that now it was all over and nothing could make any difference.

"The white folks ain never gimme a chance! They ain never give no black man a chance! There ain nothin in yo whole life yuh kin keep from em! They take yo lan! They take yo freedom! They take yo women! N then they take yo life!" He turned to her, screaming. "N then Ah gits stabbed in the back by mah own blood! When mah eyes is on the white folks to keep em from killin me, mah own blood trips me up!" He knelt in the dust again and sobbed; after a bit he looked to the sky, his face wet with tears. "Ahm gonna be hard like they is! So hep me, Gawd, Ah'm gonna be *hard*! When they come fer me Ah'm gonna *be* here! N when they git me outta here theys gonna *know* Ahm gone! Ef Gawd lets me live Ahm gonna make em *feel* it!" He stopped and tried to get his breath. "But, Lawd, Ah don wanna be this way! It don mean nothin! Yuh die ef yuh fight! Yuh die ef yuh don fight! Either way yuh die n it don mean nothin . . ."

He was lying flat on the ground, the side of his face deep in dust. Sarah stood nursing the baby with eyes black and stony. Silas pulled up slowly and stood again on the porch.

"Git on t An Peels, Sarah!"

A dull roar came from the south. They both turned. A long streak of brown dust was weaving down the hillside.

"Silas!"

"Go on cross the fiels, Sarah!"

"We kin *both* go! Git the hosses!"

He pushed her off the porch, grabbed her hand, and led

her to the rear of the house, past the well, to where a path led up a slope to the elm tree.

"Silas!"

"Yuh git on fo they ketch yuh too!"

Blind from tears, she went across the swaying fields, stumbling over blurred grass. It ain no use! She knew it was now too late to make him change his mind. The calves of her legs knotted. Suddenly her throat tightened, aching. She stopped, closed her eyes and tried to stem a flood of sorrow that drenched her. Yes, killing of white men by black men and killing of black men by white men went on in spite of the hope of white bright days and the desire of dark black nights and the long gladness of green cornfields in summer and the deep dream of sleeping grey skies in winter. And when killing started it went on, like a red river flowing. Oh, she felt sorry for Silas! Silas . . . He was following that long river of blood. Lawd, how come he wans t stay there like tha? And he did not want to die; she knew he hated dying by the way he talked of it. Yet he followed the old river of blood, knowing that it meant nothing. He followed it, cursing and whimpering. But he followed it. She stared before her at the dry, dusty grass. Somehow, men, black men and white men, land and houses, green cornfields and grey skies, gladness and dreams, were all a part of that which made life good. Yes, somehow, they were linked, like the spokes in a spinning wagon wheel. She felt they were. She knew they were. She felt it when she breathed and knew it when she looked. But she could not say how; she could not put her finger on it and when she thought hard about it it became all mixed up, like milk spilling suddenly. Or else it knotted in her throat and chest in a hard aching lump, like the one she felt now. She touched her face to the baby's face and cried again.

There was a loud blare of auto horns. The growing roar made her turn round. Silas was standing, seemingly unafraid, leaning against a post of the porch. The long line of cars came speeding in clouds of dust. Silas moved toward the door and went in. Sarah ran down the slope a piece, coming again to the elm tree. Her breath was slow and hard. The cars stopped in front of the house. There was a steady drone of motors and drifting clouds of dust. For a moment she could not see what was happening. Then on all sides white men with pistols and rifles swarmed over the fields. She dropped to her knees, unable to take her eyes away, unable it seemed to breathe. A shot rang out. A white man fell, rolling over, face downward.

"Hes gotta gun!"

"Git back!"

"Lay down!"

The white men ran back and crouched behind cars. Three more shots came from the house. She looked, her head and eyes aching. She rested the baby in her lap and shut her eyes. Her knees sank into the dust. More shots came, but it was no use looking now. She knew it all by heart. She could feel it happening even before it happened. There were men killing and being killed. Then she jerked up, being compelled to look.

"Burn the bastard out!"

"Set the sonofabitch on fire!"

"Cook the coon!"

"Smoke im out!"

She saw two white men on all fours creeping past the well. One carried a gun and the other a red tin can. When they reached the back steps the one with the tin can crept under the house and crept out again. Then both rose and ran. Shots. One fell. A yell went up. A yellow tongue of fire licked out from under the back steps.

"Burn the nigger!"

"C mon out, nigger, n git yos!"

She watched from the hill-slope; the back steps blazed. The white men fired a steady stream of bullets. Black smoke spiraled upward in the sunshine. Shots came from the house. The white men crouched out of sight, behind their cars.

"Make up yo mind, nigger!"

"C mon out er burn, yuh black bastard!"

"Yuh think yuhre white now, nigger?"

The shack blazed, flanked on all sides by whirling smoke filled with flying sparks. She heard the distant hiss of flames. White men were crawling on their stomachs. Now and then they stopped, aimed, and fired into the bulging smoke. She looked with a tense numbness; she looked, waiting for Silas to scream, or run out. But the house crackled and blazed, spouting yellow plumes to the blue sky. The white men shot again, sending a hail of bullets into the furious pillars of smoke. And still she could not see Silas running out, or hear his voice calling. Then she jumped, standing. There was a loud crash; the roof caved in. A black chimney loomed amid crumbling wood. Flames roared and black smoke billowed, hiding the house. The white men stood up, no longer afraid. Again she waited for Silas, waited to see him fight his way out, waited to hear his call. Then she breathed a long, slow breath, emptying her lungs. She knew now. Silas had killed as many as he could and had stayed on to burn, had stayed without a murmur. She filled her lungs with a quick gasp as the walls fell in; the house was hidden by eager plumes of red. She turned and ran with the baby in her arms, ran blindly across the fields, crying, "Naw, Gawd!"

IV

Fire and Cloud

I

A NAUGHTS *a naught. . . .*"

As he walked his eyes looked vacantly on the dusty road, and the words rolled without movement from his lips, each syllable floating softly up out of the depths of his body.

"*N fives a figger. . . .*"

He pulled out his pocket handkerchief and mopped his brow without lessening his pace.

"*All fer the white man. . . .*"

He reached the top of the slope and paused, head down.

"*N none fer the nigger. . . .*"

His shoulders shook in half-laugh and half-shudder. He finished mopping his brow and spat, as though to rid himself of some bitter thing. He thought, Thas the way its awways been! Wistfully he turned and looked back at the dim buildings of the town lying sprawled mistily on the crest of a far hill. Seems like the white folks jus erbout owns this whole worl! Looks like they done conquered *everthing*. We black folks is jus los in one big white fog. . . . With his eyes still on the hazy buildings, he flexed his lips slowly and spoke under his breath:

"They could do something! They could do *something*, awright! Mabbe ef five er six thousan of us marched downtown we could *scare* em inter doin something! Lawd knows, mabbe them Reds *is* right!"

He walked again and tucked his handkerchief back into his pocket. He could feel the heat of the evening over all his body, not strongly, but closely and persistently, as though he were holding his face over a tub of steaming suds. Far below him, at the bottom of the valley, lay a cluster of bleak huts with window panes red-lit from dying sunlight. Those huts were as familiar to his eyes as a nest is to the eyes of a bird, for he had lived among them all his life. He knew by sight or sound every black man, woman and child living within those huddled walls. For a moment an array of soft black faces hovered before his eyes. N whut kin Ah tell em? Whut kin Ah say t em? He stopped, looked at the ground and sighed. And then he saw himself as he had stood but a few minutes ago, facing the white woman who sat behind the brown, gleaming desk: her arms had been round, slender, snow-white, like cold marble; her hair had been the color of flowing gold and had glinted in the sunlight; her eyes had been wide and grey behind icily white spectacles. It seemed he could hear her saying in her dry, metallic voice: I'm sorry, Taylor. You'll just have to do the best you can. Explain it to them, make them understand that we cant do anything. Everybodys hongry, and after all, it's no harder on your people than it is on ours. Tell them they'll just have to wait. . . .

He wagged his head and his lips broke in a slow sick smile. Whut she know erbout bein hongry? Whut she know erbout it? He walked again, thinking, Here Ah is a man called by Gawd t preach n whut kin Ah do? Hongry folks lookin t me fer hep n whut kin Ah do? Ah done tried everthing n cant do *nuthin*! Shucks, mabbe Hadley n Greens right? They *might* be right. Gawd knows, they *might* be right.

He lifted his head and saw the wide fields plunging before him, down the hillside. The grass was dark and green. All this! he thought. All *this* n folks hongry! Good Gawd, whuts *wrong*! He saw the road running before him, winding, vanishing, the soft yellow dust filled with the ruts of wagon wheels and tiny threads of auto tires. He threw back his head and spoke out loud:

"The good Lawds gonna clean up this ol worl some day! Hes gonna make a new Heaven n a new Earth! N Hes gonna do it in a eye-twinkle change! Hes gotta do it! Things cant go on like this ferever! Gawd knows they cant!" He pulled off his coat and slung it under his left arm. "Waal, there ain nothin t do but go back n tell em. . . . Tell em the white folks wont let em eat. . . ."

The road curved, descending among the green fields that tumbled to a red sky. This was the land on which the Great God Almighty had first let him see the light of His blessed day. This was the land on which he had first taken unto himself a wife, leaving his mother and father to cleave to her. And it was on the green slopes of these struggling hills that his first-born son, Jimmy, had romped and played, growing to a strong, upright manhood. He wagged his head, musing: Lawd, them wuz the good ol days. . . . There had been plenty to eat; the blessings of God had been overflowing. He had toiled from sunup to sundown, and in the cool of the evenings his wife, May, had taught him to read and write. Then God had spoken to him, a quiet, deep voice coming out of the black night; God had called him to preach His word, to spread it to the four corners of the earth, to save His black people. And he had obeyed God and had built a church on a rock which the very gates of Hell could not prevail against. Yes, he had been like Moses, leading his people out of the wilderness into the Promised Land. He sighed, walking and taking his coat from his left arm and tucking it under his right. Yes, things had been clear-cut then. In those days there had stretched before his eyes a straight and narrow path and he had walked in it, with the help of a Gracious God. On Sundays he had preached God's Word, and on Mondays and Tuesdays and Wednesdays and Thursdays and Fridays and Saturdays he had taken old Bess, his mule, and his plow and had broke God's ground. For a moment while walking through the dust and remembering his hopes of those early years he seemed to feel again the plow handles trembling in his calloused hands and hear the earth cracking and breaking open, black, rich and damp; it seemed he could see old Bess straining forward with the plow, swishing her tail and tossing her head and snorting now and then. Yes, there had been something in those good old days when he had walked be-hind his plow, between the broad green earth and a blue sweep of sunlit sky; there had been in it all a surge of will, clean, full, joyful; the earth was his and he was the earth's; they were one; and it was that joy and will and oneness in him that God had spoken to when He had called him to preach His Word, to save His black people, to lead them, to guide them, to be a shepherd to His flock. But now the whole thing was giving way, crumbling in his hands, right before his eyes. And every time he tried to think of some way out, of some way to stop it, he saw wide grey eyes behind icily white spectacles. He mopped his brow again. Mabbe Hadley n

Greens right. . . . Lawd, Ah don know whut t do! Ef Ah fight fer things the white folk say Ahma bad nigger stirrin up trouble. N ef Ah don do nothin, we starve. . . . But somethings *gotta* be done! Mabbe ef we hada demonstration like Hadley n Green said, we could *scare* them white folks inter doin something. . . .

He looked at the fields again, half-wistfully, half-curiously. Lawd, we could make them ol fiels bloom ergin. We could make em feed us. Thas whut Gawd put em there fer. Plows could break and hoes could chop and hands could pick and arms could carry. . . . On and on that could happen and people could eat and feel as he had felt with the plow handles trembling in his hands, following old Bess, hearing the earth cracking and breaking because he wanted it to crack and break; because he willed it, because the earth was his. And they could sing as he had sung when he and May were first married; sing about picking cotton, fishing, hunting, about sun and rain. They could. . . . But whuts the usa thinkin erbout stuff like this? Its all gone now. . . . And he had to go and tell his congregation, the folks the Great God Almighty had called him to lead to the Promised Land—he had to tell them that the relief would give them no food.

That morning he had sent a committee of ten men and women from his congregation to see the mayor. Wondah how they come out? The mayor tol em something, sho! So fer hes been pretty wid me even ef he is a white man. As his feet sank softly into the dust he saw Mayor Bolton; he saw the red chin that always had a short, black stubble of beard; he saw the cigar glowing red in front of a pink, fat face. But he needs something t scare im now, he thought. Hes been runnin over us too long. . . .

He reached the bottom of the slope, turned into a cinder path, and approached the huts. N Lawd, when Ah do try t do somethin mah own folks wont stan by me, wont stick wid me. Theres ol Deacon Smith a-schemin n a-plottin, jus a-watchin me lika hawk, jus a-waitin fer me t take mah eyes off the groun sos he kin trip me up, sos he kin run t the white folks n tell em Ahm doin somethin wrong! A black snake in the grass! A black Judas! Thas all he is! Lawd, the Devils sho busy in this worl. . . .

He was walking among the crowded huts now.

hello reveren

"How yuh tonight, sonny!" Let ol Deacon Smith tell it, no matter whut Ah *do*, Ahm wrong. . . .

good evenin reveren

"Good evenin, Sistah!" Hes been a-tryin t cheat me outta mah church ever since hes been erroun here. . . .

how yuh tonight reveren taylor

"Jus fine. N how yuh tonight, Brother?" Hes awways a-whisperin berhin mah back, a-tryin t take mah congregation erway from me. . . . N when he ain doin that hes a-tryin his bes t give me wrong advice, jus like the Devil a-tryin t tempt Jesus. But Ahma gonna march on wida hepa Gawd. . . . Yeah, Ah might preach a sermon erbout tha nex Sunday.

As he turned into the street leading to his home and church, he saw a tall brown-skinned boy hurrying towards him. Here comes Jimmy! Ah bet hes lookin fer me. . . . Lawd, Ah hope ain nothin wrong. . . .

II

"Pa!" said Jimmy breathlessly when he was some twenty feet away.

Taylor stopped.

"Whuts the mattah, son?"

Jimmy came close.

"The mayors at home, waitin t see yuh," he whispered.

"The *mayor*?"

"Yeah, n two mo white men. One of em is the Chiefa Police."

"They there *now*?"

"Yeah; in the parlor."

"How long they been there?"

"Bout two-three minutes, Ah reckon. N lissen, Pa . . . Sam wuz by jus now. He say the white folks is ridin up n down the streets in their cars warnin all the black folks t stay off the streets cause theres gonna be trouble. . . ."

"Sam say tha?"

"Thas whut he tol me. N lissen, Pa . . . Ahma git Sam n Pete n Bob n Jack n some mo boys together sos ef anything happens. . . ."

Taylor gripped Jimmy's shoulders.

"Naw, son! Yuh fixin t git us *all* inter trouble now! Yuh cant do nothing like tha! Yuh gotta be careful! Ef them white folks jus *thought* we wuz doin something like that theyd crack down on us! Wed hava riot!"

"But we cant let em ride erroun n talk big n we do nothin!"

"Lissen here, son! Yuh do whut Ah tell yuh t do!" He shook Jimmy's shoulders and his voice was husky. "Yuh go tell them boys t do *nothin* till Ah see em, yuh hear me? Yuh young fools fixin t git us *all* murdered!"

"We jus as waal git killed fightin as t git killed doin nothin," said Jimmy sullenly.

"Yuh go n do whut Ah tol yuh, *hear* me? Ah gotta go n see tha mayor. . . ."

"Hes here t see yuh erbout tha demonstration," said Jimmy.

"How yuh know?"

"Cause thas whut everybodys sayin."

"Who yuh hear say tha?"

"Deacon Smiths spreadin the word."

Taylor winced as though struck by a blow and looked at the dust.

"Hes tellin alla deacons n the church membahs tha the mayors here t stop yuh," said Jimmy. "Hes tellin em yuhs mixed up wid the Reds."

"Deacon Smith there now, *too?*"

"Yeah; hes in the basement wida other deacons. Theys waitin t see yuh."

"How long they been there?"

"Bout hafa hour. N Hadley n Greens in the Bible Room, waitin t talk wid yuh, too. . . ."

Fear gripped Taylor and he stammered:

"Dddid the mmmmayor ssssee em?"

"Naw, ain nobody seen em yit. Ah brought em in thu the back do and tol em t wait fer yuh. Ahm mighty scared wid them Reds waitin fer yuh in the Bible Room and tha Chiefa Police waitin fer yuh in the parlor. Ef ol Deacon Smith knowed tha he sho would make a lotta trouble. . . ."

"Where yo ma?"

"She upstairs, sewin."

"She know whuts happenin?"

"Naw, Pa."

Taylor stood still, barely breathing.

"Whut yuh gonna do, Pa?" asked Jimmy.

"Yuh go n tell them boys not t do nothin wrong, son. Go on n tell em now! Ah got too much on mah hans now widout yuh boys stirrin up mo trouble!"

"Yessuh."

"Yuh bettah go n do it *now*!"

"Yessuh."

He watched Jimmy hurry down the street. Lawd, Ah hope tha boy don go n git inter trouble. . . .

"Yuh do whut Ah tol yuh, Jimmy!" he yelled.

"Yessuh!" Jimmy hollered back.

He saw Jimmy turn a dusty corner, and go out of sight. Hadley n Greens there in the Bible Room n the Chiefa Police is waitin in the parlor! Ah cant let them white folks see them Reds! N ef Deacon Smith tells on me theyll lynch me. . . . Ah gotta git em out of tha church widout em seein each other. . . . Good Gawd, whut a mess!

III

No sooner had he opened the door of his church than he heard a crescendo of voices. They back awready! Tha committees back! Aw, Ah bet the mayor followed em here. . . . He walked down the hall, turned into the church's waiting room, and saw a roomful of black faces.

"Reveren Taylor! The mayor run us out!"

"He put the police on us!"

The black brothers and sisters ran to Taylor and surrounded him.

"The mayor tol us t git out n don come back no mo!"

A thin black woman swung onto Taylor's arm, crying:

"Whut Ahm gonna do? Ah ain gotta mouthful of bread at home!"

"Sistahs n Brothers, jusa minute," said Taylor. "Firs, tell me whut the mayor said. . . ."

"He say he cant do *nothin*! N say fer us not t come back t his office no *mo*! N say ef we do hes gonna put us in jail!"

"In *jail?*" asked Taylor.

"Thas whut he said."

"N he tol us not t march, Reveren. He said ef we demonstrated hed put us *all* in jail."

"Who tol em yuh wuz gonna march?" asked Taylor.

"Ah bet it wuz tha ol Deacon Smith," said Sister Harris.

"The Bible says testify whut yuh see n speak whut yuh know," said Sister Davis to Sister Harris.

"Ah knows whut Ahm talkin erbout!" blazed Sister Harris.

"Sistahs n Brothers, les don start no fuss," said Taylor, sighing and dropping his shoulders.

"Whut they tell yuh at the relief station, Reveren Taylor?" asked Sister James.

"They say they cant do nothin," said Taylor.

The thin black woman came and knelt at Taylor's feet, her face in her hands.

"Reveren Taylor, it ain fer me Ahm astin! Its fer mah chillun! Theys hongry! It ain fer me, its fer them! Gawd, have mercy, theys hongry. . . ."

Taylor stepped back, ran his hand into his pocket and pulled out a palmful of loose coins.

"Here, Sistahs n Brothers, split this up between yuh all. Its ever cent Ah got in this worl, so hep me Gawd!"

He laid the coins on a small table. Brother Booker divided them as far as they would go. Then they swarmed around him again.

"Reveren, whut we gonna do?"

"Cant we make the white folks do something fer us?"

"Ahm tireda bein hongry!"

"Reveren, mah babys sick n Ah cant git her no milk!"

"Reveren, whut kin Ah tell mah wife?"

"Lawd knows, Ahm jus erbout sick of this!"

"Whut kin we do, Reveren?"

Taylor looked at them and was ashamed of his own helplessness and theirs.

"Sistahs n Brothers, les call on the great Gawd who made us n put us in this worl. . . ."

He clasped his hands in front of him, closed his eyes, and bowed his head. The room grew still and silent.

"Lawd Gawd Awmighty, Yuh made the sun n the moon n

the stars n the earth n the seas n mankind n the beasts of the fiels!"

yes jesus

"Yuh made em all, Lawd, n Yuh tol em whut t do!"

yuh made em lawd

"Yuhs strong n powerful n Yo will rules this worl!"

yuh rules it lawd

"Yuh brought the chillun of Israel outta the lan of Egypt!"

yuh sho did

"Yuh made the dry bones rise up outta the valley of death n live!"

yuh made em live lawd

"Yuh saved the Hebrew chillun in the fiery furnace!"

yes jesus

"Yuh stopped the storm n yuh made the sun stan still!"

yuh stopped it lawd

"Yuh knocked down the walls of Jericho n Yuh kept Jona in the belly of the whale!"

yuh kept im lawd

"Yuh let Yo son Jesus walk on watah n Yuh brought Im back from the dead!"

have mercy jesus

"Yuh made the lame walk!"

yuh did it lawd

"Yuh made the blin see!"

hep us now lawd

"Yuh made the deaf hear!"

glory t the mos high

"Lawd, Yuhs a rock in the tima trouble n Yuhs a shelter in the tima storm!"

he is he is

"Lawd, Yuh said Yuhd strike down the wicked men who plagued Yo chillun!"

glory t gawd

"Yuh said Yuhd destroy this ol worl n create a new Heaven n a new Earth!"

wes waitin on yuh jesus

"Lawd, Yuh said call on Yo name n Yuhd answer!"

yuh said it lawd n now wes callin

"Yuh made us n put the breatha life in us!"

yuh did lawd

"Now look down on us, Lawd! Speak t our hearts n let us know whut Yo will is! Speak t us like Yuh spoke t Jacob!"

speak lawd n our souls will be clay in yo hans

"Lawd, ack in us n well obey! Try us, Lawd, try us n watch us move t Yo will! Wes helpless at Yo feet, a-waitin fer Yo sign!"

send it lawd

"The white folks say we cant raise nothin on Yo earth! They done put the lans of the worl in their pockets! They done fenced em off n nailed em down! Theys a-tryin t take Yo place, Lawd!"

speak t em lawd

"Yuh put us in this worl n said we could live in it! Yuh said this worl wuz Yo own! Now show us the sign like Yuh showed Saul! Show us the sign n well ack! We ast this in the name of Yo son Jesus who died tha we might live! Amen!"

amen amen

Taylor stopped and opened his eyes. The room was quiet; he could hear the clock ticking softly above his head, and from the rear came the sound of children playing back of the church. The sisters and brothers rose from their knees and began talking in subdued tones.

"But, Reveren, whut kin we *do?*"

"The issues wid Gawd now, Sistahs n Brothers."

"Is we gonna march?"

"Is yuh goin wid us t the mayor?"

"Have faith, Sistahs n Brothers. Gawd takes care of His own."

"But Ahm hongry, Reveren. . . ."

"Now, Sistahs n Brothers, Ah got t go. Ah got business t tend t. . . ."

He pushed ahead of the black hands that clung to his sleeve.

"Reveren Taylor. . . ."

The thin black woman wailed, kneeling:

"Please, Reveren, cant yuh do *somethin*. . . ."

He pushed through the door, closed it, and stood for a moment with his eyes shut and his fingers slowly loosening on the knob, his ears filled with the sound of wailing voices.

IV

How come all this gotta happen at *once*? Folks a-beggin fer bread n the mayor here t see me n them Reds a-waitin in the Bible Room. . . . Ef Deacon Smith knowed tha hed ruin me sho! Ah cant let the mayor see them Reds. . . . Naw, Gawd! He looked at a door at the far end of the room, then hurried to it and opened it softly.

"May!" he called in a hoarse whisper.

"Hunh?"

"C mere, quick!"

"Whutcha wan, Dan?"

"C mon in the *room*, May!"

She edged through the half-opened door and stood in front of him, wide-eyed.

"Whutcha wan, Dan?"

"Now, lissen. . . ."

"Ain nothin wrong, is it, Dan? Ain nothin happened, is it?" He grabbed her arm.

"Naw, n don git scared!"

"Ah ain scared!"

"Yuh cant do whut Ah wan yuh t do ef yuhs scared!"

"Ah *ain* scared, Dan!"

"Lissen. . . ."

"Yeah?"

"The mayors here, in the parlor. N the Chiefa Police. . . ." She stood stock still and seemed not to breathe.

"The *mayor*?"

"Yeah. . . ."

"*Ain* nothin wrong, is it, Dan?"

"There wont be ef yuh lissen n try t do right."

"Be careful, Dan!"

"Yeah," he said, his voice low and husky. "Go in and tell them white folks Ahm sick, hear?"

She stepped back from him and shook her head.

"Gawd *ain* wid yuh when yuh lie, Dan!"

"We *gotta* lie t white folks! Theys on our necks! They *make* us lie t them! Whut kin we do but lie?"

"*Dan!*"

"Lissen t whut Ahm tellin yuh, May! Tell the mayor Ahm

gittin outta bed t see im. Tell im Ahm dressin, see? Tell im t wait a few minutes."

"Yeah?"

"Then go t the basement n tell Deacon Smith Ahm wid the mayor. Tell im n the other deacons t wait."

"Now?"

"Yeah; but Ah ain thu yit. Yuh know Hadley n Green?"

"Them *Reds*?"

"Yeah. . . ."

"Dan!" said May, her lungs suspiring in one gasp of amazed helplessness.

"May, fer Chrissakes!"

She began to cry.

"Don do nothin wrong, Dan, please! Don fergit Jimmy! Hes jus a young boy n hes gotta grow up in this town wid these white folks. Don go n do nothin n fix it so he wont hava chance. . . . Me n yuh don mattah, but thinka him, Dan, please. . . ."

Taylor swallowed and looked hard at her.

"May, yuh do whut *Ah* tell yuh t do! Ah know whut Ahm doin. Hadley n Greens downstairs, in the Bible Room. Tell em so nobody kin hear yuh, hear?—tell em aftah yuh don tol the others—tell em t come in here. Let em in thu *yo* room. . . ."

"Naw!"

She tried to get through the door. He ran to her and caught her hand again.

"Yuh do whut Ah tell yuh, May!"

"Ah ain gonna have them Reds in *here* wid tha mayor n Chiefa Police out *there*! Ah *ain*!"

"Go on n do whut Ah tell yuh, May!"

"Dan!"

"Go *erhead*, May!"

He pushed her. She went through the door, slowly, looking back at him. When the door was closed he rammed his hands deep into his pants' pockets, turned to the open window, and looked out into the street. It was profoundly quiet, save for the silvery sound of children's voices back of the church. The air was soft, warm, and full of the scent of magnolias and violets. Window panes across the street were blood-red from dying sunlight. A car sped past, lifting a great cloud of yellow-brown dust. He went to the center of the room and stood over a table littered with papers. He cocked his head, listening. He heard a door slam; footsteps echoed and ceased. A big eight-day clock above his head boomed six times; he looked and his eyes strayed up and rested on a gleaming, brass cross. Gawd, hep me now! Jus hep me t go thu wid this! Again he heard a door slam. Lawd, Ah hope May do right now. . . . N Ah hope Jimmy don go n ack a fool. . . . He crossed the floor on tiptoe, opened the door, and peeped into May's room. It was empty. A slender prism of dust-filled sunlight cut across the air. He closed the door, turned, pulled off his coat and threw it across the table. Then he loosened his collar and tie. He went to the window again and leaned with his back against the ledge, watching the door of May's room. He heard a hoarse voice rise and die. Footsteps again sounded and ceased. He frowned, listening. How come its takin May so long? He started when a timid knock came. He hurried to the door and cracked it.

V

"Hello, Reverend Taylor!" said Hadley, a white man.

"How yuh, Brother Hadley?"

"N how yuh, Reveren?" asked Green, a black man.

"Ahm fine, Brother Green. C mon in, yuh all."

Hadley and Green edged through the door.

"Say, whuts alla mystery?" asked Green.

"Ssssh! Don talk so loud," cautioned Taylor. "The mayor n the Chiefa Police is out there."

The Negro and the white man stood stone still.

"Do they know wes here?" asked Green.

"Naw, n don git scared. They done come t see me erbout tha demonstration. . . ."

Hadley and Green looked at each other.

"Pull down tha shade," whispered Green, pointing a shaking, black finger.

Quickly, Hadley moved to one side, out of range of the window. His cheeks flushed pink. Taylor lowered the shade and faced them in the semi-darkness. The eyes of the white man and the black man were upon him steadily.

"Waal?" said Green.

"Ah spose yuh know whuts up," said Taylor.

"Theyre here to scare you," said Hadley.

"Ahm trustin Gawd," sighed Taylor.

"Whut yuh gonna tell em?" asked Green.

"Thas whut Ah wanna see yuh all erbout," said Taylor.

"O.K. Whut kin we do?" asked Green.

Taylor looked around and motioned toward two chairs. "Set down, Brothers."

"Naw, this is awright," said Green, still standing.

"Come on," said Hadley. "What's on your mind?"

Taylor folded his arms and half-sat and half-leaned on the edge of the table.

"Yuh all think wes gonna have many folks out in the mawnin fer the demonstration?"

"Whut yuh mean?" asked Green.

"When Ahm talkin wid the mayor and Chiefa Police Ah wanna know how many folks Ahm talkin fer. There ain no use in us havin a demonstration ef ain but a few of us is gonna be out there. The police will try t kill us then. . . ."

"How many folks we can get out tomorrow depends a great deal on you, Reverend," said Hadley.

"Hows that?" asked Taylor.

"If you had let us use your name on those handbills, we could say five thousand easily. . . ."

Taylor turned sharply to Hadley.

"Lissen, Brother, Ah done tol yuh Ah cant do tha! N there ain no use in us talkin erbout it no mo! Ah done told yuh Ah cant let them white folks know Ahm callin folks t demonstrate. Aftah all, Ahma preacher. . . ."

"Its yo duty, Reveren," said Green. "We owes it our black folks."

"Ahm doin mah duty as Gawd lets me see it," said Taylor.

"All right, Reverend," said Hadley. "Heres what happened: Weve covered the city with fifteen thousand leaflets. Weve contacted every organization we could think of, black and white. In other words, weve done all *we* could. The rest depends on the leaders of each group. If we had their active endorsement, none of us would have to worry about a crowd tomorrow. And if we had a crowd we would not have to worry about the police. If they see the whole town turning out, theyll not start any trouble. Now, youre known. White and black in this town respect you. If you let us send out another leaflet with your name on it calling for. . . ."

Taylor turned from them and drew his hand nervously across his face. Hadley and Green were silent, watching him. Taylor went to the window and pulled back the curtain slightly and peeped out. Without turning he said softly:

"Ah done tol yuh all Ah ain scareda lettin yuh use mah name."

"We don mean *tha*," said Green hastily.

"Ef it wuz jus me who wuz takin the chance," said Taylor, "Ah wouldnt care none. But Gawd knows it ain right fer me to send them po folks out inter the streets in fronta police. Gawd knows, Ah cant do tha!"

"Honest, Reveren," said Green, touching Taylor's arm. "Ah don understan. Yuh done been thu harder things than this befo."

"N Ahll go thu wid em ergin," said Taylor proudly.

"All right!" said Hadley. "You can say the word that can make this thing a success. If you dont and we have no crowd, then youre to blame. . . ."

Taylor's eyes narrowed and when he spoke there was a note of anger in his voice.

"Gawd hep yuh ef yuhs a-tryin t say yuh gonna blame me ef things don go right!"

"Naw, Reveren!" said Green, coming hurriedly forward and spreading his black hands softly upon the air. "Don feel that way! Wes all jus in a jam. We got t do either two things: Call off this demonstration and let the folks stay hongry, er git as many as we kin together n go downtown in the mawnin. Ef we git five thousan down there the police wont bother us. Ef yuh let us send out yo name tellin the black folks. . . ."

"Naw, Brother!" said Taylor emphatically.

"Then the demonstrations going to be smashed," said Hadley. "*You* can stop it! You have the responsibility and the blame!"

Taylor sighed.

"Gawd knows Ah ain t blame. Ahm doin whut mah heart tells me t do. . . ."

"Then whats keeping you from working with us?" asked Hadley. "Im a white man and Im here willing to fight for your peoples rights!"

"Ahm wid yuh, Brother!" said Taylor in a voice which carried a deep note of pleading. "Ahm wid yuh no mattah whut yuh *think*! But yuh *cant* use mah name! Ef them white folks knowed Ah wuz callin mah folks in the streets t demonstrate, they wouldnt never gimme a chance t git something fer mah folks ergin. . . ."

"Thats just it, Reverend," said Hadley. "Dont be afraid of their turning you down because youre fighting for your people. If they knew youd really fight, theyd dislike you; yes? But you can *make* them give something to *all* of your people, not just to *you*. Dont you see, Taylor, youre standing *between* your people and the white folks. You can make them give something to *all* of them. And the poor, hungry white folks will be with you."

"Ah cant lead mah folks t go ergin them white folks like tha," said Taylor. "Thas *war!*"

Hadley came close to Taylor.

"Reverend, cant you see thats just the way the white folks *want* you to feel? Are you leading your folks just because the white folks *say* you should, or are you leading them because you *want* to? Dont you believe in what youre doing? What kind of leaders are black people to have if the white folks pick them and tell them what to do?"

"Brothers, Ahma Christian, n whut yuhs astin fer is something tha makes blood!" thundered Taylor.

Hadley and Green looked at each other.

"Waal, whut yuh gonna tell the mayor?" asked Green.

Taylor stood in the center of the room with his hands in his pockets, looking down at his feet. His voice came low, as though he were talking to himself, trying to convince himself.

"Ahma tell em mah folks is hongry. Ahma tell em they wanna march. Ahma tell em ef they march Ahma march wid em. Ahma tell em they wan bread. . . ."

"Reverend," asked Hadley, "why do you feel that this is so

different from all the other times youve gone straight to the white folks and *demanded* things for your people?"

"It is different!" said Taylor.

"You didnt say that when you saved Scott from that *mob*!"

"Tha wuz different, Brother Hadley."

"I dont see it."

Taylor's voice came low.

"Ah feels differently erbout it, Brothers."

"You saved Scotts life. All right, youre saving the lives of your congregation now. Scott was one man, but there are five hundred starving people in your church."

"We ain facin no mob now, Brother Hadley."

"Then what in Gods name are we facing, Reverend? If those police wholl be out there in the morning with their guns and clubs arent a *legal* mob, then what. . . ."

"Its more than a mob, Brother Hadley."

Hadley and Green shook their heads.

"Ah don understan yuh, Reveren," said Green.

"When Ah saved Scott from tha mob, Ah wuz goin ergin *some* of the white folks. But this thing is going ergin em *all*! This is too much like war!"

"You mean youre going against the ones with *money* now!" said Hadley. "Over three thousand of the poor white folks will be with *us*. . . ."

"But, Brother Hadley, the white folks whos got moneys got *everthing*! This is jus like civil war!"

"Reverend," said Hadley, "cant you see that if they were not afraid they wouldnt be here asking to *talk* with you? Go in and talk with them, speak to them in the name of five thousand hungry people. Tell the mayor and the Chief of Police that if they dont give the relief back we will demonstrate."

"Ah cant do tha, Brothers. Ah cant let these white folks think Ahm leadin mah folks tha way. Ah tol yuh brothers when Ah ergreed t work wid yuh Ahd go as fer as Ah could. Waal, Ah done done tha. Now, yuh here astin me t threaten this whole town n Ah ain gonna do tha!" said Taylor.

"Yuh astin fer bread, Reveren," said Green.

"Its threatenin, Brothers," said Taylor. "N tha ain Gawds way!"

"So youll let your folks starve before youll stand up and talk to those white folks?" asked Hadley.

"Ahm ackin as Gawd gives me the light t see," said Taylor. There was silence. Then Hadley laughed, noiselessly.

"Well," he said. "I didn't know you felt this way, Reverend. I thought we could count on you. You know the Party will stand behind you no matter what happens."

"Ahm sorry, Brother Hadley," said Taylor.

"When kin we see yuh t fin out whut the mayor n Chiefa Police say?" asked Green.

Taylor looked at his watch.

"Its a little aftah six now. Make it half-pas six. Thall gimme time t see the Deacon Board."

Green sighed.

"O.K."

"O.K."

Taylor held the door for them. Then he stood in the center of the room and looked miles through the floor. Lawd, Ah hope Ahm doin right. N they think Ahm scared. . . . He flushed hot with shame and anger. He sat in a chair for a moment, then got right up. He drummed his fingers on the corner of the table. Shucks, Ah jus as waal see them white folks now n git it over wid. Ah knowed this wuz comin up! Ah knowed it! He went through May's room, walking slowly, softly, seeing in his mind the picture of the fat, pink face of Mayor Bolton and the lean, red face of Chief of Police Bruden. As he turned into the narrow hall that led to the parlor he heard children yelling in the playground. He went down a stairway, opened a door, and walked through his hushed, dim-lit church. Pale rose light fell slantwise through stained windows and glinted on mahogany pews. He lifted his eyes and saw the figure of Christ on a huge snow-white cross. Gawd, hep me now! Lemme do the right thing! He followed a red carpet to a door that opened into the parlor. He paused and passed his tongue over his dry lips. He could feel his heart beating. Ahll let them do all the talkin. Ahll jus tell em mah folks is hongry. Thas all Ah kin do. Slowly, he turned the knob, his lips half-parted in dread.

VI

"Why, hello, Dan!"

"Good evenin, Mistah Mayor."

"Howve you been, Dan?"

"Fairly well, wid the hepa Gawd, suh."

Taylor shook hands with a tall, fat white man in a blue serge suit.

"Its been a long time since Ive seen you, Dan."

"Yessuh. It sho has, yo Honah."

"Hows Jimmy?"

"Jus fine, suh."

"Thats a fine boy youve got, Dan."

"Ahm sho glad yuh think so, suh."

"If you raise that boy right he will be a leader of his people some day, Dan."

"Thas the one hope of mah life, suh," said Taylor with deep emotion.

"May was tellin me youre sick," said the mayor.

"Aw, it ain nothin, suh. Jusa summer col, suh."

"I didnt mean to bother you if youre sick, Dan."

"Thas awright, suh. Ahm feelin much bettah now, suh."

"Oh, youll pull through all right; itll take a lot more than a summer cold to kill old war-horses like you and me, eh, Dan?"

The mayor laughed and winked.

"Ahm hopin Gawd spares me a few mo years, suh," said Taylor.

"But at least you look all right now," said the mayor. "Say, Dan, I want you to meet Chief Bruden. This is Dan, Chief, the boy I was telling you about."

"How yuh, Mistah Chief?" asked Taylor.

A black cigar burned red in Bruden's mouth. He shifted his thin body and growled:

"Hello, boy."

"And, Dan, this is Mr. Lowe, head of our fine Industrial Squad."

"How yuh, suh?" asked Taylor.

Lowe nodded with half-closed eyes.

"Sit down, Dan," said the mayor.

"Yessuh."

Taylor sat on the edge of a chair and rested his palms lightly on his knees.

"Maybe our little visit is a surprise, hunh?" asked the mayor.

"Yessuh. It is. But Ahm glad to be of any hep Ah kin, suh."

"Good! I knew youd talk that way. Now, Dan, we want you to help us. Youre a responsible man in this community; thats why we are here."

"Ah tries t do mah duty as Gawd shows it t me, suh."

"Thats the spirit, Dan!" The mayor patted Taylor's knee. "Now, Im going to be perfectly frank with you, Dan." The mayor peeled a wrapper from a black cigar. "Here, have one."

"Thank yuh, suh." Taylor put the cigar into his vest pocket. "Ahll smoke it aftah dinner, suh."

There was a silence during which the three white men looked at Taylor.

"Dan," began the mayor, "its not every nigger Id come to and talk this way. Its not every nigger Id trust as Im about to trust you." The mayor looked straight at Taylor. "Im doing this because Ive faith in you. Ive known you for twenty-five years, Dan. During that time I think Ive played pretty fair with you, havent I?"

Taylor swallowed.

"Ahll have t say yuh have, yo Honah."

"Mister Lowe and the Chief here had another plan," said the mayor. "But I wouldnt hear of it. I told them Id work this thing *my* way. I thought *my* way would be much better. After all, Dan, you and I have worked together in the past and I dont see why we cant work together now. Ive backed you up in a lot of things, Dan. Ive backed you even when other white folks said you were wrong. But I believe in doing the right thing. After all, we are human beings, arent we?"

"Yessuh."

"What Ive done for you in the past Im willing to do again. You remember Scott, dont you?"

"Yessuh. Yuhs been a big hep t me n mah folks, suh."

"Well, Dan, my office is always open to you when you want to see me about any of your problems or the problems of your people," said the mayor.

"N Gawd knows Ah sho thanks yuh, suh!"

The mayor bit off the tip of his cigar and spat it into a brass spittoon.

"I'm not going to beat about the bush, Dan."

The mayor paused again. There was silence. Taylor felt called upon to say something.

"Yessuh. Ah sho preciates tha, suh."

"You know these Goddam Reds are organizing a demonstration for to-morrow, dont you?" asked the mayor.

Taylor licked his lips before he answered.

"Yessuh. Ah done heard a lotta folks talkin erbout it, suh."

"Thats too bad, Dan," said the mayor.

"Folks is talking erbout it everwhere. . . ." began Taylor.

"What *folks*?" interjected Bruden.

"Waal, mos everbody, suh."

Bruden leaned forward and shook his finger in Taylor's face.

"Listen, boy! I want you to get this straight! Reds aint *folks*! Theyre Goddam sonofabitching lousy bastard rats trying to wreck our country, see? Theyre stirring up race hate! Youre old enough to understand that!"

"Hes telling you straight, boy," said Lowe. "And furthermore. . . ."

"Say, whats all this?" demanded the mayor, turning to Lowe and Bruden. "Wait a minute! Whats the big idea of talking to Dan like that? Hes not mixed up in anything like that. Save that kind of talk for bad niggers. . . ."

"The quicker all you niggers get sense enough in your Goddam thick skulls to keep away from them Reds the better off youll be!" said Bruden, ignoring the mayor.

"Aw, c mon," said the mayor. "Dans all right. Aint that right, Dan?"

Taylor looked down and saw at his feet a sharp jutting angle of sunshine falling obliquely through a window. His neck felt hot. This is the show-down, he thought. Theys tryin t trap me. . . . He cleared his throat and looked up slowly and saw the mayor gazing at him with cold grey eyes. He shifted his body slightly and saw the glint of Chief Bruden's police star; he saw Lowe's red lips twisted in half-smile and half-leer.

"Isnt that right, Dan?" the mayor asked again.

"Yessuh. Whut yuh white folks say is right. N Ah ergrees wid yuh. But Ah ain foolin wid nobody thas tryin t stir up race hate; naw, *suh*! Ah ain never done nothin like tha n Ah never will, so hep me Gawd! Now, erbout this demonstration: Yessuh, Ah heard erbout it. Thas all everbodys been talking erbout erroun here fer a week, yo Honah. Waal, suh, Ahll tell yuh. Theys jus hongry. Theys marchin cause they don know whut else t do, n thas the truth from here t Heaven! Mistah Mayor, theys hongry! Jus plain *hongry*! Ah give mah las dime today t a woman wid eight chillun. . . ."

"We know all about that, Dan," said the mayor.

"Everybodys hungry," said Bruden.

"Boy, cant you see we are all in the *same* boat?" asked Lowe.

"Waal. . . ." drawled Taylor.

"Thingsll be straightened out soon, Dan," interjected the mayor soothingly. "We will see that nobody starves."

"Ah beg yo pardon, suh. A man died jus the other day from starvation. . . ."

Taylor's voice died in his throat and he looked at the floor. He knew that he had said too much.

"I reckon that makes you out a liar, don't it?" Bruden asked the mayor.

"Aw, naw, suh!" said Taylor eagerly. "Ah ain disputin nobodys word, suh. Ah jus thought yuh hadnt heard erbout it. . . ."

"We know all about it," said Bruden, turning his head away and looking out of the window; as though he was through with the conversation, as though his mind was made up.

"What do they think theyre going to get by marching?" asked Lowe.

"They think they kin git some bread," said Taylor.

"It wont get em a Goddam crumb!" said Lowe.

There was silence. Taylor looked again at the jutting angle of sunshine and heard the mayor's shoes shifting uneasily on the brown carpet. A match struck; he heard it drop with an angry hiss into the spittoon.

"I dont see why we cant get along, Dan," drawled the mayor.

"Ahm willin t git erlong, Mistah Mayor!" protested Taylor.

"Dan, here we all are, living in good old Dixie. There are

twenty-five thousand people in this town. Ten thousand of those people are black, Dan. Theyre your people. Now, its our job to keep order among the whites, and we would like to think of you as being a responsible man to keep order among the blacks. Lets get together, Dan. You know these black people better than we do. We want to feel we can depend on you. Why dont you look at this thing the right way? You know Ill never turn you down if you do the right thing. . . ."

"Mistah Mayor, as Gawds mah judge, Ahm doin right when Ah tell yuh mah folks is hongry. . . ."

"Youre not doing right when you act like a Goddam Red!" said Lowe.

"These niggers around here trust you, Dan," said the mayor. "Theyll do what you tell them to do."

"Speak to them," urged Lowe. "Tell them whats right."

"Mistah Mayor, Gawd in Heaven knows mah people is hongry," said Taylor humbly.

The mayor threw his body forward in the chair and rested his hands on his knees.

"Listen, Dan. I know just how you feel. We *all* feel that way. White people are hungry, too. But weve got to be prudent and do this thing right. Dan, youre a leader and youve got great influence over your congregation here." The mayor paused to let the weight of his words sink in. "Dan, I helped you to get that influence by doing your people a lot of favors through *you* when you came into my office a number of times." The mayor looked at Taylor solemnly. "Im asking you now to use that influence and tell your people to stay *off* the streets tomorrow!"

When Taylor spoke he seemed to be outside of himself, listening to his own words, aghast and fearful.

"Ahm sho thankful as Gawd knows fer all yuh done done fer me n mah people, suh. But mah word don go so fer in times like these, yo Honah. These folks is lookin t me fer bread n Ah cant give it t em. They hongry n Ah cant tell em where t eat. Theys gonna march no mattah whut Ah say. . . ."

"Youve got influence here, Dan, and you can use it!"

"They wouldnt be marchin ef they wuznt hongry, yo Honah!"

"Thats Red talk, nigger!" said Lowe, standing.

"Aw, thas all right, Lowe," said the mayor, placatingly.

"Im not going to sit here and let this Goddam nigger insult me to my face!" said Lowe.

Taylor stood up.

"Ahm sorry, suh!"

"You *will* be sorry when you find a Goddam rope around your neck!" said Lowe.

"Now, now," said the mayor, laying his hand on Lowe's arm. He turned to Taylor. "You dont mean you wont speak to em, do you, Dan?"

"There ain nothin Ah kin say t em, Mistah Mayor. . . ."

"Youre doing the wrong thing, Dan!"

"Ahm lettin Gawd be mah judge, suh!"

"If you dont do the right thing *we* will be your judges!" said Lowe.

"Ahm trustin Gawd, suh."

"Well, Goddammit, you better let Him guide you right!" said Bruden, jumping to his feet.

"But white folks!" pleaded Taylor. "Mah folks cant plant nothin! Its ergin the law! They cant git no work! Whut they gonna do? They don wan no trouble. . . ."

"Youre heading for a plenty right now!" said Bruden.

The mayor spoke and his voice was low and resigned.

"Ive done all I could, Dan. You wouldnt follow my advice, now the rest is up to Mister Lowe and Chief Bruden here."

Bruden's voice came with a shout:

"A niggers a nigger! I was against coming here talking to this nigger like he was a white man in the first place. He needs his teeth kicked down his throat!" Bruden poked the red tip of his cigar at Taylor's face. "Im the Chief of Police of this town, and Im here to see that orders kept! The Chamber of Commerce says therell be no demonstration tomorrow. Therell be three hundred police downtown in the morning to see that thats done. If you send them niggers down there, or if you let these Goddam Reds fool you into it, Ill not be responsible for whatll happen! Weve never had a riot in this town, but youre plotting one right now when you act like this! And you know wholl get the worst of it!"

"Can't yuh do something, Mistah Mayor? Can't yuh fix it sos we kin git some relief?"

The mayor did not answer; Lowe came close to him.

"We know youve been seeing Hadley and Green! We know whats going on! So watch yourself, nigger!"

"Suh?"

They went out. Taylor stood at the window and saw them get into their car and disappear in a cloud of dust around a corner. He sat down, feeling sweat over all his body. Gawd knows whut t do. . . . He brought Lowe n Bruden here t threaten me. . . . N they know erbout Hadley and Green. . . . Somebody tol. . . . He looked up, hearing the soft boom of a clock. Hadley n Greens comin back here at six-thirty. . . . He went down the hall thinking, Lawd, ef Ah only knowed whut t do. . . .

VII

May met him in the hall.

"Whut they say, Dan?" she asked with suppressed hysteria.

"Don bother me now, May!"

"There wont be no trouble, will it, Dan?"

"Naw, May! Now, please! Yuh worryin me!"

"Yuhll spoil things fer Jimmy, Dan! Don do nothin wrong! Its fer Jimmy Ahm astin!"

"Itll be awright! Now, lemme go!"

He hurried down the hallway, leaving her crying. Good Gawd! How come she wont leave me erlone. Firs, its Jimmy; then its her. . . . Ef it ain one its the other. . . . He went to the end of the hall, down the steps, turned, and came to the door of the Deacon Room. He heard subdued voices. He knew that the deacons were waiting for him, waiting for some definite word. Shucks, Ahm willin t go thu wid tha march ef they is. Them white folks cant kill us *all*. . . . He pushed the door in. The voices ceased. He saw a dense cloud of tobacco smoke and a circle of black faces. He forced a wan smile.

"Good evenin, Brothers!" he said.

"How yuh, Reveren?" asked Deacon Bonds.

"Ahm sorry Ahm late," said Taylor.

"Wuz tha the mayor out there?" asked Deacon Williams.

Taylor paused and pulled out his handkerchief.

"Yeah, Brothers, it wuz the mayor. N the Chiefa Police n tha man Lowe from the Red Squad. . . ."

"RED SQUAD!" shouted Deacon Smith, jumping to his feet with an outraged look.

"Whut they say, Reveren?" asked Deacon Williams quietly, ignoring Deacon Smith.

Taylor sighed and looked at the floor. For a moment he loathed them because he knew they were expecting an answer to their questions. They were expecting him to speak now as he had always spoken, to the point, confidently, and finally. He had wanted them to do the talking, and now they were silent, waiting for him to speak. Lawd, Ah hope Ahm doin right. Ah don wanna lead these folks wrong. . . .

"They know all erbout tha demonstration," he said.

"But whut they *say*?" asked Deacon Bonds.

"Shucks, man! Yuh *know* whut they said!" said Deacon Smith. "Yuh *know* how them white folks feel erbout this thing!"

"They don wan us t march," said Taylor. "They said ef we march theyll put the police on us. . . ."

Deacon Smith leveled his forefinger at Taylor and intoned: "AH TOL YUH SO!"

"They said therell be a riot," Taylor went on stubbornly.

"Yessuh! Brothers, wes gotta do *right*!" said Deacon Smith, banging his open palm down on the table. "Ah awways said wes gotta do *right*, Reveren!"

"Ahm prayin t Gawd t guide us right," said Taylor.

"Yuh sho don ack like it!" said Deacon Smith.

"Let the Reveren finish, will yuh?" asked Deacon Bonds.

"Wes gotta do right!" said Deacon Smith again, sitting down, folding his arms, crossing his legs and turning his face sternly away.

"Whut else they say, Reveren?" asked Deacon Bonds.

Taylor sighed.

"They say wes mixed up wid the Reds. . . ."

"N by Gawd we *is*!" bawled Deacon Smith. "At least *yuh* is! Ah tol yuh t leave them Reds erlone! They don mean *no*body *no* good! When men starts t deny Gawd, nothin good kin come from em!"

"Brother Smith, let the Reveren talk, will yuh?" asked Deacon Williams.

"He ain talkin *sense!*" said Deacon Smith.

"They say therell be three hundred police downtown in the mawnin," said Taylor, ignoring Smith. "They say only Washington kin do something erbout relief, n tha we mus wait. . . ."

"N Gawd Awmighty knows thas all we kin do: wait!" said Deacon Smith.

"Fer Chrissakes, Brother Smith, let im talk!" said Deacon Williams. "We all know *yuhs* scared!"

"Ah ain scared! Ah got *sense!* Ah. . . ."

"Yuh sho don ack like it, the way yuh shoot off yo mouth!" said Deacon Williams.

Deacon Smith stood up.

"Yuh cant talk tha way t me!"

"Then keep yo big mouth shut!" said Deacon Williams.

"Whos gonna make me?"

"Brothers, please!" begged Taylor.

"A fool kin see tha the white folks is scared!" said Deacon Williams.

"N jus cause theys *scared*, theyll kill *any*body whuts fool ernuff t go downtown in the mawnin," said Deacon Smith.

"Shucks, Ahm willin t taka chance," said Deacon Hilton.

"Me too!"

"We ain got nothin t lose!"

"Any *fool* kin git his head busted!" said Deacon Smith.

"Brothers, fer the lova Gawd, quit fussin!" said Taylor.

They were silent. Taylor looked at them, letting his eyes rove from face to face.

"Brothers, this is the case," he said finally. "They threatenin us not t march, but they ain sayin our folks kin git no relief. Now, Ah figgers ef we hada big crowd downtown in the mawnin they wont bother us. . . ."

"Thas whut *yuh* think," sneered Deacon Smith.

"N ef we don hava big crowd, theyll smash us. Now, its up t us. . . ."

"Reveren, do the *po* white folks say they gonna be *wid* us?" asked Deacon Jones.

"Brother Hadley tol me theys gonna be wid us," said Taylor.

"Tha Hadley is a lie n the trutha Gawd ain in im!" shouted

Deacon Smith. "Tha white man is jus tryin t trick yuh, Ahm tellin yuh!"

"Waal, we kin never know less we try n see," said Deacon Bonds.

"Yeah, but they ain gonna let yuh try but *once*," said Deacon Smith.

"Waal, Ah ain got but *one* time t die!" said Deacon Bonds.

"Ah think the white folksll be there," said Taylor. "Theys hongry, too. . . ."

"Yuhll wake up *some* day!" said Deacon Smith.

"Whut yuh gonna do, Reveren?" asked Deacon Williams.

"Do the congregation wanna march?" asked Taylor.

"They say theys *gonna* march!"

"Waal, Ahll march wid em," said Taylor quietly. "They wont march erlone. . . ."

Deacon Smith waved his arms and screamed.

"Yeah yuhll march! But yuhs scared t let em use yo name! Whut kinda leader *is* yuh? Ef yuhs gonna ack a fool n be a Red, then how come yuh wont come on out n say so sos we kin all hear it? Naw, yuh ain man ernuff t say whut yuh is! Yuh wanna stan in wid the white folks! Yuh wanna stan in wid the Reds! Yuh wanna stan in wid the congregation! Yuh wanna stan in wid the Deacon Board! Yuh wanna stan in wid *ever*body n yuh stan in wid *no*body!"

"Ahm ackin accordin t mah lights!" said Taylor.

"Waal, they ain lettin yuh see fer!" said Deacon Smith.

"Ef yuh gotta plan bettah than mine, Brother Smith, tell us erbout it!"

"AH SAY WE OUGHTNT MARCH!"

"Then, whut we gonna do?"

"Wait n see how things come out!"

"Ahm tireda waitin," said Taylor.

"How come yuh didnt send yo name out on them leaflets?" demanded Deacon Smith. Without waiting for Taylor to answer, he flared: "Ahll tell yuh why yuh didnt! Yuh *scared*! Yuh didnt wan them white folks t know yuhs mixed up in this demonstration. Yuh wanted em t think yuh wuz being pushed erlong by other folks n yuh couldnt help whut wuz happenin! But, Reveren, as sho as theres a Gawd in Heaven yuh ain foolin nobody!"

Taylor stood up.

"Brother Smith, Ah knows whut yuhs up t! Yuh tryin t run me outta mah church, but yuh cant! Gawd Awmighty Himself put me here n Ahm stayin till He says fer me t go! Yuh been schemin t git me out, but yuh cant do it this way! It ain right n Gawd knows it ain! Yeah; ef mah folks marches in the mawnin Ahm marchin wid em!"

"Thas the time, Reveren!"

"We kin show tha ol mayor something!"

"N therell be white folks wid us, too!"

"Ahll go wid the Reveren n the congregation!"

"Ahll go!"

"N me too!"

"Gawd ain wid yuh when yuh ain in the right!" said Deacon Smith.

"Gawd didnt mean fer folks t be hongry!" said Deacon Bonds.

"But He ain wid yuh when yuh stirrin up trouble, makin blood n riots!" said Deacon Smith. "N any man whut sets here n calls himself a leader called by Gawd t preach n leads his folks the wrong way is a fool n the spirita Gawd ain in im!"

"Now, wait a minute there, Brother Smith!" said Taylor. "Yuhs talkin *dangerous!*"

"Ah say any man whut leads his folks inter guns n police. . . ."

"Ain nobody leadin us *nowhere!*" said Deacon Bonds.

"We gwine *ourselves!*" said Deacon Williams.

"Ah ain in this!" said Deacon Smith, jumping again to his feet. "Ah ain in this n Ahm gonna do whut Ah kin t hep mah people!"

The room grew quiet.

"Whut yuh mean, Brother Smith?" asked Taylor.

"Ah say Ahm gonna hep mah people!" said Deacon Smith again.

Taylor walked over to him.

"Is yuh gonna tell the white folks on us?"

Deacon Smith did not answer.

"Talk, Brother Smith!" said Taylor. "Tell us whut yuh mean!"

"Ah means whut Ah means!" said Deacon Smith; and he clamped his teeth tight, sat again, crossed his legs, folded his arms and stared at the blank wall.

Taylor swallowed and looked at the floor. Lawd, Ah don know whut t do! Ah wish this wuz over. . . . This niggers gonna tell on us! Hes gonna tell the white folks sos he kin stan in wid em. . . .

"Brother Smith. . . ." began Taylor.

The door opened and Jimmy stepped into the room.

"Say, Pa!"

"Whut yuh wan, son?"

"Somebodys out front t see yuh. Theys in a car. Theys white folks."

"Scuse me, Brothers," said Taylor. "Ahll be right back."

"Wes gonna set right here till yuh git back," said Deacon Smith.

When outside the door, Taylor turned to Jimmy.

"Who is they, Jimmy? How come they wouldnt come in?"

"Ah dunno, Pa. The car drove up jus as Ah wuz comin thu the gate. They white men. They said fer yuh t come right out."

"Awright. N, son, yuh bettah go see bout yo ma."

"Whuts the mattah?"

"Shes jus upset erbout the demonstration."

"Is they gonna march, Pa?"

"Ah reckon so."

"Is many gonna be out?"

"Ah dunno, son. Ah hope so. Yuh bettah go see erbout yo ma now."

"Yessuh."

"Yuh tell them boys whut Ah tol yuh?"

"Yessuh."

Taylor paused at the front door and peeped out from behind a curtain. In front of his gate was a long black car. Who kin tha be? For a moment he thought the mayor had come back. But his cars grey. . . . He opened the door and walked slowly down the steps. Lawd, mabbe we oughtnt go thu wid this demonstration aftah all? We might all be sorry ef somebodys killed in the mawnin. . . . He walked along a flower-bordered path that smelt of violets and magnolias. Dust rested filmily on tree leaves. The sun was almost gone. As he came to the car a white face looked out.

"You Taylor?"

"Yessuh," answered Taylor, smiling.

The rear door of the car opened and the white man stepped to the ground.

"So youre Taylor, hunh?"

"Yessuh," said Taylor again, still smiling, but puzzled. "Kin Ah be of service t yuh, suh?"

Taylor saw it coming, but could do nothing. He remembered afterward that he had wanted to ask, Whut yuh doin? The blow caught him flush on the point of the jaw, sending him flying backward. His head struck the edge of the runningboard; a flash of red shot before his eyes. He rolled, face downward, into a bed of thick violets. Dazed, he turned his head, trying to speak. He felt a hand grab the back of his collar and jerk him up.

"Get in the car, nigger!"

"Say, whut yuh. . . ."

"Shut up and get in the car, Goddam you!"

A blow came to his right eye. There were three white men now. They lifted him and rammed him down on the floor in the back of the car.

"Say, yuh cant do this!"

"Get your Goddam mouth shut, you bastard!"

A hard palm slapped him straight across his face. He struggled up, protesting.

"You. . . ."

The heel of a shoe came hard into his solar plexus. He doubled up, like a jackknife. His breath left, and he was rigid, half-paralyzed.

"You think you can run this whole Goddam town, don't you? You think a nigger can run over white folks and get away with it?"

He lay still, barely breathing, looking at blurred white faces in the semi-darkness of the roaring car.

VIII

The moment he tried to tell the direction in which the car was moving he knew he had waited too long. He remembered dimly that they had turned corners at least three times. He lay with closed eyes and wondered what they were going to do with him. She gonna be worried t death, he thought, thinking of May. And then he thought of Jimmy and said to himself, Ah hope he don go n ack a fool now. . . . The numbness which had deadened most of his stomach and chest was leaving. He felt sweat on his back and forehead. The car slowed, turned; then it ran fast again. He knew by the way the rocks crunched beneath the humming rubber tires that they were speeding over gravel. Whut roads this? He could not tell. There were so many gravel roads leading out of town. He tried to recall how long he had lain there half-paralyzed from that kick in the solar plexus. He was confused; it might have been five minutes or it might have been an hour. The car slowed again, turning. He smelt the strong scent of a burning cigarette and heard the toll of a far off church bell. The car stopped; he heard the sound of other cars, gears shifting and motors throbbing. We mus be at some crossroads. But he could not guess which one. He had an impulse to call for help. But there would not be any use in his doing that now. Mabbe they white folks anyhow. He would be better off as he was; even six white men were better than a mob of white men. The car was speeding again, lurching. He smelt dust, clay dust. Then he heard a hard, rasping voice:

"How is he?"

"O.K."

"Keep im quiet!"

"O.K."

He said nothing. He began to wonder how many of them were in the car. Yes, he should have been watching for something like this. They been threatenin me fer a long time. Now this is it. The car was gradually slowing with that long slow slowing preceding a final stop. He felt the rubber tires turning over rough ground; his head rocked from side to side, hitting against the lower back of the front seat. Then the car stopped; the motor stopped; for a moment there was complete silence. Then he heard wind sighing in trees. Wes out in the country somewhere. In the woods, he thought.

"O.K.?"

"O.K.!"

He heard a door open.

"C mon, nigger! Get up and watch yourself!"

He pulled up and caught a glimpse of starry sky. As his feet hit the ground his head began to ache. He had lain cramped so long the blood had left his limbs; he took a step, kicking out his legs to restore circulation. His arms were grabbed from behind and he felt the pressure of a kneecap in the center of his spine. He gasped and reeled backward.

"Where you think youre going?"

He rested on his knees, his body full of pain. He heard a car door slam.

"Awright, nigger! Lets go! Straight ahead!"

He got up and twisted his head about to see who had spoken. He saw four blurred white faces and then they were blotted out. He reeled backward again, his head striking the ground. A pain knotted in his temple.

"Get up, nigger! Keep your eyes in front, and walk, God-dammit!"

He pulled up and limped off, his head down. Mabbe they gonna shoot me? His feet and the feet behind him made a soft *cush-cush* in the dew-wet grass and leaves.

"Aw right, nigger!"

He stopped. Slowly he raised his eyes; he saw a tall white man holding a plaited leather whip in his hand, hitting it gently against his trousers' leg.

"You know what this is, nigger?"

He said nothing.

"Wont talk, hunh? Well, this is a nigger-lesson!"

The whip flashed in faint starlight. The blow numbed his lips. He tasted blood.

"You know what this is? Im asking you again, nigger?"

"Nawsuh," he whispered.

"This is a nigger-whip!"

The leather whacked across his shoulders.

"Mistah, Ah ain done nothin!"

"Aw, naw! You aint done nothing! You aint never done a Goddam thing, have you?" White men were standing close around him now. "All you ever do is play around with Reds, dont you? All you ever do is get crowds of niggers together to threaten white folks, dont you? When we get through with you tonight youll know how to stay in a niggers place! C mon! Get that Goddam vest off!"

He did not move. The whip wrapped itself around his neck, leaving a ring of fire.

"You want me to *beat* it off you?"

He pulled off the vest and held it in his hands.

"C mon! Get that shirt and undershirt off!"

He stripped to his waist and stood trembling. A night wind cooled his sweaty body; he was conscious of his back as he had never been before, conscious of every square inch of black skin there. One of the white men walked off a few paces and stopped.

"Bring im over here!"

"O.K.!"

They guided him with prods and kicks.

"On your knees, nigger!"

He did not move. Again his arms were caught from behind and a kneecap came into the center of his back. Breathless, he dropped, his hands and knees cooling in the wet grass. He lifted his fingers to feel his swelling lips; he felt his wrists being grabbed and carried around the trunk of a tree. He held stiffly and struggled against a rope.

"Let go!"

His arms went limp. He rested his face against a cold tree-trunk. A rope cut into his wrists. They tied his feet together, drawing the rope tight about his ankles. He looked around; they stood watching.

"Well, nigger, what do you know?"

"Nothin, suh."

"Youre a preacher, aint you?"

"Yessuh."

"Well, lets hear you pray some!"

He said nothing. The whip lashed across his bare back, *whick!* He flinched and struggled against the rope that cut his wrists to the bone. The leather thong hummed again, *whick!* and his spine arched inward, like a taut bow.

"Goddam your black soul, pray!"

He twisted his face around, pleading:

"Please, Mistah! Don whip me! Ah ain done nothin. . . ."

Another lash came across his half-turned cheek, *whick!* He jerked around and sheltered his face against the tree-trunk. The lash hit his back, *whick!*

"*Hit* that black bastard, Bob!"

"Let me have that whip!"

"Naw, wait a minute!"

He said nothing. He clenched his teeth, his whole body quivering and waiting. A split second after each blow his body would lurch, as though absorbing the shock.

"You going to pray? You want me to beat you till you *cant* pray?"

He said nothing. He was expecting each blow now; he could almost feel them before they came, stinging, burning. Each flick came straight on his back and left a streak of fire, a streak that merged with the last streak, making his whole back a sheet of living flame. He felt his strength ebbing; he could not clench his teeth any more. His mouth hung open.

"Let me have it, Bob?"

"Naw, its my turn!"

There was a pause. Then the blows came again; the pain burned its way into his body, wave upon wave. It seemed that when he held his muscles taut the blows hurt less; but he could not hold taut long. Each blow weakened him; each blow told him that soon he would give out. Warm blood seeped into his trousers, ran down his thighs. He felt he could not stand it any longer; he held his breath, his lungs swelling. Then he sagged, his back a leaping agony of fire; leaping as of itself, as though it were his but he could not control it any longer. The weight of his body rested on his arms; his head dropped to one side.

"Ahhlll pppprray," he sobbed.

"Pray, then! Goddam you, pray!"

He tried to get his breath, tried to form words, hearing trees sighing somewhere. The thong flicked again, *whick!*

"Aint you going to pray!"

"Yyyyyessuh. . . ."

He struggled to draw enough air into his lungs to make his words sound.

"Ooour Fffather. . . ."

The whip cut hard, *whick!* pouring fire and fire again.

"Have mercy, Lawd!" he screamed.

"Pray, nigger! Pray like you *mean* it!"

". . . wwwhich aaaaart in hheaven . . . hhhallowed bbe Tttthy nname. . . ." The whip struck, *whick!* "Ahm prayin, Mmmmistah!"

"Goddam your black heart, *pray!*"

". . . Tttthine kkkindom ccome . . . Ttthy wwill bbe ddddone. . . ."

He sobbed, his breath leaving his lungs, going out from him, not wanting to stay to give sound to his words. The whip brought more fire and he could not stand it any longer; his heart seemed about to burst. He screamed, stretched his knees out and twisted his arms till he lay sideways, half on his stomach. The whip came into his stomach, *whick!* He turned over; it came on his back again, *whick!* He stopped struggling and hung limply, his weight suspended on arms he could not feel. Then fire flamed over all his body; he stiffened, glaring upward, wild-eyed.

"Whats the matter, nigger? You hurt?"

"Awright, kill me! Tie me n kill me! Yuh white trash cowards, kill me!"

"Youre tough, aint you? Just wait! We'll kill you, you black sonofabitch!"

"Lemme have that whip!"

"C mon, now! Its my turn!"

"Give me that whip, Ellis!"

He was taut, but not feeling the effort to be taut.

"We'll git yuh white trash some day! So hep me Gawd, we'll git yuh!"

The whip stopped.

"Say that again, Goddam you!"

The whip lashed, *whick!* but there was no streak of fire now; there was only one sheet of pain stretching all over his body, leaping, jumping, blazing in his flesh.

"Say it!"

He relaxed and closed his eyes. He stretched his legs out, slowly, not listening, not waiting for the whip to fall. *say it whick! say it whick! say it whick!* He groaned. Then he dropped his head and could not feel any more.

IX

Moonlight pained his eyeballs and the rustle of tree leaves thundered in his ears. He seemed to have only a head that hurt, a back that blazed, and eyes that ached. In him was a feeling that some power had sucked him deep down into the

black earth, had drained all strength from him. He was waiting for that power to go away so he could come back to life,
to light. His eyes were half-open, but his lids did not move.
He was thirsty; he licked his lips, wanting water. Then the
thunder in his ears died, rolling away. He moved his hand
and touched his forehead; his arm fell limply in the wet grass
and he lay waiting to feel that he wanted to move. As his
blood began to flow swiftly again he felt sweat breaking out
over his body. It seemed he could hear a tiny, faraway sound
whispering over and over like a voice in an empty room: Ah
got fever. . . . His back rested on a bed of fire, the imprint
of leaves and grass searing him with a scalding persistence.
He turned over on his stomach and groaned. Then he jerked
up, half-sitting. He was fully conscious now, fighting for his
strength, remembering the curses, the prayer and the whip.
The voice whispered again, this time louder: Ah gotta git
home. . . . With fumbling fingers he untied the rope from
his ankles and wrists. They didnt kill me, he thought. He
stood up and the dark earth swayed and the stars blurred.
Lawd, have mercy! He found himself on his knees; he had
not known when he had started falling; he just found himself
on his knees. Lawd, Ahm weak! He stood up again, more
slowly this time, holding onto a tree. He would have to get
his shirt; he could not go through the streets with a naked
and bleeding back. He put one foot in front of the other with
conscious effort, holding his body stiffly. Each slight twist of
his shoulders sent a wave of liquid metal over him. In the
grass at his feet his shirt was smeared like a white blur. He
touched it; it was wet. He held it, instinctively fearing to put
it on. When it did touch, his whole back blazed with a pain so
intense that it seemed to glow white hot. No, he could not
put it on now. Stiffly, he went among the trees, holding the
shirt in his hands, looking at the ground.

He stopped at the edge of a dirt road, conscious of the cool
steady stars and the fire that smoldered in his back. Whut
roads this? He could not tell. Then he heard a clock striking
so faintly that it seemed to be tolling in his own mind. He
counted, Wun, Tuh. . . . Its tuh erclock, he thought. He
could not stay here all night; he had to go in one direction or
another. He watched the brown dusty road winding away in

the darkness, like a twisting ribbon. Then he ducked his head, being seared again with fire and feeling a slight rush of air brush across his face. A small bird wheeled past his eyes and fluttered dizzily in the starlight. He watched it veer and dip, then crash softly into a tree limb. It fell to the ground, flapping tiny wings blindly. Then the bird twittered in fright and sailed straight upward into the starlight, vanishing. He walked northward, not going anywhere in particular, but walked northward because the bird had darted in that direction.

The road curved, turned to gravel, crunching under his shoes. This mus be the way, he thought. There were fences along the sides of the road now. He went faster, holding his legs stiffly to avoid pulling the muscles in his back. A church steeple loomed in the starlight, slender and faint. Yeah, thas Houstons church. N Ah gotta go thu a white neighborhood, he thought with despair. He saw houses, white, serene and cool in the night. Spose Ah go to Houston? Naw, hes white. *White*. . . . Even tho he preaches the gospel Ah preaches, he might not take me in. . . . He passed a small graveyard surrounded by a high iron picket fence. A *white* graveyard, he thought and snickered bitterly. Lawd Gawd in Heaven, even the dead cant be together! He stopped and held his shirt in his hands. He dreaded trying to put it on, but he had to. Ah cant go thu the streets like this. Gingerly, he draped the shirt over his shoulders; the whole mass of bruised and mangled flesh flamed, glowed white. With a convulsive movement he rammed his arms into the sleeves, thinking that the faster he did it the less pain there would be. The fire raged so he had a wild impulse to run, feeling that he would have no time then to suffer. But he could not run in a white neighborhood. To run would mean to be shot, for a burglar, or anything. Stiff-legged, he went down a road that turned from brown dust to black asphalt. Ahead street lamps glowed in round, rosy hazes.

Far down the shadow-dappled pavement he heard the sound of feet. He walked past a white man, then he listened to the white man's footsteps dying away behind him. He stopped at a corner and held onto a telephone pole. It would be better to keep in the residential district than to go through town. He would be stopped and questioned in town surely. And jailed maybe. Three blocks later on a white boy came upon him so softly and suddenly that he started in panic. After the boy had gone he turned to look; he saw the boy turning, looking at him. He walked on hurriedly. A block later a white woman appeared. When she was some fifty feet away she crossed to the other side of the street. Hate tightened his throat, then he emptied his lungs in a short, silent, bitter laugh. Ah ain gonna bother yuh, white lady. Ah only wan t git home. . . .

Like a pillar of fire he went through the white neighborhood. Some day theys gonna burn! some day theys gonna burn in Gawd Awmightys fire! How come they make us suffer so? The worls got too mucha everthing! Yit they bleed us! They fatten on us like leeches! There ain no groun yuh kin walk on tha they don own! N Gawd knows tha ain right! He made the earth fer us all! He ain tol no lie when He put us in this worl n said be fruitful n multiply. . . . Fire fanned his hate; he stopped and looked at the burning stars. "Gawd, ef yuh gimme the strength Ahll tear this ol buildin down! Tear it down, Lawd! Tear it down like ol Samson tore the temple down!" He walked again, mumbling. "Lawd, tell me whut t do! Speak t me, Lawd!" He caught his breath; a dark figure came out of the shadows in front of him. He saw a glint of metal; it was a policeman. He held erect and walked rapidly. Ahll stop, he thought. He wont have t ast me t stop. . . . He saw the white face drawing closer. He stopped and waited.

"Put your hands up, nigger!"

"Yessuh."

He lifted his arms. The policeman patted his hips, his sides. His back blazed, but he bit his lips and held still.

"Who you work for?"

"Ahma preacher, suh."

"A *preacher*?"

"Yessuh."

"What you doing out here this time of night?"

"Ah wuz visitin a sick man, a janitah, suh, whut comes t mah church. He works fer Miz Harvey. . . ."

"Who?"

"Miz Harvey, suh."

"Never heard of her, and Ive been on this beat for ten years."

"She lives right back there, suh," he said, half-turning and pointing.

"Well, you look all right. You can go on. But keep out of here at night."

"Yessuh."

He was near his own people now. Across a grassy square he could see the top of the round-house glinting dully in the moonlight. The black asphalt turned to cinders and the houses were low, close together, squatting on the ground as though hiding in fear. He saw his church and relaxed. He came to the steps, caught hold of a bannister and rested a moment.

When inside he went quietly down a hall, mounted the stairs, and came to the door of his room. He groped in the dark and felt the bed. He tried to pull off the shirt. It had stuck. He peeled it. Then he eased onto the bed and lay on his stomach. In the darkness his back seemed to take new fire. He went to the kitchen and wet a cloth with cold water. He lay down again with the cloth spread over him. That helped some. Then he began to shake. He was crying.

X

The door creaked.

"Tha yuh, Pa?"

"Son?"

"Good Gawd, wes been lookin all over fer yuh! Where yuh been? Mas worried t death!"

"C mon in, son, n close the do."

"Don yuh wanna light?"

"Naw; close the do."

There was a short silence.

"Whuts the mattah, Pa? Yuh sick?"

"Close the do n set down, son!"

Taylor could hear Jimmy's breathing, then a chair scraping over the floor and the soft rustle of Jimmy's clothes as he sat.

"Whuts the mattah, Pa? Whut happened?"

Taylor stared in the darkness and slowly licked his swollen lips. He wanted to speak, but somehow could not. Then he stiffened, hearing Jimmy rise.

"Set *down*, son!"

"But, Pa. . . ."

Fire seethed not only in Taylor's back, but all over, inside and out. It was the fire of shame. The questions that fell from Jimmy's lips burned as much as the whip had. There rose in him a memory of all the times he had given advice, counsel, and guidance to Jimmy. And he wanted to talk to him now as he had in the past. But his impulses were deadlocked. Then suddenly he heard himself speaking, hoarsely, faintly. His voice was like a whisper rising from his whole body.

"They whipped me, son. . . ."

"Whipped yuh? Who?"

Jimmy ran to the bed and touched him.

"Son, set *down*!"

Taylor's voice was filled with a sort of tense despair. He felt Jimmy's fingers leaving him slowly. There was a silence in which he could hear only his own breath struggling in his throat.

"Yuh mean the *white* folks?"

Taylor buried his face in his pillow and tried to still the heaving in his chest.

"They beat me, son. . . ."

"Ahll git a doctah!"

"Naw!"

"But yuhs hurt!"

"Naw; lock the do! Don let May in here. . . ."

"Goddam them white bastards!"

"Set down, son!"

"Who wuz they, Pa?"

"Yuh cant do nothin, son. Yuhll have t wait. . . ."

"Wes been waitin too long! All we do is wait, *wait*!"

Jimmy's footsteps scuffed across the floor. Taylor sat up.

"Son?"

"Ahma git mah gun n git Pete n Bob n Joe n Sam! Theyll see they cant do this t us!"

Taylor groped in the darkness; he found Jimmy's shoulders.

"C mon, son! Ahm awright. . . ."

"Thas the reason why they kill us! We take everthing they put on us! We take everthing! *Everthing!*"

"Yuh cant do nothin *erlone*, Jimmy!"

Jimmy's voice was tense, almost hysterical.

"But we kin *make* em know they cant do this t us widout us doin *some*thing! Aw, hell, Pa! Is we gonna be dogs *all* the time?"

"But theyll kill yuh, son!"

"Somebody *has* t die!"

Taylor wanted to tell Jimmy something, but he could not find the words. What he wanted to say boiled in him, but it seemed too big to come out. He flinched from pain, pressing his fingers to his mouth, holding his breath.

"Pa?"

"Yeah, son?"

"Hadley n Green wuz here t see yuh three-fo times."

"Yeah?"

Jimmy said nothing. Taylor twisted around, trying to see his son's face in the darkness.

"Whut they say, son?"

"Aw, hell! It don mattah. . . ."

"Tell me whut they *said*!"

"Ttthey ssaid. . . . Aw, Pa, they didn't know!"

"Whut they *say*?"

"They said yuh had done run out on em. . . ."

"Run *out*?"

"Everbody wuz astin where yuh wuz," said Jimmy. "Nobody knowed. So they tol em yuh run out. N Brother Smith had the Deacon Board t vote yuh outta the church. . . ."

"Vote me *out*?"

"They said they didn't wan yuh fer pastah no mo. It wuz Smith who made em do it. He tol em yuh had planned a demonstration n lef em holdin the bag. He fussed n stormed at em. They thought they wuz doin right. . . ."

Taylor lay on his bed of fire in the darkness and cried. He felt Jimmy's fingers again on his face.

"Its awright, Pa. We'll git erlong somehow. . . ."

"Seems like Gawds done lef me! Ahd die fer mah people ef Ah only knowed how. . . ."

"Pa. . . ."

"How come Ah cant never do nothin? All mah life Ah done tried n cant do nothin! *Nothin!*"

"Its awright, Pa!"

"Ah done lived all mah life on mah knees, a-beggin n a-pleadin wid the white folks. N all they gimme wuz crumbs! All they did wuz kick me! N then they come wida gun n ast me t give mah own soul! N ef Ah so much as talk lika man they try t kill me. . . ."

He buried his face in the pillow, trying to sink himself into something so deeply that he could never feel again. He heard Jimmy turning the key in the lock.

"Son!"

Again he ran to Jimmy and held him.

"*Don* do tha, son!"

"Thingsll awways be like this less we *fight!*"

"Set down, son! Yo po ol pas a-*beggin* yuh t set down!"

He pulled Jimmy back to the bed. But even then it did not seem he could speak as he wanted to. He felt what he wanted to say, but it was elusive and hard to formulate.

"Son. . . ."

"Ah ain gonna live this way, Pa!"

He groped for Jimmy's shoulders in the darkness and squeezed them till the joints of his fingers cracked. And when words came they seemed to be tearing themselves from him, as though they were being pushed upward like hot lava out of a mountain from deep down.

"Don be a fool, son! Don thow you life erway! We cant do nothin erlone."

"But theys gonna treat us this way as long as we *let* em!"

He had to make Jimmy understand; for it seemed that in making him understand, in telling him, he, too, would understand.

"We gotta git wid the *people*, son. Too long we done tried t do this thing our way n when we failed we wanted t run out n pay-off the white folks. Then they kill us up like flies. Its the *people*, son! Wes too much erlone this way! Wes los when wes erlone! Wes gotta be wid our folks. . . ."

"But theys killin us!"

"N theyll keep on killin us less we learn how t fight! Son, its the people we mus gid wid us! Wes empty n weak this way! The reason we cant do nothin is cause wes so much erlone. . . ."

"Them Reds wuz right," said Jimmy.

"Ah dunno," said Taylor. "But let nothin come tween yuh n *yo* people. Even the Reds cant do nothin ef yuh lose yo people. . . ." Fire burned him as he talked, and he talked as though trying to escape it. "Membah whut Ah tol yuh prayer wuz, son?"

There was silence, then Jimmy answered slowly:

"Yuh mean lettin Gawd be so real in yo life tha everthing yuh do is cause of Im?"

"Yeah, but its different now, son. Its the *people*! Theys the ones whut mus be real t us! Gawds wid the people! N the peoples gotta be real as Gawd t us! We cant hep ourselves er the people when wes erlone. Ah been wrong erbout a lotta things Ah tol yuh, son. Ah tol yuh them things cause Ah thought they wuz right. Ah tol yuh t work hard n climb t the top. Ah tol yuh folks would lissen t yuh then. But they wont, son! All the will, all the strength, all the power, all the numbahs is in the people! Yuh cant live by yoself! When they beat me tonight, they beat *me*. . . . There wuznt nothin Ah could do but lay there n hate n pray n cry. . . . Ah couldnt *feel* mah people, Ah couldn't *see* mah people, Ah couldn't *hear* mah people. . . . All Ah could feel wuz tha whip cuttin mah blood out. . . ."

In the darkness he imagined he could see Jimmy's face as he had seen it a thousand times, looking eagerly, his eyes staring before him, fashioning his words into images, into life. He hoped Jimmy was doing that now.

"Ahll awways hate them bastards! Ahll *aw*ways hate em!"

"Theres other ways, son."

"Yuhs sick, Pa. . . ."

"Wes all sick, son. Wes gotta think erbout the people, night n day, think erbout em so hard tha our po selves is fergotten. . . . Whut they suffer is whut Ah suffered las night when they whipped me. Wes gotta keep the people wid us."

Jimmy was silent. A soft knock came at the door.

XI

"Dan!"

"Thas ma," said Jimmy.

Taylor heard Jimmy rise to his feet; he gripped Jimmy's hands.

"Please, Pa! Let her come in n hep yuh!"

"Naw."

"Dan!"

Jimmy broke from him; he heard the key turn in the lock. The door opened.

"Dan! Fer Gawds sake, whuts the mattah?"

Jimmy switched on the light. Taylor lay blinking at May's anxious face. He felt shame again, knowing that he should not feel it, but feeling it anyway. He turned over and buried his face in his hands.

"Dan!"

She ran and knelt at the side of the bed.

"They tried t kill im, Ma! They beat im!" said Jimmy.

"Ah knowed them white folks wuz gonna do something like this! Ah knowed it," sobbed May.

Taylor sat up.

"Yuh be still! Lay down!" said May.

She pushed him back onto the bed.

"Cant yuh do something fer im, Ma? Hes sufferin tha way."

Taylor heard May leave the room and come back.

"Hol still, Dan. This ain gonna hurt yuh. . . ."

He felt warm water laving him, then something cool that smelled of oil. He heard Jimmy moving to and fro, getting things for May. When his back was dressed he felt the bed sink as May sat on the edge of it. The heavy odors of violets and magnolias came to him; he was slowly coming back to the world again. He was the same man, but he was coming back somehow changed. He wondered at the strange peace that seeped into his mind and body there in the room with May and Jimmy, with the white folks far off in the darkness.

"Feel bettah, Dan?"

"Ahm awright."

"Yuh hongry?"

"Naw."

He wanted to talk to Jimmy again, to tell him about the black people. But he could not think of words that would say what he wanted to say. He would tell it somehow later on.

He began to toss, moving jerkily, more now from restlessness of mind than from the dying fire that still lingered in his body.

XII

Suddenly the doorbell pealed. Taylor turned and saw May and Jimmy looking at each other.

"Somebody at the do," said Jimmy in a tense voice.

"Yuh reckon they white folks?" asked May.

"Yuh bettah go down, Jimmy," said Taylor.

"Ef its any white folks tell em Dans out," said May.

Jimmy's footsteps died away on the stairs. A door slammed. There were faint sounds of voices. Footsteps echoed, came on the stairs, grew loud. Taylor knew that more than one person was coming up. He lifted himself and sat on the edge of the bed.

"Dan, yuh cant git up! Youhll make yoself sick!"

He ignored her. The door opened and Jimmy ran in.

"Its Brother Bonds, Pa!"

Bonds stood in the doorway with his head wrapped in blood-stained bandages. His face twitched and his eyes stared at something beyond the walls of the room, as though his attention had been riveted once and for always upon one fixed spot.

"Whut happened, Brother?" asked Taylor.

Bonds stared, dazed, with hunched and beaten shoulders. Then he sank to the floor, sobbing softly:

"They beat me! They beat mah chillun! They beat mah wife! They beat us all cause Ah tol em t git outta mah house! Lawd, how long Yuh gonna let em treat us this way? How long Yuh gonna let em make us suffer?"

May sobbed. Jimmy ran out of the room. Taylor caught him on the stairs.

"Don be a fool, boy! Yuh c mon back here, *now*!"

Jimmy flopped on the edge of a chair and mumbled to himself. The room was quiet save for the rustle of tree leaves that drifted in from the outside and the sound of Bonds sobbing on the floor. As Taylor stood his own suffering was drowned in a sense of widening horror. There was in his mind a vivid picture of all the little dingy huts where black men and women were crouched, afraid to stir out of doors. Bonds stopped crying and looked at Taylor; again that sense of shame spread over Taylor, inside and out. It stirred him to speech.

"Who else they beat, Brother?"

"Seem like everbody, Reveren! Them two Commoonists got beat something terrible n they put em in jail. N Ah heard they kilt one black man whut tried t fight back. They ketchin everbody they kin on the streets n lettin em have it. They ridin up n down in cars. . . ."

Jimmy cursed. The doorbell pealed again.

"Git me a shirt, May!"

"Dan, yuh ain able t do nothin!"

The doorbell pealed again, then again. Taylor started toward the dresser; but May got there before he did and gave him a shirt.

"Dan, be careful!"

"C mon downstairs, Brother Bonds. N yuh, too, Jimmy," said Taylor.

XIII

The church's waiting room was full. Black men and women sat and stood, saying nothing, waiting. Arms were in slings; necks were wrapped in white cloth; legs were bound in blood-stained rags.

"LOOK AT WHUT YUH DONE DONE!" a voice bawled.

It was Deacon Smith. Taylor's eyes went from face to face; he knew them all. Every Sunday they sat in the pews of his church, praying, singing, and trusting the God he gave them. The mute eyes and silent lips pinned him to a fiery spot of loneliness. He wa   d to protest that loneliness, wanted to break it down; but he did not know how. No parables sprang to his lips now to give form and meaning to his words; alone and naked, he stood ashamed. Jimmy came through the door and placed his hand on his shoulder.

"Its daylight, Pa. The folks is gatherin in the playground! theys waitin fer yuh. . . ."

Taylor went into the yard with the crowd at his heels. It

was broad daylight and the sun shone. The men in their overalls and the women with children stood about him on all sides, silent. A fat black woman elbowed her way in and faced him.

"Waal, Reveren, we done got beat up. Now, is we gonna march?"

"Yuh wanna march?" asked Taylor.

"It don make no difference wid me," she said. "Them white folks cant do no mo than theys awready done."

The crowd chimed in.

"N Gawd knows they cant!"

"Ahll go ef the nex one goes!"

"Ah gotta die sometime, so Ah jus as waal die now!"

"They cant kill us but once!"

"Ahm tired anyhow! Ah don care!"

"The white folks says theys gonna meet us at the park!"

Taylor turned to Jimmy.

"Son, git yo boys together n tell em t roun up everbody!"

"Yessuh!"

May was pulling at his sleeve.

"Dan, yuh *cant* do this. . . ."

Deacon Smith pushed his way in and faced him.

"Yuhll never set foot in a church ergin ef yuh lead them po black folks downtown t be killed!"

The crowd surged.

"Ain nobody leadin us nowhere!"

"We goin ourselves!"

"Is we gonna march, Reveren?"

"Yeah; soon as the crowd gits together," said Taylor.

"Ain nobody t blame but yuh ef yuh carry em t their *death*!" warned Deacon Smith.

"How come yuh don shut yo old big mouth n let the Reveren talk?" asked the fat woman.

"Sistah, Ah got as much right t speak as yuh!"

"Waal, don speak to me, yuh hear!"

"Somebody has t say something when ain *nobody* got no sense!"

"Man, don yuh tell me Ah ain got no sense!"

"Yuh sho don ack like it!"

"Ah got as much sense as yuh got!"

"How come yuh don use it?"

The fat sister slapped Deacon Smith straight across his face. Taylor ran between them and pried them apart. The crowd surged and screamed.

"Ef he touches Sistah Henry ergin Ahll kill im!"

"He ain got no bisness talkin tha way t a woman!"

Taylor dragged the fat woman toward the gate. The crowd followed, yelling. He stopped and faced them. They circled around, tightly, asking questions. May had hold of his sleeve. Jimmy came to him.

"Pa, theys comin!"

Taylor turned and walked across the yard with the crowd following. He took two planks and laid them upon the ends of two saw-horses and made a solid platform. He climbed up and stood in the quiet sunshine. He did not know exactly what it was he wanted to say, but whatever it was he would say it when they were quiet. He felt neither fear nor joy, just an humble confidence in himself, as though he were standing before his mirror in his room. Then he was conscious that they were quiet; he took one swift look over their heads, heads that stretched away to the street and beyond, a solid block of black, silent faces; then he looked down, not to the dust, but just a slight lowering of eyes, as though he were no longer looking at them, but at something within himself.

"Sistahs n Brothers, they tell me the Deacon Boards done voted me outta the church. Ef thas awright wid yuh, its awright wid me. The white folks says Ahma bad nigger n they don wanna have nothin else t do wid me. N thas awright, too. But theres one thing Ah wanna say. Ah knows how yuh feel erbout bein hongry. N how yuh feel is no different from how Ah feel. Yuh been waitin a week fer me t say whut yuh ought t do. Yuh been wonderin how come Ah didnt tell yuh whut yuh oughta do. Waal. . . ."

He paused and looked over the silent crowd; then again his eyes, his gaze, went inward.

"Sistahs n Brothers, the reason Ah didnt say nothin is cause Ah didnt know *whut* t say. N the only reason Ahm speakin now is cause Ah *do* know. Ah know whut t do. . . ."

He paused again, swallowing. The same feeling which gripped him so hard last night when he had been talking to

Jimmy seized him. He opened his mouth to continue; his lips moved several times before words came; and when they did come they fell with a light and hoarse whisper.

"Sistahs n Brothers, las night the white folks took me out t the woods. They took me out cause Ah tol em yuh wuz hongry. They ast me t tell yuh not t march, n Ah tol em Ah wouldnt. Then they beat me. They tied me t a tree n beat me till Ah couldnt feel no mo. They beat me cause Ah wouldnt tell yuh not t ast fer bread. They said yuhd blieve everthing Ah said. All the time they wuz hepin me, all the time they been givin me favors, they wuz doin it sos *they* could tell *me* t tell *yuh* how t ack! Sistahs n Brothers, as Gawds mah judge, Ah thought Ah wuz doin right when Ah did tha. Ah thought Ah wuz doin right when Ah tol yuh t do the things they said. N cause Ah wouldnt do it this time, they tied me t a tree n beat me till mah blood run. . . ."

Mist covered his eyes. He heard the crowd murmuring; but he did not care if they were murmuring for or against him; he wanted to finish, to say what he had been trying so hard to say for many long hours.

"Sistahs n Brothers, they whipped me n made me take the name of *Gawd* in vain! They made me say mah prayers n beat me n laughed! They beat me till Ah couldnt membah nothin! All last night Ah wuz lyin stretched out on the groun wid mah back burnin. . . . All this mawnin befo day Ah wuz limpin thu white folks streets. Sistahs n Brothers, Ah *know* now! Ah done seen the *sign*! Wes gotta git together. Ah know whut yo life is! Ah done felt it! Its *fire*! Its like the fire that burned me las night! Its sufferin! Its hell! Ah cant bear this fire erlone! Ah know now whut t do! Wes gotta git close t one ernother! Gawds done spoke! Gawds done sent His sign. Now its fer us t ack. . . ."

The crowd started yelling:

"We'll go ef yuh go!"

"Wes ready!"

"The white folks says theyll meet us at the park!"

The fat black woman started singing:

"So the sign of the fire by night
N the sign of the cloud by day
A-hoverin oer

Jus befo
As we journey on our way. . . ."

Taylor got down. He moved with the crowd slowly toward the street. May went with him, looking, wondering, saying nothing. Jimmy was at his side. They sang as they marched. More joined along the way. When they reached the park that separated the white district from the black, the poor whites were waiting. Taylor trembled when he saw them join, swelling the mass that moved toward the town. He looked ahead and saw black and white marching; he looked behind and saw black and white marching. And still they sang:

"So the sign of the fire by night. . . ."

They turned into the street that led to town.

"N the sign of the cloud by day. . . ."

Taylor saw blue-coated policemen standing lined along the curb.

"A-hoverin o'er. . . ."

Taylor felt himself moving between the silent lines of blue-coated white men, moving with a sea of placards and banners, moving under the sun like a pregnant cloud. He said to himself, They ain gonna bother us! They bettah *not* bother us. . . .

"Jus befo. . . ."

Across a valley, in front of him, he could see the buildings of the town sprawled on a hill.

"As we journey on our way. . . ."

They were tramping on pavement now. And the blue-coated men stood still and silent. Taylor saw Deacon Smith standing on the curb, and Smith's face merged with the faces of the others, meaningless, lost. Ahead was the City Hall, white and clean in the sunshine. The autos stopped at the street corners while the crowd passed; and as they entered the downtown section people massed quietly on the sidewalks. Then the crowd began to slow, barely moving. Taylor looked ahead and wondered what was about to happen; he wondered without fear; as though whatever would or could happen could not hurt this many-limbed, many-legged, many-handed crowd that was he. He felt May clinging to his sleeve. Jimmy was peering ahead. A policeman came running up to him.

"You Taylor?"

"Yessuh," he said, quietly, his gaze straight and steady.

"The mayors down front; he wants to see you!"

"Tell im Ahm back here," said Taylor.

"But he wants to see the leader up front!"

"Tell im Ahm back here," said Taylor again.

The man hesitated, then left; they waited, quiet, still. Then the crowd parted. Taylor saw Mayor Bolton hurrying toward him, his face beet-red.

"Dan, tell your people not to make any trouble! We dont want any trouble, Dan. . . ."

"There ain gonna be no trouble, yo Honah!"

"Well, tell them they can get food if they go back home, peacefully. . . ."

"Yuh tell em, yo Honah!"

They looked at each other for a moment. Then the mayor turned and walked back. Taylor saw him mount the rear seat of an auto and lift his trembling hands high above the crowd, asking for silence, his face a pasty white.

A baptism of clean joy swept over Taylor. He kept his eyes on the sea of black and white faces. The song swelled louder and vibrated through him. This is the way! he thought. Gawd ain no lie! He ain no lie! His eyes grew wet with tears, blurring his vision: the sky trembled; the buildings wavered as if about to topple; and the earth shook. . . . He mumbled out loud, exultingly:

"Freedom belongs t the strong!"

V

Bright and Morning Star

I

S HE STOOD with her black face some six inches from the moist windowpane and wondered when on earth would it ever stop raining. It might keep up like this all week, she thought. She heard rain droning upon the roof and high up in the wet sky her eyes followed the silent rush of a bright shaft of yellow that swung from the airplane beacon in far off Memphis. Momently she could see it cutting through the rainy dark; it would hover a second like a gleaming sword above her head, then vanish. She sighed, troubling, Johnny-Boys been trampin in this slop all day wid no decent shoes on his feet. . . . Through the window she could see the rich black earth sprawling outside in the night. There was more rain than the clay could soak up; pools stood everywhere. She yawned and mumbled: "Rains good n bad. It kin make seeds bus up thu the groun, er it kin bog things down lika watah-soaked coffin." Her hands were folded loosely over her stomach and the hot air of the kitchen traced a filmy veil of sweat on her forehead. From the cook stove came the soft singing of burning wood and now and then a throaty bubble rose from a pot of simmering greens.

"Shucks, Johnny-Boy coulda let somebody else do all tha runnin in the rain. Theres others bettah fixed fer it than he is. But, naw! Johnny-Boy ain the one t trust nobody t do nothing. Hes gotta do it *all* hissef. . . ."

She glanced at a pile of damp clothes in a zinc tub. Waal, Ah bettah git t work. She turned, lifted a smoothing iron with a thick pad of cloth, touched a spit-wet finger to it with a quick, jerking motion: *smiiitz!* Yeah; its hot! Stooping, she took a blue work-shirt from the tub and shook it out. With a deft twist of her shoulder she caught the iron in her right hand; the fingers of her left hand took a piece of wax from a tin box and a frying sizzle came as she smeared the bottom. She was thinking of nothing now; her hands followed a life-

407

long ritual of toil. Spreading a sleeve, she ran the hot iron to
and fro until the wet cloth became stiff. She was deep in the
midst of her work when a song rose up out of the far off days
of her childhood and broke through half-parted lips:

> *Hes the Lily of the Valley, the Bright n Mawnin Star*
> *Hes the Fairest of Ten Thousan t mah soul . . .*

A gust of wind dashed rain against the window. Johnny-
Boy oughta c mon home n eat his suppah. Aw, Lawd! Itd be
fine ef Sug could eat wid us tonight! Itd be like ol times!
Mabbe aftah all it wont be long fo he comes back. Tha lettah
Ah got from im las week said *Don give up hope.* . . . Yeah; we
gotta live in hope. Then both of her sons, Sug and Johnny-
Boy, would be back with her.

With an involuntary nervous gesture, she stopped and
stood still, listening. But the only sound was the lulling fall
of rain. Shucks, ain no usa me ackin this way, she thought.
Ever time they gits ready to hol them meetings Ah gits jump-
ity. Ah been a lil scared ever since Sug went t jail. She heard
the clock ticking and looked. Johnny-Boys a *hour* late! He
sho mus be havin a time doin all tha trampin, trampin thu the
mud. . . . But her fear was a quiet one; it was more like
an intense brooding than a fear; it was a sort of hugging of
hated facts so closely that she could feel their grain, like letting cold water run over her hand from a faucet on a winter
morning.

She ironed again, faster now, as if she felt the more she
engaged her body in work the less she would think. But how
could she forget Johnny-Boy out there on those wet fields
rounding up white and black Communists for a meeting tomorrow? And that was just what Sug had been doing when
the sheriff had caught him, beat him, and tried to make him
tell who and where his comrades were. Po Sug! They sho
musta beat the boy somethin awful! But, thank Gawd, he
didnt talk! He ain no weaklin, Sug ain! Hes been lion-hearted
all his life long.

That had happened a year ago. And now each time those
meetings came around the old terror surged back. While
shoving the iron a cluster of toiling days returned; days of

washing and ironing to feed Johnny-Boy and Sug so they could do party work; days of carrying a hundred pounds of white folks' clothes upon her head across fields sometimes wet and sometimes dry. But in those days a hundred pounds was nothing to carry carefully balanced upon her head while stepping by instinct over the corn and cotton rows. The only time it had seemed heavy was when she had heard of Sug's arrest. She had been coming home one morning with a bundle upon her head, her hands swinging idly by her sides, walking slowly with her eyes in front of her, when Bob, Johnny-Boy's pal, had called from across the fields and had come and told her that the sheriff had got Sug. That morning the bundle had become heavier than she could ever remember.

And with each passing week now, though she spoke of it to no one, things were becoming heavier. The tubs of water and the smoothing iron and the bundle of clothes were becoming harder to lift, with her back aching so; and her work was taking longer, all because Sug was gone and she didn't know just when Johnny-Boy would be taken too. To ease the ache of anxiety that was swelling her heart, she hummed, then sang softly:

> *He walks wid me, He talks wid me*
> *He tells me Ahm His own. . . .*

Guiltily, she stopped and smiled. Looks like Ah jus cant seem t fergit them ol songs, no mattah how hard Ah tries. . . . She had learned them when she was a little girl living and working on a farm. Every Monday morning from the corn and cotton fields the slow strains had floated from her mother's lips, lonely and haunting; and later, as the years had filled with gall, she had learned their deep meaning. Long hours of scrubbing floors for a few cents a day had taught her who Jesus was, what a great boon it was to cling to Him, to be like Him and suffer without a mumbling word. She had poured the yearning of her life into the songs, feeling buoyed with a faith beyond this world. The figure of the Man nailed in agony to the Cross, His burial in a cold grave, His transfigured Resurrection, His being breath and clay, God and

Man—all had focused her feelings upon an imagery which had swept her life into a wondrous vision.

But as she had grown older, a cold white mountain, the white folks and their laws, had swum into her vision and shattered her songs and their spell of peace. To her that white mountain was temptation, something to lure her from her Lord, a part of the world God had made in order that she might endure it and come through all the stronger, just as Christ had risen with greater glory from the tomb. The days crowded with trouble had enhanced her faith and she had grown to love hardship with a bitter pride; she had obeyed the laws of the white folks with a soft smile of secret knowing.

After her mother had been snatched up to heaven in a chariot of fire, the years had brought her a rough workingman and two black babies, Sug and Johnny-Boy, all three of whom she had wrapped in the charm and magic of her vision. Then she was tested by no less than God; her man died, a trial which she bore with the strength shed by the grace of her vision; finally even the memory of her man faded into the vision itself, leaving her with two black boys growing tall, slowly into manhood.

Then one day grief had come to her heart when Johnny-Boy and Sug had walked forth demanding their lives. She had sought to fill their eyes with her vision, but they would have none of it. And she had wept when they began to boast of the strength shed by a new and terrible vision.

But she had loved them, even as she loved them now; bleeding, her heart had followed them. She could have done no less, being an old woman in a strange world. And day by day her sons had ripped from her startled eyes her old vision, and image by image had given her a new one, different, but great and strong enough to fling her into the light of another grace. The wrongs and sufferings of black men had taken the place of Him nailed to the Cross; the meager beginnings of the party had become another Resurrection; and the hate of those who would destroy her new faith had quickened in her a hunger to feel how deeply her new strength went.

"Lawd, Johnny-Boy," she would sometimes say, "Ah just wan them white folks t try t make me tell *who* is *in* the party n who *ain*! Ah just wan em t try, n Ahll show em somethin they never thought a black woman could have!"

But sometimes like tonight, while lost in the forgetfulness of work, the past and the present would become mixed in her; while toiling under a strange star for a new freedom the old songs would slip from her lips with their beguiling sweetness.

The iron was getting cold. She put more wood into the fire, stood again at the window and watched the yellow blade of light cut through the wet darkness. Johnny-Boy ain here yit. . . . Then, before she was aware of it, she was still, listening for sounds. Under the drone of rain she heard the slosh of feet in mud. Tha ain Johnny-Boy. She knew his long, heavy footsteps in a million. She heard feet come on the porch. Some woman. . . . She heard bare knuckles knock three times, then once. Thas some of them comrades! She unbarred the door, cracked it a few inches, and flinched from the cold rush of damp wind.

"Whos tha?"

"Its me!"

"Who?"

"Me, Reva!"

She flung the door open.

"Lawd, chile, c mon in!"

She stepped to one side and a thin, blond-haired white girl ran through the door; as she slid the bolt she heard the girl gasping and shaking her wet clothes. Somethings wrong! Reva wouldna walked a mile t mah house in all this slop fer nothin! Tha gals stuck onto Johnny-Boy. Ah wondah ef anything happened t im?

"Git on inter the kitchen, Reva, where its warm."

"Lawd, Ah sho is wet!"

"How yuh reckon yuhd be, in all tha rain?"

"Johnny-Boy ain here *yit*?" asked Reva.

"Naw! N ain no usa yuh worryin bout im. Jus yuh git them shoes off! Yuh wanna ketch yo deatha col?" She stood looking absently. Yeah; its somethin about the party er Johnny-Boy thas gone wrong. Lawd, Ah wondah ef her pa knows how she feels bout Johnny-Boy? "Honey, yuh hadnt oughta come out in sloppy weather like this."

"Ah had t come, An Sue."

She led Reva to the kitchen.

"Git them shoes off n git close t the stove so yuhll git dry!"

"An Sue, Ah got somethin t tell yuh . . ."

The words made her hold her breath. Ah bet its somethin bout Johnny-Boy!

"Whut, honey?"

"The sheriff wuz by our house tonight. He come t see pa."

"Yeah?"

"He done got word from somewheres bout tha meetin tomorrow."

"Is it Johnny-Boy, Reva?"

"Aw, naw, An Sue! Ah ain hearda word bout im. Ain yuh seen im tonight?"

"He ain come home t eat yit."

"Where kin he be?"

"Lawd knows, chile."

"Somebodys gotta tell them comrades tha meetings off," said Reva. "The sheriffs got men watchin our house. Ah had t slip out t git here widout em followin me."

"Reva?"

"Hunh?"

"Ahma ol woman n Ah wans yuh t tell me the truth."

"Whut, An Sue?"

"Yuh ain tryin t fool me, is yuh?"

"*Fool* yuh?"

"Bout Johnny-Boy?"

"Lawd, naw, An Sue!"

"Ef theres anythin wrong jus tell me, chile. Ah kin stan it."

She stood by the ironing board, her hands as usual folded loosely over her stomach, watching Reva pull off her water-clogged shoes. She was feeling that Johnny-Boy was already lost to her; she was feeling the pain that would come when she knew it for certain; and she was feeling that she would have to be brave and bear it. She was like a person caught in a swift current of water and knew where the water was sweeping her and did not want to go on but had to go on to the end.

"It ain nothin bout Johnny-Boy, An Sue," said Reva. "But we gotta do somethin er we'll all git inter trouble."

"How the sheriff know about tha meetin?"

"Thas whut pa wans t know."

"Somebody done turned Judas."

"Sho looks like it."

"Ah bet it wuz some of them new ones," she said.

"Its hard t tell," said Reva.

"Lissen, Reva, yuh oughta stay here n git dry, but yuh bet-tah git back n tell yo pa Johnny-Boy ain here n Ah don know when hes gonna show up. *Some*bodys gotta tell them com-rades t stay erway from yo pas house."

She stood with her back to the window, looking at Reva's wide, blue eyes. Po critter! Gotta go back thu all tha slop! Though she felt sorry for Reva, not once did she think that it would not have to be done. Being a woman, Reva was not suspect; she would *have* to go. It was just as natural for Reva to go back through the cold rain as it was for her to iron night and day, or for Sug to be in jail. Right now, Johnny-Boy was out there on those dark fields trying to get home. Lawd, don let em git im tonight! In spite of herself her feel-ings became torn. She loved her son and, loving him, she loved what he was trying to do. Johnny-Boy was happiest when he was working for the party, and her love for him was for his happiness. She frowned, trying hard to fit something together in her feelings: for her to try to stop Johnny-Boy was to admit that all the toil of years meant nothing; and to let him go meant that sometime or other he would be caught, like Sug. In facing it this way she felt a little stunned, as though she had come suddenly upon a blank wall in the dark. But outside in the rain were people, white and black, whom she had known all her life. Those people depended upon Johnny-Boy, loved him and looked to him as a man and leader. Yeah; hes gotta keep on; he cant stop now. . . . She looked at Reva; she was crying and pulling her shoes back on with reluctant fingers.

"Whut yuh carryin on tha way fer, chile?"

"Yuh done los Sug, now yuh sendin Johnny-Boy . . ."

"Ah got t, honey."

She was glad she could say that. Reva believed in black folks and not for anything in the world would she falter be-fore her. In Reva's trust and acceptance of her she had found

her first feelings of humanity; Reva's love was her refuge from
shame and degradation. If in the early days of her life the
white mountain had driven her back from the earth, then in
her last days Reva's love was drawing her toward it, like the
beacon that swung through the night outside. She heard
Reva sobbing.

"Hush, honey!"

"Mah brothers in jail too! Ma cries ever day . . ."

"Ah know, honey."

She helped Reva with her coat; her fingers felt the scant
flesh of the girl's shoulders. She don git ernuff t eat, she
thought. She slipped her arms around Reva's waist and held
her close for a moment.

"Now, yuh stop that cryin."

"A-a-ah c-c-cant hep it. . . ."

"Everythingll be awright; Johnny-Boyll be back."

"Yuh think so?"

"Sho, chile. Cos he will."

Neither of them spoke again until they stood in the doorway. Outside they could hear water washing through the ruts
of the street.

"Be sho n send Johnny-Boy t tell the folks t stay erway from
pas house," said Reva.

"Ahll tell im. Don yuh worry."

"Good-bye!"

"Good-bye!"

Leaning against the door jamb, she shook her head slowly
and watched Reva vanish through the falling rain.

II

She was back at her board, ironing, when she heard feet sucking in the mud of the back yard; feet she knew from long years
of listening were Johnny-Boy's. But tonight, with all the rain
and fear, his coming was like a leaving, was almost more than
she could bear. Tears welled to her eyes and she blinked them
away. She felt that he was coming so that she could give him
up; to see him now was to say good-bye. But it was a good-bye
she knew she could never say; they were not that way toward
each other. All day long they could sit in the same room and not

speak; she was his mother and he was her son. Most of the time a nod or a grunt would carry all the meaning that she wanted to convey to him, or he to her. She did not even turn her head when she heard him come stomping into the kitchen. She heard him pull up a chair, sit, sigh, and draw off his muddy shoes; they fell to the floor with heavy thuds. Soon the kitchen was full of the scent of his drying socks and his burning pipe. Tha boys hongry! She paused and looked at him over her shoulder; he was puffing at his pipe with his head tilted back and his feet propped up on the edge of the stove; his eyelids drooped and his wet clothes steamed from the heat of the fire. Lawd, tha boy gits mo like his pa ever day he lives, she mused, her lips breaking in a slow faint smile. Hols tha pipe in his mouth just like his pa usta hol his. Wondah how they woulda got erlong ef his pa hada lived? They oughta liked each other, they so much alike. She wished there could have been other children besides Sug, so Johnny-Boy would not have to be so much alone. A man needs a woman by his side. . . . She thought of Reva; she liked Reva; the brightest glow her heart had ever known was when she had learned that Reva loved Johnny-Boy. But beyond Reva were cold white faces. Ef theys caught it means *death*. . . . She jerked around when she heard Johnny-Boy's pipe clatter to the floor. She saw him pick it up, smile sheepishly at her, and wag his head.

"Gawd, Ahm sleepy," he mumbled.

She got a pillow from her room and gave it to him.

"Here," she said.

"Hunh," he said, putting the pillow between his head and the back of the chair.

They were silent again. Yes, she would have to tell him to go back out into the cold rain and slop; maybe to get caught; maybe for the last time; she didn't know. But she would let him eat and get dry before telling him that the sheriff knew of the meeting to be held at Lem's tomorrow. And she would make him take a big dose of soda before he went out; soda always helped to stave off a cold. She looked at the clock. It was eleven. Theres time yit. Spreading a newspaper on the apron of the stove, she placed a heaping plate of greens upon it, a knife, a fork, a cup of coffee, a slab of cornbread, and a dish of peach cobbler.

"Yo suppahs ready," she said.

"Yeah," he said.

He did not move. She ironed again. Presently, she heard him eating. When she could no longer hear his knife tinkling against the edge of the plate, she knew he was through. It was almost twelve now. She would let him rest a little while longer before she told him. Till one er'clock, mabbe. Hes so tired. . . . She finished her ironing, put away the board, and stacked the clothes in her dresser drawer. She poured herself a cup of black coffee, drew up a chair, sat down and drank.

"Yuh almos dry," she said, not looking around.

"Yeah," he said, turning sharply to her.

The tone of voice in which she had spoken had let him know that more was coming. She drained her cup and waited a moment longer.

"Reva wuz here."

"Yeah?"

"She lef bout a hour ergo."

"Whut she say?"

"She said ol man Lem hada visit from the sheriff today."

"Bout the meetin?"

"Yeah."

She saw him stare at the coals glowing red through the crevices of the stove and run his fingers nervously through his hair. She knew he was wondering how the sheriff had found out. In the silence he would ask a wordless question and in the silence she would answer wordlessly. Johnny-Boys too trustin, she thought. Hes trying t make the party big n hes takin in folks fastern he kin git t know em. You cant trust ever white man yuh meet. . . .

"Yuh know, Johnny-Boy, yuh been takin in a lotta them white folks lately . . ."

"Aw, ma!"

"But, Johnny-Boy . . ."

"Please, don talk t me bout tha now, ma."

"Yuh ain t ol t lissen n learn, son," she said.

"Ah know whut yuh gonna say, ma. N yuh wrong. Yuh cant judge folks jus by how yuh feel bout em n by how long yuh done knowed em. Ef we start tha we wouldnt have *no*body in the party. When folks pledge they word t be with us, then we gotta take em in. Wes too weak t be choosy."

He rose abruptly, rammed his hands into his pockets, and stood facing the window; she looked at his back in a long silence. She knew his faith; it was deep. He had always said that black men could not fight the rich bosses alone; a man could not fight with every hand against him. But he believes so hard hes blind, she thought. At odd times they had had these arguments before; always she would be pitting her feelings against the hard necessity of his thinking, and always she would lose. She shook her head. Po Johnny-Boy; he don know . . .

"But ain nona our folks tol, Johnny-Boy," she said.

"How yuh know?" he asked. His voice came low and with a tinge of anger. He still faced the window and now and then the yellow blade of light flicked across the sharp outline of his black face.

"Cause Ah know em," she said.

"*Any*body mighta tol," he said.

"It wuznt nona *our* folks," she said again.

She saw his hand sweep in a swift arc of disgust.

"*Our* folks! Ma, who in Gawds name is *our* folks?"

"The folks we wuz born n raised wid, son. The folks we *know*!"

"We cant make the party grow tha way, ma."

"It mighta been Booker," she said.

"Yuh don know."

". . . er Blattberg . . ."

"Fer Chrissakes!"

". . . er any of the fo-five others whut joined las week."

"Ma, yuh jus don wan me t go out tonight," he said.

"Yo ol ma wans yuh t be careful, son."

"Ma, when yuh start doubtin folks in the party, then there ain no end."

"Son, Ah knows ever black man n woman in this parta the county," she said, standing too. "Ah watched em grow up; Ah even heped birth n nurse some of em; Ah knows em *all* from way back. There ain none of em that *coulda* tol! The folks Ah know jus don open they dos n ast death t walk in!

Son, it wuz some of them *white* folks! Yuh jus mark mah word n wait n see!"

"Why is it gotta be *white* folks?" he asked. "Ef they tol, then theys jus Judases, thas all."

"Son, look at whuts befo yuh."

He shook his head and sighed.

"Ma, Ah done tol yuh a hundred times. Ah cant see white n Ah cant see black," he said. "Ah sees rich men n Ah sees po men."

She picked up his dirty dishes and piled them in a pan. Out of the corners of her eyes she saw him sit and pull on his wet shoes. *Hes goin!* When she put the last dish away he was standing fully dressed, warming his hands over the stove. *Jus a few mo minutes now n he'll be gone, like Sug, mabbe.* Her throat tightened. *This black mans fight takes* ever*thin! Looks like Gawd put us in this worl jus t beat us down!*

"Keep this, ma," he said.

She saw a crumpled wad of money in his outstretched fingers.

"Naw; yuh keep it. Yuh might need it."

"It ain mine, ma. It berlongs t the party."

"But, Johnny-Boy, yuh might hafta go erway!"

"Ah kin make out."

"Don fergit yosef too much, son."

"Ef Ah don come back theyll need it."

He was looking at her face and she was looking at the money.

"Yuh keep tha," she said slowly. "Ahll give em the money."

"From where?"

"Ah got some."

"Where yuh git it from?"

She sighed.

"Ah been savin a dollah a week fer Sug ever since hes been in jail."

"Lawd, ma!"

She saw the look of puzzled love and wonder in his eyes. Clumsily, he put the money back into his pocket.

"Ahm gone," he said.

"Here; drink this glass of soda watah."

She watched him drink, then put the glass away.

"Waal," he said.

"Take the stuff outta yo pockets!"

She lifted the lid of the stove and he dumped all the papers from his pocket into the fire. She followed him to the door and made him turn round.

"Lawd, yuh tryin to maka revolution n yuh cant even keep yo coat buttoned." Her nimble fingers fastened his collar high around his throat. "There!"

He pulled the brim of his hat low over his eyes. She opened the door and with the suddenness of the cold gust of wind that struck her face, he was gone. She watched the black fields and the rain take him, her eyes burning. When the last faint footstep could no longer be heard, she closed the door, went to her bed, lay down, and pulled the cover over her while fully dressed. Her feelings coursed with the rhythm of the rain: Hes gone! Lawd, Ah *know* hes gone! Her blood felt cold.

III

She was floating in a grey void somewhere between sleeping and dreaming and then suddenly she was wide awake, hearing and feeling in the same instant the thunder of the door crashing in and a cold wind filling the room. It was pitch black and she stared, resting on her elbows, her mouth open, not breathing, her ears full of the sound of tramping feet and booming voices. She knew at once: They lookin fer im! Then, filled with her will, she was on her feet, rigid, waiting, listening.

"The lamps burnin!"

"Yuh see her?"

"Naw!"

"Look in the kitchen!"

"Gee, this place smells like niggers!"

"Say, somebodys here er been here!"

"Yeah; theres fire in the stove!"

"Mabbe hes been here n gone?"

"Boy, look at these jars of jam!"

"Niggers make good jam!"

"Git some bread!"

"Heres some cornbread!"

"Say, lemme git some!"

"Take it easy! Theres plenty here!"

"Ahma take some of this stuff home!"

"Look, heres a pota greens!"

"N some hot cawffee!"

"Say, yuh guys! C mon! Cut it out! We didnt come here fer a feas!"

She walked slowly down the hall. They lookin fer im, but they ain got im yit! She stopped in the doorway, her gnarled, black hands as always folded over her stomach, but tight now, so tightly the veins bulged. The kitchen was crowded with white men in glistening raincoats. Though the lamp burned, their flashlights still glowed in red fists. Across her floor she saw the muddy tracks of their boots.

"Yuh white folks git outta mah house!"

There was quick silence; every face turned toward her. She saw a sudden movement, but did not know what it meant until something hot and wet slammed her squarely in the face. She gasped, but did not move. Calmly, she wiped the warm, greasy liquor of greens from her eyes with her left hand. One of the white men had thrown a handful of greens out of the pot at her.

"How they taste, ol bitch?"

"Ah ast yuh t git outta mah house!"

She saw the sheriff detach himself from the crowd and walk toward her.

"Now, Anty . . ."

"White man, don yuh *Anty* me!"

"Yuh ain got the right sperit!"

"Sperit hell! Yuh git these men outta mah house!"

"Yuh ack like yuh don like it!"

"Naw, Ah don like it, n yuh knows dam waal Ah don!"

"Whut yuh gonna do bout it?"

"Ahm tellin yuh t git outta mah house!"

"Gittin sassy?"

"Ef telling yuh t git outta mah house is sass, then Ahm sassy!"

Her words came in a tense whisper; but beyond, back of them, she was watching, thinking, judging the men.

"Listen, Anty," the sheriff's voice came soft and low. "Ahm here t hep yuh. How come yuh wanna ack this way?"

"Yuh ain never heped yo *own* sef since yuh been born," she flared. "How kin the likes of yuh hep me?"

One of the white men came forward and stood directly in front of her.

"Lissen, nigger woman, yuh talkin t *white* men!"

"Ah don care who Ahm talkin t!"

"Yuhll wish some day yuh did!"

"Not t the likes of yuh!"

"Yuh need somebody t teach yuh how t be a good nigger!"

"*Yuh* cant teach it t me!"

"Yuh gonna change yo tune."

"Not longs mah bloods warm!"

"Don git smart now!"

"Yuh git outta mah house!"

"Spose we don go?" the sheriff asked.

They were crowded around her. She had not moved since she had taken her place in the doorway. She was thinking only of Johnny-Boy as she stood there giving and taking words; and she knew that they, too, were thinking of Johnny-Boy. She knew they wanted him, and her heart was daring them to take him from her.

"Spose we don go?" the sheriff asked again.

"Twenty of yuh runnin over one ol woman! Now, ain yuh white men glad yuh so brave?"

The sheriff grabbed her arm.

"C mon, now! Yuh done did ernuff sass fer one night. Wheres tha nigger son of yos?"

"Don yuh wished yuh knowed?"

"Yuh wanna git slapped?"

"Ah ain never seen one of yo kind tha wuznt too low fer . . ."

The sheriff slapped her straight across her face with his open palm. She fell back against a wall and sank to her knees.

"Is tha whut white men do t nigger women?"

She rose slowly and stood again, not even touching the place that ached from his blow, her hands folded over her stomach.

"Ah ain never seen one of yo kind tha wuznt too low fer . . ."

He slapped her again; she reeled backward several feet and fell on her side.

"Is tha whut we too low t do?"

She stood before him again, dry-eyed, as though she had not been struck. Her lips were numb and her chin was wet with blood.

"Aw, let her go! Its the nigger we wan!" said one.

"Wheres that nigger son of yos?" the sheriff asked.

"Find im," she said.

"By Gawd, ef we hafta find im we'll kill im!"

"He wont be the only nigger yuh ever killed," she said.

She was consumed with a bitter pride. There was nothing on this earth, she felt then, that they could not do to her but that she could take. She stood on a narrow plot of ground from which she would die before she was pushed. And then it was, while standing there feeling warm blood seeping down her throat, that she gave up Johnny-Boy, gave him up to the white folks. She gave him up because they had come tramping into her heart demanding him, thinking they could get him by beating her, thinking they could scare her into making her tell where he was. She gave him up because she wanted them to know that they could not get what they wanted by bluffing and killing.

"Wheres this meetin gonna be?" the sheriff asked.

"Don yuh wish yuh knowed?"

"Ain there gonna be a meetin?"

"How come yuh astin me?"

"There *is* gonna be a meetin," said the sheriff.

"Is it?"

"Ah gotta great mind t choke it outta yuh!"

"Yuh so smart," she said.

"We ain playin wid yuh!"

"Did Ah say yuh wuz?"

"Tha nigger son of yos is erroun here somewheres n we aim t find im," said the sheriff. "Ef yuh tell us where he is n ef he talks, mabbe he'll git off easy. But ef we hafta find im, we'll kill im! Ef we hafta find im, then yuh git a sheet t put over im in the mawnin, see? Git yuh a sheet, cause hes gonna be dead!"

"He wont be the only nigger yuh ever killed," she said again.

The sheriff walked past her. The others followed. Yuh didnt git whut yuh wanted! she thought exultingly. N yuh ain gonna *never* git it! Hotly, something ached in her to make them feel the intensity of her pride and freedom; her heart groped to turn the bitter hours of her life into words of a kind that would make them feel that she had taken all they had done to her in her stride and could still take more. Her faith surged so strongly in her she was all but blinded. She walked behind them to the door, knotting and twisting her fingers. She saw them step to the muddy ground. Each whirl of the yellow beacon revealed glimpses of slanting rain. Her lips moved, then she shouted:

"Yuh didnt git whut yuh wanted! N yuh ain gonna nevah git it!"

The sheriff stopped and turned; his voice came low and hard.

"Now, by Gawd, thas ernuff outta yuh!"

"Ah know when Ah done said ernuff!"

"Aw, naw, yuh don!" he said. "Yuh don know when yuh done said ernuff, but Ahma teach yuh ternight!"

He was up the steps and across the porch with one bound. She backed into the hall, her eyes full on his face.

"Tell me when yuh gonna stop talkin!" he said, swinging his fist.

The blow caught her high on the cheek; her eyes went blank; she fell flat on her face. She felt the hard heel of his wet shoes coming into her temple and stomach.

"Lemme hear yuh talk some mo!"

She wanted to, but could not; pain numbed and choked her. She lay still and somewhere out of the grey void of un-consciousness she heard someone say: *aw fer chrissakes leave her erlone its the nigger we wan. . . .*

IV

She never knew how long she had lain huddled in the dark hallway. Her first returning feeling was of a nameless fear crowding the inside of her, then a deep pain spreading from her temple downward over her body. Her ears were filled with the drone of rain and she shuddered from the cold wind blowing through the door. She opened her eyes and at first saw nothing. As if she were imagining it, she knew she was half-lying and half-sitting in a corner against a wall. With difficulty she twisted her neck and what she saw made her hold her breath—a vast white blur was suspended directly above her. For a moment she could not tell if her fear was from the blur or if the blur was from her fear. Gradually the blur resolved itself into a huge white face that slowly filled her vision. She was stone still, conscious really of the effort to breathe, feeling somehow that she existed only by the mercy of that white face. She had seen it before; its fear had gripped her many times; it had for her the fear of all the white faces she had ever seen in her life. *Sue . . .* As from a great distance, she heard her name being called. She was regaining consciousness now, but the fear was coming with her. She looked into the face of a white man, wanting to scream out for him to go; yet accepting his presence because she felt she had to. Though some remote part of her mind was active, her limbs were powerless. It was as if an invisible knife had split her in two, leaving one half of her lying there helpless, while the other half shrank in dread from a forgotten but familiar enemy. *Sue its me Sue its me . . .* Then all at once the voice came clearly.

"Sue, its me! Its Booker!"

And she heard an answering voice speaking inside of her, Yeah, its Booker . . . The one whut jus joined . . . She roused herself, struggling for full consciousness; and as she did so she transferred to the person of Booker the nameless fear she felt. It seemed that Booker towered above her as a challenge to her right to exist upon the earth.

"Yuh awright?"

She did not answer; she started violently to her feet and fell.

"Sue, yuh hurt!"

"Yeah," she breathed.

"Where they hit yuh?"

"Its mah head," she whispered.

She was speaking even though she did not want to; the fear that had hold of her compelled her.

"They beat yuh?"

"Yeah."

"Them bastards! Them Gawddam bastards!"

She heard him saying it over and over; then she felt herself being lifted.

"Naw!" she gasped.

"Ahma take yuh t the kitchen!"

"Put me down!"

"But yuh cant stay here like this!"

She shrank in his arms and pushed her hands against his body; when she was in the kitchen she freed herself, sank into a chair, and held tightly to its back. She looked wonderingly at Booker. There was nothing about him that should frighten her so, but even that did not ease her tension. She saw him go to the water bucket, wet his handkerchief, wring it, and offer it to her. Distrustfully, she stared at the damp cloth.

"Here; put this on yo fohead . . ."

"Naw!"

"C mon; itll make yuh feel bettah!"

She hesitated in confusion. What right had she to be afraid when someone was acting as kindly as this toward her? Reluctantly, she leaned forward and pressed the damp cloth to her head. It helped. With each passing minute she was catching hold of herself, yet wondering why she felt as she did.

"Whut happened?"

"Ah don know."

"Yuh feel bettah?"

"Yeah."

"Who all wuz here?"

"Ah don know," she said again.

"Yo head still hurt?"

"Yeah."

"Gee, Ahm sorry."

"Ahm awright," she sighed and buried her face in her hands.

She felt him touch her shoulder.

"Sue, Ah got some bad news fer yuh . . ."

She knew; she stiffened and grew cold. It had happened; she stared dry-eyed, with compressed lips.

"Its mah Johnny-Boy," she said.

"Yeah; Ahm awful sorry t hafta tell yuh this way. But Ah thought yuh oughta know . . ."

Her tension eased and a vacant place opened up inside of her. A voice whispered, Jesus, hep me!

"W-w-where is he?"

"They got im out t Foleys Woods tryin t make im tell who the others is."

"He ain gonna tell," she said. "They just as waal kill im, cause he ain gonna nevah tell."

"Ah hope he don," said Booker. "But he didnt hava chance t tell the others. They grabbed im jus as he got t the woods."

Then all the horror of it flashed upon her; she saw flung out over the rainy countryside an array of shacks where white and black comrades were sleeping; in the morning they would be rising and going to Lem's; then they would be caught. And that meant terror, prison, and death. The comrades would have to be told; she would have to tell them; she could not entrust Johnny-Boy's work to another, and especially not to Booker as long as she felt toward him as she did. Gripping the bottom of the chair with both hands, she tried to rise; the room blurred and she swayed. She found herself resting in Booker's arms.

"Lemme go!"

"Sue, yuh too weak t walk!"

"Ah gotta tell em!" she said.

"Set down, Sue! Yuh hurt! Yuh sick!"

When seated, she looked at him helplessly.

"Sue, lissen! Johnny-Boys caught. Ahm here. Yuh tell me who they is n Ahll tell em."

She stared at the floor and did not answer. Yes; she was too weak to go. There was no way for her to tramp all those miles through the rain tonight. But should she tell Booker? If only she had somebody like Reva to talk to! She did not want to decide alone; she must make no mistake about this. She felt Booker's fingers pressing on her arm and it was as though the white mountain was pushing her to the edge of a sheer height; she again exclaimed inwardly, Jesus, hep me! Booker's white face was at her side, waiting. Would she be doing right to tell him? Suppose she did not tell and then the comrades were caught? She could not ever forgive herself for doing a thing like that. But maybe she was wrong; maybe her fear was what Johnny-Boy had always called "jus foolishness." She remembered his saying, Ma we cant make the party grow ef we start doubtin everbody. . . .

"Tell me who they is, Sue, n Ahll tell em. Ah jus joined n Ah don know who they is."

"Ah don know who they is," she said.

"Yuh *gotta* tell me who they is, Sue!"

"Ah tol yuh Ah don know!"

"Yuh *do* know! C mon! Set up n talk!"

"Naw!"

"Yuh wan em all t git *killed*?"

She shook her head and swallowed. Lawd, Ah don blieve in this man!

"Lissen, Ahll call the names n yuh tell me which ones is in the party n which ones ain, see?"

"Naw!"

"Please, Sue!"

"Ah don know," she said.

"Sue, yuh ain doin right by em. Johnny-Boy wouldnt wan yuh t be this way. Hes out there holdin up his end. Les hol up ours . . ."

"Lawd, Ah don know . . ."

"Is yuh scareda me cause Ahm *white*? Johnny-Boy ain like tha. Don let all the work we done go fer nothin."

She gave up and bowed her head in her hands.

"Is it Johnson? Tell me, Sue?"

"Yeah," she whispered in horror; a mounting horror of feeling herself being undone.

"Is it Green?"

"Yeah."

"Murphy?"

"Lawd, Ah don know!"

"Yuh gotta tell me, Sue!"

"Mistah Booker, please leave me erlone . . ."

"Is it Murphy?"

She answered yes to the names of Johnny-Boy's comrades; she answered until he asked her no more. Then she thought, How he know the sheriffs men is watchin Lems house? She stood up and held onto her chair, feeling something sure and firm within her.

"How yuh know bout Lem?"

"Why . . . How Ah know?"

"Whut yuh doin here this tima night? How yuh know the sheriff got Johnny-Boy?"

"Sue, don yuh blieve in me?"

She did not, but she could not answer. She stared at him until her lips hung open; she was searching deep within herself for certainty.

"You meet Reva?" she asked.

"Reva?"

"Yeah; Lems gal?"

"Oh, yeah. Sho, Ah met Reva."

"She tell yuh?"

She asked the question more of herself than of him; she longed to believe.

"Yeah," he said softly. "Ah reckon Ah oughta be goin t tell em now."

"Who?" she asked. "Tell *who*?"

The muscles of her body were stiff as she waited for his answer; she felt as though life depended upon it.

"The comrades," he said.

"Yeah," she sighed.

She did not know when he left; she was not looking or listening. She just suddenly saw the room empty and from her the thing that had made her fearful was gone.

V

For a space of time that seemed to her as long as she had been upon the earth, she sat huddled over the cold stove. One minute she would say to herself, They both gone now; Johnny-Boy n Sug . . . Mabbe Ahll never see em ergin. Then a surge of guilt would blot out her longing. "Lawd, Ah shouldna tol!" she mumbled. "But no man kin be so low-down as t do a thing like tha . . ." Several times she had an impulse to try to tell the comrades herself; she was feeling a little better now. But what good would that do? She had told Booker the names. He jus couldnt be a Judas t po folks like us . . . He *couldnt*!

"An Sue!"

Thas Reva! Her heart leaped with an anxious gladness. She

rose without answering and limped down the dark hallway. Through the open door, against the background of rain, she saw Reva's face lit now and then to whiteness by the whirling beams of the beacon. She was about to call, but a thought checked her. Jesus, hep me! Ah gotta tell her bout Johnny-Boy . . . Lawd, Ah cant!

"An Sue, yuh there?"

"C mon in, chile!"

She caught Reva and held her close for a moment without speaking.

"Lawd, Ahm sho glad yuh here," she said at last.

"Ah thought somethin had happened t yuh," said Reva, pulling away. "Ah saw the do open . . . Pa tol me to come back n stay wid yuh tonight . . ." Reva paused and started. "W-w-whuts the mattah?"

She was so full of having Reva with her that she did not understand what the question meant.

"Hunh?"

"Yo neck . . ."

"Aw, it ain nothin, chile. C mon in the kitchen."

"But theres blood on yo neck!"

"The sheriff wuz here . . ."

"Them fools! Whut they wanna bother yuh fer? Ah could kill em! So hep me Gawd, Ah could!"

"It ain nothin," she said.

She was wondering how to tell Reva about Johnny-Boy and Booker. Ahll wait a lil while longer, she thought. Now that Reva was here, her fear did not seem as awful as before.

"C mon, lemme fix yo head, An Sue. Yuh hurt."

They went to the kitchen. She sat silent while Reva dressed her scalp. She was feeling better now; in just a little while she would tell Reva. She felt the girl's finger pressing gently upon her head.

"Tha hurt?"

"A lil, chile."

"Yuh po thing."

"It ain nothin."

"Did Johnny-Boy come?"

She hesitated.

"Yeah."

"He done gone t tell the others?"

Reva's voice sounded so clear and confident that it mocked her. Lawd, Ah cant tell this chile . . .

"Yuh tol im, didnt yuh, An Sue?"

"Y-y-yeah . . ."

"Gee! Thas good! Ah tol pa he didnt hafta worry ef Johnny-Boy got the news. Mabbe thingsll come out awright."

"Ah hope . . ."

She could not go on; she had gone as far as she could. For the first time that night she began to cry.

"Hush, An Sue! Yuh awways been brave. Itll be awright!"

"Ain nothin awright, chile. The worls jus too much fer us, Ah reckon."

"Ef yuh cry that way itll make me cry."

She forced herself to stop. Naw; Ah cant carry on this way in fronta Reva . . . Right now she had a deep need for Reva to believe in her. She watched the girl get pine-knots from behind the stove, rekindle the fire, and put on the coffee pot.

"Yuh wan some cawffee?" Reva asked.

"Naw, honey."

"Aw, c mon, An Sue."

"Jusa lil, honey."

"Thas the way to be. Oh, say, Ah fergot," said Reva, measuring out spoonsful of coffee. "Pa tol me t tell yuh t watch out fer tha Booker man. Hes a stool."

She showed not one sign of outward movement or expression, but as the words fell from Reva's lips she went limp inside.

"Pa tol me soon as Ah got back home. He got word from town . . ."

She stopped listening. She felt as though she had been slapped to the extreme outer edge of life, into a cold darkness. She knew now what she had felt when she had looked up out of her fog of pain and had seen Booker. It was the image of all the white folks, and the fear that went with them, that she had seen and felt during her lifetime. And again, for the second time that night, something she had felt had come true. All she could say to herself was, Ah didnt like im! Gawd knows, Ah didnt! Ah tol Johnny-Boy it wuz some of them white folks . . .

"Here; drink yo cawffee . . ."

She took the cup; her fingers trembled, and the steaming liquid spilt onto her dress and leg.

"Ahm sorry, An Sue!"

Her leg was scalded, but the pain did not bother her.

"Its awright," she said.

"Wait; lemme put some lard on tha burn!"

"It don hurt."

"Yuh worried bout somethin."

"Naw, honey."

"Lemme fix yuh so mo cawffee."

"Ah don wan nothin now, Reva."

"Waal, buck up. Don be tha way . . ."

They were silent. She heard Reva drinking. No; she would not tell Reva; Reva was all she had left. But she had to do something, some way, somehow. She was undone too much as it was; and to tell Reva about Booker or Johnny-Boy was more than she was equal to; it would be too coldly shameful. She wanted to be alone and fight this thing out with herself.

"Go t bed, honey. Yuh tired."

"Naw; Ahm awright, An Sue."

She heard the bottom of Reva's empty cup clank against the top of the stove. Ah *got* t make her go t bed! Yes; Booker would tell the names of the comrades to the sheriff. If she could only stop him some way! That was the answer, the point, the star that grew bright in the morning of new hope. Soon, maybe half an hour from now, Booker would reach Foley's Woods. Hes boun t go the long way, cause he don know no short cut, she thought. Ah could wade the creek n beat im there. . . . But what would she do after that?

"Reva, honey, go t bed. Ahm awright. Yuh need res."

"Ah ain sleepy, An Sue."

"Ah knows whuts bes fer yuh, chile. Yuh tired n wet."

"Ah wanna stay up wid yuh."

She forced a smile and said:

"Ah don think they gonna hurt Johnny-Boy . . ."

"Fer *real*, An Sue?"

"Sho, honey."

"But Ah wanna wait up wid yuh."

"Thas mah job, honey. Thas whut a mas fer, t wait up fer her chullun."

"Good night, An Sue."

"Good night, honey."

She watched Reva pull up and leave the kitchen; presently she heard the shucks in the mattress whispering, and she knew that Reva had gone to bed. She was alone. Through the cracks of the stove she saw the fire dying to grey ashes; the room was growing cold again. The yellow beacon continued to flit past the window and the rain still drummed. Yes; she was alone; she had done this awful thing alone; she must find some way out, alone. Like touching a festering sore, she put her finger upon that moment when she had shouted her defiance to the sheriff, when she had shouted to feel her strength. She had lost Sug to save others; she had let Johnny-Boy go to save others; and then in a moment of weakness that came from too much strength she had lost all. If she had not shouted to the sheriff, she would have been strong enough to have resisted Booker; she would have been able to tell the comrades herself. Something tightened in her as she remembered and understood the fit of fear she had felt on coming to herself in the dark hallway. A part of her life she thought she had done away with forever had had hold of her then. She had thought the soft, warm past was over; she had thought that it did not mean much when now she sang: *Hes the Lily of the Valley, the Bright n Mawnin Star"* . . . The days when she had sung that song were the days when she had not hoped for anything on this earth, the days when the cold mountain had driven her into the arms of Jesus. She had thought that Sug and Johnny-Boy had taught her to forget Him, to fix her hope upon the fight of black men for freedom. Through the gradual years she had believed and worked with them, had felt strength shed from the grace of their terrible vision. That grace had been upon her when she had let the sheriff slap her down; it had been upon her when she had risen time and again from the floor and faced him. But she had trapped herself with her own hunger; to water the long dry thirst of her faith her pride had made a bargain which her flesh could not keep. Her having told the names of Johnny-Boy's comrades was but an incident in a deeper horror. She stood up and looked at the floor while call and counter-call, loyalty and counter-loyalty struggled in her soul. Mired she was between two abandoned worlds, living, but dying without the strength of the grace that either gave. The clearer she felt it the fuller did something well up from the depths of her for release; the more urgent did she feel the need to fling into her black sky another star, another hope, one more terrible vision to give her the strength to live and act. Softly and restlessly she walked about the kitchen, feeling herself naked against the night, the rain, the world; and shamed whenever the thought of Reva's love crossed her mind. She lifted her empty hands and looked at her writhing fingers. Lawd, whut kin Ah do now? She could still wade the creek and get to Foley's Woods before Booker. And then what? How could she manage to see Johnny-Boy or Booker? Again she heard the sheriff's threatening voice: Git yuh a sheet, cause hes gonna be dead! The sheet! Thas it, the *sheet*! Her whole being leaped with will; the long years of her life bent toward a moment of focus, a point. Ah kin go wid mah sheet! Ahll be doin whut he said! Lawd Gawd in Heaven, Ahma go lika nigger woman wid mah windin sheet t git mah dead son! But then what? She stood straight and smiled grimly; she had in her heart the whole meaning of her life; her entire personality was poised on the brink of a total act. Ah know! Ah *know*! She thought of Johnny-Boy's gun in the dresser drawer. Ahll hide the gun in the sheet n go aftah Johnny-Boys body. . . . She tiptoed to her room, eased out the dresser drawer, and got a sheet. Reva was sleeping; the darkness was filled with her quiet breathing. She groped in the drawer and found the gun. She wound the gun in the sheet and held them both under her apron. Then she stole to the bedside and watched Reva. Lawd, hep her! But mabbe shes bettah off. This had t happen sometimes . . . She n Johnny-Boy couldna been together in this here South . . . N Ah couldnt tell her bout Booker. Itll come out awright n she wont nevah know. Reva's trust would never be shaken. She caught her breath as the shucks in the mattress rustled dryly; then all was quiet and she breathed easily again. She tiptoed to the door, down the hall, and stood on the porch. Above her the yellow beacon whirled through the rain. She went over muddy ground, mounted a slope, stopped and looked back at her house. The lamp glowed in her window, and the yellow beacon that swung every few seconds seemed to feed it with light. She turned and started across the fields, holding the gun and sheet tightly, thinking, Po Reva . . . Po critter . . . Shes fas ersleep . . .

VI

For the most part she walked with her eyes half shut, her lips tightly compressed, leaning her body against the wind and the driving rain, feeling the pistol in the sheet sagging cold and heavy in her fingers. Already she was getting wet; it seemed that her feet found every puddle of water that stood between the corn rows.

She came to the edge of the creek and paused, wondering at what point was it low. Taking the sheet from under her apron, she wrapped the gun in it so that her finger could be upon the trigger. Ahll cross here, she thought. At first she did not feel the water; her feet were already wet. But the water grew cold as it came up to her knees; she gasped when it reached her waist. Lawd, this creeks high! When she had passed the middle, she knew that she was out of danger. She came out of the water, climbed a grassy hill, walked on, turned a bend and saw the lights of autos gleaming ahead. Yeah; theys still there! She hurried with her head down. Wondah did Ah beat im here? Lawd, Ah *hope* so! A vivid image of Booker's white face hovered a moment before her eyes and a surging will rose up in her so hard and strong that it vanished. She was among the autos now. From nearby came the hoarse voices of the men.

"Hey, yuh!"

She stopped, nervously clutching the sheet. Two white men with shotguns came toward her.

"Whut in hell yuh doin out here?"

She did not answer.

"Didnt yuh hear somebody speak t yuh?"

"Ahm comin aftah mah son," she said humbly.

"Yo *son*?"

"Yessuh."

"Whut yo son doin out here?"

"The sheriffs got im."

"Holy Scott! Jim, its the niggers ma!"

"Whut yuh got there?" asked one.

"A sheet."

"A *sheet*?"

"Yessuh."

"Fer whut?"

"The sheriff tol me t bring a sheet t git his body."

"Waal, waal . . ."

"Now, ain tha somethin?"

The white men looked at each other.

"These niggers sho love one ernother," said one.

"N tha ain no lie," said the other.

"Take me t the sheriff," she begged.

"Yuh ain givin us *orders*, is yuh?"

"Nawsuh."

"We'll take yuh when wes good n ready."

"Yessuh."

"So yuh wan his body?"

"Yessuh."

"Waal, he ain dead yit."

"They gonna kill im," she said.

"Ef he talks they wont."

"He ain gonna talk," she said.

"How yuh know?"

"Cause he ain."

"We got ways of makin niggers talk."

"Yuh ain got no way fer im."

"Yuh thinka lot of that black Red, don yuh?"

"Hes mah son."

"Why don yuh teach im some sense?"

"Hes mah son," she said again.

"Lissen, ol nigger woman, yuh stand there wid yo hair white. Yuh got bettah sense than t blieve tha niggers kin make a revolution . . ."

"A black republic," said the other one, laughing.

"Take me t the sheriff," she begged.

"Yuh his ma," said one. "Yuh kin make im talk n tell whos in this thing wid im."

"He ain gonna talk," she said.

"Don yuh wan im t live?"

She did not answer.

"C mon, les take her t Bradley."

They grabbed her arms and she clutched hard at the sheet and gun; they led her toward the crowd in the woods. Her feelings were simple; Booker would not tell; she was there with the gun to see to that. The louder became the voices of the men the deeper became her feeling of wanting to right the mistake she had made; of wanting to fight her way back to solid ground. She would stall for time until Booker showed up. Oh, ef theyll only lemme git close t Johnny-Boy! As they led her near the crowd she saw white faces turning and looking at her and heard a rising clamor of voices.

"Whos tha?"

"A nigger woman!"

"Whut she doin out here?"

"This is his ma!" called one of the men.

"Whut she wans?"

"She brought a sheet t cover his body!"

"He ain dead yit!"

"They tryin t make im talk!"

"But he will be dead soon ef he don open up!"

"Say, look! The niggers ma brought a sheet t cover up his body!"

"Now, ain that sweet?"

"Mabbe she wans t hol a prayer meetin!"

"Did she git a preacher?"

"Say, go git Bradley!"

"O.K.!"

The crowd grew quiet. They looked at her curiously; she felt their cold eyes trying to detect some weakness in her. Humbly, she stood with the sheet covering the gun. She had already accepted all that they could do to her.

The sheriff came.

"So yuh brought yo sheet, hunh?"

"Yessuh," she whispered.

"Looks like them slaps we gave yuh learned yuh some sense, didnt they?"

She did not answer.

"Yuh don need tha sheet. Yo son ain dead yit," he said, reaching toward her.

She backed away, her eyes wide.

"Naw!"

"Now, lissen, Anty!" he said. "There ain no use in yuh ackin a fool! Go in there n tell tha nigger son of yos t tell us whos in this wid im, see? Ah promise we wont kill im ef he talks. We'll let im git outta town."

"There ain nothin Ah kin tell im," she said.

"Yuh wan us t kill im?"

She did not answer. She saw someone lean toward the sheriff and whisper.

"Bring her erlong," the sheriff said.

They led her to a muddy clearing. The rain streamed down through the ghostly glare of the flashlights. As the men formed a semi-circle she saw Johnny-Boy lying in a trough of mud. He was tied with rope; he lay hunched and one side of his face rested in a pool of black water. His eyes were staring questioningly at her.

"Speak t im," said the sheriff.

If she could only tell him why she was here! But that was impossible; she was close to what she wanted and she stared straight before her with compressed lips.

"Say, nigger!" called the sheriff, kicking Johnny-Boy. "Heres yo ma!"

Johnny-Boy did not move or speak. The sheriff faced her again.

"Lissen, Anty," he said. "Yuh got mo say wid im than any-body. Tell im t talk n hava chance. Whut he wanna pertect the other niggers n white folks fer?"

She slid her finger about the trigger of the gun and looked stonily at the mud.

"Go t him," said the sheriff.

She did not move. Her heart was crying out to answer the amazed question in Johnny-Boy's eyes. But there was no way now.

"Waal, yuhre astin fer it. By Gawd, we gotta way to *make* yuh talk t im," he said, turning away. "Say, Tim, git one of them logs n turn that nigger upside-down n put his legs on it!"

A murmur of assent ran through the crowd. She bit her lips; she knew what that meant.

"Yuh wan yo nigger son crippled?" she heard the sheriff ask.

She did not answer. She saw them roll the log up; they lifted Johnny-Boy and laid him on his face and stomach, then they pulled his legs over the log. His knee-caps rested on the sheer top of the log's back and the toes of his shoes pointed groundward. So absorbed was she in watching that she felt that it was she who was being lifted and made ready for torture.

"Git a crowbar!" said the sheriff.

A tall, lank man got a crowbar from a nearby auto and stood over the log. His jaws worked slowly on a wad of tobacco.

"Now, its up t yuh, Anty," the sheriff said. "Tell the man whut t do!"

She looked into the rain. The sheriff turned.

"Mabbe she think wes playin. Ef she don say nothin, then break em at the knee-caps!"

"O.K., Sheriff!"

She stood waiting for Booker. Her legs felt weak; she wondered if she would be able to wait much longer. Over and over she said to herself, Ef he came now Ahd kill em both!

"She ain sayin nothin, Sheriff!"

"Waal, Gawddammit, let im have it!"

The crowbar came down and Johnny-Boy's body lunged in the mud and water. There was a scream. She swayed, holding tight to the gun and sheet.

"Hol im! Git the other leg!"

The crowbar fell again. There was another scream.

"Yuh break em?" asked the sheriff.

The tall man lifted Johnny-Boy's legs and let them drop limply again, dropping rearward from the knee-caps. Johnny-Boy's body lay still. His head had rolled to one side and she could not see his face.

"Jus lika broke sparrow wing," said the man, laughing softly.

Then Johnny-Boy's face turned to her; he screamed.

"Go way, ma! Go way!"

It was the first time she had heard his voice since she had

come out to the woods; she all but lost control of herself. She started violently forward, but the sheriff's arm checked her.

"Aw, naw! Yuh had yo chance!" He turned to Johnny-Boy. "She kin go ef yuh talk."

"Mistah, he ain gonna talk," she said.

"Go way, ma!" said Johnny-Boy.

"Shoot im! Don make im suffah so," she begged.

"He'll either talk or he'll never hear yuh ergin," the sheriff said. "Theres other things we kin do t im."

She said nothing.

"What yuh come here fer, ma?" Johnny-Boy sobbed.

"Ahm gonna split his eardrums," the sheriff said. "Ef yuh got anythin t say t im yuh bettah say it *now!*"

She closed her eyes. She heard the sheriff's feet sucking in mud. Ah could save im! She opened her eyes; there were shouts of eagerness from the crowd as it pushed in closer.

"Bus em, Sheriff!"

"Fix im so he cant hear!"

"He knows how t do it, too!"

"He busted a Jew boy tha way once!"

She saw the sheriff stoop over Johnny-Boy, place his flat palm over one ear and strike his fist against it with all his might. He placed his palm over the other ear and struck again. Johnny-Boy moaned, his head rolling from side to side, his eyes showing white amazement in a world without sound.

"Yuh wouldnt talk t im when yuh had the chance," said the sheriff. "Try n talk now."

She felt warm tears on her cheeks. She longed to shoot Johnny-Boy and let him go. But if she did that they would take the gun from her, and Booker would tell who the others were. Lawd, hep me! The men were talking loudly now, as though the main business was over. It seemed ages that she stood there watching Johnny-Boy roll and whimper in his world of silence.

"Say, Sheriff, heres somebody lookin fer yuh!"

"Who is it?"

"Ah don know!"

"Bring em in!"

She stiffened and looked around wildly, holding the gun tight. Is tha Booker? Then she held still, feeling that her

excitement might betray her. Mabbe Ah kin shoot em both!
Mabbe Ah kin shoot *twice*! The sheriff stood in front of her,
waiting. The crowd parted and she saw Booker hurrying
forward.

"Ah know em all, Sheriff!" he called.

He came full into the muddy clearing where Johnny-Boy lay.

"Yuh mean yuh got the names?"

"Sho! The ol nigger . . ."

She saw his lips hang open and silent when he saw her. She
stepped forward and raised the sheet.

"Whut . . ."

She fired, once; then, without pausing, she turned, hearing
them yell. She aimed at Johnny-Boy, but they had their arms
around her, bearing her to the ground, clawing at the sheet in
her hand. She glimpsed Booker lying sprawled in the mud, on
his face, his hands stretched out before him; then a cluster of
yelling men blotted him out. She lay without struggling,
looking upward through the rain at the white faces above her.
And she was suddenly at peace; they were not a white mountain now; they were not pushing her any longer to the edge
of life. Its awright . . .

"She shot Booker!"

"She hada gun in the sheet!"

"She shot im right thu the head!"

"Whut she shoot im fer?"

"Kill the bitch!"

"Ah *thought* somethin wuz wrong bout her!"

"Ah wuz fer givin it t her from the firs!"

"Thas whut yuh git fer treatin a nigger nice!"

"Say, Bookers dead!"

She stopped looking into the white faces, stopped listening.
She waited, giving up her life before they took it from her;
she had done what she wanted. Ef only Johnny-Boy . . .
She looked at him; he lay looking at her with tired eyes. Ef
she could only tell im! But he lay already buried in a grave of
silence.

"Whut yuh kill im fer, hunh?"

It was the sheriff's voice; she did not answer.

"Mabbe she wuz shootin at yuh, Sheriff?"

"Whut yuh kill im fer?"

She felt the sheriff's foot come into her side; she closed her eyes.

"Yuh black bitch!"

"Let her have it!"

"Yuh reckon she foun out bout Booker?"

"She mighta."

"Jesus Chris, whut yuh dummies *waitin* on!"

"Yeah; kill her!"

"Kill em *both*!"

"Let her know her nigger sons dead firs!"

She turned her head toward Johnny-Boy; he lay looking puzzled in a world beyond the reach of voices. At leas he cant hear, she thought.

"C mon, let im have it!"

She listened to hear what Johnny-Boy could not. They came, two of them, one right behind the other; so close together that they sounded like one shot. She did not look at Johnny-Boy now; she looked at the white faces of the men, hard and wet in the glare of the flashlights.

"Yuh hear tha, nigger woman?"

"Did tha surprise im? Hes in hell now wonderin whut hit im!"

"C mon! Give it t her, Sheriff!"

"Lemme shoot her, Sheriff! It wuz mah pal she shot!"

"Awright, Pete! Thas fair ernuff!"

She gave up as much of her life as she could before they took it from her. But the sound of the shot and the streak of fire that tore its way through her chest forced her to live again, intensely. She had not moved, save for the slight jarring impact of the bullet. She felt the heat of her own blood warming her cold, wet back. She yearned suddenly to talk. "Yuh didnt git whut yuh wanted! N yuh ain gonna nevah git it! Yuh didnt kill me; Ah come here by mahsef . . ." She felt rain falling into her wide-open, dimming eyes and heard faint voices. Her lips moved soundlessly. *Yuh didnt git yuh didnt yuh didnt* . . . Focused and pointed she was, buried in the depths of her star, swallowed in its peace and strength; and not feeling her flesh growing cold, cold as the rain that fell from the invisible sky upon the doomed living and the dead that never dies.

NATIVE SON

Even today is my complaint rebellious,
My stroke is heavier than my groaning.
                                        —Job

BOOK ONE

FEAR

BRRRRRRRIIIIIIIIIIIIIIIIIIIINNG!

An alarm clock clanged in the dark and silent room. A bed spring creaked. A woman's voice sang out impatiently:

"Bigger, shut that thing off!"

A surly grunt sounded above the tinny ring of metal. Naked feet swished dryly across the planks in the wooden floor and the clang ceased abruptly.

"Turn on the light, Bigger."

"Awright," came a sleepy mumble.

Light flooded the room and revealed a black boy standing in a narrow space between two iron beds, rubbing his eyes with the backs of his hands. From a bed to his right the woman spoke again:

"Buddy, get up from there! I got a big washing on my hands today and I want you-all out of here."

Another black boy rolled from bed and stood up. The woman also rose and stood in her nightgown.

"Turn your heads so I can dress," she said.

The two boys averted their eyes and gazed into a far corner of the room. The woman rushed out of her nightgown and put on a pair of step-ins. She turned to the bed from which she had risen and called:

"Vera! Get up from there!"

"What time is it, Ma?" asked a muffled, adolescent voice from beneath a quilt.

"Get up from there, I say!"

"O.K., Ma."

A brown-skinned girl in a cotton gown got up and stretched her arms above her head and yawned. Sleepily, she sat on a chair and fumbled with her stockings. The two boys kept their faces averted while their mother and sister put on enough clothes to keep them from feeling ashamed; and the mother and sister did the same while the boys dressed. Abruptly, they all paused, holding their clothes in their

hands, their attention caught by a light tapping in the thinly
plastered walls of the room. They forgot their conspiracy
against shame and their eyes strayed apprehensively over the
floor.

"There he is again, Bigger!" the woman screamed, and the
tiny, one-room apartment galvanized into violent action. A
chair toppled as the woman, half-dressed and in her stocking
feet, scrambled breathlessly upon the bed. Her two sons,
barefoot, stood tense and motionless, their eyes searching
anxiously under the bed and chairs. The girl ran into a corner,
half-stooped and gathered the hem of her slip into both of her
hands and held it tightly over her knees.

"Oh! Oh!" she wailed.

"There he goes!"

The woman pointed a shaking finger. Her eyes were round
with fascinated horror.

"Where?"

"I don't see 'im!"

"Bigger, he's behind the trunk!" the girl whimpered.

"Vera!" the woman screamed. "Get up here on the bed!
Don't let that thing *bite* you!"

Frantically, Vera climbed upon the bed and the woman
caught hold of her. With their arms entwined about each
other, the black mother and the brown daughter gazed open-
mouthed at the trunk in the corner.

Bigger looked round the room wildly, then darted to a curtain and swept it aside and grabbed two heavy iron skillets
from a wall above a gas stove. He whirled and called softly to
his brother, his eyes glued to the trunk.

"Buddy!"

"Yeah?"

"Here; take this skillet."

"O.K."

"Now, get over by the door!"

"O.K."

Buddy crouched by the door and held the iron skillet by its
handle, his arm flexed and poised. Save for the quick, deep
breathing of the four people, the room was quiet. Bigger
crept on tiptoe toward the trunk with the skillet clutched
stiffly in his hand, his eyes dancing and watching every inch

of the wooden floor in front of him. He paused and, without moving an eye or muscle, called:

"Buddy!"

"Hunh?"

"Put that box in front of the hole so he can't get out!"

"O.K."

Buddy ran to a wooden box and shoved it quickly in front of a gaping hole in the molding and then backed again to the door, holding the skillet ready. Bigger eased to the trunk and peered behind it cautiously. He saw nothing. Carefully, he stuck out his bare foot and pushed the trunk a few inches.

"There he is!" the mother screamed again.

A huge black rat squealed and leaped at Bigger's trouser-leg and snagged it in his teeth, hanging on.

"Goddamn!" Bigger whispered fiercely, whirling and kicking out his leg with all the strength of his body. The force of his movement shook the rat loose and it sailed through the air and struck a wall. Instantly, it rolled over and leaped again. Bigger dodged and the rat landed against a table leg. With clenched teeth, Bigger held the skillet; he was afraid to hurl it, fearing that he might miss. The rat squeaked and turned and ran in a narrow circle, looking for a place to hide; it leaped again past Bigger and scurried on dry rasping feet to one side of the box and then to the other, searching for the hole. Then it turned and reared upon its hind legs.

"Hit 'im, Bigger!" Buddy shouted.

"Kill 'im!" the woman screamed.

The rat's belly pulsed with fear. Bigger advanced a step and the rat emitted a long thin song of defiance, its black beady eyes glittering, its tiny forefeet pawing the air restlessly. Bigger swung the skillet; it skidded over the floor, missing the rat, and clattered to a stop against a wall.

"Goddamn!"

The rat leaped. Bigger sprang to one side. The rat stopped under a chair and let out a furious screak. Bigger moved slowly backward toward the door.

"Gimme that skillet, Buddy," he asked quietly, not taking his eyes from the rat.

Buddy extended his hand. Bigger caught the skillet and lifted it high in the air. The rat scuttled across the floor and stopped again at the box and searched quickly for the hole; then it reared once more and bared long yellow fangs, piping shrilly, belly quivering.

Bigger aimed and let the skillet fly with a heavy grunt. There was a shattering of wood as the box caved in. The woman screamed and hid her face in her hands. Bigger tip-toed forward and peered.

"I got 'im," he muttered, his clenched teeth bared in a smile. "By God, I got 'im."

He kicked the splintered box out of the way and the flat black body of the rat lay exposed, its two long yellow tusks showing distinctly. Bigger took a shoe and pounded the rat's head, crushing it, cursing hysterically:

"You sonofa*bitch!*"

The woman on the bed sank to her knees and buried her face in the quilts and sobbed:

"Lord, Lord, have mercy. . . ."

"Aw, Mama," Vera whimpered, bending to her. "Don't cry. It's dead now."

The two brothers stood over the dead rat and spoke in tones of awed admiration.

"Gee, but he's a big bastard."

"That sonofabitch could cut your throat."

"He's over a foot long."

"How in hell do they get so big?"

"Eating garbage and anything else they can get."

"Look, Bigger, there's a three-inch rip in your pant-leg."

"Yeah; he was after me, all right."

"Please, Bigger, take 'im out," Vera begged.

"Aw, don't be so scary," Buddy said.

The woman on the bed continued to sob. Bigger took a piece of newspaper and gingerly lifted the rat by its tail and held it out at arm's length.

"Bigger, take 'im out," Vera begged again.

Bigger laughed and approached the bed with the dangling rat, swinging it to and fro like a pendulum, enjoying his sister's fear.

"Bigger!" Vera gasped convulsively; she screamed and swayed and closed her eyes and fell headlong across her mother and rolled limply from the bed to the floor.

"Bigger, for God's sake!" the mother sobbed, rising and bending over Vera. "Don't do that! Throw that rat out!"

He laid the rat down and started to dress.

"Bigger, help me lift Vera to the bed," the mother said.

He paused and turned round.

"What's the matter?" he asked, feigning ignorance.

"Do what I asked you, will you, boy?"

He went to the bed and helped his mother lift Vera. Vera's eyes were closed. He turned away and finished dressing. He wrapped the rat in a newspaper and went out of the door and down the stairs and put it into a garbage can at the corner of an alley. When he returned to the room his mother was still bent over Vera, placing a wet towel upon her head. She straightened and faced him, her cheeks and eyes wet with tears and her lips tight with anger.

"Boy, sometimes I wonder what makes you act like you do."

"What I do now?" he demanded belligerently.

"Sometimes you act the biggest fool I ever saw."

"What you talking about?"

"You scared your sister with that rat and she *fainted*! Ain't you got no sense at *all*?"

"Aw, I didn't know she was that scary."

"Buddy!" the mother called.

"Yessum."

"Take a newspaper and spread it over that spot."

"Yessum."

Buddy opened out a newspaper and covered the smear of blood on the floor where the rat had been crushed. Bigger went to the window and stood looking out abstractedly into the street. His mother glared at his back.

"Bigger, sometimes I wonder why I birthed you," she said bitterly.

Bigger looked at her and turned away.

"Maybe you oughtn't've. Maybe you ought to left me where I was."

"You shut your sassy mouth!"

"Aw, for Chrissakes!" Bigger said, lighting a cigarette.

"Buddy, pick up them skillets and put 'em in the sink," the mother said.

"Yessum."

Bigger walked across the floor and sat on the bed. His mother's eyes followed him.

"We wouldn't have to live in this garbage dump if you had any manhood in you," she said.

"Aw, don't start that again."

"How you feel, Vera?" the mother asked.

Vera raised her head and looked about the room as though expecting to see another rat.

"Oh, Mama!"

"You poor thing!"

"I couldn't help it. Bigger scared me."

"Did you hurt yourself?"

"I bumped my head."

"Here; take it easy. You'll be all right."

"How come Bigger acts that way?" Vera asked, crying again.

"He's just crazy," the mother said. "Just plain dumb black crazy."

"I'll be late for my sewing class at the Y.W.C.A.," Vera said.

"Here; stretch out on the bed. You'll feel better in a little while," the mother said.

She left Vera on the bed and turned a pair of cold eyes upon Bigger.

"Suppose you wake up some morning and find your sister dead? What would you think then?" she asked. "Suppose those rats cut our veins at night when we sleep? Naw! Nothing like that ever bothers you! All you care about is your own pleasure! Even when the relief offers you a job you won't take it till they threaten to cut off your food and starve you! Bigger, honest, you the most no-countest man I ever seen in all my life!"

"You done told me that a thousand times," he said, not looking round.

"Well, I'm telling you agin! And mark my word, some of these days you going to set down and *cry*. Some of these days you going to wish you had made something out of yourself, instead of just a tramp. But it'll be too late then."

"Stop prophesying about me," he said.

"I prophesy much as I please! And if you don't like it, you

can get out. We can get along without you. We can live in one room just like we living now, even with you gone," she said.

"Aw, for Chrissakes!" he said, his voice filled with nervous irritation.

"You'll regret how you living some day," she went on. "If you don't stop running with that gang of yours and do right you'll end up where you never thought you would. You think I don't know what you boys is doing, but I do. And the gallows is at the end of the road you traveling, boy. Just remember that." She turned and looked at Buddy. "Throw that box outside, Buddy."

"Yessum."

There was silence. Buddy took the box out. The mother went behind the curtain to the gas stove. Vera sat up in bed and swung her feet to the floor.

"Lay back down, Vera," the mother said.

"I feel all right now, Ma. I got to go to my sewing class."

"Well, if you feel like it, set the table," the mother said, going behind the curtain again. "Lord, I get so tired of this I don't know what to do," her voice floated plaintively from behind the curtain. "All I ever do is try to make a home for you children and you don't care."

"Aw, Ma," Vera protested. "Don't say that."

"Vera, sometimes I just want to lay down and quit."

"Ma, please don't say that."

"I can't last many more years, living like this."

"I'll be old enough to work soon, Ma."

"I reckon I'll be dead then. I reckon God'll call me home."

Vera went behind the curtain and Bigger heard her trying to comfort his mother. He shut their voices out of his mind. He hated his family because he knew that they were suffering and that he was powerless to help them. He knew that the moment he allowed himself to feel to its fulness how they lived, the shame and misery of their lives, he would be swept out of himself with fear and despair. So he held toward them an attitude of iron reserve; he lived with them, but behind a wall, a curtain. And toward himself he was even more exacting. He knew that the moment he allowed what his life meant to enter fully into his consciousness, he would either kill himself or someone else. So he denied himself and acted tough.

He got up and crushed his cigarette upon the window sill.
Vera came into the room and placed knives and forks upon
the table.

"Get ready to eat, you-all," the mother called.

He sat at the table. The odor of frying bacon and boiling
coffee drifted to him from behind the curtain. His mother's
voice floated to him in song.

> *Life is like a mountain railroad*
> *With an engineer that's brave*
> *We must make the run successful*
> *From the cradle to the grave. . . .*

The song irked him and he was glad when she stopped and
came into the room with a pot of coffee and a plate of crin-
kled bacon. Vera brought the bread in and they sat down. His
mother closed her eyes and lowered her head and mumbled,

"Lord, we thank Thee for the food You done placed before
us for the nourishment of our bodies. Amen." She lifted her
eyes and without changing her tone of voice, said, "You
going to have to learn to get up earlier than this, Bigger, to
hold a job."

He did not answer or look up.

"You want me to pour you some coffee?" Vera asked.

"Yeah."

"You going to take the job, ain't you, Bigger?" his mother
asked.

He laid down his fork and stared at her.

"I told you last night I was going to take it. How many
times you want to ask me?"

"Well, don't bite her head off," Vera said. "She only asked
you a question."

"Pass the bread and stop being smart."

"You know you have to see Mr. Dalton at five-thirty," his
mother said.

"You done said that ten times."

"I don't want you to forget, son."

"And you know how you can forget," Vera said.

"Aw, lay off Bigger," Buddy said. "He told you he was
going to take the job."

"Don't tell 'em nothing," Bigger said.

"You shut your mouth, Buddy, or get up from this table," the mother said. "I'm not going to take any stinking sass from you. One fool in the family's enough."

"Lay off, Ma," Buddy said.

"Bigger's setting here like he ain't glad to get a job," she said.

"What you want me to do? Shout?" Bigger asked.

"Oh, Bigger!" his sister said.

"I wish you'd keep your big mouth out of this!" he told his sister.

"If you get that job," his mother said in a low, kind tone of voice, busy slicing a loaf of bread, "I can fix up a nice place for you children. You could be comfortable and not have to live like pigs."

"Bigger ain't decent enough to think of nothing like that," Vera said.

"God, I wish you-all would let me eat," Bigger said.

His mother talked on as though she had not heard him and he stopped listening.

"Ma's talking to you, Bigger," Vera said.

"So *what?*"

"Don't be that way, Bigger!"

He laid down his fork and his strong black fingers gripped the edge of the table; there was silence save for the tinkling of his brother's fork against a plate. He kept staring at his sister till her eyes fell.

"I wish you'd let me eat," he said again.

As he ate he felt that they were thinking of the job he was to get that evening and it made him angry; he felt that they had tricked him into a cheap surrender.

"I need some carfare," he said.

"Here's all I got," his mother said, pushing a quarter to the side of his plate.

He put the quarter in his pocket and drained his cup of coffee in one long swallow. He got his coat and cap and went to the door.

"You know, Bigger," his mother said, "if you don't take that job the relief'll cut us off. We won't have any food."

"I told you I'd take it!" he shouted and slammed the door.

He went down the steps into the vestibule and stood looking out into the street through the plate glass of the front
door. Now and then a street car rattled past over steel tracks.
He was sick of his life at home. Day in and day out there was
nothing but shouts and bickering. But what could he do?
Each time he asked himself that question his mind hit a blank
wall and he stopped thinking. Across the street directly in
front of him, he saw a truck pull to a stop at the curb and two
white men in overalls got out with pails and brushes. Yes, he
could take the job at Dalton's and be miserable, or he could
refuse it and starve. It maddened him to think that he did not
have a wider choice of action. Well, he could not stand here
all day like this. What was he to do with himself? He tried to
decide if he wanted to buy a ten-cent magazine, or go to a
movie, or go to the poolroom and talk with the gang, or just
loaf around. With his hands deep in his pockets, another cigarette slanting across his chin, he brooded and watched the
men at work across the street. They were pasting a huge colored poster to a signboard. The poster showed a white face.

"That's Buckley!" He spoke softly to himself. "He's running for State's Attorney again." The men were slapping the
poster with wet brushes. He looked at the round florid face
and wagged his head. "I bet that sonofabitch rakes off a million bucks in graft a year. Boy, if I was in his shoes for just
one day I'd *never* have to worry again."

When the men were through they gathered up their pails
and brushes and got into the truck and drove off. He looked
at the poster: the white face was fleshy but stern; one hand
was uplifted and its index finger pointed straight out into the
street at each passer-by. The poster showed one of those faces
that looked straight at you when you looked at it and all the
while you were walking and turning your head to look at it it
kept looking unblinkingly back at you until you got so far
from it you had to take your eyes away, and then it stopped,
like a movie blackout. Above the top of the poster were tall
red letters: YOU CAN'T WIN!

He snuffed his cigarette and laughed silently. "You crook,"
he mumbled, shaking his head. "You let whoever pays *you* off
win!" He opened the door and met the morning air. He went
along the sidewalk with his head down, fingering the quarter

in his pocket. He stopped and searched all of his pockets; in his vest pocket he found a lone copper cent. That made a total of twenty-six cents, fourteen cents of which would have to be saved for carfare to Mr. Dalton's; that is, if he decided to take the job. In order to buy a magazine and go to the movies he would have to have at least twenty cents more. "Goddammit, I'm always broke!" he mumbled.

He stood on the corner in the sunshine, watching cars and people pass. He needed more money; if he did not get more than he had now he would not know what to do with himself for the rest of the day. He wanted to see a movie; his senses hungered for it. In a movie he could dream without effort; all he had to do was lean back in a seat and keep his eyes open.

He thought of Gus and G.H. and Jack. Should he go to the poolroom and talk with them? But there was no use in his going unless they were ready to do what they had been long planning to do. If they could, it would mean some sure and quick money. From three o'clock to four o'clock in the afternoon there was no policeman on duty in the block where Blum's Delicatessen was and it would be safe. One of them could hold a gun on Blum and keep him from yelling; one could watch the front door; one could watch the back; and one could get the money from the box under the counter. Then all four of them could lock Blum in the store and run out through the back and duck down the alley and meet an hour later, either at Doc's poolroom or at the South Side Boys' Club, and split the money.

Holding up Blum ought not take more than two minutes, at the most. And it would be their last job. But it would be the toughest one that they had ever pulled. All the other times they had raided newsstands, fruit stands, and apartments. And, too, they had never held up a white man before. They had always robbed Negroes. They felt that it was much easier and safer to rob their own people, for they knew that white policemen never really searched diligently for Negroes who committed crimes against other Negroes. For months they had talked of robbing Blum's, but had not been able to bring themselves to do it. They had the feeling that the robbing of Blum's would be a violation of ultimate taboo; it would be a trespassing into territory where the full wrath of an alien white world would be turned loose upon them; in short, it would be a symbolic challenge of the white world's rule over them; a challenge which they yearned to make, but were afraid to. Yes; if they could rob Blum's, it would be a real hold-up, in more senses than one. In comparison, all of their other jobs had been play.

"Good-bye, Bigger."

He looked up and saw Vera passing with a sewing kit dangling from her arm. She paused at the corner and came back to him.

"Now, what you want?"

"Bigger, please. . . . You're getting a good job now. Why don't you stay away from Jack and Gus and G.H. and keep out of trouble?"

"You keep your big mouth out of my business!"

"But, Bigger!"

"Go on to school, will you!"

She turned abruptly and walked on. He knew that his mother had been talking to Vera and Buddy about him, telling them that if he got into any more trouble he would be sent to prison and not just to the reform school, where they sent him last time. He did not mind what his mother said to Buddy about him. Buddy was all right. Tough, plenty. But Vera was a sappy girl; she did not have any more sense than to believe everything she was told.

He walked toward the poolroom. When he got to the door he saw Gus half a block away, coming toward him. He stopped and waited. It was Gus who had first thought of robbing Blum's.

"Hi, Bigger!"

"What you saying, Gus?"

"Nothing. Seen G.H. or Jack yet?"

"Naw. You?"

"Naw. Say, got a cigarette?"

"Yeah."

Bigger took out his pack and gave Gus a cigarette; he lit his and held the match for Gus. They leaned their backs against the red-brick wall of a building, smoking, their cigarettes slanting white across their black chins. To the east Bigger saw the sun burning a dazzling yellow. In the sky above him a few big white clouds drifted. He puffed silently, relaxed, his mind pleasantly vacant of purpose. Every slight movement in the street evoked a casual curiosity in him. Automatically, his eyes followed each car as it whirred over the smooth black asphalt. A woman came by and he watched the gentle sway of her body until she disappeared into a doorway. He sighed, scratched his chin and mumbled,

"Kinda warm today."

"Yeah," Gus said.

"You get more heat from this sun than from them old radiators at home."

"Yeah; them old white landlords sure don't give much heat."

"And they always knocking at your door for money."

"I'll be glad when summer comes."

"Me too," Bigger said.

He stretched his arms above his head and yawned; his eyes moistened. The sharp precision of the world of steel and stone dissolved into blurred waves. He blinked and the world grew hard again, mechanical, distinct. A weaving motion in the sky made him turn his eyes upward; he saw a slender streak of billowing white blooming against the deep blue. A plane was writing high up in the air.

"Look!" Bigger said.

"What?"

"That plane writing up there," Bigger said, pointing.

"Oh!"

They squinted at a tiny ribbon of unfolding vapor that spelled out the word: USE. . . . The plane was so far away that at times the strong glare of the sun blanked it from sight.

"You can hardly see it," Gus said.

"Looks like a little bird," Bigger breathed with childlike wonder.

"Them white boys sure can fly," Gus said.

"Yeah," Bigger said, wistfully. "They get a chance to do everything."

Noiselessly, the tiny plane looped and veered, vanishing and appearing, leaving behind it a long trail of white plumage, like coils of fluffy paste being squeezed from a tube; a plume-coil that grew and swelled and slowly began to fade into the air at the edges. The plane wrote another word: SPEED. . . .

"How high you reckon he is?" Bigger asked.

"I don't know. Maybe a hundred miles; maybe a thousand."

"I could fly one of them things if I had a chance," Bigger mumbled reflectively, as though talking to himself.

Gus pulled down the corners of his lips, stepped out from the wall, squared his shoulders, doffed his cap, bowed low and spoke with mock deference:

"Yessuh."

"You go to hell," Bigger said, smiling.

"Yessuh," Gus said again.

"I *could* fly a plane if I had a chance," Bigger said.

"If you wasn't black and if you had some money and if they'd let you go to that aviation school, you *could* fly a plane," Gus said.

For a moment Bigger contemplated all the "ifs" that Gus had mentioned. Then both boys broke into hard laughter, looking at each other through squinted eyes. When their laughter subsided, Bigger said in a voice that was half-question and half-statement:

"It's funny how the white folks treat us, ain't it?"

"It better be funny," Gus said.

"Maybe they right in not wanting us to fly," Bigger said. " 'Cause if I took a plane up I'd take a couple of bombs along and drop 'em as sure as hell. . . ."

They laughed again, still looking upward. The plane sailed and dipped and spread another word against the sky: GASO-LINE. . . .

"Use Speed Gasoline," Bigger mused, rolling the words slowly from his lips. "God, I'd like to fly up there in that sky."

"God'll let you fly when He gives you your wings up in heaven," Gus said.

They laughed again, reclining against the wall, smoking, the lids of their eyes drooped softly against the sun. Cars whizzed past on rubber tires. Bigger's face was metallically black in the strong sunlight. There was in his eyes a pensive, brooding amusement, as of a man who had been long confronted and tantalized by a riddle whose answer seemed always just on the verge of escaping him, but prodding him irresistibly on to seek its solution. The silence irked Bigger; he was anxious to do something to evade looking so squarely at this problem.

"Let's play 'white,'" Bigger said, referring to a game of play-acting in which he and his friends imitated the ways and manners of white folks.

"I don't feel like it," Gus said.

"General!" Bigger pronounced in a sonorous tone, looking at Gus expectantly.

"Aw, hell! I don't want to play," Gus whined.

"You'll be court-martialed," Bigger said, snapping out his words with military precision.

"Nigger, you nuts!" Gus laughed.

"General!" Bigger tried again, determinedly.

Gus looked wearily at Bigger, then straightened, saluted and answered:

"Yessuh."

"Send your men over the river at dawn and attack the enemy's left flank," Bigger ordered.

"Yessuh."

"Send the Fifth, Sixth, and Seventh Regiments," Bigger said, frowning. "And attack with tanks, gas, planes, and infantry."

"Yessuh!" Gus said again, saluting and clicking his heels.

For a moment they were silent, facing each other, their shoulders thrown back, their lips compressed to hold down the mounting impulse to laugh. Then they guffawed, partly at themselves and partly at the vast white world that sprawled and towered in the sun before them.

"Say, what's a 'left flank'?" Gus asked.

"I don't know," Bigger said. "I heard it in the movies."

They laughed again. After a bit they relaxed and leaned against the wall, smoking. Bigger saw Gus cup his left hand to his ear, as though holding a telephone receiver; and cup his right hand to his mouth, as though talking into a transmitter.

"Hello," Gus said.

"Hello," Bigger said. "Who's this?"

"This is Mr. J. P. Morgan speaking," Gus said.

"Yessuh, Mr. Morgan," Bigger said; his eyes filled with mock adulation and respect.

"I want you to sell twenty thousand shares of U. S. Steel in the market this morning," Gus said.

"At what price, suh?" Bigger asked.

"Aw, just dump 'em at any price," Gus said with casual irritation. "We're holding too much."

"Yessuh," Bigger said.

"And call me at my club at two this afternoon and tell me if the President telephoned," Gus said.

"Yessuh, Mr. Morgan," Bigger said.

Both of them made gestures signifying that they were hanging up telephone receivers; then they bent double, laughing.

"I bet that's *just* the way they talk," Gus said.

"I wouldn't be surprised," Bigger said.

They were silent again. Presently, Bigger cupped his hand to his mouth and spoke through an imaginary telephone transmitter.

"Hello."

"Hello," Gus answered. "Who's this?"

"This is the President of the United States speaking," Bigger said.

"Oh, yessuh, Mr. President," Gus said.

"I'm calling a cabinet meeting this afternoon at four o'clock and you, as Secretary of State, *must* be there."

"Well, now, Mr. President," Gus said, "I'm pretty busy. They raising sand over there in Germany and I got to send 'em a note. . . ."

"But this is important," Bigger said.

"What you going to take up at this cabinet meeting?" Gus asked.

"Well, you see, the niggers is raising sand all over the country," Bigger said, struggling to keep back his laughter. "We've got to do something with these black folks. . . ."

"Oh, if it's about the niggers, I'll be right there, Mr. President," Gus said.

They hung up imaginary receivers and leaned against the wall and laughed. A street car rattled by. Bigger sighed and swore.

"Goddammit!"

"What's the matter?"

"They don't let us do *nothing*."

"Who?"

"The *white* folks."

"You talk like you just now finding that out," Gus said.

"Naw. But I just can't get used to it," Bigger said. "I swear to God I can't. I know I oughtn't think about it, but I can't help it. Every time I think about it I feel like somebody's poking a red-hot iron down my throat. Goddammit, look! We live here and they live there. We black and they white. They got things and we ain't. They do things and we can't. It's just like living in jail. Half the time I feel like I'm on the outside of the world peeping in through a knot-hole in the fence. . . ."

"Aw, ain't no use feeling that way about it. It don't help none," Gus said.

"You know one thing?" Bigger said.

"What?"

"Sometimes I feel like something awful's going to happen to me," Bigger spoke with a tinge of bitter pride in his voice.

"What you mean?" Gus asked, looking at him quickly. There was fear in Gus's eyes.

"I don't know. I just feel that way. Every time I get to thinking about me being black and they being white, me being here and they being there, I feel like something awful's going to happen to me. . . ."

"Aw, for Chrissakes! There ain't nothing you can do about it. How come you want to worry yourself? You black and they make the laws. . . ."

"Why they make us live in one corner of the city? Why don't they let us fly planes and run ships. . . ."

Gus hunched Bigger with his elbow and mumbled good-naturedly, "Aw, nigger, quit thinking about it. You'll go nuts."

The plane was gone from the sky and the white plumes of floating smoke were thinly spread, vanishing. Because he was restless and had time on his hands, Bigger yawned again and hoisted his arms high above his head.

"Nothing ever happens," he complained.

"What you want to happen?"

"Anything," Bigger said with a wide sweep of his dingy palm, a sweep that included all the possible activities of the world.

Then their eyes were riveted; a slate-colored pigeon swooped down to the middle of the steel car tracks and began strutting to and fro with ruffled feathers, its fat neck bobbing with regal pride. A street car rumbled forward and the pigeon rose swiftly through the air on wings stretched so taut and sheer that Bigger could see the gold of the sun through their translucent tips. He tilted his head and watched the slate-colored bird flap and wheel out of sight over the edge of a high roof.

"Now, if I could only do that," Bigger said.

Gus laughed.

"Nigger, you nuts."

"I reckon we the only things in this city that can't go where we want to go and do what we want to do."

"Don't think about it," Gus said.

"I can't help it."

"That's why you feeling like something awful's going to happen to you," Gus said. "You think too much."

"What in hell can a man do?" Bigger asked, turning to Gus.

"Get drunk and sleep it off."

"I can't. I'm broke."

Bigger crushed his cigarette and took out another one and offered the package to Gus. They continued smoking. A huge truck swept past, lifting scraps of white paper into the sunshine; the bits settled down slowly.

"Gus?"

"Hunh?"

"You know where the white folks live?"

"Yeah," Gus said, pointing eastward. "Over across the 'line'; over there on Cottage Grove Avenue."

"Naw; they don't," Bigger said.

"What you mean?" Gus asked, puzzled. "Then, where do they live?"

Bigger doubled his fist and struck his solar plexus.

"Right down here in my stomach," he said.

Gus looked at Bigger searchingly, then away, as though ashamed.

"Yeah; I know what you mean," he whispered.

"Every time I think of 'em, I *feel* 'em," Bigger said.

"Yeah; and in your chest and throat, too," Gus said.
"It's like fire."

"And sometimes you can't hardly breathe. . . ."

Bigger's eyes were wide and placid, gazing into space.

"That's when I feel like something awful's going to happen to me. . . ." Bigger paused, narrowed his eyes. "Naw; it ain't like something going to happen to me. It's. . . . It's like I was going to do something I can't help. . . ."

"Yeah!" Gus said with uneasy eagerness. His eyes were full of a look compounded of fear and admiration for Bigger. "Yeah; I know what you mean. It's like you going to fall and don't know where you going to land. . . ."

Gus's voice trailed off. The sun slid behind a big white cloud and the street was plunged in cool shadow; quickly the sun edged forth again and it was bright and warm once more. A long sleek black car, its fenders glinting like glass in the sun, shot past them at high speed and turned a corner a few blocks away. Bigger pursed his lips and sang:

"Zooooooooooom!"

"They got everything," Gus said.

"They own the world," Bigger said.

"Aw, what the hell," Gus said. "Let's go in the poolroom."

"O.K."

They walked toward the door of the poolroom.

"Say, you taking that job you told us about?" Gus asked.

"I don't know."

"You talk like you don't want it."

"Oh, hell, yes! I want the job," Bigger said.

They looked at each other and laughed. They went inside. The poolroom was empty, save for a fat, black man who held a half-smoked, unlit cigar in his mouth and leaned on the front counter. To the rear burned a single green-shaded bulb.

"Hi, Doc," Bigger said.

"You boys kinda early this morning," Doc said.

"Jack or G.H. around yet?" Bigger asked.

"Naw," Doc said.

"Let's shoot a game," Gus said.

"I'm broke," Bigger said.

"I got some money."

"Switch on the light. The balls are racked," Doc said.

Bigger turned on the light. They lagged for first shot. Bigger won. They started playing. Bigger's shots were poor; he was thinking of Blum's, fascinated with the idea of the robbery, and a little afraid of it.

"Remember what we talked about so much?" Bigger asked in a flat, neutral tone.

"Naw."

"Old Blum."

"Oh," Gus said. "We ain't talked about that for a month. How come you think of it all of a sudden?"

"Let's clean the place out."

"I don't know."

"It was your plan from the start," Bigger said.

Gus straightened and stared at Bigger, then at Doc who was looking out of the front window.

"You going to tell Doc? Can't you never learn to talk low?"

"Aw, I was just asking you, do you want to try it?"

"Naw."

"How come? You scared 'cause he's a white man?"

"Naw. But Blum keeps a gun. Suppose he beats us to it?"

"Aw, you scared; that's all. He's a white man and you scared."

"The hell I'm scared," Gus, hurt and stung, defended himself.

Bigger went to Gus and placed an arm about his shoulders.

"Listen, you won't have to go in. You just stand at the door and keep watch, see? Me and Jack and G.H.'ll go in. If anybody comes along, you whistle and we'll go out the back way. That's all."

The front door opened; they stopped talking and turned their heads.

"Here comes Jack and G.H. now," Bigger said.

Jack and G.H. walked to the rear of the poolroom.

"What you guys doing?" Jack asked.

"Shooting a game. Wanna play?" Bigger asked.

"You asking 'em to play and I'm paying for the game," Gus said.

They all laughed and Bigger laughed with them but stopped quickly. He felt that the joke was on him and he took a seat alongside the wall and propped his feet upon the rungs of a chair, as though he had not heard. Gus and G.H. kept on laughing.

"You niggers is crazy," Bigger said. "You laugh like monkeys and you ain't got nerve enough to do nothing but talk."

"What you mean?" G.H. asked.

"I got a haul all figured out," Bigger said.

"What haul?"

"Old Blum's."

There was silence. Jack lit a cigarette. Gus looked away, avoiding the conversation.

"If old Blum was a black man, you-all would be itching to go. 'Cause he's white, everybody's scared."

"I ain't scared," Jack said. "I'm with you."

"You say you got it all figured out?" G.H. asked.

Bigger took a deep breath and looked from face to face. It seemed to him that he should not have to explain.

"Look, it'll be easy. There ain't nothing to be scared of. Between three and four ain't nobody in the store but the old man. The cop is way down at the other end of the block. One of us'll stay outside and watch. Three of us'll go in, see? One of us'll throw a gun on old Blum; one of us'll make for the cash box under the counter; one of us'll make for the back door and have it open so we can make a quick get-away down the back alley. . . . That's all. It won't take three minutes."

"I thought we said we wasn't never going to use a gun," G.H. said. "And we ain't bothered no white folks before."

"Can't you see? This is something *big*," Bigger said.

He waited for more objections. When none were forthcoming, he talked again.

"We can do it, if you niggers ain't scared."

Save for the sound of Doc's whistling up front, there was silence. Bigger watched Jack closely; he knew that the situation was one in which Jack's word would be decisive. Bigger was afraid of Gus, because he knew that Gus would not hold out if Jack said yes. Gus stood at the table, toying with a cue stick, his eyes straying lazily over the billiard balls scattered about the table in the array of an unfinished game. Bigger rose and sent the balls whirling with a sweep of his hand, then looked straight at Gus as the gleaming balls kissed and rebounded from the rubber cushions, zig-zagging across the table's green cloth. Even though Bigger had asked Gus to be with him in the robbery, the fear that Gus would really go made the muscles of Bigger's stomach tighten; he was hot all over. He felt as if he wanted to sneeze and could not; only it was more nervous than wanting to sneeze. He grew hotter, tighter; his nerves were taut and his teeth were on edge. He felt that something would soon snap within him.

"Goddammit! Say something, somebody!"

"I'm in," Jack said again.

"I'll go if the rest goes," G.H. said.

Gus stood without speaking and Bigger felt a curious sensation—half-sensual, half-thoughtful. He was divided and pulled against himself. He had handled things just right so far; all but Gus had consented. The way things stood now there were three against Gus, and that was just as he had wanted it to be. Bigger was afraid of robbing a white man and he knew that Gus was afraid, too. Blum's store was small and Blum was alone, but Bigger could not think of robbing him without being flanked by his three pals. But even with his pals he was afraid. He had argued all of his pals but one into consenting to the robbery, and toward the lone man who held out he felt a hot hate and fear; he had transferred his fear of the whites to Gus. He hated Gus because he knew that Gus was afraid, as even he was; and he feared Gus because he felt that Gus would consent and then he would be compelled to go through with the robbery. Like a man about to shoot himself and dreading to shoot and yet knowing that he has to shoot and feeling it all at once and powerfully, he watched Gus and waited for him to say yes. But Gus did not speak. Bigger's teeth clamped so tight that his jaws ached. He edged toward Gus, not looking at Gus, but feeling the presence of Gus over all his body, through him, in and out of him, and hating himself and Gus because he felt it. Then he could not stand it any longer. The hysterical tensity of his nerves urged him to speak, to free himself. He faced Gus, his eyes red with anger and fear, his fists clenched and held stiffly to his sides.

"You black sonofabitch," he said in a voice that did not vary in tone. "You scared 'cause he's a white man."

"Don't cuss me, Bigger," Gus said quietly.

"I *am* cussing you!"

"You don't have to cuss me," Gus said.

"Then why don't you use that black tongue of yours?" Bigger asked. "Why don't you say what you going to do?"

"I don't have to use my tongue unless I *want* to!"

"You bastard! You scared bastard!"

"You ain't my boss," Gus said.

"You yellow!" Bigger said. "You scared to rob a white man."

"Aw, Bigger. Don't say that," G.H. said. "Leave 'im alone."

"He's yellow," Bigger said. "He won't go with us."

"I didn't say I wouldn't go," Gus said.

"Then, for Chrissakes, say what you going to do," Bigger said.

Gus leaned on his cue stick and gazed at Bigger and Bigger's stomach tightened as though he were expecting a blow and were getting ready for it. His fists clenched harder. In a split second he felt how his fist and arm and body would feel if he hit Gus squarely in the mouth, drawing blood; Gus would fall and he would walk out and the whole thing would be over and the robbery would not take place. And his thinking and feeling in this way made the choking tightness rising from the pit of his stomach to his throat slacken a little.

"You see, Bigger," began Gus in a tone that was a compromise between kindness and pride. "You see, Bigger, you the cause of all the trouble we ever have. It's your hot temper. Now, how come you want to cuss me? Ain't I got a right to make up my mind? Naw; that ain't your way. You start cussing. You say I'm scared. It's *you* who's scared. You scared I'm going to say yes and you'll have to go through with the job. . . ."

"Say that again! Say that again and I'll take one of these balls and sink it in your Goddamn mouth," Bigger said, his pride wounded to the quick.

"Aw, for Chrissakes," Jack said.

"You *see* how he is," Gus said.

"Why don't you say what you going to do?" Bigger demanded.

"Aw, I'm going with you-all," Gus said in a nervous tone

that sought to hide itself; a tone that hurried on to other things. "I'm going, but Bigger don't have to act like that. He don't have to cuss me."

"Why didn't you say that at first?" Bigger asked; his anger amounted almost to frenzy. "You make a man want to sock you!"

". . . . I'll help on the haul," Gus continued, as though Bigger had not spoken. "I'll help just like I always help. But I'll be Goddamn if I'm taking orders from *you*, Bigger! You just a scared coward! You calling me scared so nobody'll see how scared *you* is!"

Bigger leaped at him, but Jack ran between them. G.H. caught Gus's arm and led him aside.

"Who's asking you to take orders?" Bigger said. "I never want to give orders to a piss-sop like you!"

"You boys cut out that racket back there!" Doc called.

They stood silently about the pool table. Bigger's eyes followed Gus as Gus put his cue stick in the rack and brushed chalk dust from his trousers and walked a little distance away. Bigger's stomach burned and a hazy black cloud hovered a moment before his eyes, and left. Mixed images of violence ran like sand through his mind, dry and fast, vanishing. He could stab Gus with his knife; he could slap him; he could kick him; he could trip him up and send him sprawling on his face. He could do a lot of things to Gus for making him feel this way.

"Come on, G.H.," Gus said.

"Where we going?"

"Let's walk."

"O.K."

"What we gonna do?" Jack asked. "Meet here at three?"

"Sure," Bigger said. "Didn't we just decide?"

"I'll be here," Gus said, with his back turned.

When Gus and G.H. had gone Bigger sat down and felt cold sweat on his skin. It was planned now and he would have to go through with it. His teeth gritted and the last image he had seen of Gus going through the door lingered in his mind. He could have taken one of the cue sticks and gripped it hard and swung it at the back of Gus's head, feeling the impact of the hard wood cracking against the bottom of the skull. The tight feeling was still in him and he knew that it would remain until they were actually doing the job, until they were in the store taking the money.

"You and Gus sure don't get along none," Jack said, shaking his head.

Bigger turned and looked at Jack; he had forgotten that Jack was still there.

"Aw, that yellow black bastard," Bigger said.

"He's all right," Jack said.

"He's scared," Bigger said. "To make him ready for a job, you have to make him scared two ways. You have to make him more scared of what'll happen to him if he don't do the job than of what'll happen to him if he pulls the job."

"If we going to Blum's today, we oughtn't fuss like this," Jack said. "We got a job on our hands, a real job."

"Sure. Sure, I know," Bigger said.

Bigger felt an urgent need to hide his growing and deepening feeling of hysteria; he had to get rid of it or else he would succumb to it. He longed for a stimulus powerful enough to focus his attention and drain off his energies. He wanted to run. Or listen to some swing music. Or laugh or joke. Or read a *Real Detective Story Magazine*. Or go to a movie. Or visit Bessie. All that morning he had lurked behind his curtain of indifference and looked at things, snapping and glaring at whatever had tried to make him come out into the open. But now he was out; the thought of the job at Blum's and the tilt he had had with Gus had snared him into things and his self-trust was gone. Confidence could only come again now through action so violent that it would make him forget. These were the rhythms of his life: indifference and violence; periods of abstract brooding and periods of intense desire; moments of silence and moments of anger—like water ebbing and flowing from the tug of a far-away, invisible force. Being this way was a need of his as deep as eating. He was like a strange plant blooming in the day and wilting at night; but the sun that made it bloom and the cold darkness that made it wilt were never seen. It was his own sun and darkness, a private and personal sun and darkness. He was bitterly proud of his swiftly changing moods and boasted when he had to suffer the results of them. It was the way he was, he would say; he could not help it, he would say, and his head would wag. And it was his sullen stare and the violent action that followed that made Gus and Jack and G.H. hate and fear him as much as he hated and feared himself.

"Where you want to go?" Jack asked. "I'm tired of setting."

"Let's walk," Bigger said.

They went to the front door. Bigger paused and looked round the poolroom with a wild and exasperated expression, his lips tightening with resolution.

"Goin'?" Doc asked, not moving his head.

"Yeah," Bigger said.

"See you later," Jack said.

They walked along the street in the morning sunshine. They waited leisurely at corners for cars to pass; it was not that they feared cars, but they had plenty of time. They reached South Parkway smoking freshly lit cigarettes.

"I'd like to see a movie," Bigger said.

"*Trader Horn's* running again at the Regal. They're bringing a lot of old pictures back."

"How much is it?"

"Twenty cents."

"O.K. Let's see it."

They walked six blocks in silence. It was eleven-thirty when they reached Forty-seventh Street and South Parkway and the Regal was just opening. They bought tickets and walked into the darkened movie and took seats. The picture had not yet started and they sat listening to the pipe organ playing low and soft. Bigger moved restlessly and his breath quickened; he looked round in the shadows to see if any attendant was near, then slouched far down in his seat. He glanced at Jack and saw that Jack was watching him out of the corners of his eyes. They both laughed.

"You at it again?" Jack asked.

"I'm polishing my nightstick," Bigger said.

They giggled.

"I'll beat you," Jack said.

"Go to hell."

The organ played for a long moment on a single note, then died away.

"I'll bet you ain't even hard yet," Jack whispered.

"I'm getting hard."

"Mine's like a rod," Jack said with intense pride.

"I wished I had Bessie here now," Bigger said.

"I could make old Clara moan now."

They sighed.

"I believe that woman who passed saw us."

"So what?"

"If she comes back I'll throw it in her."

"You a killer."

"If she saw it she'd faint."

"Or grab it, maybe."

"Yeah."

Bigger saw Jack lean forward and stretch out his legs, rigidly.

"You gone?"

"Yee-eeah. . . ."

"You pull off fast. . . ."

Again they were silent. Then Bigger leaned forward, breathing hard.

"I'm gone. . . . God. . . . damn. . . ."

They sat still for five minutes, slumped down in their seats. Finally, they straightened.

"I don't know where to put my feet now," Bigger said, laughing. "Let's take another seat."

"O.K."

They moved to other seats. The organ still played. Now and then they glanced back up to the projector's room high in the rear of the theatre. They were impatient for the picture to start. When they spoke again their voices were throaty, drawling, tinged with uneasiness.

"You reckon it'll go all right?" Bigger asked.

"Maybe."

"I'd just as soon go to jail as take that relief job."

"Don't say that."

"I don't give a damn."

"Let's think about how we'll do it, not about how we'll get caught."

"Scared?"

"Hell, naw."

They listened to the pipe organ. It was humming so low

that it could scarcely be heard. There were times when it seemed to stop altogether; then it would surge forth again, mellow, nostalgic, sweet.

"We better take our guns this time," Bigger said.

"O.K. But we gotta be careful. We don't wanna kill nobody."

"Yeah, but I'll feel safer with a gun this time."

"Gee, I wished it was three now. I wished it was over."

"Me too."

The organ stopped and the screen flashed with the rhythm of moving shadows. Bigger sat looking at the first picture; it was a newsreel. As the scenes unfolded his interest was caught and he leaned forward. He saw images of smiling, dark-haired white girls lolling on the gleaming sands of a beach. The background was a stretch of sparkling water. Palm trees stood near and far. The voice of the commentator ran with the movement of the film: *Here are the daughters of the rich taking sunbaths in the sands of Florida! This little collection of debutantes represents over four billion dollars of America's wealth and over fifty of America's leading families. . . .*

"Some babies," Jack said.

"Yeah, man!"

"I'd like to be there."

"You can," Bigger said. "But you'd be hanging from a tree like a bunch of bananas. . . ."

They laughed softly and easily, listening to the commentator's voice. The scene shifted to and fro over the glittering sands. Then Bigger saw in close-up the picture of a slight, smiling white girl whose waist was encircled by the arms of a man. He heard the commentator's voice: *Mary Dalton, daughter of Chicago's Henry Dalton, 4605 Drexel Boulevard, shocks society by spurning the boys of La Salle Street and the Gold Coast and accepting the attentions of a well-known radical while on her recent winter vacation in Florida. . . .* The close-up showed the smiling girl kissing the man, who lifted her up and swung her round from the camera.

"Say, Jack?"

"Hunh?"

"That gal. . . . That gal there in that guy's arms. . . . That's the daughter of the guy I'm going to work for. They live at 4605 Drexel. . . . That's where I'm going tonight to see about that job. . . ."

"For real?"

"Sure!"

The close-up faded and the next scene showed only the girl's legs running over the sparkling sands; they were followed by the legs of the man running in pursuit. The words droned on: *Ha! He's after her! There! He's got her! Oh, boy, don't you wish you were down here in Florida?* The close-up faded and another came, showing two pairs of legs standing close together. *Oh, boy!* said the voice. Slowly, the girl's legs strained upward until only the tips of her toes touched the sand. *Ah, the naughty rich!* There was a slow fade-out, while the commentator's voice ran on: *Shortly after a scene like this, shocked Mama and Papa Dalton summoned Mary home by wire from her winter vacation and denounced her Communist friend.*

"Say, Jack?"

"Yeah."

"What's a Communist?"

"Damn if I know. It's a race of people who live in Russia, ain't it?"

"That guy who was kissing old man Dalton's daughter was a Communist and her folks didn't like it."

"Rich people don't like Communists."

"She was a hot-looking number, all right."

"Sure," said Jack. "When you start working there you gotta learn to stand in with her. Then you can get everything you want, see? These rich folks do their dirt on the sly. I bet the reason the old man was so mad about that Communist was 'cause his gal was too open about it. . . ."

"Yeah; maybe so," said Bigger.

"Shucks, my ma use to work for rich white folks and you ought to hear the tales she used to tell. . . ."

"What kind of tales?" Bigger asked eagerly.

"Ah, them rich white women'll go to bed with anybody, from a poodle on up. They even have their chauffeurs. Say," Jack said, punching Bigger in the ribs, "if you run across anything too much for you to handle at that place, let me know."

They laughed. Bigger turned his eyes to the screen, but he did not look. He was filled with a sense of excitement about his new job. Was what he had heard about rich white people really true? Was he going to work for people like you saw in the movies? If he were, then he'd see a lot of things from the inside; he'd get the dope, the low-down. He looked at *Trader Horn* unfold and saw pictures of naked black men and women whirling in wild dances and heard drums beating and then gradually the African scene changed and was replaced by images in his own mind of white men and women dressed in black and white clothes, laughing, talking, drinking and dancing. Those were smart people; they knew how to get hold of money, millions of it. Maybe if he were working for them something would happen and he would get some of it. He would see just how they did it. Sure, it was all a game and white people knew how to play it. And rich white people were not so hard on Negroes; it was the poor whites who hated Negroes. They hated Negroes because they didn't have their share of the money. His mother had always told him that rich white people liked Negroes better than they did poor whites. He felt that if he were a poor white and did not get his share of the money, then he would deserve to be kicked. Poor white people were stupid. It was the rich white people who were smart and knew how to treat people. He remembered hearing somebody tell a story of a Negro chauffeur who had married a rich white girl and the girl's family had shipped the couple out of the country and had supplied them with money.

Yes, his going to work for the Daltons was something big. Mr. Dalton was a millionaire. Maybe Mary Dalton was a hot kind of girl; maybe she spent lots of money; maybe she'd like to come to the South Side and see the sights sometimes. Or maybe she had a secret sweetheart and only he would know about it because he would have to drive her around; maybe she would give him money not to tell.

He was a fool for wanting to rob Blum's just when he was about to get a good job. Why hadn't he thought of that before? Why take a fool's chance when other things, big things, could happen? If something slipped up this afternoon he would be out of a job and in jail, maybe. And he wasn't so hot about robbing Blum's, anyway. He frowned in the darkened movie, hearing the roll of tom-toms and the screams of black men and women dancing free and wild, men and women who were adjusted to their soil and at home in their world, secure from fear and hysteria.

"Come on, Bigger," Jack said. "We gotta go."

"Hunh?"

"It's twenty to three."

He rose and walked down the dark aisle over the soft, invisible carpet. He had seen practically nothing of the picture, but he did not care. As he walked into the lobby his insides tightened again with the thought of Gus and Blum's.

"Swell, wasn't it?"

"Yeah; it was a killer," Bigger said.

He walked alongside Jack briskly until they came to Thirty-ninth Street.

"We better get our guns," Bigger said.

"Yeah."

"We got about fifteen minutes."

"O.K."

"So long."

He walked home with a mounting feeling of fear. When he reached his doorway, he hesitated about going up. He didn't want to rob Blum's; he was scared. But he had to go through with it now. Noiselessly, he went up the steps and inserted his key in the lock; the door swung in silently and he heard his mother singing behind the curtain.

> *Lord, I want to be a Christian,*
> *In my heart, in my heart,*
> *Lord, I want to be a Christian,*
> *In my heart, in my heart. . . .*

He tiptoed into the room and lifted the top mattress of his bed and pulled forth the gun and slipped it inside of his shirt. Just as he was about to open the door his mother paused in her singing.

"That you, Bigger?"

He stepped quickly into the outer hallway and slammed the door and bounded headlong down the stairs. He went to the vestibule and swung through the door into the street, feeling that ball of hot tightness growing larger and heavier in his stomach and chest. He opened his mouth to breathe. He

headed for Doc's and came to the door and looked inside.
Jack and G.H. were shooting pool at a rear table. Gus was not
there. He felt a slight lessening of nervous tension and swallowed. He looked up and down the street; very few people
were out and the cop was not in sight. A clock in a window
across the street told him that it was twelve minutes to three.
Well, this was it; he had to go in. He lifted his left hand and
wiped sweat from his forehead in a long slow gesture. He
hesitated a moment longer at the door, then went in, walking
with firm steps to the rear table. He did not speak to Jack or
G.H., nor they to him. He lit a cigarette with shaking fingers
and watched the spinning billiard balls roll and gleam and
clack over the green stretch of cloth, dropping into holes after
bounding to and fro from the rubber cushions. He felt impelled to say something to ease the swelling in his chest. Hurriedly, he flicked his cigarette into a spittoon and, with twin
eddies of blue smoke jutting from his black nostrils, shouted
hoarsely,

"Jack, I betcha two bits you can't make it!"

Jack did not answer; the ball shot straight across the table
and vanished into a side pocket.

"You would've lost," Jack said.

"Too late now," Bigger said. "You wouldn't bet, so *you*
lost."

He spoke without looking. His entire body hungered for
keen sensation, something exciting and violent to relieve the
tautness. It was now ten minutes to three and Gus had not
come. If Gus stayed away much longer, it would be too late.
And Gus knew that. If they were going to do anything, it
certainly ought to be done before folks started coming into
the streets to buy their food for supper, and while the cop
was down at the other end of the block.

"That bastard!" Bigger said. "I knew it!"

"Oh, he'll be along," Jack said.

"Sometimes I'd like to cut his yellow heart out," Bigger
said, fingering the knife in his pocket.

"Maybe he's hanging around some meat," G.H. said.

"He's just scared," Bigger said. "Scared to rob a white
man."

The billiard balls clacked. Jack chalked his cue stick and the metallic noise made Bigger grit his teeth until they ached. He didn't like that noise; it made him feel like cutting something with his knife.

"If he makes us miss this job, I'll fix 'im, so help me," Bigger said. "He oughtn't be late. Every time somebody's late, things go wrong. Look at the big guys. You don't ever hear of them being late, do you? Naw! They work like clocks!"

"Ain't none of us got more guts'n Gus," G.H. said. "He's been with us every time."

"Aw, shut your trap," Bigger said.

"There you go again, Bigger," G.H. said. "Gus was just talking about how you act this morning. You get too nervous when something's coming off. . . ."

"Don't tell me I'm nervous," Bigger said.

"If we don't do it today, we can do it tomorrow," Jack said.

"Tomorrow's Sunday, fool!"

"Bigger, for Chrissakes! Don't holler!" Jack said tensely.

Bigger looked at Jack hard and long, then turned away with a grimace.

"Don't tell the world what we're trying to do," Jack whispered in a mollifying tone.

Bigger walked to the front of the store and stood looking out of the plate glass window. Then, suddenly, he felt sick. He saw Gus coming along the street. And his muscles stiffened. He was going to do something to Gus; just what, he did not know. As Gus neared he heard him whistling: "The Merry-Go-Round Broke Down. . . ." The door swung in.

"Hi, Bigger," Gus said.

Bigger did not answer. Gus passed him and started toward the rear tables. Bigger whirled and kicked him hard. Gus flopped on his face with a single movement of his body. With a look that showed that he was looking at Gus on the floor and at Jack and G.H. at the rear table and at Doc—looking at them all at once in a kind of smiling, roving, turning-slowly glance—Bigger laughed, softly at first, then harder, louder, hysterically; feeling something like hot water bubbling inside of him and trying to come out. Gus got up and stood, quiet, his mouth open and his eyes dead-black with hate.

"Take it easy, boys," Doc said, looking up from behind his counter, and then bending over again.

"What you kick me for?" Gus asked.

" 'Cause I wanted to," Bigger said.

Gus looked at Bigger with lowered eyes. G.H. and Jack leaned on their cue sticks and watched silently.

"I'm going to fix you one of these days," Gus threatened.

"Say that again," Bigger said.

Doc laughed, straightening and looking at Bigger.

"Lay off the boy, Bigger."

Gus turned and walked toward the rear tables. Bigger, with an amazing bound, grabbed him in the back of his collar.

"I asked you to say that again!"

"Quit, Bigger!" Gus spluttered, choking, sinking to his knees.

"Don't tell me to quit!"

The muscles of his body gave a tightening lunge and he saw his fist come down on the side of Gus's head; he had struck him really before he was conscious of doing so.

"Don't hurt 'im," Jack said.

"I'll kill 'im," Bigger said through shut teeth, tightening his hold on Gus's collar, choking him harder.

"T-turn m-m-m-me l-l-loose," Gus gurgled, struggling.

"Make me!" Bigger said, drawing his fingers tighter.

Gus was very still, resting on his knees. Then, like a taut bow finding release, he sprang to his feet, shaking loose from Bigger and turning to get away. Bigger staggered back against the wall, breathless for a moment. Bigger's hand moved so swiftly that nobody saw it; a gleaming blade flashed. He made a long step, as graceful as an animal leaping, threw out his left foot and tripped Gus to the floor. Gus turned over to rise, but Bigger was on top of him, with the knife open and ready.

"Get up! Get up and I'll slice your tonsils!"

Gus lay still.

"That's all right, Bigger," Gus said in surrender. "Lemme up."

"You trying to make a fool out of me, ain't you?"

"Naw," Gus said, his lips scarcely moving.

"You Goddamn right you ain't," Bigger said.

His face softened a bit and the hard glint in his bloodshot eyes died. But he still knelt with the open knife. Then he stood.

"Get up!" he said.

"Please, Bigger!"

"You want me to slice you?"

He stooped again and placed the knife at Gus's throat. Gus did not move and his large black eyes looked pleadingly. Bigger was not satisfied; he felt his muscles tightening again.

"Get up! I ain't going to ask you no more!"

Slowly, Gus stood. Bigger held the open blade an inch from Gus's lips.

"Lick it," Bigger said, his body tingling with elation.

Gus's eyes filled with tears.

"Lick it, I said! You think I'm playing?"

Gus looked round the room without moving his head, just rolling his eyes in a mute appeal for help. But no one moved. Bigger's left fist was slowly lifting to strike. Gus's lips moved toward the knife; he stuck out his tongue and touched the blade. Gus's lips quivered and tears streamed down his cheeks.

"Hahahaha!" Doc laughed.

"Aw, leave 'im alone," Jack called.

Bigger watched Gus with lips twisted in a crooked smile.

"Say, Bigger, ain't you scared 'im enough?" Doc asked.

Bigger did not answer. His eyes gleamed hard again, pregnant with another idea.

"Put your hands up, way up!" he said.

Gus swallowed and stretched his hands high along the wall.

"Leave 'im alone, Bigger," G.H. called weakly.

"I'm doing this," Bigger said.

He put the tip of the blade into Gus's shirt and then made an arc with his arm, as though cutting a circle.

"How would you like me to cut your belly button out?"

Gus did not answer. Sweat trickled down his temples. His lips hung wide, loose.

"Shut them liver lips of yours!"

Gus did not move a muscle. Bigger pushed the knife harder into Gus's stomach.

"Bigger!" Gus said in a tense whisper.

"Shut your mouth!"

Gus shut his mouth. Doc laughed. Jack and G.H. laughed. Then Bigger stepped back and looked at Gus with a smile.

"You clown," he said. "Put your hands down and set on that chair." He watched Gus sit. "That ought to teach you not to be late next time, see?"

"We ain't late, Bigger. We still got time. . . ."

"Shut up! It *is* late!" Bigger insisted commandingly.

Bigger turned aside; then, hearing a sharp scrape on the floor, stiffened. Gus sprang from the chair and grabbed a billiard ball from the table and threw it with a half-sob and half-curse. Bigger flung his hands upward to shield his face and the impact of the ball struck his wrist. He had shut his eyes when he had glimpsed the ball sailing through the air toward him and when he opened his eyes Gus was flying through the rear door and at the same time he heard the ball hit the floor and roll away. A hard pain throbbed in his hand. He sprang forward, cursing.

"You sonofabitch!"

He slipped on a cue stick lying in the middle of the floor and tumbled forward.

"That's enough now, Bigger," Doc said, laughing.

Jack and G.H. also laughed. Bigger rose and faced them, holding his hurt hand. His eyes were red and he stared with speechless hate.

"Just keep laughing," he said.

"Behave yourself, boy," Doc said.

"Just keep laughing," Bigger said again, taking out his knife.

"Watch what you're doing now," Doc cautioned.

"Aw, Bigger," Jack said, backing away toward the rear door.

"You done spoiled things now," G.H. said. "I reckon that was what you wanted. . . ."

"You go to hell!" Bigger shouted, drowning out G.H.'s voice.

Doc bent down behind the counter and when he stood up he had something in his hand which he did not show. He stood there laughing. White spittle showed at the corners of Bigger's lips. He walked to the billiard table, his eyes on Doc. Then he began to cut the green cloth on the table with long sweeping strokes of his arm. He never took his eyes from Doc's face.

"Why, you sonofabitch!" Doc said. "I ought to shoot you, so help me God! Get out, before I call a cop!"

Bigger walked slowly past Doc, looking at him, not hurrying, and holding the open knife in his hand. He paused in the
doorway and looked back. Jack and G.H. were gone.

"Get out of here!" Doc said, showing a gun.

"Don't you like it?" Bigger asked.

"Get out before I shoot you!" Doc said. "And don't you
ever set your black feet inside here again!"

Doc was angry and Bigger was afraid. He shut the knife
and slipped it in his pocket and swung through the door to
the street. He blinked his eyes from the bright sunshine; his
nerves were so taut that he had difficulty in breathing. Halfway down the block he passed Blum's store; he looked out of
the corners of his eyes through the plate glass window and
saw that Blum was alone and the store was empty of customers. Yes; they would have had time to rob the store; in
fact, they still had time. He had lied to Gus and G.H. and
Jack. He walked on; there was not a policeman in sight. Yes;
they could have robbed the store and could have gotten away.
He hoped the fight he had had with Gus covered up what he
was trying to hide. At least the fight made him feel the equal
of them. And he felt the equal of Doc, too; had he not
slashed his table and dared him to use his gun?

He had an overwhelming desire to be alone; he walked to
the middle of the next block and turned into an alley. He
began to laugh, softly, tensely; he stopped still in his tracks
and felt something warm roll down his cheek and he brushed
it away. "Jesus," he breathed. "I laughed so hard I cried."
Carefully, he dried his face on his coat sleeve, then stood for
two whole minutes staring at the shadow of a telephone
pole on the alley pavement. Suddenly he straightened and
walked on with a single expulsion of breath. "What the hell!"
He stumbled violently over a tiny crack in the pavement.
"Goddamn!" he said. When he reached the end of the alley, he
turned into a street, walking slowly in the sunshine, his hands
jammed deep into his pockets, his head down, depressed.

He went home and sat in a chair by the window, looking
out dreamily.

"That you, Bigger?" his mother called from behind the
curtain.

"Yeah," he said.

"What you run in here and run out for, a little while ago?"

"Nothing."

"Don't you go and get into no trouble, now, boy."

"Aw, Ma! Leave me alone."

He listened awhile to her rubbing clothes on the metal washboard, then he gazed abstractedly into the street, thinking of how he had felt when he fought Gus in Doc's poolroom. He was relieved and glad that in an hour he was going to see about that job at the Dalton place. He was disgusted with the gang; he knew that what had happened today put an end to his being with them in any more jobs. Like a man staring regretfully but hopelessly at the stump of a cut-off arm or leg, he knew that the fear of robbing a white man had had hold of him when he started that fight with Gus; but he knew it in a way that kept it from coming to his mind in the form of a hard and sharp idea. His confused emotions had made him feel instinctively that it would be better to fight Gus and spoil the plan of the robbery than to confront a white man with a gun. But he kept this knowledge of his fear thrust firmly down in him; his courage to live depended upon how successfully his fear was hidden from his consciousness. He had fought Gus because Gus was late; that was the reason his emotions accepted and he did not try to justify himself in his own eyes, or in the eyes of the gang. He did not think enough of them to feel that he had to; he did not consider himself as being responsible to them for what he did, even though they had been involved as deeply as he in the planned robbery. He felt that same way toward everyone. As long as he could remember, he had never been responsible to anyone. The moment a situation became so that it exacted something of him, he rebelled. That was the way he lived; he passed his days trying to defeat or gratify powerful impulses in a world he feared.

.   .   .   .

Outside his window he saw the sun dying over the rooftops in the western sky and watched the first shade of dusk fall. Now and then a street car ran past. The rusty radiator hissed at the far end of the room. All day long it had been springlike; but now dark clouds were slowly swallowing the sun. All at once the street lamps came on and the sky was black and close to the house-tops.

Inside his shirt he felt the cold metal of the gun resting against his naked skin; he ought to put it back between the mattresses. No! He would keep it. He would take it with him to the Dalton place. He felt that he would be safer if he took it. He was not planning to use it and there was nothing in particular that he was afraid of, but there was in him an uneasiness and distrust that made him feel that he ought to have it along. He was going among white people, so he would take his knife and his gun; it would make him feel that he was the equal of them, give him a sense of completeness. Then he thought of a good reason why he should take it; in order to get to the Dalton place, he had to go through a white neighborhood. He had not heard of any Negroes being molested recently, but he felt that it was always possible.

Far away a clock boomed five times. He sighed and got up and yawned and stretched his arms high above his head to loosen the muscles of his body. He got his overcoat, for it was growing cold outdoors; then got his cap. He tiptoed to the door, wanting to slip out without his mother hearing him. Just as he was about to open it, she called,

"Bigger!"

He stopped and frowned.

"Yeah, Ma."

"You going to see about that job?"

"Yeah."

"Ain't you going to eat?"

"I ain't got time now."

She came to the door, wiping her soapy hands upon an apron.

"Here; take this quarter and buy you something."

"O.K."

"And be careful, son."

He went out and walked south to Forty-sixth Street, then eastward. Well, he would see in a few moments if the Daltons for whom he was to work were the ones he had seen and heard about in the movie. But while walking through this quiet and spacious white neighborhood, he did not feel the pull and mystery of the thing as strongly as he had in the movie. The houses he passed were huge; lights glowed softly in windows. The streets were empty, save for an occasional car that zoomed past on swift rubber tires. This was a cold and distant world; a world of white secrets carefully guarded. He could feel a pride, a certainty, and a confidence in these streets and houses. He came to Drexel Boulevard and began to look for 4605. When he came to it, he stopped and stood before a high, black, iron picket fence, feeling constricted inside. All he had felt in the movie was gone; only fear and emptiness filled him now.

Would they expect him to come in the front way or back? It was queer that he had not thought of that. Goddamn! He walked the length of the picket fence in front of the house, seeking for a walk leading to the rear. But there was none. Other than the front gate, there was only a driveway, the entrance to which was securely locked. Suppose a police saw him wandering in a white neighborhood like this? It would be thought that he was trying to rob or rape somebody. He grew angry. Why had he come to take this goddamn job? He could have stayed among his own people and escaped feeling this fear and hate. This was not his world; he had been foolish in thinking that he would have liked it. He stood in the middle of the sidewalk with his jaws clamped tight; he wanted to strike something with his fist. Well. . . . God-damn! There was nothing to do but go in the front way. If he were doing wrong, they could not kill him, at least; all they could do was to tell him that he could not get the job.

Timidly, he lifted the latch on the gate and walked to the steps. He paused, waiting for someone to challenge him. Nothing happened. Maybe nobody was home? He went to the door and saw a dim light burning in a shaded niche above a doorbell. He pushed it and was startled to hear a soft gong sound within. Maybe he had pushed it too hard? Aw, what the hell! He had to do better than this; he relaxed his taut muscles and stood at ease, waiting. The doorknob turned. The door opened. He saw a white face. It was a woman.

"Hello!"

"Yessum," he said.

"You want to see somebody?"

"Er. . . . Er. . . . I want to see Mr. Dalton."

"Are you the Thomas boy?"

"Yessum."

"Come in."

He edged through the door slowly, then stopped halfway. The woman was so close to him that he could see a tiny mole at the corner of her mouth. He held his breath. It seemed that there was not room enough for him to pass without actually touching her.

"Come on in," the woman said.

"Yessum," he whispered.

He squeezed through and stood uncertainly in a softly lighted hallway.

"Follow me," she said.

With cap in hand and shoulders sloped, he followed, walking over a rug so soft and deep that it seemed he was going to fall at each step he took. He went into a dimly lit room.

"Take a seat," she said. "I'll tell Mr. Dalton that you're here and he'll be out in a moment."

"Yessum."

He sat and looked up at the woman; she was staring at him and he looked away in confusion. He was glad when she left. That old bastard! What's so damn funny about me? I'm just like she is. . . . He felt that the position in which he was sitting was too awkward and found that he was on the very edge of the chair. He rose slightly to sit farther back; but when he sat he sank down so suddenly and deeply that he thought the chair had collapsed under him. He bounded halfway up, in fear; then, realizing what had happened, he sank distrustfully down again. He looked round the room; it was lit by dim lights glowing from a hidden source. He tried to find them by roving his eyes, but could not. He had not expected anything like this; he had not thought that this world would be so utterly different from his own that it would intimidate him. On the smooth walls were several paintings whose nature he tried to make out, but failed. He would have liked to examine them, but dared not. Then he listened; a faint sound of piano music floated to him from somewhere. He was sitting in a white home; dim lights burned round him; strange objects challenged him; and he was feeling angry and uncomfortable.

"All right. Come this way."

He started at the sound of a man's voice.

"Suh?"

"Come this way."

Misjudging how far back he was sitting in the chair, his first attempt to rise failed and he slipped back, resting on his side. Grabbing the arms of the chair, he pulled himself upright and found a tall, lean, white-haired man holding a piece of paper in his hand. The man was gazing at him with an amused smile that made him conscious of every square inch of skin on his black body.

"Thomas?" the man asked. "Bigger Thomas?"

"Yessuh," he whispered; not speaking, really; but hearing his words roll involuntarily from his lips.

"Come this way."

"Yessuh."

He followed the man out of the room and down a hall. The man stopped abruptly. Bigger paused, bewildered; then he saw coming slowly toward him a tall, thin, white woman, walking silently, her hands lifted delicately in the air and touching the walls to either side of her. Bigger stepped back to let her pass. Her face and hair were completely white; she seemed to him like a ghost. The man took her arm gently and held her for a moment. Bigger saw that she was old and her grey eyes looked stony.

"Are you all right?" the man asked.

"Yes," she answered.

"Where's Peggy?"

"She's preparing dinner. I'm quite all right, Henry."

The man let go of the woman and she walked on slowly, the long white fingers of her hands just barely touching the walls. Behind the woman, following at the hem of her dress, was a big white cat, pacing without sound. She's blind! Bigger thought in amazement.

"Come on; this way," the man said.

"Yessuh."

He wondered if the man had seen him staring at the woman. He would have to be careful here. There were so many strange things. He followed the man into a room.

"Sit down."

"Yessuh," he said, sitting.

"That was Mrs. Dalton," the man said. "She's blind."

"Yessuh."

"She has a very deep interest in colored people."

"Yessuh," Bigger whispered. He was conscious of the effort to breathe; he licked his lips and fumbled nervously with his cap.

"Well, I'm Mr. Dalton."

"Yessuh."

"Do you think you'd like driving a car?"

"Oh, yessuh."

"Did you bring the paper?"

"Suh?"

"Didn't the relief give you a note to me?"

"Oh, yessuh!"

He had completely forgotten about the paper. He stood to reach into his vest pocket and, in doing so, dropped his cap. For a moment his impulses were deadlocked; he did not know if he should pick up his cap and then find the paper, or find the paper and then pick up his cap. He decided to pick up his cap.

"Put your cap here," said Mr. Dalton, indicating a place on his desk.

"Yessuh."

Then he was stone-still; the white cat bounded past him and leaped upon the desk; it sat looking at him with large placid eyes and mewed plaintively.

"What's the matter, Kate?" Mr. Dalton asked, stroking the cat's fur and smiling. Mr. Dalton turned back to Bigger. "Did you find it?"

"Nawsuh. But I got it here, somewhere."

He hated himself at that moment. Why was he acting and feeling this way? He wanted to wave his hand and blot out the white man who was making him feel this. If not that, he wanted to blot himself out. He had not raised his eyes to the level of Mr. Dalton's face once since he had been in the house. He stood with his knees slightly bent, his lips partly open, his shoulders stooped; and his eyes held a look that went only to the surface of things. There was an organic conviction in him that this was the way white folks wanted him to be when in their presence; none had ever told him that in so many words, but their manner had made him feel that they did. He laid the cap down, noticing that Mr. Dalton was watching him closely. Maybe he was not acting right? God-damn! Clumsily, he searched for the paper. He could not find it at first and he felt called upon to say something for taking so long.

"I had it right here in my vest pocket," he mumbled.

"Take your time."

"Oh, here it is."

He drew the paper forth. It was crumpled and soiled. Nervously, he straightened it out and handed it to Mr. Dalton, holding it by its very tip end.

"All right, now," said Mr. Dalton. "Let's see what you've got here. You live at 3721 Indiana Avenue?"

"Yessuh."

Mr. Dalton paused, frowned, and looked up at the ceiling.

"What kind of a building is that over there?"

"You mean where I live, suh?"

"Yes."

"Oh, it's just an old building."

"Where do you pay rent?"

"Down on Thirty-first Street."

"To the South Side Real Estate Company?"

"Yessuh."

Bigger wondered what all these questions could mean; he had heard that Mr. Dalton owned the South Side Real Estate Company, but he was not sure.

"How much rent do you pay?"

"Eight dollars a week."

"For how many rooms?"

"We just got one, suh."

"I see. . . . Now, Bigger, tell me, how old are you?"

"I'm twenty, suh."

"Married?"

"Nawsuh."

"Sit down. You needn't stand. And I won't be long."

"Yessuh."

He sat. The white cat still contemplated him with large, moist eyes.

"Now, you have a mother, a brother, and a sister?"

"Yessuh."

"There are four of you?"

"Yessuh, there's four of us," he stammered, trying to show that he was not as stupid as he might appear. He felt a need to speak more, for he felt that maybe Mr. Dalton expected it. And he suddenly remembered the many times his mother had told him not to look at the floor when talking with white folks or asking for a job. He lifted his eyes and saw Mr. Dalton watching him closely. He dropped his eyes again.

"They call you Bigger?"

"Yessuh."

"Now, Bigger, I'd like to talk with you a little. . . ."

Yes, Goddammit! He knew what was coming. He would be asked about that time he had been accused of stealing auto tires and had been sent to the reform school. He felt guilty, condemned. He should not have come here.

"The relief people said some funny things about you. I'd like to talk to you about them. Now, you needn't feel ashamed with me," said Mr. Dalton, smiling. "I was a boy myself once and I think I know how things are. So just be yourself. . . ." Mr. Dalton pulled out a package of cigarettes. "Here; have one."

"Nawsuh; thank you, suh."

"You don't smoke?"

"Yessuh. But I just don't want one now."

"Now, Bigger, the relief people said you were a very good worker when you were interested in what you were doing. Is that true?"

"Well, I do my work, suh."

"But they said you were always in trouble. How do you explain that?"

"I don't know, suh."

"Why did they send you to the reform school?"

His eyes glared at the floor.

"They said I was stealing!" he blurted defensively. "But I wasn't."

"Are you sure?"

"Yessuh."

"Well, how did you get mixed up in it?"

"I was with some boys and the police picked us up."

Mr. Dalton said nothing. Bigger heard a clock ticking somewhere behind him and he had a foolish impulse to look at it. But he restrained himself.

"Well, Bigger, how do you feel about it now?"

"Suh? 'Bout what?"

"If you had a job, would you steal now?"

"Oh, nawsuh. I don't steal."

"Well," said Mr. Dalton, "they say you can drive a car and I'm going to give you a job."

He said nothing.

"You think you can handle it?"

"Oh, yessuh."

"The pay calls for $20 a week, but I'm going to give you $25. The extra $5 is for yourself, for you to spend as you like. You will get the clothes you need and your meals. You're to sleep in the back room, above the kitchen. You can give the $20 to your mother to keep your brother and sister in school. How does that sound?"

"It sounds all right. Yessuh."

"I think we'll get along."

"Yessuh."

"I don't think we'll have any trouble."

"Nawsuh."

"Now, Bigger," said Mr. Dalton, "since that's settled, let's see what you'll have to do every day. I leave every morning for my office at nine. It's a twenty-minute drive. You are to be back at ten and take Miss Dalton to school. At twelve, you call for Miss Dalton at the University. From then until night you are more or less free. If either Miss Dalton or I go out at night, of course, you do the driving. You work every day, but we don't get up till noon on Sundays. So you will have Sunday mornings to yourself, unless something unexpected happens. You get one full day off every two weeks."

"Yessuh."

"You think you can handle that?"

"Oh, yessuh."

"And any time you're bothered about anything, come and see me. Let's talk it over."

"Yessuh."

"Oh, Father!" a girl's voice sang out.

"Yes, Mary," said Mr. Dalton.

Bigger turned and saw a white girl walk into the room. She was very slender.

"Oh, I didn't know you were busy."

"That's all right, Mary. What is it?"

Bigger saw that the girl was looking at him. Yes; she was the same girl he had seen in the movie.

"Is this the new chauffeur, Father?"

"What do you want, Mary?"

"Will you get the tickets for the Thursday concert?"

"At Orchestra Hall?"

"Yes."

"Yes. I'll get them."

"Is this the new chauffeur?"

"Yes," said Mr. Dalton. "This is Bigger Thomas."

"Hello, Bigger," the girl said.

Bigger swallowed. He looked at Mr. Dalton, then felt that he should not have looked.

"Good evening, mam."

The girl came close to him and stopped just opposite his chair.

"Bigger, do you belong to a union?" she asked.

"Now, Mary!" said Mr. Dalton, frowning.

"Well, Father, he should," the girl said, turning to him, then back to Bigger. "Do you?"

"Mary. . . ." said Mr. Dalton.

"I'm just asking him a question, Father!"

Bigger hesitated. He hated the girl then. Why did she have to do this when he was trying to get a job?

"No'm," he mumbled, his head down and his eyes glowering.

"And why not?" the girl asked.

Bigger heard Mr. Dalton mumble something. He wished Mr. Dalton would speak and end this thing. He looked up and saw Mr. Dalton staring at the girl. She's making me lose my job! he thought. Goddamn! He knew nothing about unions, except that they were considered bad. And what did she mean by talking to him this way in front of Mr. Dalton, who, surely, didn't like unions?

"We can settle about the union later, Mary," said Mr. Dalton.

"But you wouldn't mind belonging to a union, would you?" the girl asked.

"I don't know, mam," Bigger said.

"Now, Mary, you can see that the boy is new," said Mr. Dalton. "Leave him alone."

The girl turned and poked out a red tongue at him.

"All right, Mr. Capitalist!" She turned again to Bigger. "Isn't he a capitalist, Bigger?"

Bigger looked at the floor and did not answer. He did not know what a capitalist was.

The girl started to leave, but stopped.

"Oh, Father, if he hasn't anything else to do, let him drive me to my lecture at the University tonight."

"I'm talking to him now, Mary. He'll be through in a moment."

The girl picked up the cat and walked from the room. There was a short interval of silence. Bigger wished the girl had not said anything about unions. Maybe he would not be hired now? Or, if hired, maybe he would be fired soon if she kept acting like that. He had never seen anyone like her before. She was not a bit the way he had imagined she would be.

"Oh, Mary!" Mr. Dalton called.

"Yes, Father," Bigger heard her answer from the hallway.

Mr. Dalton rose and left the room. He sat still, listening. Once or twice he thought he heard the girl laugh, but he was not sure. The best thing he could do was to leave that crazy girl alone. No wonder they called her a Communist in the movies. She was crazy, all right. He had heard about unions; in his mind unions and Communists were linked. He relaxed a little, then stiffened when he heard Mr. Dalton walk back into the room. Wordlessly, the white man sat behind the desk and picked up the paper and looked at it in a long silence. Bigger watched him with lowered eyes; he knew that Mr. Dalton was thinking of something other than that paper. In his heart he cursed the crazy girl. Maybe Mr. Dalton was deciding not to hire him? Goddamn! Maybe he would not get the extra five dollars a week now? *Goddamn that woman!* She spoiled everything! Maybe Mr. Dalton would feel that he could not trust him.

"Oh, Bigger," said Mr. Dalton.

"Yessuh."

"I want you to know why I'm hiring you."

"Yessuh."

"You see, Bigger, I'm a supporter of the National Association for the Advancement of Colored People. Did you ever hear of that organization?"

"Nawsuh."

"Well, it doesn't matter," said Mr. Dalton. "Have you had your dinner?"

"Nawsuh."

"Well, I think you'll do."

Mr. Dalton pushed a button. There was silence. The woman who had answered the front door came in.

"Yes, Mr. Dalton."

"Peggy, this is Bigger. He's going to drive for us. Give him something to eat, and show him where he's to sleep and where the car is."

"Yes, Mr. Dalton."

"And, Bigger, at eight-thirty, drive Miss Dalton out to the University and wait for her," said Mr. Dalton.

"Yessuh."

"That's all now."

"Yessuh."

"Come with me," Peggy said.

Bigger rose and got his cap and followed the woman through the house to the kitchen. The air was full of the scent of food cooking and pots bubbled on the stove.

"Sit here," Peggy said, clearing a place for him at a white-topped table. He sat and rested his cap on his knees. He felt a little better now that he was out of the front part of the house, but still not quite comfortable.

"Dinner isn't quite ready yet," Peggy said. "You like bacon and eggs?"

"Yessum."

"Coffee?"

"Yessum."

He sat looking at the white walls of the kitchen and heard the woman stir about behind him.

"Did Mr. Dalton tell you about the furnace?"

"No'm."

"Well, he must have forgotten it. You're supposed to attend to that, too. I'll show you where it is before you go."

"You mean I got to keep the fire going, mam?"

"Yes. But it's easy. Did you ever fire before?"

"No'm."

"You can learn. There's nothing to it."

"Yessum."

Peggy seemed kind enough, but maybe she was being kind in order to shove her part of the work on him. Well, he would wait and see. If she got nasty, he would talk to Mr. Dalton about her. He smelt the odor of frying bacon and realized that he was very hungry. He had forgotten to buy a sandwich with the quarter his mother had given him, and he had not eaten since morning. Peggy placed a plate, knife, fork, spoon, sugar, cream, and bread before him; then she dished up the bacon and eggs.

"You can get more if you want it."

The food was good. This was not going to be a bad job. The only thing bad so far was that crazy girl. He chewed his bacon and eggs while some remote part of his mind considered in amazement how different the girl had seemed in the movie. On the screen she was not dangerous and his mind could do with her as it liked. But here in her home she walked over everything, put herself in the way. He had quite forgotten that Peggy was in the kitchen and when his plate was empty he took a soft piece of bread and began to sop it clean, carrying the bread to his mouth in huge chunks.

"You want some more?"

He stopped chewing and laid the bread aside. He had not wanted to let her see him do that; he did that only at home.

"No'm," he said. "I got a plenty."

"You reckon you'll like it here?" Peggy asked.

"Yessum. I hope so."

"This is a swell place," Peggy said. "About as good as you'll find anywhere. The last colored man who worked for us stayed ten years."

Bigger wondered why she said "us." She must stand in with the old man and old woman pretty good, he thought.

"Ten years?" he said.

"Yes; ten years. His name was Green. He was a good man, too."

"How come he to leave?"

"Oh, he was smart, that Green was. He took a job with the government. Mrs. Dalton made him go to night school. Mrs. Dalton's always trying to help somebody."

Yes; Bigger knew that. But he was not going to any night school. He looked at Peggy; she was bent over the sink, washing dishes. Her words had challenged him and he felt he had to say something.

"Yessum, he was smart," he said. "And ten years is a long time."

"Oh, it wasn't so long," Peggy said. "I've been here twenty years myself. I always was one for sticking to a job. I always say when you get a good place, then stick there. A rolling stone gathers no moss, and it's true."

Bigger said nothing.

"Everything's simple and nice around here," Peggy said. "They've got millions, but they live like human beings. They don't put on airs and strut. Mrs. Dalton believes that people should be that way."

"Yessum."

"They're Christian people and believe in everybody working hard. And living a clean life. Some people think we ought to have more servants than we do, but we get along. It's just like one big family."

"Yessum."

"Mr. Dalton's a fine man," Peggy said.

"Oh, yessum. He is."

"You know, he does a lot for your people."

"My people?" asked Bigger, puzzled.

"Yes, the colored people. He gave over five million dollars to colored schools."

"Oh!"

"But Mrs. Dalton's the one who's really nice. If it wasn't for her, he would not be doing what he does. She made him rich. She had millions when he married her. Of course, he made a lot of money himself afterwards out of real estate. But most of the money's hers. She's blind, poor thing. She lost her sight ten years ago. Did you see her yet?"

"Yessum."

"Was she alone?"

"Yessum."

"Poor thing! Mrs. Patterson, who takes care of her, is away for the week-end and she's all alone. Isn't it too bad, about her?"

"Oh, yessum," he said, trying to get into his voice some of the pity for Mrs. Dalton that he thought Peggy expected him to feel.

"It's really more than a job you've got here," Peggy went on. "It's just like home. I'm always telling Mrs. Dalton that this is the only home I'll ever know. I wasn't in this country but two years before I started working here. . . ."

"Oh," said Bigger, looking at her.

"I'm Irish, you know," she said. "My folks in the old country feel about England like the colored folks feel about this country. So I know something about colored people. Oh, these are fine people, fine as silk. Even the girl. Did you meet her yet?"

"Yessum."

"Tonight?"

"Yessum."

Peggy turned and looked at him sharply.

"She's a sweet thing," she said. "I've known her since she was two years old. But she's kind of wild, she is. Always in hot water. Keeps her folks worried. The Lord only knows where she got her wild ways. But she's got 'em. If you stay around here long, you'll get to know her."

Bigger wanted to ask about the girl, but thought that he had better not do that now.

"If you're through, I'll show you the furnace and the car, and where your room is," she said and turned the fire low under the pots on the stove.

"Yessum."

He rose and followed her out of the kitchen, down a narrow stairway at the end of which was the basement. It was dark; Bigger heard a sharp click and the light came on.

"This way. . . . What did you say your name was?"

"Bigger, mam."

"What?"

"Bigger."

He smelt the scent of coal and ashes and heard fire roaring. He saw a red bed of embers glowing in the furnace.

"This is the furnace," she said.

"Yessum."

"Every morning you'll find the garbage here; you burn it and put the bucket on the dumb-waiter."

"Yessum."

"You never have to use a shovel for coal. It's a self-feeder. Look, see?"

Peggy pulled a lever and there came a loud rattle of fine lumps of coal sliding down a metal chute. Bigger stooped and saw, through the cracks of the furnace, the coal spreading out fanwise over the red bed of fire.

"That's fine," he mumbled in admiration.

"And you don't have to worry about water, either. It fills itself."

Bigger liked that; it was easy; it would be fun, almost.

"Your biggest trouble will be taking out the ashes and sweeping. And keep track of how the coal runs; when it's low, tell me or Mr. Dalton and we'll order some more."

"Yessum. I can handle it."

"Now, to get to your room all you have to do is go up these back stairs. Come on."

He followed up a stretch of stairs. She opened a door and switched on a light and Bigger saw a large room whose walls were covered with pictures of girls' faces and prize fighters.

"This was Green's room. He was always one for pictures. But he kept things neat and nice. It's plenty warm here. Oh, yes; before I forget. Here are the keys to the room and the garage and the car. Now, I'll show you the garage. You have to get to it from the outside."

He followed her down the steps and outside into the drive-way. It was much warmer.

"Looks like snow," Peggy said.

"Yessum."

"This is the garage," she said, unlocking and pushing open a door which, as it swung in, made lights come on automatically. "You always bring the car out and wait at the side door for the folks. Let's see. You say you're driving Miss Dalton tonight?"

"Yessum."

"Well, she leaves at eight-thirty. So you're free until then. You can look over your room if you want to."

"Yessum. I reckon I will."

Bigger went behind Peggy down the stairs and back into the basement. She went to the kitchen and he went to his room. He stood in the middle of the floor, looking at the walls. There were pictures of Jack Johnson, Joe Louis, Jack Dempsey, and Henry Armstrong; there were others of Ginger Rogers, Jean Harlow, and Janet Gaynor. The room was large and had two radiators. He felt the bed; it was soft. Gee! He would bring Bessie here some night. Not right at once; he would wait until he had learned the ropes of the place. A room all to himself! He could bring a pint of liquor up here and drink it in peace. He would not have to slip around any more. He would not have to sleep with Buddy and stand Buddy's kicking all night long. He lit a cigarette and stretched himself full length upon the bed. Ohhhh. . . . This was not going to be bad at all. He looked at his dollar watch; it was seven. In a little while he would go down and examine the car. And he would buy himself another watch, too. A dollar watch was not good enough for a job like this; he would buy a gold one. There were a lot of new things he would get. Oh, boy! This would be an easy life. Everything was all right, except that girl. She worried him. She might cause him to lose his job if she kept talking about unions. She was a funny girl, all right. Never in his life had he met anyone like her. She puzzled him. She was rich, but she didn't act like she was rich. She acted like. . . . Well, he didn't know exactly what she did act like. In all of the white women he had met, mostly on jobs and at relief stations, there was always a certain coldness and reserve; they stood their distance and spoke to him from afar. But this girl waded right in and hit him between the eyes with her words and ways. Aw, hell! What good was there in thinking about her like this? Maybe she was all right. Maybe he would just have to get used to her; that was all. I bet she spends a plenty of dough, he thought. And the old man had given five million dollars to colored people. If a man could give five million dollars away, then millions must be as common to him as nickels. He rose up and sat on the edge of the bed.

What make of car was he to drive? He had not thought to look when Peggy had opened the garage door. He hoped it would be a Packard, or a Lincoln, or a Rolls Royce. Boy! Would he drive! Just wait! Of course, he would be careful when he was driving Miss or Mr. Dalton. But when he was alone he would burn up the pavement; he would make those tires smoke!

He licked his lips; he was thirsty. He looked at his watch; it was ten past eight. He would go to the kitchen and get a drink of water and then drive the car out of the garage. He went down the steps, through the basement to the stairs leading to the kitchen door. Though he did not know it, he walked on tiptoe. He eased the door open and peeped in. What he saw made him suck his breath in; Mrs. Dalton in flowing white clothes was standing stone-still in the middle of the kitchen floor. There was silence, save for the slow ticking of a large clock on a white wall. For a moment he did not know if he should go in or go back down the steps; his thirst was gone. Mrs. Dalton's face was held in an attitude of intense listening and her hands were hanging loosely at her sides. To Bigger her face seemed to be capable of hearing in every pore of the skin and listening always to some low voice speaking. Sitting quietly on the floor beside her was the white cat, its large black eyes fastened upon him. It made him uneasy just to look at her and that white cat; he was about to close the door and tiptoe softly back down the stairs when she spoke.

"Are you the new boy?"

"Yessum."

"Did you want something?"

"I didn't mean to disturb you, mam. I—I. . . . I just wanted a drink of water."

"Well, come on in. I think you'll find a glass somewhere."

He went to the sink, watching her as he walked, feeling that she could see him even though he knew that she was blind. His skin tingled. He took a glass from a narrow shelf and filled it from a faucet. As he drank he stole a glance at her over the rim of the glass. Her face was still, tilted, waiting. It reminded him of a dead man's face he had once seen. Then he realized that Mrs. Dalton had turned and listened to the sound of his feet as he had walked. She knows exactly where I'm standing, he thought.

"You like your room?" she asked; and as she spoke he realized that she had been standing there waiting to hear the sound of his glass as it had clinked on the sink.

"Oh, yessum."

"I hope you're a careful driver."

"Oh, yessum. I'll be careful."

"Did you ever drive before?"

"Yessum. But it was a grocery truck."

He had the feeling that talking to a blind person was like talking to someone whom he himself could scarcely see.

"How far did you go in school, Bigger?"

"To the eighth grade, mam."

"Do you ever think of going back?"

"Well, I gotta work now, mam."

"Suppose you had the chance to go back?"

"Well, I don't know, mam."

"The last man who worked here went to night school and got an education."

"Yessum."

"What would you want to be if you had an education?"

"I don't know, mam."

"Did you ever think about it?"

"No'm."

"You would rather work?"

"I reckon I would, mam."

"Well, we'll talk about that some other time. I think you'd better get the car for Miss Dalton now."

"Yessum."

He left her standing in the middle of the kitchen floor, exactly as he had found her. He did not know just how to take her; she made him feel that she would judge all he did harshly but kindly. He had a feeling toward her that was akin to that which he held toward his mother. The difference in his feelings toward Mrs. Dalton and his mother was that he felt that his mother wanted him to do the things *she* wanted him to do, and he felt that Mrs. Dalton wanted him to do the things she felt that *he* should have wanted to do. But he did not want to go to night school. Night school was all right; but he had other plans. Well, he didn't know just what they were right now, but he was working them out.

The night air had grown warmer. A wind had risen. He lit a cigarette and unlocked the garage; the door swung in and again he was surprised and pleased to see the lights spring on automatically. These people's got everything, he mused. He examined the car; it was a dark blue Buick, with steel spoke wheels and of a new make. He stepped back from it and looked it over; then he opened the door and looked at the dashboard. He was a little disappointed that the car was not so expensive as he had hoped, but what it lacked in price was more than made up for in color and style. "It's all right," he said half-aloud. He got in and backed it into the driveway and turned it round and pulled it up to the side door.

"Is that you, Bigger?"

The girl stood on the steps.

"Yessum."

He got out and held the rear door open for her.

"Thank you."

He touched his cap and wondered if it were the right thing to do.

"Is it that university-school out there on the Midway, mam?"

Through the rear mirror above him he saw her hesitate before answering.

"Yes; that's the one."

He pulled the car into the street and headed south, driving about thirty-five miles an hour. He handled the car expertly, picking up speed at the beginning of each block and slowing slightly as he approached each street intersection.

"You drive well," she said.

"Yessum," he said proudly.

He watched her through the rear mirror as he drove; she was kind of pretty, but very little. She looked like a doll in a show window: black eyes, white face, red lips. And she was not acting at all now as she had acted when he first saw her. In fact, she had a remote look in her eyes. He stopped the car at Forty-seventh Street for a red light; he did not have to stop again until he reached Fifty-first Street where a long line of cars formed in front of him and a long line in back. He held the steering wheel lightly, waiting for the line to move forward. He had a keen sense of power when driving; the feel of a car added something to him. He loved to press his foot against a pedal and sail along, watching others stand still, seeing the asphalt road unwind under him. The lights flashed from red to green and he nosed the car forward.

"Bigger!"

"Yessum."

"Turn at this corner and pull up on a side street."

"Here, mam?"

"Yes; here."

Now, what on earth did this mean? He pulled the car off Cottage Grove Avenue and drew to a curb. He turned to look at her and was startled to see that she was sitting on the sheer edge of the back seat, her face some six inches from his.

"I scare you?" she asked softly, smiling.

"Oh, no'm," he mumbled, bewildered.

He watched her through the mirror. Her tiny white hands dangled over the back of the front seat and her eyes looked out vacantly.

"I don't know how to say what I'm going to say," she said.

He said nothing. There was a long silence. What in all hell did this girl want? A street car rumbled by. Behind him, reflected in the rear mirror, he saw the traffic lights flash from green to red, and back again. Well, whatever she was going to say, he wished she would say it and get it over. This girl was strange. She did the unexpected every minute. He waited for her to speak. She took her hands from the back of the front seat and fumbled in her purse.

"Gotta match?"

"Yessum."

He dug a match from his vest pocket.

"Strike it," she said.

He blinked. He struck the match and held the flame for her. She smoked awhile in silence.

"You're not a tattle-tale, are you?" she asked with a smile.

He opened his mouth to reply, but no words came. What she had asked and the tone of voice in which she had asked it made him feel that he ought to have answered in some way; but what?

"I'm not going to the University," she said at last. "But you can forget that. I want you to drive me to the Loop. But if anyone should ask you, then I went to the University, see, Bigger?"

"Yessum; it's all right with me," he mumbled.

"I think I can trust you."

"Yessum."

"After all, I'm on your side."

Now, what did *that* mean? She was on *his* side. What side was he on? Did she mean that she liked colored people? Well, he had heard that about her whole family. Was she really crazy? How much did her folks know of how she acted? But if she were really crazy, why did Mr. Dalton let him drive her out?

"I'm going to meet a friend of mine who's also a friend of yours," she said.

"Friend of mine!" he could not help exclaiming.

"Oh, you don't know him yet," she said, laughing.

"Oh."

"Go to the Outer Drive and then to 16 Lake Street."

"Yessum."

Maybe she was talking about the Reds? *That* was it! But none of his friends were Reds. What was all this? If Mr. Dalton should ask him if he had taken her to the University, he would have to say yes and depend upon her to back him up. But suppose Mr. Dalton had someone watching, someone who would tell where he had really taken her? He had heard that many rich people had detectives working for them. If only he knew what this was all about he would feel much better. And she had said that she was going to meet someone who was a friend of his. He didn't want to meet any Communists. They didn't have any money. He felt that it was all right for a man to go to jail for robbery, but to go to jail for fooling around with Reds was bunk. Well, he would drive her; that was what he had been hired for. But he was going to watch his step in this business. The only thing he hoped was that she would not make him lose his job. He pulled the car off the Outer Drive at Seventh Street, drove north on Michigan Boulevard to Lake Street, then headed west for two blocks, looking for number 16.

"It's right here, Bigger."

"Yessum."

He pulled to a stop in front of a dark building.

"Wait," she said, getting out of the car.

He saw her smiling broadly at him, almost laughing. He felt that she knew every feeling and thought he had at that moment and he turned his head away in confusion. Goddamn that woman!

"I won't be long," she said.

She started off, then turned back.

"Take it easy, Bigger. You'll understand it better bye and bye."

"Yessum," he said, trying to smile; but couldn't.

"Isn't there a song like that, a song your people sing?"

"Like what, mam?"

"We'll understand it better bye and bye?"

"Oh, yessum."

She was an odd girl, all right. He felt something in her over and above the fear she inspired in him. She responded to him as if he were human, as if he lived in the same world as she. And he had never felt that before in a white person. But why? Was this some kind of game? The guarded feeling of freedom he had while listening to her was tangled with the hard fact that she was white and rich, a part of the world of people who told him what he could and could not do.

He looked at the building into which she had gone; it was old and unpainted; there were no lights in the windows or doorway. Maybe she was meeting her sweetheart? If that was all, then things would straighten out. But if she had gone to meet those Communists? And what were Communists like, anyway? Was *she* one? What made people Communists? He remembered seeing many cartoons of Communists in newspapers and always they had flaming torches in their hands and wore beards and were trying to commit murder or set things on fire. People who acted that way were crazy. All he could recall having heard about Communists was associated in his mind with darkness, old houses, people speaking in whispers, and trade unions on strike. And this was something like it.

He stiffened; the door into which she had gone opened. She came out, followed by a young white man. They walked to the car; but, instead of getting into the back seat, they came to the side of the car and stood, facing him. At once Bigger recognized the man as the one he had seen in the newsreel in the movie.

"Oh, Bigger, this is Jan. And Jan, this is Bigger Thomas."

Jan smiled broadly, then extended an open palm toward him. Bigger's entire body tightened with suspense and dread.

"How are you, Bigger?"

Bigger's right hand gripped the steering wheel and he wondered if he ought to shake hands with this white man.

"I'm fine," he mumbled.

Jan's hand was still extended. Bigger's right hand raised itself about three inches, then stopped in mid-air.

"Come on and shake," Jan said.

Bigger extended a limp palm, his mouth open in astonishment. He felt Jan's fingers tighten about his own. He tried to pull his hand away, ever so gently, but Jan held on, firmly, smiling.

"We may as well get to know each other," Jan said. "I'm a friend of Mary's."

"Yessuh," he mumbled.

"First of all," Jan continued, putting his foot upon the running-board, "don't say *sir* to me. I'll call you Bigger and you'll call me Jan. That's the way it'll be between us. How's that?"

Bigger did not answer. Mary was smiling. Jan still gripped his hand and Bigger held his head at an oblique angle, so that he could, by merely shifting his eyes, look at Jan and then out into the street whenever he did not wish to meet Jan's gaze. He heard Mary laughing softly.

"It's all right, Bigger," she said. "Jan *means* it."

He flushed warm with anger. Goddamn her soul to hell! Was she laughing at him? Were they making fun of him? What was it that they wanted? Why didn't they leave him alone? He was not bothering them. Yes, anything could happen with people like these. His entire mind and body were painfully concentrated into a single sharp point of attention. He was trying desperately to understand. He felt foolish sitting behind the steering wheel like this and letting a white man hold his hand. What would people passing along the street think?

He was very conscious of his black skin and there was in him a prodding conviction that Jan and men like him had made it so that he would be conscious of that black skin. Did not white people despise a black skin? Then why was Jan doing this? Why was Mary standing there so eagerly, with shining eyes? What could they get out of this? Maybe they did not despise him? But they made him feel his black skin by just standing there looking at him, one holding his hand and the other smiling. He felt he had no physical existence at all right then; he was something he hated, the badge of shame which he knew was attached to a black skin. It was a shadowy region, a No Man's Land, the ground that separated the white world from the black that he stood upon. He felt naked, transparent; he felt that this white man, having helped to put him down, having helped to deform him, held him up now to look at him and be amused. At that moment he felt toward Mary and Jan a dumb, cold, and inarticulate hate.

"Let me drive awhile," Jan said, letting go of his hand and opening the door.

Bigger looked at Mary. She came forward and touched his arm.

"It's all right, Bigger," she said.

He turned in the seat to get out, but Jan stopped him.

"No; stay in and move over."

He slid over and Jan took his place at the wheel. He was still feeling his hand strangely; it seemed that the pressure of Jan's fingers had left an indelible imprint. Mary was getting into the front seat, too.

"Move over, Bigger," she said.

He moved closer to Jan. Mary pushed herself in, wedging tightly between him and the outer door of the car. There were white people to either side of him; he was sitting between two vast white looming walls. Never in his life had he been so close to a white woman. He smelt the odor of her hair and felt the soft pressure of her thigh against his own. Jan headed the car back to the Outer Drive, weaving in and out of the line of traffic. Soon they were speeding along the lake front, past a huge flat sheet of dully gleaming water. The sky was heavy with snow clouds and the wind was blowing strong.

"Isn't it glorious tonight?" she asked.

"God, yes!" Jan said.

Bigger listened to the tone of their voices, to their strange accents, to the exuberant phrases that flowed so freely from their lips.

"That sky!"

"And that water!"

"It's so beautiful it makes you ache just to look at it," said Mary.

"This is a beautiful world, Bigger," Jan said, turning to him. "Look at that skyline!"

Bigger looked without turning his head; he just rolled his eyes. Stretching to one side of him was a vast sweep of tall buildings flecked with tiny squares of yellow light.

"We'll own all that some day, Bigger," Jan said with a wave of his hand. "After the revolution it'll be ours. But we'll have to fight for it. What a world to win, Bigger! And when that day comes, things'll be different. There'll be no white and no black; there'll be no rich and no poor."

Bigger said nothing. The car whirred along.

"We seem strange to you, don't we, Bigger?" Mary asked.

"Oh, no'm," he breathed softly, knowing that she did not believe him, but finding it impossible to answer her in any other way.

His arms and legs were aching from being cramped into so small a space, but he dared not move. He knew that they would not have cared if he had made himself more comfortable, but his moving would have called attention to himself and his black body. And he did not want that. These people made him feel things he did not want to feel. If he were white, if he were like them, it would have been different. But he was black. So he sat still, his arms and legs aching.

"Say, Bigger," asked Jan, "where can we get a good meal on the South Side?"

"Well," Bigger said, reflectively.

"We want to go to a *real* place," Mary said, turning to him gayly.

"You want to go to a night club?" Bigger asked in a tone that indicated that he was simply mentioning names and not recommending places to go.

"No; we want to eat."

"Look, Bigger. We want one of those places where colored people eat, not one of those show places."

What *did* these people want? When he answered his voice was neutral and toneless.

"Well, there's Ernie's Kitchen Shack. . . ."

"That sounds good!"

"Let's go there, Jan," Mary said.

"O.K.," Jan said. "Where is it?"

"It's at Forty-seventh Street and Indiana," Bigger told them.

Jan swung the car off the Outer Drive at Thirty-first Street and drove westward to Indiana Avenue. Bigger wanted Jan to drive faster, so that they could reach Ernie's Kitchen Shack in the shortest possible time. That would allow him a chance to sit in the car and stretch out his cramped and aching legs while they ate. Jan turned onto Indiana Avenue and headed south. Bigger wondered what Jack and Gus and G.H. would say if they saw him sitting between two white people in a car like this. They would tease him about such a thing as long as they could remember it. He felt Mary turn in her seat. She placed her hand on his arm.

"You know, Bigger, I've long wanted to go into these houses," she said, pointing to the tall, dark apartment buildings looming to either side of them, "and just *see* how your people live. You know what I mean? I've been to England, France and Mexico, but I don't know how people live ten blocks from me. We know so *little* about each other. I just want to *see*. I want to *know* these people. Never in my life have I been inside of a Negro home. Yet they *must* live like we live. They're *human*. . . . There are twelve million of them. . . . They live in our country. . . . In the same city with us. . . ." her voice trailed off wistfully.

There was silence. The car sped through the Black Belt, past tall buildings holding black life. Bigger knew that they were thinking of his life and the life of his people. Suddenly he wanted to seize some heavy object in his hand and grip it with all the strength of his body and in some strange way rise up and stand in naked space above the speeding car and with one final blow blot it out—with himself and them in it. His heart was beating fast and he struggled to control his breath. This thing was getting the better of him; he felt that he should not give way to his feelings like this. But he could not help it. Why didn't they leave him alone? What had he done to them? What good could they get out of sitting here making him feel so miserable?

"Tell me where it is, Bigger," Jan said.

"Yessuh."

Bigger looked out and saw that they were at Forty-sixth Street.

"It's at the end of the next block, suh."

"Can I park along here somewhere?"

"Oh; yessuh."

"Bigger, *please!* Don't say *sir* to me. . . . I don't *like* it. You're a man just like I am; I'm no better than you. Maybe other white men like it. But I don't. Look, Bigger. . . ."

"Yes. . . ." Bigger paused, swallowed, and looked down at his black hands. "O.K.," he mumbled, hoping that they did not hear the choke in his voice.

"You see, Bigger. . . ." Jan began.

Mary reached her hand round back of Bigger and touched Jan's shoulder.

"Let's get out," she said hurriedly.

Jan pulled the car to the curb and opened the door and stepped out. Bigger slipped behind the steering wheel again, glad to have room at last for his arms and legs. Mary got out of the other door. Now, he could get some rest. So intensely taken up was he with his own immediate sensations, that he did not look up until he felt something strange in the long silence. When he did look he saw, in a split second of time, Mary turn her eyes away from his face. She was looking at Jan and Jan was looking at her. There was no mistaking the meaning of the look in their eyes. To Bigger it was plainly a bewildered and questioning look, a look that asked: What on earth is wrong with him? Bigger's teeth clamped tight and he stared straight before him.

"Aren't you coming with us, Bigger?" Mary asked in a sweet tone that made him want to leap at her.

The people in Ernie's Kitchen Shack knew him and he did not want them to see him with these white people. He knew that if he went in they would ask one another: *Who're them white folks Bigger's hanging around with?*

"I—I. . . . I don't want to go in. . . ." he whispered breathlessly.

"Aren't you hungry?" Jan asked.

"Naw; I ain't hungry."

Jan and Mary came close to the car.

"Come and sit with us anyhow," Jan said.

"I. . . . I. . . ." Bigger stammered.

"It'll be all right," Mary said.

"I can stay here. Somebody has to watch the car," he said.

"Oh, to hell with the car!" Mary said. "Come on in."

"I don't want to eat," Bigger said stubbornly.

"Well," Jan sighed. "If that's the way you feel about it, we won't go in."

Bigger felt trapped. Oh, Goddamn! He saw in a flash that he could have made all of this very easy if he had simply acted from the beginning as if they were doing nothing unusual. But he did not understand them; he distrusted them, really hated them. He was puzzled as to why they were treating him this way. But, after all, this was his job and it was just as painful to sit here and let them stare at him as it was to go in.

"O.K.," he mumbled angrily.

He got out and slammed the door. Mary came close to him and caught his arm. He stared at her in a long silence; it was the first time he had ever looked directly at her, and he was able to do so only because he was angry.

"Bigger," she said, "you don't have to come in unless you really want to. Please, don't think. . . . Oh, Bigger. . . . We're not trying to make you feel badly. . . ."

Her voice stopped. In the dim light of the street lamp Bigger saw her eyes cloud and her lips tremble. She swayed against the car. He stepped backward, as though she were contaminated with an invisible contagion. Jan slipped his arm about her waist, supporting her. Bigger heard her sob softly. Good God! He had a wild impulse to turn around and walk away. He felt ensnared in a tangle of deep shadows, shadows as black as the night that stretched above his head. The way he had acted had made her cry, and yet the way she had acted had made him feel that he had to act as he had toward her. In his relations with her he felt that he was riding a seesaw; never were they on a common level; either he or she was up in the air. Mary dried her eyes and Jan whispered something to her. Bigger wondered what he could say to his mother, or the relief, or Mr. Dalton, if he left them. They would be sure to ask why he had walked off his job, and he would not be able to tell.

"I'm all right, now, Jan," he heard Mary say. "I'm sorry. I'm just a fool, I suppose. . . . I acted a ninny." She lifted her eyes to Bigger. "Don't mind me, Bigger. I'm just silly, I guess. . . ."

He said nothing.

"Come on, Bigger," Jan said in a voice that sought to cover up everything. "Let's eat."

Jan caught his arm and tried to pull him forward, but Bigger hung back. Jan and Mary walked toward the entrance of the café and Bigger followed, confused and resentful. Jan went to a small table near a wall.

"Sit down, Bigger."

Bigger sat. Jan and Mary sat in front of him.

"You like fried chicken?" Jan asked.

"Yessuh," he whispered.

He scratched his head. How on earth could he learn not to say *yessuh* and *yessum* to white people in one night when he had been saying it all his life long? He looked before him in such a way that his eyes would not meet theirs. The waitress came and Jan ordered three beers and three portions of fried chicken.

"Hi, Bigger!"

He turned and saw Jack waving at him, but staring at Jan and Mary. He waved a stiff palm in return. Goddamn! Jack walked away hurriedly. Cautiously, Bigger looked round; the waitresses and several people at other tables were staring at him. They all knew him and he knew that they were wondering as he would have wondered if he had been in their places. Mary touched his arm.

"Have you ever been here before, Bigger?"

He groped for neutral words, words that would convey information but not indicate any shade of his own feelings.

"A few times."

"It's very nice," Mary said.

Somebody put a nickel in an automatic phonograph and they listened to the music. Then Bigger felt a hand grab his shoulder.

"Hi, Bigger! Where you been?"

He looked up and saw Bessie laughing in his face.

"Hi," he said gruffly.

"Oh, 'scuse me. I didn't know you had company," she said, walking away with her eyes upon Jan and Mary.

"Tell her to come over, Bigger," Mary said.

Bessie had gone to a far table and was sitting with another girl.

"She's over there now," Bigger said.

The waitress brought the beer and chicken.

"This is simply grand!" Mary exclaimed.

"You got something there," Jan said, looking at Bigger. "Did I say that right, Bigger?"

Bigger hesitated.

"That's the way they say it," he spoke flatly.

Jan and Mary were eating. Bigger picked up a piece of chicken and bit it. When he tried to chew he found his mouth dry. It seemed that the very organic functions of his body had altered; and when he realized why, when he understood the cause, he could not chew the food. After two or three bites, he stopped and sipped his beer.

"Eat your chicken," Mary said. "It's good!"

"I ain't hungry," he mumbled.

"Want some more beer?" Jan asked after a long silence.

Maybe if he got a little drunk it would help him.

"I don't mind," he said.

Jan ordered another round.

"Do they keep anything stronger than beer here?" Jan asked.

"They got anything you want," Bigger said.

Jan ordered a fifth of rum and poured a round. Bigger felt the liquor warming him. After a second drink Jan began to talk.

"Where were you born, Bigger?"

"In the South."

"Whereabouts?"

"Mississippi."

"How far did you go in school?"

"To the eighth grade."

"Why did you stop?"

"No money."

"Did you go to school in the North or South?"

"Mostly in the South. I went two years up here."

"How long have you been in Chicago?"

"Oh, about five years."

"You like it here?"

"It'll do."

"You live with your people?"

"My mother, brother, and sister."

"Where's your father?"

"Dead."

"How long ago was that?"

"He got killed in a riot when I was a kid—in the South."

There was silence. The rum was helping Bigger.

"And what was done about it?" Jan asked.

"Nothing, far as I know."

"How do you feel about it?"

"I don't know."

"Listen, Bigger, that's what we want to *stop*. That's what we Communists are fighting. We want to stop people from treating others that way. I'm a member of the Party. Mary sympathizes. Don't you think if we got together we could stop things like that?"

"I don't know," Bigger said; he was feeling the rum rising to his head. "There's a lot of white people in the world."

"You've read about the Scottsboro boys?"

"I heard about 'em."

"Don't you think we did a good job in helping to keep 'em from killing those boys?"

"It was all right."

"You know, Bigger," said Mary, "we'd like to be friends of yours."

He said nothing. He drained his glass and Jan poured another round. He was getting drunk enough to look straight at them now. Mary was smiling at him.

"You'll get used to us," she said.

Jan stoppered the bottle of rum.

"We'd better go," he said.

"Yes," Mary said. "Oh, Bigger, I'm going to Detroit at nine in the morning and I want you to take my small trunk down to the station. Tell father and he'll let you make up your time. You better come for the trunk at eight-thirty."

"I'll take it down."

Jan paid the bill and they went back to the car. Bigger got behind the steering wheel. He was feeling good. Jan and Mary got into the back seat. As Bigger drove he saw her resting in Jan's arms.

"Drive around in the park awhile, will you, Bigger?"

"O.K."

He turned into Washington Park and pulled the car slowly round and round the long gradual curves. Now and then he watched Jan kiss Mary in the reflection of the rear mirror above his head.

"You got a girl, Bigger?" Mary asked.

"I got a girl," he said.

"I'd like to meet her some time."

He did not answer. Mary's eyes stared dreamily before her, as if she were planning future things to do. Then she turned to Jan and laid her hand tenderly upon his arm.

"How was the demonstration?"

"Pretty good. But the cops arrested three comrades."

"Who were they?"

"A Y. C. L.-er and two Negro women. Oh, by the way, Mary. We need money for bail badly."

"How much?"

"Three thousand."

"I'll mail you a check."

"Swell."

"Did you work hard today?"

"Yeah. I was at a meeting until three this morning. Max and I've been trying to raise bail money all day today."

"Max is a darling, isn't he?"

"He's one of the best lawyers we've got."

Bigger listened; he knew that they were talking Communism and he tried to understand. But he couldn't.

"Jan."

"Yes, honey."

"I'm coming out of school this spring and I'm going to join the Party."

"*Gee,* you're a brick!"

"But I'll have to be careful."

"Say, how's about your working with me, in the office?"

"No, I want to work among Negroes. That's where people are needed. It seems as though they've been pushed out of everything."

"That's true."

"When I see what they've done to those people, it makes me *so* mad. . . ."

"Yes; it's awful."

"And I feel so helpless and useless. I want to *do* something."

"I knew all along you'd come through."

"Say, Jan, do you know many Negroes? I want to meet some."

"I don't know any very well. But you'll meet them when you're in the Party."

"They have so much *emo*tion! What a people! If we could ever get them going. . . ."

"We can't have a revolution without 'em," Jan said. "They've got to be organized. They've got spirit. They'll give the Party something it needs."

"And their songs—the spirituals! Aren't they marvelous?" Bigger saw her turn to him. "Say, Bigger, can you sing?"

"I can't sing," he said.

"Aw, Bigger," she said, pouting. She tilted her head, closed her eyes and opened her mouth.

> "*Swing low, sweet chariot,*
> *Coming fer to carry me home. . . .*"

Jan joined in and Bigger smiled derisively. Hell, that ain't the tune, he thought.

"Come on, Bigger, and help us sing it," Jan said.

"I can't sing," he said again.

They were silent. The car purred along. Then he heard Jan speaking in low tones.

"Where's the bottle?"

"Right here."

"I want a sip."

"I'll take one, too, honey."

"Going heavy tonight, ain't you?"

"About as heavy as you."

They laughed. Bigger drove in silence. He heard the faint, musical gurgle of liquor.

"Jan!"

"What?"

"That was a *big* sip!"

"Here; you get even."

Through the rear mirror he saw her tilt the bottle and drink.

"Maybe Bigger wants another one, Jan. Ask him."

"Oh, say, Bigger! Here; take a swig!"

He slowed the car and reached back for the bottle; he tilted it twice, taking two huge swallows.

"Woooow!" Mary laughed.

"You took a *swig*, all right," Jan said.

Bigger wiped his mouth with the back of his hand and continued driving slowly through the dark park. Now and then he heard the half-empty bottle of rum gurgling. They getting plastered, he thought, feeling the effect of the rum creeping outward to his fingers and upward to his lips. Presently, he heard Mary giggle. Hell, she's plastered already! The car rolled slowly round and round the sloping curves. The rum's soft heat was spreading fanwise out from his stomach, engulfing his whole body. He was not driving; he was simply sitting and floating along smoothly through darkness. His hands rested lightly on the steering wheel and his body slouched lazily down in the seat. He looked at the mirror; Mary was lying flat on her back in the rear seat and Jan was bent over her. He saw a faint sweep of white thigh. They plastered, all right, he thought. He pulled the car softly round the curves, looking at the road before him one second and up at the mirror the next. He heard Jan whispering; then he heard them both sigh. Filled with a sense of them, his muscles grew gradually taut. He sighed and sat up straight, fighting off the stiffening feeling in his loins. But soon he was slouched again. His lips were numb. I'm almost drunk, he thought. His sense of the city and park fell away; he was floating in the car and Jan and Mary were in back, kissing, spooning. A long time passed. Jan sat up and pulled Mary with him.

"It's one o'clock, honey," Mary said. "I better go in."

"O.K. But let's drive a little more. It's great here."

"Father says I'm a bad girl."

"I'm sorry, darling."

"I'll call you in the morning before I go."

"Sure. What time?"

"About eight-thirty."

"Gee, but I hate to see you go to Detroit."

"I hate to go too. But I got to. You see, honey, I got to make up for being bad with you down in Florida. I got to do what Mother and Father say for awhile."

"I hate to see you go just the same."

"I'll be back in a couple of days."

"A couple of days is a long time."

"You're silly, but you're sweet," she said, laughing and kissing him.

"You better drive on, Bigger," Jan called.

He swung the car out of the park and headed for Forty-sixth Street.

"I'll get out here, Bigger!"

He stopped the car. Bigger heard them speak in whispers.

"Good-bye, Jan."

"Good-bye, honey."

"I'll call you tomorrow?"

"Sure."

Jan stood at the front door of the car and held out his palm. Bigger shook timidly.

"It's been great meeting you, Bigger," Jan said.

"O.K.," Bigger mumbled.

"I'm damn glad I know you. Look. Have another drink."

Bigger took a big swallow.

"You better give me one, too, Jan. It'll make me sleep," Mary said.

"You're sure you haven't had enough?"

"Aw, come on, honey."

She got out of the car and stood on the curb. Jan gave her the bottle and she tilted it.

"Whoa!" Jan said.

"What's the matter?"

"I don't want you to pass out."

"I can hold it."

Jan tilted the bottle and emptied it, then laid it in the gutter. He fumbled clumsily in his pockets for something. He swayed; he was drunk.

"You lose something, honey?" Mary lisped; she, too, was drunk.

"Naw; I got some stuff here I want Bigger to read. Listen, Bigger, I got some pamphlets here. I want you to read 'em, see?"

Bigger held out his hand and received a small batch of booklets.

"O.K."

"I really want you to read 'em, now. We'll have a talk 'bout 'em in a coupla days. . . ." His speech was thick.

"I'll read 'em," Bigger said, stifling a yawn and stuffing the booklets into his pocket.

"I'll see that he reads 'em," Mary said.

Jan kissed her again. Bigger heard a Loop-bound car rumbling far down the avenue.

"Well, good-bye," he said.

"Goo'-bye, honey," Mary said. "I'm gonna ride up front with Bigger."

She got into the front seat. The street car clanged to a stop. Jan swung onto it and it started north. Bigger drove toward Drexel Boulevard. Mary slumped down in the seat and sighed. Her legs sprawled wide apart. The car rolled along. Bigger's head was spinning.

"You're very nice, Bigger," she said.

He looked at her. Her face was pasty white. Her eyes were glassy. She was very drunk.

"I don't know," he said.

"My! But you say the *fun*niest things," she giggled.

"Maybe," he said.

She leaned her head on his shoulder.

"You don't mind, do you?"

"I don't mind."

"You know, for *three* hours you haven't said *yes* or *no*."

She doubled up with laughter. He tightened with hate. Again she was looking inside of him and he did not like it. She sat up and dabbed at her eyes with a handkerchief. He kept his eyes straight in front of him and swung the car into the driveway and brought it to a stop. He got out and opened the door. She did not move. Her eyes were closed.

"We're here," he said.

She tried to get up and slipped back into the seat.

"Aw, shucks!"

She's drunk, *really* drunk, Bigger thought. She stretched out her hand.

"Here; gimme a lift. I'm wobbly. . . ."

She was resting on the small of her back and her dress was pulled up so far that he could see where her stockings ended on her thighs. He stood looking at her for a moment; she raised her eyes and looked at him. She laughed.

"Help me, Bigger. I'm stuck."

He helped her and his hands felt the softness of her body as she stepped to the ground. Her dark eyes looked at him feverishly from deep sockets. Her hair was in his face, filling him with its scent. He gritted his teeth, feeling a little dizzy.

"Where's my hat? I dropped it somewhere. . . ."

She swayed as she spoke and he tightened his arms about her, holding her up. He looked round; her hat was lying on the running board.

"Here it is," he said.

As he picked it up he wondered what a white man would think seeing him here with her like this. Suppose old man Dalton saw him now? Apprehensively, he looked up at the big house. It was dark and silent.

"Well," Mary sighed. "I suppose I better go to bed. . . ."

He turned her loose, but had to catch her again to keep her off the pavement. He led her to the steps.

"Can you make it?"

She looked at him as though she had been challenged.

"Sure. Turn me loose. . . ."

He took his arm from her and she mounted the steps firmly and then stumbled loudly on the wooden porch. Bigger made a move toward her, but stopped, his hands outstretched, frozen with fear. Good God, she'll wake up everybody! She was

half-bent over, resting on one knee and one hand, looking
back at him in amused astonishment. That girl's crazy! She
pulled up and walked slowly back down the steps, holding
onto the railing. She swayed before him, smiling.

"I sure am drunk. . . ."

He watched her with a mingled feeling of helplessness, admiration, and hate. If her father saw him here with her now,
his job would be over. But she was beautiful, slender, with an
air that made him feel that she did not hate him with the hate
of other white people. But, for all of that, she was white and
he hated her. She closed her eyes slowly, then opened them;
she was trying desperately to take hold of herself. Since she
was not able to get to her room alone, ought he to call Mr.
Dalton or Peggy? Naw. . . . That would betray her. And,
too, in spite of his hate for her, he was excited standing here
watching her like this. Her eyes closed again and she swayed
toward him. He caught her.

"I'd better help you," he said.

"Let's go the back way, Bigger. I'll stumble sure as hell
. . . . and wake up everybody . . . . if we go up the
front. . . ."

Her feet dragged on the concrete as he led her to the basement. He switched on the light, supporting her with his free
hand.

"I didn't know I was sho drunk," she mumbled.

He led her slowly up the narrow stairs to the kitchen door,
his hand circling her waist and the tips of his fingers feeling
the soft swelling of her breasts. Each second she was leaning
more heavily against him.

"Try to stand up," he whispered fiercely as they reached the
kitchen door.

He was thinking that perhaps Mrs. Dalton was standing in
flowing white and staring with stony blind eyes in the middle
of the floor, as she had been when he had come for the glass
of water. He eased the door back and looked. The kitchen
was empty and dark, save for a faint blue hazy light that
seeped through a window from the winter sky.

"Come on."

She pulled heavily on him, her arm about his neck. He
pushed the door in and took a step inside and stopped, waiting,

listening. He felt her hair brush his lips. His skin glowed warm and his muscles flexed; he looked at her face in the dim light, his senses drunk with the odor of her hair and skin. He stood for a moment, then whispered in excitement and fear:

"Come on; you got to get to your room."

He led her out of the kitchen into the hallway; he had to walk her a step at a time. The hall was empty and dark; slowly he half-walked and half-dragged her to the back stairs. Again he hated her; he shook her.

"Come on; wake up!"

She did not move or open her eyes; finally she mumbled something and swayed limply. His fingers felt the soft curves of her body and he was still, looking at her, enveloped in a sense of physical elation. This little bitch! he thought. Her face was touching his. He turned her round and began to mount the steps, one by one. He heard a slight creaking and stopped. He looked, straining his eyes in the gloom. But there was no one. When he got to the top of the steps she was completely limp and was still trying to mumble something. Goddamn! He could move her only by lifting her bodily. He caught her in his arms and carried her down the hall, then paused. Which was her door? Goddamn!

"Where's your room?" he whispered.

She did not answer. Was she completely out? He could not leave her here; if he took his hands from her she would sink to the floor and lie there all night. He shook her hard, speaking as loudly as he dared.

"Where's your room?"

Momentarily, she roused herself and looked at him with blank eyes.

"Where's your room?" he asked again.

She rolled her eyes toward a door. He got her as far as the door and stopped. Was this really her room? Was she too drunk to know? Suppose he opened the door to Mr. and Mrs. Dalton's room? Well, all they could do was fire him. It wasn't his fault that she was drunk. He felt strange, possessed, or as if he were acting upon a stage in front of a crowd of people. Carefully, he freed one hand and turned the knob of the door. He waited; nothing happened. He pushed the door in quietly; the room was dark and silent. He felt along the wall with his fingers for the electric switch and could not find it. He stood, holding her in his arms, fearful, in doubt. His eyes were growing used to the darkness and a little light seeped into the room from the winter sky through a window. At the far end of the room he made out the shadowy form of a white bed. He lifted her and brought her into the room and closed the door softly.

"Here; wake up, now."

He tried to stand her on her feet and found her weak as jelly. He held her in his arms again, listening in the darkness. His senses reeled from the scent of her hair and skin. She was much smaller than Bessie, his girl, but much softer. Her face was buried in his shoulder; his arms tightened about her. Her face turned slowly and he held his face still, waiting for her face to come round, in front of his. Then her head leaned backward, slowly, gently; it was as though she had given up. Her lips, faintly moist in the hazy blue light, were parted and he saw the furtive glints of her white teeth. Her eyes were closed. He stared at her dim face, the forehead capped with curly black hair. He eased his hand, the fingers spread wide, up the center of her back and her face came toward him and her lips touched his, like something he had imagined. He stood her on her feet and she swayed against him. He tightened his arms as his lips pressed tightly against hers and he felt her body moving strongly. The thought and conviction that Jan had had her a lot flashed through his mind. He kissed her again and felt the sharp bones of her hips move in a hard and veritable grind. Her mouth was open and her breath came slow and deep.

He lifted her and laid her on the bed. Something urged him to leave at once, but he leaned over her, excited, looking at her face in the dim light, not wanting to take his hands from her breasts. She tossed and mumbled sleepily. He tightened his fingers on her breasts, kissing her again, feeling her move toward him. He was aware only of her body now; his lips trembled. Then he stiffened. The door behind him had creaked.

He turned and a hysterical terror seized him, as though he were falling from a great height in a dream. A white blur was standing by the door, silent, ghostlike. It filled his eyes and gripped his body. It was Mrs. Dalton. He wanted to knock her out of his way and bolt from the room.

"Mary!" she spoke softly, questioningly.

Bigger held his breath. Mary mumbled again; he bent over her, his fists clenched in fear. He knew that Mrs. Dalton could not see him; but he knew that if Mary spoke she would come to the side of the bed and discover him, touch him. He waited tensely, afraid to move for fear of bumping into something in the dark and betraying his presence.

"Mary!"

He felt Mary trying to rise and quickly he pushed her head back to the pillow.

"She must be asleep," Mrs. Dalton mumbled.

He wanted to move from the bed, but was afraid he would stumble over something and Mrs. Dalton would hear him, would know that someone besides Mary was in the room. Frenzy dominated him. He held his hand over her mouth and his head was cocked at an angle that enabled him to see Mary and Mrs. Dalton by merely shifting his eyes. Mary mumbled and tried to rise again. Frantically, he caught a corner of the pillow and brought it to her lips. He had to stop her from mumbling, or he would be caught. Mrs. Dalton was moving slowly toward him and he grew tight and full, as though about to explode. Mary's fingernails tore at his hands and he caught the pillow and covered her entire face with it, firmly. Mary's body surged upward and he pushed downward upon the pillow with all of his weight, determined that she must not move or make any sound that would betray him. His eyes were filled with the white blur moving toward him in the shadows of the room. Again Mary's body heaved and he held the pillow in a grip that took all of his strength. For a long time he felt the sharp pain of her fingernails biting into his wrists. The white blur was still.

"Mary? Is that you?"

He clenched his teeth and held his breath, intimidated to the core by the awesome white blur floating toward him. His muscles flexed taut as steel and he pressed the pillow, feeling the bed give slowly, evenly, but silently. Then suddenly her fingernails did not bite into his wrists. Mary's fingers loosened. He did not feel her surging and heaving against him. Her body was still.

"Mary! Is that *you*?"

He could see Mrs. Dalton plainly now. As he took his hands from the pillow he heard a long slow sigh go up from the bed into the air of the darkened room, a sigh which afterwards, when he remembered it, seemed final, irrevocable.

"Mary! Are you ill?"

He stood up. With each of her movements toward the bed his body made a movement to match hers, away from her, his feet not lifting themselves from the floor, but sliding softly and silently over the smooth deep rug, his muscles flexed so taut they ached. Mrs. Dalton now stood over the bed. Her hands reached out and touched Mary.

"Mary! Are you asleep? I heard you moving about. . . ."

Mrs. Dalton straightened suddenly and took a quick step back.

"You're dead drunk! You *stink* with whiskey!"

She stood silently in the hazy blue light, then she knelt at the side of the bed. Bigger heard her whispering. She's praying, he thought in amazement and the words echoed in his mind as though someone had spoken them aloud. Finally, Mrs. Dalton stood up and her face tilted to that upward angle at which she always held it. He waited, his teeth clamped, his fists clenched. She moved slowly toward the door; he could scarcely see her now. The door creaked; then silence.

He relaxed and sank to the floor, his breath going in a long gasp. He was weak and wet with sweat. He stayed crouched and bent, hearing the sound of his breathing filling the darkness. Gradually, the intensity of his sensations subsided and he was aware of the room. He felt that he had been in the grip of a weird spell and was now free. The fingertips of his right hand were pressed deeply into the soft fibers of the rug and his whole body vibrated from the wild pounding of his heart. He had to get out of the room, and quickly. Suppose that had been *Mr.* Dalton? His escape had been narrow enough, as it was.

He stood and listened. Mrs. Dalton might be out there in the hallway. How could he get out of the room? He all but shuddered with the intensity of his loathing for this house and all it had made him feel since he had first come into it. He reached his hand behind him and touched the wall; he was glad to have something solid at his back. He looked at the shadowy bed and remembered Mary as some person he had not seen in a long time. She was still there. Had he hurt her? He went to the bed and stood over her; her face lay sideways on the pillow. His hand moved toward her, but stopped in mid-air. He blinked his eyes and stared at Mary's face; it was darker than when he had first bent over her. Her mouth was open and her eyes bulged glassily. Her bosom, her bosom, her—her bosom was not moving! He could not hear her breath coming and going now as he had when he had first brought her into the room! He bent and moved her head with his hand and found that she was relaxed and limp. He snatched his hand away. Thought and feeling were balked in him; there was something he was trying to tell himself, desperately, but could not. Then, convulsively, he sucked his breath in and huge words formed slowly, ringing in his ears: *She's dead.* . . .

The reality of the room fell from him; the vast city of white people that sprawled outside took its place. She was dead and he had killed her. He was a murderer, a Negro murderer, a black murderer. He had killed a white woman. He had to get away from here. Mrs. Dalton had been in the room while he was there, but she had not known it. But, *had* she? No! Yes! Maybe she had gone for help? No. If she had known she would have screamed. She didn't know. He had to slip out of the house. Yes. He could go home to bed and tomorrow he could tell them that he had driven Mary home and had left her at the side door.

In the darkness his fear made live in him an element which he reckoned with as "them." He had to construct a case for "them." But, *Jan!* Oh. . . . Jan would give him away. When it was found that she was dead Jan would say that he had left them together in the car at Forty-sixth Street and Cottage Grove Avenue. But he would tell them that that was not true. And, after all, was not Jan a *Red*? Was not his word as good as Jan's? He would say that Jan had come home with them. No one must know that he was the last person who had been with her.

Fingerprints! He had read about them in magazines. His fingerprints would give him away, surely! They could prove that he had been inside of her room! But suppose he told

them that he had come to get the trunk? That was it! The
trunk! His fingerprints had a right to be here. He looked
round and saw her trunk on the other side of the bed, open,
the top standing up. He could take the trunk to the basement
and put the car into the garage and then go home. *No!* There
was a better way. He would not put the car into the garage!
He would say that Jan had come to the house and he had left
Jan outside in the car. But there was still a *better way!* Make
them think that Jan did it. Reds'd do anything. Didn't the
papers say so? He would tell them that he had brought Jan
and Mary home in the car and Mary had asked him to go
with her to her room to get the trunk—and Jan was *with*
them!—and he had got the trunk and had taken it to the
basement and when he had gone he had left Mary and Jan—
who had come back down—sitting in the car, kissing. . . .
That's it!

He heard a clock ticking and searched for it with his eyes; it
was at the head of Mary's bed, its white dial glowing in the
blue darkness. It was five minutes past three. Jan had left them
at Forty-sixth Street and Cottage Grove. *Jan didn't leave at
Forty-sixth Street; he rode with us.* . . .

He went to the trunk and eased the top down and dragged
it over the rug to the middle of the floor. He lifted the top
and felt inside; it was half-empty.

Then he was still, barely breathing, filled with another idea.
Hadn't Mr. Dalton said that they did not get up early on
Sunday mornings? Hadn't Mary said that she was going to
Detroit? If Mary were missing when they got up, would they
not think that she had already gone to Detroit? He. . . . *Yes!*
He could, he could put her *in* the trunk! She was small. Yes;
put her in the trunk. She had said that she would be gone for
three days. For three days, then, maybe no one would know.
He would have three days of time. She was a crazy girl any-
how. She was always running around with Reds, wasn't she?
Anything could happen to her. People would think that she
was up to some of her crazy ways when they missed her. Yes,
Reds'd do anything. Didn't the papers say so?

He went to the bed; he would have to lift her into the
trunk. He did not want to touch her, but he knew he had
to. He bent over. His hands were outstretched, trembling in

mid-air. He had to touch her and lift her and put her in the trunk. He tried to move his hands and could not. It was as though he expected her to scream when he touched her. Goddamn! It all seemed foolish! He wanted to laugh. It was unreal. Like a nightmare. He had to lift a dead woman and was afraid. He felt that he had been dreaming of something like this for a long time, and then, suddenly, it was true. He heard the clock ticking. Time was passing. It would soon be morning. He had to act. He could not stand here all night like this; he might go to the electric chair. He shuddered and something cold crawled over his skin. Goddamn!

He pushed his hand gently under her body and lifted it. He stood with her in his arms; she was limp. He took her to the trunk and involuntarily jerked his head round and saw a white blur standing at the door and his body was instantly wrapped in a sheet of blazing terror and a hard ache seized his head and then the white blur went away. *I thought that was her. . . .* His heart pounded.

He stood with her body in his arms in the silent room and cold facts battered him like waves sweeping in from the sea: she was dead; she was white; she was a woman; he had killed her; he was black; he might be caught; he did not want to be caught; if he were they would kill him.

He stooped to put her in the trunk. Could he get her in? He looked again toward the door, expecting to see the white blur; but nothing was there. He turned her on her side in his arms; he was breathing hard and his body trembled. He eased her down, listening to the soft rustle of her clothes. He pushed her head into a corner, but her legs were too long and would not go in.

He thought he heard a noise and straightened; it seemed to him that his breathing was as loud as wind in a storm. He listened and heard nothing. He had to get her legs in! Bend her legs at the knees, he thought. Yes, almost. A little more. . . . He bent them some more. Sweat dripped from his chin onto his hands. He doubled her knees and pushed her completely into the trunk. That much was done. He eased the top down and fumbled in the darkness for the latch and heard it click loudly.

He stood up and caught hold of one of the handles of the

trunk and pulled. The trunk would not move. He was weak and his hands were slippery with sweat. He gritted his teeth and caught the trunk with both hands and pulled it to the door. He opened the door and looked into the hall; it was empty and silent. He stood the trunk on end and carried his right hand over his left shoulder and stooped and caught the strap and lifted the trunk to his back. Now, he would have to stand up. He strained; the muscles of his shoulders and legs quivered with effort. He rose, swaying, biting his lips.

Putting one foot carefully before the other, he went down the hall, down the stairs, then through another hall to the kitchen and paused. His back ached and the strap cut into his palm like fire. The trunk seemed to weigh a ton. He expected the white blur to step before him at any moment and hold out its hand and touch the trunk and demand to know what was in it. He wanted to put the trunk down and rest; but he was afraid that he would not be able to lift it again. He walked across the kitchen floor, down the steps, leaving the kitchen door open behind him. He stood in the darkened basement with the trunk upon his back and listened to the roaring draft of the furnace and saw the coals burning red through the cracks. He stooped, waiting to hear the bottom of the trunk touch the concrete floor. He bent more and rested on one knee. Goddamn! His hand, seared with fire, slipped from the strap and the trunk hit the floor with a loud clatter. He bent forward and squeezed his right hand in his left to still the fiery pain.

He stared at the furnace. He trembled with another idea. He—he could, he—he could put her, he could put her *in* the furnace. He would *burn* her! That was the safest thing of all to do. He went to the furnace and opened the door. A huge red bed of coals blazed and quivered with molten fury.

He opened the trunk. She was as he had put her: her head buried in one corner and her knees bent and doubled toward her stomach. He would have to lift her again. He stooped and caught her shoulders and lifted her in his arms. He went to the door of the furnace and paused. The fire seethed. Ought he to put her in head or feet first? Because he was tired and scared, and because her feet were nearer, he pushed her in, feet first. The heat blasted his hands.

He had all but her shoulders in. He looked into the furnace; her clothes were ablaze and smoke was filling the interior so that he could scarcely see. The draft roared upward,
droning in his ears. He gripped her shoulders and pushed
hard, but the body would not go any farther. He tried again,
but her head still remained out. Now. . . . Goddamn! He
wanted to strike something with his fist. What could he do?
He stepped back and looked.

A noise made him whirl; two green burning pools—pools
of accusation and guilt—stared at him from a white blur that
sat perched upon the edge of the trunk. His mouth opened in
a silent scream and his body became hotly paralyzed. It was
the white cat and its round green eyes gazed past him at the
white face hanging limply from the fiery furnace door. *God!*
He closed his mouth and swallowed. Should he catch the cat
and kill it and put it in the furnace, too? He made a move.
The cat stood up; its white fur bristled; its back arched. He
tried to grab it and it bounded past him with a long wail of
fear and scampered up the steps and through the door and
out of sight. Oh! He had left the kitchen door open. *That* was
it. He closed the door and stood again before the furnace,
thinking, Cats can't talk. . . .

He got his knife from his pocket and opened it and stood
by the furnace, looking at Mary's white throat. Could he do
it? He had to. Would there be blood? Oh, Lord! He looked
round with a haunted and pleading look in his eyes. He saw
a pile of old newspapers stacked carefully in a corner. He got
a thick wad of them and held them under the head. He
touched the sharp blade to the throat, just touched it, as if
expecting the knife to cut the white flesh of itself, as if he
did not have to put pressure behind it. Wistfully, he gazed at
the edge of the blade resting on the white skin; the gleaming
metal reflected the tremulous fury of the coals. Yes; he *had*
to. Gently, he sawed the blade into the flesh and struck a
bone. He gritted his teeth and cut harder. As yet there was no
blood anywhere but on the knife. But the bone made it difficult. Sweat crawled down his back. Then blood crept outward
in widening circles of pink on the newspapers, spreading
quickly now. He whacked at the bone with the knife. The
head hung limply on the newspapers, the curly black hair

dragging about in blood. He whacked harder, but the head would not come off.

He paused, hysterical. He wanted to run from the basement and go as far as possible from the sight of this bloody throat. But he could not. He must not. He *had* to burn this girl. With eyes glazed, with nerves tingling with excitement, he looked about the basement. He saw a hatchet. *Yes!* That would do it. He spread a neat layer of newspapers beneath the head, so that the blood would not drip on the floor. He got the hatchet, held the head at a slanting angle with his left hand and, after pausing in an attitude of prayer, sent the blade of the hatchet into the bone of the throat with all the strength of his body. The head rolled off.

He was not crying, but his lips were trembling and his chest was heaving. He wanted to lie down upon the floor and sleep off the horror of this thing. But he had to get out of here. Quickly, he wrapped the head in the newspapers and used the wad to push the bloody trunk of the body deeper into the furnace. Then he shoved the head in. The hatchet went next.

Would there be coal enough to burn the body? No one would come down here before ten o'clock in the morning, maybe. He looked at his watch. It was four o'clock. He got another piece of paper and wiped his knife with it. He put the paper into the furnace and the knife into his pocket. He pulled the lever and coal rattled against the sides of the tin chute and he saw the whole furnace blaze and the draft roared still louder. When the body was covered with coal, he pushed the lever back. Now!

He shut the trunk and pushed it into a corner. In the morning he would take it to the station. He looked around to see if he had left anything that would betray him; he saw nothing.

He went out of the back door; a few fine flakes of snow were floating down. It had grown colder. The car was still in the driveway. Yes; he would leave it there.

Jan and Mary were sitting in the car, kissing. They said, Good night, Bigger. . . . And he said, Good night. . . . And he touched his hand to his cap. . . .

As he passed the car he saw that the door was still open.

Mary's purse was on the floor. He took it and closed the door. Naw! Leave it open; he opened it and went on down the driveway.

The streets were empty and silent. The wind chilled his wet body. He tucked the purse under his arm and walked. What would happen now? Ought he to run away? He stopped at a street corner and looked into the purse. There was a thick roll of bills; tens and twenties. . . . Good! He would wait until morning to decide what to do. He was tired and sleepy.

He hurried home and ran up the steps and went on tiptoe into the room. His mother and brother and sister breathed regularly in sleep. He began to undress, thinking, *I'll tell 'em I left her with Jan in the car after I took the trunk down in the basement. In the morning I'll take the trunk to the station, like she told me. . . .*

He felt something heavy sagging in his shirt; it was the gun. He took it out; it was warm and wet. He shoved it under the pillow. *They can't say I did it. If they do, they can't prove it.*

He eased the covers of the bed back and slipped beneath them and stretched out beside Buddy; in five minutes he was sound asleep.

BOOK TWO

FLIGHT

IT SEEMED to Bigger that no sooner had he closed his eyes than he was wide awake again, suddenly and violently, as though someone had grabbed his shoulders and had shaken him. He lay on his back, in bed, hearing and seeing nothing. Then, like an electric switch being clicked on, he was aware that the room was filled with pale daylight. Somewhere deep in him a thought formed: It's morning. Sunday morning. He lifted himself on his elbows and cocked his head in an attitude of listening. He heard his mother and brother and sister breathing softly, in deep sleep. He saw the room and saw snow falling past the window; but his mind formed no image of any of these. They simply existed, unrelated to each other; the snow and the daylight and the soft sound of breathing cast a strange spell upon him, a spell that waited for the wand of fear to touch it and endow it with reality and meaning. He lay in bed, only a few seconds from deep sleep, caught in a deadlock of impulses, unable to rise to the land of the living.

Then, in answer to a foreboding call from a dark part of his mind, he leaped from bed and landed on his bare feet in the middle of the room. His heart raced; his lips parted; his legs trembled. He struggled to come fully awake. He relaxed his taut muscles, feeling fear, remembering that he had killed Mary, had smothered her, had cut her head off and put her body in the fiery furnace.

This was Sunday morning and he had to take the trunk to the station. He glanced about and saw Mary's shiny black purse lying atop his trousers on a chair. Good God! Though the air of the room was cold, beads of sweat broke onto his forehead and his breath stopped. Quickly, he looked round; his mother and sister were still sleeping. Buddy slept in the bed from which he had just arisen. Throw that purse away! Maybe he had forgotten other things? He searched the pockets of his trousers with nervous fingers and found the knife. He snapped it open and tiptoed to the window. Dried ridges of black blood were on the blade! He had to get rid of these at once. He put the knife into the purse and dressed hurriedly and silently. Throw the knife and purse into a garbage can. That's it! He put on his coat and found stuffed in a pocket the pamphlets Jan had given him. Throw these away, too! Oh, but. . . . Naw! He paused and gripped the pamphlets in his black fingers as his mind filled with a cunning idea. Jan had given him these pamphlets and he would keep them and show them to the police if he were ever questioned. That's it! He would take them to his room at Dalton's and put them in a dresser drawer. He would say that he had not even opened them and had not wanted to. He would say that he had taken them only because Jan had insisted. He shuffled the pamphlets softly, so that the paper would not rustle, and read the titles: *Race Prejudice on Trial. The Negro Question in the United States. Black and White Unite and Fight.* But that did not seem so dangerous. He looked at the bottom of a pamphlet and saw a black and white picture of a hammer and a curving knife. Below it he read a line that said: *Issued by the Communist Party of the United States.* Now, *that* did seem dangerous. He looked further and saw a pen-and-ink drawing of a white hand clasping a black hand in solidarity and remembered the moment when Jan had stood on the running board of the car and had shaken hands with him. That had been an awful moment of hate and shame. Yes, he would tell them that he was afraid of Reds, that he had not wanted to sit in the car with Jan and Mary, that he had not wanted to eat with them. He would say that he had done so only because it had been his job. He would tell them that it was the first time he had ever sat at a table with white people.

He stuffed the pamphlets into his coat pocket and looked at his watch. It was ten minutes until seven. He had to hurry and pack his clothes. He had to take that trunk to the station at eight-thirty.

Then fear rendered his legs like water. Suppose Mary had not burned? Suppose she was still there, exposed to view? He wanted to drop everything and rush back and see. But maybe even something worse had happened; maybe they had discovered that she was dead and maybe the police were looking for him? Should he not leave town right now? Gripped by the same impelling excitement that had had hold of him when he was carrying Mary up the stairs, he stood in the middle of the room. *No;* he would stay. Things were with him; no one suspected that she was dead. He would carry through and blame the thing upon Jan. He got his gun from beneath the pillow and put it in his shirt.

He tiptoed from the room, looking over his shoulder at his mother and sister and brother sleeping. He went down the steps to the vestibule and into the street. It was white and cold. Snow was falling and an icy wind blew. The streets were empty. Tucking the purse under his arm, he walked to an alley where a garbage can stood covered with snow. Was it safe to leave it here? The men on the garbage trucks would empty the can early in the morning and no one would be prying round on a day like this, with all the snow and its being Sunday. He lifted the top of the can and pushed the purse deep into a frozen pile of orange peels and mildewed bread. He replaced the top and looked round; no one was in sight.

He went back to the room and got his suitcase from under the side of the bed. His folks were still sleeping. In order to pack his clothes, he had to get to the dresser on the other side of the room. But how could he get there, with the bed on which his mother and sister slept standing squarely in the way? Goddamn! He wanted to wave his hand and blot them out. They were always too close to him, so close that he could never have any way of his own. He eased to the bed and stepped over it. His mother stirred slightly, then was still. He pulled open a dresser drawer and took out his clothes and piled them in the suitcase. While he worked there hovered before his eyes an image of Mary's head lying on the wet newspapers, the curly black ringlets soaked with blood.

"Bigger!"

He sucked his breath in and whirled about, his eyes glaring. His mother was leaning on her elbow in bed. He knew at once that he should not have acted frightened.

"What's the matter, boy?" she asked in a whisper.

"Nothing," he answered, whispering too.

"You jumped like something bit you."

"Aw, leave me alone. I got to pack."

He knew that his mother was waiting for him to give an

account of himself, and he hated her for that. Why couldn't she wait until he told her of his own accord? And yet he knew that if she waited, he would never tell her.

"You get the job?"

"Yeah."

"What they paying you?"

"Twenty."

"You started already?"

"Yeah."

"When?"

"Last night."

"I wondered what made you so late."

"I had to work," he drawled with impatience.

"You didn't get in until after four."

He turned and looked at her.

"I got in at *two*."

"It was after *four*, Bigger," she said, turning and straining her eyes to look at an alarm clock above her head. "I tried to wait up for you, but I couldn't. When I heard you come in, I looked up at the clock and it was after four."

"*I* know when I got in, Ma."

"But, Bigger, it was after *four*."

"It was just a little after *two*."

"Oh, Lord! If you *want* it two, then let it be two, for all I care. You act like you scared of something."

"Now, what you want to start a fuss for?"

"A fuss? *Boy!*"

"Before I get out of bed, you pick on me."

"Bigger, I'm not picking on you, honey. I'm glad you got the job."

"You don't talk like it."

He felt that his acting in this manner was a mistake. If he kept on talking about the time he had gotten in last night, he would so impress it upon her that she would remember it and perhaps say something later on that would hurt him. He turned away and continued packing. He had to do better than this; he had to control himself.

"You want to eat?"

"Yeah."

"I'll fix you something."

"O.K."

"You going to stay on the place?"

"Yeah."

He heard her getting out of bed; he did not dare look round now. He had to keep his head turned while she dressed.

"How you like the people, Bigger?"

"They all right."

"You don't act like you glad."

"Oh, Ma! For Chrissakes! You want me to *cry!*"

"Bigger, sometimes I wonder what makes you act like you do."

He had spoken in the wrong tone of voice; he had to be careful. He fought down the anger rising in him. He was in trouble enough without getting into a fuss with his mother.

"You got a good job, now," his mother said. "You ought to work hard and keep it and try to make a man out of yourself. Some day you'll want to get married and have a home of your own. You got your chance now. You always said you never had a chance. Now, you got one."

He heard her move about and he knew that she was dressed enough for him to turn round. He strapped the suitcase and set it by the door; then he stood at the window, looking wistfully out at the feathery flakes of falling snow.

"Bigger, what's wrong with you?"

He whirled.

"Nothing," he said, wondering what change she saw in him. "Nothing. You just worry me, that's all," he concluded, feeling that even if he did say something wrong he had to fight her off him now. He wondered just how his words *really* did sound. Was the tone of his voice this morning different from other mornings? Was there something unusual in his voice since he had killed Mary? Could people tell he had done something wrong by the way he acted? He saw his mother shake her head and go behind the curtain to prepare breakfast. He heard a yawn; he looked and saw that Vera was leaning on her elbow, smiling at him.

"You get the job?"

"Yeah."

"How much you making?"

"Aw, Vera. Ask Ma. I done told her everything."

"Goody! Bigger got a job!" sang Vera.

"Aw, shut up," he said.

"Leave him alone, Vera," the mother said.

"What's the matter?"

"What's the matter with 'im *all* the time?" asked the mother.

"Oh, Bigger," said Vera, tenderly and plaintively.

"That boy just ain't got no sense, that's all," the mother said. "He won't even speak a decent word to you."

"Turn your head so I can dress," Vera said.

Bigger looked out of the window. He heard someone say, "Aw!" and he knew that Buddy was awake.

"Turn your head, Buddy," Vera said.

"O.K."

Bigger heard his sister rushing into her clothes.

"You can look now," Vera said.

He saw Buddy sitting up in bed, rubbing his eyes. Vera was sitting on the edge of a chair, with her right foot hoisted upon another chair, buckling her shoes. Bigger stared vacantly in her direction. He wished that he could rise up through the ceiling and float away from this room, forever.

"I wish you wouldn't look at me," Vera said.

"Hunh?" said Bigger, looking in surprise at her pouting lips. Then he noticed what she meant and poked out his lips at her. Quickly, she jumped up and threw one of her shoes at him. It sailed past his head and landed against the window, rattling the panes.

"I told you not to look at me!" Vera screamed.

Bigger stood up, his eyes red with anger.

"I just wish you had hit me," he said.

"You, Vera!" the mother called.

"Ma, make 'im stop looking at me," Vera wailed.

"Wasn't nobody looking at her," Bigger said.

"You looked under my dress when I was buttoning my shoes!"

"I just *wish* you had hit me," Bigger said again.

"I ain't no dog!" Vera said.

"Come on in the kitchen and dress, Vera," the mother said.

"He makes me feel like a dog," Vera sobbed with her face buried in her hands, going behind the curtain.

"Boy," said Buddy, "I tried to keep awake till you got in last night, but I couldn't. I had to go to bed at three. I was so sleepy I could hardly keep my eyes open."

"I was here before then," Bigger said.

"Aw, naw! I was up. . . ."

"*I* know when I got in!"

They looked at each other in silence.

"O.K.," Buddy said.

Bigger was uneasy. He felt that he was not handling himself right.

"You get the job?" Buddy asked.

"Yeah."

"Driving?"

"Yeah."

"What kind of a car is it?"

"A Buick."

"Can I ride with you some time?"

"Sure; soon as I get settled."

Buddy's questions made him feel a little more at ease; he always liked the adoration Buddy showed him.

"Gee! That's the kind of job I want," Buddy said.

"It's easy."

"Will you see if you can find me one?"

"Sure. Give me time."

"Got a cigarette?"

"Yeah."

They were silent, smoking. Bigger was thinking of the furnace. Had Mary burned? He looked at his watch; it was seven o'clock. Ought he go over right now, without waiting for breakfast? Maybe he had left something lying round that would let them know Mary was dead. But if they slept late on Sunday mornings, as Mr. Dalton had said, they would have no reason to be looking round down there.

"Bessie was by last night," Buddy said.

"Yeah?"

"She said she saw you in Ernie's Kitchen Shack with some white folks."

"Yeah. I was driving 'em last night."

"She was talking about you and her getting married."

"Humph!"

"How come gals that way, Bigger? Soon's a guy get a good job, they want to marry?"

"Damn if I know."

"You got a good job now. You can get a better gal than Bessie," Buddy said.

Although he agreed with Buddy, he said nothing.

"I'm going to tell Bessie!" Vera called.

"If you do, I'll break your neck," Bigger said.

"Hush that kind of talk in here," the mother said.

"Oh, yeah," Buddy said. "I met Jack last night. He said you almost murdered old Gus."

"I ain't having nothing to do with that gang no more," Bigger said emphatically.

"But Jack's all right," Buddy said.

"Well, Jack, but none of the rest."

Gus and G.H. and Jack seemed far away to Bigger now, in another life, and all because he had been in Dalton's home for a few hours and had killed a white girl. He looked round the room, seeing it for the first time. There was no rug on the floor and the plastering on the walls and ceiling hung loose in many places. There were two worn iron beds, four chairs, an old dresser, and a drop-leaf table on which they ate. This was much different from Dalton's home. Here all slept in one room; there he would have a room for himself alone. He smelt food cooking and remembered that one could not smell food cooking in Dalton's home; pots could not be heard rattling all over the house. Each person lived in one room and had a little world of his own. He hated this room and all the people in it, including himself. Why did he and his folks have to live like this? What had they ever done? Perhaps they had not done anything. Maybe they had to live this way precisely because none of them in all their lives had ever done anything, right or wrong, that mattered much.

"Fix the table, Vera. Breakfast's ready," the mother called.

"Yessum."

Bigger sat at the table and waited for food. Maybe this would be the last time he would eat here. He felt it keenly and it helped him to have patience. Maybe some day he would be eating in jail. Here he was sitting with them and they did not know that he had murdered a white girl and cut her head off and burnt her body. The thought of what he had done, the awful horror of it, the daring associated with such actions, formed for him for the first time in his fear-ridden life a barrier of protection between him and a world he feared. He had murdered and had created a new life for himself. It was something that was all his own, and it was the first time in his life he had had anything that others could not take from him. Yes; he could sit here calmly and eat and not be concerned about what his family thought or did. He had a natural wall from behind which he could look at them. His crime was an anchor weighing him safely in time; it added to him a certain confidence which his gun and knife did not. He was outside of his family now, over and beyond them; they were incapable of even thinking that he had done such a deed. And he had done something which even he had not thought possible.

Though he had killed by accident, not once did he feel the need to tell himself that it had been an accident. He was black and he had been alone in a room where a white girl had been killed; therefore he had killed her. That was what everybody would say anyhow, no matter what he said. And in a certain sense he knew that the girl's death had not been accidental. He had killed many times before, only on those other times there had been no handy victim or circumstance to make visible or dramatic his will to kill. His crime seemed natural; he felt that all of his life had been leading to something like this. It was no longer a matter of dumb wonder as to what would happen to him and his black skin; he knew now. The hidden meaning of his life—a meaning which others did not see and which he had always tried to hide—had spilled out. No; it was no accident, and he would never say that it was. There was in him a kind of terrified pride in feeling and thinking that some day he would be able to say publicly that he had done it. It was as though he had an obscure but deep debt to fulfil to himself in accepting the deed.

Now that the ice was broken, could he not do other things? What was there to stop him? While sitting there at the table waiting for his breakfast, he felt that he was arriving at something which had long eluded him. Things were becoming clear; he would know how to act from now on. The thing to do was to act just like others acted, live like they lived, and while they were not looking, do what you wanted. They would never know. He felt in the quiet presence of his mother, brother, and sister a force, inarticulate and unconscious, making for living without thinking, making for peace and habit, making for a hope that blinded. He felt that they wanted and yearned to see life in a certain way; they needed a certain picture of the world; there was one way of living they preferred above all others; and they were blind to what did not fit. They did not want to see what others were doing if that doing did not feed their own desires. All one had to do was be bold, do something nobody thought of. The whole thing came to him in the form of a powerful and simple feeling; there was in everyone a great hunger to believe that made him blind, and if he could see while others were blind, then he could get what he wanted and never be caught at it. Now, who on earth would think that he, a black timid Negro boy, would murder and burn a rich white girl and would sit and wait for his breakfast like this? Elation filled him.

He sat at the table watching the snow fall past the window and many things became plain. No, he did not have to hide behind a wall or a curtain now; he had a safer way of being safe, an easier way. What he had done last night had proved that. Jan was blind. Mary had been blind. Mr. Dalton was blind. And Mrs. Dalton was blind; yes, blind in more ways than one. Bigger smiled slightly. Mrs. Dalton had not known that Mary was dead while she had stood over the bed in that room last night. She had thought that Mary was drunk, because she was used to Mary's coming home drunk. And Mrs. Dalton had not known that he was in the room with her; it would have been the last thing she would have thought of. He was black and would not have figured in her thoughts on such an occasion. Bigger felt that a lot of people were like Mrs. Dalton, blind. . . .

"Here you are, Bigger," his mother said, setting a plate of grits on the table.

He began to eat, feeling much better after thinking out what had happened to him last night. He felt he could control himself now.

"Ain't you-all eating?" he asked, looking round.

"You go on and eat. You got to go. We'll eat later," his mother said.

He did not need any money, for he had the money he had gotten from Mary's purse; but he wanted to cover his tracks carefully.

"You got any money, Ma?"

"Just a little, Bigger."

"I need some."

"Here's a half. That leaves me exactly one dollar to last till Wednesday."

He put the half-dollar in his pocket. Buddy had finished dressing and was sitting on the edge of the bed. Suddenly, he saw Buddy, saw him in the light of Jan. Buddy was soft and vague; his eyes were defenseless and their glance went only to the surface of things. It was strange that he had not noticed that before. Buddy, too, was blind. Buddy was sitting there longing for a job like his. Buddy, too, went round and round in a groove and did not see things. Buddy's clothes hung loosely compared with the way Jan's hung. Buddy seemed aimless, lost, with no sharp or hard edges, like a chubby puppy. Looking at Buddy and thinking of Jan and Mr. Dalton, he saw in Buddy a certain stillness, an isolation, meaninglessness.

"How come you looking at me that way, Bigger?"

"Hunh?"

"You looking at me so funny."

"I didn't know it. I was thinking."

"What?"

"Nothing."

His mother came into the room with more plates of food and he saw how soft and shapeless she was. Her eyes were tired and sunken and darkly ringed from a long lack of rest. She moved about slowly, touching objects with her fingers as she passed them, using them for support. Her feet dragged over the wooden floor and her face held an expression of tense effort. Whenever she wanted to look at anything, even though it was near her, she turned her entire head and body to see it and did not shift her eyes. There was in her heart, it seemed, a heavy and delicately balanced burden whose weight she did not want to assume by disturbing it one whit. She saw him looking at her.

"Eat your breakfast, Bigger."

"I'm eating."

Vera brought her plate and sat opposite him. Bigger felt that even though her face was smaller and smoother than his mother's, the beginning of the same tiredness was already there. How different Vera was from Mary! He could see it in the very way Vera moved her hand when she carried the fork to her mouth; she seemed to be shrinking from life in every gesture she made. The very manner in which she sat showed a fear so deep as to be an organic part of her; she carried the food to her mouth in tiny bits, as if dreading its choking her, or fearing that it would give out too quickly.

"Bigger!" Vera wailed.

"Hunh?"

"You stop now," Vera said, laying aside her fork and slapping her hand through the air at him.

"What?"

"Stop looking at me, Bigger!"

"Aw, shut up and eat your breakfast!"

"Ma, make 'im stop looking at me!"

"I ain't looking at her, Ma!"

"You *is!*" Vera said.

"Eat your breakfast, Vera, and hush," said the mother.

"He just keeps watching me, Ma!"

"Gal, you crazy!" said Bigger.

"I ain't no crazy'n you!"

"Now, *both* of you hush," said the mother.

"I ain't going to eat with him watching me," Vera said, getting up and sitting on the edge of the bed.

"Go on and eat your grub!" Bigger said, leaping to his feet and grabbing his cap. "I'm getting out of here."

"What's wrong with you, Vera?" Buddy asked.

" 'Tend to your business!" Vera said, tears welling to her eyes.

"Will you children *please* hush," the mother wailed.

"Ma, you oughtn't let 'im treat me that way," Vera said.

Bigger picked up his suitcase. Vera came back to the table, drying her eyes.

"When will I see you again, Bigger?" the mother asked.

"I don't know," he said, slamming the door.

He was halfway down the steps when he heard his name called.

"Say, Bigger!"

He stopped and looked back. Buddy was running down the steps. He waited, wondering what was wrong.

"What you want?"

Buddy stood before him, diffident, smiling.

"I—I. . . ."

"What's the matter?"

"Shucks, I just thought. . . ."

Bigger stiffened with fright.

"Say, what you so excited about?"

"Aw, I reckon it ain't nothing. I just thought maybe you was in trouble. . . ."

Bigger mounted the steps and stood close to Buddy.

"Trouble? What you mean?" he asked in a frightened whisper.

"I—I just thought you was kind of nervous. I wanted to help you, that's all. I—I just thought. . . ."

"How come you think that?"

Buddy held out a roll of bills in his hand.

"You dropped it on the floor," he said.

Bigger stepped back, thunder-struck. He felt in his pocket for the money; it was not there. He took the money from Buddy and stuffed it hurriedly in his pocket.

"Did Ma see it?"

"Naw."

He gazed at Buddy in a long silence. He knew that Buddy was yearning to be with him, aching to share his confidence; but that could not happen now. He caught Buddy's arm in a tight grip.

"Listen, don't tell nobody, see? Here," he said, taking out the roll and peeling off a bill. "Here; take this and buy something. But don't tell *no*body."

"Gee! Thanks. I—I won't tell. But can I help you?"

"Naw; naw. . . ."

Buddy started back up the steps.

"Wait," Bigger said.

Buddy came back and stood facing him, his eyes eager, shining. Bigger looked at him, his body as taut as that of an animal about to leap. But his brother would not betray him. He could trust Buddy. He caught Buddy's arm again and squeezed it until Buddy flinched with pain.

"Don't you tell *no*body, hear?"

"Naw; naw. . . . I *won't*. . . ."

"Go on back, now."

Buddy ran up the steps, out of sight. Bigger stood brooding in the shadows of the stairway. He thrust the feeling from him, not with shame, but with impatience. He had felt toward Buddy for an instant as he had felt toward Mary when she lay upon the bed with the white blur moving toward him in the hazy blue light of the room. But he won't tell, he thought.

He went down the steps and into the street. The air was cold and the snow had stopped. Overhead the sky was clearing a little. As he neared the corner drug store, which stayed open all night, he wondered if any of the gang was around. Maybe Jack or G.H. was hanging out and had not gone home, as they sometimes did. Though he felt he was cut off from them forever, he had a strange hankering for their presence. He wanted to know how he would feel if he saw them again. Like a man reborn, he wanted to test and taste each thing now to see how it went; like a man risen up well from a long illness, he felt deep and wayward whims.

He peered through the frosted glass; yes, G.H. was there. He opened the door and went in. G.H. sat at the fountain, talking to the soda-jerker. Bigger sat next to him. They did not speak. Bigger bought two packages of cigarettes and shoved one of them to G.H., who looked at him in surprise.

"This for *me*?" G.H. asked.

Bigger waved his palm and pulled down the corners of his lips.

"Sure."

G.H. opened the pack.

"Jesus, I sure needed one. Say, you working now?"

"Yeah."

"How you like it?"

"Swell."

"Jack was telling me you saw the gal in the movie you suppose to drive around. Did you?"

"Sure."

"How is she?"

"Aw, we like that," Bigger said, crossing his fingers. He was trembling with excitement; sweat was on his forehead. He was excited and something was impelling him to become more excited. It was like a thirst springing from his blood. The door opened and Jack came in.

"Say, how is it, Bigger?"

Bigger wagged his head.

"Honky dory," he said. "Here; gimme another pack of cigarettes," he told the clerk. "This is for you, Jack."

"Jesus, you in clover, sure 'nough," Jack said, glimpsing the thick roll of bills.

"Where's Gus?" Bigger asked.

"He'll be along in a minute. We been hanging out at Clara's all night."

The door opened again; Bigger turned and saw Gus step inside. Gus paused.

"Now, you-all don't fight," Jack said.

Bigger bought another package of cigarettes and tossed it toward Gus. Gus caught it and stood, bewildered.

"Aw, come on, Gus. Forget it," Bigger said.

Gus came forward slowly; he opened the package and lit one.

"Bigger, you sure is crazy," Gus said with a shy smile.

Bigger knew that Gus was glad that the fight was over. Bigger was not afraid of them now; he sat with his feet propped upon his suitcase, looking from one to the other with a quiet smile.

"Lemme have a dollar," Jack said.

Bigger peeled off a dollar bill for each of them.

"Don't say I never give you nothing," he said, laughing.

"Bigger, you sure is one more crazy nigger," Gus said again, laughing with joy.

But he had to go; he could not stay here talking with them. He ordered three bottles of beer and picked up his suitcase.

"Ain't you going to drink one, too?" G.H. asked.

"Naw; I got to go."

"We'll be seeing you!"

"So long!"

He waved at them and swung through the door. He walked over the snow, feeling giddy and elated. His mouth was open and his eyes shone. It was the first time he had ever been in their presence without feeling fearful. He was following a strange path into a strange land and his nerves were hungry to see where it led. He lugged his suitcase to the end of the block, and stood waiting for a street car. He slipped his fingers into his vest pocket and felt the crisp roll of bills. Instead of going to Dalton's, he could take a street car to a railway station and leave town. But what would happen if he left? If he ran away now it would be thought at once that he knew something about Mary, as soon as she was missed. No; it would be far better to stick it out and see what happened. It might be a long time before anyone would think that Mary was killed and a still longer time before anyone would think that he had done it. And when Mary was missed, would they not think of the Reds first?

The street car rumbled up and he got on and rode to Forty-seventh Street, where he transferred to an eastbound car. He looked anxiously at the dim reflection of his black face in the sweaty windowpane. Would any of the white faces all about him think that he had killed a rich white girl? No! They might think he would steal a dime, rape a woman, get drunk, or cut somebody; but to kill a millionaire's daughter and burn her body? He smiled a little, feeling a tingling sensation enveloping all his body. He saw it all very sharply and simply: act like other people thought you ought to act, yet do what you wanted. In a certain sense he had been doing just that in a loud and rough manner all his life, but it was only last night when he had smothered Mary in her room while her blind mother had stood with outstretched arms that he had seen how clearly it could be done. Although he was trembling a little, he was not really afraid. He was eager, tremendously excited. I can take care of them, he thought, thinking of Mr. and Mrs. Dalton.

There was only one thing that worried him; he had to get that lingering image of Mary's bloody head lying on those newspapers from before his eyes. If that were done, then he would be all right. Gee, what a fool she was, he thought, remembering how Mary had acted. Carrying on that way! Hell, she

made me do it! I couldn't help it! She should've known better! She should've left me alone, Goddammit! He did not feel
sorry for Mary; she was not real to him, not a human being;
he had not known her long or well enough for that. He felt
that his murder of her was more than amply justified by the
fear and shame she had made him feel. It seemed that her
actions had evoked fear and shame in him. But when he
thought hard about it it seemed impossible that they could
have. He really did not know just where that fear and shame
had come from; it had just been there, that was all. Each time
he had come in contact with her it had risen hot and hard.

It was not Mary he was reacting to when he felt that fear
and shame. Mary had served to set off his emotions, emotions
conditioned by many Marys. And now that he had killed
Mary he felt a lessening of tension in his muscles; he had shed
an invisible burden he had long carried.

As the car lurched over the snow he lifted his eyes and saw
black people upon the snow-covered sidewalks. Those people
had feelings of fear and shame like his. Many a time he had
stood on street corners with them and talked of white people
as long sleek cars zoomed past. To Bigger and his kind white
people were not really people; they were a sort of great natural force, like a stormy sky looming overhead, or like a deep
swirling river stretching suddenly at one's feet in the dark. As
long as he and his black folks did not go beyond certain limits, there was no need to fear that white force. But whether
they feared it or not, each and every day of their lives they
lived with it; even when words did not sound its name, they
acknowledged its reality. As long as they lived here in this
prescribed corner of the city, they paid mute tribute to it.

There were rare moments when a feeling and longing for
solidarity with other black people would take hold of him. He
would dream of making a stand against that white force, but
that dream would fade when he looked at the other black
people near him. Even though black like them, he felt there
was too much difference between him and them to allow for a
common binding and a common life. Only when threatened
with death could that happen; only in fear and shame, with
their backs against a wall, could that happen. But never could
they sink their differences in hope.

As he rode, looking at the black people on the sidewalks, he felt that one way to end fear and shame was to make all those black people act together, rule them, tell them what to do, and make them do it. Dimly, he felt that there should be one direction in which he and all other black people could go whole-heartedly; that there should be a way in which gnaw-ing hunger and restless aspiration could be fused; that there should be a manner of acting that caught the mind and body in certainty and faith. But he felt that such would never hap-pen to him and his black people, and he hated them and wanted to wave his hand and blot them out. Yet, he still hoped, vaguely. Of late he had liked to hear tell of men who could rule others, for in actions such as these he felt that there was a way to escape from this tight morass of fear and shame that sapped at the base of his life. He liked to hear of how Japan was conquering China; of how Hitler was running the Jews to the ground; of how Mussolini was invading Spain. He was not concerned with whether these acts were right or wrong; they simply appealed to him as possible avenues of escape. He felt that some day there would be a black man who would whip the black people into a tight band and to-gether they would act and end fear and shame. He never thought of this in precise mental images; he felt it; he would feel it for a while and then forget. But hope was always wait-ing somewhere deep down in him.

It was fear that had made him fight Gus in the poolroom. If he had felt certain of himself and of Gus, he would not have fought. But he knew Gus, as he knew himself, and he knew that one of them might fail through fear at the decisive moment. How could he think of going to rob Blum's that way? He distrusted and feared Gus and he knew that Gus distrusted and feared him; and the moment he tried to band himself and Gus together to do something, he would hate Gus and himself. Ultimately, though, his hate and hope turned outward from himself and Gus: his hope toward a vague benevolent something that would help and lead him, and his hate toward the whites; for he felt that they ruled him, even when they were far away and not thinking of him, ruled him by conditioning him in his relations to his own people.

The street car crawled through the snow; Drexel Boulevard was the next stop. He lifted the suitcase and stood at the door. In a few minutes he would know if Mary had burned. The car stopped; he swung off and walked through snow as deep as his ankles, heading for Dalton's.

When he got to the driveway he saw that the car was standing just as he had left it, but all covered with a soft coat of snow. The house loomed white and silent. He unlatched the gate and went past the car, seeing before his eyes an image of Mary, her bloody neck just inside the furnace and her head with its curly black hair lying upon the soggy newspapers. He paused. He could turn round now and go back. He could get into the car and be miles from here before anybody knew it. But why run away unless there was good reason? He had some money to make a run for it when the time came. And he had his gun. His fingers trembled so that he had difficulty in unlocking the door; but they were not trembling from fear. It was a kind of eagerness he felt, a confidence, a fulness, a freedom; his whole life was caught up in a supreme and meaningful act. He pushed the door in, then was stone-still, sucking his breath in softly. In the red glare of the furnace stood a shadowy figure. Is that Mrs. Dalton? But it was taller and stouter than Mrs. Dalton. Oh, it was Peggy! She stood with her back to him, a little bent. She seemed to be peering hard into the furnace. She didn't hear me come in, he thought. *Maybe I ought to go!* But before he could move Peggy turned round.

"Oh, good morning, Bigger."

He did not answer.

"I'm glad you came. I was just about to put more coal into the fire."

"I'll fix it, mam."

He came forward, straining his eyes to see if any traces of Mary were in the furnace. When he reached Peggy's side he saw that she was staring through the cracks of the door at the red bed of livid coals.

"The fire was very hot last night," Peggy said. "But this morning it got low."

"I'll fix it," Bigger said, standing and not daring to open the door of the furnace while she stood there beside him in the red darkness.

He heard the dull roar of the draft going upwards and wondered if she suspected anything. He knew that he should have turned on the light; but what if he did and the light revealed parts of Mary in the furnace?

"I'll fix it, mam," he said again.

Quickly, he wondered if he would have to kill her to keep her from telling if she turned on the light and saw something that made her think that Mary was dead? Without turning his head he saw an iron shovel resting in a near-by corner. His hands clenched. Peggy moved from his side toward a light that swung from the ceiling at the far end of the room near the stairs.

"I'll give you some light," she said.

He moved silently and quickly toward the shovel and waited to see what would happen. The light came on, blindingly bright; he blinked. Peggy stood near the steps holding her right hand tightly over her breast. She had on a kimono and was trying to hold it closely about her. Bigger understood at once. She was not even thinking of the furnace; she was just a little ashamed of having been seen in the basement in her kimono.

"Has Miss Dalton come down yet?" she asked over her shoulder as she went up the steps.

"No'm. I haven't seen her."

"You just come?"

"Yessum."

She stopped and looked back at him.

"But the car, it's in the driveway."

"Yessum," he said simply, not volunteering any information.

"Then it stayed out all night?"

"I don't know, mam."

"Didn't you put it in the garage?"

"No'm. Miss Dalton told me to leave it out."

"Oh! Then it *did* stay out all night. That's why it's covered with snow."

"I reckon so, mam."

Peggy shook her head and sighed.

"Well, I suppose she'll be ready for you to take her to the station in a few minutes."

"Yessum."

"I see you brought the trunk down."

"Yessum. She told me to bring it down last night."

"Don't forget it," she said, going through the kitchen door.

For a long time after she had gone he did not move from his tracks. Then, slowly, he looked round the basement, turning his head like an animal with eyes and ears alert, searching to see if anything was amiss. The room was exactly as he had left it last night. He walked about, looking closer. All at once he stopped, his eyes widening. Directly in front of him he saw a small piece of blood-stained newspaper lying in the livid reflection cast by the cracks in the door of the furnace. Had Peggy seen that? He ran to the light and turned it out and ran back and looked at the piece of paper. He could barely see it. That meant that Peggy had not seen it. How about Mary? Had she burned? He turned the light back on and picked up the piece of paper. He glanced to the left and right to see if anyone was watching, then opened the furnace door and peered in, his eyes filled with the vision of Mary and her bloody throat. The inside of the furnace breathed and quivered in the grip of fiery coals. But there was no sign of the body, even though the body's image hovered before his eyes, between his eyes and the bed of coals burning hotly. Like the oblong mound of fresh clay of a newly made grave, the red coals revealed the bent outline of Mary's body. He had the feeling that if he simply touched that red oblong mound with his finger it would cave in and Mary's body would come into full view, unburnt. The coals had the appearance of having burnt the body beneath, leaving the glowing embers formed into a shell of red hotness with a hollowed space in the center, keeping still in the embrace of the quivering coals the huddled shape of Mary's body. He blinked his eyes and became aware that he still held the piece of paper in his hand. He lifted it to the level of the door and the draft sucked it from his fingers; he watched it fly into the red trembling heat, smoke, turn black, blaze, then vanish.

He shut the door and pulled the lever for more coal. The rattling of the tiny lumps against the tin sides of the chute came loudly to his ears as the oblong mound of red fire turned gradually black and blazed from the fanwise spreading of coal whirling into the furnace. He shut off the lever and stood up; things were all right so far. As long as no one poked round in that fire, things would be all right. He himself did not want to poke in it, for fear that some part of Mary was still there. If things could go on like this until afternoon, Mary would be burned enough to make him safe. He turned and looked at the trunk again. Oh! He must not forget! He had to put those Communist pamphlets in his room right away. He ran back of the furnace, up the steps to his room and placed the pamphlets smoothly and neatly in a corner of his dresser drawer. Yes, they would have to be stacked neatly. No one must think that he had read them.

He went back to the basement, dragged the trunk to the door, lifted it to his back, carried it to the car and fastened it to the running board. He looked at his watch; it was eight-twenty. Now, he would have to wait for Mary to come out. He took his seat at the steering wheel and waited for five minutes. He would ring the bell for her. He looked at the steps leading up to the side door of the house, remembering how Mary had stumbled last night and how he had held her up. Then, involuntarily, he started in fright as a full blast of intense sunshine fell from the sky, making the snow leap and glitter and sparkle about him in a world of magic whiteness without sound. It's getting late! He would have to go in and ask for Miss Dalton. If he stayed here too long it would seem that he was not expecting her to come down. He got out of the car and walked up the steps to the side door. He looked through the glass; no one was in sight. He tried to open the door and found it locked. He pushed the bell, hearing the gong sound softly within. He waited a moment, then saw Peggy hurrying down the hall. She opened the door.

"Hasn't she come out yet?"

"No'm. And it's getting late."

"Wait. I'll call her."

Peggy, still dressed in the kimono, ran up the stairs, the same stairs up which he had half-dragged Mary and the same stairs down which he had stumbled with the trunk last night. Then he saw Peggy coming back down the stairs, much slower than she had gone up. She came to the door.

"She ain't here. Maybe she's gone. What did she tell you?"

"She said to drive her to the station and to take her trunk, mam."

"Well, she ain't in her room and she ain't in Mrs. Dalton's room. And Mr. Dalton's asleep. Did she tell you she was going this morning?"

"That's what she told me last night, mam."

"She told you to bring the trunk down last night?"

"Yessum."

Peggy thought a moment, looking past him at the snow-covered car.

"Well, you better take the trunk on. Maybe she didn't stay here last night."

"Yessum."

He turned and started down the steps.

"Bigger!"

"Yessum."

"You say she told you to leave the car out, all *night*?"

"Yessum."

"Did she say she was going to use it again?"

"No'm. You see," Bigger said, feeling his way, "he was in it. . . ."

"*Who?*"

"The gentleman."

"Oh; yes. Take the trunk on. I suppose Mary was up to some of her pranks."

He got into the car and pulled it down the driveway to the street, then headed northward over the snow. He wanted to look back and see if Peggy was watching him, but dared not. That would make her think that he thought that something was wrong, and he did not want to give that impression now. Well, at least he had one person thinking it as he wanted it thought.

He reached the La Salle Street Station, pulled the car to a platform, backed into a narrow space between other cars, hoisted the trunk up, and waited for a man to give him a ticket for the trunk. He wondered what would happen if no one called for it. Maybe they would notify Mr. Dalton. Well, he would wait and see. He had done his part. Miss Dalton had asked him to take the trunk to the station and he had done it.

He drove as hurriedly back to the Dalton's as the snow-covered streets would allow him. He wanted to be back on the spot to see what would happen, to be there with his fingers on the pulse of time. He reached the driveway and nosed the car into the garage, locked it, and then stood wondering if he ought to go to his room or to the kitchen. It would be better to go straight to the kitchen as though nothing had happened. He had not as yet eaten his breakfast as far as Peggy was concerned, and his coming into the kitchen would be thought natural. He went through the basement, pausing to look at the roaring furnace, and then went to the kitchen door and stepped in softly. Peggy stood at the gas stove with her back to him. She turned and gave him a brief glance.

"You make it all right?"

"Yessum."

"You see her down there?"

"No'm."

"Hungry?"

"A little, mam."

"A little?" Peggy laughed. "You'll get used to how this house is run on Sundays. Nobody gets up early and when they do they're almost famished."

"I'm all right, mam."

"That was the only kick Green had while he was working here," Peggy said. "He swore we starved him on Sundays."

Bigger forced a smile and looked down at the black and white linoleum on the floor. What would she think if she knew? He felt very kindly toward Peggy just then; he felt he had something of value which she could never take from him even if she despised him. He heard a phone ring in the hallway. Peggy straightened and looked at him as she wiped her hands on her apron.

"Who on earth's calling here this early on a Sunday morning?" she mumbled.

She went out and he sat, waiting. Maybe that was Jan asking about Mary. He remembered that Mary had promised to call him. He wondered how long it took to go to Detroit. Five or six hours? It was not far. Mary's train had already gone. About four o'clock she would be due in Detroit. Maybe someone had planned to meet her? If she was not on the train, would they call or wire about it? Peggy came back, went to the stove and continued cooking.

"Things'll be ready in a minute," she said.

"Yessum."

Then she turned to him.

"Who was the gentleman with Miss Dalton last night?"

"I don't know, mam. I think she called him Jan, or something like that."

"Jan? He just called," Peggy said. She tossed her head and her lips tightened. "He's a no-good one, if there ever was one. One of them anarchists who's agin the government."

Bigger listened and said nothing.

"What on earth a good girl like Mary wants to hang around with that crazy bunch for, God only knows. Nothing good'll come of it, just you mark my word. If it wasn't for that Mary and her wild ways, this household would run like a clock. It's such a pity, too. Her mother's the very soul of goodness. And there never was a finer man than Mr. Dalton. . . . But later on Mary'll settle down. They all do. They think they're missing something unless they kick up their heels when they're young and foolish. . . ."

She brought a bowl of hot oatmeal and milk to him and he began to eat. He had difficulty in swallowing, for he had no appetite. But he forced the food down. Peggy talked on and he wondered what he should say to her; he found that he could say nothing. Maybe she was not expecting him to say anything. Maybe she was talking to him because she had no one else to talk to, like his mother did sometimes. Yes; he would see about the fire again when he got to the basement. He would fill that furnace as full of coal as it would get and make sure that Mary burned in a hurry. The hot cereal was making him sleepy and he suppressed a yawn.

"What all I got to do today, mam?"

"Just wait on call. Sunday's a dull day. Maybe Mr. or Mrs. Dalton'll go out."

"Yessum."

He finished the oatmeal.

"You want me to do anything now?"

"No. But you're not through eating. You want some ham and eggs?"

"No'm. I got a plenty."

"Well, it's right here for you. Don't be afraid to ask for it."

"I reckon I'll see about the fire now."

"All right, Bigger. Just you listen for the bell about two o'clock. Till then I don't think there'll be anything."

He went to the basement. The fire was blazing. The embers glowed red and the draft droned upward. It did not need any coal. Again he looked round the basement, into every nook and corner, to see if he had left any trace of what had happened last night. There was none.

He went to his room and lay on the bed. Well; here he was now. What would happen? The room was quiet. No! He heard something! He cocked his head, listening. He caught faint sounds of pots and pans rattling in the kitchen below. He got up and walked to the far end of the room; the sounds came louder. He heard the soft but firm tread of Peggy as she walked across the kitchen floor. She's right under me, he thought. He stood still, listening. He heard Mrs. Dalton's voice, then Peggy's. He stooped and put his ear to the floor. Were they talking about Mary? He could not make out what they were saying. He stood up and looked round. A foot from him was the door of the clothes closet. He opened it; the voices came clearly. He went into the closet and the planks squeaked; he stopped. Had they heard him? Would they think he was snooping? Oh! He had an idea! He got his suitcase and opened it and took out an armful of clothes. If anyone came into the room it would seem that he was putting his clothes away. He went into the closet and listened.

". . . . you mean the car stayed out all *night* in the drive-way?"

"Yes; he said she told him to leave it there."

"What time was that?"

"I don't know, Mrs. Dalton. I didn't ask him."

"I don't understand this at all."

"Oh, she's all right. I don't think you need worry."

"But she didn't even leave a note, Peggy. That's not like Mary. Even when she ran away to New York that time she at least left a note."

"Maybe she hasn't gone. Maybe something came up and she stayed out all night, Mrs. Dalton."

"But why would she leave the car out?"

"I don't know."

"And he said a man was with her?"

"It was that Jan, I think, Mrs. Dalton."

"Jan?"

"Yes; the one who was with her in Florida."

"She just *won't* leave those awful people alone."

"He called here this morning, asking for her."

"Called *here*?"

"Yes."

"And what did he say?"

"He seemed sort of peeved when I told him she was gone."

"What can that poor child be up to? She told me she was not seeing him any more."

"Maybe *she* had him to call, Mrs. Dalton. . . ."

"What do you mean?"

"Well, mam, I was kind of thinking that maybe she's with him again, like that time she was in Florida. And maybe she had him to call to see if we knew she was gone. . . ."

"Oh, Peggy!"

"Oh, I'm sorry, mam. . . . Maybe she stayed with some friends of hers?"

"But she was in her *room* at two o'clock this morning, Peggy. Whose house would she go to at that hour?"

"Mrs. Dalton, I noticed something when I went to her room this morning."

"What?"

"Well, mam, it looks like her bed wasn't slept in at all. The cover wasn't even pulled back. Looks like somebody had just stretched out awhile and then got up. . . ."

"Oh!"

Bigger listened intently, but there was silence. They knew that something was wrong now. He heard Mrs. Dalton's voice again, quavering with doubt and fear.

"Then she *didn't* sleep here last night?"

"Looks like she didn't."

"Did that boy say Jan was in the car?"

"Yes. I thought something was strange about the car being left out in the snow all night, and so I asked him. He said she told him to leave the car there and he said Jan was in it."

"Listen, Peggy. . . ."

"Yes, Mrs. Dalton."

"Mary was drunk last night. I hope nothing's happened to her."

"Oh, what a pity!"

"I went to her room just after she came in. . . . She was too drunk to talk. She was *drunk*, I tell you. I never thought she'd come home in that condition."

"She'll be all right, Mrs. Dalton. I *know* she will."

There was another long silence. Bigger wondered if Mrs. Dalton was on her way to his room. He went back to the bed and lay down, listening. There were no sounds. He lay a long time, hearing nothing; then he heard footsteps in the kitchen again. He hurried into the closet.

"Peggy!"

"Yes, Mrs. Dalton."

"Listen, I just felt around in Mary's room. Something's wrong. She didn't finish packing her trunk. At least half of her things are still there. She said she was planning to go to some dances in Detroit and she didn't take the new things she bought."

"Maybe she didn't go to Detroit."

"But where *is* she?"

Bigger stopped listening, feeling fear for the first time. He had not thought that the trunk was not fully packed. How could he explain that she had told him to take a half-packed trunk to the station? Oh, shucks! The girl was drunk. That was it. Mary was so drunk that she didn't know what she was doing. He would say that she had told him to take it and he had just taken it; that's all. If someone asked him why he had taken a half-packed trunk to the station, he would tell them that that was no different from all the other foolish things that Mary had told him to do that night. Had not people seen him eating with her and Jan in Ernie's Kitchen Shack? He would say that both of them were drunk and that he had done what they told him because it was his job. He listened again to the voices.

". . . . and after a while send that boy to me. I want to talk to him."

"Yes, Mrs. Dalton."

Again he lay on the bed. He would have to go over his story and make it foolproof. Maybe he had done wrong in taking that trunk? Maybe it would have been better to have carried Mary down in his arms and burnt her? But he had put her in the trunk because of the fear of someone's seeing her in his arms. That was the only way he could have gotten her down out of the room. Oh, hell, what had happened had happened and he would stick to his story. He went over the story again, fastening every detail firmly in his mind. He would say that she had been drunk, sloppy drunk. He lay on the soft bed in the warm room listening to the steam hiss in the radiator and thinking drowsily and lazily of how drunk she had been and of how he had lugged her up the steps and of how he had pushed the pillow over her face and of how he had put her in the trunk and of how he had struggled with the trunk on the dark stairs and of how his fingers had burned while he had stumbled down the stairs with the heavy trunk going *bump-bump-bump* so loud that surely all the world must have heard it. . . .

He jumped awake, hearing a knock at the door. His heart raced. He sat up and stared sleepily around the room. Had someone knocked? He looked at his watch; it was three o'clock. Gee! He must have slept through the bell that was to ring at two. The knock came again.

"O.K.!" he mumbled.

"This is Mrs. Dalton!"

"Yessum. Just a minute."

He reached the door in two long steps, then stood a moment trying to collect himself. He blinked his eyes and wet his lips. He opened the door and saw Mrs. Dalton smiling before him, dressed in white, her pale face held as it had been when she was standing in the darkness while he had smothered Mary on the bed.

"Y-y-yes, mam," he stammered. "I—I was asleep. . . ."

"You didn't get much sleep last night, did you?"

"No'm," he drawled, afraid of what she might mean.

"Peggy rang for you three times, and you didn't answer."

"I'm sorry, mam. . . ."

"That's all right. I wanted to ask you about last night. . . . Oh, you took the trunk to the station, didn't you?" she asked.

"Yessum. This morning," he said, detecting hesitancy and confusion in her voice.

"I see," said Mrs. Dalton. She stood with her face tilted upward in the semi-darkness of the hallway. He had his hand on the doorknob, waiting, his muscles taut. He had to be careful with his answers now. And yet he knew he had a certain protection; he knew that a certain element of shame would keep Mrs. Dalton from asking him too much and letting him know that she was worried. He was a boy and she was an old woman. He was the hired and she was the hirer. And there was a certain distance to be kept between them.

"You left the car in the driveway last night, didn't you?"

"Yessum. I was about to put it up," he said, indicating that his only concern was with keeping his job and doing his duties. "But she told me to leave it."

"And was someone with her?"

"Yessum. A gentleman."

"That must have been pretty late, wasn't it?"

"Yessum. A little before two, mam."

"And you took the trunk down a little before two?"

"Yessum. She told me to."

"She took you to her room?"

He did not want her to think that he had been alone in the room with Mary. Quickly, he recast the story in his mind.

"Yessum. They went up. . . ."

"Oh, *he* was with her?"

"Yessum."

"I see. . . ."

"Anything wrong, mam?"

"Oh, no! I—I—I. . . . No; there's nothing wrong."

She stood in the doorway and he looked at her light-grey blind eyes, eyes almost as white as her face and hair and dress. He knew that she was really worried and wanted to ask him more questions. But he knew that she would not want to hear him tell of how drunk her daughter had been. After all, he was black and she was white. He was poor and she was rich. She would be ashamed to let him think that something was so wrong in her family that she had to ask him, a black servant, about it. He felt confident.

"Will there be anything right now, mam?"

"No. In fact, you may take the rest of the day off, if you like. Mr. Dalton is not feeling well and we're not going out."

"Thank you, mam."

She turned away and he shut the door; he stood listening to the soft whisper of her shoes die away down the hall, then on the stairs. He pictured her groping her way, her hands touching the walls. She must know this house like a book, he thought. He trembled with excitement. She was white and he was black; she was rich and he was poor; she was old and he was young; she was the boss and he was the worker. He was safe; yes. When he heard the kitchen door open and shut he went to the closet and listened again. But there were no sounds.

Well, he would go out. To go out now would be the answer to the feeling of strain that had come over him while talking to Mrs. Dalton. He would go and see Bessie. That was it! He got his cap and coat and went to the basement. The suction of air through the furnace moaned and the fire was white-hot; there was enough coal to last until he came back.

He went to Forty-seventh Street and stood on the corner to wait for a car. Yes, Bessie was the one he wanted to see now. Funny, he had not thought of her much during the last day and night. Too many exciting things had been happening. He had had no need to think of her. But now he had to forget and relax and he wanted to see her. She was always home on Sunday afternoons. He wanted to see her very badly; he felt that he would be stronger to go through to-morrow if he saw her.

The street car came and he got on, thinking of how things had gone that day. No; he did not think they would suspect him of anything. He was black. Again he felt the roll of crisp bills in his pocket; if things went wrong he could always run away. He wondered how much money was in the roll; he had not even counted it. He would see when he got to Bessie's. No; he need not be afraid. He felt the gun nestling close to his skin. That gun could always make folks stand away and think twice before bothering him.

But of the whole business there was one angle that bothered him; he should have gotten more money out of it; he should have *planned* it. He had acted too hastily and accidentally. Next time things would be much different; he would plan and arrange so that he would have money enough to keep him a long time. He looked out of the car window and then round at the white faces near him. He wanted suddenly to stand up and shout, telling them that he had killed a rich white girl, a girl whose family was known to all of them. Yes; if he did that a look of startled horror would come over their faces. But, no. He would not do that, even though the satisfaction would be keen. He was so greatly outnumbered that he would be arrested, tried, and executed. He wanted the keen thrill of startling them, but felt that the cost was too great. He wished that he had the power to say what he had done without fear of being arrested; he wished that he could be an idea in their minds; that his black face and the image of his smothering Mary and cutting off her head and burning her could hover before their eyes as a terrible picture of reality which they could see and feel and yet not destroy. He was not satisfied with the way things stood now; he was a man who had come in sight of a goal, then had won it, and in winning it had seen just within his grasp another goal, higher, greater. He had learned to shout and had shouted and no ear had heard him; he had just learned to walk and was walking but could not see the ground beneath his feet; he had long been yearning for weapons to hold in his hands and suddenly found that his hands held weapons that were invisible.

The car stopped a block from Bessie's home and he got off. When he reached the building in which she lived, he looked up to the second floor and saw a light burning in her window. The street lamps came on suddenly, lighting up the snow-covered sidewalks with a yellow sheen. It had gotten dark early. The lamps were round hazy balls of light frozen into motionlessness, anchored in space and kept from blowing away in the icy wind by black steel posts. He went in and rang the bell and, in answer to a buzzer, mounted the stairs and found Bessie smiling at him in her door.

"Hello, stranger!"

"Hi, Bessie."

He stood face to face with her, then reached for her hands. She shied away.

"What's the matter?"

"You know what's the matter."

"Naw, I don't."

"What you reaching for me for?"

"I want to kiss you, honey."

"You don't want to kiss me."

"Why?"

"I ought to be asking *you* that."

"What's the matter?"

"I saw you with your white friends last night."

"Aw; they wasn't my friends."

"Who was they?"

"I work for 'em."

"And you eat with 'em."

"Aw, Bessie. . . ."

"You didn't even *speak* to me."

"I *did*!"

"You just growled and waved your hand."

"Aw, baby. I was working then. You understand."

"I thought maybe you was 'shamed of me, sitting there with that white gal all dressed in silk and satin."

"Aw, hell, Bessie. Come on. Don't act that way."

"You really want to kiss me?"

"Sure. What you think I came here for?"

"How come you so long seeing me, then?"

"I told you I been working, honey. You saw me last night. Come on. Don't act this way."

"I don't know," she said, shaking her head.

He knew that she was trying to see how badly he wanted her, trying to see how much power she still had over him. He grabbed her arm and pulled her to him, kissing her long and hard, feeling as he did so that she was not responding. When he took his lips away he looked at her with eyes full of reproach and at the same time he felt his teeth clamping and his lips tingling slightly with rising passion.

"Let's go in," he said.

"If you want to."

"Sure I want to."

"You stayed away so long."

"Aw, don't be that way."

They went in.

"How come you acting so cold tonight?" he asked.

"You could have dropped me a postcard," she said.

"Aw, I just forgot it."

"Or you could've phoned."

"Honey, I was busy."

"Looking at that old white gal, I reckon."

"Aw, hell!"

"You don't love me no more."

"The hell I don't."

"You could've come by just for five minutes."

"Baby, I was busy."

When he kissed her this time she responded a little. To let her know that he wanted her he allowed her to draw his tongue into her mouth.

"I'm tired tonight," she sighed.

"Who *you* been seeing?"

"*No*body."

"What you doing tired?"

"If you want to talk that way you can leave right now. I didn't ask you who you been seeing to make you stay away this long, did I?"

"You all on edge tonight."

"You could have just said, 'Hello, dog!' "

"Really, honey. I was busy."

"You was setting there at that table with them white folks like you was a lawyer or something. You wouldn't even look at me when I spoke to you."

"Aw, forget it. Let's talk about something else."

He attempted to kiss her again and she shied away.

"Come on, honey."

"Who *you* been with?"

"Nobody. I swear. I been working. And I been thinking hard about you. I been missing you. Listen, I got a room all my own where I'm working. Some nights you can stay there with me, see? Gee, I been missing you awful, honey. Soon's I got time I came right over."

He stood looking at her in the dim light of the room. She was teasing him and he liked it. At least it took him away from that terrible image of Mary's head lying on the bloody newspaper. He wanted to kiss her again, but deep down he did not really mind her standing off from him; it made him hunger more keenly for her. She was looking at him wistfully, half-leaning against a wall, her hands on her hips. Then suddenly he knew how to draw her out, to drive from her mind all thought of her teasing him. He reached into his pocket and drew forth the roll of bills. Smiling, he held it in his palm and spoke as though to himself:

"Well, I reckon somebody else might like this if you don't."

She came a step forward.

"Bigger! Gee! Where you get all that money from?"

"Wouldn't you like to know?"

"How much is it?"

"What you care?"

She came to his side.

"How much is it, really?"

"What you want to know for?"

"Let me see it. I'll give it back to you."

"I'll let you see it, but it'll have to stay in *my* hand, see?"

He watched the expression of coyness on her face change to one of amazement as she counted the bills.

"Lord, Bigger! Where you get this money from?"

"Wouldn't you like to know?" he said, slipping his arm about her waist.

"Is it yours?"

"What in hell you reckon I'm doing with it?"

"Tell me where you get it from, honey."

"You going to be sweet to me?"

He felt her body growing gradually less stiff; but her eyes were searching his face.

"You ain't got into nothing, is you?"

"You going to be sweet to me?"

"Oh, Bigger!"

"Kiss me, honey."

He felt her relax completely; he kissed her and she drew him to the bed. They sat down. Gently, she took the money from his hand.

"How much is it?" he asked.

"Don't you know?"

"Naw."

"Didn't you *count* it?"

"Naw."

"Bigger, where you get this money from?"

"Maybe I'll tell you some day," he said, leaning back and resting his head on the pillow.

"You into something."

"How much is there?"

"A hundred and twenty-five dollars."

"You going to be sweet to me?"

"But, Bigger, *where* you get this money from?"

"What do that matter?"

"You going to buy me something?"

"Sure."

"What?"

"Anything you want."

They were silent for a moment. Finally, his arm about her waist felt her body relax into a softness he knew and wanted. She rested her head on the pillow; he put the money in his pocket and leaned over her.

"Gee, honey. I been wanting you bad."

"For real?"

"Honest to God."

He placed his hands on her breasts just as he had placed them on Mary's last night and he was thinking of that while he kissed her. He took his lips away for breath and heard Bessie say:

"Don't stay away so long from me, hear, honey?"

"I won't."

"You love me?"

"Sure."

He kissed her again and he felt her arm lifting above his head and he heard the click as the light went out. He kissed her again, hard.

"Bessie?"

"Hunh?"

"Come on, honey."

They were still a moment longer; then she rose. He waited. He heard her clothes rustling in the darkness; she was undressing. He got up and began to undress. Gradually, he began to see in the darkness; she was on the other side of the bed, her dark body like a shadow in the denser darkness surrounding her. He heard the bed creak as she lay down. He went to her, folding her in his arms, mumbling.

"Gee, kid."

He felt two soft palms holding his face tenderly and the thought and image of the whole blind world which had made him ashamed and afraid fell away as he felt her as a fallow field beneath him stretching out under a cloudy sky waiting for rain, and he slept in her body, rising and sinking with the ebb and flow of her blood, being willingly dragged into a warm night sea to rise renewed to the surface to face a world he hated and wanted to blot out of existence, clinging close to a fountain whose warm waters washed and cleaned his senses, cooled them, made them strong and keen again to see and smell and touch and taste and hear, cleared them to end the tiredness and to reforge in him a new sense of time and space;—after he had been tossed to dry upon a warm sunlit rock under a white sky he lifted his hand slowly and heavily and touched Bessie's lips with his fingers and mumbled,

"Gee, kid."

"Bigger."

He took his hand away and relaxed. He did not feel that he wanted to step forth and resume where he had left off living; not just yet. He was lying at the bottom of a deep dark pit upon a pallet of warm wet straw and at the top of the pit he could see the cold blue of the distant sky. Some hand had reached inside of him and had laid a quiet finger of peace upon the restless tossing of his spirit and had made him feel that he did not need to long for a home now. Then, like the long withdrawing sound of a receding wave, the sense of night and sea and warmth went from him and he lay looking in the darkness at the shadowy outline of Bessie's body, hearing his and her breathing.

"Bigger?"

"Hunh?"

"You like your job?"

"Yeah. Why?"

"I just asked."

"You swell."

"You mean that?"

"Sure."

"Where you working?"

"Over on Drexel."

"Where?"

"In the 4600 block."

"Oh!"

"What?"

"Nothing."

"But, what?"

"Oh, I just happen to think of something."

"Tell me. What is it?"

"It ain't nothing, Bigger, honey."

What did she mean by asking all these questions? He wondered if she had detected anything in him. Then he wondered
if he were not letting fear get the better of him by thinking
always in terms of Mary and of her having been smothered
and burnt. But he wanted to know why she had asked where
he worked.

"Come on, honey. Tell me what you thinking."

"It ain't nothing much, Bigger. I used to work over in that
section, not far from where the Loeb folks lived."

"Loeb?"

"Yeah. One of the families of one of the boys that killed
that Franks boy. Remember?"

"Naw; what you mean?"

"You remember hearing people talk about Loeb and
Leopold."

"Oh!"

"The ones who killed the boy and then tried to get money
from the boy's family. . . .

. . . . *by sending notes to them* Bigger was not listening. The
world of sound fell abruptly away from him and a vast picture
appeared before his eyes, a picture teeming with so much
meaning that he could not react to it all at once. He lay, his
eyes unblinking, his heart pounding, his lips slightly open, his
breath coming and going so softly that it seemed he was not
breathing at all. *you remember them aw you ain't even listening*
He said nothing. *how come you won't listen when I talk to you*
Why could he, why could he not, not send a letter to the
Daltons, asking for money? *Bigger* He sat up in bed, staring
into the darkness. *what's the matter honey* He could ask for ten

thousand, or maybe twenty. *Bigger what's the matter I'm talk-ing to you* He did not answer; his nerves were taut with the hard effort to remember something. Now! Yes, Loeb and Leopold had planned to have the father of the murdered boy get on a train and throw the money out of the window while passing some spot. He leaped from bed and stood in the middle of the floor. *Bigger* He could, yes, he could have them pack the money in a shoe box and have them throw it out of a car somewhere on the South Side. He looked round in the darkness, feeling Bessie's fingers on his arm. He came to him-self and sighed.

"What's the matter, honey?" she asked.

"Hunh?"

"What's on your mind?"

"Nothing."

"Come on and tell me. You worried?"

"Naw; naw. . . ."

"Now, I told *you* what was on my mind, but you won't tell me what's on *yours*. That ain't fair."

"I just forgot something. That's all."

"That ain't what you was thinking about," she said.

He sat back on the bed, feeling his scalp tingle with excite-ment. Could he do it? This was what had been missing and this was what would make the thing complete. But this thing was so big he would have to take time and think it over care-fully.

"Honey, tell me where you get that money?"

"What money?" he asked in a tone of feigned surprise.

"Aw, Bigger. I know something's wrong. You worried. You got something on your mind. I can tell it."

"You want me to make up something to tell you?"

"All right; if that's the way you feel about it."

"Aw, Bessie. . . ."

"You didn't have to come here tonight."

"Maybe I shouldn't've come."

"You don't have to come no more."

"Don't you love me?"

"About as much as you love me."

"How much is that?"

"You ought to know."

"Aw, let's stop fussing," he said.

He felt the bed sag gently and heard the bed-covers rustling as she pulled them over her. He turned his head and stared at the dim whites of her eyes in the darkness. Maybe, yes, maybe he could, maybe he could use her. He leaned and stretched himself on the bed beside her; she did not move. He put his hand upon her shoulder, pressing it just softly enough to let her know that he was thinking about her. His mind tried to grasp and encompass as much of her life as it could, tried to understand and weigh it in relation to his own, as his hand rested on her shoulder. Could he trust her? How much could he tell her? Would she act with him, blindly, believing his word?

"Come on. Let's get dressed and go out and get something to drink," she said.

"O.K."

"You ain't acting like you always act tonight."

"I got something on my mind."

"Can't you tell me?"

"I don't know."

"Don't you trust me?"

"Sure."

"Then why don't you tell me?"

He did not answer. Her voice had come in a whisper, a whisper he had heard many times when she wanted something badly. It brought to him a full sense of her life, what he had been thinking and feeling when he had placed his hand upon her shoulder. The same deep realization he had had that morning at home at the breakfast table while watching Vera and Buddy and his mother came back to him; only it was Bessie he was looking at now and seeing how blind she was. He felt the narrow orbit of her life: from her room to the kitchen of the white folks was the farthest she ever moved. She worked long hours, hard and hot hours seven days a week, with only Sunday afternoons off; and when she did get off she wanted fun, hard and fast fun, something to make her feel that she was making up for the starved life she led. It was her hankering for sensation that he liked about her. Most nights she was too tired to go out; she only wanted to get drunk. She wanted liquor and he wanted her. So he would give her the liquor and she would give him herself. He had heard her complain about how hard the white folks worked her; she had told him over and over again that she lived their lives when she was working in their homes, not her own. That was why, she told him, she drank. He knew why she liked him; he gave her money for drinks. He knew that if he did not give it to her someone else would; she would see to that. Bessie, too, was very blind. What ought he tell her? She might come in just handy. Then he realized that whatever he chose to tell her ought not to be anything that would make her feel in any way out of it; she ought to be made to feel that she knew it all. Goddamn! He just simply could not get used to acting like he ought. He should not have made her think that something was happening that he did not want her to know.

"Give me time, honey, and I'll tell you," he said, trying to straighten things out.

"You don't have to unless you want to."

"Don't be that way."

"You just can't treat me any old way, Bigger."

"I ain't trying to, honey."

"You can't play me cheap."

"Take it easy. I know what I'm doing."

"I hope you do."

"For Chrissakes!"

"Aw, come on. I want a drink."

"Naw; listen. . . ."

"Keep your business. You don't have to tell me. But don't you come running to me when you need a friend, see?"

"When we get a couple of drinks, I'll tell you all about it."

"Suit yourself."

He saw her waiting at the door for him; he put on his coat and cap and they walked slowly down the stairs, saying nothing. It seemed warmer outside, as though it were going to snow again. The sky was low and dark. The wind blew. As he walked beside Bessie his feet sank into the soft snow. The streets were empty and silent, stretching before him white and clean under the vanishing glow of a long string of street lamps. As he walked he saw out of the corners of his eyes Bessie striding beside him, and it seemed that his mind could feel the soft swing of her body as it went forward. He yearned suddenly to be back in bed with her, feeling her body warm and pliant to his. But the look on her face was a hard and distant one; it separated him from her body by a great suggestion of space. He had not really wanted to go out with her tonight; but her questions and suspicions had made him say yes when she had wanted to go for a drink. As he walked beside her he felt that there were two Bessies: one a body that he had just had and wanted badly again; the other was in Bessie's face; it asked questions; it bargained and sold the other Bessie to advantage. He wished he could clench his fist and swing his arm and blot out, kill, sweep away the Bessie on Bessie's face and leave the other helpless and yielding before him. He would then gather her up and put her in his chest, his stomach, some place deep inside him, always keeping her there even when he slept, ate, talked; keeping her there just to feel and know that she was his to have and hold whenever he wanted to.

"Where we going?"

"Wherever you want to."

"Let's go to the Paris Grill."

"O.K."

They turned a corner and walked to the middle of the block to the grill, and went in. An automatic phonograph was playing. They went to a rear table. Bigger ordered two sloe gin fizzes. They sat silent, looking at each other, waiting. He saw Bessie's shoulders jerking in rhythm to the music. Would she help him? Well, he would ask her; he would frame the story so that she would not have to know everything. He knew that he should have asked her to dance, but the excitement that had hold of him would not let him. He was feeling different tonight from every other night; he did not need to dance and sing and clown over the floor in order to blot out a day and night of doing nothing. He was full of excitement. The waitress brought the drinks and Bessie lifted hers.

"Here's to you, even if you don't want to talk and even if you is acting queer."

"Bessie, I'm worried."

"Aw, come on and drink," she said.

"O.K."

They sipped.

"Bigger?"

"Hunh?"

"Can't I help you in what you doing?"

"Maybe."

"I want to."

"You trust me?"

"I have so far."

"I mean now?"

"Yes; if you tell me what to trust you for?"

"Maybe I can't do that."

"Then you don't trust me."

"It's got to be that way, Bessie."

"If I trusted you, would you tell me?"

"Maybe."

"Don't say 'maybe,' Bigger."

"Listen, honey," he said, not liking the way he was talking to her, but afraid of telling her outright. "The reason I'm acting this way is I got something big on."

"What?"

"It'll mean a lot of money."

"I wish you'd either tell me or quit talking about it."

They were silent; he saw Bessie drain her glass.

"I'm ready to go," she said.

"Aw. . . ."

"I want to get some sleep."

"You mad?"

"Maybe."

He did not want her to be that way. How could he make her stay? How much could he tell her? Could he make her trust him without telling everything? He suddenly felt she would come closer to him if he made her feel that he was in danger. That's it! Make her feel concerned about him.

"Maybe I'll have to get out of town soon," he said.

"The police?"

"Maybe."

"What you do?"

"I'm planning to do it now."

"But where you get that money?"

"Look, Bessie, if I had to leave town and wanted dough, would you help me if I split with you?"

"If you took me with you, you wouldn't have to split."

He was silent; he had not thought of Bessie's being with him. A woman was a dangerous burden when a man was running away. He had read of how men had been caught because of women, and he did not want that to happen to him. But, if, yes, but if he told her, yes, just enough to get her to work with him?

"O.K.," he said. "I'll say this much. I'll take you if you help me."

"You really mean that?"

"Sure."

"Then you going to tell me?"

Yes, he could dress the story up. Why even mention Jan? Why not tell it so that if she were ever questioned she would say the things that he wanted her to say, things that would help him? He lifted the glass and drained the liquor and set it down and leaned forward and toyed with the cigarette in his fingers. He spoke with bated breath.

"Listen, here's the dope, see? The gal where I'm working, the daughter of the old man who's rich, a millionaire, has done run off with a Red, see?"

"Eloped?"

"Hunh? Er. . . . Yeah; eloped."

"With a *Red*?"

"Yeah; one of them Communists."

"Oh! What's wrong with her?"

"Aw; she's crazy. Nobody don't know she's gone, so last night I took the money from her room, see?"

"Oh!"

"They don't know where she is."

"But what you going to do?"

"They don't know where she is," he said again.

"What you mean?"

He sucked his cigarette; he saw her looking at him, her black eyes wide with eager interest. He liked that look. In one way, he hated to tell her, because he wanted to keep her guessing. He wanted to take as long as possible in order to see that look of complete absorption upon her face. It made him feel alive and gave him a heightened sense of the value of himself.

"I got an idea," he said.

"Oh, Bigger, *tell* me!"

"Don't talk so loud!"

"Well, *tell* me!"

"They don't know where the girl is. They might think she's kidnapped, see?" His whole body was tense and as he spoke his lips trembled.

"Oh, that was what you was so excited about when I told you about Loeb and Leopold. . . ."

"Well, what you think?"

"Would they *really* think she's kidnapped?"

"We can *make* 'em think it."

She looked into her empty glass. Bigger beckoned the waitress and ordered two more drinks. He took a deep swallow and said,

"The gal's gone, see? They don't know where she is. Don't nobody know. But they might think somebody did if they was told, see?"

"You mean. . . . You mean we could say *we* did it? You mean write to 'em. . . ."

". . . . and ask for money, sure," he said. "And get it, too. You see, we cash in, 'cause nobody else is trying to."

"But suppose she shows up?"

"She won't."

"How you know?"

"I just know she won't."

"Bigger, you *know* something about that girl. You know where she is?"

"That's all right about where she is. I know we won't have to worry about her showing up, see?"

"Oh, Bigger, this is *crazy*!"

"Then, hell, we won't talk about it no more!"

"Oh, I don't mean that."

"Then what *do* you mean?"

"I mean we got to be careful."

"We can get ten thousand dollars."

"How?"

"We can have 'em leave the money somewhere. They'll think they can get the girl back. . . ."

"Bigger, you know where that girl is?" she said, giving her voice a tone of half-question and half-statement.

"Naw."

"Then it'll be in the papers. She'll show up."

"She won't."

"How you know?"

"She just won't."

He saw her lips moving, then heard her speak softly, leaning toward him.

"Bigger, you ain't done nothing to that girl, is you?"

He stiffened with fear. He felt suddenly that he wanted something in his hand, something solid and heavy: his gun, a knife, a brick.

"If you say that again, I'll slap you back from this table!"

"Oh!"

"Come on, now. Don't be a fool."

"Bigger, you oughtn't've done it. . . ."

"You going to help me? Say yes or no."

"Gee, Bigger. . . ."

"You scared? You scared after letting me take that silver from Mrs. Heard's home? After letting me get Mrs. Macy's radio? You scared now?"

"I don't know."

"You wanted me to tell you; well, I told you. That's a woman, always. You want to know something, then you run like a rabbit."

"But we'll get *caught*."

"Not if we do right."

"But how could we do it, Bigger?"

"I'll figure it out."

"But I want to know."

"It'll be easy."

"But how?"

"I can fix it so you can pick up the money and nobody'll bother you."

"They catch people who do things like that."

"If you scared they *will* catch you."

"How could I pick up the money?"

"We'll tell 'em where to leave it."

"But they'll have police watching."

"Not if they want the gal back. We got a club over 'em, see? And I'll be watching, too. I work in the house where they live. If they try to doublecross us, I'll let you know."

"You reckon we could do it?"

"We could have 'em throw the money out of a car. You could be in some spot to see if they send anybody to watch. If you see anybody around, then you don't touch the money, see? But they want the gal; they won't watch."

There was a long silence.

"Bigger, I don't know," she said.

"We could go to New York, to Harlem, if we had money. New York's a real town. We could lay low for awhile."

"But suppose they mark the money?"

"They won't. And if they do, I'll tell you. You see, I'm right there in the house."

"But if we run off, they'll think we did it. They'll be looking for us for years, Bigger. . . ."

"We won't run right away. We'll lay low for awhile."

"I don't know, Bigger."

He felt satisfied; he could tell by the way she looked that if he pushed her hard enough she would come in with him. She was afraid and he could handle her through her fear. He looked at his watch; it was getting late. He ought to go back and have a look at that furnace.

"Listen, I got to go."

He paid the waitress and they went out. There was another way to bind her to him. He drew forth the roll of bills, peeled off one for himself, and held out the rest of the money toward her.

"Here," he said. "Get you something and save the rest for me."

"Oh!"

She looked at the money and hesitated.

"Don't you want it?"

"Yeah," she said, taking the roll.

"If you string along with me you'll get plenty more."

They stopped in front of her door; he stood looking at her.

"Well," he said. "What you think?"

"Bigger, honey. I—I don't know," she said plaintively.

"You wanted me to tell you."

"I'm scared."

"Don't you trust me?"

"But we ain't never done nothing like this before. They'll

look everywhere for us for something like this. It ain't like coming to where I work at night when the white folks is gone out of town and stealing something. It ain't. . . ."

"It's up to you."

"I'm scared, Bigger."

"Who on earth'll think *we* did it?"

"I don't know. You really think they don't know where the girl is?"

"I know they don't."

"*You* know?"

"Naw."

"She'll turn up."

"She won't. And, anyhow, she's a crazy girl. They might even think she's in it herself, just to get money from her family. They might think the Reds is doing it. They won't think *we* did. They don't think we got enough guts to do it. They think niggers is too scared. . . ."

"I don't know."

"Did I ever tell you wrong?"

"Naw; but we ain't never done nothing like this before."

"Well, I ain't wrong now."

"When do you want to do it?"

"Soon as they begin to worry about the gal."

"You really reckon we could?"

"I told you what I think."

"Naw; Bigger! I ain't going to do it. I think you. . . ."

He turned abruptly and walked away from her.

"Bigger!"

She ran over the snow and tugged at his sleeve. He stopped, but did not turn round. She caught his coat and pulled him about. Under the yellow sheen of a street lamp they confronted each other, silently. All about them was the white snow and the night; they were cut off from the world and were conscious only of each other. He looked at her without expression, waiting. Her eyes were fastened fearfully and distrustfully upon his face. He held his body in an attitude that suggested that he was delicately balanced upon a hairline, waiting to see if she would push him forward or draw him back. Her lips smiled faintly and she lifted her hand and touched his face with her fingers. He knew that she was fighting out in her feelings the question of just how much he meant to her. She grabbed his hand and squeezed it, telling him in the pressure of her fingers that she wanted him.

"But, Bigger, honey. . . . Let's don't do that. We getting along all right like we is now. . . ."

He drew his hand away.

"I'm going," he said.

"When I'll see you, honey?"

"I don't know."

He started off again and she overtook him and encircled him with her arms.

"Bigger, honey. . . ."

"Come on, Bessie. What you going to do?"

She looked at him with round, helpless black eyes. He was still poised, wondering if she would pull him toward her, or let him fall alone. He was enjoying her agony, seeing and feeling the worth of himself in her bewildered desperation. Her lips trembled and she began to cry.

"What you going to do?" he asked again.

"If I do it, it's 'cause you want me to," she sobbed.

He put his arm about her shoulders.

"Come on, Bessie," he said. "Don't cry."

She stopped and dried her eyes; he looked at her closely. She'll do it, he thought.

"I got to go," he said.

"I ain't going in right now."

"Where you going?"

He found that he was afraid of what she did, now that she was working with him. His peace of mind depended upon knowing what she did and why.

"I'm going to get a pint."

That was all right; she was feeling as he knew she always felt.

"Well, I'll see you tomorrow night, hunh?"

"O.K., honey. But be careful."

"Look, Bessie, don't you worry none. Just trust me. No matter what happens, they won't catch us. And they won't even know you had anything to do with it."

"If they start after us, where could we hide, Bigger? You know we's black. We can't go just *any*where."

He looked round the lamp-lit, snow-covered street.

"There's plenty of places," he said. "I know the South Side from A to Z. We could even hide out in one of those old buildings, see? Like I did last time. Nobody ever looks into 'em."

He pointed across the street to a black, looming empty apartment building.

"Well," she sighed.

"I'm going," he said.

"So long, honey."

He walked toward the car line; when he looked back he saw her still standing in the snow; she had not moved. She'll be all right, he thought. She'll go along.

Snow was falling again; the streets were long paths leading through a dense jungle, lit here and there with torches held high in invisible hands. He waited ten minutes for a car and none came. He turned the corner and walked, his head down, his hands dug into his pockets, going to Dalton's.

He was confident. During the last day and night new fears had come, but new feelings had helped to allay those fears. The moment when he had stood above Mary's bed and found that she was dead the fear of electrocution had entered his flesh and blood. But at home at the breakfast table with his mother and sister and brother, seeing how blind they were; and overhearing Peggy and Mrs. Dalton talking in the kitchen, a new feeling had been born in him, a feeling that all but blotted out the fear of death. As long as he moved carefully and knew what he was about, he could handle things, he thought. As long as he could take his life into his own hands and dispose of it as he pleased, as long as he could decide just when and where he would run to, he need not be afraid.

He felt that he had his destiny in his grasp. He was more alive than he could ever remember having been; his mind and attention were pointed, focused toward a goal. For the first time in his life he moved consciously between two sharply defined poles: he was moving away from the threatening penalty of death, from the deathlike times that brought him that tightness and hotness in his chest; and he was moving toward that sense of fulness he had so often but inadequately felt in magazines and movies.

The shame and fear and hate which Mary and Jan and Mr. Dalton and that huge rich house had made rise so hard and hot in him had now cooled and softened. Had he not done what they thought he never could? His being black and at the bottom of the world was something which he could take with a new-born strength. What his knife and gun had once meant to him, his knowledge of having secretly murdered Mary now meant. No matter how they laughed at him for his being black and clownlike, he could look them in the eyes and not feel angry. The feeling of being always enclosed in the stifling embrace of an invisible force had gone from him.

As he turned into Drexel Boulevard and headed toward Dalton's, he thought of how restless he had been, how he was consumed always with a body hunger. Well, in a way he had settled that tonight; as time passed he would make it more definite. His body felt free and easy now that he had lain with Bessie. That she would do what he wanted was what he had sealed in asking her to work with him in this thing. She would be bound to him by ties deeper than marriage. She would be his; her fear of capture and death would bind her to him with all the strength of her life; even as what he had done last night had bound him to this new path with all the strength of his own life.

He turned off the sidewalk and walked up the Dalton driveway, went into the basement and looked through the bright cracks of the furnace door. He saw a red heap of seething coals and heard the upward hum of the draft. He pulled the lever, hearing the rattle of coal against tin and seeing the quivering embers grow black. He shut off the coal and stooped and opened the bottom door of the furnace. Ashes were piling up. He would have to take the shovel and clean them out in the morning and make sure that no unburnt bones were left. He had closed the door and started to the rear of the furnace, going to his room, when he heard Peggy's voice.

"Bigger!"

He stopped and before answering he felt a keen sensation of excitement flush over all his skin. She was standing at the head of the stairs, in the door leading to the kitchen.

"Yessum."

He went to the bottom of the steps and looked upward.

"Mrs. Dalton wants you to pick up the trunk at the station. . . ."

"The *trunk*?"

He waited for Peggy to answer his surprised question. Perhaps he should not have asked it in that way?

"They called up and said that no one had claimed it. And Mr. Dalton got a wire from Detroit. Mary never got there."

"Yessum."

She came all the way down the stairs and looked round the basement, as though seeking some missing detail. He stiffened; if she saw something that would make her ask him about Mary he would take the iron shovel and let her have it straight across her head and then take the car and make a quick getaway.

"Mr. Dalton's worried," Peggy said. "You know, Mary didn't pack the new clothes she bought to take with her on the trip. And poor Mrs. Dalton's been pacing the floor and phoning Mary's friends all day."

"Don't nobody know where she is?" Bigger asked.

"*No*body. Did Mary tell you to take the trunk like it *was*?"

"Yessum," he said, knowing that this was the first hard hurdle. "It was locked and standing in a corner. I took it down and put it right where you saw it this morning."

"Oh, Peggy!" Mrs. Dalton's voice called.

"Yes!" Peggy answered.

Bigger looked up and saw Mrs. Dalton at the head of the stairs, standing in white as usual and with her face tilted trustingly upward.

"Is the boy back yet?"

"He's down here now, Mrs. Dalton."

"Come in the kitchen a moment, will you, Bigger?" she asked.

"Yessum."

He followed Peggy into the ktichen. Mrs. Dalton had her hands clasped tightly in front of her and her face was still tilted, higher now, and her white lips were parted.

"Peggy told you about picking up the trunk?"

"Yessum. I'm on my way now."

"What time did you leave here last night?"

"A little before two, mam."

"And she told you to take the trunk down?"

"Yessum."

"And she told you not to put the car up?"

"Yessum."

"And it was just where you left it last night when you came this morning?"

"Yessum."

Mrs. Dalton turned her head as she heard the inner kitchen door open; Mr. Dalton stood in the doorway.

"Hello, Bigger."

"Good day, suh."

"How are things?"

"Fine, suh."

"The station called about the trunk a little while ago. You'll have to pick it up."

"Yessuh. I'm on my way now, suh."

"Listen, Bigger. What happened last night?"

"Well, nothing, suh. Miss Dalton told me to take the trunk down so I could take it to the station this morning; and I did."

"Was Jan *with* you?"

"Yessuh. All three of us went upstairs when I brought 'em in in the car. We went to the room to get the trunk. Then I took it down and put it in the basement."

"Was Jan drunk?"

"Well, I don't know, suh. They was drinking. . . ."

"And what happened?"

"Nothing, suh. I just took the trunk to the basement and left. Miss Dalton told me to leave the car out. She said Mr. Jan would take care of it."

"What were they talking about?"

Bigger hung his head.

"I don't know, suh."

He saw Mrs. Dalton lift her right hand and he knew that she meant for Mr. Dalton to stop questioning him so closely. He felt her shame.

"That's all right, Bigger," Mrs. Dalton said. She turned to Mr. Dalton. "Where do you suppose this Jan would be now?"

"Maybe he's at the Labor Defender office."

"Can you get in touch with him?"

"Well," said Mr. Dalton, standing near Bigger and looking hard at the floor. "I could. But I'd rather wait. I still think Mary's up to some of her foolish pranks. Bigger, you'd better get that trunk."

"Yessuh."

He got the car and drove through the falling snow toward the Loop. In answering their questions he felt that he had succeeded in turning their minds definitely in the direction of Jan. If things went at this pace he would have to send the ransom note right away. He would see Bessie tomorrow and get things settled. Yes; he would ask for ten thousand dollars. He would have Bessie stand in the window of an old building at some well-lighted street corner with a flashlight. In the note he would tell Mr. Dalton to put the money in a shoe box and drop it in the snow at the curb; he would tell him to keep his car moving and his lights blinking and not to drop the money until he saw the flashlight blink three times in the window. . . . Yes; that's how it would be. Bessie would see the lights of Mr. Dalton's car blinking and after the car was gone she would pick up the box of money. It would be easy.

He pulled the car into the station, presented the ticket, got the trunk, hoisted it to the running board, and headed again for the Dalton home. When he reached the driveway the snow was falling so thickly that he could not see ten feet in front of him. He put the car into the garage, set the trunk in the snow, locked the garage door, lifted the trunk to his back and carried it to the entrance of the basement. Yes; the trunk was light; it was half-empty. No doubt they would question him again about that. Next time he would have to go into details and he would try to fasten hard in his mind the words he spoke so that he could repeat them a thousand times, if necessary. He could, of course, set the trunk in the snow right now and take a street car and get the money from Bessie and leave town. But why do that? He could handle this thing. It was going his way. They were not suspecting him and he would be able to tell the moment their minds turned in his direction. And, too, he was glad he had let Bessie keep that money. Suppose he were searched here on the job? For them to find money on him was alone enough to fasten suspicion upon him definitely. He unlocked the door and took the trunk inside; his back was bent beneath its weight and he walked slowly with his eyes on the wavering red shadows on the floor. He heard the fire singing in the furnace. He took the trunk to the corner in which he had placed it the night before. He put it down and stood looking at it. He had an impulse to open it and look inside. He stooped to fumble with the metal clasp, then started violently, jerking upright.

"Bigger!"

Without answering and before he realized what he was doing, he whirled, his eyes wide with fear and his hand half-raised, as though to ward off a blow. The moment of whirling brought him face to face with what seemed to his excited senses an army of white men. His breath stopped and he blinked his eyes in the red darkness, thinking that he should be acting more calmly. Then he saw Mr. Dalton and another white man standing at the far end of the basement; in the red shadows their faces were white discs of danger floating still in the air.

"Oh!" he said softly.

The white man at Mr. Dalton's side was squinting at him; he felt that tight, hot, choking fear returning. The white man clicked on the light. He had a cold, impersonal manner that told Bigger to be on his guard. In the very look of the man's eyes Bigger saw his own personality reflected in narrow, re-stricted terms.

"What's the matter, boy?" the man asked.

Bigger said nothing; he swallowed, caught hold of himself and came forward slowly. The white man's eyes were steadily upon him. Panic seized Bigger as he saw the white man lower his head, narrow his eyes still more, sweep back his coat and ram his hands into his pants' pockets, revealing as he did so a shining badge on his chest. Words rang in Bigger's mind: This is a cop! He could not take his eyes off the shining bit of metal. Abruptly, the man changed his attitude and expression, took his hands from his pocket and smiled a smile that Bigger did not believe.

"I'm not the law, boy. So don't be scared."

Bigger clamped his teeth; he had to control himself. He should not have let that man see him staring at his badge.

"Yessuh," he said.

"Bigger, this is Mr. Britten," Mr. Dalton said. "He's a private investigator attached to the staff of my office. . . ."

"Yessuh," Bigger said again, his tension slackening.

"He wants to ask you some questions. So just be calm and try to tell him whatever he wants to know."

"Yessuh."

"First of all, I want to have a look at that trunk," Britten said.

Bigger stood aside as they passed him. He glanced quickly at the furnace. It was still very hot, droning. Then he, too, went to the trunk, standing discreetly to one side, away from the two white men, looking with surface eyes at what they were doing. He shoved his hands deep into his pockets; he stood in a peculiar attitude that allowed him to respond at once to whatever they said or did and at the same time to be outside and away from them. He watched Britten turn the trunk over and bend to it and try to work the lock. I got to be careful, Bigger thought. One little slip now and I'll spoil the whole thing. Sweat came onto his neck and face. Britten could not unlock the trunk and he looked upward, at Bigger.

"It's locked. You got a key, boy?"

"Nawsuh."

Bigger wondered if this were a trap; he decided to play safe and speak only when he was spoken to.

"You mind if I break it?"

"Go right ahead," Mr. Dalton said. "Say, Bigger, get Mr. Britten the hatchet."

"Yessuh," he answered mechanically.

He thought rapidly, his entire body stiff. Should he tell them that the hatchet was somewhere in the house and offer to go after it and take the opportunity and run away? How much did they really suspect him? Was this whole thing a ruse to confuse and trap him? He glanced sharply and intently at their faces; they seemed to be waiting only for the hatchet. Yes; he would take a chance and stay; he would lie his way out of this. He turned and went to the spot where the hatchet had been last night, the spot from which he had taken it to cut off Mary's head. He stopped and pretended to search. Then he straightened.

"It ain't here now. . . . . I—I saw it about here yesterday," he mumbled.

"Well, never mind," Britten said. "I think I can manage."

Bigger eased back toward them, waiting, watching. Britten lifted his foot and gave the lock a short, stout kick with the heel of his shoe and it sprang open. He lifted out the tray and looked inside. It was half-empty and the clothes were disarrayed and tumbled.

"You see?" Mr. Dalton said. "She didn't take all of her things."

"Yes. In fact, she didn't need a trunk at all from the looks of this," Britten said.

"Bigger, was the trunk locked when she told you to take it down?" Mr. Dalton asked.

"Yessuh," Bigger said, wondering if that answer was the safest.

"Was she too drunk to know what she was doing, Bigger?"

"Well, they went into the room," he said. "I went in after them. Then she told me to take the trunk down. That's all happened."

"She could have put these things into a small suitcase," Britten said.

The fire sang in Bigger's ears and he saw the red shadows dance on the walls. Let them try to find out who did it! His teeth were clamped hard, until they ached.

"Sit down, Bigger," Britten said.

Bigger looked at Britten, feigning surprise.

"Sit on the trunk," Britten said.

"Me?"

"Yeah. Sit down."

He sat.

"Now, take your time and think hard. I want to ask you some questions."

"Yessuh."

"What time did you take Miss Dalton from here last night?"

"About eight-thirty, suh."

Bigger knew that this was it. This man was here to find out everything. This was an examination. He would have to point his answers away from himself quite definitely. He would have to tell his story. He would let each of the facts of his story fall slowly, as though he did not realize the significance of them. He would answer only what was asked.

"You drove her to school?"

He hung his head and did not answer.

"Come on, boy!"

"Well, mister, you see, I'm just working here. . . ."

"What do you mean?"

Mr. Dalton came close and looked hard into his face.

"Answer his questions, Bigger."

"Yessuh."

"You drove her to school?" Britten asked again.

Still, he did not answer.

"I asked you a question, boy!"

"Nawsuh. I didn't drive her to school."

"Where did you take her?"

"Well, suh. She told me, after I got as far as the park, to turn round and take her to the Loop."

"She didn't go to *school?*" Mr. Dalton asked, his lips hanging open in surprise.

"Nawsuh."

"Why didn't you tell me this before, Bigger?"

"She told me not to."

There was silence. The furnace droned. Huge red shadows swam across the walls.

"Where did you take her, then?" Britten asked.

"To the Loop, suh."

"Whereabouts in the Loop?"

"To Lake Street, suh."

"Do you remember the number?"

"Sixteen, I think, suh."

"Sixteen Lake Street?"

"Yessuh."

"That's the Labor Defender office," Mr. Dalton said, turning to Britten. "This Jan's a Red."

"How long was she in there?" Britten asked.

"About half-hour, I reckon, suh."

"Then what happened?"

"Well, I waited in the car. . . ."

"She stayed there till *you* brought her home?"

"Nawsuh."

"She came out. . . ."

"*They* came out. . . ."

"This man Jan was with her, then?"

"Yessuh. He was with her. Seems to me she went in there to get him. She didn't say anything; she just went in and stayed awhile and then came out with him."

"Then you drove 'em. . . ."

"*He* drove," Bigger said.

"Weren't *you* driving?"

"Yessuh. But he wanted to drive and she told me to let him."

There was another silence. They wanted him to draw the picture and he would draw it like he wanted it. He was trembling with excitement. In the past had they not always drawn the picture for him? He could tell them anything he wanted and what could they do about it? It was his word against Jan's, and Jan was a Red.

"You waited somewhere for 'em?" Britten asked; the tone of curt hostility had suddenly left his voice.

"Nawsuh. I was in the car. . . ."

"And where did they go?"

He wanted to tell of how they had made him sit between them; but he thought that he would tell that later on, when he was telling how Jan and Mary had made him feel.

"Well, Mr. Jan asked me where was a good place to eat. The only one I knew about where white folks," he said "white folks" very slowly, so that they would know that he was conscious of what was meant, "ate on the South Side was Ernie's Kitchen Shack."

"You took them there?"

"Mr. Jan drove the car, suh."

"How long did they stay there?"

"Well, we must've stayed. . . ."

"Weren't you waiting in the car?"

"Nawsuh. You see, mister, I did what they told me. I was only working for 'em. . . ."

"Oh!" Britten said. "I suppose he made you *eat* with 'im?"

"I didn't want to, mister. I swear I didn't. He kept worrying me till I went in."

Britten walked away from the trunk, running the fingers of his left hand nervously through his hair. Again he turned to Bigger.

"They got drunk, hunh?"

"Yessuh. They was drinking."

"What did this Jan say to you?"

"He talked about the Communists. . . ."

"How much did they drink?"

"It seemed like a lot to me, suh."

"Then you brought 'em home?"

"I drove 'em through the park, suh."

"*Then* you brought 'em home?"

"Yessuh. That was nearly two."

"How drunk was Miss Dalton?"

"Well, she couldn't hardly stand up, suh. When we got home, he had to lift her up the steps," Bigger said with lowered eyes.

"That's all right, boy. You can talk to us about it," Britten said. "Just how drunk was she?"

"She passed out," Bigger said.

Britten looked at Dalton.

"She could not have left this house by herself," Britten said. "If Mrs. Dalton's right, then she could *not* have left." Britten stared at Bigger and Bigger felt that some deeper question was on Britten's mind.

"What else happened?"

He would shoot now; he would let them have some of it.

"Well, I told you Miss Dalton told me to take the trunk. I said that 'cause she told me not to tell about me taking her to the Loop. It was Mr. Jan who told me to take the trunk down and not put the car away."

"*He* told you not to put the car away and to take the trunk?"

"Yessuh. That's right."

"Why didn't you tell us this before, Bigger?" asked Mr. Dalton.

"She told me not to, suh."

"How was this Jan acting?" Britten asked.

"He was drunk," said Bigger, feeling that now was the time to drag Jan in definitely. "Mr. Jan was the one who told me to take the trunk down and leave the car in the snow. I told you Miss Dalton told me that, but he told me. I would've been giving the whole thing away if I had told about Mr. Jan."

Britten walked toward the furnace and back again; the furnace droned as before. Bigger hoped that no one would try to look into it now; his throat grew dry. Then he started nervously as Britten whirled and pointed his finger into his face.

"What did he say about the Party?"

"Suh?"

"Aw, come on, boy! Don't stall! Tell me what he said about the Party!"

"The party? He asked me to sit at his table. . . ."

"I mean the *Party!*"

"It wasn't a party, mister. He made me sit at his table and he bought chicken and told me to eat. I didn't want to, but he made me and it was my job."

Britten came close to Bigger and narrowed his grey eyes.

"What unit are you in?"

"Suh?"

"Come on, *Comrade*, tell me what unit you are in?"

Bigger gazed at him, speechless, alarmed.

"Who's your organizer?"

"I don't know what you mean," Bigger said, his voice quavering.

"Don't you read the *Daily?*"

"Daily what?"

"Didn't you know Jan before you came to work here?"

"Nawsuh. *Naw*suh!"

"Didn't they send you to Russia?"

Bigger stared and did not answer. He knew now that Britten was trying to find out if he were a Communist. It was something he had not counted on, ever. He stood up, trembling. He had not thought that this thing could cut two ways. Slowly, he shook his head and backed away.

"Nawsuh. You got me wrong. I ain't never fooled around with them folks. Miss Dalton and Mr. Jan was the first ones I ever met, so help me God!"

Britten followed Bigger till Bigger's head struck the wall. Bigger looked squarely into his eyes. Britten, with a movement so fast that Bigger did not see it, grabbed him in the

collar and rammed his head hard against the wall. He saw a
flash of red.

"You *are* a Communist, *you goddamn* black sonofabitch!
And you're going to tell me about Miss Dalton and that Jan
bastard!"

"*Naw*suh! I ain't no Communist! *Naw*suh!"

"Well, what's *this?*" Britten jerked from his pocket the small
packet of pamphlets that Bigger had put in his dresser drawer,
and held them under his eyes. "You know you're lying! Come
on, talk!"

"Nawsuh! You got me wrong! Mr. Jan gave me them
things! He and Miss Dalton told me to read 'em. . . ."

"Didn't you know Miss Dalton before?"

"Nawsuh!"

"Wait, Britten!" Mr. Dalton laid his hand on Britten's
arm. "Wait. There's something to what he says. She tried to
talk to him about unions when she first saw him yesterday. If
that Jan gave him those pamphlets, then he knows nothing
about it."

"You're sure?"

"I'm positive. I thought at first, when you brought me
those pamphlets, that he must have known something. But I
don't think he does. And there's no use blaming him for
something he didn't do."

Britten loosened his fingers from Bigger's collar and
shrugged his shoulders. Bigger relaxed, still standing, his
head resting against the wall, aching. He had not thought
that anyone would dare think that he, a black Negro, would
be Jan's partner. Britten was his enemy. He knew that the
hard light in Britten's eyes held him guilty because he was
black. He hated Britten so hard and hot, while standing there
with sleepy eyes and parted lips, that he would gladly have
grabbed the iron shovel from the corner and split his skull in
two. For a split second a roaring noise in his ears blotted out
sound. He struggled to control himself; then he heard Britten
talking.

". . . . got to get hold of that Jan."

"That seems to be the next thing," said Mr. Dalton,
sighing.

Bigger felt that if he said something directly to Mr. Dalton, he could swing things round again in his favor; but he did not know just how to put it.

"You suppose she ran off?" he heard Britten ask.

"I don't know," Mr. Dalton said.

Britten turned to Bigger and looked at him; Bigger kept his eyes down.

"Boy, I just want to know, are you telling the truth?"

"Yessuh. I'm telling the truth. I just started to work here last night. I ain't done nothing. I did just what they told me to do."

"You sure he's all right?" Britten asked Dalton.

"He's all right."

"If you don't want me to work for you, Mr. Dalton," Bigger said, "I'll go home. I didn't want to come here," he continued, feeling that his words would awaken in Mr. Dalton a sense of why he was here, "but they sent me anyhow."

"That's true," Mr. Dalton told Britten. "He's referred to me from the relief. He's been in a reform school and I'm giving him a chance. . . ." Mr. Dalton turned to Bigger. "Just forget it, Bigger. We had to make sure. Stay on and do your work. I'm sorry this had to happen. Don't let it break you down."

"Yessuh."

"O.K.," said Britten. "If you say he's O.K., then it's O.K. with me."

"Go on to your room, Bigger," said Mr. Dalton.

"Yessuh."

Head down, he walked to the rear of the furnace and upstairs into his room. He turned the latch on the door and hurried to the closet to listen. The voices came clearly. Britten and Mr. Dalton had come into the kitchen.

"My, but it was hot down there," said Mr. Dalton.

"Yes."

". . . . I'm a little sorry you bothered him. He's here to try to get a new slant on things."

"Well, you see 'em one way and I see 'em another. To me, a nigger's a nigger."

"But he's sort of a problem boy. He's not really bad."

"You got to be rough with 'em, Dalton. See how I got that dope out of 'im? He wouldn't've told you that."

"But I don't want to make a mistake here. It wasn't his fault. He was doing what that crazy daughter of mine told him. I don't want to do anything I'll regret. After all, these black boys never get a chance. . . ."

"They don't need a chance, if you ask me. They get in enough trouble without it."

"Well, as long as they do their work, let's let 'em be."

"Just as you say. You want me to stay on the job?"

"Sure. We must see this Jan. I can't understand Mary's going away and not saying anything."

"I can have 'im picked up."

"No, no! Not that way. Those Reds'll get hold of it and they'll raise a stink in the papers."

"Well, what do you want me to do?"

"I'll try to get 'im to come here. I'll phone his office, and if he's not there I'll phone his home."

Bigger heard their footsteps dying away. A door slammed and then all was quiet. He came out of the closet and looked in the dresser drawer where he had put the pamphlets. Yes, Britten had searched his room; his clothes were mussed and tumbled. He would know how to handle Britten next time. Britten was familiar to him; he had met a thousand Brittens in his life. He stood in the center of the room, thinking. When Britten questioned Jan, would Jan deny having been with Mary at all, in order to protect her? If he did, that would be in his favor. If Britten wanted to check on his story about Mary's not going to school last night, he could. If Jan said that they had not been drinking it could be proved that they had been drinking by folks in the café. If Jan lied about one thing, it would be readily believed that he would lie about others. If Jan said that he had not come to the house, who would believe him after it was seen that he had lied about his not drinking and about Mary's going to school? If Jan tried to protect Mary, as he thought he would, he would only succeed in making a case against himself.

Bigger went to the window and looked out at the white curtain of falling snow. He thought of the kidnap note. Should he try to get money from them now? Hell, yes! He would show that Britten bastard! He would work fast. But he would wait until after Jan had told his story. He should see

Bessie tonight. And he ought to pick out the pencil and paper he would use. And he must not forget to use gloves when he wrote the note so that no fingerprints would be on the paper. He'd give that Britten something to worry about, all right. Just wait.

Because he could go now, run off if he wanted to and leave it all behind, he felt a certain sense of power, a power born of a latent capacity to live. He was conscious of this quiet, warm, clean, rich house, this room with this bed so soft, the wealthy white people moving in luxury to all sides of him, whites living in a smugness, a security, a certainty that he had never known. The knowledge that he had killed a white girl they loved and regarded as their symbol of beauty made him feel the equal of them, like a man who had been somehow cheated, but had now evened the score.

The more the sense of Britten seeped into him the more did he feel the need to face him once again and let him try to get something from him. Next time he would do better; he had let Britten trap him on that Communist business. He should have been on the lookout for that; but the lucky thing was that he knew that Britten had done all his tricks at once, had shot his bolt, had played all his cards. Now that the thing was out in the open, he would know how to act. And furthermore, Britten might want him as a witness against Jan. He smiled while he lay in the darkness. If that happened, he would be safe in sending the ransom note. He could send it just when they thought they had pinned the disappearance of Mary upon Jan. That would throw everything into confusion and would make them want to reply and give the money at once and save the girl.

The warm room lulled his blood and a deepening sense of fatigue drugged him with sleep. He stretched out more fully on the bed, sighed, turned on his back, swallowed, and closed his eyes. Out of the surrounding silence and darkness came the quiet ringing of a distant church bell, thin, faint, but clear. It tolled, soft, then loud, then still louder, so loud that he wondered where it was. It sounded suddenly directly above his head and when he looked it was not there but went on tolling and with each passing moment he felt an urgent need to run and hide as though the bell were sounding a warning and he stood on a street corner in a red glare of light like that which came from the furnace and he had a big package in his arms so wet and slippery and heavy that he could scarcely hold onto it and he wanted to know what was in the package and he stopped near an alley corner and unwrapped it and the paper fell away and he saw—it was his *own* head—his own head lying with black face and half-closed eyes and lips parted with white teeth showing and hair wet with blood and the red glare grew brighter like light shining down from a red moon and red stars on a hot summer night and he was sweating and breathless from running and the bell clanged so loud that he could hear the iron tongue clapping against the metal sides each time it swung to and fro and he was running over a street paved with black coal and his shoes kicked tiny lumps rattling against tin cans and he knew that very soon he had to find some place to hide but there was no place and in front of him white people were coming to ask about the head from which the newspapers had fallen and which was now slippery with blood in his naked hands and he gave up and stood in the middle of the street in the red darkness and cursed the booming bell and the white people and felt that he did not give a damn what happened to him and when the people closed in he hurled the bloody head squarely into their faces *dongdongdong*. . . .

He opened his eyes and looked about him in the darkened room, hearing a bell ring. He sat up. The bell sounded again. How long had it been ringing? He got to his feet, swaying from stiffness, trying to shake off sleep and that awful dream.

"Yessum," he mumbled.

The bell rang again, insistently. He fumbled in the dark for the light chain and pulled it. Excitement quickened within him. Had something happened? Was this the police?

"Bigger!" a muffled voice called.

"Yessuh."

He braced himself for whatever was coming and stepped to the door. As he opened it he felt it being pushed in by some-one who seemed determined to get in in a hurry. Bigger backed away, blinking his eyes.

"We want to talk to you," said Britten.

"Yessuh."

He did not hear what Britten said after that, for he saw directly behind Britten a face that made him hold his breath. It was not fear he felt, but a tension, a supreme gathering of all the forces of his body for a showdown.

"Go on in, Mr. Erlone," Mr. Dalton said.

Bigger saw Jan's eyes looking at him steadily. Jan stepped into the room and Mr. Dalton followed. Bigger stood with his lips slightly parted, his hands hanging loosely by his sides, his eyes watchful, but veiled.

"Sit down, Erlone," Britten said.

"This is all right," Jan said. "I'll stand."

Bigger saw Britten pull from his coat pocket the packet of pamphlets and hold them under Jan's eyes. Jan's lips twisted into a faint smile.

"Well," Jan said.

"You're one of those tough Reds, hunh?" Britten asked.

"Come on. Let's get this over with," Jan said. "What do you want?"

"Take it easy," Britten said. "You got plenty of time. I know your kind. You like to rush and have things your way."

Bigger saw Mr. Dalton standing to one side, looking anxiously from one to the other. Several times Mr. Dalton made as if to say something, then checked himself, as though uncertain.

"Bigger," Britten asked, "is this the man Miss Dalton brought here last night?"

Jan's lips parted. He stared at Britten, then at Bigger.

"Yessuh," Bigger whispered, struggling to control his feelings, hating Jan violently because he knew he was hurting him; wanting to strike Jan with something because Jan's wide, incredulous stare made him feel hot guilt to the very core of him.

"You didn't bring me here, Bigger!" Jan said. "Why do you tell them that?"

Bigger did not answer; he decided to talk only to Britten and Mr. Dalton. There was silence. Jan was staring at Bigger; Britten and Mr. Dalton were watching Jan. Jan made a move toward Bigger, but Britten's arm checked him.

"Say, what *is* this!" Jan demanded. "What're you making this boy lie for?"

"I suppose you're going to tell us you weren't drunk last night, hunh?" asked Britten.

"What business is that of yours?" Jan shot at him.

"Where's Miss Dalton?" Britten asked.

Jan looked round the room, puzzled.

"She's in Detroit," he said.

"You know your story by heart, don't you?" Britten said.

"Say, Bigger, what're they doing to you? Don't be afraid. Speak *up*!" said Jan.

Bigger did not answer; he looked stonily at the floor.

"Where did Miss Dalton tell you she was going?" Britten asked.

"She told me she was going to Detroit."

"Did you see her last night?"

Jan hesitated.

"No."

"You didn't give these pamphlets to this boy last night?"

Jan shrugged his shoulders, smiled and said:

"All right. I saw her. So what? You know why I didn't say so in the first place. . . ."

"No. We *don't* know," Britten said.

"Well, Mr. Dalton here doesn't like Reds, as you call 'em, and I didn't want to get Miss Dalton in trouble."

"Then, you *did* meet her last night?"

"Yes."

"Where is she?"

"If she's not in Detroit, then I don't know where she is."

"You gave these pamphlets to this boy?"

"Yes; I did."

"You and Miss Dalton were drunk last night. . . ."

"Aw, come on! We weren't drunk. We had a little to drink. . . ."

"You brought her home about two?"

Bigger stiffened and waited.

"Yeah."

"You told the boy to take her trunk down to the basement?"

Jan opened his mouth, but no words came. He looked at Bigger, then back to Britten.

"Say, what is this?"

"Where's my daughter, Mr. Erlone?" Mr. Dalton asked.

"I tell you I don't know."

"Listen, let's be frank, Mr. Erlone," said Mr. Dalton. "We know my daughter was drunk last night when you brought her here. She was too drunk to leave here by herself. Do you know where she is?"

"I—I didn't come here last night," Jan stammered.

Bigger sensed that Jan had said that he had come home with Mary last night in order to make Mr. Dalton believe that he would not have left his daughter alone in a car with a strange chauffeur. And Bigger felt that after Jan admitted that they had been drinking, he was bound to say that he had brought the girl home. Unwittingly, Jan's desire to protect Mary had helped him. Jan's denial of having come to the home would not be believed now; it would make Mr. Dalton and Britten feel that he was trying to cover up something of even much greater seriousness.

"You didn't come *home* with her?" Mr. Dalton asked.

"No!"

"You didn't tell the boy to take the trunk down?"

"Hell, no! Who says I did? I left the car and took a trolley home." Jan turned and faced Bigger. "Bigger, what're you telling these people?"

Bigger did not answer.

"He's just told us what you did last night," Britten said.

"Where's Mary. . . . Where's Miss Dalton?" Jan asked.

"We're waiting for you to tell us," said Britten.

"D-d-didn't she go to Detroit?" Jan stammered.

"No," said Mr. Dalton.

"I called her this morning and Peggy told me she had."

"You called her just to see if the family had missed her, didn't you?" asked Britten.

Jan walked over to Bigger.

"Leave 'im alone!" Britten said.

"Bigger," Jan said, "why did you tell these men I came here?"

"You say you didn't come here at *all* last night?" Mr. Dalton asked again.

"Absolutely not. Bigger, *tell* 'em when I left the car."

Bigger said nothing.

"Come on, Erlone. I don't know what you're up to, but you've been lying ever since you've been in this room. You said you didn't come here last night, and then you say you did. You said you weren't drunk last night, then you say you were. You said you didn't see Miss Dalton last night, then you say you did. Come on, now. Tell us where Miss Dalton is. Her father and mother want to know."

Bigger saw Jan's bewildered eyes.

"Listen, I've told you all I know," said Jan, putting his hat back on. "Unless you tell me what this joke's all about, I'm getting on back home. . . ."

"Wait a minute," said Mr. Dalton.

Mr. Dalton came forward a step, and fronted Jan.

"You and I don't agree. Let's forget that. I want to know where my daughter is. . . ."

"Is this a game?" asked Jan.

"No; no. . . ." said Mr. Dalton. "I want to know. I'm worried. . . ."

"I tell you, I don't know!"

"Listen, Mr. Erlone. Mary's the only girl we've got. I don't want her to do anything rash. Tell her to come back. Or you bring her back."

"Mr. Dalton, I'm telling you the truth. . . ."

"Listen," Mr. Dalton said. "I'll make it all right with you. . . ."

Jan's face reddened.

"What do you mean?" he asked.

"I'll make it worth your while. . . ."

"You son. . . ." Jan stopped. He walked to the door.

"Let 'im go," said Britten. "He can't get away. I'll phone and have 'im picked up. He knows more than he's telling. . . ."

Jan paused in the doorway, looking at all three of them. Then he went out. Bigger sat on the edge of the bed and heard Jan's feet run down the stairs. A door slammed; then silence. Bigger saw Mr. Dalton gazing at him queerly. He did not like that look. But Britten was jotting something on a pad, his face pale and hard in the yellow glare of the suspended electric bulb.

"You're telling us the truth about all this, aren't you, Bigger?" Mr. Dalton asked.

"Yessuh."

"He's all right," Britten said. "Come on; let's get to a phone. I'm having that guy picked up for questioning. It's the only thing to do. And I'll have some men go over Miss Dalton's room. We'll find out what happened. I'll bet my right arm that goddamn Red's up to something!"

Britten went out and Mr. Dalton followed, leaving Bigger still on the edge of the bed. When he heard the door slam, he got up and grabbed his cap and went softly down the stairs into the basement. He stood a moment looking through the cracks into the humming fire, blindingly red now; then he went into the driveway, through the falling snow to the street. He had to see Bessie at once; the kidnap note had to be sent right away; there was no time to lose. If Mr. Dalton, Britten or Peggy missed him and asked him where he had been, he would say that he had gone out to get a package of cigarettes. But with all of the excitement, no one would probably think of him. And they were after Jan now; he was safe.

"Bigger!"

He stopped, whirled, his hand reaching inside of his shirt for his gun. He saw Jan standing in the doorway of a store. As Jan came forward Bigger backed away. Jan stopped.

"For Chrissakes! Don't be afraid of me. I'm not going to hurt you."

In the pale yellow sheen of the street lamp they faced each other; huge wet flakes of snow floated down slowly, forming a delicate screen between them. Bigger had his hand inside of his shirt, on his gun. Jan stood staring, his mouth open.

"What's all this about, Bigger? I haven't done anything to you, have I? Where's Mary?"

Bigger felt guilty; Jan's presence condemned him. Yet he knew of no way to atone for his guilt; he felt he had to act as he was acting.

"I don't want to talk to you," he mumbled.

"But what have I done to you?" Jan asked desperately.

Jan had done nothing to him, and it was Jan's innocence that made anger rise in him. His fingers tightened about the gun.

"I don't want to talk to you," he said again.

He felt that if Jan continued to stand there and make him

feel this awful sense of guilt, he would have to shoot him in spite of himself. He began to tremble, all over; his lips parted and his eyes widened.

"Go 'way," Bigger said.

"Listen, Bigger, if these people are bothering you, just tell me. Don't be scared. I'm used to this sort of thing. Listen, now. Let's go somewhere and get a cup of coffee and talk this thing over."

Jan came forward again and Bigger drew his gun. Jan stopped; his face whitened.

"For God's sake, man! What're you doing? Don't shoot. . . . I haven't bothered you. . . . Don't. . . ."

"Leave me alone," Bigger said, his voice tense and hysterical. "Leave me alone! Leave me alone!"

Jan backed away from him.

"Leave me alone!" Bigger's voice rose to a scream.

Jan backed farther away, then turned and walked rapidly off, looking back over his shoulder. When he reached the corner he ran through the snow, out of sight. Bigger stood still, the gun in hand. He had utterly forgotten where he was; his eyes were still riveted on that point in space where he had last seen Jan's retreating form. The tension in him slackened and he lowered the gun until it hung at his side, loosely in his fingers. He was coming back into possession of himself; for the past three minutes it seemed he had been under a strange spell, possessed by a force which he hated, but which he had to obey. He was startled when he heard soft footsteps coming toward him in the snow. He looked and saw a white woman. The woman saw him and paused; she turned abruptly and ran across the street. Bigger shoved the gun in his pocket and ran to the corner. He looked back; the woman was vanishing through the snow, in the opposite direction.

In him as he walked was a cold, driving will. He would go through with this; he would work fast. He had encountered in Jan a much stronger determination than he had thought would be there. If he sent the kidnap note, it would have to be done before Jan could prove that he was completely inno- cent. At that moment he did not care if he was caught. If only he could cower Jan and Britten into awe, into fear of him and his black skin and his humble manners!

He reached a corner and went into a drug store. A white clerk came to him.

"Give me a envelope, some paper and a pencil," he said.

He paid the money, put the package into his pocket and went out to the corner to wait for a car. One came; he got on and rode eastward, wondering what kind of note he would write. He rang the bell for the car to stop, got off and walked through the quiet Negro streets. Now and then he passed an empty building, white and silent in the night. He would make Bessie hide in one of these buildings and watch for Mr. Dalton's car. But the ones he passed were too old; if one went into them they might collapse. He walked on. He had to find a building where Bessie could stand in a window and see the package of money when it was thrown from the car. He reached Langley Avenue and walked westward to Wabash Avenue. There were many empty buildings with black windows, like blind eyes, buildings like skeletons standing with snow on their bones in the winter winds. But none of them were on corners. Finally, at Michigan Avenue and East Thirty-sixth Place, he saw the one he wanted. It was tall, white, silent, standing on a well-lighted corner. By looking from any of the front windows Bessie would be able to see in all four directions. Oh! He had to have a flashlight! He went to a drug store and bought one for a dollar. He felt in the inner pocket of his coat for his gloves. Now, he was ready. He crossed the street and stood waiting for a car. His feet were cold and he stamped them in the snow, surrounded by people waiting, too, for a car. He did not look at them; they were simply blind people, blind like his mother, his brother, his sister, Peggy, Britten, Jan, Mr. Dalton, and the sightless Mrs. Dalton and the quiet empty houses with their black gaping windows.

He looked round the street and saw a sign on a building: THIS PROPERTY IS MANAGED BY THE SOUTH SIDE REAL ESTATE COMPANY. He had heard that Mr. Dalton owned the South Side Real Estate Company, and the South Side Real Estate Company owned the house in which he lived. He paid eight dollars a week for one rat-infested room. He had never seen Mr. Dalton until he had come to work for him; his mother always took the rent to the real estate office. Mr. Dalton was somewhere far away, high up, distant, like a god. He owned property all over the Black Belt, and he owned property where white folks lived, too. But Bigger could not live in a building across the "line." Even though Mr. Dalton gave millions of dollars for Negro education, he would rent houses to Negroes only in this prescribed area, this corner of the city tumbling down from rot. In a sullen way Bigger was conscious of this. Yes; he would send the kidnap note. He would jar them out of their senses.

When the car came he rode south and got off at Fifty-first Street and walked to Bessie's. He had to ring five times before the buzzer answered. Goddammit, I bet she's drunk! he thought. He mounted the steps and saw her peering at him through the door with eyes red from sleep and alcohol. His doubt of her made him fearful and angry.

"Bigger?" she asked.

"Get on back in the room," he said.

"What's the matter?" she asked, backing away, her mouth open.

"Let me in! Open the door!"

She threw the door wide, almost stumbling as she did so.

"Turn on the light."

"What's the matter, Bigger?"

"How many times do you want me to ask you to turn on the light?"

She turned it on.

"Pull them shades."

She lowered the shades. He stood watching her. Now, I don't want any trouble out of her. He went to the dresser and pushed her jars and combs and brushes aside and took the package from his pocket and laid it in the cleared space.

"Bigger?"

He turned and looked at her.

"What?"

"You ain't really planning to do that, sure 'nough?"

"What the hell you think?"

"Bigger, naw!"

He caught her arm and squeezed it in a grip of fear and hate.

"You ain't going to turn away from me now! Not now, Goddamn you!"

She said nothing. He took off his cap and coat and threw them on the bed.

"They're wet, Bigger!"

"So what?"

"I ain't doing this," she said.

"Like hell you ain't!"

"You can't make me!"

"You done helped me to steal enough from the folks you worked for to put you in jail already."

She did not answer; he turned from her and got a chair and pulled it up to the dresser. He unwrapped the package and balled the paper into a knot and threw it into a corner of the room. Instinctively, Bessie stooped to pick it up. Bigger laughed and she straightened suddenly. Yes; Bessie was blind. He was about to write a kidnap note and she was worried about the cleanliness of her room.

"What's the matter?" she asked.

"Nothing."

He was smiling grimly. He took out the pencil; it was not sharpened.

"Gimme a knife."

"Ain't you got one?"

"Hell, naw! Get me a knife!"

"What you do with your knife?"

He stared at her, remembering that she knew that he had had a knife. An image of blood gleaming on the metal blade in the glare of the furnace came before his eyes and fear rose in him hotly.

"You want me to slap you?"

She went behind a curtain. He sat looking at the paper and pencil. She came back with a butcher knife.

"Bigger, please. . . . I don't want to do it."

"Got any liquor?"

"Yeah. . . ."

"Get you a shot and set on that bed and keep quiet."

She stood undecided, then got the bottle from under a pillow and drank. She lay on the bed, on her stomach, her face turned so that she could see him. He watched her through the looking-glass of the dresser. He sharpened the pencil and spread out the piece of paper. He was about to write when he remembered that he did not have his gloves on. Goddamn!

"Gimme my gloves."

"Hunh?"

"Get my gloves out of the inside of my coat pocket."

She swayed to her feet and got the gloves and stood back of his chair, holding them limply in her hands.

"Give 'em here."

"Bigger. . . ."

"Give me the gloves and get back on that bed, will you?"

He snatched them from her and gave her a shove and turned back to the dresser.

"Bigger. . . ."

"I ain't asking you but once more to shut up!" he said, pushing the knife out of the way so he could write.

He put on the gloves and took up the pencil in a trembling hand and held it poised over the paper. He should disguise his handwriting. He changed the pencil from his right to his left hand. He would not write it; he would print it. He swallowed with dry throat. Now, what would be the best kind of note? He thought, I want you to put ten thousand. . . . Naw; that would not do. Not "I." It would be better to say "we." *We got your daughter,* he printed slowly in big round letters. That was better. He ought to say something to let Mr. Dalton think that Mary was still alive. He wrote: *She is safe.* Now, tell him not to go to the police. No! Say something about Mary first! He bent and wrote: *She wants to come home.* . . . Now, tell him not to go to the police. *Don't go to the police if you want your daughter back safe.* Naw; that ain't good. His scalp tingled with excitement; it seemed that he could feel each strand of hair upon his head. He read the line over and crossed out "safe" and wrote "alive." For a moment he was frozen, still. There was in his stomach a slow, cold, vast rising movement, as though he held within the embrace of his bowels the swing of planets through space. He was giddy. He caught hold of himself, focused his attention to write again. Now, about the money. How much? Yes; make it ten thousand. *Get ten thousand in 5 and 10 bills and put it in a shoe box.* . . . That's good. He had read that somewhere. . . . *and tomorrow night ride your car up and down Michigan Avenue from 35th Street to 40th Street.* That would make it hard for anybody to tell just where Bessie would be hiding. He wrote: *Blink your headlights some. When you see a light in a window blink three times throw the box in the snow and drive off. Do what this letter say.* Now, he would sign it. But how? It should be signed in some way that would throw them off the trail. Oh, yes! Sign "Red." He printed, *Red.* Then, for some reason, he thought that that was not enough. Oh, yes. He would make one of those signs, like the ones he had seen on the Communist pamphlets. He wondered how they were made. There was a hammer and a round kind of knife. He drew a hammer, then a curving knife. But it did not look right. He examined it and discovered that he had left the handle off the knife. He sketched it in. Now, it was complete. He read it over. Oh! He had left out something. He had to put in the time when he wanted them to bring the money. He bent and printed again: *p.s. Bring the money at midnight.* He sighed, lifted his eyes and saw Bessie standing behind him. He turned and looked at her.

"Bigger, you ain't really going to do that?" she whispered in horror.

"Sure."

"*Where's* that girl?"

"I don't know."

"You *do* know. You wouldn't be doing this if you didn't know."

"Aw, what difference do it make?"

She looked straight into his eyes and whispered,

"Bigger, did you kill that girl?"

His jaw clamped tight and he stood up. She turned from him and flung herself upon the bed, sobbing. He began to feel cold; he discovered that his body was covered with sweat. He heard a soft rustle and looked down at his hand; the kidnap note was shaking in his trembling fingers. But I ain't scared, he told himself. He folded the note, put it into an envelope, sealed it by licking the flap, and shoved it in his pocket. He lay down on the bed beside Bessie and took her in his arms. He tried to speak to her and found his throat so husky that no words came.

"Come on, kid," he whispered finally.

"Bigger, what's happened to you?"

"It ain't nothing. You ain't got much to do."

"I don't *want* to."

"Don't be scared."

"You told me you was never going to kill nobody."

"I ain't killed nobody."

"You *did*! I see it in your eyes. I see it all over you."

"Don't you trust me, baby?"

"Where's that girl, Bigger?"

"I don't know."

"How you know she won't turn up?"

"She just won't."

"You *did* kill her."

"Aw, forget the girl."

She stood up.

"If you killed *her* you'll kill *me*," she said. "I ain't in this."

"Don't be a fool. I love you."

"You told me you *never* was going to kill."

"All right. They white folks. They done killed plenty of us."

"That don't make it right."

He began to doubt her; he had never heard this tone in her voice before. He saw her tear-wet eyes looking at him in stark fear and he remembered that no one had seen him leave his room. To stop Bessie who now knew too much would be easy. He could take the butcher knife and cut her throat. He had to make certain of her, one way or the other, before he went back to Dalton's. Quickly, he stooped over her, his fists clenched. He was feeling as he had felt when he stood over Mary's bed with the white blur drawing near; an iota more of fear would have sent him plunging again into murder.

"I don't want no playing from you now."

"I'm scared, Bigger," she whimpered.

She tried to get up; he knew she had seen the mad light in his eyes. Fear sheathed him in fire. His words came in a thick whisper.

"Keep still, now. I ain't playing. Pretty soon they'll be after me, maybe. And I ain't going to let 'em catch me, see? I ain't going to let 'em! The first thing they'll do in looking for me is to come to you. They'll grill you about me and you, you drunk fool, you'll tell! You'll tell if you ain't in it, too. If you ain't in it for your life, you'll tell."

"Naw; Bigger!" she whimpered tensely. At that moment she was too scared even to cry.

"You going to do what *I* say?"

She wrenched herself free and rolled across the bed and stood up on the other side. He ran round the bed and followed her as she backed into a corner. His voice hissed from his throat:

"I ain't going to leave you behind to snitch!"

"I ain't going to snitch! I *swear* I ain't."

He held his face a few inches from hers. He had to bind her to him.

"Yeah; I killed the girl," he said. "Now, you know. You got to help me. You in it as deep as me! You done spent some of the money. . . ."

She sank to the bed again, sobbing, her breath catching in her throat. He stood looking down at her, waiting for her to quiet. When she had control of herself, he lifted her and stood her upon her feet. He reached under the pillow and brought out the bottle and took out the stopper and put his hand round her and tilted her head.

"Here; take a shot."

"Naw."

"*Drink.* . . ."

He carried the bottle to her lips; she drank a small swallow. When he attempted to put the bottle away, she took it from him.

"That's enough, now. You don't want to get sloppy drunk."

He turned her loose and she lay back on the bed, limp, whimpering. He bent to her.

"Listen, Bessie."

"Bigger, please! Don't do this to me! *Please!* All I do is work, work like a dog! From morning till night. I ain't got no happiness. I ain't never had none. I ain't got nothing and you do this to me. After how good I been to you. Now you just spoil my whole life. I've done everything for you I know how and you do this to me. *Please,* Bigger. . . ." She turned her head away and stared at the floor. "Lord, don't let this happen to me! I ain't done nothing for this to come to me! I just work! I ain't had no happiness, no nothing. I just work. I'm black and I work and don't bother nobody. . . ."

"Go on," Bigger said, nodding his head affirmatively; he knew the truth of all she spoke without her telling it. "Go on and see what that gets you."

"But I don't want to do it, Bigger. They'll catch us. God *knows* they will."

"I ain't going to leave you here to snitch on me."

"I won't tell. Honest, I won't. I cross my heart and swear by God, I won't. You can run away. . . ."

"I ain't got no money."

"You *have* got money. I paid rent out of what you gave me and I bought some liquor. But the rest is there."

"That ain't enough. I got to have some real dough."

She cried again. He got the knife and stood over her.

"I can stop it all right now," he said.

She started up, her mouth opening to scream.

"If you scream, I'll *have* to kill you. So help me God!"

"Naw; naw! Bigger, don't! *Don't!*"

Slowly, his arm relaxed and hung at his side; she fell to sobbing again. He was afraid that he would have to kill her before it was all over. She would not do to take along, and he could not leave her behind.

"All right," he said. "But you better do the right thing."

He put the knife on the dresser and got the flashlight from his overcoat pocket and then stood over her with the letter and flashlight in his hand.

"Come on," he said. "Get your coat on."

"Not tonight, Bigger! Not tonight. . . ."

"It won't be tonight. But I got to show you what to do."

"But it's cold. It's snowing. . . ."

"Sure. And nobody'll see us. Come *on!*"

She pulled up; he watched her struggle into her coat. Now and then she paused and looked at him, blinking back her tears. When she was dressed, he put on his coat and cap and led her to the street. The air was thick with snow. The wind blew hard. It was a blizzard. The street lamps were faint smudges of yellow. They walked to the corner and waited for a car.

"I'd rather do anything but this," she said.

"Stop now. We're in it."

"Bigger, honey, I'd run off with you. I'd work for you, baby. We don't have to do this. Don't you believe I love you?"

"Don't try that on me now."

The car came; he helped her on and sat down beside her and looked past her face at the silent snow flying white and wild outside the window. He brought his eyes farther round and looked at her; she was staring with blank eyes, like a blind woman waiting for some word to tell her where she was going. Once she cried and he gripped her shoulder so tightly that she stopped, more absorbed in the painful pressure of steel-like fingers than in her fate. They got off at Thirty-sixth Place and walked over to Michigan Avenue. When they reached the corner, Bigger stopped and made her stop by gripping her arm again. They were in front of the high, white, empty building with black windows.

"Where we going?"

"Right here."

"Bigger," she whimpered.

"Come on, now. Don't start that!"

"But I don't *want* to."

"You *got* to."

He looked up and down the street, past ghostly lamps that shed a long series of faintly shimmering cones of yellow against the snowy night. He took her to the front entrance which gave into a vast pool of inky silence. He brought out the flashlight and focused the round spot on a rickety stairway leading upward into a still blacker darkness. The planks creaked as he led her up. Now and then he felt his shoes sink into a soft, cushy substance. Cobwebs brushed his face. All round him was the dank smell of rotting timber. He stopped abruptly as something with dry whispering feet flitted across his path, emitting as the rush of its flight died a thin, piping wail of lonely fear.

"Ooow!"

Bigger whirled and centered the spot of light on Bessie's face. Her lips were drawn back, her mouth was open, and her hands were lifted midway to white-rimmed eyes.

"What you trying to do?" he asked. "Tell the whole world we in here?"

"Oh, Bigger!"

"Come on!"

After a few feet he stopped and swung the light. He saw dusty walls, walls almost like those of the Dalton home. The doorways were wider than those of any house in which he had ever lived. Some rich folks lived here once, he thought. Rich white folks. That was the way most houses on the South Side were, ornate, old, stinking; homes once of rich white people, now inhabited by Negroes or standing dark and empty with yawning black windows. He remembered that bombs had been thrown by whites into houses like these when Negroes had first moved into the South Side. He swept the disc of yellow and walked gingerly down a hall and into a room at the front of the house. It was feebly lit from the street lamps outside; he switched off the flashlight and looked round. The room had six large windows. By standing close to any of them, the streets in all four directions were visible.

"See, Bessie. . . ."

He turned to look at her and found that she was not there. He called tensely:

"Bessie!"

There was no answer; he bounded to the doorway and switched on the flashlight. She was leaning against a wall, sobbing. He went to her, caught her arm and yanked her back into the room.

"Come on! You got to do better than this."

"I'd rather have you kill me right now," she sobbed.

"Don't you say that again!"

She was silent. His black open palm swept upward in a swift narrow arc and smacked solidly against her face.

"You want me to wake you up?"

She bent her head to her knees; he caught hold of her arm again and dragged her to the window. He spoke like a man who had been running and was out of breath:

"Now, look. All you got to do is come here tomorrow night, see? Ain't nothing going to bother you. I'm seeing to everything. Don't you worry none. You just do what I say. You come here and just watch. About twelve o'clock a car'll come along. It'll be blinking its headlights, see? When it comes, you just raise this flashlight and blink it three times, see? Like this. Remember that. Then watch that car. It'll throw out a package. Watch that package, 'cause the money'll be in it. It'll go into the snow. Look and see if anybody's about. If you see nobody, then go and get the package and go home. But don't go straight home. Make sure nobody's watching you, nobody's following you, see? Ride three or four street cars and transfer fast. Get off about five blocks from home and look behind you as you walk, see? Now, look. You can see up and down Michigan and Thirty-sixth. You can see if anybody's watching. I'll be in the white folks' house all day tomorrow. If they put anybody out to watch, I'll let you know not to come."

"Bigger. . . ."

"Come on, now."

"Take me home."

"You going to do it?"

She did not answer.

"You already in it," he said. "You got part of the money."

"I reckon it don't make no difference," she sighed.

"It'll be easy."

"It won't. I'll get caught. But it don't make no difference. I'm lost anyhow. I was lost when I took up with you. I'm lost and it don't matter. . . ."

"Come on."

He led her back to the car stop. He said nothing as they waited in the whirling snow. When he heard the car coming, he took her purse from her, opened it and put the flashlight inside. The car stopped; he helped her on, put seven cents in her trembling hand and stood in the snow watching her black face through the window white with ice as the car moved off slowly through the night.

He walked to Dalton's through the snow. His right hand was in his coat pocket, his fingers about the kidnap note. When he reached the driveway, he looked about the street carefully. There was no one. He looked at the house; it was white, huge, silent. He walked up the steps and stood in front of the door. He waited a moment to see what would happen. So deeply conscious was he of violating dangerous taboo, that he felt that the very air or sky would suddenly speak, commanding him to stop. He was sailing fast into the face of a cold wind that all but sucked his breath from him; but he liked it. Around him were silence and night and snow falling, falling as though it had fallen from the beginning of time and would always fall till the end of the world. He took the letter out of his pocket and slipped it under the door. Turning, he ran down the steps and round the house. I done it! I done it now! They'll see it tonight or in the morning. . . . He went to the basement door, opened it and looked inside; no one was there. Like an enraged beast, the furnace throbbed with heat, suffusing a red glare over everything. He stood in front of the cracks and watched the restless embers. Had Mary burned completely? He wanted to poke round in the coals to see, but dared not; he flinched from it even in thought. He pulled the lever for more coal, then went to his room.

When he stretched out on his bed in the dark he found that his whole body was trembling. He was cold and hungry. While lying there shaking, a hot bath of fear, hotter than his blood, engulfed him, bringing him to his feet. He stood in the middle of the floor, seeing vivid images of his gloves, his pencil, and paper. How on earth had he forgotten them? He had to burn them. He would do it right now. He pulled on the light and went to his overcoat and got the gloves and pencil and paper and stuffed them into his shirt. He went to the door, listened a moment, then went into the hall and down the stairs to the furnace. He stood a moment before the gleaming cracks. Hurriedly, he opened the door and dumped the gloves and pencil and paper in; he watched them smoke, blaze; he closed the door and heard them burn in a furious whirlwind of draft.

A strange sensation enveloped him. Something tingled in his stomach and on his scalp. His knees wobbled, giving way. He stumbled to the wall and leaned against it weakly. A wave of numbness spread fanwise from his stomach over his entire body, including his head and eyes, making his mouth gap. Strength ebbed from him. He sank to his knees and pressed his fingers to the floor to keep from tumbling over. An organic sense of dread seized him. His teeth chattered and he felt sweat sliding down his armpits and back. He groaned,

holding as still as possible. His vision was blurred; but gradually it cleared. Again he saw the furnace. Then he realized
that he had been on the verge of collapse. Soon the glare and
drone of the fire came to his eyes and ears. He closed his
mouth and gritted his teeth; the peculiar paralyzing numbness
was leaving.

When he was strong enough to stand without support, he
rose to his feet and wiped his forehead on his sleeve. He had
strained himself from a too long lack of sleep and food; and
the excitement was sapping his energy. He should go to the
kitchen and ask for his dinner. Surely, he should not starve
like this. He mounted the steps to the door and knocked timidly; there was no answer. He turned the knob and pushed
the door in and saw the kitchen flooded with light. On a table
were spread several white napkins under which was something that looked like plates of food. He stood gazing at it,
then went to the table and lifted the corners of the napkins.
There were sliced bread and steak and fried potatoes and
gravy and string beans and spinach and a huge piece of chocolate cake. His mouth watered. Was this for him? He wondered if Peggy was around. Ought he try to find her? But he
disliked the thought of looking for her; that would bring attention to himself, something which he hated. He stood in
the kitchen, wondering if he ought to eat, but afraid to do so.
He rested his black fingers on the edge of the white table and
a silent laugh burst from his parted lips as he saw himself for a
split second in a lurid objective light: he had killed a rich
white girl and had burned her body after cutting her head off
and had lied to throw the blame on someone else and had
written a kidnap note demanding ten thousand dollars and
yet he stood here afraid to touch food on the table, food
which undoubtedly was his own.

"Bigger?"

"Hunh?" he answered before he knew who had called.

"Where've you been? Your dinner's been waiting for you
since five o'clock. There's a chair. Eat. . . ."

as much as you want. . . . He stopped listening. In Peggy's
hand was the kidnap note. *I'll heat your coffee go ahead and eat*
Had she opened it? Did she know what was in it? No; the
envelope was still sealed. She came to the table and removed

the napkins. His knees were shaking with excitement and sweat broke out on his forehead. His skin felt as though it were puckering up from a blast of heat. *don't you want the steak warmed* the question reached him from far away and he shook his head without really knowing what she meant. *don't you feel well*

"This is all right," he murmured.

"You oughtn't starve yourself that way."

"I wasn't hungry."

"You're hungrier than you think," she said.

She set a cup and saucer at his plate, then laid the letter on the edge of the table. It held his attention as though it were a steel magnet and his eyes were iron. She got the coffee pot and poured his cup full. No doubt she had just gotten the letter from under the door and had not yet had time to give it to Mr. Dalton. She placed a small jar of cream at his plate and took up the letter again.

"I've got to give this to Mr. Dalton," she said. "I'll be back in a moment."

"Yessum," he whispered.

She left. He stopped chewing and stared before him, his mouth dry. But he *had* to eat. Not to eat now would create suspicion. He shoved the food in and chewed each mouthful awhile, then washed it down with swallows of hot coffee. When the coffee gave out, he used cold water. He strained his ears to catch sounds. But none came. Then the door swung in silently and Peggy came back. He could see nothing in her round red face. Out of the corners of his eyes he watched her go to the stove and putter with pots and pans.

"Want more coffee?"

"No'm."

"You ain't scared of all this trouble we're having round here, are you, Bigger?"

"Oh, no'm," he said, wondering if something in his manner had made her ask that.

"That poor Mary!" Peggy sighed. "She acts like such a ninny. Imagine a girl keeping her parents worried sick all the time. But there are children for you these days."

He hurried with his eating, saying nothing; he wanted to get out of the kitchen. The thing was in the open now; not all

of it, but some of it. Nobody knew about Mary yet. He saw
in his mind a picture of the Dalton family distraught and hor-
rified when they found that Mary was kidnapped. That would
put them a certain distance from him. They would think that
white men did it; they would never think that a black, timid
Negro did that. They would go after Jan. The "Red" he had
signed to the letter and the hammer and curving knife would
make them look for Communists.

"You got enough?"

"Yessum."

"You better clean the ashes out of the furnace in the morning, Bigger."

"Yessum."

"And be ready for Mr. Dalton at eight."

"Yessum."

"Your room all right?"

"Yessum."

The door swung in violently. Bigger started in fright. Mr.
Dalton came into the kitchen, his face ashy. He stared at
Peggy and Peggy, holding a dish towel in her hand, stared at
him. In Mr. Dalton's hand was the letter, opened.

"What's the matter, Mr. Dalton?"

"Who. . . . Where did. . . . Who gave you this?"

"What?"

"This *letter*."

"Why, nobody. I got it from the door."

"When?"

"A few minutes ago. Anything wrong?"

Mr. Dalton looked round the entire kitchen, not at anything in particular, but just round the entire stretch of four
walls, his eyes wide and unseeing. He looked back at Peggy; it
was as if he had thrown himself upon her mercy; was waiting
for her to say some word that would take the horror away.

"W-what's the matter, Mr. Dalton?" Peggy asked again.

Before Mr. Dalton could answer, Mrs. Dalton groped her
way into the kitchen, her white hands held high. Bigger
watched her fingers tremble through the air till they touched
Mr. Dalton's shoulder. They gripped his coat hard enough to
tear it from his body. Bigger, without moving an eyelid, felt
his skin grow hot and his muscles stiffen.

"Henry! Henry!" Mrs. Dalton called. "What's the matter?"
Mr. Dalton did not hear her; he still stared at Peggy.

"Did you see who left this letter?"

"No, Mr. Dalton."

"You, Bigger?"

"Nawsuh," he whispered, his mouth full of dry food.

"Henry, tell me! *Please!* For Heaven's sake!"

Mr. Dalton put his arm about Mrs. Dalton's waist and held her close to him.

"It's. . . . It's about Mary. . . . It's. . . . She. . . ."

"What? Where is she?"

"They. . . . They got her! They kidnapped her!"

"Henry! No!" Mrs. Dalton screamed.

"Oh, no!" Peggy whimpered, running to Mr. Dalton.

"My baby," Mrs. Dalton sobbed.

"She's been kidnapped," Mr. Dalton said, as though he had to say the words over again to convince himself.

Bigger's eyes were wide, taking in all three of them in one constantly roving glance. Mrs. Dalton continued to sob and Peggy sank into a chair, her face in her hands. Then she sprang up and ran out of the room, crying:

"Lord, don't let them kill her!"

Mrs. Dalton swayed. Mr. Dalton lifted her and staggered, trying to get her through the door. As he watched Mr. Dalton there flashed through Bigger's mind a quick image of how he had lifted Mary's body in his arms the night before. He rose and held the door open for Mr. Dalton and watched him walk unsteadily down the dim hallway with Mrs. Dalton in his arms.

He was alone in the kitchen now. Again the thought that he had the chance to walk out of here and be clear of it all came to him, and again he brushed it aside. He was tensely eager to stay and see how it would all end, even if that end swallowed him in blackness. He felt that he was living upon a high pinnacle where bracing winds whipped about him. There came to his ears a muffled sound of sobs. Then suddenly there was silence. What's happening? Would Mr. Dalton phone the police now? He strained to listen, but no sounds came. He went to the door and took a few steps into the hallway. There were still no sounds. He looked about to make sure that no one was watching him, then crept on tiptoe down the hall. He heard voices. Mr. Dalton was talking to someone. He crept farther; yes, he could hear. . . . *I want to talk to Britten please.* Mr. Dalton was phoning. *come right over please yes at once something awful has happened I don't want to talk about it over the phone* That meant that when Britten came back he would be questioned again. *yes right away I'll be waiting*

He had to get back to his room. He tiptoed along the hall, through the kitchen, down the steps and into the basement. The torrid cracks of the furnace gleamed in the crimson darkness and he heard the throaty undertone of the draft devouring the air. Was she burnt? But even if she were not, who would think of looking in the furnace for her? He went to his room, into the closet, closed the door and listened. Silence. He came out, left the door open and, in order to get to the closet quickly and without sound, pulled off his shoes. He lay again on the bed, his mind whirling, with images born of a multitude of impulses. He could run away; he could remain; he could even go down and confess what he had done. The mere thought that these avenues of action were open to him made him feel free, that his life was his, that he held his future in his hands. But they would never think that he had done it; not a meek black boy like him.

He bounded off the bed, listening, thinking that he had heard voices. He had been so deeply taken up with his own thoughts that he did not know if he had actually heard anything or had imagined it. Yes; he heard faint footsteps below. He hurried to the closet. The footsteps ceased. There came to him the soft sound of sobbing. It was Peggy. Her sobbing quieted, then rose to a high pitch. He stood for a long time, listening to Peggy's sobs and the long moan of the wind sweeping through the night outside. Peggy's sobs ceased and her footsteps sounded once more. Was she going to answer the doorbell? Footsteps came again; Peggy had gone to the front of the house for something and had come back. He heard a heavy voice, a man's. At first he could not identify it; then he realized that it was Britten's.

". . . . and you found the note?"

"Yes."

"How long ago?"

"About an hour."

"You're sure you didn't see anyone leave it?"

"It was sticking under the door."

"Think, now. Did you see anybody about the house or driveway?"

"No. The boy and me, that's all that's been around here."

"And where's the boy now?"

"Upstairs in his room, I think."

"Did you ever see this handwriting before?"

"No, Mr. Britten."

"Can you guess, can you think, imagine who would send such a note?"

"No. Not a soul in this whole wide world, Mr. Britten," Peggy wailed.

Britten's voice ceased. There was the sound of other heavy feet. Chairs scraped over the floor. More people were in the kitchen. Who were they? Their movements sounded like those of men. Then Bigger heard Britten speaking again.

"Listen, Peggy. Tell me, how *does* this boy act?"

"What do you mean, Mr. Britten?"

"Does he seem intelligent? Does he seem to be *acting*?"

"I don't know, Mr. Britten. He's just like all the other colored boys."

"Does he say 'yes mam' and 'no mam'?"

"Yes, Mr. Britten. He's polite."

"But does he seem to be trying to appear like he's more ignorant than he *really* is?"

"I don't know, Mr. Britten."

"Have you missed anything around the house since he's been here?"

"No; nothing."

"Has he ever insulted you, or anything?"

"Oh, no! No!"

"What kind of a boy is he?"

"He's just a quiet colored boy. That's all I can say. . . ."

"Did you ever see him reading anything?"

"No, Mr. Britten."

"Does he speak more intelligently at some times than at others?"

"No, Mr. Britten. He talked always the same, to me."

"Has he ever done anything that would make you think he knows something about this note?"

"No, Mr. Britten."

"When you speak to him, does he hesitate before he answers, as though he's thinking up what to say?"

"No, Mr. Britten. He talks and acts natural-like."

"When he talks, does he wave his hands around a lot, like he's been around a lot of Jews?"

"I never noticed, Mr. Britten."

"Did you ever hear 'im call anybody *comrade?*"

"No, Mr. Britten."

"Does he pull off his cap when he comes in the house?"

"I never noticed. I think so, Mr. Britten."

"Has he ever sat down in your presence without being asked, like he was used to being around white people?"

"No, Mr. Britten. Only when I told him to."

"Does he speak first, or does he wait until he's spoken to?"

"Well, Mr. Britten. He seemed always to wait until we spoke to him before he said anything."

"Now, listen, Peggy. Think and try to remember if his voice goes *up* when he talks, like Jews when they talk. Know what I mean? You see, Peggy, I'm trying to find out if he's been around Communists. . . ."

"No, Mr. Dalton. He talks just like all other colored folks to me."

"Where did you say he is now?"

"Upstairs in his room."

When Britten's voice ceased Bigger was smiling. Yes; Britten was trying to trap him, trying to make out a case against him; but he could not find anything to go upon. Was Britten coming to talk to him now? There came the sound of other voices.

"It's a ten-to-one chance that she's dead."

"Yeah. They usually bump 'em off. They're scared of 'em after they get 'em. They think they might identify them afterwards."

"Did the old man say he was going to pay?"

"Sure. He wants his daughter back."

"That's just ten thousand dollars shot to hell, if you ask me."

"But he wants the girl."

"Say, I bet it's those Reds trying to raise money."

"Yeah!"

"Maybe that's how they get their dough. They say that guy, Bruno Hauptmann, the one who snatched the Lindy baby, did it for the Nazis. They needed the money."

"I'd like to shoot every one of them goddamn bastards, Red or no Red."

There was the sound of a door opening and more footsteps.

"You have any luck with the old man?"

"Not yet." It was Britten's voice.

"He's pretty washed up, eh?"

"Yeah; and who wouldn't be?"

"He won't call the cops?"

"Naw; he's scared stiff."

"It might seem hard on the family, but if you let them snatchers know they can't scare money out of you, they'll stop."

"Say, Brit, try 'im again."

"Yeah; tell 'im there ain't nothing to do now but to call the cops."

"Aw, I don't know. I hate to worry 'im."

"Well, after all, it's *his* daughter. Let him handle it."

"But, listen, Brit. When they pick up this Erlone fellow, he's going to tell the cops and the papers'll have the story anyway. So call 'em now. The sooner they get started the better."

"Naw; I'll wait for the old man to give the signal."

Bigger knew that Mr. Dalton had not wanted to notify the police; that much was certain. But how long would he hold out? The police would know everything as soon as Jan was picked up, for Jan would tell enough to make the police and the newspapers investigate. But if Jan were confronted with the fact of the kidnapping of Mary, what would happen? Could Jan prove an alibi? If he did, then the police would start looking for someone else. They would start questioning him again; they would want to know why he had lied about Jan's being in the house. But would not the word "Red" which he had signed to the ransom note throw them off the track and make them still think that Jan or his comrades did it? Why would anybody want to think that Bigger had kidnapped Mary? Bigger came out of the closet and wiped sweat from his forehead with his sleeve. He had knelt so long that his blood had almost stopped and needle-like pains shot from the bottom of his feet to the calves of his legs. He went to the window and looked out at the swirling snow. He could hear wind rising; it was a blizzard all right. The snow moved in no given direction, but filled the world with a vast white storm of flying powder. The sharp currents of wind could be seen in whorls of snow twisting like miniature tornadoes.

The window overlooked an alley, to the right of which was Forty-fifth Street. He tried the window to see if it would open; he lifted it a few inches, then all the way with a loud and screechy sound. Had anyone heard him? He waited; nothing happened. Good! If the worst came to the worst, he could jump out of this window, right here, and run away. It was two stories to the ground and there was a deep drift of soft snow just below him. He lowered the window and lay again on the bed, waiting. The sound of firm feet came on the stairs. Yes; someone was coming up! His body grew rigid. A knock came at the door.

"Yessuh!"

"Open up!"

He pulled on the light, opened the door and met a white face.

"They want you downstairs."

"Yessuh!"

The man stepped to one side and Bigger went past him on down the hall and down the steps into the basement, feeling the eyes of the white man on his back, and hearing as he neared the furnace the muffled breathing of the fire and seeing directly before his eyes Mary's bloody head with its jet-black curly hair, shining and wet with blood on the crumpled newspapers. He saw Britten standing near the furnace with three white men.

"Hello, Bigger."

"Yessuh," Bigger said.

"You heard what happened?"

"Yessuh."

"Listen, boy. You're talking just to me and my men here. Now, tell me, do you think Jan's mixed up in this?"

Bigger's eyes fell. He did not want to answer in a hurry and he did not want to blame Jan definitely, for that would make them question him too closely. He would hint and point in Jan's direction.

"I don't know, suh," he said.

"Just tell me what you *think*."

"I don't know, suh," Bigger said again.

"You *really* saw him here last night, didn't you?"

"Oh, yessuh."

"You'd swear he told you to take that trunk down and leave the car out in the snow."

"I—I'd swear to what's true, suh," said Bigger.

"Did he act like he had anything up his sleeve?"

"I don't know, suh."

"What time did you say you left?"

"A little before two, suh."

Britten turned to the other men, one of whom stood near the furnace with his back to the fire, warming his hands behind him. The man's legs were sprawled wide apart and a cigar glowed in a corner of his mouth.

"It must've been that Red," Britten said to him.

"Yeah," said the man at the furnace. "What would he have the boy take the trunk down for and leave the car out? It was to throw us off the scent."

"Listen, Bigger," said Britten. "Did you see this guy act in any way out of the ordinary? I mean, sort of nervous, say? Just what *did* he talk about?"

"He talked about Communists. . . ."

"Did he ask you to join?"

"He gave me that stuff to read."

"Come on. Tell us some of the things he said."

Bigger knew the things that white folks hated to hear Negroes ask for; and he knew that these were the things the Reds were always asking for. And he knew that white folks did not like to hear these things asked for even by whites who fought for Negroes.

"Well," Bigger said, feigning reluctance, "he told me that

some day there wouldn't be no rich folks and no poor folks. . . ."

"Yeah?"

"And he said a black man would have a chance. . . ."

"Go on."

"And he said there would be no more lynching. . . ."

"And what was the girl saying?"

"She agreed with 'im."

"How did you feel toward them?"

"I don't know, suh."

"I mean, did you like 'em?"

He knew that the average white man would not approve of his liking such talk.

"It was my job. I just did what they told me," he mumbled.

"Did the girl act in any way scared?"

He sensed what kind of a case they were trying to build against Jan and he remembered that Mary had cried last night when he had refused to go into the café with her to eat.

"Well, I don't know, suh. She was crying once. . . ."

"*Crying?*"

The men crowded about him.

"Yessuh."

"Did he hit her?"

"I didn't see that."

"What did he do then?"

"Well, he put his arms around her and she stopped."

Bigger had his back to a wall. The crimson luster of the fire gleamed on the white men's faces. The sound of air being sucked upward through the furnace mingled in Bigger's ears with the faint whine of the wind outside in the night. He was tired; he closed his eyes a long second and then opened them, knowing that he had to keep alert and answer questions to save himself.

"Did this fellow Jan say anything to you about white women?"

Bigger tightened with alarm.

"Suh?"

"Did he say he would let you meet some white women if you joined the Reds?"

He knew that sex relations between blacks and whites were repulsive to most white men.

"Nawsuh," he said, simulating abashment.

"Did Jan lay the girl?"

"I don't know, suh."

"Did you take them to a room or a hotel?"

"Nawsuh. Just to the park."

"They were in the back seat?"

"Yessuh."

"How long were you in the park?"

"Well, about two hours, I reckon, suh."

"Come on, now, boy. Did he lay the girl?"

"I don't know, suh. They was back there kissing and going on."

"Was she lying down?"

"Well, yessuh. She was," said Bigger, lowering his eyes because he felt that it would be better to do so. He knew that whites thought that all Negroes yearned for white women, therefore he wanted to show a certain fearful deference even when one's name was mentioned in his presence.

"They were drunk, weren't they?"

"Yessuh. They'd been drinking a lot."

He heard the sound of autos coming into the driveway. Was this the police?

"Who's that?" Britten asked.

"I don't know," said one of the men.

"I'd better see," Britten said.

Bigger saw, after Britten had opened the door, four cars standing in the snow with headlights glowing.

"Who's that?" Britten called.

"The press!"

"There's nothing here for you!" Britten called in an uneasy voice.

"Don't stall us!" a voice answered. "Some of it's already in the papers. You may as well tell the rest."

"What's in the papers?" Britten asked as the men entered the basement.

A tall red-faced man shoved his hand into his pocket and brought forth a newspaper and handed it to Britten.

"The Reds say you're charging 'em with spiriting away the old man's daughter."

Bigger darted a glance at the paper from where he was; he saw: RED NABBED AS GIRL VANISHES.

"Goddamn!" said Britten.

"Phew!" said the tall red-faced man. "What a night! Red arrested! Snowstorm. And this place down here looks like somebody's been murdered."

"Come on, you," said Britten. "You're in Mr. Dalton's house now."

"Oh, I'm sorry."

"Where's the old man?"

"Upstairs. He doesn't want to be bothered."

"Is that girl really missing, or is this just a stunt?"

"I can't tell you anything," Britten said.

"Who's this boy, here?"

"Keep quiet, Bigger," Britten said.

"Is he the one Erlone said accused him?"

Bigger stood against the wall and looked round vaguely.

"You going to pull the dumb act on us?" asked one of the men.

"Listen, you guys," said Britten. "Take it easy. I'll go and see if the old man will see you."

"That's the time. We're waiting. All the wires are carrying this story."

Britten went up the steps and left Bigger standing with the crowd of men.

"Your name's Bigger Thomas?" the red-faced man asked.

"Keep quiet, Bigger," said one of Britten's men.

Bigger said nothing.

"Say, what's all this? This boy can talk if he wants to."

"This smells like something big to me," said one of the men.

Bigger had never seen such men before; he did not know how to act toward them or what to expect of them. They were not rich and distant like Mr. Dalton, and they were harder than Britten, but in a more impersonal way, a way that maybe was more dangerous than Britten's. Back and forth they walked across the basement floor in the glare of the furnace with their hats on and with cigars and cigarettes in their mouths. Bigger felt in them a coldness that disregarded everybody. They seemed like men out for keen sport. They would be around a long time now that Jan had been arrested and questioned. Just what did they think of what he had told

about Jan? Was there any good in Britten's telling him not to talk to them? Bigger's eyes watched the balled newspaper in a white man's gloved hand. If only he could read that paper! The men were silent, waiting for Britten to return. Then one of them came and leaned against the wall, near him. Bigger looked out of the corners of his eyes and said nothing. He saw the man light a cigarette.

"Smoke, kid?"

"Nawsuh," he mumbled.

He felt something touch the center of his palm. He made a move to look, but a whisper checked him.

"Keep still. It's for you. I want you to give me the dope."

Bigger's fingers closed over a slender wad of paper; he knew at once that it was money and that he would give it back. He held the money and watched his chance. Things were happening so fast that he felt he was not doing full justice to them. He was tired. Oh, if only he could go to sleep! If only this whole thing could be postponed for a few hours, until he had rested some! He felt that he would have been able to handle it then. Events were like the details of a tortured dream, happening without cause. At times it seemed that he could not quite remember what had gone before and what it was he was expecting to come. At the head of the stairs the door opened and he saw Britten. While the others were looking off, Bigger shoved the money back into the man's hand. The man looked at him, shook his head and flicked his cigarette away and walked to the center of the floor.

"I'm sorry, boys," Britten said. "But the old man won't be able to see you till Tuesday."

Bigger thought quickly; that meant that Mr. Dalton was going to pay the money and was not going to call in the police.

"Tuesday?"

"Aw, come on!"

"Where *is* the girl?"

"I'm sorry," said Britten.

"You're putting us in the position of having to print anything we can get about this case," said one of the men.

"You all know Mr. Dalton," Britten explained. "You

wouldn't do that. For God's sake, give the man a chance. I can't tell you why now, but it's important. He'd do as much for you some time."

"Is the girl *missing*?"

"I don't know."

"Is she *here* in the house?"

Britten hesitated.

"No; I don't think she is."

"When did she leave?"

"I don't know."

"When will she be back?"

"I can't say."

"Is this Erlone fellow telling the truth?" asked one of the men. "He said that Mr. Dalton's trying to slander the Communist Party by having him arrested. And he says it's an attempt to break up his relationship with Miss Dalton."

"I don't know," Britten said.

"Erlone was picked up and taken to police headquarters and questioned," the man continued. "He claimed that this boy here lied about his being in the home last night. Is *that* true?"

"Really, I can't say anything about that," Britten said.

"Did Mr. Dalton forbid Erlone to see Miss Dalton?"

"I don't know," Britten said, whipping out a handkerchief and wiping his forehead. "Honest to God, boys, I can't tell you anything. You'll have to see the old man."

All eyes lifted at once. Mr. Dalton stood at the head of the stairs in the doorway, white-faced, holding a piece of paper in his fingers. Bigger knew at once that it was the kidnap note. What was going to happen now? All of the men talked at once, shouting questions, asking to take pictures.

"Where's Miss Dalton?"

"Did you swear out a warrant for the arrest of Erlone?"

"Were they engaged?"

"Did you forbid her to see him?"

"Did you object to his politics?"

"Don't you want to make a statement, Mr. Dalton?"

Bigger saw Mr. Dalton lift his hand for silence, then walk slowly down the steps and stand near the men, just a few feet above them. They gathered closer, raising their silver bulbs.

"Do you wish to comment on what Erlone said about your chauffeur?"

"What did he say?" Mr. Dalton asked.

"He said the chauffeur had been paid to lie about him."

"That's not true," Mr. Dalton said firmly.

Bigger blinked as lightning shot past his eyes. He saw the men lowering the silver bulbs.

"Gentlemen," said Mr. Dalton. "Please! Give me just a moment. I do want to make a statement." Mr. Dalton paused, his lips quivering. Bigger could see that he was very nervous. "Gentlemen," Mr. Dalton said again, "I want to make a statement and I want you to take it carefully. The way you men handle this will mean life or death to someone, someone close to this family, to me. Someone. . . ." Mr. Dalton's voice trailed off. The basement filled with murmurs of eagerness. Bigger heard the kidnap note crackling faintly in Mr. Dalton's fingers. Mr. Dalton's face was dead-white and his blood-shot eyes were deep set in his head above patches of dark-colored skin. The fire in the furnace was low and the draft was but a whisper. Bigger saw Mr. Dalton's white hair glisten like molten silver from the pale sheen of the fire.

Then, suddenly, so suddenly that the men gasped, the door behind Mr. Dalton filled with a flowing white presence. It was Mrs. Dalton, her white eyes held wide and stony, her hands lifted sensitively upward toward her lips, the fingers long and white and wide apart. The basement was lit up with the white flash of a dozen silver bulbs.

Ghostlike, Mrs. Dalton moved noiselessly down the steps until she came to Mr. Dalton's side, the big white cat following her. She stood with one hand lightly touching a banister and the other held in mid-air. Mr. Dalton did not move or look round; he placed one of his hands over hers on the banister, covering it, and faced the men. Meanwhile, the big white cat bounded down the steps and leaped with one movement upon Bigger's shoulder and sat perched there. Bigger was still, feeling that the cat had given him away, had pointed him out as the murderer of Mary. He tried to lift the cat down; but its claws clutched his coat. The silver lightning flashed in his eyes and he knew that the men had taken pictures of him with the cat poised upon his shoulder. He tugged at the cat once more and managed to get it down. It landed on its feet with a long whine, then began to rub itself against Bigger's legs. Goddamn! Why can't that cat leave me alone? He heard Mr. Dalton speaking.

"Gentlemen, you may take pictures, but wait a moment. I've just phoned the police and asked that Mr. Erlone be released immediately. I want it known that I do not want to prefer charges against him. It is important that this be understood. I hope your papers will carry the story."

Bigger wondered if this meant that suspicion was now pointing away from Jan? He wondered what would happen if he tried to leave the house? Were they watching him?

"Further," Mr. Dalton went on, "I want to announce publicly that I apologize for his arrest and inconvenience." Mr. Dalton paused, wet his lips with his tongue, and looked down over the small knot of men whose hands were busy jotting his words down upon their white pads of paper. "And, gentlemen, I want to announce that Miss Dalton, our daughter. . . . Miss Dalton. . . ." Mr. Dalton's voice faltered. Behind him, a little to one side, stood Mrs. Dalton; she placed her white hand upon his arm. The men lifted their silver bulbs and again lightning flashed in the red gloom of the basement. "I—I want to announce," Mr. Dalton said in a quiet voice that carried throughout the room, though it was spoken in a tense whisper, "that Miss Dalton has been kidnapped. . . ."

"Kidnapped?"

"Oh!"

"When?"

"We think it happened last night," said Mr. Dalton.

"What are they asking?"

"Ten thousand dollars."

"Have you any idea who it is?"

"We know nothing."

"Have you had any word from her, Mr. Dalton?"

"No; not directly. But we've had a letter from the kidnappers. . . ."

"Is that it there?"

"Yes. This is the letter."

"When did you get it?"

"Tonight."

"Through the mail?"

"No; someone left it under our door."

"Are you going to pay the ransom?"

"Yes," said Mr. Dalton. "I'm going to pay. Listen, gentlemen, you can help me and perhaps save my daughter's life by saying in your stories that I'll pay as I've been instructed. And, too, what's most important, tell the kidnappers through your papers that I shall not call in the police. Tell them I'll do everything they ask. Tell them to return our daughter. Tell them, for God's sake, not to kill her, that they will get what they want. . . ."

"Have you any idea, Mr. Dalton, who they are?"

"I have not."

"Can we see that letter?"

"I'm sorry, but you can't. The instructions for the delivery of the money are here, and I have been cautioned not to make them public. But say in your papers that these instructions will be followed."

"When was Miss Dalton last seen?"

"Sunday morning, about two o'clock."

"Who saw her?"

"My chauffeur and my wife."

Bigger stared straight before him, not allowing his eyes to move.

"Please, don't ask him any questions," said Mr. Dalton. "I'm speaking for my whole family. I don't want a lot of crazy versions of this story going around. We want our daughter back; that's all that matters now. Tell her in the papers that we're doing all we can to get her back and that everything is forgiven. Tell her that we. . . ." Again his voice broke and he could not go on.

"Please, Mr. Dalton," begged one man. "Just let us take one shot of that note. . . ."

"No; no. . . . I can't do that."

"How is it signed?"

Mr. Dalton looked straight before him. Bigger wondered if he would tell. He saw Mr. Dalton's lips moving silently, debating something.

"Yes; I'll tell you how it's signed," said the old man, his

hands trembling. Mrs. Dalton's face turned slightly toward him and her fingers gripped in his coat. Bigger knew that Mrs. Dalton was asking him silently if he had not better keep the signature of the note from the papers; and he knew, too, that Mr. Dalton seemed to have reasons of his own for wanting to tell. Maybe it was to let the Reds know that he had received their note.

"Yes," Mr. Dalton said. "It's signed 'Red.' That's all."

"*Red?*"

"Yes."

"Do you know the identity?"

"No."

"Have you any suspicions?"

"Beneath the signature is a scrawled emblem of the Communist Party, the hammer and the sickle," said Mr. Dalton.

The men were silent. Bigger saw the astonishment on their faces. Several did not wait to hear more; they rushed out of the basement to telephone their stories in.

"Do you think the Communists did it?"

"I don't know. I'm not positively blaming anybody. I'm only releasing this information to let the public and the kidnappers know that I've received this note. If they'll return my daughter, I'll ask no questions of anyone."

"Was your daughter mixed up with those people, Mr. Dalton?"

"I know nothing about that."

"Didn't you forbid your daughter to associate with this Erlone?"

"I hope this has nothing to do with that."

"You think Erlone's mixed in this?"

"I don't know."

"Why did you have him released?"

"I ordered his arrest before I received this note."

"Do you feel that maybe he'll return the girl if he's out?"

"I don't know. I don't know if he's got our daughter. I only know that Mrs. Dalton and I want our daughter back."

"Then why did you have Erlone released?"

"Because I have no charges to prefer against him," said Mr. Dalton stubbornly.

"Mr. Dalton, hold the letter up, and hold your hand out,

like you're making an appeal. Good! Now, put your hand out, too, Mrs. Dalton. Like that. O.K., *hold* it!"

Bigger watched the silver bulbs flash again. Mr. and Mrs. Dalton were standing upon the steps: Mrs. Dalton in white and Mr. Dalton with the letter in his hand and his eyes looking straight back to the rear wall of the basement. Bigger heard the soft whisper of the fire in the furnace and saw the men adjusting their cameras. Others were standing round, still scribbling nervously upon their pads of paper. The bulbs flashed again and Bigger was startled to see that they were pointed in his direction. He wanted to duck his head, or throw his hands in front of his face, but it was too late. They had enough pictures of him now to know him by sight in a crowd. A few more of the men left and Mr. and Mrs. Dalton turned and walked slowly up the stairs and disappeared through the kitchen door, the big white cat following close behind them. Bigger still stood with his back to the wall, watching and trying to value every move in relation to himself and his chances of getting the money.

"You suppose we can use Mr. Dalton's phone?" one of the men asked Britten.

"Sure."

Britten led a group of them up the stairs into the kitchen. The three men who had come with Britten sat on the steps and stared gloomily at the floor. Soon the men who had gone to phone their stories in came back. Bigger knew that they wanted to talk to him. Britten also came back and sat upon the steps.

"Say, can't you give us any more dope on this?" one of the reporters asked Britten.

"Mr. Dalton's told you everything," Britten said.

"This is a big story," said one of the men. "Say, how did Mrs. Dalton take this?"

"She collapsed," said Britten.

For awhile nobody said anything. Then Bigger saw the men, one by one, turn and stare at him. He lowered his eyes; he knew that they were longing to ask him questions and he did not want that. His eyes roved the room and saw the crumpled copy of the newspaper lying forgotten in a corner. He wanted ever so badly to read it; he would get at it the first opportunity and find out just what Jan had said. Presently, the men began to wander aimlessly about the basement, looking into corners, examining the shovel, the garbage pail, and the trunk. Bigger watched one man stand in front of the furnace. The man's hand reached out and opened the door; a feeble red glare lit the man's face as he stooped and looked inside at the bed of smoldering coals. Suppose he poked deeply into them? Suppose Mary's bones came into view? Bigger held his breath. But the man would not poke into that fire; nobody suspected him. He was just a black clown. He breathed again as the man closed the door. The muscles of Bigger's face jerked violently, making him feel that he wanted to laugh. He turned his head aside and fought to control himself. He was full of hysteria.

"Say, how about a look at the girl's room?" asked one of the men.

"Sure. Why not?" Britten said.

All of the men followed Britten up the stairs and Bigger was left alone. At once his eyes went to the newspaper; he wanted to pick it up, but was afraid. He stepped to the back door and made sure that it was locked; then he went to the top of the stairs and looked hurriedly into the kitchen; he saw no one. He bounded down the steps and snatched up the paper. He opened it and saw a line of heavy black type stretched across the top of the front page: SEEK HYDE PARK HEIRESS MISSING FROM HOME SINCE SATURDAY. GIRL BELIEVED HIDING OUT WITH COMMUNISTS. POLICE NAB LOCAL RED LEADER; GRILLED ON RELATIONSHIP WITH MARY DALTON. AUTHORITIES ACT ON TIP SUPPLIED BY GIRL'S FATHER.

And there was the picture of Jan in the center of page one. It was Jan all right. Just like him. He turned to the story, reading,

Did the foolish dream of solving the problem of human misery and poverty by dividing her father's real estate millions among the lowly force Mary Dalton to leave the palatial Hyde Park home of her parents, Mr. and Mrs. Henry G. Dalton, 4605 Drexel Boulevard, and take up life under an assumed name with her long-haired friends in the Communist movement?

This was the question that police sought to answer late tonight as they grilled Jan Erlone, executive secretary of the Labor Defenders, a Communist "front" organization in which it was said that Mary Dalton held a membership in defiance of her father's wishes.

The story went on to say that Jan was being held for investigation at the Eleventh Street Police Station and that Mary had been missing from her home since eight o'clock Saturday night. It also mentioned that Mary had been in the "company of Erlone until early Sunday morning at a notorious South Side café in the Black Belt."

That was all. He had expected more. He looked further. No; here was something else. It was a picture of Mary. It was so lifelike that it reminded him of how she had looked the first time he had seen her; he blinked his eyes. He was looking again in sweaty fear at her head lying upon the sticky newspapers with blood oozing outward toward the edges. Above the picture was a caption: IN DUTCH WITH PA. Bigger lifted his eyes and looked at the furnace; it seemed impossible that she was there in the fire, burning. . . . The story in the paper had not been as alarming as he had thought it would be. But as soon as they heard of Mary's being kidnapped, what would happen? He heard footsteps and dropped the paper back in the corner and stood just as he had before, his back against the wall, his eyes vacant and sleepy. The door opened and the men came down the steps, talking in low, excited tones. Again Bigger noticed that they were watching him. Britten also came back.

"Say, why can't we talk to this boy?" one demanded.

"There's nothing he can tell you," Britten said.

"But he can tell us what he saw. After all, he drove the car last night."

"O.K. with me," Britten said. "But Mr. Dalton's told you everything."

One of the men walked over to Bigger.

"Say, Mike, you think this Erlone fellow did this?"

"My name ain't Mike," Bigger said, resentfully.

"Oh, I don't mean no harm," the man said. "But do you think he did it?"

"Answer his questions, Bigger," Britten said.

Bigger was sorry he had taken offense. He could not afford

to get angry now. And he had no need to be angry. Why should he be angry with a lot of fools? They were looking for the girl and the girl was ten feet from them, burning. He had killed her and they did not know it. He would let them call him "Mike."

"I don't know, suh," he said.

"Come on; tell us what happened."

"I only work here, suh," Bigger said.

"Don't be afraid. Nobody's going to hurt you."

"Mr. Britten can tell you," Bigger said.

The men shook their heads and walked away.

"Good God, Britten!" said one of the men. "All we've got on this kidnapping is that a letter was found, Erlone's to be released, the letter was signed by 'Red,' and there was a hammer and sickle emblem on it. That doesn't make sense. Give us some more details."

"Listen, you guys," Britten said. "Give the old man a chance. He's trying to get his daughter back, alive. He's given you a big story; now wait."

"Tell us straight now; when was that girl last seen?"

Bigger listened to Britten tell the story all over again. He listened carefully to every word Britten said and to the tone of voice in which the men asked their questions, for he wanted to know if any of them suspected him. But they did not. All of their questions pointed to Jan.

"But Britten," asked one of the men, "why did the old man want this Erlone released?"

"Figure it out for yourself," Britten said.

"Then he thinks Erlone had something to do with the snatching of his daughter and wanted him out so he could give her back?"

"I don't know," Britten said.

"Aw, come on, Britten,"

"Use your imagination," Britten said.

Two more of the men buttoned their coats, pulled their hats low over their eyes and left. Bigger knew that they were going to phone in more information to their papers; they were going to tell about Jan's trying to convert him to Communism, the Communist literature Jan had given him, the rum, the half-packed trunk being taken down to the station, and lastly, about the kidnap note and the demand for ten thousand dollars. The men looked round the basement with flashlights. Bigger still leaned against the wall. Britten sat on the steps. The fire whispered in the furnace. Bigger knew that soon he would have to clean the ashes out, for the fire was not burning as hotly as it should. He would do that as soon as some of the excitement died down and all of the men left.

"It's pretty bad, hunh, Bigger?" Britten asked.

"Yessuh."

"I'd bet a million dollars that this is Jan's smart idea."

Bigger said nothing. He was limp all over; he was standing up here against this wall by some strength not his own. Hours past he had given up trying to exert himself any more; he could no longer call up any energy. So he just forgot it and found himself coasting along.

It was getting a little chilly; the fire was dying. The draft could scarcely be heard. Then the basement door burst open suddenly and one of the men who had gone to telephone came in, his mouth open, his face wet and red from the snow.

"Say!" he called.

"Yeah?"

"What is it?"

"My city editor just told me that that Erlone fellow won't leave jail."

For a moment the strangeness of the news made them all stare silently. Bigger roused himself and tried to make out just what it meant. Then someone asked the question he longed to ask.

"Won't leave? What you mean?"

"Well, this Erlone refused to go when they told him that Mr. Dalton had requested his release. It seems he had got wind of the kidnapping and said that he didn't want to go out."

"That means he's guilty!" said Britten. "He doesn't want to leave jail because he knows they'll shadow him and find out where the girl is, see? He's *scared*."

"What else?"

"Well, this Erlone says he's got a dozen people to swear that he did not come here last night."

Bigger's body stiffened and he leaned forward slightly.

"That's a lie!" Britten said. "This boy here saw him."

"Is that right, boy?"

Bigger hesitated. He suspected a trap. But if Jan really had an alibi, then he had to talk; he had to steer them away from himself.

"Yessuh."

"Well, somebody's lying. That Erlone fellow says that he can prove it."

"Prove hell!" Britten said. "He's just got some of his Red friends to lie for him; that's all."

"But what in hell's the good of his not wanting to leave jail?" asked one of the men.

"He says if he stays in they can't possibly say he's mixed up in this kidnapping business. He said this boy's lying. He claims they told him to say these things in order to blacken his name and reputation. He swears the family knows where the girl is and that this thing is a stunt to raise a cry against the Reds."

The men gathered round Bigger.

"Say, boy, come on with the dope now. Was that guy really here last night?"

"Yessuh; he was here all right."

"You *saw* 'im?"

"Yessuh."

"Where?"

"I drove him and Miss Dalton up here in the car. We went upstairs together to get the trunk."

"And you *left* him here?"

"Yessuh."

Bigger's heart was pounding, but he tried to keep his face and voice under control. He did not want to seem unduly excited over these new developments. He was wondering if Jan could really prove that he had not been here last night; and he was thinking the question in his own mind when he heard someone ask,

"Who has this Erlone got to prove he was not here last night?"

"He says he met some friend of his when he got on the street car last night. And he says he went to a party after he left Miss Dalton at two-thirty."

"Where was the party?"

"Somewhere on the North Side."

"Say, if what he says is true, then there's something fishy here."

"Naw," said Britten. "I'll bet he went to his pals, the ones he planned all of this with. Sure; why wouldn't they alibi for 'im?"

"So *you* really think he did it?"

"Hell, yes!" Britten said. "These Reds'll do anything and they stick together. Sure; he's got an alibi. Why shouldn't he have one? He's got enough pals working for 'im. His wanting to stay in jail's nothing but a dodge, but he's not so smart. He thinks that his gag'll work and leave him free of suspicion, but it won't."

The talk stopped abruptly as the door at the head of the stairs opened. Peggy's head came through.

"You gentlemen want some coffee?" she asked.

"Sure!"

"Atta gal!"

"I'll bring some down in just a minute," she said, closing the door.

"Who is she?"

"Mrs. Dalton's cook and housekeeper," Britten said.

"She know anything about all this?"

"Naw."

Again the men turned to Bigger. He felt this time he had to say something more to them. Jan was saying that he was lying and he had to wipe out doubt in their minds. They would think that he knew more than he was telling if he did not talk. After all, their attitude toward him so far made him feel that they did not consider him as being mixed up in the kidnapping. He was just another black ignorant Negro to them. The main thing was to keep their minds turned in another direction, Jan's direction, or that of Jan's friends.

"Say," one of the men asked, coming close to him and placing a foot upon the edge of the trunk. "Did this Erlone fellow talk to you about Communism?"

"Yessuh."

"Oh!" Britten exclaimed.

"What?"

"I forgot! Let me show you fellows the stuff he gave the boy to read."

Britten stood up, his face flushed with eagerness. He ran his hand into his pocket and pulled forth the batch of pamphlets that Jan had given Bigger and held them up for all to see. The men again got their bulbs and flashed their lightning to take pictures of the pamphlets. Bigger could hear their hard breathing; he knew that they were excited. When they finished, they turned to him again.

"Say, boy, was this guy drunk?"

"Yessuh."

"And the girl, too?"

"Yessuh."

"He took the girl upstairs when they got here?"

"Yessuh."

"Say, boy, what do you think of public ownership? Do you think the government ought to build houses for people to live in?"

Bigger blinked.

"Suh?"

"Well, what do you think of private property?"

"I don't own any property. Nawsuh," Bigger said.

"Aw, he's a dumb cluck. He doesn't know anything," one of the men whispered in a voice loud enough for Bigger to hear.

There was a silence. Bigger leaned against the wall, hoping that this would satisfy them for a time, at least. The draft could not be heard in the furnace now at all. The door opened again and Peggy came into view carrying a pot of coffee in one hand and a folding card table in the other. One of the men went up the steps and met her, took the table, opened it, and placed it for her. She set the pot upon it. Bigger saw a thin spout of steam jutting from the pot and smelt the good scent of coffee. He wanted some, but he knew that he should not ask with the white men waiting to drink.

"Thank you, sirs," Peggy mumbled, looking humbly round at the strange faces of the men. "I'll get the sugar and cream and some cups."

"Say, boy," Britten said. "Tell the men how Jan made you eat with 'im."

"Yeah; tell us about it."

"Is it true?"

"Yessuh."

"You didn't want to eat with 'im, did you?"

"Nawsuh."

"Did you ever eat with white people before?"

"Nawsuh."

"Did this guy Erlone say anything to you about white women?"

"Oh, nawsuh."

"How did you feel, eating with him and Miss Dalton?"

"I don't know, suh. It was my job."

"You didn't feel just right, did you?"

"Well, suh. They told me to eat and I ate. It was my job."

"In other words, you felt you had to eat or lose your job?"

"Yessuh," said Bigger, feeling that this ought to place him in the light of a helpless, bewildered man.

"Good God!" said one of the men. "What a story! Don't you see it? These Negroes want to be left alone and these Reds are forcing 'em to live with 'em, see? Every wire in the country'll carry it!"

"This is better than Loeb and Leopold," said one.

"Say, I'm slanting this to the primitive Negro who doesn't want to be disturbed by white civilization."

"A swell idea!"

"Say, is this Erlone really a citizen?"

"That's an angle."

"Mention his foreign-sounding name."

"Is he Jewish?"

"I don't know."

"This is good enough as it is. You can't have everything you want."

"It's classic!"

"It's a natural!"

Then, before Bigger knew it, the men had their bulbs in their hands again, aiming at him. He hung his head slowly, slowly so as not to let them know that he was trying to dodge them.

"Hold up a little, boy!"

"Stand straight!"

"Look over this way. Now, that's it!"

Yes; the police would certainly have enough pictures of him. He thought it rather bitterly, smiling a smile that did not reach his lips or eyes.

Peggy came back with her arms full of cups, saucers, spoons, a jar of cream and a bowl of sugar.

"Here it is, sirs. Help yourselves."

She turned to Bigger.

"There's not enough heat upstairs. You'd better clean those ashes out and make a better fire."

"Yessum."

Clean the fire out! Good God! Not now, not with the men standing round. He did not move from his place beside the wall; he watched Peggy walk back up the stairs and close the door behind her. Well, he had to do something. Peggy had spoken to him in the presence of these men, and for him not to obey would seem odd. And even if they did not say anything about it, Peggy herself would soon come back and ask about the fire. Yes, he had to do something. He walked to the door of the furnace and opened it. The low bed of fire was red-hot, but he could tell from the weak blast of heat upon his face that it was not as hot as it ought to be, not as hot as it had been when he had shoved Mary in. He was trying to make his tired brain work fast. What could he do to avoid bothering with the ashes? He stooped and opened the lower door; the ashes, white and grey, were piled almost level with the lower grate. No air could get through. Maybe he could sift the ashes down more and make that do until the men left? He would try it. He caught hold of the handle and worked it to and fro, seeing white ashes and red embers falling into the bottom of the furnace. Behind him he could hear the men's talk and the tinkle of their spoons against the cups. Well, there. He had gotten some of the ashes down out of the stove, but they choked the lower bin and still no air could get through. He would put some coal in. He shut the doors of the furnace and pulled the lever for coal; there was the same loud rattle of coal against the tin sides of the chute. The interior of the furnace grew black with coal. But the draft did not roar and the coal did not blaze. Goddamn! He stood up and looked helplessly into the furnace. Ought he to try to slip out of here and leave this whole foolish thing right now? Naw! There was no use of being scared; he had a chance to get that money. Put more coal in; it would burn after awhile. He pulled the lever for still more coal. Inside the furnace he saw the coal beginning to smoke; there were faint wisps of white smoke at first, then the smoke drew dark, bulging out. Bigger's eyes smarted, watered; he coughed.

The smoke was rolling from the furnace now in heavy billowing grey clouds, filling the basement. Bigger backed away, catching a lungful of smoke. He bent over, coughing. He heard the men coughing. He had to do something about those ashes, and quickly. With his hands stretched before him, he groped in the corner for the shovel, found it, and opened the lower door of the furnace. The smoke surged out, thick and acrid. Goddamn!

"You'd better do something about those ashes, boy!" one of the men called.

"That fire can't get any air, Bigger!" It was Britten's voice.

"Yessuh," Bigger mumbled.

He could scarcely see. He stood still, his eyes closed and stinging, his lungs heaving, trying to expel the smoke. He held onto the shovel, wanting to move, to do something; but he did not know what.

"Say, you! Get some of those ashes out of there!"

"What're you trying to do, smother us?"

"I'm getting 'em out," Bigger mumbled, not moving from where he stood.

He heard a cup smash on the concrete floor and a man cursed.

"I can't see! The smoke's got my eyes!"

Bigger heard someone near him; then someone was tugging at the shovel in his hands. He held onto it desperately, not wanting to let it go, feeling that if he did so he was surrendering his secret, his life.

"Here! Give me that shovel! I'll h-h-help y-you. . . ." a man coughed.

"Nawsuh. I-I-I can d-do it," Bigger said.

"C-come on. L-let go!"

His fingers loosened about the shovel.

"Yessuh," he said, not knowing what else to say.

Through the clouds of smoke he heard the man clanging the shovel round inside of the ash bin. He coughed and stepped back, his eyes blazing as though fire had leaped into them. Behind him the other men were coughing. He opened his eyes and strained to see what was happening. He felt that there was suspended just above his head a huge weight that would soon fall and crush him. His body, despite the smoke and his burning eyes and heaving chest, was flexed taut. He wanted to lunge at the man and take the shovel from him, lam him across the head with it and bolt from the basement. But he stood still, hearing the babble of voices and the clanging of the shovel against iron. He knew that the man was digging frantically at the ashes in the bin, trying to clean as much out as possible so that air could pass up through the grates, pipes, chimney and out into the night. He heard the man yell:

"Open that door! I'm choking!"

There was a scuffle of feet. Bigger felt the icy wind of the night sweep over him and he discovered that he was wet with sweat. Somehow something had happened and now things were out of his hands. He was nervously poised, waiting for what the new flow of events would bring. The smoke drifted past him toward the open door. The room was clearing; the smoke thinned to a grey pall. He heard the man grunting and saw him bent over, digging at the ashes in the bin. He wanted to go to him and ask for the shovel; he wanted to say that he could take care of it now. But he did not move. He felt that he had let things slip through his hands to such an extent that he could not get at them again. Then he heard the draft, this time a long low sucking of air that grew gradually to a drone, then a roar. The air passage was clear.

"There was a hell of a lot of ashes in there, boy," the man gasped. "You shouldn't let it get that way."

"Yessuh," Bigger whispered.

The draft roared loud now; the air passage was completely clear.

"Shut that door, boy! It's cold in here!" one of the men called.

He wanted to go to the door and keep right on out of it and shut it behind him. But he did not move. One of the men closed it and Bigger felt the cold air fall away from his wet body. He looked round; the men were still standing about the table, red-eyed, sipping coffee.

"What's the matter, boy?" one of them asked.

"Nothing," Bigger said.

The man with the shovel stood in front of the furnace and looked down into the ashes strewn over the floor. What's he doing? Bigger wondered. He saw the man stoop and poke the shovel into the ashes. *What's he looking at?* Bigger's muscles twitched. He wanted to run to the man's side and see what it was he was looking at; he had in his mind an image of Mary's head lying there bloody and unburnt before the man's eyes. Suddenly, the man straightened, only to stoop again, as though unable to decide if the evidence of his eyes was true. Bigger edged forward, his lungs not taking in or letting out air; he himself was a huge furnace now through which no air could go; and the fear that surged into his stomach, filling him, choking him, was like the fumes of smoke that had belched from the ash bin.

"Say. . . ." the man called; his voice sounded tentative, dubious.

"What?" one man at the table answered.

"Come here! Look!" The man's voice was low, excited, tense; but what it lacked in volume was more than made up for in the breathless manner in which he spoke. The words had rolled without effort from his lips.

The men set their cups down and ran to the pile of ashes. Bigger, doubtful and uncertain, paused as the men ran past him.

"What is it?"

"What's the matter?"

Bigger tiptoed and looked over their shoulders; he did not know how he got strength enough to go and look; he just found himself walking and then found himself standing and peering over the men's shoulders. He saw a pile of scattered ashes, nothing else. But there must be something, or why would the men be looking?

"What is it?"

"See? *This!*"

"What?"

"Look! It's. . . ."

The man's voice trailed off and he stooped again and poked the shovel deeper. Bigger saw come into full view on the surface of the ashes several small pieces of white bone. Instantly, his whole body was wrapped in a sheet of fear.

"It's bone. . . ."

"Aw," one of the men said. "That's just some garbage they're burning. . . ."

"Naw! Wait; let's *see* that!"

"Toorman, come here. You studied medicine once. . . ."

The man called Toorman reached out his foot and kicked an oblong bone from the ashes; it slid a few inches over the concrete floor.

"My God! It's from a *body*. . . ."

"And look! Here's something. . . ."

One of them stooped and picked up a bit of round metal and held it close to his eyes.

"It's an earring. . . ."

There was silence. Bigger stared without a thought or an image in his mind. There was just the old feeling, the feeling that he had had all his life: he was black and had done wrong; white men were looking at something with which they would soon accuse him. It was the old feeling, hard and constant again now, of wanting to grab something and clutch it in his hands and swing it into someone's face. He knew. They were looking at the bones of Mary's body. Without its making a clear picture in his mind, he understood how it had happened. Some of the bones had not burnt and had fallen into the lower bin when he had worked the handle to sift the ashes. The white man had poked in the shovel to clear the air passage and had raked them out. And now there they lay, tiny, oblong pieces of white bone, cushioned in grey ashes. He could not stay here now. At any moment they would begin to suspect him. They would hold him; they would not let him go even if they were not certain whether he had done it or not. And Jan was still in jail, swearing that he had an alibi. They would know that Mary was dead; they had stumbled upon the white bones of her body. They would be looking for the murderer. The men were silent, bent over, poking into the pile of grey ashes. Bigger saw the hatchet blade come into view. God! The whole world was tumbling down. Quickly, Bigger's eyes looked at their bent backs; they were not watching him. The red glare of the fire lit their faces and the draft of the furnace drummed. Yes; he would go, now! He tiptoed to the rear of the furnace and stopped, listening. The men were whispering in tense tones of horror.

"It's the girl!"

"Good God!"

"Who do you suppose did it?"

Bigger tiptoed up the steps, one at a time, hoping that the roar of the furnace and the men's voices and the scraping of the shovel would drown out the creaking sounds his feet made. He reached the top of the steps and breathed deeply, his lungs aching from holding themselves full of air so long. He stole to the door of his room and opened it and went in and pulled on the light. He turned to the window and put his hands under the upper ledge and lifted; he felt a cold rush of air laden with snow. He heard muffled shouts downstairs and the inside of his stomach glowed white-hot. He ran to the door and locked it and then turned out the light. He groped to the window and climbed into it, feeling again the chilling blast of snowy wind. With his feet upon the bottom ledge, his legs bent under him, his sweaty body shaken by wind, he looked into the snow and tried to see the ground below; but he could not. Then he leaped, headlong, sensing his body twisting in the icy air as he hurtled. His eyes were shut and his hands were clenched as his body turned, sailing through the snow. He was in the air a moment; then he hit. It seemed at first that he hit softly, but the shock of it went through him, up his back to his head and he lay buried in a cold pile of snow, dazed. Snow was in his mouth, eyes, ears; snow was seeping down his back. His hands were wet and cold. Then he felt all of the muscles of his body contract violently, caught in a spasm of reflex action, and at the same time he felt his groin laved with warm water. It was his urine. He had not been able to control the muscles of his hot body against the chilled assault of the wet snow over all his skin. He lifted his head, blinking his eyes, and looked above him. He sneezed. He was himself now; he struggled against the snow, pushing it away from him. He got to his feet, one at a time, and pulled himself out. He walked, then tried to run; but he felt too weak. He went down Drexel Boulevard, not knowing just where he was heading, but knowing that he had to get out of this white neighborhood. He avoided the car line, turned down dark streets, walking more rapidly now, his eyes before him, but turning now and then to look behind.

Yes, he would have to tell Bessie not to go to that house. It was all over. He had to save himself. But it was familiar, this running away. All his life he had been knowing that sooner or later something like this would come to him. And now, here it was. He had always felt outside of this white world, and now it was true. It made things simple. He felt in his shirt. Yes; the gun was still there. He might have to use it. He would shoot before he would let them take him; it meant death either way, and he would die shooting every slug he had.

He came to Cottage Grove Avenue and walked southward. He could not make any plans until he got to Bessie's and got the money. He tried to shut out of his mind the fear of being caught. He lowered his head against the driving snow and tramped through the icy streets with clenched fists. Although his hands were almost frozen, he did not want to put them in his pockets, for that would have made him feel that he would not have been ready to defend himself were the police to accost him suddenly. He went on past street lamps covered with thick coatings of snow, gleaming like huge frosted moons above his head. His face ached from the sub-zero cold and the wind cut into his wet body like a long sharp knife going to the heart of him with pain.

He was in sight of Forty-seventh Street now. He saw, through a gauzelike curtain of snow, a boy standing under an awning selling papers. He pulled his cap visor lower and slipped into a doorway to wait for a car. Back of the newsboy was a stack of papers piled high upon a newsstand. He wanted to see the tall black headline, but the driving snow would not let him. The papers ought to be full of him now. It did not seem strange that they should be, for all his life he had felt that things had been happening to him that should have gone into them. But only after he had acted upon feelings which he had had for years would the papers carry the story, *his* story. He felt that they had not wanted to print it as long as it had remained buried and burning in his own heart. But now that he had thrown it out, thrown it at those who made him live as they wanted, the papers were printing it. He fished three cents out of his pocket; he went over to the boy with averted face.

"*Tribune.*"

He took the paper into a doorway. His eyes swept the streets above the top of it; then he read in tall black type: MILLIONAIRE HEIRESS KIDNAPPED. ABDUCTORS DEMAND $10,000 IN RANSOM NOTE. DALTON FAMILY ASK RELEASE OF COMMUNIST SUSPECT. Yes; they had it now. Soon they would have the story of her death, of the reporters' finding her bones in the furnace, of her head being cut off, of his running away during the excitement. He looked up, hearing the approach of a car. When it heaved into sight he saw that it was almost empty of passengers. Good! He ran into the street and reached the steps just as the last man got on. He paid his fare, watching to see if the conductor was noticing him; then went through the car, watching to see if any face was turned to him. He stood on the front platform, back of the motorman. If anything happened he could get off quickly here. The car started and he opened the paper again, reading:

A servant's discovery early yesterday evening of a crudely penciled ransom note demanding $10,000 for the return of Mary Dalton, missing Chicago heiress, and the Dalton family's sudden demand for the release of Jan Erlone, Communist leader held in connection with the girl's disappearance, were the startling developments in a case which is baffling local and state police.

The note, bearing the signature of "Red" and the famed hammer and sickle emblem of the Communist Party, was found sticking under the front door by Peggy O'Flagherty, a cook and housekeeper in the Henry Dalton residence in Hyde Park.

Bigger read a long stretch of type in which was described the "questioning of a Negro chauffeur," "the half-packed trunk," "the Communist pamphlets," "drunken sexual orgies," "the frantic parents," and "the radical's contradictory story." Bigger's eyes skimmed the words: "clandestine meetings offered opportunities for abduction," "police asked not to interfere in case," "anxious family trying to contact kidnappers"; and:

It was conjectured that perhaps the family had information to the effect that Erlone knew of the whereabouts of Miss Dalton, and certain police officials assigned that as the motive behind the family's request for the radical's release.

Reiterating that police had framed him as a part of a drive to oust Communists from Chicago, Erlone demanded that the charges upon which he had been originally held be made public. Failing to obtain a satisfactory answer, he refused to leave jail, whereupon police again remanded him to his cell upon a charge of disorderly conduct.

Bigger lifted his eyes and looked about; no one was watching him. His hand was shaking with excitement. The car moved lumberingly through the snow and he saw that he was near Fiftieth Street. He stepped to the door and said,

"Out."

The car stopped and he swung off into the driving snow. He was almost in front of Bessie's now. He looked up to her window; it was dark. The thought that she might not be in her room, but out drinking with friends, made him angry. He went into the vestibule. A dim light glowed and his body was thankful for the meager warmth. He could finish reading the paper now. He unfolded it; then, for the first time, he saw his picture. It was down in the lower left-hand corner of page two. Above it he read: REDS TRIED TO SNARE HIM. It was a small picture and his name was under it; he looked solemn and black and his eyes gazed straight and the white cat sat perched upon his right shoulder, its big round black eyes twin pools of secret guilt. And, oh! Here was a picture of Mr. and Mrs. Dalton standing upon the basement steps. That the image of Mr. and Mrs. Dalton which he had seen but two hours ago should be seen again so soon made him feel that this whole vague white world which could do things this quickly was more than a match for him, that soon it would track him down and have it out with him. The white-haired old man and the white-haired old woman standing on the steps with their arms stretched forth pleadingly were a powerful symbol of helpless suffering and would stir up a lot of hate against him when it was found out that a Negro had killed Mary.

Bigger's lips tightened. There was no chance of his getting that money now. They had found Mary and would stop at nothing to get the one who had killed her. There would be a thousand white policemen on the South Side searching for him or any black man who looked like him.

He pressed the bell and waited for the buzzer to ring. Was she there? Again he pressed the bell, holding his finger hard upon it until the door buzzed. He bounded up the steps, sucking his breath in sharply at each lift of his knees. When he reached the second landing he was breathing so hard that he stopped, closed his eyes and let his chest heave itself to stillness. He glanced up and saw Bessie staring sleepily at him through the half-opened door. He went in and stood for a moment in the darkness.

"Turn on the light," he said.

"Bigger! What's happened?"

"Turn on the light!"

She said nothing and did not move. He groped forward, sweeping the air with his open palm for the cord; he found it and jerked on the light. Then he whirled and looked about him, expecting to see someone lurking in the corners of the room.

"What's happened?" She came forward and touched his clothes. "You're wet."

"It's all off," he said.

"I don't have to do it?" she asked eagerly.

Yes; she was thinking only of herself now. He was alone.

"Bigger, tell me what happened?"

"They know all about it. They'll be after me soon."

Her eyes were too filled with fear to cry. He walked about aimlessly and his shoes left rings of dirty water on the wooden floor.

"Tell me, Bigger! Please!"

She was wanting the word that would free her of this nightmare; but he would not give it to her. No; let her be with him; let somebody be with him now. She caught hold of his coat and he felt her body trembling.

"Will they come for me, too, Bigger? I didn't want to do it!"

Yes; he would let her know, let her know everything; but let her know it in a way that would bind her to him, at least a little longer. He did not want to be alone now.

"They found the girl," he said.

"What we going to do, Bigger? Look what you done to me. . . ."

She began to cry.

"Aw, come on, kid."

"You *really* killed her?"

"She's dead," he said. "They found her."

She ran to the bed, fell upon it and sobbed. With her mouth all twisted and her eyes wet, she asked in gasps:

"Y-y-you d-didn't send the l-letter?"

"Yeah."

"Bigger," she whimpered.

"There ain't no help for it now."

"Oh, Lord! They'll come for me. They'll know you did it and they'll go to your home and talk to your ma and brother and everybody. They'll come for me now sure."

That was true. There was no way for her but to come with him. If she stayed here they would come to her and she would simply lie on the bed and sob out everything. She would not be able to help it. And what she would tell them about him, his habits, his life, would help them to track him down.

"You got the money?"

"It's in my dress pocket."

"How much is it?"

"Ninety dollars."

"Well, what you planning to do?" he asked.

"I wish I could kill myself."

"Ain't no use talking that way."

"There ain't no way else to talk."

It was a shot in the dark, but he decided to try it.

"If you don't act better'n this, I'll just leave."

"Naw; naw. . . . Bigger!" she cried, rising and running to him.

"Well, snap out of it," he said, backing to a chair. He sat down and felt how tired he was. Some strength he did not know he possessed had enabled him to run away, to stand here and talk with her; but now he felt that he would not have strength enough to run even if the police should suddenly burst into the room.

"You h-hurt?" she asked, catching hold of his shoulder.

He leaned forward in the chair and rested his face in the palms of his hands.

"Bigger, what's the matter?"

"I'm tired and awful sleepy," he sighed.

"Let me fix you something to eat."

"I need a drink."

"Naw; no whiskey. You need some hot milk."

He waited, hearing her move about. It seemed that his body had turned to a piece of lead that was cold and heavy and wet and aching. Bessie switched on her electric stove, emptied a bottle of milk into a pan and set it upon the glowing red circle. She came back to him and placed her hands upon his shoulders, her eyes wet with fresh tears.

"I'm scared, Bigger."

"You can't be scared now."

"You oughtn't've killed her, honey."

"I didn't mean to. I couldn't help it. I swear!"

"What happened? You never told me."

"Aw, hell. I was in her room. . . ."

"*Her* room?"

"Yeah. She was drunk. She passed out. I. . . . I took her there."

"What she do?"

"She. . . . Nothing. She didn't do anything. Her ma came in. She's blind. . . ."

"The girl?"

"Naw; her ma. I didn't want her to find me there. Well, the girl was trying to say something and I was scared. I just put the edge of the pillow in her mouth and. . . . I didn't mean to kill her. I just pulled the pillow over her face and she died. Her ma came into the room and the girl was trying to say something and her ma had her hands stretched out, like this, see? I was scared she was going to touch me. I just sort of pushed the pillow hard over the girl's face to keep her from yelling. Her ma didn't touch me; I got out of the way. But when she left I went to the bed and the girl. . . . She. . . . She was dead. . . . That was all. She was dead. . . . I didn't mean. . . ."

"You didn't plan to kill her?"

"Naw; I swear I didn't. But what's the use? Nobody'll believe me."

"Honey, don't you see?"

"What?"

"They'll say. . . ."

Bessie cried again. He caught her face in his hands. He was concerned; he wanted to see this thing through her eyes at that moment.

"What?"

"They'll. . . . They'll say you raped her."

Bigger stared. He had entirely forgotten the moment when he had carried Mary up the stairs. So deeply had he pushed it all back down into him that it was not until now that its real meaning came back. They would say he had raped her and there would be no way to prove that he had not. That fact had not assumed importance in his eyes until now. He stood up, his jaws hardening. Had he raped her? Yes, he had raped her. Every time he felt as he had felt that night, he raped. But rape was not what one did to women. Rape was what one felt when one's back was against a wall and one had to strike out, whether one wanted to or not, to keep the pack from killing one. He committed rape every time he looked into a white face. He was a long, taut piece of rubber which a thousand white hands had stretched to the snapping point, and when he snapped it was rape. But it was rape when he cried out in hate deep in his heart as he felt the strain of living day by day. That, too, was rape.

"They found her?" Bessie asked.

"Hunh?"

"They found her?"

"Yeah. Her bones. . . ."

"Bones?"

"Aw, Bessie. I didn't know what to do. I put her in the furnace."

Bessie flung her face to his wet coat and wailed violently.

"Bigger!"

"Hunh?"

"What we going to do?"

"I don't know."

"They'll be looking for us."

"They got my picture."

"Where can we hide?"

"We can stay in some of them old houses for awhile."

"But they might find us there."

"There's plenty of 'em. It'll be like hiding in a jungle."

The milk on the stove boiled over. Bessie rose, her lips still twisted with sobs, and turned off the electric switch. She poured out a glass of milk and brought it to him. He sipped it, slowly, then set the glass aside and leaned over again. They were silent. Bessie gave him the glass once more and he drank it down, then another glass. He stood up, his legs and entire body feeling heavy and sleepy.

"Get your clothes on. And get them blankets and quilts. We got to get out of here."

She went to the bed and rolled the covers back, rolling the pillows with them; as she worked Bigger went to her and put his hands on her shoulders.

"Where's the bottle?"

She got it from her purse and gave it to him; he drank a long swallow and she put it back.

"Hurry up," he said.

She sobbed softly as she worked, pausing now and then to wipe tears from her eyes. Bigger stood in the middle of the floor, thinking, Maybe they searching at home now; maybe they talking to Ma and Vera and Buddy. He crossed the floor and twitched back the curtains and looked out. The streets were white and empty. He turned and saw Bessie bent motionless over the pile of bedclothing.

"Come on; we got to get out of here."

"I don't care what happens."

"Come on. You can't act like that."

What could he do with her? She would be a dangerous burden. It would be impossible to take her if she were going to act like this, and yet he could not leave her here. Coldly, he knew that he had to take her with him, and then at some future time settle things with her, settle them in a way that would not leave him in any danger. He thought of it calmly, as if the decision were being handed down to him by some logic not his own, over which he had no control, but which he had to obey.

"You want me to leave you here?"

"Naw; naw. . . . *Bigger!*"

"Well, come on. Get your hat and coat."

She was facing him, then she sank to her knees.

"Oh, Lord," she moaned. "What's the use of running? They'll catch us anywhere. I should've known this would happen." She clenched her hands in front of her and rocked to and fro with her eyes closed upon gushing tears. "All my life's been full of hard trouble. If I wasn't hungry, I was sick. And if I wasn't sick, I was in trouble. I ain't never bothered nobody. I just worked hard every day as long as I can remember, till I was tired enough to drop; then I had to get drunk to forget it. I had to get drunk to sleep. That's all I ever did. And now I'm in this. They looking for me and when they catch me they'll kill me." She bent her head to the floor. "God only knows why I ever let you treat me this way. I wish to God I never seen you. I wish one of us had died before we was born. God knows I do! All you ever caused me was trouble, just plain black trouble. All you ever did since we been knowing each other was to get me drunk so's you could have me. That was all! I see it now. I ain't drunk now. I see everything you ever did to me. I didn't want to see it before. I was too busy thinking about how good I felt when I was with you. I thought I was happy, but deep down in me I knew I wasn't. But you got me into this murder and I see it all now. I been a fool, just a blind dumb black drunk fool. Now I got to run away and I know deep down in your heart you really don't care."

She stopped, choked. He had not listened to what she had said. Her words had made leap to consciousness in him a thousand details of her life which he had long known and they made him see that she was in no condition to be taken along and at the same time in no condition to be left behind. It was not with anger or regret that he thought this, but as a man seeing what he must do to save himself and feeling resolved to do it.

"Come on, Bessie. We can't stay here like this."

He stooped and with one hand caught hold of her arm and with the other he lifted the bundle of bedclothes. He dragged her across the threshold, and pulled the door after him. He

went down the steps; she came stumbling behind, whimpering. When he reached the vestibule, he got his gun from inside his shirt and put it in the pocket of his coat. He might
have to use it any minute now. The moment he stepped out
of that door he would have his life in his hands. Whatever
happened now depended upon him; and when he felt it that
way some of his fear left; it was simple again. He opened the
door and an icy blast of wind struck his face. He drew back
and turned to Bessie.

"Where's the bottle?"

She held out her purse; he got the bottle and took a deep
drink.

"Here," he said. "You better take one."

She drank and put the bottle back into the purse. They
went into the snow, over the frozen streets, through the
sweeping wind. Once she stopped and began to cry. He
grabbed her arm.

"Shut up, now! Come on!"

They stopped in front of a tall, snow-covered building
whose many windows gaped blackly, like the eye-sockets of
empty skulls. He took the purse from her and got the flashlight. He clutched her arm and pulled her up the steps to the
front door. It was half-ajar. He put his shoulder to it and gave
a stout shove; it yielded grudgingly. It was black inside and
the feeble glow of the flashlight did not help much. A sharp
scent of rot floated to him and he heard the scurrying of
quick, dry feet over the wooden floor. Bessie sucked in her
breath deeply, about to scream; but Bigger gripped her arm
so hard that she bent halfway over and moaned. As he went
up the steps there came frequently to his ears a slight creak, as
of a tree bending in wind. With one hand he held her wrist,
the bundle of bedclothes under his arm; with the other he
beat off the clinging filmy spider webs that came thick onto
his lips and eyes. He walked to the third floor and into a
room that had a window opening to a narrow air-shaft. It
stank of old timber. He circled the spot of the flashlight; the
floor was carpeted with black dirt and he saw two bricks lying
in corners. He looked at Bessie; her hands covered her face
and he could see the damp of tears on her black fingers. He
dropped the bundle of bedclothes.

"Unroll 'em and spread 'em out."

She obeyed. He placed the two pillows near the window, so that when he lay down the window would be just above his head. He was so cold that his teeth chattered. Bessie stood by a wall, leaning against it, crying.

"Take it easy," he said.

He hoisted the window and looked up the air-shaft; snow flew above the roof of the house. He looked downward and saw nothing but black darkness into which now and then a few flakes of white floated from the sky, falling slowly in the dim glow of the flashlight. He lowered the window and turned back to Bessie; she had not moved. He crossed the floor and took the purse from her and got the half-filled flask and drained it. It was good. It burned in his stomach and took his mind off the cold and the sound of the wind outside. He sat on the edge of the pallet and lit a cigarette. It was the first one he had smoked in a long time; he sucked the hot smoke deep into his lungs and blew it out slowly. The whiskey heated him all over, making his head whirl. Bessie cried, softly, piteously.

"Come on and lay down," he said.

He took the gun from his coat pocket and put it where he could reach it.

"Come on, Bessie. You'll freeze standing there like that."

He stood up and pulled off his overcoat and spread it upon the top of the blanket for additional cover; then switched off the flashlight. The whiskey lulled him, numbed his senses. Bessie's soft whimpers came to him through the cold. He took a long last draw from the cigarette and crushed it. Bessie's shoes creaked over the floor. He lay quietly, feeling the warmth of the alcohol spreading through him. He was tense inside; it was as though he had been compelled to hold himself in a certain awkward posture for a long time and then when he had the chance to relax he could not. He was tense with desire, but as long as he knew that Bessie was standing there in the room, he kept it from his mind. Bessie was worried and not to her should his mind turn now in that way. But that part of him which always made him at least outwardly adjusted to what was expected of him made him now keep what his body wanted out of full consciousness. He heard Bessie's clothes rustling in the darkness and he knew that she was pulling off her coat. Soon she would be lying here beside him. He waited for her. After a few moments he felt her fingers pass lightly over his face; she was seeking for the pallet. He reached out, groping, and found her arm.

"Here; lay down."

He held the cover for her; she slid down beside him and stretched out. Now that she was close to him the whiskey made him whirl faster and the tensity of his body mounted. A gust of wind rattled the windowpane and made the old building creak. He felt snug and warm, even though he knew he was in danger. The building might fall upon him as he slept, but the police might get him if he were anywhere else. He laid his fingers upon Bessie's shoulders; slowly he felt the stiffness go out of her body and as it left the tensity in his own rose and his blood grew hot.

"Cold?" he asked in a soft whisper.

"Yeah," she breathed.

"Get close to me."

"I never thought I'd be like this."

"It won't be like this always."

"I'd just as soon die right now."

"Don't say that."

"I'm cold all over. I feel like I'll never get warm."

He drew her closer, till he felt her breath coming full in his face. The wind swept against the windowpane and the building, whining, then whispered out into silence. He turned from his back and lay face to face with her, on his side. He kissed her; her lips were cold. He kept kissing her until her lips grew warm and soft. A huge warm pole of desire rose in him, insistent and demanding; he let his hand slide from her shoulder to her breasts, feeling one, then the other; he slipped his other arm beneath her head, kissing her again, hard and long.

"Please, Bigger. . . ."

She tried to turn from him, but his arm held her tightly; she lay still, whimpering. He heard her sigh, a sigh he knew, for he had heard it many times before; but this time he heard in it a sigh deep down beneath the familiar one, a sigh of resignation, a giving up, a surrender of something more than her body. Her head lay limp in the crook of his arm and his hand reached for the hem of her dress, caught it in his fingers and gathered it up slowly. His cold fingers touched her warm flesh, and sought still warmer and softer flesh. Bessie was still, unresisting, without response. His icy fingers touched inside of her and at once she spoke, not a word, but a sound that gave forth a meaning of horror accepted. Her breath went out of her lungs in long soft gasps that turned to a whisper of pleading.

"Bigger. . . . *Don't!*"

Her voice came to him now from out of a deep, far-away silence and he paid her no heed. The loud demand of the tensity of his own body was a voice that drowned out hers. In the cold darkness of the room it seemed that he was on some vast turning wheel that made him want to turn faster and faster; that in turning faster he would get warmth and sleep and be rid of his tense fatigue. He was conscious of nothing now but her and what he wanted. He flung the cover back, ignoring the cold, and not knowing that he did it. Bessie's hands were on his chest, her fingers spreading protestingly open, pushing him away. He heard her give a soft moan that seemed not to end even when she breathed in or out; a moan which he heard, too, from far away and without heeding. He had to now. Yes. Bessie. His desire was naked and hot in his hand and his fingers were touching her. Yes. Bessie. Now. He had to now. *don't Bigger don't* He was sorry, but he had to. He. He could not help it. Help it. Sorry. Help it. Sorry. Help it. Sorry. Help it now. She should. Look! She should should should look. Look at how he was. He. He was. He was feeling bad about how she would feel but he could not help it now. Feeling. *Bessie.* Now. All. He heard her breathing heavily and heard his own breath going and coming heavily. *Bigger.* Now. All. All. Now. All. *Bigger.* . . .

He lay still, feeling rid of that hunger and tenseness and hearing the wail of the night wind over and above his and her breathing. He turned from her and lay on his back again, stretching his legs wide apart. He felt the tenseness flow gradually from him. His breathing grew less and less heavy and rapid until he could no longer hear it, then so slow and steady that the consciousness of breathing left him entirely. He was not at all sleepy and he lay, feeling Bessie lying there beside him. He turned his head in the darkness toward her. Her breath came to him slowly. He wondered if she were sleeping; somewhere deep in him he knew that he was lying here waiting for her to go to sleep. Bessie did not figure in what was before him. He remembered that he had seen two bricks lying on the floor of the room as he had entered. He tried to recall just where they were, but could not. But he was sure they were there somewhere; he would have to find them, at least one of them. It would have been much better if he had not said anything to Bessie about the murder. Well, it was her own fault. She had bothered him so much that he had had to tell her. And how on earth could he have known that they would find Mary's bones in the furnace so soon? He felt no regret as the image of the smoking furnace and the white pieces of bone came back to him. He had gazed straight at those bones for almost a full minute and had not been able to realize that they were the bones of Mary's body. He had thought that they might find out some other way and then suddenly confront him with the evidence. Never did he think that he could stand and look at the evidence and not know it.

His thoughts came back to the room. What about Bessie? He listened to her breathing. He could not take her with him and he could not leave her behind. Yes. She was asleep. He reconstructed in his mind the details of the room as he had seen them by the glow of the flashlight when he had first come in. The window was directly behind him, above his head. The flashlight was at his side; the gun was lying beside the flashlight, the handle pointing toward him, so he could get it quickly and be in a position to use it. But he could not use the gun; that would make too much noise. He would have to use a brick. He remembered hoisting the window; it had not been hard. Yes, that was what he could do with it, throw it out of the window, down the narrow air-shaft where nobody would find it until, perhaps, it had begun to smell.

He could not leave her here and he could not take her with him. If he took her along she would be crying all the time; she would be blaming him for all that had happened; she would be wanting whiskey to help her to forget and there would be times when he could not get it for her. The room was black-dark and silent; the city did not exist. He sat up slowly, holding his breath, listening. Bessie's breath was deep, regular. He could not take her and he could not leave her. He stretched out his hand and caught the flashlight. He listened again; her breath came like the sleep of the tired. He was holding the covers off her by sitting up this way and he did not want her to get cold and awaken. He eased the covers back; she still slept. His finger pressed a button on the flashlight and a dim spot of yellow leaped to life on the opposite wall. Quickly, he lowered it to the floor, for fear that it might disturb her; and as he did so there passed before his eyes in a split second of time one of the bricks he had glimpsed when he had first come into the room.

He stiffened; Bessie stirred restlessly. Her deep, regular breathing had stopped. He listened, but could not hear it. He saw her breath as a white thread stretching out over a vast black gulf and felt that he was clinging to it and was waiting to see if the ravel in the white thread which had started would continue and let him drop to the rocks far below. Then he heard her breathing again, in, out; in, out. He, too, breathed again, struggling now with his own breath to control it, to keep it from sounding so loud in his throat that it would awaken her. The fear that had gripped him when she had stirred made him realize that it would have to be quick and sure. Softly, he poked his legs from beneath the blanket, then waited. Bessie breathed, slow, long, heavy, regular. He lifted his arm and the blanket fell away. He stood up and his muscles lifted his body in slow motion. Outside in the cold night the wind moaned and died down, like an idiot in an icy black pit. Turning, he centered the disc of light where he thought Bessie's face must be. Yes. She was asleep. Her black face, stained with tears, was calm. He switched off the light, turned toward the wall and his fingers felt over the cold floor for the brick. He found it, gripped it in his hand and tiptoed back to the pallet. Her breath guided him in the darkness; he stopped where he thought her head must be. He couldn't take her and he couldn't leave her; so he would have to kill her. It was his life against hers. Quickly, to make certain where he must strike, he switched on the light, fearing as he did so that it might awaken her; then switched it off again, retaining as an image before his eyes her black face calm in deep sleep.

He straightened and lifted the brick, but just at that moment the reality of it all slipped from him. His heart beat wildly, trying to force its way out of his chest. No! Not this! His breath swelled deep in his lungs and he flexed his muscles, trying to impose his will over his body. He had to do better than this. Then, as suddenly as the panic had come, it left. But he had to stand here until that picture came back, that motive, that driving desire to escape the law. Yes. It *must* be this way. A sense of the white blur hovering near, of Mary burning, of Britten, of the law tracking him down, came back. Again, he was ready. The brick was in his hand. In his mind his hand traced a quick invisible arc through the cold air of the room; high above his head his hand paused in fancy and imaginatively swooped down to where he thought her head must be. He was rigid; not moving. This was the way it *had* to be. Then he took a deep breath and his hand gripped the brick and shot upward and paused a second and then plunged downward through the darkness to the accompaniment of a deep short grunt from his chest and landed with a thud. *Yes!* There was a dull gasp of surprise, then a moan. No, that must not be! He lifted the brick again and again, until in falling it struck a sodden mass that gave softly but stoutly to each landing blow. Soon he seemed to be striking a wet wad of cotton, of some damp substance whose only life was the jarring of the brick's impact. He stopped, hearing his own breath heaving in and out of his chest. He was wet all over, and cold. How many times he had lifted the brick and brought it down he did not know. All he knew was that the room was quiet and cold and that the job was done.

In his left hand he still held the flashlight, gripping it for sheer life. He wanted to switch it on and see if he had really done it, but could not. His knees were slightly bent, like a runner's poised for a race. Fear was in him again; he strained his ears. Didn't he hear her breathing? He bent and listened. It was his own breathing he heard; he had been breathing so loud that he had not been able to tell if Bessie was still breathing or not.

His fingers on the brick began to ache; he had been gripping it for some minutes with all the strength of his body. He was conscious of something warm and sticky on his hand and his sense of it covered him, all over; it cast a warm glow that enveloped the surface of his skin. He wanted to drop the brick, wanted to be free of this warm blood that crept and grew powerful with each passing moment. Then a dreadful thought rendered him incapable of action. Suppose Bessie was not as she had sounded when the brick hit her? Suppose, when he turned on the flashlight, he would see her lying there staring at him with those round large black eyes, her bloody mouth open in awe and wonder and pain and accusation? A cold chill, colder than the air of the room, closed about his shoulders like a shawl whose strands were woven of ice. It became unbearable and something within him cried out in silent agony; he stooped until the brick touched the floor, then loosened his fingers, bringing his hand to his stomach where he wiped it dry upon his coat. Gradually his breath subsided until he could no longer hear it and he knew for certain that Bessie was not breathing. The room was filled with quiet and cold and death and blood and the deep moan of the night wind.

But he had to look. He lifted the flashlight to where he thought her head must be and pressed the button. The yellow spot sprang wide and dim on an empty stretch of floor; he moved it over a circle of crumpled bedclothes. There! Blood and lips and hair and face turned to one side and blood running slowly. She seemed limp; he could act now. He turned off the light. Could he leave her here? No. Somebody might find her.

Avoiding her, he stepped to the far side of the pallet, then turned in the dark. He centered the spot of light where he thought the window must be. He walked to the window and stopped, waiting to hear someone challenge his right to do what he was doing. Nothing happened. He caught hold of the window, hoisted it slowly up and the wind blasted his face. He turned to Bessie again and threw the light upon the face of death and blood. He put the flashlight in his pocket and stepped carefully in the dark to her side. He would have to lift her in his arms; his arms hung loose and did not move; he just stood. But he had to move her. He had to get her to the window. He stooped and slid his hands beneath her body, expecting to touch blood, but not touching it. Then he lifted her, feeling the wind screaming a protest against him. He stepped to the window and lifted her into it; he was working fast now that he had started. He pushed her as far out in his arms as possible, then let go. The body hit and bumped against the narrow sides of the air-shaft as it went down into blackness. He heard it strike the bottom.

He turned the light upon the pallet, half-expecting her to still be there; but there was only a pool of warm blood, a faint veil of vapor hovering in the air above it. Blood was on the pillows too. He took them and threw them out of the window, down the air-shaft. It was over.

He eased the window down. He would take the pallet into another room; he wished he could leave it here, but it was cold and he needed it. He rolled the quilts and blanket into a bundle and picked it up and went into the hall. Then he stopped abruptly, his mouth open. *Good God!* Goddamn, yes, it was in her dress pocket! Now, he was in for it. He had thrown Bessie down the air-shaft and the money was in the pocket of her dress! What could he do about it? Should he go down and get it? Anguish gripped him. *Naw!* He did not want to see her again. He felt that if he should ever see her face again he would be overcome with a sense of guilt so deep as to be unbearable. That was a dumb thing to do, he thought. Throwing her away with all that money in her pocket. He sighed and went through the hall and entered another room. Well, he would have to do without money; that was all. He spread the quilts upon the floor and rolled himself into them. He had seven cents between him and starvation and the law and the long days ahead.

He closed his eyes, longing for a sleep that would not come. During the last two days and nights he had lived so fast and hard that it was an effort to keep it all real in his mind. So close had danger and death come that he could not feel that it was he who had undergone it all. And, yet, out of it all, over and above all that had happened, impalpable but real, there remained to him a queer sense of power. *He* had done this. *He* had brought all this about. In all of his life these two murders were the most meaningful things that had ever happened to him. He was living, truly and deeply, no matter what others might think, looking at him with their blind eyes. Never had he had the chance to live out the consequences of his actions; never had his will been so free as in this night and day of fear and murder and flight.

He had killed twice, but in a true sense it was not the first time he had ever killed. He had killed many times before, but only during the last two days had this impulse assumed the form of actual killing. Blind anger had come often and he had either gone behind his curtain or wall, or had quarreled and fought. And yet, whether in running away or in fighting, he had felt the need of the clean satisfaction of facing this thing in all its fulness, of fighting it out in the wind and sunlight, in front of those whose hate for him was so unfathomably deep that, after they had shunted him off into a corner of the city to rot and die, they could turn to him, as Mary had that night in the car, and say: "I'd like to know how your people live."

But what was he after? What did he want? What did he love and what did he hate? He did not know. There was something he *knew* and something he *felt*; something the *world* gave him and something he *himself* had; something spread out in *front* of him and something spread out in *back*; and never in all his life, with this black skin of his, had the two worlds, thought and feeling, will and mind, aspiration and satisfaction, been together; never had he felt a sense of wholeness. Sometimes, in his room or on the sidewalk, the world seemed to him a strange labyrinth even when the streets were straight and the walls were square; a chaos which made him feel that something in him should be able to understand it, divide it, focus it. But only under the stress of hate was the conflict resolved. He had been so conditioned in a cramped environment that hard words or kicks alone knocked him upright and made him capable of action—action that was futile because the world was too much for him. It was then that he closed his eyes and struck out blindly, hitting what or whom he could, not looking or caring what or who hit back.

And, under it all, and this made it hard for him, he did not want to make believe that it was solved, make believe that he was happy when he was not. He hated his mother for that

way of hers which was like Bessie's. What his mother had was
Bessie's whiskey, and Bessie's whiskey was his mother's religion. He did not want to sit on a bench and sing, or lie in a
corner and sleep. It was when he read the newspapers or magazines, went to the movies, or walked along the streets with
crowds, that he felt what he wanted: to merge himself with
others and be a part of this world, to lose himself in it so he
could find himself, to be allowed a chance to live like others,
even though he was black.

He turned restlessly on his hard pallet and groaned. He had
been caught up in a whirl of thought and feeling which had
swept him onward and when he opened his eyes he saw that
daylight stood outside of a dirty window just above his head.
He jumped up and looked out. The snow had stopped falling
and the city, white, still, was a vast stretch of roof-tops and
sky. He had been thinking about it for hours here in the dark
and now there it was, all white, still. But what he had thought
about it had made it real with a reality it did not have now in
the daylight. When lying in the dark thinking of it, it seemed
to have something which left it when it was looked at. Why
should not this cold white world rise up as a beautiful dream
in which he could walk and be at home, in which it would be
easy to tell what to do and what not to do? If only someone
had gone before and lived or suffered or died—made it so
that it could be understood! It was too stark, not redeemed,
not made real with the reality that was the warm blood of life.
He felt that there was something missing, some road which, if
he had once found it, would have led him to a sure and quiet
knowledge. But why think of that now? A chance for that was
gone forever. He had committed murder twice and had
created a new world for himself.

.   .   .   .

He left the room and went down to a window on the first
floor and looked out. The street was quiet and no cars were
running. The tracks were buried under snow. No doubt the
blizzard had tied up traffic all over the city.

He saw a little girl pick her way through the snow and stop
at a corner newsstand; a man hurried out of a drug store and
sold the girl a paper. Could he snatch a paper while the man
was inside? The snow was so soft and deep he might get

caught trying to get away. Could he find an empty building
in which to hide after he had snatched the paper? Yes; that
was just the thing. He looked carefully up and down the
street; no one was in sight. He went through the door and
the wind was like a branding-iron on his face. The sun came
out, suddenly, so strong and full that it made him dodge as
from a blow; a million bits of sparkle pained his eyes. He
went to the newsstand and saw a tall black headline. HUNT
BLACK IN GIRL'S DEATH. Yes; they had the story. He
walked on and looked for a place to hide after he had
snatched the paper. At the corner of an alley he saw an empty
building with a gaping window on the first floor. Yes; this
was a good place. He mapped out a careful plan of action; he
did not want it said that he had done all the things he had
and then had got caught stealing a three-cent newspaper.

He went to the drug store and looked inside at the man
leaning against a wall, smoking. Yes. Like this! He reached
out and grabbed a paper and in the act of grabbing it he
turned and looked at the man who was looking at him, a
cigarette slanting whitely across his black chin. Even before he
moved from his tracks, he ran; he felt his legs turn, start, then
slip in snow. Goddamn! The white world tilted at a sharp
angle and the icy wind shot past his face. He fell flat and the
crumbs of snow ate coldly at his fingers. He got up, on one
knee, then on both; when he was on his feet he turned toward the drug store, still clutching the paper, amazed and
angry with himself for having been so clumsy. The drug store
door opened. He ran.

"Hey!"

As he ducked down the alley he saw the man standing in
the snow looking at him and he knew that the man would not
follow.

"Hey, you!"

He scrambled to the window, pitched the paper in before
him, caught hold and heaved himself upward onto the ledge
and then inside. He landed on his feet and stood peering
through the window into the alley; all was white and quiet.
He picked up the paper and walked down the hallway to
the steps and up to the third floor, using the flashlight and
hearing his footsteps echo faintly in the empty building. He

stopped, clutched his pocket in panic as his mouth flew open.
Yes; he had it. He thought that he had dropped the gun when
he had fallen in the snow, but it was still there. He sat on the
top step of the stairs and opened out the paper, but for quite
awhile he did not read. He listened to the creaking of the
building caused by the wind sweeping over the city. Yes; he
was alone; he looked down and read, REPORTERS FIND
DALTON GIRL'S BONES IN FURNACE. NEGRO
CHAUFFEUR DISAPPEARS. FIVE THOUSAND PO-
LICE SURROUND BLACK BELT. AUTHORITIES
HINT SEX CRIME. COMMUNIST LEADER PROVES
ALIBI. GIRL'S MOTHER IN COLLAPSE. He paused and
reread the line, AUTHORITIES HINT SEX CRIME. Those
words excluded him utterly from the world. To hint that he
had committed a sex crime was to pronounce the death sentence; it meant a wiping out of his life even before he was captured; it meant death before death came, for the white men
who read those words would at once kill him in their hearts.

The Mary Dalton kidnapping case was dramatically cracked wide
open when a group of local newspaper reporters accidentally discovered several bones, later positively established as those of the missing
heiress, in the furnace of the Dalton home late today. . . .

.   .   .   .

Search of the Negro's home, 3721 Indiana Avenue, in the heart of
the South Side, failed to reveal his whereabouts. Police expressed
belief that Miss Dalton met her death at the hands of the Negro,
perhaps in a sex crime, and that the white girl's body was burned to
destroy evidence.

Bigger looked up. His right hand twitched. He wanted a
gun in that hand. He got his gun from his pocket and held it.
He read again:

Immediately a cordon of five thousand police, augmented by more
than three thousand volunteers, was thrown about the Black Belt.
Chief of Police Glenman said this morning that he believed that the
Negro was still in the city, since all roads leading in and out of
Chicago were blocked by a record-breaking snowfall.

Indignation rose to white heat last night as the news of the Negro's rape and murder of the missing heiress spread through the city.

Police reported that many windows in the Negro sections were
smashed.

Every street car, bus, el train and auto leaving the South Side is being stopped and searched. Police and vigilantes, armed with rifles, tear gas, flashlights, and photos of the killer, began at 18th Street this morning and are searching every Negro home under a blanket warrant from the Mayor. They are making a careful search of all abandoned buildings, which are said to be hideouts for Negro criminals.

Maintaining that they feared for the lives of their children, a delegation of white parents called upon Superintendent of City Schools Horace Minton, and begged that all schools be closed until the Negro rapist and murderer was captured.

Reports were current that several Negro men were beaten in various North and West Side neighborhoods.

In the Hyde Park and Englewood districts, men organized vigilante groups and sent word to Chief of Police Glenman offering aid.

Glenman said this morning that the aid of such groups would be accepted. He stated that a woefully undermanned police force together with recurring waves of Negro crime made such a procedure necessary.

Several hundred Negroes resembling Bigger Thomas were rounded up from South Side "hot spots"; they are being held for investigation.

In a radio broadcast last night Mayor Ditz warned of possible mob violence and exhorted the public to maintain order. "Every effort is being made to apprehend this fiend," he said.

It was reported that several hundred Negro employees throughout the city had been dismissed from jobs. A well-known banker's wife phoned this paper that she had dismissed her Negro cook, "for fear that she might poison the children."

Bigger's eyes were wide and his lips were parted; he scanned the print quickly: "handwriting experts busy," "Erlone's fingerprints not found in Dalton home," "radical still in custody"; and then a sentence leaped at Bigger, like a blow:

Police are not yet satisfied with the account Erlone has given of himself and are of the conviction that he may be linked to the Negro as an accomplice; they feel that the plan of the murder and kidnapping was too elaborate to be the work of a Negro mind.

At that moment he wanted to walk out into the street and up to a policeman and say, "No! Jan didn't help me! He didn't have a damn thing to do with it! I—I did it!" His lips twisted in a smile that was half-leer and half-defiance.

Holding the paper in taut fingers, he read phrases: "Negro

ordered to clean out ashes . . . . reluctant to respond . . . .
dreading discovery . . . . smoke-filled basement . . . . trag-
edy of Communism and racial mixture . . . . possibility that
kidnap note was work of Reds. . . ."

Bigger looked up. The building was quiet save for the continual creaking caused by the wind. He could not stay here.
There was no telling when they were coming into this neighborhood. He could not leave Chicago; all roads were blocked,
and all trains, buses and autos were being stopped and
searched. It would have been much better if he had tried to
leave town at once. He should have gone to some other place,
perhaps Gary, Indiana, or Evanston. He looked at the paper
and saw a black-and-white map of the South Side, around the
borders of which was a shaded portion an inch deep. Under
the map ran a line of small print:

Shaded portion shows area already covered by police and vigilantes in search for Negro rapist and murderer. White portion shows
area yet to be searched.

He was trapped. He would have to get out of this building.
But where could he go? Empty buildings would serve only as
long as he stayed within the white portion of the map, and
the white portion was shrinking rapidly. He remembered that
the paper had been printed last night. That meant that the
white portion was now much smaller than was shown here.
He closed his eyes, calculating: he was at Fifty-third Street
and the hunt had started last night at Eighteenth Street. If
they had gone from Eighteenth Street to Twenty-eighth
Street last night, then they would have gone from Twenty-
eighth Street to Thirty-eighth Street since then. And by midnight tonight they would be at Forty-eighth Street, or right
here.

He wondered about empty flats. The paper had not mentioned them. Suppose he found a small, empty kitchenette flat
in a building where many people lived? That was by far the
safest thing.

He went to the end of the hall and flashed the light on a
dirty ceiling and saw a wooden stairway leading to the roof.
He climbed and pulled himself up into a narrow passage at
the end of which was a door. He kicked at the door several

times, each kick making it give slightly until he saw snow, sunshine, and an oblong strip of sky. The wind came stinging into his face and he remembered how weak and cold he was. How long could he keep going this way? He squeezed through and stood in the snow on the roof. Before him was a maze of white, sun-drenched roof-tops.

He crouched behind a chimney and looked down into the street. At the corner he saw the newsstand from which he had stolen the paper; the man who had shouted at him was standing by it. Two black men stopped at the newsstand and bought a paper, then walked into a doorway. One of them leaned eagerly over the other's shoulder. Their lips moved and they pointed their black fingers at the paper and shook their heads as they talked. Two more men joined them and soon there was a small knot of them standing in the doorway, talking and pointing at the paper. They broke up abruptly and went away. Yes; they were talking about him. Maybe all of the black men and women were talking about him this morning; maybe they were hating him for having brought this attack upon them.

He had crouched so long in the snow that when he tried to move he found that his legs had lost all feeling. A fear that he was freezing seized him. He kicked out his legs to restore circulation of his blood, then crawled to the other side of the roof. Directly below him, one floor away, through a window without shades, he saw a room in which were two small iron beds with sheets dirty and crumpled. In one bed sat three naked black children looking across the room to the other bed on which lay a man and woman, both naked and black in the sunlight. There were quick, jerky movements on the bed where the man and woman lay, and the three children were watching. It was familiar; he had seen things like that when he was a little boy sleeping five in a room. Many mornings he had awakened and watched his father and mother. He turned away, thinking: Five of 'em sleeping in one room and here's a great big empty building with just me in it. He crawled back to the chimney, seeing before his eyes an image of the room of five people, all of them blackly naked in the strong sunlight, seen through a sweaty pane: the man and woman moving jerkily in tight embrace, and the three children watching.

Hunger came to his stomach; an icy hand reached down his throat and clutched his intestines and tied them into a cold, tight knot that ached. The memory of the bottle of milk Bessie had heated for him last night came back so strongly that he could almost taste it. If he had that bottle of milk now he would make a fire out of a newspaper and hold the bottle over the flame until it was warm. He saw himself take the top off the white bottle, with some of the warm milk spilling over his black fingers, and then lift the bottle to his mouth and tilt his head and drink. His stomach did a slow flip-flop and he heard it growl. He felt in his hunger a deep sense of duty, as powerful as the urge to breathe, as intimate as the beat of his heart. He felt like dropping to his knees and lifting his face to the sky and saying: "I'm hungry!" He wanted to pull off his clothes and roll in the snow until something nourishing seeped into his body through the pores of his skin. He wanted to grip something in his hands so hard that it would turn to food. But soon his hunger left; soon he was taking it a little easier; soon his mind rose from the desperate call of his body and concerned itself with the danger that lurked about him. He felt something hard at the corners of his lips and touched it with his fingers; it was frozen saliva.

He crawled back through the door into the narrow passage and lowered himself down the shallow wooden steps into the hallway. He went to the first floor and stood at the window through which he had first climbed. He had to find an empty apartment in some building where he could get warm; he felt that if he did not get warm soon he would simply lie down and close his eyes. Then he had an idea; he wondered why he had not thought of it before. He struck a match and lit the newspaper; as it blazed he held one hand over it awhile, and then the other. The heat came to his skin from far off. When the paper had burned so close that he could no longer hold it, he dropped it to the floor and stamped it out with his shoes. At least he could feel his hands now; at least they ached and let him know that they were his.

He climbed through the window and walked to the street, turned northward, joining the people passing. No one recognized him. He looked for a building with a "For Rent" sign. He walked two blocks and saw none. He knew that empty flats were scarce in the Black Belt; whenever his mother wanted to move she had to put in requests long months in advance. He remembered that his mother had once made him tramp the streets for two whole months looking for a place to live. The rental agencies had told him that there were not enough houses for Negroes to live in, that the city was condemning houses in which Negroes lived as being too old and too dangerous for habitation. And he remembered the time when the police had come and driven him and his mother and his brother and sister out of a flat in a building which had collapsed two days after they had moved. And he had heard it said that black people, even though they could not get good jobs, paid twice as much rent as whites for the same kind of flats. He walked five more blocks and saw no "For Rent" sign. Goddamn! Would he freeze trying to find a place in which to get warm? How easy it would be for him to hide if he had the whole city in which to move about! They keep us bottled up here like wild animals, he thought. He knew that black people could not go outside of the Black Belt to rent a flat; they had to live on their side of the "line." No white real estate man would rent a flat to a black man other than in the sections where it had been decided that black people might live.

His fists clenched. What was the use of running away? He ought to stop right here in the middle of the sidewalk and shout out what this was. It was so wrong that surely all the black people round him would do something about it; so wrong that all the white people would stop and listen. But he knew that they would simply grab him and say that he was crazy. He reeled through the streets, his bloodshot eyes looking for a place to hide. He paused at a corner and saw a big black rat leaping over the snow. It shot past him into a doorway where it slid out of sight through a hole. He looked wistfully at that gaping black hole through which the rat had darted to safety.

He passed a bakery and wanted to go in and buy some rolls with the seven cents he had. But the bakery was empty of customers and he was afraid that the white proprietor would recognize him. He would wait until he came to a Negro business establishment, but he knew that there were not many of them. Almost all businesses in the Black Belt were owned by Jews, Italians, and Greeks. Most Negro businesses were funeral parlors; white undertakers refused to bother with dead black bodies. He came to a chain grocery store. Bread sold here for five cents a loaf, but across the "line" where white folks lived, it sold for four. And now, of all times, he could not cross that "line." He stood looking through the plate glass at the people inside. Ought he to go in? He had to. He was starving. They trick us every breath we draw! he thought. They gouge our eyes out! He opened the door and walked to the counter. The warm air made him dizzy; he caught hold of a counter in front of him and steadied himself. His eyes blurred and there swam before him a vast array of red and blue and green and yellow cans stacked high upon shelves. All about him he heard the soft voices of men and women.

"You waited on, sir?"

"A loaf of bread," he whispered.

"Anything else, sir?"

"Naw."

The man's face went away and came again; he heard paper rustling.

"Cold out, isn't it?"

"Hunh? Oh, yessuh."

He laid the nickel on the counter; he saw the blurred loaf being handed to him.

"Thank you. Call again."

He walked unsteadily to the door with the loaf under his arm. Oh, Lord! If only he could get into the street! In the doorway he met people coming in; he stood to one side to let them pass, then went into the cold wind, looking for an empty flat. At any moment he expected to hear his name shouted; expected to feel his arms being grabbed. He walked five blocks before he saw a two-story flat building with a "For Rent" sign in a window. Smoke bulged out of chimneys and he knew that it was warm inside. He went to the front door and read the little vacancy notice pasted on the glass and saw that the flat was a rear one. He went down the alley to the rear steps and mounted to the second floor. He tried a window and it slid up easily. He was in luck. He hoisted himself through and dropped into a warm room, a kitchen. He was suddenly tense, listening. He heard voices; they seemed to be coming from the room in front of him. Had he made a mistake? No. The kitchen was not furnished; no one, it seemed, lived in here. He tiptoed to the next room and found it empty; but he heard the voices even more clearly now. He saw still another room leading farther; he tiptoed and looked. That room, too, was empty, but the sound of the voices was coming so loud that he could make out the words. An argument was going on in the front flat. He stood with the loaf of bread in his hands, his legs wide apart, listening.

"Jack, yuh mean t' stan' there 'n' say yuh'd give tha' nigger up t' the white folks?"

"Damn right Ah would!"

"But, Jack, s'pose he ain' guilty?"

"Whut in hell he run off fer then?"

"Mabbe he thought they wuz gonna blame the murder on *him*!"

"Lissen, Jim. Ef he wuzn't guilty, then he oughta stayed 'n' faced it. Ef Ah knowed where tha' nigger wuz Ah'd turn im up 'n' git these white folks off me."

"But, Jack, *ever'* nigger looks guilty t' white folks when somebody's done a crime."

"Yeah; tha's 'cause so many of us ack like Bigger Thomas; tha's all. When yuh ack like Bigger Thomas yuh stir up trouble."

"But, Jack, who's stirring up trouble now? The papers say they beatin' us up all over the city. They don't care whut black man they git. We's all dogs in they sight! Yuh gotta stan' up 'n' fight these folks."

" 'N' git killed? Hell, naw! Ah gotta family. Ah gotta wife 'n' baby. Ah ain't startin' no fool fight. Yuh can't git no justice pertectin' men who kill. . . ."

"We's *all* murderers t' them, Ah tell yuh!"

"Lissen, Jim. Ah'm a hard-workin' man. Ah fixes the streets wid a pick 'n' shovel ever' day, when Ah git a chance. But the boss tol' me he didn't wan' me in them streets wid this mob feelin' among the white folks. . . . He says Ah'll git killed. So he lays me off. Yuh see, tha' Goddamn nigger Bigger Thomas made me lose mah job. . . . He made the white folks think we's *all* jus' like him!"

"But, Jack, Ah tell yuh they think it awready. Yuh's a good man, but tha' ain' gonna keep 'em from comin' t' yo' home, is it? Hell, naw! We's all black 'n' we jus' as waal *ack* black, don' yuh see?"

"Aw, Jim, it's awright t' git mad, but yuh gotta look at things straight. Tha' guy made me lose mah job. Tha' ain' fair! How is Ah gonna eat? Ef Ah knowed where the black sonofabitch wuz Ah'd call the cops 'n' let 'em come 'n' git 'im!"

"Waal, Ah wouldn't. Ah'd die firs'!"

"Man, yuh crazy! Don' yuh wan' a home 'n' wife 'n' chillun? Whut's fightin' gonna git yuh? There's *mo'* of them than us. They could kill us all. Yuh gotta learn t' live 'n' git erlong wid people."

"When folks hate me, Ah don' wanna git erlong."

"But we gotta *eat*! We gotta *live*!"

"Ah don' care! Ah'd die firs'!"

"Aw, hell! Yuh crazy!"

"Ah don' care whut yuh say. Ah'd die 'fo' Ah'd let 'em scare me inter tellin' on tha' man. Ah tell yuh, Ah'd die firs'!"

He tiptoed back into the kitchen and took out his gun. He would stay here and if his own people bothered him he would use it. He turned on the water faucet and put his mouth under the stream and the water exploded in his stomach. He sank to his knees and rolled in agony. Soon the pain ceased and he drank again. Then, slowly, so that the paper would not rustle, he unwrapped the loaf of bread and chewed a piece. It tasted good, like cake, with a sweetish and smooth flavor he had never thought bread could have. As he ate his hunger returned in full force and he sat on the floor and held a fistful of bread in each hand, his cheeks bulging and his jaws working and his Adam's apple going up and down with each swallow. He could not stop until his mouth became so dry that the bread balled on his tongue; he held it there, savoring the taste.

He stretched out on the floor and sighed. He was drowsy, but when he was on the verge of sleep he jerked abruptly to a dull wakefulness. Finally, he slept, then sat up, half-awake, following an unconscious prompting of fear. He groaned and his hands flayed the air to ward off an invisible danger. Once

he got up completely and walked a few steps with outstretched hands and then lay down in a spot almost ten feet
from where he had originally slept. There were two Biggers:
one was determined to get rest and sleep at any cost; and the
other shrank from images charged with terror. There came a
long space of time in which he did not move; he lay on his
back, his hands folded upon his chest, his mouth and eyes
open. His chest rose and fell so slowly and gently that it
seemed that during the intervals when it did not move he
would never breathe again. A wan sun came onto his face,
making the black skin shine like dull metal; the sun left and
the quiet room filled with deep shadows.

As he slept there stole into his consciousness a disturbing,
rhythmic throbbing which he tried to fight off to keep from
waking up. His mind, protecting him, wove the throb into
patterns of innocent images. He thought he was in the Paris
Grill listening to the automatic phonograph playing; but that
was not satisfying. Next, his mind told him that he was at
home in bed and his mother was singing and shaking the
mattress, wanting him to get up. But this image, like the
others, failed to quiet him. The throb pulsed on, insistent,
and he saw hundreds of black men and women beating drums
with their fingers. But that, too, did not answer the question.
He tossed restlessly on the floor, then sprang to his feet, his
heart pounding, his ears filled with the sound of singing and
shouting.

He went to the window and looked out; in front of him,
down a few feet, through a window, was a dim-lit church. In
it a crowd of black men and women stood between long rows
of wooden benches, singing, clapping hands, and rolling their
heads. Aw, them folks go to church every day in the week, he
thought. He licked his lips and got another drink of water.
How near were the police? What time was it? He looked at
his watch and found that it had stopped running; he had forgotten to wind it. The singing from the church vibrated
through him, suffusing him with a mood of sensitive sorrow.
He tried not to listen, but it seeped into his feelings, whispering of another way of life and death, coaxing him to lie down
and sleep and let them come and get him, urging him to believe that all life was a sorrow that had to be accepted. He

shook his head, trying to rid himself of the music. How long had he slept? What were the papers saying now? He had two cents left; that would buy a *Times*. He picked up what remained of the loaf of bread and the music sang of surrender, resignation. *Steal away, Steal away, Steal away to Jesus. . . .* He stuffed the bread into his pockets; he would eat it some time later. He made sure that his gun was still intact, hearing, *Steal away, Steal away home, I ain't got long to stay here. . . .* It was dangerous to stay here, but it was also dangerous to go out. The singing filled his ears; it was complete, self-contained, and it mocked his fear and loneliness, his deep yearning for a sense of wholeness. Its fulness contrasted so sharply with his hunger, its richness with his emptiness, that he recoiled from it while answering it. Would it not have been better for him had he lived in that world the music sang of? It would have been easy to have lived in it, for it was his mother's world, humble, contrite, believing. It had a center, a core, an axis, a heart which he needed but could never have unless he laid his head upon a pillow of humility and gave up his hope of living in the world. And he would never do that.

He heard a street car passing in the street; they were running again. A wild thought surged through him. Suppose the police had already searched this neighborhood and had overlooked him? But sober judgment told him that that was impossible. He patted his pocket to make sure the gun was there, then climbed through the window. Cold wind smote his face. It must be below zero, he thought. At both ends of the alley the street lamps glowed through the murky air, refracted into mammoth balls of light. The sky was dark blue and far away. He walked to the end of the alley and turned onto the sidewalk, joining the passing stream of people. He waited for someone to challenge his right to walk there, but no one did.

At the end of the block he saw a crowd of people and fear clutched hard at his stomach. What were they doing? He slowed and saw that they were gathered about a newsstand. They were black people and they were buying papers to read about how the white folks were trying to track him to earth. He lowered his head and went forward and slipped into the crowd. The people were talking excitedly. Cautiously, he held out two cents in his cold fingers. When he was close enough, he saw the front page; his picture was in the center of it. He bent his head lower, hoping that no one would see him closely enough to see that it was he who was pictured there.

"*Times*," he said.

He tucked the paper under his arm, edged out of the crowd and walked southward, looking for an empty flat. At the next corner he saw a "For Rent" sign in a building which he knew was cut up into small kitchenette flats. This was what he wanted. He went to the door and read the sign; there was an empty flat on the fourth floor. He walked to the alley and began to mount the outside rear stairs, his feet softly crunching in snow. He heard a door open; he stopped, got his gun and waited, kneeling in the snow.

"Who's that?"

It was a woman's voice. Then a man's voice sounded.

"What's the matter, Ellen?"

"I thought I heard someone out here on the porch."

"Ah, you're simply nervous. You're scared of all this stuff you've been reading in the papers."

"But I'm sure I heard somebody."

"Aw, empty the garbage and shut the door. It's cold."

Bigger flattened against the building, in the dark. He saw a woman come out of a door, pause, look round; she went to the far end of the porch and dumped something into a garbage pail and went back inside. I would've had to kill 'em both if she saw me, he thought. He tiptoed up to the fourth floor and found two windows, both of them dark. He tried to lift the screen in one of them and found it frozen. Gently, he shook it to and fro until it loosened; then he lifted it out and laid it on the porch in the snow. Inch by inch, he raised the window, breathing so loud that he thought surely people must hear him even in the streets. He climbed through into a dark room and struck a match. An electric light was on the other side of the room and he went to it and pulled the chain. He put his cap over the bulb so that no light would seep through to the outside, then opened the paper. Yes; here was a large picture of him. At the top of the picture ran a tall line of black type: 24-HOUR SEARCH FAILS TO UNEARTH RAPIST. In another column he saw: RAID 1,000 NEGRO

HOMES. INCIPIENT RIOT QUELLED AT 47TH AND HALSTED. There was another map of the South Side. This time the shaded area had deepened from both the north and south, leaving a small square of white in the middle of the oblong Black Belt. He stood looking at that tiny square of white as though gazing down into the barrel of a gun. He was there on that map, in that white spot, standing in a room waiting for them to come. Dead-set, his eyes stared above the top of the paper. There was nothing left for him but to shoot it out. He examined the map again; the police had come from the north as far south as Fortieth Street; and they had come from the south as far north as Fiftieth Street. That meant that he was somewhere in between, and they were minutes away. He read:

Today and last night eight thousand armed men combed cellars, old buildings and more than one thousand Negro homes in the Black Belt in a vain effort to apprehend Bigger Thomas, 20-year-old Negro rapist and killer of Mary Dalton, whose bones were found last Sunday night in a furnace.

Bigger's eyes went down the page, snatching at what he thought most important: "word spread that the slayer had been captured, but was immediately denied," "before night police and vigilantes will have covered the entire Black Belt," "raiding numerous Communist headquarters throughout the city," "the arrest of hundreds of Reds failed, however, to uncover any clues," "public warned by Mayor against 'boring from within,' . . . ." Then:

A curious sidelight was revealed today when it became known that the apartment building in which the Negro killer lived is owned and managed by a sub-firm of the Dalton Real Estate Company.

He lowered the paper; he could read no more. The one fact to remember was that eight thousand men, white men, with guns and gas, were out there in the night looking for him. According to this paper, they were but a few blocks away. Could he get to the roof of this building? If so, maybe he could crouch there until they passed. He thought of burying himself deep in the snow of the roof, but he knew that that was impossible. He pulled the chain again and plunged the room in darkness. Using the flashlight, he went to the door and opened it and looked into the hall. It was empty and a dim light burned at the far end. He put out the flashlight and tiptoed, looking at the ceiling, searching for a trapdoor leading to the roof. Finally, he saw a pair of wooden steps leading upward. Suddenly, his muscles stiffened as though a wire strung through his body had jerked him. A siren shriek entered the hallway. And immediately he heard voices, excited, low, tense. From somewhere down below a man called,

"They's comin'!"

There was nothing to do now but go up; he clutched the wooden steps above him and climbed, wanting to get out of sight before anyone came into the hall. He reached the trapdoor and pushed against it with his head; it opened. He grabbed something solid in the darkness above him and hoisted himself upward, hoping as he did so that it would hold him and not let him go crashing down upon the hall floor. He rested on his knees, his chest heaving. Then he eased the door shut, peering just in time to see a door in the hall opening. That was close! The siren sounded again; it was outside in the street. It seemed to sound a warning that no one could hide from it; that action to escape was futile; that soon the men with guns and gas would come and penetrate where the siren sound had penetrated.

He listened; there were throbs of motors; shouts rose from the streets; there were screams of women and curses of men. He heard footsteps on the stairs. The siren died and began again, on a high, shrill note this time. It made him want to clutch at his throat; as long as it sounded it seemed that he could not breathe. He had to get to the roof! He switched on the flashlight and crawled through a narrow loft till he came to an opening. He put his shoulder to it and heaved; it gave so suddenly and easily that he drew back in fear. He thought that someone had snatched it open from above and in the same instant of its opening he saw an expanse of gleaming white snow against the dark smudge of night and a stretch of luminous sky. A medley of crashing sounds came, louder than he had thought that sound could be: horns, sirens, screams. There was hunger in those sounds as they crashed over the roof-tops and chimneys; but under it, low and distinct, he heard voices of fear: curses of men and cries of children.

Yes; they were looking for him in every building and on every floor and in every room. They wanted him. His eyes jerked upward as a huge, sharp beam of yellow light shot into the sky. Another came, crossing it like a knife. Then another. Soon the sky was full of them. They circled slowly, hemming him in; bars of light forming a prison, a wall between him and the rest of the world; bars weaving a shifting wall of light into which he dared not go. He was in the midst of it now; this was what he had been running from ever since that night Mrs. Dalton had come into the room and had charged him with such fear that his hands had gripped the pillow with fingers of steel and had cut off the air from Mary's lungs.

Below him was a loud, heavy pounding, like a far-away rumble of thunder. He had to get to the roof; he struggled upward, then fell flat, in deep soft snow, his eyes riveted upon a white man across the street upon another roof. Bigger watched the man whirl the beam of a flashlight. Would the man look in his direction? Could the beam of a flashlight make him visible from where the man was? He watched the man walk round awhile and then disappear.

Quickly, he rose and shut the trapdoor. To leave it open would create suspicion. Then he fell flat again, listening. There was the sound of many running feet below him. It seemed that an army was thundering up the stairs. There was nowhere he could run to now; either they caught him or they did not. The thundering grew louder and he knew that the men were nearing the top floor. He lifted his eyes and looked in all directions, watching roofs to the left and right of him. He did not want to be surprised by someone creeping upon him from behind. He saw that the roof to his right was not joined to the one upon which he lay; that meant that no one could steal upon him from that direction. The one to his left was joined to the roof of the building upon which he lay, making it one long icy runway. He lifted his head and looked; there were other roofs joined, too. He could run over those roofs, over the snow and round those chimneys until he came to the building that dropped to the ground. Then that would be all. Would he jump off and kill himself? He did not know.

He had an almost mystic feeling that if he were ever cornered something in him would prompt him to act the right way, the right way being the way that would enable him to die without shame.

He heard a noise close by; he looked round just in time to see a white face, a head, then shoulders pull into view upon the roof to the right of him. A man stood up, cut sharply against the background of roving yellow lights. He watched the man twirl a pencil of light over the snow. Bigger raised his gun and trained it upon the man and waited; if the light reached him, he would shoot. What would he do afterwards? He did not know. But the yellow spot never reached him. He watched the man go down, feet first, then shoulders and head; he was gone.

He relaxed a bit; at least the roof to his right was safe now. He waited to hear sounds that would tell him that someone was climbing up through the trapdoor. The rumbling below him rose in volume with the passing seconds, but he could not tell if the men were coming closer or receding. He waited and held his gun. Above his head the sky stretched in a cold, dark-blue oval, cupping the city like an iron palm covered with silk. The wind blew, hard, icy, without ceasing. It seemed to him that he had already frozen, that pieces could be broken off him, as one chips bits from a cake of ice. In order to know that he still had the gun in his hand he had to look at it, for his hand no longer had any feeling.

Then he was stiff with fear. There were pounding feet right below him. They were on the top floor now. Ought he to run to the roof to his left? But he had seen no one search that roof; if he ran he might come face to face with someone coming up out of another trapdoor. He looked round, thinking that maybe someone was creeping upon him; but there was nobody. The sound of feet came louder. He put his ear to the naked ice and listened. Yes; they were walking about in the hallway; there were several of them directly under him, near the trapdoor. He looked again to the roof on his left, wanting to run to it and hide; but was afraid. Were they coming up? He listened; but there were so many voices he could not make out the words. He did not want them to surprise him. Whatever happened, he wanted to go down looking into the faces of those that would kill him. Finally, under the terror-song of the siren, the voices came so close that he could hear words clearly.

"God, but I'm tired!"

"I'm cold!"

"I believe we're just wasting time."

"Say, Jerry! You going to the roof this time?"

"Yeah; I'll go."

"That nigger might be in New York by now."

"Yeah. But we better look."

"Say, did you see that brown gal in there?"

"The one that didn't have much on?"

"Yeah."

"Boy, she was a peach, wasn't she?"

"Yeah; I wonder what on earth a nigger wants to kill a white woman for when he has such good-looking women in his own race. . . ."

"Boy, if she'd let me stay here I'd give up this goddamn hunt."

"Come on. Give a lift. You'd better hold this ladder. It seems rickety."

"O.K."

"Hurry up. Here comes the captain."

Bigger was set. Then he was not set. He clung to a chimney that stood a foot from the trapdoor. Ought he to stay flat or stand up? He stood up, pushing against the chimney, trying to merge with it. He held the gun and waited. Was the man coming up? He looked to the roof to his left; it was still empty. But if he ran to it he might meet someone. He heard footsteps in the passage of the loft. Yes; the man was coming. He waited for the trapdoor to open. He held the gun tightly; he wondered if he was holding it too tightly, so tightly that it would go off before he wanted it to. His fingers were so cold that he could not tell how much pressure he was putting behind the trigger. Then, like a shooting star streaking across a black sky, the fearful thought came to him that maybe his fingers were frozen so stiff that he could not pull the trigger. Quickly, he felt his right hand with his left; but even that did not tell him anything. His right hand was so cold that all he felt was one cold piece of flesh touching another. He had to wait and see. He had to have faith. He had to trust himself; that was all.

The trapdoor opened, slightly at first, then wide. He watched it, his mouth open, staring through the blur of tears which the cold wind had whipped into his eyes. The door came all the way open, cutting off his view for a moment, then it fell back softly upon the snow. He saw the bare head of a white man—the back of the head—framed in the narrow opening, stenciled against the yellow glare of the restless bars of light. Then the head turned slightly and Bigger saw the side of a white face. He watched the man, moving like a figure on the screen in close-up slow motion, come out of the hole and stand with his back to him, flashlight in hand. The idea took hold swiftly. Hit him. Hit him! In the head. Whether it would help or not, he did not know and it did not matter. He had to hit this man before he turned that spot of yellow on him and then yelled for the others. In the split second that he saw the man's head, it seemed that an hour passed, an hour filled with pain and doubt and anguish and suspense, filled with the sharp throb of life lived upon a needle-point. He lifted his left hand, caught the gun which he held in his right, took it into the fingers of his left hand, turned it round, caught it again in his right and held it by the barrel: all one motion, swift, silent; done in one breath with eyes staring unblinkingly. *Hit him!* He lifted it, high, by the barrel. Yes. *Hit him!* His lips formed the words as he let it come down with a grunt which was a blending of a curse, a prayer and a groan.

He felt the impact of the blow throughout the length of his arm, jarring his flesh slightly. His hand stopped in mid-air, at the point where the metal of the gun had met the bone of the skull; stopped, frozen, still, as though again about to lift and descend. In the instant, almost of the blow being struck, the white man emitted something like a soft cough; his flashlight fell into the snow, a fast flick of vanishing light. The man fell away from Bigger, on his face, full length in the cushion of snow, like a man falling soundlessly in a deep dream. Bigger was aware of the clicking sound of the metal against the bone of the skull; it stayed on in his ears, faint but distinct, like a sharp bright point lingering on in front of the eyes when a light has gone out suddenly and darkness is everywhere—so the click of the gun handle against the man's head stayed on in his ears. He had not moved from his tracks; his right hand was still extended, upward, in mid-air; he lowered it, looking at the man, the sound of the metal against bone fading in his ears like a dying whisper.

The sound of the siren had stopped at some time which he did not remember; then it started again, and the interval in which he had not heard it seemed to hold for him some preciously hidden danger, as though for a dreadful moment he had gone to sleep at his post with an enemy near. He looked through the whirling spokes of light and saw a trapdoor open upon the roof to his left. He stood rigid, holding the gun, watching, waiting. If only the man did not see him when he came up! A head came into view; a white man climbed out of the trapdoor and stood in the snow.

He flinched; someone was crawling in the loft below him. Would he be trapped? A voice, a little afraid, called from the open hole through which the man whom he had struck had climbed.

"Jerry!"

The voice sounded clearly in spite of the siren and the clang of the fire wagons.

"Jerry!"

The voice was a little louder now. It was the man's partner. Bigger looked back to the roof to his left; the man was still standing there, flashing a light round. If he would only leave! He had to get away from this trapdoor here. If that man came up to see about his partner and found him sprawled in the snow he would yell before he got a chance to hit him. He squeezed against the chimney, looking at the man on the roof to his left, holding his breath. The man turned, walked toward the trapdoor and climbed through. He waited to hear the door shut; it did. Now, that roof was clear! He breathed a silent prayer.

"Jeeerry!"

With gun in hand, Bigger crept across the roof. He came to a small mound of brick, where the upjutting ridge of the building's flat top joined that of the other. He paused and looked back. The hole was still empty. If he tried to climb

over, would the man come out of the hole just in time to see
him? He had to take the chance. He grabbed the ledge,
hoisted himself upon it, and lay flat for a moment on the ice,
then slid to the other side, rolling over. He felt snow in his
face and eyes; his chest heaved. He crawled to another chimney and waited; it was so cold that he had a wild wish to
merge into the icy bricks of the chimney and have it all over.
He heard the voice again, this time loud, insistent:

"Jerry!"

He looked out from behind the chimney. The hole was still
empty. But the next time the voice came he knew that the
man was coming out, for he could feel the tremor of the
voice, as though it were next to him.

"Jerry!"

Then he saw the man's face come through; it was stuck like
a piece of white pasteboard above the top of the hole and
when the man's voice sounded again Bigger knew that he had
seen his partner in the snow.

"Jerry! *Say!*"

Bigger lifted his gun and waited.

"Jerry. . . ."

The man came out of the hole and stood over his partner,
then scrambled in again, screaming:

"Say! Say!"

Yes; the man would spread the word. Ought he to run?
Suppose he went down into the trapdoor of another roof?
Naw! There would be people standing in the hallways and
they would be afraid; they would scream at the sight of him
and he would be caught. They would be glad to give him up
and put an end to this terror. It would be better to run farther
over the roofs. He rose; then, just as he was about to run, he
saw a head bob up in the hole. Another man came through
and stood over Jerry. He was tall and he stooped over Jerry's
form and seemed to be putting his hand upon his face. Then
another came through. One of the men centered his flashlight
on Jerry's body and Bigger saw one bend and roll the body
over. The spotlight lit Jerry's face. One of the men ran to the
sheer edge of the roof, overlooking the street; his hand went
to his mouth and Bigger heard the sound of a whistle, sharp,
thin. The roar in the street died; the siren stopped; but the

circling columns of yellow continued to whirl. In the peace and quiet of the sudden calm, the man yelled,

"Surround the block!"

Bigger heard an answering shout.

"You got a line on 'im?"

"I think he's round here!"

A wild yell went up. Yes; they felt that they were near him now. He heard the man's shrill whistle sounding again. It got quiet, but not so quiet as before. There were shouts of wild joy floating up.

"Send up a stretcher and a detail of men!"

"O.K.!"

The man turned and went back to Jerry lying in the snow. Bigger heard snatches of talk.

". . . . how do you suppose it happened?"

"Looks like he was hit. . . ."

". . . . maybe he's about. . . ."

"Quick! Take a look over the roof!"

He saw one of the men rise and flash a light. The circling beams lit the roof to a daylight brightness and he could see that one man held a gun. He would have to cross to other roofs before this man or others came upon him. They were suspicious and would comb every inch of space on top of these houses. On all fours, he scrambled to the next ledge and then turned and looked back; the man was still standing, throwing the spot of yellow about over the snow. Bigger grabbed the icy ledge, hoisted himself flat upon it, and slid over. He did not think now of how much strength was needed to climb and run; the fear of capture made him forget even the cold, forget even that he had no strength left. From somewhere in him, out of the depths of flesh and blood and bone, he called up energy to run and dodge with but one impulse: he had to elude these men. He was crawling to the other ledge, over the snow, on his hands and knees, when he heard the man yell,

"There he is!"

The three words made him stop; he had been listening for them all night and when they came he seemed to feel the sky crashing soundlessly about him. What was the use of running? Would it not be better to stop, stand up, and lift his hands high above his head in surrender? Hell, naw! He continued to crawl.

"Stop, *you!*"

A shot rang out, whining past his head. He rose and ran to the ledge, leaped over; ran to the next ledge, leaped over it. He darted among the chimneys so that no one could see him long enough to shoot. He looked ahead and saw something huge and round and white looming up in the dark: a bulk rising up sheer from the snow of the roof and swelling in the night, glittering in the glare of the searching knives of light. Soon he would not be able to go much farther, for he would reach that point where the roof ended and dropped to the street below. He wove among the chimneys, his feet slipping and sliding over snow, keeping in mind that white looming bulk which he had glimpsed ahead of him. Was it something that would help him? Could he get upon it, or behind it, and hold them off? He was listening and expecting more shots as he ran, but none came.

He stopped at a ledge and looked back; he saw in the lurid glare of the slashing lances of light a man stumbling over the snow. Ought he to stop and shoot? Naw! More would be coming in a moment and he would only waste time. He had to find some place to hide, some ambush from which he could fight. He ran to another ledge, past the white looming bulk which now towered directly above him, then stopped, blinking: deep down below was a sea of white faces and he saw himself falling, spinning straight down into that ocean of boiling hate. He gripped the icy ledge with his fingers, thinking that if he had been running any faster he would have gone right off the roof, hurtling four floors.

Dizzily, he drew back. This was the end. There were no more roofs over which to run and dodge. He looked; the man was still coming. Bigger stood up. The siren was louder than before and there were more shouts and screams. Yes; those in the streets knew now that the police and vigilantes had trapped him upon the roofs. He remembered the quick glimpse he had had of the white looming bulk; he looked up. Directly above him, white with snow, was a high water tank with a round flat top. There was a ladder made of iron whose slick rungs were coated with ice that gleamed like neon in the circling blades of yellow. He caught hold and climbed. He did not know where he was going; he knew only that he had to hide.

He reached the top of the tank and three shots sang past his head. He lay flat, on his stomach, in snow. He was high above the roof-tops and chimneys now and he had a wide view. A man was climbing over a near-by ledge, and beyond him was a small knot of men, their faces lit to a distinct whiteness by the swinging pencils of light. Men were coming up out of the trapdoor far in front of him and were moving toward him, dodging behind chimneys. He raised the gun, leveled it, aimed, and shot; the men stopped but no one fell. He had missed. He shot again. No one fell. The knot of men broke up and disappeared behind ledges and chimneys. The noise in the street rose in a flood of strange joy. No doubt the sound of the pistol shots made them think that he was shot, captured, or dead.

He saw a man running toward the water tank in the open; he shot again. The man ducked behind a chimney. He had missed. Perhaps his hands were too cold to shoot straight? Maybe he ought to wait until they were closer? He turned his head just in time to see a man climbing over the edge of the roof, from the street side. The man was mounting a ladder which had been hoisted up the side of the building from the ground. He leveled the gun to shoot, but the man got over and left his line of vision, disappearing under the tank.

Why could he not shoot straight and fast enough? He looked in front of him and saw two men running under the tank. There were three men beneath the tank now. They were surrounding him, but they could not come for him without exposing themselves.

A small black object fell near his head in the snow, hissing, shooting forth a white vapor, like a blowing plume, which was carried away from him by the wind. Tear gas! With a movement of his hand he knocked it off the tank. Another came and he knocked it off. Two more came and he shoved them off. The wind blew strong, from the lake. It carried the gas away from his eyes and nose. He heard a man yell,

"Stop it! The wind's blowing it away! He's throwing 'em back!"

The bedlam in the street rose higher; more men climbed through trapdoors to the roof. He wanted to shoot, but remembered that he had but three bullets left. He would shoot when they were closer and he would save one bullet for himself. They would not take him alive.

"Come on down, boy!"

He did not move; he lay with gun in hand, waiting. Then, directly under his eyes, four white fingers caught hold of the icy edge of the water tank. He gritted his teeth and struck the white fingers with the butt of the gun. They vanished and he heard a thud as a body landed on the snow-covered roof. He lay waiting for more attempts to climb up, but none came.

"It's no use fighting, boy! You're caught! Come on down!"

He knew that they were afraid, and yet he knew that it would soon be over, one way or another: they would either capture or kill him. He was surprised that he was not afraid. Under it all some part of his mind was beginning to stand aside; he was going behind his curtain, his wall, looking out with sullen stares of contempt. He was outside of himself now, looking on; he lay under a winter sky lit with tall gleams of whirling light, hearing thirsty screams and hungry shouts, defiant, unafraid.

"Tell 'em to hurry with the hose! The nigger's armed!"

What did that mean? His eyes roved, watching for a moving object to shoot at; but none appeared. He was not conscious of his body now; he could not feel himself at all. He knew only that he was lying here with a gun in his hand, surrounded by men who wanted to kill him. Then he heard a hammering noise near by; he looked. Behind the edge of a chimney he saw a trapdoor open.

"All right, boy!" a hoarse voice called. "We're giving you your last chance. Come on down!"

He lay still. What was coming? He knew that they were not going to shoot, for they could not see him. Then what? And while wondering, he knew: a furious whisper of water, gleaming like silver in the bright lights, streaked above his head with vicious force, passing him high in the air and hitting the roof beyond with a thudding drone. They had turned on the water hose; the fire department had done that. They were trying to drive him into the open. The stream of water was coming from behind the chimney where the trapdoor had opened, but as yet the water had not touched him. Above him the rushing stream jerked this way and that; they were trying to reach him with it. Then the water hit him, in the side; it was like the blow of a pile driver. His breath left and he felt a dull pain in his side that spread, engulfing him. The water was trying to push him off the tank; he gripped the edges hard, feeling his strength ebbing. His chest heaved and he knew from the pain that throbbed in him that he would not be able to hold on much longer with water pounding at his body like this. He felt cold, freezing; his blood turned to ice, it seemed. He gasped, his mouth open. Then the gun loosened in his fingers; he tried to grip it again and found that he could not. The water left him; he lay gasping, spent.

"Throw that gun down, boy!"

He gritted his teeth. The icy water clutched again at his body like a giant hand; the chill of it squeezed him like the circling coils of a monstrous boa constrictor. His arms ached. He was behind his curtain now, looking down at himself freezing under the impact of water in sub-zero winds. Then the stream of water veered from his body.

"Throw that gun down, boy!"

He began to shake all over; he let go of the gun completely. Well, this was all. Why didn't they come for him? He gripped the edges of the tank again, digging his fingers into the snow and ice. His strength left. He gave up. He turned over on his back and looked weakly up into the sky through the high shifting lattices of light. This was all. They could shoot him now. Why didn't they shoot? Why didn't they come for him?

"Throw that gun down, boy!"

They wanted the gun. He did not have it. He was not afraid any more. He did not have strength enough to be.

"Throw that gun down, boy!"

Yes; take the gun and shoot it at them, shoot it empty. Slowly, he stretched out his hand and tried to pick up the gun, but his fingers were too stiff. Something laughed in him, cold and hard; he was laughing at himself. Why didn't they come for him? They were afraid. He rolled his eyes, looking longingly at the gun. Then, while he was looking at it, the stream of hissing silver struck it and whirled it off the tank, out of sight. . . .

"There it is!"

"Come on down, boy! You're through!"

"Don't go up there! He might have another gun!"

"Come on down, boy!"

He was outside of it all now. He was too weak and cold to hold onto the edges of the tank any longer; he simply lay atop the tank, his mouth and eyes open, listening to the stream of water whir above him. Then the water hit him again, in the side; he felt his body sliding over the slick ice and snow. He wanted to hold on, but could not. His body teetered on the edge; his legs dangled in air. Then he was falling. He landed on the roof, on his face, in snow, dazed.

He opened his eyes and saw a circle of white faces, but he was outside of them, behind his curtain, his wall, looking on. He heard men talking and their voices came to him from far away.

"That's him, all right!"

"Get 'im down to the street!"

"The water did it!"

"He seems half-frozen!"

"All right, get 'im down to the street!"

He felt his body being dragged across the snow of the roof. Then he was lifted and put, feet first, into a trapdoor.

"You got 'im?"

"Yeah! Let 'im drop on!"

"O.K.!"

He dropped into rough hands inside of the dark loft. They were dragging him by his feet. He closed his eyes and his head slid along over rough planking. They struggled him through the last trapdoor and he knew that he was inside of a building, for warm air was on his face. They had him by his legs again and were dragging him down a hall, over smooth carpet.

There was a short stop, then they started down the stairs with him, his head bumping along the steps. He folded his wet arms about his head to save himself, but soon the steps had pounded his elbows and arms so hard that all of his strength left. He relaxed, feeling his head bounding painfully

down the steps. He shut his eyes and tried to lose consciousness. But he still felt it, drumming like a hammer in his brain.
Then it stopped. He was near the street; he could hear shouts
and screams coming to him like the roar of water. He was in
the street now, being dragged over snow. His feet were up in
the air, grasped by strong hands.

"Kill 'im!"

"Lynch 'im!"

"That black sonofabitch!"

They let go of his feet; he was in the snow, lying flat on his
back. Round him surged a sea of noise. He opened his eyes a
little and saw an array of faces, white and looming.

"Kill that black ape!"

Two men stretched his arms out, as though about to
crucify him; they placed a foot on each of his wrists, making
them sink deep down in the snow. His eyes closed, slowly,
and he was swallowed in darkness.

BOOK THREE

FATE

THERE WAS no day for him now, and there was no night; there was but a long stretch of time, a long stretch of time that was very short; and then—the end. Toward no one in the world did he feel any fear now, for he knew that fear was useless; and toward no one in the world did he feel any hate now, for he knew that hate would not help him.

Though they carried him from one police station to another, though they threatened him, persuaded him, bullied him, and stormed at him, he steadfastly refused to speak. Most of the time he sat with bowed head, staring at the floor; or he lay full length upon his stomach, his face buried in the crook of an elbow, just as he lay now upon a cot with the pale yellow sunshine of a February sky falling obliquely upon him through the cold steel bars of the Eleventh Street Police Station.

Food was brought to him upon trays and an hour later the trays were taken away, untouched. They gave him packages of cigarettes, but they lay on the floor, unopened. He would not even drink water. He simply lay or sat, saying nothing, not noticing when anyone entered or left his cell. When they wanted him to go from one place to another, they caught him by the wrist and led him; he went without resistance, walking always with dragging feet, head down. Even when they snatched him up by the collar, his weak body easily lending itself to be manhandled, he looked without hope or resentment, his eyes like two still pools of black ink in his flaccid face. No one had seen him save the officials and he had asked to see no one. Not once during the three days following his capture had an image of what he had done come into his mind. He had thrust the whole thing back of him, and there it lay, monstrous and horrible. He was not so much in a stupor, as in the grip of a deep physiological resolution not to react to anything.

Having been thrown by an accidental murder into a position where he had sensed a possible order and meaning in his relations with the people about him; having accepted the moral guilt and responsibility for that murder because it had made him feel free for the first time in his life; having felt in his heart some obscure need to be at home with people and having demanded ransom money to enable him to do it— having done all this and failed, he chose not to struggle any more. With a supreme act of will springing from the essence of his being, he turned away from his life and the long train of disastrous consequences that had flowed from it and looked wistfully upon the dark face of ancient waters upon which some spirit had breathed and created him, the dark face of the waters from which he had been first made in the image of a man with a man's obscure need and urge; feeling that he wanted to sink back into those waters and rest eternally.

And yet his desire to crush all faith in him was in itself built upon a sense of faith. The feelings of his body reasoned that if there could be no merging with the men and women about him, there should be a merging with some other part of the natural world in which he lived. Out of the mood of renunciation there sprang up in him again the will to kill. But this time it was not directed outward toward people, but inward, upon himself. Why not kill that wayward yearning within him that had led him to this end? He had reached out and killed and had not solved anything, so why not reach inward and kill that which had duped him? This feeling sprang up of itself, organically, automatically; like the rotted hull of a seed forming the soil in which it should grow again.

And, under and above it all, there was the fear of death before which he was naked and without defense; he had to go forward and meet his end like any other living thing upon the earth. And regulating his attitude toward death was the fact that he was black, unequal, and despised. Passively, he hungered for another orbit between two poles that would let him live again; for a new mode of life that would catch him up with the tension of hate and love. There would have to hover above him, like the stars in a full sky, a vast configuration of images and symbols whose magic and power could lift him up and make him live so intensely that the dread of being black and unequal would be forgotten; that even death would not matter, that it would be a victory. This would have to happen before he could look them in the face again: a new pride and a new humility would have to be born in him, a humility springing from a new identification with some part of the world in which he lived, and this identification forming the basis for a new hope that would function in him as pride and dignity.

But maybe it would never come; maybe there was no such thing for him; maybe he would have to go to his end just as he was, dumb, driven, with the shadow of emptiness in his eyes. Maybe this was all. Maybe the confused promptings, the excitement, the tingling, the elation—maybe they were false lights that led nowhere. Maybe they were right when they said that a black skin was bad, the covering of an apelike animal. Maybe he was just unlucky, a man born for dark doom, an obscene joke happening amid a colossal din of siren screams and white faces and circling lances of light under a cold and silken sky. But he could not feel that for long; just as soon as his feelings reached such a conclusion, the conviction that there was some way out surged back into him, strong and powerful, and, in his present state, condemning and paralyzing.

And then one morning a group of men came and caught him by the wrists and led him into a large room in the Cook County Morgue, in which there were many people. He blinked from the bright lights and heard loud and excited talking. The compact array of white faces and the constant flashing of bulbs for pictures made him stare in mounting amazement. His defense of indifference could protect him no longer. At first he thought that it was the trial that had begun, and he was prepared to sink back into his dream of nothingness. But it was not a court room. It was too informal for that. He felt crossing his feelings a sensation akin to the same one he had had when the reporters had first come into Mr. Dalton's basement with their hats on, smoking cigars and cigarettes, asking questions; only now it was much stronger. There was in the air a silent mockery that challenged him. It was not their hate he felt; it was something deeper than that. He sensed that in their attitude toward him they had gone beyond hate. He heard in the sound of their voices a patient

certainty; he saw their eyes gazing at him with calm conviction. Though he could not have put it into words, he felt that
not only had they resolved to put him to death, but that they
were determined to make his death mean more than a mere
punishment; that they regarded him as a figment of that black
world which they feared and were anxious to keep under control. The atmosphere of the crowd told him that they were
going to use his death as a bloody symbol of fear to wave
before the eyes of that black world. And as he felt it, rebellion
rose in him. He had sunk to the lowest point this side of
death, but when he felt his life again threatened in a way that
meant that he was to go down the dark road a helpless spec-
tacle of sport for others, he sprang back into action, alive,
contending.

He tried to move his hands and found that they were
shackled by strong bands of cold steel to white wrists of
policemen sitting to either side of him. He looked round; a
policeman stood in front of him and one in back. He heard
a sharp, metallic click and his hands were free. There was a
rising murmur of voices and he sensed that it was caused by
his movements. Then his eyes became riveted on a white face,
tilted slightly upward. The skin had a quality of taut anxiety
and around the oval of white face was a framework of whiter
hair. It was Mrs. Dalton, sitting quietly, her frail, waxen
hands folded in her lap. Bigger remembered as he looked at
her that moment of stark terror when he had stood at the side
of the bed in the dark blue room hearing his heart pound
against his ribs with his fingers upon the pillow pressing
down upon Mary's face to keep her from mumbling.

Sitting beside Mrs. Dalton was Mr. Dalton, looking
straight before him with wide-open, unblinking eyes. Mr.
Dalton turned slowly and looked at Bigger and Bigger's eyes
fell.

He saw Jan: blond hair; blue eyes; a sturdy, kind face looking squarely into his own. Hot shame flooded him as the
scene in the car came back; he felt again the pressure of Jan's
fingers upon his hand. And then shame was replaced by guilty
anger as he recalled Jan's confronting him upon the sidewalk
in the snow.

He was getting tired; the more he came to himself, the

more a sense of fatigue seeped into him. He looked down at
his clothes; they were damp and crumpled and the sleeves of
his coat were drawn halfway up his arms. His shirt was open
and he could see the black skin of his chest. Suddenly, he felt
the fingers of his right hand throb with pain. Two fingernails
were torn off. He could not remember how it had happened.
He tried to move his tongue and found it swollen. His lips
were dry and cracked and he wanted water. He felt giddy.
The lights and faces whirled slowly, like a merry-go-round.
He was falling swiftly through space. . . .

When he opened his eyes he was stretched out upon a cot.
A white face loomed above him. He tried to lift his body and
was pushed back.

"Take it easy, boy. Here; drink this."

A glass touched his lips. Ought he to drink? But what difference did it make? He swallowed something warm; it was
milk. When the glass was empty he lay upon his back and
stared at the white ceiling; the memory of Bessie and the milk
she had warmed for him came back strongly. Then the image
of her death came and he closed his eyes, trying to forget. His
stomach growled; he was feeling better. He heard a low
drone of voices. He gripped the edge of the cot and sat up.

"Hey! How're you feeling, boy?"

"Hunh?" he grunted. It was the first time he had spoken
since they had caught him.

"How're you feeling?"

He closed his eyes and turned his head away, sensing that
they were white and he was black, that they were the captors
and he the captive.

"He's coming out of it."

"Yeah. That crowd must've got 'im."

"Say, boy! You want something to eat?"

He did not answer.

"Get 'im something. He doesn't know what he wants."

"You better lie down, boy. You'll have to go back to the
inquest this afternoon."

He felt their hands pushing him back onto the cot. The
door closed; he looked round. He was alone. The room was
quiet. He had come out into the world again. He had not
tried to; it had just happened. He was being turned here and

there by a surge of strange forces he could not understand. It was not to save his life that he had come out; he did not care what they did to him. They could place him in the electric chair right now, for all he cared. It was to save his pride that he had come. He did not want them to make sport of him. If they had killed him that night when they were dragging him down the steps, that would have been a deed born of their strength over him. But he felt they had no right to sit and watch him, to use him for whatever they wanted.

The door opened and a policeman brought in a tray of food, set it on a chair next to him and left. There was steak and fried potatoes and coffee. Gingerly, he cut a piece of steak and put it into his mouth. It tasted so good that he tried to swallow it before he chewed it. He sat on the edge of the cot and drew the chair forward so that he could reach the food. He ate so fast that his jaws ached. He stopped and held the food in his mouth, feeling the juices of his glands flowing round it. When he was through, he lit a cigarette, stretched out upon the cot and closed his eyes. He dozed off to an uneasy sleep.

Then suddenly he sat upright. He had not seen a newspaper in a long time. What were they saying now? He got up; he swayed and the room lurched. He was still weak and giddy. He leaned against the wall and walked slowly to the door. Cautiously, he turned the knob. The door swung in and he looked into the face of a policeman.

"What's the matter, boy?"

He saw a heavy gun sagging at the man's hip. The policeman caught him by the wrist and led him back to the cot.

"Here; take it easy."

"I want a paper," he said.

"Hunh? A paper?"

"I want to read the paper."

"Wait a minute. I'll see."

The policeman went out and presently returned with an armful of papers.

"Here you are, boy. You're in 'em all."

He did not turn to the papers until after the man had left the room. Then he spread out the *Tribune* and saw: NEGRO RAPIST FAINTS AT INQUEST. He understood now; it

was the inquest he had been taken to. He had fainted and
they had brought him here. He read:

Overwhelmed by the sight of his accusers, Bigger Thomas, Negro
sex-slayer, fainted dramatically this morning at the inquest of Mary
Dalton, millionaire Chicago heiress.

Emerging from a stupor for the first time since his capture last
Monday night, the black killer sat cowed and fearful as hundreds
sought to get a glimpse of him.

"He looks exactly like an ape!" exclaimed a terrified young white
girl who watched the black slayer being loaded onto a stretcher after
he had fainted.

Though the Negro killer's body does not seem compactly built, he
gives the impression of possessing abnormal physical strength. He is
about five feet, nine inches tall and his skin is exceedingly black. His
lower jaw protrudes obnoxiously, reminding one of a jungle beast.

His arms are long, hanging in a dangling fashion to his knees. It is
easy to imagine how this man, in the grip of a brain-numbing sex
passion, overpowered little Mary Dalton, raped her, murdered her,
beheaded her, then stuffed her body into a roaring furnace to destroy the evidence of his crime.

His shoulders are huge, muscular, and he keeps them hunched, as
if about to spring upon you at any moment. He looks at the world
with a strange, sullen, fixed-from-under stare, as though defying all
efforts of compassion.

All in all, he seems a beast utterly untouched by the softening
influences of modern civilization. In speech and manner he lacks the
charm of the average, harmless, genial, grinning southern darky so
beloved by the American people.

The moment the killer made his appearance at the inquest, there
were shouts of "Lynch 'im! Kill 'im!"

But the brutish Negro seemed indifferent to his fate, as though
inquests, trials, and even the looming certainty of the electric chair
held no terror for him. He acted like an earlier missing link in the
human species. He seemed out of place in a white man's civilization.

An Irish police captain remarked with deep conviction: "I'm convinced that death is the only cure for the likes of him."

For three days the Negro has refused all nourishment. Police believe that he is either trying to starve himself to death and cheat the
chair, or that he is trying to excite sympathy for himself.

From Jackson, Mississippi, came a report yesterday from Edward Robertson, editor of the *Jackson Daily Star*, regarding Bigger
Thomas' boyhood there. The editor wired:

"Thomas comes of a poor darky family of a shiftless and immoral variety. He was raised here and is known to local residents as an irreformable sneak thief and liar. We were unable to send him to the chain gang because of his extreme youth.

"Our experience here in Dixie with such depraved types of Negroes has shown that only the death penalty, inflicted in a public and dramatic manner, has any influence upon their peculiar mentality. Had that nigger Thomas lived in Mississippi and committed such a crime, no power under Heaven could have saved him from death at the hands of indignant citizens.

"I think it but proper to inform you that in many quarters it is believed that Thomas, despite his dead-black complexion, may have a minor portion of white blood in his veins, a mixture which generally makes for a criminal and intractable nature.

"Down here in Dixie we keep Negroes firmly in their places and we make them know that if they so much as touch a white woman, good or bad, they cannot live.

"When Negroes become resentful over imagined wrongs, nothing brings them to their senses so quickly as when citizens take the law into their hands and make an example out of a trouble-making nigger.

"Crimes such as the Bigger Thomas murders could be lessened by segregating all Negroes in parks, playgrounds, cafés, theatres, and street cars. Residential segregation is imperative. Such measures tend to keep them as much as possible out of direct contact with white women and lessen their attacks against them.

"We of the South believe that the North encourages Negroes to get more education than they are organically capable of absorbing, with the result that northern Negroes are generally more unhappy and restless than those of the South. If separate schools were maintained, it would be fairly easy to limit the Negroes' education by regulating the appropriation of moneys through city, county, and state legislative bodies.

"Still another psychological deterrent can be attained by conditioning Negroes so that they have to pay deference to the white person with whom they come in contact. This is done by regulating their speech and actions. We have found that the injection of an element of constant fear has aided us greatly in handling the problem."

He lowered the paper; he could not read any more. Yes, of course; they were going to kill him; but they were having this sport with him before they did it. He held very still; he was trying to make a decision; not thinking, but feeling it out. Ought he to go back behind his wall? *Could* he go back now?

He felt that he could not. But would not any effort he made now turn out like the others? Why go forward and meet more hate? He lay on the cot, feeling as he had felt that night when his fingers had gripped the icy edges of the water tank under the roving flares of light, knowing that men crouched below him with guns and tear gas, hearing the screams of sirens and shouts rising thirstily from ten thousand throats. . . .

Overcome with drowsiness, he closed his eyes; then opened them abruptly. The door swung in and he saw a black face. Who was this? A tall, well-dressed black man came forward and paused. Bigger pulled up and leaned on his elbow. The man came all the way to the cot and stretched forth a dingy palm, touching Bigger's hand.

"Mah po' boy! May the good Lawd have mercy on yuh."

He stared at the man's jet-black suit and remembered who he was: Reverend Hammond, the pastor of his mother's church. And at once he was on guard against the man. He shut his heart and tried to stifle all feeling in him. He feared that the preacher would make him feel remorseful. He wanted to tell him to go; but so closely associated in his mind was the man with his mother and what she stood for that he could not speak. In his feelings he could not tell the difference between what this man evoked in him and what he had read in the papers; the love of his own kind and the hate of others made him feel equally guilty now.

"How yuh feel, son?" the man asked; he did not answer and the man's voice hurried on: "Yo' ma ast me t' come 'n' see yuh. She wants t' come too."

The preacher knelt upon the concrete floor and closed his eyes. Bigger clamped his teeth and flexed his muscles; he knew what was coming.

"Lawd Jesus, turn Yo' eyes 'n' look inter the heart of this po' sinner! Yuh said mercy wuz awways Yo's 'n' ef we ast fer it on bended knee Yuh'd po' it out inter our hearts 'n' make our cups run over! We's astin' Yuh t' po' out Yo' mercy now, Lawd! Po' it out fer this po' sinner boy who stan's in deep need of it! Ef his sins be as scarlet, Lawd, wash 'em white as snow! Fergive 'im fer whutever he's done, Lawd! Let the light of Yo' love guide 'im th'u these dark days! 'N' he'p them who's a-tryin' to he'p 'im, Lawd! Enter inter they hearts 'n'

breathe compassion on they sperits! We ast this in the nama
Yo' Son Jesus who died on the cross 'n' gave us the mercy of
Yo' love! Ahmen. . . ."

Bigger stared unblinkingly at the white wall before him as
the preacher's words registered themselves in his consciousness. He knew without listening what they meant; it was the
old voice of his mother telling of suffering, of hope, of love
beyond this world. And he loathed it because it made him feel
as condemned and guilty as the voice of those who hated
him.

"Son. . . ."

Bigger glanced at the preacher, and then away.

"Fergit ever'thing but yo' soul, son. Take yo' mind off
ever'thing but eternal life. Fergit whut the newspapers say.
Fergit yuh's black. Gawd looks past yo' skin 'n inter yo' soul,
son. He's lookin' at the only parta yuh tha's *His*. He wants
yuh 'n' He loves yuh. Give yo'se'f t' 'Im, son. Lissen, lemme
tell yuh why yuh's here; lemme tell yuh a story tha'll make yo'
heart glad. . . ."

Bigger sat very still, listening and not listening. If someone
had afterwards asked him to repeat the preacher's words, he
would not have been able to do so. But he felt and sensed
their meaning. As the preacher talked there appeared before
him a vast black silent void and the images of the preacher
swam in that void, grew large and powerful; familiar images
which his mother had given him when he was a child at her
knee; images which in turn aroused impulses long dormant,
impulses that he had suppressed and sought to shunt from
his life. They were images which had once given him a reason
for living, had explained the world. Now they sprawled before his eyes and seized his emotions in a spell of awe and
wonder.

. . . . an endless reach of deep murmuring waters upon
whose face was darkness and there was no form no shape no
sun no stars and no land and a voice came out of the darkness
and the waters moved to obey and there emerged slowly a
huge spinning ball and the voice said *let there be light* and
there was light and it was good light and the voice said *let
there be a firmament* and the waters parted and there was a
vast space over the waters which formed into clouds stretching

above the waters and like an echo the voice came from far away saying *let dry land appear* and with thundering rustling the waters drained off and mountain peaks reared into view and there were valleys and rivers and the voice called the dry land *earth* and the waters *seas* and the earth grew grass and trees and flowers that gave off seed that fell to the earth to grow again and the earth was lit by the light of a million stars and for the day there was a sun and for the night there was a moon and there were days and weeks and months and years and the voice called out of the twilight and moving creatures came forth out of the great waters whales and all kinds of living creeping things and on the land there were beasts and cattle and the voice said *let us make man in our own image* and from the dusty earth a man rose up and loomed against the day and the sun and after him a woman rose up and loomed against the night and the moon and they lived as one flesh and there was no Pain no Longing no Time no Death and Life was like the flowers that bloomed round them in the garden of earth and out of the clouds came a voice saying *eat not of the fruit of the tree in the midst of the garden, neither touch it, lest ye die. . . .*

The preacher's words ceased droning. Bigger looked at him out of the corners of his eyes. The preacher's face was black and sad and earnest and made him feel a sense of guilt deeper than that which even his murder of Mary had made him feel. He had killed within himself the preacher's haunting picture of life even before he had killed Mary; that had been his first murder. And now the preacher made it walk before his eyes like a ghost in the night, creating within him a sense of exclusion that was as cold as a block of ice. Why should this thing rise now to plague him after he had pressed a pillow of fear and hate over its face to smother it to death? To those who wanted to kill him he was not human, not included in that picture of Creation; and that was why he had killed it. To live, he had created a new world for himself, and for that he was to die.

Again the preacher's words seeped into his feelings:

"Son, yuh know whut tha' tree wuz? It wuz the tree of knowledge. It wuzn't enuff fer man t' be like Gawd, he wanted t' know *why*. 'N' all Gawd wanted 'im t' do wuz bloom like the flowers in the fiel's, live as chillun. Man wanted t' know why 'n' he fell from light t' darkness, from love t' damnation, from blessedness t' shame. 'N' Gawd cast 'em outa the garden 'n' tol' the man he had t' git his bread by the sweat of his brow 'n' tol' the woman she had t' bring fo'th her chillun in pain 'n' sorrow. The worl' turned ergin 'em 'n' they had t' fight the worl' fer life. . . ."

. . . the man and the woman walked fearfully among trees their hands covering their nakedness and back of them high in the twilight against the clouds an angel waved a flaming sword driving them out of the garden into the wild night of cold wind and tears and pain and death and the man and woman took their food and burnt it to send smoke to the sky begging forgiveness. . . .

"Son, fer thousan's of years we been prayin' for Gawd t' take tha' cuss off us. Gawd heard our prayers 'n' said He'd show us a way back t' 'Im. His Son Jesus came down t' earth 'n' put on human flesh 'n' lived 'n' died t' show us the way. Jesus let men crucify 'Im; but His death wuz a victory. He showed us tha' t' live in this worl' wuz t' be crucified by it. This worl' ain' our home. Life ever' day is a crucifixion. There ain' but one way out, son, 'n' tha's Jesus' way, the way of love 'n' fergiveness. Be like Jesus. Don't resist. Thank Gawd tha' He done chose this way fer yuh t' come t' 'Im. It's love tha's gotta save yuh, son. Yuh gotta b'lieve tha' Gawd gives eternal life th'u the love of Jesus. Son, look at me. . . ."

Bigger's black face rested in his hands and he did not move.

"Son, promise me yuh'll stop hatin' long enuff fer Gawd's love t' come inter yo' heart."

Bigger said nothing.

"Won't yuh promise, son?"

Bigger covered his eyes with his hands.

"Jus' say yuh'll *try*, son."

Bigger felt that if the preacher kept asking he would leap up and strike him. How could he believe in that which he had killed? He was guilty. The preacher rose, sighed, and drew from his pocket a small wooden cross with a chain upon it.

"Look, son. Ah'm holdin' in mah hands a wooden cross taken from a tree. A tree is the worl', son. 'N' nailed t' this

tree is a sufferin' man. Tha's whut life is, son. Sufferin'. How
kin yuh keep from b'lievin' the word of Gawd when Ah'm
holdin' befo' yo' eyes the only thing tha' gives a meanin' t' yo'
life? Here, lemme put it roun' yo' neck. When yuh git alone,
look at this cross, son, 'n' b'lieve. . . ."

They were silent. The wooden cross hung next to the skin
of Bigger's chest. He was feeling the words of the preacher,
feeling that life was flesh nailed to the world, a longing spirit
imprisoned in the days of the earth.

He glanced up, hearing the doorknob turn. The door
opened and Jan stood framed in it, hesitating. Bigger sprang
to his feet, galvanized by fear. The preacher also stood, took a
step backward, bowed, and said,

"Good mawnin', suh."

Bigger wondered what Jan could want of him now. Was he
not caught and ready for trial? Would not Jan get his revenge?
Bigger stiffened as Jan walked to the middle of the floor and
stood facing him. Then it suddenly occurred to Bigger that he
need not be standing, that he had no reason to fear bodily
harm from Jan here in jail. He sat and bowed his head; the
room was quiet, so quiet that Bigger heard the preacher and
Jan breathing. The white man upon whom he had tried to
blame his crime stood before him and he sat waiting to hear
angry words. Well, why didn't he speak? He lifted his eyes;
Jan was looking straight at him and he looked away. But Jan's
face was not angry. If he were not angry, then what did he
want? He looked again and saw Jan's lips move to speak, but
no words came. And when Jan did speak his voice was low
and there were long pauses between the words; it seemed to
Bigger that he was listening to a man talk to himself.

"Bigger, maybe I haven't the words to say what I want to
say, but I'm going to try. . . . This thing hit me like a bomb.
It t-t-took me all week to get myself together. They had me in
jail and I couldn't for the life of me figure out what was happening. . . . I—I don't want to worry you, Bigger. I know
you're in trouble. But there's something I just got to
say. . . . You needn't talk to me unless you want to, Bigger. I
think I know something of what you're feeling now. I'm not
dumb, Bigger; I can understand, even if I didn't seem to
understand that night. . . ." Jan paused, swallowed, and lit a

cigarette. "Well, you jarred me. . . . I see now. I was kind of blind. I—I just wanted to come here and tell you that I'm not angry. . . . I'm not angry and I want you to let me help you. I don't hate you for trying to blame this thing on me. . . . Maybe you had good reasons. . . . I don't know. And maybe in a certain sense, I'm the one who's really guilty. . . ." Jan paused again and sucked long and hard at his cigarette, blew the smoke out slowly and nervously bit his lips. "Bigger, I've never done anything against you and your people in my life. But I'm a white man and it would be asking too much to ask you not to hate me, when every white man you see hates you. I—I know my. . . . my face looks like theirs to you, even though I don't feel like they do. But I didn't know we were so far apart until that night. . . . I can understand now why you pulled that gun on me when I waited outside that house to talk to you. It was the only thing you could have done; but I didn't know my white face was making you feel guilty, condemning you. . . ." Jan's lips hung open, but no words came from them; his eyes searched the corners of the room.

Bigger sat silently, bewildered, feeling that he was on a vast blind wheel being turned by stray gusts of wind. The preacher came forward.

"Is yuh Mistah Erlone?"

"Yes," said Jan, turning.

"Tha' wuz a mighty fine thing you jus' said, suh. Ef anybody needs he'p, this po' boy sho does. Ah'm Reveren' Hammon'."

Bigger saw Jan and the preacher shake hands.

"Though this thing hurt me, I got something out of it," Jan said, sitting down and turning to Bigger. "It made me see deeper into men. It made me see things I knew, but had forgotten. I—I lost something, but I got something, too. . . ." Jan tugged at his tie and the room was silent, waiting for him to speak. "It taught me that it's your right to hate me, Bigger. I see now that you couldn't do anything else but that; it was all you had. But, Bigger, if I say you got the right to hate me, then that ought to make things a little different, oughtn't it? Ever since I got out of jail I've been thinking this thing over and I felt that I'm the one who ought to be in jail for murder instead of you. But that can't be, Bigger. I can't take upon myself the blame for what one hundred million people have done." Jan leaned forward and stared at the floor. "I'm not trying to make up to you, Bigger. I didn't come here to feel sorry for you. I don't suppose you're so much worse off than the rest of us who get tangled up in this world. I'm here because I'm trying to live up to this thing as I see it. And it isn't easy, Bigger. I—I loved that girl you killed. I—I loved. . . ." His voice broke and Bigger saw his lips tremble. "I was in jail grieving for Mary and then I thought of all the black men who've been killed, the black men who had to grieve when their people were snatched from them in slavery and since slavery. I thought that if they could stand it, then I ought to." Jan crushed the cigarette with his shoe. "At first, I thought old man Dalton was trying to frame me, and I wanted to kill him. And when I heard that you'd done it, I wanted to kill you. And then I got to thinking. I saw if I killed, this thing would go on and on and never stop. I said, 'I'm going to help that guy, if he lets me.' "

"May Gawd in heaven bless yuh, son," the preacher said.

Jan lit another cigarette and offered one to Bigger; but Bigger refused by keeping his hands folded in front of him and staring stonily at the floor. Jan's words were strange; he had never heard such talk before. The meaning of what Jan had said was so new that he could not react to it; he simply sat, staring, wondering, afraid even to look at Jan.

"Let me be on your side, Bigger," Jan said. "I can fight this thing with you, just like you've started it. I can come from all of those white people and stand here with you. Listen, I got a friend, a lawyer. His name is Max. He understands this thing and wants to help you. Won't you talk to him?"

Bigger understood that Jan was not holding him guilty for what he had done. Was this a trap? He looked at Jan and saw a white face, but an honest face. This white man believed in him, and the moment he felt that belief he felt guilty again; but in a different sense now. Suddenly, this white man had come up to him, flung aside the curtain and walked into the room of his life. Jan had spoken a declaration of friendship that would make other white men hate him: a particle of white rock had detached itself from that looming mountain of white hate and had rolled down the slope, stopping still at his

feet. The word had become flesh. For the first time in his life a
white man became a human being to him; and the reality of
Jan's humanity came in a stab of remorse: he had killed what
this man loved and had hurt him. He saw Jan as though someone had performed an operation upon his eyes, or as though
someone had snatched a deforming mask from Jan's face.

Bigger started nervously; the preacher's hand came to his
shoulder.

"Ah don't wanna break in 'n' meddle where Ah ain' got no
bisness, suh," the preacher said in a tone that was militant,
but deferring. "But there ain' no usa draggin' no Communism
in this thing, Mistah. Ah respecks yo' feelin's powerfully, suh;
but whut yuh's astin' jus' stirs up mo' hate. Whut this po' boy
needs is understandin'. . . ."

"But he's got to fight for it," Jan said.

"Ah'm wid yuh when yuh wanna change men's hearts," the
preacher said. "But Ah can't go wid yuh when yuh wanna stir
up mo' hate. . . ."

Bigger sat looking from one to the other, bewildered.

"How on earth are you going to change men's hearts when
the newspapers are fanning hate into them every day?" Jan
asked.

"Gawd kin change 'em!" the preacher said fervently.

Jan turned to Bigger.

"Won't you let my friend help you, Bigger?"

Bigger's eyes looked round the room, as if seeking a means
of escape. What could he say? He was guilty.

"Forget me," he mumbled.

"I can't," Jan said.

"It's over for me," Bigger said.

"Don't you believe in yourself?"

"Naw," Bigger whispered tensely.

"You believed enough to kill. You thought you were settling something, or you wouldn't've killed," Jan said.

Bigger stared and did not answer. Did this man believe in
him *that* much?

"I want you to talk to Max," Jan said.

Jan went to the door. A policeman opened it from the outside. Bigger sat, open-mouthed, trying to feel where all this
was bearing him. He saw a man's head come into the door, a

head strange and white, with silver hair and a lean white face that he had never seen before.

"Come on in," Jan said.

"Thanks."

The voice was quiet, firm, but kind; there was about the man's thin lips a faint smile that seemed to have always been there. The man stepped inside; he was tall.

"How are you, Bigger?"

Bigger did not answer. He was doubtful again. Was this a trap of some kind?

"This is Reverend Hammond, Max," Jan said.

Max shook hands with the preacher, then turned to Bigger.

"I want to talk with you," Max said. "I'm from the Labor Defenders. I want to help you."

"I ain't got no money," Bigger said.

"I know that. Listen, Bigger, don't be afraid of me. And don't be afraid of Jan. We're not angry with you. I want to represent you in court. Have you spoken to any other lawyer?"

Bigger looked at Jan and Max again. They seemed all right. But how on earth could they help him? He wanted help, but dared not think that anybody would want to do anything for him now.

"Nawsuh," he whispered.

"How have they treated you? Did they beat you?"

"I been sick," Bigger said, knowing that he had to explain why he had not spoken or eaten in three days. "I been sick and I don't know."

"Are you willing to let us handle your case?"

"I ain't got no money."

"Forget about that. Listen, they're taking you back to the inquest this afternoon. But you don't have to answer any questions, see? Just sit and say nothing. I'll be there and you won't have to be scared. After the inquest they'll take you to the Cook County Jail and I'll be over to talk with you."

"Yessuh."

"Here; take these cigarettes."

"Thank you, suh."

The door swung in and a tall, big-faced man with grey eyes came forward hurriedly. Max and Jan and the preacher stood to one side. Bigger stared at the man's face; it teased him. Then he remembered: it was Buckley, the man whose face he had seen the workmen pasting upon a billboard a few mornings ago. Bigger listened to the men talk, feeling in the tones of their voices a deep hostility toward one another.

"So, you're horning in again, hunh, Max?"

"This boy's my client and he's signing no confessions," Max said.

"What the hell do I want with his confession?" Buckley asked. "We've got enough evidence on him to put him in a dozen electric chairs."

"I'll see that his rights are protected," Max said.

"Hell, man! You can't do him any good."

Max turned to Bigger.

"Don't let these people scare you, Bigger."

Bigger heard, but did not answer.

"What in hell you Reds can get out of bothering with a black thing like that, God only knows," Buckley said, rubbing his hands across his eyes.

"You're afraid that you won't be able to kill this boy before the April elections, if we handle his case, aren't you, Buckley?" Jan asked.

Buckley whirled.

"Why in God's name can't you pick out somebody decent to defend sometimes? Somebody who'll appreciate it. Why do you Reds take up with scum like this . . . ?"

"You and your tactics have forced us to defend this boy," Max said.

"What do you mean?" Buckley asked.

"If you had not dragged the name of the Communist Party into this murder, I'd not be here," Max said.

"Hell, this boy signed the name of the Communist Party to the kidnap note. . . ."

"I realize that," Max said. "The boy got the idea from the newspapers. I'm defending this boy because I'm convinced that men like you made him what he is. His trying to blame the Communists for his crime was a natural reaction for him. He had heard men like you lie about the Communists so much that he believed them. If I can make the people of this country understand why this boy acted like he did, I'll be doing more than defending him."

Buckley laughed, bit off the tip of a fresh cigar, lit it and stood puffing. He advanced to the center of the room, cocked his head to one side, took the cigar out of his mouth and squinted at Bigger.

"Boy, did you ever think you'd be as important a man as you are right now?"

Bigger had been on the verge of accepting the friendship of Jan and Max, and now this man stood before him. What did the puny friendship of Jan and Max mean in the face of a million men like Buckley?

"I'm the State's Attorney," Buckley said, walking from one end of the room to the other. His hat was on the back of his head. A white silk handkerchief peeped from the breast pocket of his black coat. He paused by the cot, towering over Bigger. How soon were they going to kill him, Bigger wondered. The breath of warm hope which Jan and Max had blown so softly upon him turned to frost under Buckley's cold gaze.

"Boy, I'd like to give you a piece of good advice. I'm going to be honest with you and tell you that you don't have to talk to me unless you want to, and I'll tell you that whatever you say to me might be used against you in court, see? But, boy, you're *caught*! That's the first thing you want to understand. We know what you've done. We got the evidence. So you might as well talk."

"He'll decide that with me," Max said.

Buckley and Max faced each other.

"Listen, Max. You're wasting your time. You'll never get this boy off in a million years. Nobody can commit a crime against a family like the Daltons and sneak out of it. Those poor old parents are going to be in that court room to see that this boy *burns*! This boy killed the *only* thing they had. If you want to save your face, you and your buddy can leave now and the papers won't know you were in here. . . ."

"I reserve the right to determine whether I should defend him or not," Max said.

"Listen, Max. You think I'm trying to hoodwink you, don't you?" Buckley asked, turning and going to the door. "Let me show you something."

A policeman opened the door and Buckley said,

"Tell 'em to come in."

"O.K."

The room was silent. Bigger sat on the cot, looking at the floor. He hated this; if anything could be done in his behalf, he himself wanted to do it; not others. The more he saw others exerting themselves, the emptier he felt. He saw the policeman fling the door wide open. Mr. and Mrs. Dalton walked in slowly and stood; Mr. Dalton was looking at him, his face white. Bigger half-rose in dread, then sat again, his eyes lifted, but unseeing. He sank back to the cot.

Swiftly, Buckley crossed the room and shook hands with Mr. Dalton, and, turning to Mrs. Dalton, said:

"I'm dreadfully sorry, madam."

Bigger saw Mr. Dalton look at him, then at Buckley.

"Did he say who was in this thing with him?" Mr. Dalton asked.

"He's just come out of it," Buckley said. "And he's got a lawyer now."

"I have charge of his defense," Max said.

Bigger saw Mr. Dalton look briefly at Jan.

"Bigger, you're a foolish boy if you don't tell who was in this thing with you," Mr. Dalton said.

Bigger tightened and did not answer. Max walked over to Bigger and placed a hand on his shoulder.

"I will talk to him, Mr. Dalton," Max said.

"I'm not here to bully this boy," Mr. Dalton said. "But it'll go easier with him if he tells all he knows."

There was silence. The preacher came forward slowly, hat in hand, and stood in front of Mr. Dalton.

"Ah'ma preacher of the gospel, suh," he said. " 'N' Ah'm mighty sorry erbout whut's done happened t' yo' daughter. Ah knows of yo' good work, suh. 'N' the likes of this should'na come t' yuh."

Mr. Dalton sighed and said wearily,

"Thank you."

"The best thing you can do is help us," Buckley said, turning to Max. "A grave wrong has been done to two people who've helped Negroes more than anybody I know."

"I sympathize with you, Mr. Dalton," Max said. "But killing this boy isn't going to help you or any of us."

"I tried to help him," Mr. Dalton said.

"We wanted to send him to school," said Mrs. Dalton faintly.

"I know," Max said. "But those things don't touch the fundamental problem involved here. This boy comes from an oppressed people. Even if he's done wrong, we must take that into consideration."

"I want you to know that my heart is not bitter," Mr. Dalton said. "What this boy has done will not influence my relations with the Negro people. Why, only today I sent a dozen ping-pong tables to the South Side Boys' Club. . . ."

"Mr. Dalton!" Max exclaimed, coming forward suddenly. "My God, man! Will ping-pong keep men from murdering? Can't you *see*? Even after losing your daughter, you're going to keep going in the *same* direction? Don't you grant as much life-feeling to other men as you have? Could *ping-pong* have kept you from making your millions? This boy and millions like him want a meaningful life, not ping-pong. . . ."

"What do you want me to do?" Mr. Dalton asked coldly. "Do you want me to die and atone for a suffering I never caused? I'm not responsible for the state of this world. I'm doing all one man can. I suppose you want me to take my money and fling it out to the millions who have nothing?"

"No; no; no. . . . Not that," Max said. "If you felt that millions of others experienced life as deeply as you, but differently, you'd see that what you're doing doesn't help. Something of a more fundamental nature. . . ."

"Communism!" Buckley boomed, pulling down the corners of his lips. "Gentlemen, let's don't be childish! This boy's going on trial for his life. My job is to enforce the laws of this state. . . ."

Buckley's voice stopped as the door opened and the policeman looked inside.

"What is it?" Buckley asked.

"The boy's folks are here."

Bigger cringed. Not this! Not here; not *now*! He did not want his mother to come in here now, with these people standing round. He looked about with a wild, pleading expression. Buckley watched him, then turned back to the policeman.

"They have a right to see 'im," Buckley said. "Let 'em come in."

Though he sat, Bigger felt his legs trembling. He was so tense in body and mind that when the door swung in he bounded up and stood in the middle of the room. He saw his mother's face; he wanted to run to her and push her back through the door. She was standing still, one hand upon the doorknob; the other hand clutched a frayed pocketbook, which she dropped and ran to him, throwing her arms about him, crying,

"My baby. . . ."

Bigger's body was stiff with dread and indecision. He felt his mother's arms tight about him and he looked over her shoulder and saw Vera and Buddy come slowly inside and stand, looking about timidly. Beyond them he saw Gus and G.H. and Jack, their mouths open in awe and fear. Vera's lips were trembling and Buddy's hands were clenched. Buckley, the preacher, Jan, Max, Mr. and Mrs. Dalton stood along the wall, behind him, looking on silently. Bigger wanted to whirl and blot them from sight. The kind words of Jan and Max were forgotten now. He felt that all of the white people in the room were measuring every inch of his weakness. He identi-fied himself with his family and felt their naked shame under the eyes of white folks. While looking at his brother and sister and feeling his mother's arms about him; while knowing that Jack and G.H. and Gus were standing awkwardly in the door-way staring at him in curious disbelief—while being con-scious of all this, Bigger felt a wild and outlandish conviction surge in him: *They ought to be glad!* It was a strange but strong feeling, springing from the very depths of his life. Had he not taken fully upon himself the crime of being black? Had he not done the thing which they dreaded above all others? Then they ought not stand here and pity him, cry over him; but look at him and go home, contented, feeling that their shame was washed away.

"Oh, Bigger, son!" his mother wailed. "We been so wor-ried. . . . We ain't slept a single night! The police is there all the time. . . . They stand outside our door. . . . They watch and follow us everywhere! Son, son. . . ."

Bigger heard her sobs; but what could he do? She ought

not to have come here. Buddy came over to him, fumbling with his cap.

"Listen, Bigger, if you didn't do it, just tell me and I'll fix 'em. I'll get a gun and kill four or five of 'em. . . ."

The room gasped. Bigger turned his head quickly and saw that the white faces along the wall were shocked and startled.

"Don't talk that way, Buddy," the mother sobbed. "You want me to die right now? I can't stand no more of this. You mustn't talk that way. . . . We in enough trouble now. . . ."

"Don't let 'em treat you bad, Bigger," Buddy said stoutly.

Bigger wanted to comfort them in the presence of the white folks, but did not know how. Desperately, he cast about for something to say. Hate and shame boiled in him against the people behind his back; he tried to think of words that would defy them, words that would let them know that he had a world and life of his own in spite of them. And at the same time he wanted those words to stop the tears of his mother and sister, to quiet and soothe the anger of his brother; he longed to stop those tears and that anger because he knew that they were futile, that the people who stood along the wall back of him had the destiny of him and his family in their hands.

"Aw, Ma, don't you-all worry none," he said, amazed at his own words; he was possessed by a queer, imperious nervous energy. "I'll be out of this in no time."

His mother gave him an incredulous stare. Bigger turned his head again and looked feverishly and defiantly at the white faces along the wall. They were staring at him in surprise. Buckley's lips were twisted in a faint smile. Jan and Max looked dismayed. Mrs. Dalton, white as the wall behind her, listened, open-mouthed. The preacher and Mr. Dalton were shaking their heads sadly. Bigger knew that no one in the room, except Buddy, believed him. His mother turned her face away and cried. Vera knelt upon the floor and covered her face with her hands.

"Bigger," his mother's voice came low and quiet; she caught his face between the palms of her trembling hands. "Bigger," she said, "tell me. Is there anything, *any*thing we can do?"

He knew that his mother's question had been prompted by

his telling her that he would get out of all this. He knew that they had nothing; they were so poor that they were depending upon public charity to eat. He was ashamed of what he had done; he should have been honest with them. It had been a wild and foolish impulse that had made him try to appear strong and innocent before them. Maybe they would remember him only by those foolish words after they had killed him. His mother's eyes were sad, skeptical; but kind, patient, waiting for his answer. Yes; he had to wipe out that lie, not only so that they might know the truth, but to redeem himself in the eyes of those white faces behind his back along the white wall. He was lost; but he would not cringe; he would not lie, not in the presence of that white mountain looming behind him.

"There ain't nothing, Ma. But I'm all right," he mumbled.

There was silence. Buddy lowered his eyes. Vera sobbed louder. She seemed so little and helpless. She should not have come here. Her sorrow accused him. If he could only make her go home. It was precisely to keep from feeling this hate and shame and despair that he had always acted hard and tough toward them; and now he was without defense. His eyes roved the room, seeing Gus and G.H. and Jack. They saw him looking at them and came forward.

"I'm sorry, Bigger," Jack said, his eyes on the floor.

"They picked us up, too," G.H. said, as though trying to comfort Bigger with the fact. "But Mr. Erlone and Mr. Max got us out. They tried to make us tell about a lot of things we didn't do, but we wouldn't tell."

"Anything we can do, Bigger?" Gus asked.

"I'm all right," Bigger said. "Say, when you go, take Ma home, will you?"

"Sure; sure," they said.

Again there was silence and Bigger's taut nerves ached to fill it up.

"How you l-l-like them sewing classes at the Y, Vera?" he asked.

Vera tightened her hands over her face.

"Bigger," his mother sobbed, trying to talk through her tears. "Bigger, honey, she won't go to school no more. She says the other girls look at and make her 'shamed. . . ."

He had lived and acted on the assumption that he was

alone, and now he saw that he had not been. What he had done made others suffer. No matter how much he would long for them to forget him, they would not be able to. His family was a part of him, not only in blood, but in spirit. He sat on the cot and his mother knelt at his feet. Her face was lifted to his; her eyes were empty, eyes that looked upward when the last hope of earth had failed.

"I'm praying for you, son. That's all I can do now," she said. "The Lord knows I did all I could for you and your sister and brother. I scrubbed and washed and ironed from morning till night, day in and day out, as long as I had strength in my old body. I did all I know how, son, and if I left anything undone, it's just 'cause I didn't know. It's just 'cause your poor old ma couldn't see, son. When I heard the news of what happened, I got on my knees and turned my eyes to God and asked Him if I had raised you wrong. I asked Him to let me bear your burden if I did wrong by you. Honey, your poor old ma can't do nothing now. I'm old and this is too much for me. I'm at the end of my rope. Listen, son, your poor old ma wants you to promise her one thing. . . . Honey, when ain't nobody round you, when you alone, get on your knees and tell God everything. Ask Him to guide you. That's all you can do now. Son, *promise* me you'll go to Him."

"Ahmen!" the preacher intoned fervently.

"Forget me, Ma," Bigger said.

"Son, I can't forget you. You're my boy. I brought you into this world."

"Forget me, Ma."

"Son, I'm worried about you. I can't help it. You got your soul to save. I won't be able to rest easy as long as I'm on this earth if I thought you had gone away from us without asking God for help. Bigger, we had a hard time in this world, but through it all, we been together, ain't we?"

"Yessum," he whispered.

"Son, there's a place where we can be together again in the great bye and bye. God's done fixed it so we can. He's fixed a meeting place for us, a place where we can live without fear. No matter what happens to us here, we can be together in God's heaven. Bigger, your old ma's a-begging you to promise her you'll pray."

"She's tellin' yuh right, son," the preacher said.

"Forget me, Ma," Bigger said.

"Don't you want to see your old ma again, son?"

Slowly, he stood up and lifted his hands and tried to touch his mother's face and tell her yes; and as he did so something screamed deep down in him that it was a lie, that seeing her after they killed him would never be. But his mother believed; it was her last hope; it was what had kept her going through the long years. And she was now believing it all the harder because of the trouble he had brought upon her. His hands finally touched her face and he said with a sigh (knowing that it would never be, knowing that his heart did not believe, knowing that when he died, it would be over, forever):

"I'll pray, Ma."

Vera ran to him and embraced him. Buddy looked grateful. His mother was so happy that all she could do was cry. Jack and G.H. and Gus smiled. Then his mother stood up and encircled him with her arms.

"Come here, Vera," she whimpered.

Vera came.

"Come here, Buddy."

Buddy came.

"Now, put your arms around your brother," she said.

They stood in the middle of the floor, crying, with their arms locked about Bigger. Bigger held his face stiff, hating them and himself, feeling the white people along the wall watching. His mother mumbled a prayer, to which the preacher chanted.

"Lord, here we is, maybe for the last time. You gave me these children, Lord, and told me to raise 'em. If I failed, Lord, I did the best I could. (*Ahmen!*) These poor children's been with me a long time and they's all I got. Lord, please let me see 'em again after the sorrow and suffering of this world! (*Hear her, Lawd!*) Lord, please let me see 'em where I can love 'em in peace. Let me see 'em again beyond the grave! (*Have mercy, Jesus!*) You said You'd heed prayer, Lord, and I'm asking this in the name of Your son."

"Ahmen 'n' Gawd bless yuh, Sistah Thomas," the preacher said.

They took their arms from round Bigger, silently, slowly;

then turned their faces away, as though their weakness made them ashamed in the presence of powers greater than themselves.

"We leaving you now with God, Bigger," his mother said. "Be sure and pray, son."

They kissed him.

Buckley came forward.

"You'll have to go now, Mrs. Thomas," he said. He turned to Mr. and Mrs. Dalton. "I'm sorry, Mrs. Dalton. I didn't mean to keep you standing there so long. But you see how things are. . . ."

Bigger saw his mother straighten suddenly and stare at the blind white woman.

"Is you Mrs. Dalton?" she asked.

Mrs. Dalton moved nervously, lifted her thin, white hands and tilted her head. Her mouth came open and Mr. Dalton placed an arm about her.

"Yes," Mrs. Dalton whispered.

"Oh, Mrs. Dalton, come right this way," Buckley said hurriedly.

"No; please," Mrs. Dalton said. "What is it, Mrs. Thomas?"

Bigger's mother ran and knelt on the floor at Mrs. Dalton's feet.

"Please, mam!" she wailed. "Please, don't let 'em kill my boy! You know how a mother feels! Please, mam. . . . We live in your house. . . . They done asked us to move. . . . We ain't got nothing. . . ."

Bigger was paralyzed with shame; he felt violated.

"*Ma!*" he shouted, more in shame than anger.

Max and Jan ran to the black woman and tried to lift her up.

"That's all right, Mrs. Thomas," Max said. "Come with me."

"Wait," Mrs. Dalton said.

"Please, mam! Don't let 'em kill my boy! He ain't never had a chance! He's just a poor boy! Don't let 'em kill 'im! I'll work for you for the rest of my life! I'll do anything you say, mam!" the mother sobbed.

Mrs. Dalton stooped slowly, her hands trembling in the air. She touched the mother's head.

"There's nothing I can do now," Mrs. Dalton said calmly.

"It's out of my hands. I did all I could, when I wanted to give your boy a chance at life. You're not to blame for this. You must be brave. Maybe it's better. . . ."

"If you speak to 'em, they'll listen to you, mam," the mother sobbed. "Tell 'em to have mercy on my boy. . . ."

"Mrs. Thomas, it's too late for me to do anything now," Mrs. Dalton said. "You must not feel like this. You have your other children to think of. . . ."

"I know you hate us, mam! You lost your daughter. . . ."

"No; no. . . . I don't hate you," Mrs. Dalton said.

The mother crawled from Mrs. Dalton to Mr. Dalton.

"You's rich and powerful," she sobbed. "Spare me my boy. . . ."

Max struggled with the black woman and got her to her feet. Bigger's shame for his mother amounted to hate. He stood with clenched fists, his eyes burning. He felt that in another moment he would have leaped at her.

"That's all right, Mrs. Thomas," Max said.

Mr. Dalton came forward.

"Mrs. Thomas, there's nothing we can do," he said. "This thing is out of our hands. Up to a certain point we can help you, but beyond that. . . . People must protect themselves. But you won't have to move. I'll tell them not to make you move."

The black woman sobbed. Finally, she quieted enough to speak.

"Thank you, sir. God knows I thank you. . . ."

She turned again toward Bigger, but Max led her from the room. Jan caught hold of Vera's arm and led her forward, then stopped in the doorway, looking at Jack and G.H. and Gus.

"You boys going to the South Side?"

"Yessuh," they said.

"Come on. I got a car downstairs. I'll take you."

"Yessuh."

Buddy lingered, looking wistfully at Bigger.

"Good-bye, Bigger," he said.

"Good-bye, Buddy," Bigger mumbled.

The preacher passed Bigger and pressed his arm.

"Gawd bless you, son."

They all left except Buckley. Bigger sat again upon the cot, weak and exhausted. Buckley stood over him.

"Now, Bigger, you see all the trouble you've caused? Now, I'd like to get this case out of the way as soon as possible. The longer you stay in jail, the more agitation there'll be for and against you. And that doesn't help you any, no matter who tells you it does. Boy, there's not but one thing for you to do, and that's to come clean. I know those Reds, Max and Erlone, have told you a lot of things about what they're going to do for you. But, don't believe 'em. They're just after publicity, boy; just after building themselves up at your expense, see? They can't do a *damn* thing for you! You're dealing with the *law* now! And if you let those Reds put a lot of fool ideas into your head, then you're gambling with your own life."

Buckley stopped and relit his cigar. He cocked his head to one side, listening.

"You hear that?" he asked softly.

Bigger looked at him, puzzled. He listened, hearing a faint din.

"Come here, boy. I want to show you something," he said, rising and catching hold of Bigger's arm.

Bigger was reluctant to follow him.

"Come on. Nobody's going to hurt you."

Bigger followed him out of the door; there were several policemen standing on guard in the hallway. Buckley led Bigger to a window through which he looked and saw the streets below crowded with masses of people in all directions.

"See that, boy? Those people would like to lynch you. That's why I'm asking you to trust me and talk to me. The quicker we get this thing over, the better for you. We're going to try to keep 'em from bothering you. But can't you see the longer they stay around here, the harder it'll be for us to handle them?"

Buckley let go of Bigger's arm and hoisted the window; a cold wind swept in and Bigger heard a roar of voices. Involuntarily, he stepped backward. Would they break into the jail? Buckley shut the window and led him back to the room. He sat upon the cot and Buckley sat opposite him.

"You look like an intelligent boy. You see what you're in. Tell me about this thing. Don't let those Reds fool you into saying you're not guilty. I'm talking to you as straight as I'd talk to a son of mine. Sign a confession and get this over with."

Bigger said nothing; he sat looking at the floor.

"Was Jan mixed up in this?"

Bigger heard the faint excited sound of mob voices coming through the concrete walls of the building.

"He proved an alibi and he's free. Tell me, did he leave you holding the bag?"

Bigger heard the far-away clang of a street car.

"If he made you do it, then sign a complaint against him."

Bigger saw the shining tip of the man's black shoes; the sharp creases in his striped trousers; the clear, icy glinting of the eyeglasses upon his high, long nose.

"Boy," said Buckley in a voice so loud that Bigger flinched, "where's Bessie?"

Bigger's eyes widened. He had not thought of Bessie but once since his capture. Her death was unimportant beside that of Mary's; he knew that when they killed him it would be for Mary's death; not Bessie's.

"Well, boy, we found her. You hit her with a brick, but she didn't die right away. . . ."

Bigger's muscles jerked him to his feet. Bessie *alive*! But the voice droned on and he sat down.

"She tried to get out of that air-shaft, but she couldn't. She froze to death. We got the brick you hit her with. We got the blanket and the quilt and the pillows you took from her room. We got a letter from her purse she had written to you and hadn't mailed, a letter telling you she didn't want to go through with trying to collect the ransom money. You see, boy, we got you. Come on, now, tell me all about it."

Bigger said nothing. He buried his face in his hands.

"You raped her, didn't you? Well, if you won't tell about Bessie, then tell me about that woman you raped and choked to death over on University Avenue last fall."

Was the man trying to scare him, or did he really think he had done other killings?

"Boy, you might just as well tell me. We've got a line on all you ever did. And how about the girl you attacked in Jackson Park last summer? Listen, boy, when you were in your cell sleeping and wouldn't talk, we brought women in to identify you. Two women swore complaints against you. One was the sister of the woman you killed last fall, Mrs. Clinton. The other woman, Miss Ashton, says you attacked her last summer by climbing through the window of her bedroom."

"I ain't bothered no woman last summer or last fall either," Bigger said.

"Miss Ashton identified you. She swears you're the one."

"I don't know nothing about it."

"But Mrs. Clinton, the sister of the woman you killed last fall, came to your cell and pointed you out. Who'll believe you when you say you didn't do it? You killed and raped two women in two days; who'll believe you when you say you didn't rape and kill the others? Come on, boy. You haven't a chance holding out."

"I don't know nothing about other women," Bigger repeated stubbornly.

Bigger wondered how much did the man really know. Was he lying about the other women in order to get him to tell about Mary and Bessie? Or were they really trying to pin other crimes upon him?

"Boy, when the newspapers get hold of what we've got on you, you're cooked. I'm not the one who's doing this. The Police Department is digging up the dirt and bringing it to me. Why don't you talk? Did you kill the other women? Or did somebody make you do it? Was Jan in this business? Were the Reds helping you? You're a fool if Jan was mixed up in this and you won't tell."

Bigger shifted his feet and listened to the faint clang of another street car passing. The man leaned forward, caught hold of Bigger's arm and spoke while shaking him.

"You're hurting nobody but yourself holding out like this, boy! Tell me, were Mary, Bessie, Mrs. Clinton's sister, and Miss Ashton the only women you raped or killed?"

The words burst out of Bigger:

"I never heard of no Miss Clinton or Miss Ashton before!"

"Didn't you attack a girl in Jackson Park last summer?"

"Naw!"

"Didn't you choke and rape a woman on University Avenue last fall?"

"Naw!"

"Didn't you climb through a window out in Englewood last fall and rape a woman?"

"Naw; naw! I tell you I didn't!"

"You're not telling the truth, boy. Lying won't get you anywhere."

"I *am* telling the truth!"

"Whose idea was the kidnap note? Jan's?"

"He didn't have nothing to do with it," said Bigger, feeling a keen desire on the man's part to have him implicate Jan.

"What's the use of your holding out, boy? Make it easy for yourself."

Why not talk and get it over with? They knew he was guilty. They could prove it. If he did not talk, then they would say he had committed every crime they could think of.

"Boy, why didn't you and your pals rob Blum's store like you'd planned to last Saturday?"

Bigger looked at him in surprise. They had found that out, too!

"You didn't think I knew about that, did you? I know a lot more, boy. I know about that dirty trick you and your friend Jack pulled off in the Regal Theatre, too. You wonder how I know it? The manager told us when we were checking up. I know what boys like you do, Bigger. Now, come on. You wrote that kidnap note, didn't you?"

"Yeah," he sighed. "I wrote it."

"Who helped you?"

"Nobody."

"Who was going to help you to collect the ransom money?"

"Bessie."

"Come on. Was it Jan?"

"Naw."

"Bessie?"

"Yeah."

"Then why did you kill her?"

Nervously, Bigger's fingers fumbled with a pack of cigarettes and got one out. The man struck a match and held a light for him, but he struck his own match and ignored the offered flame.

"When I saw I couldn't get the money, I killed her to keep her from talking," he said.

"And you killed Mary, too?"

"I didn't mean to kill her, but it don't matter now," he said.

"Did you lay her?"

"Naw."

"You laid Bessie before you killed her. The doctors said so. And now you expect me to believe you didn't lay Mary."

"I *didn't*!"

"Did Jan?"

"Naw."

"Didn't Jan lay her first and then you? . . ."

"Naw; naw. . . ."

"But Jan wrote the kidnap note, didn't he?"

"I never saw Jan before that night."

"But didn't he write the note?"

"Naw; I tell you he didn't."

"*You* wrote the note?"

"Yeah."

"Didn't Jan tell you to write it?"

"Naw."

"Why did you kill Mary?"

He did not answer.

"See here, boy. What you say doesn't make sense. You were never in the Dalton home until Saturday night. Yet, in one night a girl is raped, killed, burnt, and the next night a kidnap note is sent. Come on. Tell me everything that happened and about everybody who helped you."

"There wasn't nobody but me. I don't care what happens to me, but you can't make me say things about other people."

"But you told Mr. Dalton that Jan was in this thing, too."

"I was trying to blame it on him."

"Well, come on. Tell me everything that happened."

Bigger rose and went to the window. His hands caught the cold steel bars in a hard grip. He knew as he stood there that he could never tell why he had killed. It was not that he did not really want to tell, but the telling of it would have involved an explanation of his entire life. The actual killing of Mary and Bessie was not what concerned him most; it was knowing and feeling that he could never make anybody know what had driven him to it. His crimes were known, but what he had felt before he committed them would never be known. He would have gladly admitted his guilt if he had thought that in doing so he could have also given in the same breath a sense of the deep, choking hate that had been his life, a hate that he had not wanted to have, but could not help having. How could he do that? The impulsion to try to tell was as deep as had been the urge to kill.

He felt a hand touch his shoulder; he did not turn round; his eyes looked downward and saw the man's gleaming black shoes.

"I know how you feel, boy. You're colored and you feel that you haven't had a square deal, don't you?" the man's voice came low and soft; and Bigger, listening, hated him for telling him what he knew was true. He rested his tired head against the steel bars and wondered how was it possible for this man to know so much about him and yet be so bitterly against him. "Maybe you've been brooding about this color question a long time, hunh, boy?" the man's voice continued low and soft. "Maybe you think I don't understand? But I do. I know how it feels to walk along the streets like other people, dressed like them, talking like them, and yet excluded for no reason except that you're black. I know your people. Why, they give me votes out there on the South Side every election. I once talked to a colored boy who raped and killed a woman, just like you raped and killed Mrs. Clinton's sister. . . ."

"I didn't do it!" Bigger screamed.

"Why keep saying that? If you talk, maybe the judge'll help you. Confess it all and get it over with. You'll feel better. Say, listen, if you tell me everything, I'll see that you're sent to the hospital for an examination, see? If they say you're not responsible, then maybe you won't have to die. . . ."

Bigger's anger rose. He was not crazy and he did not want to be called crazy.

"I don't want to go to no hospital."

"It's a way out for you, boy."

"I don't want no way out."

"Listen, start at the beginning. Who was the first woman you ever killed?"

He said nothing. He wanted to talk, but he did not like the

note of intense eagerness in the man's voice. He heard the door behind him open; he turned his head just in time to see another white man look in questioningly.

"I thought you wanted me," the man said.

"Yes; come on in," Buckley said.

The man came in and took a seat, holding a pencil and paper on his knee.

"Here, Bigger," Buckley said, taking Bigger by the arm. "Sit down here and tell me all about it. Get it *over* with."

Bigger wanted to tell how he had felt when Jan had held his hand; how Mary had made him feel when she asked him about how Negroes lived; the tremendous excitement that had hold of him during the day and night he had been in the Dalton home—but there were no words for him.

"You went to Mr. Dalton's home at five-thirty that Saturday, didn't you?"

"Yessuh," he mumbled.

Listlessly, he talked. He traced his every action. He paused at each question Buckley asked and wondered how he could link up his bare actions with what he had felt; but his words came out flat and dull. White men were looking at him, waiting for his words, and all the feelings of his body vanished, just as they had when he was in the car between Jan and Mary. When he was through, he felt more lost and undone than when he was captured. Buckley stood up; the other white man rose and held out the papers for him to sign. He took the pen in hand. Well, why shouldn't he sign? He was guilty. He was lost. They were going to kill him. Nobody could help him. They were standing in front of him, bending over him, looking at him, waiting. His hand shook. He signed.

Buckley slowly folded the papers and put them into his pocket. Bigger looked up at the two men, helplessly, wonderingly. Buckley looked at the other white man and smiled.

"That was not as hard as I thought it would be," Buckley said.

"He came through like a clock," the other man said.

Buckley looked down at Bigger and said,

"Just a scared colored boy from Mississippi."

There was a short silence. Bigger felt that they had forgotten him already. Then he heard them speaking.

"Anything else, chief?"

"Naw. I'll be at my club. Let me know how the inquest turns out."

"O.K., chief."

"So long."

"I'll be seeing you, chief."

Bigger felt so empty and beaten that he slid to the floor. He heard the feet of the men walking away softly. The door opened and shut. He was alone, profoundly, inescapably. He rolled on the floor and sobbed, wondering what it was that had hold of him, why he was here.

.   .   .   .

He lay on the cold floor sobbing; but really he was stand-ing up strongly with contrite heart, holding his life in his hands, staring at it with a wondering question. He lay on the cold floor sobbing; but really he was pushing forward with his puny strength against a world too big and too strong for him. He lay on the cold floor sobbing; but really he was groping forward with fierce zeal into a welter of circum-stances which he felt contained a water of mercy for the thirst of his heart and brain.

He wept because he had once again trusted his feelings and they had betrayed him. Why should he have felt the need to try to make his feelings known? And why did not he hear resounding echoes of his feelings in the hearts of others? There were times when he did hear echoes, but always they were couched in tones which, living as a Negro, he could not answer or accept without losing face with the world which had first evoked in him the song of manhood. He feared and hated the preacher because the preacher had told him to bow down and ask for a mercy he knew he needed; but his pride would never let him do that, not this side of the grave, not while the sun shone. And Jan? And Max? They were telling him to believe in himself. Once before he had accepted com-pletely what his life had made him feel, even unto murder. He had emptied the vessel which life had filled for him and found the emptying meaningless. Yet the vessel was full again, wait-ing to be poured out. But no! Not blindly this time! He felt that he could not move again unless he swung out from the base of his own feelings; he felt that he would have to have light in order to act now.

Gradually, more from a lessening of strength than from peace of soul, his sobs ceased and he lay on his back, staring at the ceiling. He had confessed and death loomed now for certain in a public future. How could he go to his death with white faces looking on and saying that only death would cure him for having flung into their faces his feeling of being black? How could death be victory now?

He sighed, pulled up off the floor and lay on the cot, half-awake, half-asleep. The door opened and four policemen came and stood above him; one touched his shoulder.

"Come on, boy."

He rose and looked at them questioningly.

"You're going back to the inquest."

They clicked the handcuffs upon his wrists and led him into the hall, to a waiting elevator. The doors closed and he dropped downward through space, standing between four tall, silent men in blue. The elevator stopped; the doors opened and he saw a restless crowd of people and heard a babble of voices. They led him through a narrow aisle.

"That sonofa*bitch!*"

"Gee, isn't he *black!*"

"Kill 'im!"

A hard blow came to his temple and he slumped to the floor. The faces and voices left him. Pain throbbed in his head and the right side of his face numbed. He held up an elbow to protect himself; they yanked him back upon his feet. When his sight cleared he saw policemen struggling with a slender white man. Shouts rose in a mighty roar. To the front of him a white man pounded with a hammer-like piece of wood upon a table.

"Quiet! Or the room'll be cleared of everybody except witnesses!"

The clamor ceased. The policemen pushed Bigger into a chair. Stretching to the four walls of the room was a solid sheet of white faces. Standing with squared shoulders all round were policemen with clubs in hand, silver metal on their chests, faces red and stern, grey and blue eyes alert. To the right of the man at the table, in rows of three each, six men sat still and silent, their hats and overcoats on their knees. Bigger looked about and saw the pile of white bones lying atop a table; beside them lay the kidnap note, held in place by a bottle of ink. In the center of the table were white sheets of paper fastened together by a metal clasp; it was his signed confession. And there was Mr. Dalton, white-faced, white-haired; and beside him was Mrs. Dalton, still and straight, her face, as always, tilted trustingly upward, to one side. Then he saw the trunk into which he had stuffed Mary's body, the trunk which he had lugged down the stairs and had carried to the station. And, yes, there was the blackened hatchet blade and a tiny round piece of metal. Bigger felt a tap on his shoulder and looked round; Max was smiling at him.

"Take it easy, Bigger. You won't have to say anything here. It won't be long."

The man at the front table rapped again.

"Is there a member of the deceased's family here, one who can give us the family history?"

A murmur swept the room. A woman rose hurriedly and went to the blind Mrs. Dalton, caught hold of her arm, led her forward to a seat to the extreme right of the man at the table, facing the six men in the rows of chairs. That must be Mrs. Patterson, Bigger thought, remembering the woman Peggy had mentioned as Mrs. Dalton's maid.

"Will you please raise your right hand?"

Mrs. Dalton's frail, waxen hand went up timidly. The man asked Mrs. Dalton if the testimony she was about to give was the truth, the whole truth and nothing but the truth, so help you God, and Mrs. Dalton answered,

"Yes, sir; I do."

Bigger sat stolidly, trying not to let the crowd detect any fear in him. His nerves were painfully taut as he hung onto the old woman's words. Under the man's questioning, Mrs. Dalton said that her age was fifty-three, that she lived at 4605 Drexel Boulevard, that she was a retired school teacher, that she was the mother of Mary Dalton and the wife of Henry Dalton. When the man began asking questions relating to Mary, the crowd leaned forward in their seats. Mrs. Dalton said that Mary was twenty-three years of age, single; that she carried about thirty thousand dollars' worth of insurance, that she owned real estate amounting to approximately a quarter of a million dollars, and that she was active right up to the date of her death. Mrs. Dalton's voice came tense and faint and Bigger wondered how much more of this he could stand. Would it not have been much better to have stood up in the full glare of those roving knives of light and let them shoot him down? He could have cheated them out of this show, this hunt, this eager sport.

"Mrs. Dalton," the man said, "I'm the Deputy Coroner and it is with considerable anxiety that I ask you these questions. But it is necessary for me to trouble you in order to establish the identity of the deceased. . . ."

"Yes, sir," Mrs. Dalton whispered.

Carefully, the coroner lifted from the table at his side a tiny piece of blackened metal; he turned, fronted Mrs. Dalton, then paused. The room was so quiet that Bigger could hear the coroner's footsteps on the wooden floor as he walked to Mrs. Dalton's chair. Tenderly, he caught her hand in his and said,

"I'm placing in your hand a metal object which the police retrieved from the ashes of the furnace in the basement of your home. Mrs. Dalton, I want you to feel this metal carefully and tell me if you remember ever having felt it before."

Bigger wanted to turn his eyes away, but he could not. He watched Mrs. Dalton's face; he saw the hand tremble that held the blackened bit of metal. Bigger jerked his head round. A woman began to sob without restraint. A wave of murmurs rose through the room. The coroner took a quick step back to the table and rapped sharply with his knuckles. The room was instantly quiet, save for the sobbing woman. Bigger looked back to Mrs. Dalton. Both of her hands were now fumbling nervously with the piece of metal; then her shoulders shook. She was crying.

"Do you recognize it?"

"Y-y-yes. . . ."

"What is it?"

"A-a-an earring. . . ."

"When did you first come in contact with it?"

Mrs. Dalton composed her face, and, with tears on her cheeks, answered,

"When I was a girl, years ago. . . ."

"Do you remember precisely when?"

"Thirty-five years ago."

"You once owned it?"

"Yes; it was one of a pair."

"Yes, Mrs. Dalton. No doubt the other earring was destroyed in the fire. This one dropped through the grates into the bin under the furnace. Now, Mrs. Dalton, how long did you own this pair of earrings?"

"For thirty-three years."

"How did they come into your possession?"

"Well, my mother gave them to me when I was of age. My grandmother gave them to my mother when she was of age, and I in turn gave them to my daughter when she was of age. . . ."

"What do you mean, of age?"

"At eighteen."

"And when did you give them to your daughter?"

"About five years ago."

"She wore them all the time?"

"Yes."

"Are you positive that this is one of the same earrings?"

"Yes. There can be no mistake. They were a family heirloom. There are no two others like them. My grandmother had them designed and made to order."

"Mrs. Dalton, when were you last in the company of the deceased?"

"Last Saturday night, or I should say, early Sunday morning."

"At what time?"

"It was nearly two o'clock, I think."

"Where was she?"

"In her room, in bed."

"Were you in the habit of seeing, I mean, in the habit of meeting your daughter at such an hour?"

"No. I knew that she'd planned to go to Detroit Sunday morning. When I heard her come in I wanted to find out why she'd stayed out so late. . . ."

"Did you speak with her?"

"No. I called her several times, but she did not answer."

"Did you touch her?"

"Yes; slightly."

"But she did not speak to you?"

"Well, I heard some mumbling. . . ."

"Do you know who it was?"

"No."

"Mrs. Dalton, could your daughter by any means, in your judgment, have been dead then, and you not have known or suspected it?"

"I don't know."

"Do you know if your daughter was alive when you spoke to her?"

"I don't know. I assumed she was."

"Was there anyone else in the room at the time?"

"I don't know. But I felt strange there."

"Strange? What do you mean, strange?"

"I—I don't know. I wasn't satisfied, for some reason. It seemed to me that there was something I should have done, or said. But I kept saying to myself, 'She's asleep; that's all.'"

"If you felt so dissatisfied, why did you leave the room without trying to awaken her?"

Mrs. Dalton paused before answering; her thin mouth was wide open and her face tilted far to one side.

"I smelt alcohol in the room," she whispered.

"Yes?"

"I thought Mary was intoxicated."

"Had you ever encountered your daughter intoxicated before?"

"Yes; and that was why I thought she was intoxicated then. It was the same odor."

"Mrs. Dalton, if someone had possessed your daughter sexually while she lay on that bed, could you in any way have detected it?"

The room buzzed. The coroner rapped for order.

"I don't know," she whispered.

"Just a few more questions, please, Mrs. Dalton. What aroused your suspicions that something had befallen your daughter?"

"When I went to her room the next morning I felt her bed and found that she had not slept in it. Next I felt in her clothes rack and found that she had not taken the new clothes she had bought."

"Mrs. Dalton, you and your husband have given large sums of money to Negro educational institutions, haven't you?"

"Yes."

"Could you tell us roughly how much?"

"Over five million dollars."

"You bear no ill will toward the Negro people?"

"No; none whatever."

"Mrs. Dalton, please, tell us what was the last thing you did when you stood above your daughter's bed that Sunday morning?"

"I—I. . . ." She paused, lowered her head and dabbed at her eyes. "I knelt at the bedside and prayed. . . ." she said, her words coming in a sharp breath of despair.

"That is all. Thank you, Mrs. Dalton."

The room heaved a sigh. Bigger saw the woman lead Mrs. Dalton back to her seat. Many eyes in the room were fastened upon Bigger now, cold grey and blue eyes, eyes whose tense hate was worse than a shout or a curse. To get rid of that concentrated gaze, he stopped looking, even though his eyes remained open.

The coroner turned to the men sitting in rows to his right and said,

"You gentlemen, the jurors, are any of you acquainted with the deceased or are any of you members of the family?"

One of the men rose and said,

"No, sir."

"Would there be any reason why you could not render a fair and impartial verdict in this?"

"No, sir."

"Is there any objection to these men serving as jurors in this case?" the coroner asked of the entire room.

There was no answer.

"In the name of the coroner, I will ask the jurors to rise, pass by this table, and view the remains of the deceased, one Mary Dalton."

In silence the six men rose and filed past the table, each looking at the pile of white bones. When they were seated again, the coroner called,

"We will now hear Mr. Jan Erlone!"

Jan rose, came forward briskly, and was asked to swear to tell the truth, the whole truth, and nothing but the truth, so help him God. Bigger wondered if Jan would turn on him now. He wondered if he could really trust any white man, even this white man who had come and offered him his friendship. He leaned forward to hear. Jan was asked several times if he was a foreigner and Jan said no. The coroner walked close to Jan's chair and leaned the upper part of his body forward and asked in a loud voice,

"Do you believe in social equality for Negroes?"

The room stirred.

"I believe all races are equal. . . ." Jan began.

"Answer *yes* or *no*, Mr. Erlone! You're not on a soap box. *Do* you believe in social equality for Negroes?"

"Yes."

"Are you a member of the Communist Party?"

"Yes."

"In what condition was Miss Dalton when you left her last Sunday morning?"

"What do you mean?"

"Was she drunk?"

"I would not say she was drunk. She had had a few drinks."

"What time did you leave her?"

"It was about one-thirty, I think."

"Was she in the front seat of the car?"

"Yes; she was in the front seat."

"Had she been in the front seat all along?"

"No."

"Was she in the front seat when you left the café?"

"No."

"Did you put her in the front seat when you left the car?"

"No; she said she wanted to sit up front."

"You didn't *ask* her to?"

"No."

"When you left her, was she able to get out of the car alone?"

"I think so."

"Had you had any relations with her while in the back seat

that would have tended to make her, let us say, stunned, too weak to have gotten out alone?"

"No!"

"Is it not true, Mr. Erlone, that Miss Dalton was in no condition to protect herself and you lifted her into that front seat?"

"No! I didn't lift her into the front seat!"

Jan's voice sounded throughout the room. There was a quick buzzing of conversation.

"Why did you leave an unprotected white girl alone in a car with a drunken Negro?"

"I was not aware that Bigger was drunk and I did not consider Mary as being unprotected."

"Had you at any time in the past left Miss Dalton alone in the company of Negroes?"

"No."

"You had never used Miss Dalton as bait before, had you?"

Bigger was startled by a noise behind him. He turned his head; Max was on his feet.

"Mr. Coroner, I realize that this is not a trial. But the questions being asked now have no earthly relation to the cause and manner of the death of the deceased."

"Mr. Max, we are allowing plenty of latitude here. The Grand Jury will determine whether the testimony offered here has any relation or not."

"But questions of this sort inflame the public mind. . . ."

"Now, listen, Mr. Max. No question asked in this room will inflame the public mind any more than has the death of Mary Dalton, and you know it. You have the right to question any of these witnesses, but I will not tolerate any publicity-seeking by your kind here!"

"But Mr. Erlone is not on trial here, Mr. Coroner!"

"He is suspected of being implicated in this murder! And we're after the one who killed this girl and the reasons for it! If you think these questions have the wrong construction, you may question the witness when we're through. But you cannot regulate the questions asked here!"

Max sat down. The room was quiet. The coroner paced to and fro a few seconds before he spoke again; his face was red and his lips were pressed tight.

"Mr. Erlone, didn't you give that Negro material relating to the Communist Party?"

"Yes."

"What was the nature of that material?"

"I gave him some pamphlets on the Negro question."

"Material advocating the equality of whites and blacks?"

"It was material which explained. . . ."

"Did that material contain a plea for 'unity of whites and blacks'?"

"Why, yes."

"Did you, in your agitation of that drunken Negro, tell him that it was all right for him to have sexual relations with white women?"

"No!"

"Did you advise Miss Dalton to have sexual relations with him?"

"No!"

"Did you *shake hands* with that Negro?"

"Yes."

"Did you *offer* to shake hands with him?"

"Yes. It is what any decent person. . . ."

"Confine yourself to answering the questions, please, Mr. Erlone. We want none of your Communist explanations here. Tell me, did you *eat* with that Negro?"

"Why, yes."

"You *invited* him to eat?"

"Yes."

"Miss Dalton was at the table when you *invited* him to sit down?"

"Yes."

"How many times have you *eaten* with Negroes before?"

"I don't know. Many times."

"You *like* Negroes?"

"I make no distinctions. . . ."

"Do you *like* Negroes, Mr. Erlone?"

"I object!" Max shouted. "How on earth is that related to this case!"

"You cannot regulate these questions!" the coroner shouted. "I've told you that before! A woman has been foully murdered. This witness brought the deceased into contact with the last person who saw her alive. We have the right to determine what this witness' attitude was toward that girl and that Negro!" The coroner turned back to Jan. "Now, Mr. Erlone, didn't you ask that Negro to sit in the front seat of the car, *between* you and Miss Dalton?"

"No; he was already in the front seat."

"But you *didn't* ask him to get into the *back* seat, did you?"

"No."

"Why *didn't* you?"

"My God! The man is human! Why don't you ask me . . . ?"

"I'm asking these questions and you're answering them. Now, tell me, Mr. Erlone, would you have invited that Negro to sleep with you?"

"I refuse to answer that question!"

"But you didn't refuse that drunken Negro the right to sleep with that girl, did you?"

"His right to associate with her or anybody else was not in question. . . ."

"Did you try to keep that Negro *from* Miss Dalton?"

"I didn't. . . ."

"Answer yes or no!"

"No!"

"Have you a sister?"

"Why, yes."

"Where is she?"

"In New York."

"Is she married?"

"No."

"Would you consent for her to marry a Negro?"

"I have nothing to do with whom she marries."

"Didn't you tell that drunken Negro to call you Jan instead of Mr. Erlone?"

"Yes; but, . . ."

"Confine yourself to answering the questions!"

"But, Mr. Coroner, you imply. . . ."

"I'm trying to establish a motive for the murder of that innocent girl!"

"No; you're not! You're trying to indict a race of people and a political party!"

"We want no statements! Tell me, was Miss Dalton in a condition to say good-bye to you when you left her in that car with the drunken Negro?"

"Yes. She said good-bye."

"Tell me, how much liquor did you give Miss Dalton that night?"

"I don't know."

"What kind of liquor was it?"

"Rum."

"Why did you prefer rum?"

"I don't know. I just bought rum."

"Was it to stimulate the body to a great extent?"

"No."

"How much was bought?"

"A fifth of a gallon."

"Who paid for it?"

"I did."

"Did that money come from the treasury of the Communist Party?"

"No!"

"Don't they allow you a budget for recruiting expenses?"

"No!"

"How much was drunk before you bought the fifth of rum?"

"We had a few beers."

"How many?"

"I don't know."

"You don't remember much about what happened that night, do you?"

"I'm telling you all I remember."

"*All* you remember?"

"Yes."

"Is it possible that you don't remember some things?"

"I'm telling you all I remember."

"Were you too drunk to remember everything that happened?"

"No."

"You knew what you were doing?"

"Yes."

"You deliberately left the girl in that condition?"

"She was in no *condition*!"

"Just how drunk was she after the beers and rum?"

"She seemed to know what she was doing."

"Did you have any fears about her being able to defend herself?"

"No."

"Did you care?"

"Of course, I did."

"You thought that whatever would happen would be all right?"

"I thought she was all right."

"Just tell me, Mr. Erlone, how drunk was Miss Dalton?"

"Well, she was a little high, if you know what I mean."

"Feeling good?"

"Yes; you could say that."

"Receptive?"

"I don't know what you mean."

"Were you satisfied when you left her?"

"What do you mean?"

"You had enjoyed her company?"

"Why, yes."

"And after enjoying a woman like that, isn't there a let-down?"

"I don't know what you mean."

"It was late, wasn't it, Mr. Erlone? You wanted to go home?"

"Yes."

"You did not want to remain with her any longer?"

"No; I was tired."

"So you left her to the Negro?"

"I left her in the car. I didn't leave her to anybody."

"But the Negro was in the car?"

"Yes."

"And she got in the front seat with him?"

"Yes."

"And you did not try to stop her?"

"No."

"And all three of you had been drinking?"

"Yes."

"And you were satisfied to leave her like that, with a drunken Negro?"

"What do you *mean*?"

"You had no fear for her?"

"Why, no."

"You felt that she, being drunk, would be as satisfied with anyone else as she had been with you?"

"No; no. . . . Not that way. You're leading. . . ."

"Just answer the questions. Had Miss Dalton, to your knowledge, ever had sex relations with a Negro before?"

"No."

"Did you think that that would be as good a time as any for her to learn?"

"No; no. . . ."

"Didn't you promise to contact the Negro to see if he was grateful enough to join the Communist Party?"

"I didn't say I'd contact him."

"Didn't you tell him you'd contact him within two or three days?"

"No."

"Mr. Erlone, are you sure you didn't say that?"

"Oh, yes! But it was not with the construction you are putting upon it. . . ."

"Mr. Erlone, were you surprised when you heard of the death of Miss Dalton?"

"Yes. At first I was too stunned to believe it. I thought surely there was some mistake."

"You hadn't expected that drunken Negro to go that far, had you?"

"I hadn't expected anything."

"But you told that Negro to read those Communist pamphlets, didn't you?"

"I gave them to him."

"You told him to *read* them?"

"Yes."

"But you didn't expect him to go so far as to rape and kill the girl?"

"I didn't expect anything in that direction at all."

"That's all, Mr. Erlone."

Bigger watched Jan go back to his seat. He knew how Jan felt. He knew what the man had been trying to do in asking the questions. He was not the only object of hate here.

What did the Reds want that made the coroner hate Jan so?

"Will Mr. Henry Dalton please come forward?" the coroner asked.

Bigger listened as Mr. Dalton told how the Dalton family always hired Negro boys as chauffeurs, especially when those Negro boys were handicapped by poverty, lack of education, misfortune, or bodily injury. Mr. Dalton said that this was to give them a chance to support their families and go to school. He told how Bigger had come to the house, how timid and frightened he had acted, and how moved and touched the family had been for him. He told how he had not thought that Bigger had had anything to do with the disappearance of Mary, and how he had told Britten not to question him. He then told of receiving the kidnap note, and of how shocked he had been when he was informed that Bigger had fled his home, thereby indicating his guilt.

When the coroner's questioning was over, Bigger heard Max ask,

"May I direct a few questions?"

"Certainly. Go right ahead," the coroner said.

Max went forward and stood directly in front of Mr. Dalton.

"You are the president of the Dalton Real Estate Company, are you not?"

"Yes."

"Your company owns the building in which the Thomas family has lived for the past three years, does it not?"

"Well, no. My company owns the stock in a company that owns the house."

"I see. What is the name of *that* company?"

"The South Side Real Estate Company."

"Now, Mr. Dalton, the Thomas family paid you. . . ."

"Not to *me*! They pay rent to the South Side Real Estate Company."

"You own the controlling stock in the Dalton Real Estate Company, don't you?"

"Why, yes."

"And that company in turn owns the stock that controls the South Side Real Estate Company, doesn't it?"

"Why, yes."

"I think I can say that the Thomas family pays rent to *you*?"

"Indirectly, yes."

"Who formulates the policies of these two companies?"

"Why, I do."

"Why is it that you charge the Thomas family and other Negro families more rent for the same kind of houses than you charge whites?"

"I don't fix the rent scales," Mr. Dalton said.

"Who does?"

"Why, the law of supply and demand regulates the price of houses."

"Now, Mr. Dalton, it has been said that you donate millions of dollars to educate Negroes. Why is it that you exact an exorbitant rent of eight dollars per week from the Thomas family for one unventilated, rat-infested room in which four people eat and sleep?"

The coroner leaped to his feet.

"I'll not tolerate your brow-beating this witness! Have you no sense of decency? This man is one of the most respected men in this city! And your questions have no bearing. . . ."

"They *do* have a bearing!" Max shouted. "You said we could question with latitude here! I'm trying to find the guilty person, too! Jan Erlone is not the only man who's influenced Bigger Thomas! There were many others *before* him. I have as much right to determine what effect their attitude has had upon his conduct as you had to determine what Jan Erlone's had!"

"I'm willing to answer his questions if it will clear things up," Mr. Dalton said quietly.

"Thank you, Mr. Dalton. Now, tell me, why is it that you charged the Thomas family eight dollars per week for one room in a tenement?"

"Well, there's a housing shortage."

"All over Chicago?"

"No. Just here on the South Side."

"You own houses in other sections of the city?"

"Yes."

"Then why don't you rent those houses to Negroes?"

"Well. . . . Er. . . . I—I—I don't think they'd like to live any other place."

"Who told you that?"

"Nobody."

"You came to that conclusion yourself?"

"Why, yes."

"Isn't it true you *refuse* to rent houses to Negroes if those houses are in other sections of the city?"

"Why, yes."

"Why?"

"Well, it's an old custom."

"Do you think that custom is right?"

"I didn't make the custom," Mr. Dalton said.

"Do you think that custom is right?" Max asked again.

"Well, I think Negroes are happier when they're together."

"Who told you *that*?"

"Why, nobody."

"Aren't they more profitable when they're together?"

"I don't know what you mean."

"Mr. Dalton, doesn't this policy of your company tend to keep Negroes on the South Side, in one area?"

"Well, it works that way. But I didn't originate. . . ."

"Mr. Dalton, you give millions to help Negroes. May I ask why you don't charge them less rent for fire-traps and check that against your charity budget?"

"Well, to charge them less rent would be unethical."

"Unethical!"

"Why, yes. I would be underselling my competitors."

"Is there an agreement among realtors as to what Negroes should be charged for rent?"

"No. But there's a code of ethics in business."

"So, the profits you take from the Thomas family in rents, you give back to them to ease the pain of their gouged lives and to salve the ache of your own conscience?"

"That's a distortion of fact, sir!"

"Mr. Dalton, why do you contribute money to Negro education?"

"I want to see them have a chance."

"Have you ever employed any of the Negroes you helped to educate?"

"Why, no."

"Mr. Dalton, do you think that the terrible conditions under which the Thomas family lived in one of your houses may in some way be related to the death of your daughter?"

"I don't know what you mean."

"That's all," said Max.

After Mr. Dalton left the stand, Peggy came, then Britten, a host of doctors, reporters, and many policemen.

"We will now hear from Bigger Thomas!" the coroner called.

A wave of excited voices swept over the room. Bigger's fingers gripped the arms of the chair. Max's hand touched his shoulder. Bigger turned and Max whispered,

"Sit still."

Max rose.

"Mr. Coroner?"

"Yes?"

"In the capacity of Bigger Thomas' lawyer, I'd like to state that he does not wish to testify here."

"His testimony would help to clear up any doubt as to the cause of the death of the deceased," the coroner said.

"My client is already in police custody and it is his right to refuse. . . ."

"All right. All right," the coroner said.

Max sat down.

"Stay in your seat. It's all right," Max whispered to Bigger.

Bigger relaxed and felt his heart pounding. He longed for something to happen so that the white faces would stop staring at him. Finally, the faces turned away. The coroner strode to the table and lifted the kidnap note with a slow, long, delicate, and deliberate gesture.

"Gentlemen," he said, facing the six men in the rows of chairs, "you have heard the testimony of the witnesses. I think, however, that you should have the opportunity to examine the evidence gathered by the Police Department."

The coroner gave the kidnap note to one of the jurors who read it and passed it on to the others. All of the jurors examined the purse, the blood-stained knife, the blackened hatchet blade, the Communist pamphlets, the rum bottle, the trunk, and the signed confession.

"Owing to the peculiar nature of this crime, and owing to the fact that the deceased's body was all but destroyed, I deem it imperative that you examine one additional piece of evidence. It will help shed light upon the actual manner of the death of the deceased," the coroner said.

He turned and nodded in the direction of two white-coated attendants who stood at the rear door. The room was quiet. Bigger wondered how much longer it would last; he felt that he could not stand much more. Now and then the room blurred and a slight giddiness came over him; but his muscles would flex taut and it would pass. The hum of voices grew suddenly loud and the coroner rapped for order. Then a commotion broke out. Bigger heard a man's voice saying,

"Move aside, please!"

He looked and saw the two white-coated attendants pushing an oblong, sheet-covered table through the crowd and down the aisle. What's this? Bigger wondered. He felt Max's hand come on to his shoulder.

"Take it easy, Bigger. This'll soon be over."

"What they doing?" Bigger asked in a tense whisper.

For a long moment Max did not answer. Then he said uncertainly,

"I don't know."

The oblong table was pushed to the front of the room. The coroner spoke in a deep, slow voice that was charged with passionate meaning:

"As Deputy Coroner, I have decided, in the interests of justice, to offer in evidence the raped and mutilated body of one Bessie Mears, and the testimony of police officers and doctors relating to the cause and manner of her death. . . ."

The coroner's voice was drowned out. The room was in an uproar. For two minutes the police had to pound their clubs against the walls to restore quiet. Bigger sat still as stone as Max rushed past him and stopped a few feet from the sheet-covered table.

"Mr. Coroner," Max said. "This is outrageous! Your indecent exhibition of that girl's dead body serves no purpose but that of an incitement to mob violence. . . ."

"It will enable the jury to determine the exact manner of the death of Mary Dalton, who was slain by the man who slew Bessie Mears!" the coroner said in a scream that was compounded of rage and vindictiveness.

"The confession of Bigger Thomas covers all the evidence necessary for this jury!" Max said. "You are criminally appealing to mob emotion. . . ."

"That's for the Grand Jury to determine!" the coroner said. "And you cannot interrupt these proceedings any longer! If you persist in this attitude, you'll be removed from this room! I have the legal right to determine what evidence is necessary. . . ."

Slowly, Max turned and walked back to his seat, his lips a thin line, his face white, his head down.

Bigger was crushed, helpless. His lips dropped wide apart. He felt frozen, numb. He had completely forgotten Bessie during the inquest of Mary. He understood what was being done. To offer the dead body of Bessie as evidence and proof that he had murdered Mary would make him appear a monster; it would stir up more hate against him. Bessie's death had not been mentioned during the inquest and all of the white faces in the room were utterly surprised. It was not because he had thought any the less of Bessie that he had forgotten her, but Mary's death had caused him the most fear; not her death in itself, but what it meant to him as a Negro. They were bringing Bessie's body in now to make the white men and women feel that nothing short of a quick blotting out of his life would make the city safe again. They were using his having killed Bessie to kill him for his having killed Mary, to cast him in a light that would sanction any action taken to destroy him. Though he had killed a black girl and a white girl, he knew that it would be for the death of the white girl that he would be punished. The black girl was merely "evidence." And under it all he knew that the white people did not really care about Bessie's being killed. White people never searched for Negroes who killed other Negroes. He had even heard it said that white people felt it was good when one Negro killed another; it meant that they had one Negro less to contend with. Crime for a Negro was only when he harmed whites, took white lives, or injured white property. As time passed he could not help looking and listening to what was going on in the room. His eyes rested wistfully on the still oblong white draped form under the sheet on the table and he felt a deeper sympathy for Bessie than at any time when she was alive. He knew that Bessie, too, though dead, though killed by him, would resent her dead body being used in this way. Anger quickened in him: an old feeling that Bessie had often described to him when she had come from long hours of hot toil in the white folks' kitchens, a feeling of being forever commanded by others so much that thinking and feeling for one's self was impossible. Not only had he lived where they told him to live, not only had he done what they told him to do, not only had he done these things until he had killed to be quit of them; but even after obeying, after killing, they still ruled him. He was their property, heart and soul, body and blood; what they did claimed every atom of him, sleeping and waking; it colored life and dictated the terms of death.

The coroner rapped for order, then rose and stepped to the table and with one sweep of his arm flung the sheet back from Bessie's body. The sight, bloody and black, made Bigger flinch involuntarily and lift his hands to his eyes and at the same instant he saw blinding flashes of the silver bulbs flicking through the air. His eyes looked with painful effort to the back of the room, for he felt that if he saw Bessie again he would rise from his chair and sweep his arm in an attempt to blot out this room and the people in it. Every nerve of his body helped him to stare without seeing and to sit amid the noise without hearing.

A pain came to the front of his head, right above the eyes. As the slow minutes dragged, his body was drenched in cold sweat. His blood throbbed in his ears; his lips were parched and dry; he wanted to wet them with his tongue, but could not. The tense effort to keep out of his consciousness the terrible sight of Bessie and the drone of the voices would not allow him to move a single muscle. He sat still, surrounded by an invisible cast of concrete. Then he could hold out no longer. He bent forward and buried his face in his hands. He heard a far-away voice speaking from a great height. . . .

"The jury will retire to the next room."

Bigger lifted his head and saw the six men rise and file out through a rear door. The sheet had been pulled over Bessie's body and he could not see her. The voices in the room grew loud and the coroner rapped for order. The six men filed slowly back to their chairs. One of them gave the coroner a slip of paper. The coroner rose, lifted his hand for silence and read a long string of words that Bigger could not understand. But he caught phrases:

". . . . the said Mary Dalton came to her death in the bedroom of her home, located at 4605 Drexel Boulevard, from suffocation and strangulation due to external violence, said violence received when the deceased was choked by the hands of one, Bigger Thomas, during the course of criminal rape. . . .

". . . . we, the Jury, believe that the said occurrence was murder and recommend that the said Bigger Thomas be held to the Grand Jury on a charge of murder, until released by due process of law. . . ."

The voice droned on, but Bigger did not listen. This meant that he was going to jail to stay there until tried and executed. Finally, the coroner's voice stopped. The room was full of noise. Bigger heard men and women walking past him. He looked about like a man waking from a deep sleep. Max had hold of his arm.

"Bigger?"

He turned his head slightly.

"I'll see you tonight. They're taking you to the Cook County Jail. I'll come there and talk things over with you. We'll see what can be done. Meanwhile, take it easy. As soon as you can, lie down and get some sleep, hear?"

Max left him. He saw two policemen wheeling Bessie's body back through the door. The two policemen who sat to either side of him took his arms and locked his wrists to theirs. Two more policemen stood in front of him and two more stood in back.

"Come on, boy."

Two policemen walked ahead, making a path for him in the dense crowd. As he passed white men and women they were silent, but as soon as he was some few feet away, he heard their voices rise. They took him out of the front door, into the hall. He thought that they were going to take him back upstairs and he made a motion to go in the direction of the elevator, but they jerked him back roughly.

"This way!"

They led him out of the front door of the building, to the street. Yellow sunshine splashed the sidewalks and buildings. A huge throng of people covered the pavement. The wind blew hard. Out of the shrill pitch of shouts and screams he caught a few distinct words:

". . . . turn 'im loose. . . ."

". . . . give 'im what he gave that girl. . . ."

". . . . let us take care of 'im. . . ."

". . . . burn that black ape. . . ."

A narrow aisle was cleared for him across the width of the pavement to a waiting car. As far as he could see there were blue-coated white men with bright silver stars shining on their chests. They wedged him tightly into the back seat of the car, between the two policemen to whom he was handcuffed. The motor throbbed. Ahead, he saw a car swing out from the curb and roll with screaming siren down the street through the sunshine. Another followed it. Then four more. At last the car in which he sat fell in line behind them. Back of him he heard other cars pulling out from the curb, with throbbing motors and shrieking sirens. He looked at the passing buildings out of the side window, but could not recognize any familiar landmarks. To each side of him were peering white faces with open mouths. Soon, however, he knew that he was heading southward. The sirens screamed so loud that he seemed to be riding a wave of sound. The cars swerved onto State Street. At Thirty-fifth Street the neighborhood became familiar. At Thirty-seventh Street he knew that two blocks to his left was his home. What were his mother and brother and sister doing now? And where were Jack and G.H. and Gus? The rubber tires sang over the flat asphalt. There was a policeman at every corner, waving the cars on. Where were they taking him? Maybe they were going to keep him in a jail on the South Side? Maybe they were taking him to the Hyde Park Police Station? They reached Forty-seventh Street and rolled eastward, toward Cottage Grove Avenue. They came to Drexel Boulevard and swung north again. He stiffened and leaned forward. Mr. Dalton lived on this street.

What were they going to do with him? The cars slowed and
stopped directly in front of the Dalton gate. What were they
bringing him here for? He looked at the big brick house,
drenched in sunshine, still, quiet. He looked into the faces of
the two policemen who sat to either side of him; they were
staring silently ahead. Upon the sidewalks, to the front and
rear of him, were long lines of policemen with drawn guns.
White faces filled the apartment windows all round him.
People were pouring out of doors, running toward the Dalton home. A policeman with a golden star upon his chest
came to the door of the car, opened it, glanced at him briefly,
then turned to the driver.

"O.K., boys; take 'im out."

They led him to the curb. Already a solidly packed crowd
stood all over the sidewalks, the streets, on lawns, and behind
the lines of the policemen. He heard a white boy yell,

"There's the nigger that killed Miss Mary!"

They led him through the gate, down the walk, up the
steps; he stood a second facing the front door of the Dalton
home, the same door before which he had stood so humbly
with his cap in his hand a little less than a week ago. The door
opened and he was led down the hall to the rear stairs and up
to the second floor, to the door of Mary's room. It seemed
that he could not breathe. What did they bring him here for?
His body was once more wet with sweat. How long could he
stand this without collapsing again? They led him into the
room. It was crowded with armed policemen and newspapermen ready with their bulbs. He looked round; the room was
just as he had seen it *that* night. There was the bed upon
which he had smothered Mary. The clock with the glowing
dial stood on the small dresser. The same curtains were at the
windows and the shades were still far up, as far up as they had
been that night when he had stood near them and had seen
Mrs. Dalton in flowing white grope her way slowly into the
dark blue room with her hands lifted before her. He felt the
eyes of the men upon him and his body stiffened, flushing hot
with shame and anger. The man with the golden star on his
chest came to him and spoke in a soft low tone.

"Now, Bigger, be a good boy. Just relax and take it easy.
We want you to take your time and show us just what

happened that night, see? And don't mind the boys' taking pictures. Just go through the motions you went through that night. . . ."

Bigger glared; his whole body tightened and he felt that he was going to rise another foot in height.

"Come on," the man said. "Nobody's going to hurt you. Don't be afraid."

Outrage burned in Bigger.

"Come on. Show us what you did."

He stood without moving. The man caught his arm and tried to lead him to the bed. He jerked back violently, his muscles flexed taut. A hot band of fire encircled his throat. His teeth clamped so hard that he could not have spoken had he tried. He backed against a wall, his eyes lowered in a baleful glare.

"What's the matter, boy?"

Bigger's lips pulled back, showing his white teeth. Then he blinked his eyes; the flashlights went off and he knew in the instant of their flashing that they had taken his picture showing him with his back against a wall, his teeth bared in a snarl.

"Scared, boy? You weren't scared that night you were in here with that girl, were you?"

Bigger wanted to take enough air into his lungs to scream, "Yes! I was scared!" But who would believe him? He would go to his death without ever trying to tell men like these what he had felt that night. When the man spoke again, his tone had changed.

"Come on, now, boy. We've treated you pretty nice, but we can get tough if we have to, see? It's up to *you*! Get over there by that bed and show us how you raped and murdered that girl!"

"I didn't rape her," Bigger said through stiff lips.

"Aw, come on. What you got to lose now? Show us what you did."

"I don't want to."

"You *have* to!"

"I *don't* have to."

"Well, we'll *make* you!"

"You can't make me do nothing but die!"

And as he said it, he wished that they would shoot him so
that he could be free of them, forever. Another white man
with a golden star upon his chest walked over.

"Drop it. We got our case."

"You think we ought to?"

"Sure. What's the use?"

"O.K., boys. Take 'im back to the car."

They clamped the steel handcuffs on his wrists and led him
down the hall. Even before the front door was opened, he
heard the faint roar of voices. As far as he could see through
the glass panels, up and down the street, were white people
standing in the cold wind and sunshine. They took him
through the door and the roar grew louder; as soon as he was
visible the roar reached a deafening pitch and continued to
rise each second. Surrounded by policemen, he was half-
dragged and half-lifted along the narrow lane of people,
through the gate, toward the waiting car.

"You black ape!"

"Shoot that bastard!"

He felt hot spittle splashing against his face. Somebody
tried to leap at him, but was caught by the policemen and held
back. As he stumbled along a high bright object caught his eyes;
he looked up. Atop a building across the street, above the
heads of the people, loomed a flaming cross. At once he knew
that it had something to do with him. But why should they
burn a cross? As he gazed at it he remembered the sweating
face of the black preacher in his cell that morning talking intensely and solemnly of Jesus, of there being a cross for him, a
cross for everyone, and of how the lowly Jesus had carried the
cross, paving the way, showing how to die, how to love and
live the life eternal. But he had never seen a cross burning like
that one upon the roof. Were white people wanting him to
love Jesus, too? He heard the wind whipping the flames. No!
That was not right; they ought not burn a cross. He stood in
front of the car, waiting for them to push him in, his eyes
wide with astonishment, his impulses deadlocked, trying to
remember something.

"He's looking at it!"

"He sees it!"

The eyes and faces about him were not at all the way the

black preacher's had been when he had prayed about Jesus and His love, about His dying upon the cross. The cross the preacher had told him about was bloody, not flaming; meek, not militant. It had made him feel awe and wonder, not fear and panic. It had made him want to kneel and cry, but this cross made him want to curse and kill. Then he became conscious of the cross that the preacher had hung round his throat; he felt it nestling against the skin of his chest, an image of the same cross that blazed in front of his eyes high upon the roof against the cold blue sky, its darting tongues of fire lashed to a hissing fury by the icy wind.

"Burn 'im!"

"Kill 'im!"

It gripped him: that cross was not the cross of Christ, but the cross of the Ku Klux Klan. He had a cross of salvation round his throat and they were burning one to tell him that they hated him! No! He did not want that! Had the preacher trapped him? He felt betrayed. He wanted to tear the cross from his throat and throw it away. They lifted him into the waiting car and he sat between two policemen, still looking fearfully at the fiery cross. The sirens screamed and the cars rolled slowly through the crowded streets and he was feeling the cross that touched his chest, like a knife pointed at his heart. His fingers ached to rip it off; it was an evil and black charm which would surely bring him death now. The cars screamed up State Street, then westward on Twenty-sixth Street, one behind the other. People paused on the sidewalks to look. Ten minutes later they stopped in front of a huge white building; he was led up steps, down hallways and then halted in front of a cell door. He was pushed inside; the handcuffs were unlocked and the door clanged shut. The men lingered, looking at him curiously.

With bated breath he tore his shirt open, not caring who saw him. He gripped the cross and snatched it from his throat. He threw it away, cursing a curse that was almost a scream.

"I don't want it!"

The men gasped and looked at him, amazed.

"Don't throw that away, boy. That's your *cross*!"

"I can die without a cross!"

"Only God can help you now, boy. You'd better get your soul right!"

"I ain't got no soul!"

One of the men picked up the cross and brought it back.

"Here, boy; keep this. This is *God's* cross!"

"I don't care!"

"Aw, leave 'im alone!" one of the men said.

They left, dropping the cross just inside the cell door. He picked it up and threw it away again. He leaned weakly against the bars, spent. What were they trying to do to him? He lifted his head, hearing footsteps. He saw a white man coming toward him, then a black man. He straightened and stiffened. It was the old preacher who had prayed over him that morning. The white man began to unlock the door.

"I don't want you!" Bigger shouted.

"Son!" the preacher admonished.

"I don't want you!"

"What's the matter, son?"

"Take your Jesus and go!"

"But, son! Yuh don't know whut yuh's sayin'! Lemme pray fer yuh!"

"Pray for yourself!"

The white guard caught the preacher by the arm and, pointing to the cross on the floor, said,

"Look, Reverend, he threw his cross away."

The preacher looked and said:

"Son, don't spit in Gawd's face!"

"I'll spit in your face if you don't leave me alone!" Bigger said.

"The Reds've been talking to 'im," the guard said, piously touching his fingers to his forehead, his chest, his left shoulder, and then his right; making the sign of the cross.

"That's a goddamn lie!" Bigger shouted. His body seemed a flaming cross as words boiled hysterically out of him. "I told you I don't want you! If you come in here, I'll kill you! Leave me alone!"

Quietly, the old black preacher stopped and picked up the cross. The guard inserted the key in the lock and the door swung in. Bigger ran to it and caught the steel bars in his hands and swept the door forward, slamming it shut. It smashed the old black preacher squarely in the face, sending him reeling backwards upon the concrete. The echo of steel crashing against steel resounded throughout the long quiet corridor, wave upon wave, dying somewhere far away.

"You'd better leave 'im alone now," the guard said. "He seems pretty wild."

The preacher rose slowly and gathered his hat, Bible, and the cross from the floor. He stood a moment with his hand nursing his bruised face.

"Waal, son. Ah'll leave yuh t' yo' Gawd," he sighed, dropping the cross back inside the cell.

The preacher walked away. The guard followed. Bigger was alone. His emotions were so intense that he really saw and heard nothing. Finally, his hot and taut body relaxed. He saw the cross, snatched it up and held it for a long moment in fingers of steel. Then he flung it again through the bars of the cell. It hit the wall beyond with a lonely clatter.

. . . .

Never again did he want to feel anything like hope. That was what was wrong; he had let that preacher talk to him until somewhere in him he had begun to feel that maybe something could happen. Well, something *had* happened: the cross the preacher had hung round his throat had been burned in front of his eyes.

When his hysteria had passed, he got up from the floor. Through blurred eyes he saw men peering at him from the bars of other cells. He heard a low murmur of voices and in the same instant his consciousness recorded without bitterness—like a man stepping out of his house to go to work and noticing that the sun is shining—the fact that even here in the Cook County Jail Negro and white were segregated into different cell-blocks. He lay on the cot with closed eyes and the darkness soothed him some. Occasionally his muscles twitched from the hard storm of passion that had swept him. A small hard core in him resolved never again to trust anybody or anything. Not even Jan. Or Max. They were all right, maybe; but whatever he thought or did from now on would have to come from him and him alone, or not at all. He wanted no more crosses that might turn to fire while still on his chest.

His inflamed senses cooled slowly. He opened his eyes. He heard a soft tapping on a near-by wall. Then a sharp whisper:

"Say, you new guy!"

He sat up, wondering what they wanted.

"Ain't you the guy they got for that Dalton job?"

His hands clenched. He lay down again. He did not want to talk to them. They were not his kind. He felt that they were not here for crimes such as his. He did not want to talk to the whites because they were white and he did not want to talk to the Negroes because he felt ashamed. His own kind would be too curious about him. He lay a long while, empty of mind, and then he heard the steel door open. He looked and saw a white man with a tray of food. He sat up and the man brought the tray to the cot and placed it beside him.

"Your lawyer sent this, kid. You got a good lawyer," the man said.

"Say, can I see a paper?" Bigger asked.

"Well, now," the man said, scratching his head. "Oh, what the hell. Yeah; sure. Here, take mine. I'm through with it. And say, your lawyer's bringing some clothes for you. He told me to tell you."

Bigger did not hear him; he ignored the tray of food and opened out the paper. He paused, waiting to hear the door shut. When it clanged, he bent forward to read, then paused again, wondering about the man who had just left, amazed at how friendly he had acted. For a fleeting moment, while the man had been in his cell, he had not felt apprehensive, cornered. The man had acted straight, matter-of-fact. It was something he could not understand. He lifted the paper close and read: NEGRO KILLER SIGNS CONFESSIONS FOR TWO MURDERS. SHRINKS AT INQUEST WHEN CONFRONTED WITH BODY OF SLAIN GIRL. ARRAIGNED TOMORROW. REDS TAKE CHARGE OF KILLER'S DEFENSE. NOT GUILTY PLEA LIKELY. His eyes ran over the paper, looking for some clue that would tell him something of his fate.

. . . . slayer will undoubtedly pay supreme penalty for his crimes . . . . there is no doubt of his guilt . . . . what is doubtful is how many other crimes he has committed . . . . killer attacked at inquest . . . .

Then:

Expressing opinions about Communists' defending the Negro rapist and killer, Mr. David A. Buckley, State's Attorney, said: "What else can you expect from a gang like that? I'm in favor of cleaning them out lock, stock, and barrel. I'm of the conviction that if you got to the bottom of Red activity in this country, you'd find the root of many an unsolved crime."

When questioned as to what effect the Thomas trial would have upon the forthcoming April elections, in which he is a candidate to succeed himself, Mr. Buckley took his pink carnation from the lapel of his morning coat and waved the reporters away with a laugh.

A long scream sounded and Bigger dropped the paper, jumped to his feet, and ran to the barred door to see what was happening. Down the corridor he saw six white men struggling with a brown-skinned Negro. They dragged him over the floor by his feet and stopped directly in front of Bigger's cell door. As the door swung in, Bigger backed to his cot, his mouth open in astonishment. The man was turning and twisting in the white men's hands, trying desperately to free himself.

"Turn me loose! Turn me loose!" the man screamed over and over.

The men lifted him and threw him inside, locked the door, and left. The man lay on the floor for a moment, then scrambled to his feet and ran to the door.

"Give me my papers!" he screamed.

Bigger saw that the man's eyes were blood-red; the corners of his lips were white with foam. Sweat glistened on his brown face. He clutched the bars with such frenzy that when he yelled his entire body vibrated. He seemed so agonized that Bigger wondered why the men did not give him his belongings. Emotionally, Bigger sided with the man.

"You can't get away with it!" the man yelled.

Bigger went to him and placed a hand on his shoulder.

"Say, what they got of yours?" he asked.

The man ignored him, shouting,

"I'll report you to the President, you hear? Bring me my papers or let me out of here, you white bastards! You want to destroy all my evidence! You can't cover up your crimes! I'll publish them to the whole world! I know why you're putting me in jail! The Professor told you to! But he's not going to get away with it. . . ."

Bigger watched, fascinated, fearful. He had the sensation that the man was too emotionally wrought up over whatever it was that he had lost. Yet the man's emotions seemed real; they affected him, compelling sympathy.

"Come back here!" the man screamed. "Bring me my papers or I'll tell the President and have you dismissed from office. . . ."

What papers did they have of his? Bigger wondered. Who was the president the man yelled about? And who was the professor? Over the man's screams Bigger heard a voice calling from another cell.

"Say, you new guy!"

Bigger avoided the frenzied man and went to the door.

"He's balmy!" a white man said. "Make 'em take 'im outta your cell. He'll kill you. He went off his nut from studying too much at the university. He was writing a book on how colored people live and he says somebody stole all the facts he'd found. He says he's got to the bottom of why colored folks are treated bad and he's going to tell the President and have things changed, see? He's *nuts*! He swears that his university professor had him locked up. The cops picked him up this morning in his underwear; he was in the lobby of the Post Office building, waiting to speak to the President. . . ."

Bigger ran from the door to the cot. All of his fear of death, all his hate and shame vanished in face of his dread of this insane man turning suddenly upon him. The man still clutched the bars, screaming. He was about Bigger's size. Bigger had the queer feeling that his own exhaustion formed a hair-line upon which his feelings were poised, and that the man's driving frenzy would suck him into its hot whirlpool. He lay on the cot and wrapped his arms about his head, torn with a nameless anxiety, hearing the man's screams in spite of his need to escape them.

"You're afraid of me!" the man shouted. "That's why you put me in here! But I'll tell the President anyhow! I'll tell 'im you make us live in such crowded conditions on the South Side that one out of every ten of us is insane! I'll tell 'im that you dump all the stale foods into the Black Belt and sell them for more than you can get anywhere else! I'll tell 'im you tax us, but you won't build hospitals! I'll tell 'im the schools are so crowded that they breed perverts! I'll tell 'im you hire us last and fire us first! I'll tell the President and the League of Nations. . . ."

The men in other cells began to holler.

"Pipe down, you nut!"

"Take 'im away!"

"Throw 'im out!"

"The hell with you!"

"You can't scare me!" the man yelled. "I know you! They put you in here to watch me!"

The men set up a clamor. But soon a group of men dressed in white came running in with a stretcher. They unlocked the cell and grabbed the yelling man, laced him in a strait-jacket, flung him onto the stretcher and carted him away. Bigger sat up and stared before him, hopelessly. He heard voices calling from cell to cell.

"Say, what they got of his?"

"Nothing! He's nuts!"

Finally, things quieted. For the first time since his capture, Bigger felt that he wanted someone near him, something physical to cling to. He was glad when he heard the lock in his door click. He sat up; a guard loomed over him.

"Come on, boy. Your lawyer's here."

He was handcuffed and led down the hall to a small room where Max stood. He was freed of the steel links on his wrists and pushed inside; he heard the door shut behind him.

"Sit down, Bigger. Say, how do you feel?"

Bigger sat down on the edge of the chair and did not answer. The room was small. A single yellow electric globe dropped from the ceiling. There was one barred window. All about them was profound silence. Max sat opposite Bigger and Bigger's eyes met his and fell. Bigger felt that he was sitting and holding his life helplessly in his hands, waiting for

Max to tell him what to do with it; and it made him hate himself. An organic wish to cease to be, to stop living, seized him. Either he was too weak, or the world was too strong; he did not know which. Over and over he had tried to create a world to live in, and over and over he had failed. Now, once again, he was waiting for someone to tell him something; once more he was poised on the verge of action and commitment. Was he letting himself in for more hate and fear? What could Max do for him now? Even if Max tried hard and honestly, were there not thousands of white hands to stop Max? Why not tell him to go home? His lips trembled to speak, to tell Max to leave; but no words came. He felt that even in speaking in that way he would be indicating how hopeless he felt, thereby disrobing his soul to more shame.

"I bought some clothes for you," Max said. "When they give 'em to you in the morning, put 'em on. You want to look your best when you come up for arraignment."

Bigger was silent; he glanced at Max again, and then away.

"What's on your mind, Bigger?"

"Nothing," he mumbled.

"Now, listen, Bigger. I want you to tell me all about yourself. . . ."

"Mr. Max, it ain't no use in you doing nothing!" Bigger blurted.

Max eyed him sharply.

"Do you really feel that way, Bigger?"

"There ain't no way else to feel."

"I want to talk to you honestly, Bigger. I see no way out of this but a plea of guilty. We can ask for mercy, for life in prison. . . ."

"I'd rather die!"

"Nonsense. You want to live."

"For what?"

"Don't you want to fight this thing?"

"What can I do? They got me."

"You don't want to die that way, Bigger."

"It don't matter which way I die," he said; but his voice choked.

"Listen, Bigger, you're facing a sea of hate now that's no different from what you've faced all your life. And because it's that way, you've *got* to fight. If they can wipe you out, then they can wipe others out, too."

"Yeah," Bigger mumbled, resting his hands upon his knees and staring at the black floor. "But I can't win."

"First of all, Bigger. Do you trust me?"

Bigger grew angry.

"You can't help me, Mr. Max," he said, looking straight into Max's eyes.

"But do you trust me, Bigger?" Max asked again.

Bigger looked away. He felt that Max was making it very difficult for him to tell him to leave.

"I don't know, Mr. Max."

"Bigger, I know my face is white," Max said. "And I know that almost every white face you've met in your life had it in for you, even when that white face didn't know it. Every white man considers it his duty to make a black man keep his distance. He doesn't know why most of the time, but he acts that way. It's the way things are, Bigger. But I want you to know that you can trust me."

"It ain't no use, Mr. Max."

"You want me to handle your case?"

"You can't help me none. They got me."

Bigger knew that Max was trying to make him feel that he accepted the way he looked at things and it made him as self-conscious as when Jan had taken his hand and shaken it that night in the car. It made him live again in that hard and sharp consciousness of his color and feel the shame and fear that went with it, and at the same time it made him hate himself for feeling it. He trusted Max. Was Max not taking upon himself a thing that would make other whites hate him? But he doubted if Max could make him see things in a way that would enable him to go to his death. He doubted that God Himself could give him a picture for that now. As he felt at present, they would have to drag him to the chair, as they had dragged him down the steps the night they captured him. He did not want his feelings tampered with; he feared that he might walk into another trap. If he expressed belief in Max, if he acted on that belief, would it not end just as all other commitments of faith had ended? He wanted to believe; but was afraid. He felt that he should have been able to meet Max halfway; but, as always, when a white man talked to him, he was caught out in No Man's Land. He sat slumped in his chair with his head down and he looked at Max only when Max's eyes were not watching him.

"Here; take a cigarette, Bigger." Max lit Bigger's and then lit his own; they smoked awhile. "Bigger, I'm your lawyer. I want to talk to you honestly. What you say is in strictest confidence. . . ."

Bigger stared at Max. He felt sorry for the white man. He saw that Max was afraid that he would not talk at all. And he had no desire to hurt Max. Max leaned forward determinedly. Well, tell him. Talk. Get it over with and let Max go.

"Aw, I don't care what I say or do now. . . ."

"Oh, yes, you *do*!" Max said quickly.

In a fleeting second an impulse to laugh rose up in Bigger, and left. Max was anxious to help him and he had to die.

"Maybe I do care," Bigger drawled.

"If you don't care about what you say or do, then why didn't you re-enact that crime out at the Dalton home today?"

"I wouldn't do nothing for *them*."

"Why?"

"They hate black folks," he said.

"*Why*, Bigger?"

"I don't know, Mr. Max."

"Bigger, don't you know they hate others, too?"

"Who they hate?"

"They hate trade unions. They hate folks who try to organize. They hate Jan."

"But they hate black folks more than they hate unions," Bigger said. "They don't treat union folks like they do me."

"Oh, yes, they do. You think that because your color makes it easy for them to point you out, segregate you, exploit you. But they do that to others, too. They hate me because I'm trying to help you. They're writing me letters, calling me a 'dirty Jew.' "

"All I know is that they hate me," Bigger said grimly.

"Bigger, the State's Attorney gave me a copy of your confession. Now, tell me, did you tell him the truth?"

"Yeah. There wasn't nothing else to do."

"Now, tell me this, Bigger. Why did you do it?"

Bigger sighed, shrugged his shoulders and sucked his lungs full of smoke.

"I don't know," he said; smoke eddied slowly from his nostrils.

"Did you plan it?"

"Naw."

"Did anybody help you?"

"Naw."

"Had you been thinking about doing something like that for a long time?"

"Naw."

"How did it happen?"

"It just happened, Mr. Max."

"Are you sorry?"

"What's the use of being sorry? That won't help me none."

"You can't think of any reason why you did it?"

Bigger was staring straight before him, his eyes wide and shining. His talking to Max had evoked again in him that urge to talk, to tell, to try to make his feelings known. A wave of excitement flooded him. He felt that he ought to be able to reach out with his bare hands and carve from naked space the concrete, solid reasons why he had murdered. He felt them that strongly. If he could do that, he would relax; he would sit and wait until they told him to walk to the chair; and he would walk.

"Mr. Max, I don't know. I was all mixed up. I was feeling so many things at once."

"Did you rape her, Bigger?"

"Naw, Mr. Max. I didn't. But nobody'll believe me."

"Had you planned to before Mrs. Dalton came into the room?"

Bigger shook his head and rubbed his hands nervously across his eyes. In a sense he had forgotten Max was in the room. He was trying to feel the texture of his own feelings, trying to tell what they meant.

"Oh, I don't know. I was feeling a little that way. Yeah, I reckon I was. I was drunk and she was drunk and I was feeling that way."

"But, did you rape her?"

"Naw. But everybody'll say I did. What's the use? I'm

black. They say black men do that. So it don't matter if I did
or if I didn't."

"How long had you known her?"

"A few hours."

"Did you like her?"

"*Like* her?"

Bigger's voice boomed so suddenly from his throat that
Max started. Bigger leaped to his feet; his eyes widened and
his hands lifted midway to his face, trembling.

"No! No! Bigger. . . ." Max said.

"*Like* her? I *hated* her! So help me God, I hated her!" he
shouted.

"Sit down, Bigger!"

"I hate her now, even though she's dead! God knows, I
hate her right now. . . ."

Max grabbed him and pushed him back into the chair.

"Don't get excited, Bigger. Here; take it easy!"

Bigger quieted, but his eyes roved the room. Finally, he
lowered his head and knotted his fingers. His lips were
slightly parted.

"You say you hated her?"

"Yeah; and I ain't sorry she's dead."

"But what had she done to you? You say you had just met
her."

"I don't know. She didn't do nothing to me." He paused
and ran his hand nervously across his forehead. "She. . . . It
was. . . . Hell, I don't know. She asked me a lot of questions. She acted and talked in a way that made me hate her.
She made me feel like a dog. I was so mad I wanted to
cry. . . ." His voice trailed off in a plaintive whimper. He
licked his lips. He was caught in a net of vague, associative
memory: he saw an image of his little sister, Vera, sitting on
the edge of a chair crying because he had shamed her by
"looking" at her; he saw her rise and fling her shoe at him.
He shook his head, confused. "Aw, Mr. Max, she wanted me
to tell her how Negroes live. She got into the front seat of the
car where I was. . . ."

"But, Bigger, you don't hate people for that. She was being
kind to you. . . ."

"Kind, hell! She wasn't kind to me!"

"What do you mean? She accepted you as another human being."

"Mr. Max, we're all split up. What you say is kind ain't kind at all. I didn't know nothing about that woman. All I knew was that they kill us for women like her. We live apart. And then she comes and acts like that to me."

"Bigger, you should have tried to understand. She was acting toward you only as she knew how."

Bigger glared about the small room, searching for an answer. He knew that his actions did not seem logical and he gave up trying to explain them logically. He reverted to his feelings as a guide in answering Max.

"Well, I acted toward her only as I know how. She was rich. She and her kind own the earth. She and her kind say black folks are dogs. They don't let you do nothing but what they want. . . ."

"But, Bigger, *this* woman was trying to help you!"

"She didn't act like it."

"How *should* she have acted?"

"Aw, I don't know, Mr. Max. White folks and black folks is strangers. We don't know what each other is thinking. Maybe she was trying to be kind; but she didn't act like it. To me she looked and acted like all other white folks. . . ."

"But she's not to be blamed for that, Bigger."

"She's the same color as the rest of 'em," he said defensively.

"I don't understand, Bigger. You say you hated her and yet you say you felt like having her when you were in the room and she was drunk and you were drunk. . . ."

"Yeah," Bigger said, wagging his head and wiping his mouth with the back of his hand. "Yeah; that's funny, ain't it?" He sucked at his cigarette. "Yeah; I reckon it was because I knew I oughtn't 've wanted to. I reckon it was because they say we black men do that anyhow. Mr. Max, you know what some white men say we black men do? They say we rape white women when we got the clap and they say we do that because we believe that if we rape white women then we'll get rid of the clap. That's what some white men *say*. They *believe* that. Jesus, Mr. Max, when folks says things like that about you, you whipped before you born. What's the use? Yeah; I reckon I was feeling that way when I was in the room with her. They say we do things like that and they say it to kill us. They draw a line and say for you to stay on your side of the line. They don't care if there's no bread over on your side. They don't care if you die. And then they say things like that about you and when you try to come from behind your line they kill you. They feel they ought to kill you then. Everybody wants to kill you then. Yeah; I reckon I was feeling that way and maybe the reason was because they say it. Maybe that was the reason."

"You mean you wanted to defy them? You wanted to show them that you dared, that you didn't care?"

"I don't know, Mr. Max. But what I got to care about? I knew that some time or other they was going to get me for something. I'm black. I don't have to do nothing for 'em to get me. The first white finger they point at me, I'm a goner, see?"

"But, Bigger, when Mrs. Dalton came into that room, why didn't you stop right there and tell her what was wrong? You wouldn't've been in all this trouble then. . . ."

"Mr. Max, so help me God, I couldn't do nothing when I turned around and saw that woman coming to that bed. Honest to God, I didn't know what I was doing. . . ."

"You mean you went blank?"

"Naw; naw. . . . I knew what I was doing, all right. But I couldn't help it. That's what I mean. It was like another man stepped inside of my skin and started acting for me. . . ."

"Bigger, tell me, did you feel more attraction for Mary than for the women of your own race?"

"Naw. But they say that. It ain't true. I hated her then and I hate her now."

"But why did you kill Bessie?"

"To keep her from talking. Mr. Max, after killing that white woman, it wasn't hard to kill somebody else. I didn't have to think much about killing Bessie. I knew I had to kill her and I did. I had to get away. . . ."

"Did you hate Bessie?"

"Naw."

"Did you love her?"

"Naw. I was just scared. I wasn't in love with Bessie. She was just my girl. I don't reckon I was ever in love with nobody. I killed Bessie to save myself. You have to have a girl, so I had Bessie. And I killed her."

"Bigger, tell me, when did you start hating Mary?"

"I hated her as soon as she spoke to me, as soon as I saw her, I reckon I hated her before I saw her. . . ."

"But, *why?*"

"I told you. What her kind ever let us do?"

"What, exactly, Bigger, did you want to do?"

Bigger sighed and sucked at his cigarette.

"Nothing, I reckon. Nothing. But I reckon I wanted to do what other people do."

"And because you couldn't, you hated her?"

Again Bigger felt that his actions were not logical, and again he fell back upon his feelings for a guide in answering Max's questions.

"Mr. Max, a guy gets tired of being told what he can do and can't do. You get a little job here and a little job there. You shine shoes, sweep streets; anything. . . . You don't make enough to live on. You don't know when you going to get fired. Pretty soon you get so you can't hope for nothing. You just keep moving all the time, doing what other folks say. You ain't a man no more. You just work day in and day out so the world can roll on and other people can live. You know, Mr. Max, I always think of white folks. . . ."

He paused. Max leaned forward and touched him.

"Go on, Bigger."

"Well, they own everything. They choke you off the face of the earth. They like God. . . ." He swallowed, closed his eyes and sighed. "They don't even let you feel what you want to feel. They after you so hot and hard you can only feel what they doing to you. They kill you before you die."

"But, Bigger, I asked you what it was that you wanted to do so badly that you had to hate them?"

"Nothing. I reckon I didn't want to do nothing."

"But you said that people like Mary and her kind never let you do anything."

"Why should I want to do anything? I ain't got a chance. I don't know nothing. I'm just black and they make the laws."

"What would you like to have been?"

Bigger was silent for a long time. Then he laughed without

sound, without moving his lips; it was three short expulsions of breath forced upward through his nostrils by the heaving of his chest.

"I wanted to be an aviator once. But they wouldn't let me go to the school where I was suppose' to learn it. They built a big school and then drew a line around it and said that no-body could go to it but those who lived within the line. That kept all the colored boys out."

"And what else?"

"Well, I wanted to be in the army once."

"Why didn't you join?"

"Hell, it's a Jim Crow army. All they want a black man for is to dig ditches. And in the navy, all I can do is wash dishes and scrub floors."

"And was there anything else you wanted to do?"

"Oh, I don't know. What's the use now? I'm through, washed up. They got me. I'll die."

"Tell me the things you *thought* you'd have liked to do?"

"I'd like to be in business. But what chance has a black guy got in business? We ain't got no money. We don't own no mines, no railroads, no nothing. They don't want us to. They make us stay in one little spot. . . ."

"And you didn't want to stay there?"

Bigger glanced up; his lips tightened. There was a feverish pride in his blood-shot eyes.

"I *didn't*," he said.

Max stared and sighed.

"Look, Bigger. You've told me the things you could not do. But you did something. You committed these crimes. You killed two women. What on earth did you think you could get out of it?"

Bigger rose and rammed his hands into his pockets. He leaned against the wall, looking vacantly. Again he forgot that Max was in the room.

"I don't know. Maybe this sounds crazy. Maybe they going to burn me in the electric chair for feeling this way. But I ain't worried none about them women I killed. For a little while I was free. I was doing something. It was wrong, but I was feeling all right. Maybe God'll get me for it. If He do, all right. But I ain't worried. I killed 'em 'cause I was scared and mad. But I been scared and mad all my life and after I killed that first woman, I wasn't scared no more for a little while."

"What were you afraid of?"

"Everything," he breathed and buried his face in his hands.

"Did you ever hope for anything, Bigger?"

"What for? I couldn't get it. I'm black," he mumbled.

"Didn't you ever want to be happy?"

"Yeah; I guess so," he said, straightening.

"How did you think you could be happy?"

"I don't know. I wanted to do things. But everything I wanted to do I couldn't. I wanted to do what the white boys in school did. Some of 'em went to college. Some of 'em went to the army. But I couldn't go."

"But still, you wanted to be happy?"

"Yeah; sure. Everybody wants to be happy, I reckon."

"Did you think you ever would be?"

"I don't know. I just went to bed at night and got up in the morning. I just lived from day to day. I thought maybe I would be."

"How?"

"I don't know," he said in a voice that was almost a moan.

"What did you think happiness would be like?"

"I don't know. It wouldn't be like this."

"You ought to have some idea of what you wanted, Bigger."

"Well, Mr. Max, if I was happy I wouldn't always be wanting to do something I know I couldn't do."

"And why did you always want to?"

"I couldn't help it. Everybody feels that way, I reckon. And I did, too. Maybe I would've been all right if I could've done something I wanted to do. I wouldn't be scared then. Or mad, maybe. I wouldn't be always hating folks; and maybe I'd feel at home, sort of."

"Did you ever go to the South Side Boys' Club, the place where Mr. Dalton sent those ping-pong tables?"

"Yeah; but what the hell can a guy do with ping-pong?"

"Do you feel that that club kept you out of trouble?"

Bigger cocked his head.

"Kept me out of trouble?" he repeated Max's words. "Naw; that's where we planned most of our jobs."

"Did you ever go to church, Bigger?"

"Yeah; when I was little. But that was a long time ago."

"Your folks were religious?"

"Yeah; they went to church all the time."

"Why did you stop going?"

"I didn't like it. There was nothing in it. Aw, all they did was sing and shout and pray all the time. And it didn't get 'em nothing. All the colored folks do that, but it don't get 'em nothing. The white folks got everything."

"Did you ever feel happy in church?"

"Naw. I didn't want to. Nobody but poor folks get happy in church."

"But you are poor, Bigger."

Again Bigger's eyes lit with a bitter and feverish pride.

"I ain't that poor," he said.

"But Bigger, you said that if you were where people did not hate you and you did not hate them, you could be happy. Nobody hated you in church. Couldn't you feel at home there?"

"I wanted to be happy in this world, not out of it. I didn't want that kind of happiness. The white folks like for us to be religious, then they can do what they want to with us."

"A little while ago you spoke of God 'getting you' for killing those women. Does that mean you believe in Him?"

"I don't know."

"Aren't you afraid of what'll happen to you after you die?"

"Naw. But I don't want to die."

"Didn't you know that the penalty for killing that white woman would be death?"

"Yeah; I knew it. But I felt like she was killing me, so I didn't care."

"If you could be happy in religion now, would you want to be?"

"Naw. I'll be dead soon enough. If I was religious, I'd be dead now."

"But the church promises eternal life?"

"That's for whipped folks."

"You don't feel like you've had a chance, do you?"

"Naw; but I ain't asking nobody to be sorry for me. Naw; I

ain't asking that at all. I'm black. They don't give black people a chance, so I took a chance and lost. But I don't care none now. They got me and it's all over."

"Do you feel, Bigger, that somehow, somewhere, or sometime or other you'll have a chance to make up for what you didn't get here on earth?"

"Hell, naw! When they strap me in that chair and turn on the heat, I'm through, for always."

"Bigger, I want to ask you something about your race. Do you love your people?"

"I don't know, Mr. Max. We all black and the white folks treat us the same."

"But Bigger, your race is doing things for you. There are Negroes leading your people."

"Yeah; I know. I heard about 'em. They all right, I guess."

"Don't you know any of 'em?"

"Naw."

"Bigger, are there many Negro boys like you?"

"I reckon so. All of 'em I know ain't got nothing and ain't going nowhere."

"Why didn't you go to some of the leaders of your race and tell them how you and others boys felt?"

"Aw, hell, Mr. Max. They wouldn't listen to me. They rich, even though the white folks treat them almost like they do me. They almost like the white people, when it comes to guys like me. They say guys like me make it hard for them to get along with white folks."

"Did you ever hear any of your leaders make speeches?"

"Yeah, sure. At election time."

"What did you think of them?"

"Aw, I don't know. They all the same. They wanted to get elected to office. They wanted money, like everybody else. Mr. Max, it's a game and they play it."

"Why didn't you play it?"

"Hell, what do I know? I ain't got nothing. Nobody'll pay any attention to me. I'm just a black guy with nothing. I just went to grammar school. And politics is full of big shots, guys from colleges."

"Didn't you trust them?"

"I don't reckon they wanted anybody to trust 'em. They wanted to get elected to office. They paid you to vote."

"Did you ever vote?"

"Yeah; I voted twice. I wasn't old enough, so I put my age up so I could vote and get the five dollars."

"You didn't mind selling your vote?"

"Naw; why should I?"

"You didn't think politics could get you anything?"

"It got me five dollars on election day."

"Bigger, did any white people ever talk to you about labor unions?"

"Naw; nobody but Jan and Mary. But she oughtn't done it. . . . But I couldn't help what I did. And Jan. I reckon I did him wrong by signing 'Red' to that ransom note."

"Do you believe he's your friend now?"

"Well, he ain't against me. He didn't turn against me today when they was questioning him. I don't think he hates me like the others. I suppose he's kind of hurt about Miss Dalton, though."

"Bigger, did you think you'd ever come to this?"

"Well, to tell the truth, Mr. Max, it seems sort of natural-like, me being here facing that death chair. Now I come to think of it, it seems like something like this just had to be."

They were silent. Max stood up and sighed. Bigger watched to see what Max was thinking, but Max's face was white and blank.

"Well, Bigger," Max said. "We'll enter a plea of not guilty at the arraignment tomorrow. But when the trial comes up we'll change it to a plea of guilty and ask for mercy. They're rushing the trial; it may be held in two or three days. I'll tell the judge all I can of how you feel and why. I'll try to get him to make it life in prison. That's all I can see under the circumstances. I don't have to tell you how they feel toward you, Bigger. You're a Negro; you know. Don't hope for too much. There's an ocean of hot hate out there against you and I'm going to try to sweep some of it back. They want your life; they want revenge. They felt they had you fenced off so that you could not do what you did. Now they're mad because deep down in them they believe that they made you do it. When people feel that way, you can't reason with 'em. Then, too, a lot depends upon what judge we have. Any twelve white men in this state will have already condemned you; we can't trust a jury. Well, Bigger, I'll do the best I can."

They were silent. Max gave him another cigarette and took one for himself. Bigger watched Max's head of white hair, his long face, the deep-grey, soft, sad eyes. He felt that Max was kind, and he felt sorry for him.

"Mr. Max, if I was you I wouldn't worry none. If all folks was like you, then maybe I wouldn't be here. But you can't help that now. They going to hate you for trying to help me. I'm gone. They got me."

"Oh, they'll hate me, yes," said Max. "But I can take it. That's the difference. I'm a Jew and they hate me, but I know why and I can fight. But sometimes you can't win no matter how you fight; that is, you can't win if you haven't got time. And they're pressing us now. But you need not worry about their hating me for defending you. The fear of hate keeps many whites from trying to help you and your kind. Before I can fight your battle, I've got to fight a battle with them." Max snuffed out his cigarette. "I got to go now," Max said. He turned and faced Bigger. "Bigger, how do you feel?"

"I don't know. I'm just setting here waiting for 'em to come and tell me to walk to that chair. And I don't know if I'll be able to walk or not."

Max averted his face and opened the door. A guard came and caught Bigger by the wrist.

"I'll see you in the morning, Bigger," Max called.

Back in his cell, Bigger stood in the middle of the floor, not moving. He was not stoop-shouldered now, nor were his muscles taut. He breathed softly, wondering about the cool breath of peace that hovered in his body. It was as though he were trying to listen to the beat of his own heart. All round him was darkness and there were no sounds. He could not remember when he had felt as relaxed as this before. He had not thought of it or felt it while Max was speaking to him; it was not until after Max had gone that he discovered that he had spoken to Max as he had never spoken to anyone in his life; not even to himself. And his talking had eased from his shoulders a heavy burden. Then he was suddenly and violently angry. Max had tricked him! But no. Max had not compelled him to talk; he had talked of his own accord, prodded by excitement, by a curiosity about his own feelings. Max had only sat and listened, had only asked questions. His anger passed and fear took its place. If he were as confused as this when his time came, they really *would* have to drag him to the chair. He had to make a decision: in order to walk to that chair he had to weave his feelings into a hard shield of either hope or hate. To fall between them would mean living and dying in a fog of fear.

He was balanced on a hair-line now, but there was no one to push him forward or backward, no one to make him feel that he had any value or worth—no one but himself. He brushed his hands across his eyes, hoping to untangle the sensations fluttering in his body. He lived in a thin, hard core of consciousness; he felt time slipping by; the darkness round him lived, breathed. And he was in the midst of it, wanting again to let his body taste of that short respite of rest he had felt after talking with Max. He sat down on the cot; he had to grasp this thing.

Why had Max asked him all those questions? He knew that Max was seeking facts to tell the judge; but in Max's asking of those questions he had felt a recognition of his life, of his feelings, of his person that he had never encountered before. What was this? Had he done wrong? Had he left himself in for another betrayal? He felt as though he had been caught off his guard. But this, this—confidence? He had no right to be proud; yet he had spoken to Max as a man who *had* something. He had told Max that he did not want religion, that he had not stayed in his place. He had no right to feel that, no right to forget that he was to die, that he was black, a murderer; he had no right to forget that, not even for a second. Yet he had.

He wondered if it were possible that after all everybody in the world felt alike? Did those who hated him have in them the same thing Max had seen in him, the thing that had made Max ask him those questions? And what motive could Max have in helping? Why would Max risk that white tide of hate to help him? For the first time in his life he had gained a pinnacle of feeling upon which he could stand and see vague relations that he had never dreamed of. If that white looming

mountain of hate were not a mountain at all, but people, people like himself, and like Jan—then he was faced with a high
hope the like of which he had never thought could be, and a
despair the full depths of which he knew he could not stand
to feel. A strong counter-emotion waxed in him, urging him,
warning him to leave this newly-seen and newly-felt thing
alone, that it would lead him to but another blind alley, to
deeper hate and shame.

Yet he saw and felt but one life, and that one life was more
than a sleep, a dream; life was all life had. He knew that he
would not wake up some time later, after death, and sigh at
how simple and foolish his dream had been. The life he saw
was short and his sense of it goaded him. He was seized with
a nervous eagerness. He stood up in the middle of the cell
floor and tried to see himself in relation to other men, a thing
he had always feared to try to do, so deeply stained was his
own mind with the hate of others for him. With this new
sense of the value of himself gained from Max's talk, a sense
fleeting and obscure, he tried to feel that if Max had been able
to see the man in him beneath those wild and cruel acts of his,
acts of fear and hate and murder and flight and despair, then
he *too* would hate, if *he* were *they*, just as now *he* was hating
them and *they* were hating *him*. For the first time in his life he
felt ground beneath his feet, and he wanted it to stay there.

He was tired, sleepy, and feverish; but he did not want to
lie down with this war raging in him. Blind impulses welled
up in his body, and his intelligence sought to make them
plain to his understanding by supplying images that would
explain them. Why was all this hate and fear? Standing trembling in his cell, he saw a dark vast fluid image rise and float;
he saw a black sprawling prison full of tiny black cells in
which people lived; each cell had its stone jar of water and a
crust of bread and no one could go from cell to cell and there
were screams and curses and yells of suffering and nobody
heard them, for the walls were thick and darkness was everywhere. Why were there so many cells in the world? But was
this true? He wanted to believe, but was afraid. Dare he flat-
ter himself that much? Would he be struck dead if he made
himself the equal of others, even in fancy?

He was too weak to stand any longer. He sat again on the

edge of the cot. How could he find out if this feeling of his was true, if others had it? How could one find out about life when one was about to die? Slowly he lifted his hands in the darkness and held them in mid-air, the fingers spread weakly open. If he reached out with his hands, and if his hands were electric wires, and if his heart were a battery giving life and fire to those hands, and if he reached out with his hands and touched other people, reached out through these stone walls and felt other hands connected with other hearts—if he did that, would there be a reply, a shock? Not that he wanted those hearts to turn their warmth to him; he was not wanting that much. But just to know that they were there and warm! Just that, and no more; and it would have been enough, more than enough. And in that touch, response of recognition, there would be union, identity; there would be a supporting oneness, a wholeness which had been denied him all his life.

Another impulse rose in him, born of desperate need, and his mind clothed it in an image of a strong blinding sun sending hot rays down and he was standing in the midst of a vast crowd of men, white men and black men and all men, and the sun's rays melted away the many differences, the colors, the clothes, and drew what was common and good upward toward the sun. . . .

He stretched out full length upon the cot and groaned. Was he foolish in feeling this? Was it fear and weakness that made this desire come to him now that death was near? How could a notion that went so deep and caught up so much of him in one swoop of emotion be wrong? Could he trust bare, naked feeling this way? But he had; all his life he had hated on the basis of bare sensation. Why should he not accept this? Had he killed Mary and Bessie and brought sorrow to his mother and brother and sister and put himself in the shadow of the electric chair only to find out this? Had he been blind all along? But there was no way to tell now. It was too late. . . .

He would not mind dying now if he could only find out what this meant, what he was in relation to all the others that lived, and the earth upon which he stood. Was there some battle everybody was fighting, and he had missed it? And if he had missed it, were not the whites to blame for it? Were they not the ones to hate even now? Maybe. But he was not interested in hating them now. He had to die. It was more important to him to find out what this new tingling, this new elation, this new excitement meant.

He felt he wanted to live now—not escape paying for his crime—but live in order to find out, to see if it were true, and to feel it more deeply; and, if he had to die, to die within it. He felt that he would have lost all if he had to die without fully feeling it, without knowing for certain. But there was no way now. It was too late. . . .

He lifted his hands to his face and touched his trembling lips. Naw. . . . Naw. . . . He ran to the door and caught the cold steel bars in his hot hands and gripped them tightly, holding himself erect. His face rested against the bars and he felt tears roll down his cheeks. His wet lips tasted salt. He sank to his knees and sobbed: "I don't want to die. . . . I don't want to die. . . ."

.   .   .   .

Having been bound over to the Grand Jury and indicted by it, having been arraigned and having pled not guilty to the charge of murder and been ordered to trial—all in less than a week, Bigger lay one sunless grey morning on his cot, staring vacantly at the black steel bars of the Cook County Jail.

Within an hour he would be taken to court where they would tell him if he was to live or die, and when. And with but a few minutes between him and the beginning of judgment, the obscure longing to possess the thing which Max had dimly evoked in him was still a motive. He felt he *had* to have it now. How could he face that court of white men without something to sustain him? Since that night when he had stood alone in his cell, feeling the high magic which Max's talk had given him, he was more than ever naked to the hot blasts of hate.

There were moments when he wished bitterly that he had not felt those possibilities, when he wished that he could go again behind his curtain. But that was impossible. He had been lured into the open, and trapped, twice trapped; trapped by being in jail for murder, and again trapped by being stripped of emotional resources to go to his death.

In an effort to recapture that high moment, he had tried to talk with Max, but Max was preoccupied, busy preparing his plea to the court to save his life. But Bigger wanted to save his *own* life. Yet he knew that the moment he tried to put his feelings into words, his tongue would not move. Many times, when alone after Max had left him, he wondered wistfully if there was not a set of words which he had in common with others, words which would evoke in others a sense of the same fire that smoldered in him.

He looked out upon the world and the people about him with a double vision: one vision pictured death, an image of him, alone, sitting strapped in the electric chair and waiting for the hot current to leap through his body; and the other vision pictured life, an image of himself standing amid throngs of men, lost in the welter of their lives with the hope of emerging again, different, unafraid. But so far only the certainty of death was his; only the unabating hate of the white faces could be seen; only the same dark cell, the long lonely hours, only the cold bars remained.

Had his will to believe in a new picture of the world made him act a fool and thoughtlessly pile horror upon horror? Was not his old hate a better defense than this agonized uncertainty? Was not an impossible hope betraying him to this end? On how many fronts could a man fight at once? Could he fight a battle within as well as without? Yet he felt that he could not fight the battle for his life without first winning the one raging within him.

His mother and Vera and Buddy had come to visit him and again he had lied to them, telling them that he was praying, that he was at peace with the world and men. But that lie had only made him feel more shame for himself and more hate for them; it had hurt because he really yearned for that certainty of which his mother spoke and prayed, but he could not get it on the terms on which he felt he had to have it. After they had left, he told Max not to let them come again.

A few moments before the trial, a guard came to his cell and left a paper.

"Your lawyer sent this," he said and left.

He unfolded the *Tribune* and his eyes caught a headline: TROOPS GUARD NEGRO KILLER'S TRIAL. Troops?

He bent forward and read: PROTECT RAPIST FROM
MOB ACTION. He went down the column:

Fearing outbreaks of mob violence, Gov. H. M. O'Dorsey ordered
out two regiments of the Illinois National Guard to keep public
peace during the trial of Bigger Thomas, Negro rapist and killer, it
was announced from Springfield, the capital, this morning.

His eyes caught phrases: "sentiment against killer still rising," "public opinion demands death penalty," "fear uprising
in Negro sector," and "city tense."

Bigger sighed and stared into space. His lips hung open
and he shook his head slowly. Was he not foolish in even
listening when Max talked of saving his life? Was he not
heightening the horror of his own end by straining after a
flickering hope? Had not this voice of hate been sounding
long before he was born; and would it not still sound long
after he was dead?

He read again, catching phrases: "the black killer is fully
aware that he is in danger of going to the electric chair,"
"spends most of his time reading newspaper accounts of his
crime and eating luxurious meals sent to him by Communist
friends," "killer not sociable or talkative," "Mayor lauds police
for bravery," and "a vast mass of evidence assembled against
killer."

Then:

In relation to the Negro's mental condition, Dr. Calvin H. Rob-
inson, a psychiatric attaché of the police department, declared:
"There is no question but that Thomas is more alert mentally and
more cagy than we suspect. His attempt to blame the Communists
for the murder and kidnap note and his staunch denial of having
raped the white girl indicate that he may be hiding many other
crimes."

Professional psychologists at University of Chicago pointed out
this morning that white women have an unusual fascination for
Negro men. "They think," said one of the professors who requested
that his name not be mentioned in connection with the case, "that
white women are more attractive than the women of their own race.
They just can't help themselves."

It was said that Boris A. Max, the Negro's Communistic lawyer,
will enter a plea of not guilty and try to free his client through a long
drawn-out jury trial.

Bigger dropped the paper, stretched out upon the cot and closed his eyes. It was the same thing over and over again. What was the use of reading it?

"Bigger!"

Max was standing outside of the cell. The guard opened the door and Max walked in.

"Well, Bigger, how do you feel?"

"All right, I reckon," he mumbled.

"We're on our way to court."

Bigger rose and looked vacantly round the cell.

"Are you ready?"

"Yeah," Bigger sighed. "I reckon I am."

"Listen, son. Don't be nervous. Just take it easy."

"Will I be setting near you?"

"Sure. Right at the same table. I'll be there throughout the entire trial. So don't be scared."

A guard led him outside the door. The corridor was lined with policemen. It was silent. He was placed between two policemen and his wrists were shackled to theirs. Black and white faces peered at him from behind steel bars. He walked stiffly between the two policemen; ahead of him walked six more; and he heard many more walking in back. They led him to an elevator that took him to an underground passage. They walked through a long stretch of narrow tunnel; the sound of their feet echoed loudly in the stillness. They reached another elevator and rode up and walked along a hallway crowded with excited people and policemen. They passed a window and Bigger caught a quick glimpse of a vast crowd of people standing behind closely formed lines of khaki-clad troops. Yes, those were the troops and the mob the paper had spoken of.

He was taken into a room. Max led the way to a table. After the handcuffs were unlocked, Bigger sat, flanked by policemen. Softly, Max laid his right hand upon Bigger's knee.

"We've got just a few minutes," Max said.

"Yeah," Bigger mumbled. His eyes were half-closed; his head leaned slightly to one side and his eyes looked beyond Max at some point in space.

"Here," Max said. "Straighten your tie."

Bigger tugged listlessly at the knot.

"Now, maybe you'll have to say something just once, see. . . ."

"You mean in the court room?"

"Yes; but I'll. . . ."

Bigger's eyes widened with fear.

"Naw!"

"Now, listen, son. . . ."

"But I don't want to say nothing."

"I'm trying to save your life. . . ."

Bigger's nerves gave way and he spoke hysterically:

"They going to *kill* me! You *know* they going to kill me. . . ."

"But you'll *have* to, Bigger. Now, listen. . . ."

"Can't you fix it so I won't have to say nothing?"

"It's only a word or two. When the judge asks how you want to plead, say guilty."

"Will I have to stand up?"

"Yes."

"I don't want to."

"Don't you realize I'm trying to save your life? Help me just this little bit. . . ."

"I reckon I don't care. I reckon you can't save it."

"You mustn't feel that way. . . ."

"I can't help it."

"Here's another thing. The court'll be full, see? Just go in and sit down. You'll be right by me. And let the judge see that you notice what's going on."

"I hope Ma won't be there."

"I asked her to come. I want the judge to see her," Max said.

"She'll feel bad."

"All of this is for you, Bigger."

"I reckon I ain't worth it."

"Well, this thing's bigger than you, son. In a certain sense, every Negro in America's on trial out there today."

"They going to kill me anyhow."

"Not if we fight. Not if I tell them how you've had to live."

A policeman walked over to Max, tapped him lightly on the shoulder, and said,

"The judge's waiting."

"All right," Max said. "Come on, Bigger. Let's go. Keep your chin up."

They stood and were surrounded by policemen. Bigger walked beside Max down a hallway and then through a door. He saw a huge room crowded with men and women. Then he saw a small knot of black faces, over to one side of the room, behind a railing. A deep buzzing of voices came to him. Two policemen pushed the people to one side, making a path for Max and Bigger. Bigger moved forward slowly, feeling Max's hand tugging at the sleeve of his coat. They reached the front of the room.

"Sit down," Max whispered.

As Bigger sat the lightning of silver bulbs flashed in his eyes; they were taking more pictures of him. He was so tense in mind and body that his lips trembled. He did not know what to do with his hands; he wanted to put them into his coat pockets; but that would take too much effort and would attract attention. He kept them lying on his knees, palms up. There was a long and painful wait. The voices behind him still buzzed. Pale yellow sunshine fell through high windows and slashed the air.

He looked about. Yes; there were his mother and brother and sister; they were staring at him. There were many of his old school mates. There was his teacher, two of them. And there was G.H. and Jack and Gus and Doc. Bigger lowered his eyes. These were the people to whom he had once boasted, acted tough; people whom he had once defied. Now they were watching him as he sat here. They would feel that they were right and he was wrong. The old, hot choking sensation came back to his stomach and throat. Why could they not just shoot him and get it over with? They were going to kill him anyhow, so why make him go through with this? He was startled by the sound of a deep, hollow voice booming and a banging on a wooden table.

"Everybody rise, please . . . ."

Everybody stood up. Bigger felt Max's hand touching his arm and he rose and stood with Max. A man, draped in long black robes and with a dead-white face, came through a rear door and sat behind a high pulpit-like railing. That's the judge, Bigger thought, easing back into his seat.

"Hear ye, hear ye. . . ." Bigger heard the hollow voice booming again. He caught snatches of phrases: ". . . . this Honorable Branch of the Cook County Criminal Court . . . . now in session . . . . pursuant to adjournment . . . . the Honorable Chief Justice Alvin C. Hanley, presiding. . . ."

Bigger saw the judge look toward Buckley and then toward him and Max. Buckley rose and went to the foot of the railing; Max also rose and went forward. They talked a moment to the judge in low voices and then each went back to his seat. A man sitting just below the judge rose and began reading a long paper in a voice so thick and low that Bigger could only hear some of the words.

". . . . indictment number 666-983 . . . . the People of the State of Illinois vs. Bigger Thomas. . . . The Grand Jurors chosen, selected and sworn in and for the said County of Cook, present that Bigger Thomas did rape and inflict sexual injury upon the body . . . . strangulation by hand . . . . smother to death and dispose of body by burning same in furnace . . . . did with knife and hatchet sever head from body . . . . said acts committed upon one Mary Dalton, and contrary to the form of the statute in such case made and provided, against the peace and dignity of the People of the State of Illinois. . . ."

The man pronounced Bigger's name over and over again and Bigger felt that he was caught up in a vast but delicate machine whose wheels would whir no matter what was pitted against them. Over and over the man said that he had killed Mary and Bessie; that he had beheaded Mary; that he had battered Bessie with a brick; that he had raped both Mary and Bessie; that he had shoved Mary in the furnace; that he had thrown Bessie down the air-shaft and left her to freeze to death; and that he had stayed on in the Dalton home when Mary's body was burning and had sent a kidnap note. When the man finished, a gasp of astonishment came from the court room and Bigger saw faces turning and looking in his direction. The judge rapped for order and asked,

"Is the defendant ready to enter a plea to this indictment?" Max rose.

"Yes, Your Honor. The defendant, Bigger Thomas, pleads guilty."

Immediately Bigger heard a loud commotion. He turned his head and saw several men pushing through the crowd toward the door. He knew that they were newspapermen. The judge rapped again for order. Max tried to continue speaking, but the judge stopped him.

"Just a minute, Mr. Max. We must have order!"

The room grew quiet.

"Your Honor," Max said, "after long and honest deliberation, I have determined to make a motion in this court to withdraw our plea of not guilty and enter a plea of guilty.

"The laws of this state allow the offering of evidence in mitigation of punishment, and I shall request, at such time as the Court deems best, that I be given the opportunity to offer evidence as to the mental and emotional attitude of this boy, to show the degree of responsibility he had in these crimes. Also, I want to offer evidence as to the youth of this boy. Further, I want to prevail upon this Court to consider this boy's plea of guilty as evidence mitigating his punishment. . . ."

"Your Honor!" Buckley shouted.

"Allow me to finish," Max said.

Buckley came to the front of the room, his face red.

"You cannot plead that boy both guilty and insane," Buckley said. "If you claim Bigger Thomas is insane, the State will demand a jury trial. . . ."

"Your Honor," Max said, "I do not claim that this boy is legally insane. I shall endeavor to show, through the discussion of evidence, the mental and emotional attitude of this boy and the degree of responsibility he had in these crimes."

"That's a defense of insanity!" Buckley shouted.

"I'm making no such defense," Max said.

"A man is either sane or insane," Buckley said.

"There are degrees of insanity," Max said. "The laws of this state permit the hearing of evidence to ascertain the degree of responsibility. And, also, the law permits the offering of evidence toward the mitigation of punishment."

"The State will submit witnesses and evidence to establish the legal sanity of the defendant," Buckley said.

There was a long argument which Bigger did not understand. The judge called both lawyers forward to the railing and they talked for over an hour. Finally, they went back to their seats and the judge looked toward Bigger and said,

"Bigger Thomas, will you rise?"

His body flushed hot. As he had felt when he stood over the bed with the white blur floating toward him; as he had felt when he had sat in the car between Jan and Mary; as he had felt when he had seen Gus coming through the door of Doc's poolroom—so he felt now: constricted, taut, in the grip of a powerful, impelling fear. At that moment it seemed that any action under heaven would have been preferable to standing. He wanted to leap from his chair and swing some heavy weapon and end this unequal fight. Max caught his arm.

"Stand up, Bigger."

He rose, holding on to the edge of the table, his knees trembling so that he thought that they would buckle under him. The judge looked at him a long time before speaking. Behind him Bigger heard the room buzzing with the sound of voices. The judge rapped for order.

"How far did you get in school?" the judge asked.

"Eighth grade," Bigger whispered, surprised at the question.

"If your plea is guilty, and the plea is entered in this case," the judge said and paused, "the Court may sentence you to death," the judge said and paused again, "or the Court may sentence you to the penitentiary for the term of your natural life," the judge said and paused yet again, "or the Court may sentence you to the penitentiary for a term of not less than fourteen years.

"Now, do you understand what I have said?"

Bigger looked at Max; Max nodded to him.

"Speak up," the judge said. "If you do not understand what I have said, then say so."

"Y-y-yessuh; I understand," he whispered.

"Then, realizing the consequences of your plea, do you still plead guilty?"

"Y-y-yessuh," he whispered again; feeling that it was all a wild and intense dream that must end soon, somehow.

"That's all. You may sit down," the judge said.

He sat.

"Is the State prepared to present its evidence and witnesses?" the judge asked.

"We are, Your Honor," said Buckley, rising and half-facing the judge and the crowd.

"Your Honor, my statement at this time will be very brief. There is no need for me to picture to this Court the horrible details of these dastardly crimes. The array of witnesses for the State, the confession made and signed by the defendant himself, and the concrete evidence will reveal the unnatural aspect of this vile offense against God and man more eloquently than I could ever dare. In more than one respect, I am thankful that this is the case, for some of the facts of this evil crime are so fantastic and unbelievable, so utterly beast-like and foreign to our whole concept of life, that I feel incapable of communicating them to this Court.

"Never in my long career as an officer of the people have I been placed in a position where I've felt more unalterably certain of my duty. There is no room here for evasive, theoretical, or fanciful interpretations of the law." Buckley paused, surveyed the court room, then stepped to the table and lifted from it the knife with which Bigger had severed Mary's head from her body. "This case is as clean-cut as this murderer's knife, the knife that dismembered an innocent girl!" Buckley shouted. He paused again and lifted from the table the brick with which Bigger had battered Bessie in the abandoned building. "Your Honor, this case is as solid as this brick, the brick that battered a poor girl's brains out!" Buckley again looked at the crowd in the court room. "It is not often," Buckley continued, "that a representative of the people finds the masses of the citizens who elected him to office standing literally at his back, waiting for him to enforce the law. . . ." The room was quiet as a tomb. Buckley strode to the window and with one motion of his hand hoisted it up. The rumbling mutter of the vast mob swept in. The court room stirred.

"Kill 'im now!"

"Lynch 'im!"

The judge rapped for order.

"If this is not stopped, I'll order the room cleared!" the judge said.

Max was on his feet.

"I object!" Max said. "This is highly irregular. In effect, it is an attempt to intimidate this Court."

"Objection sustained," the judge said. "Proceed in a fashion more in keeping with the dignity of your office and this Court, Mr. State's Attorney."

"I'm very sorry, Your Honor," Buckley said, going toward the railing and wiping his face with a handkerchief. "I was laboring under too much emotion. I merely wanted to impress the Court with the urgency of this situation. . . ."

"The Court is waiting to hear your plea," the judge said.

"Yes; of course, Your Honor," Buckley said. "Now, what are the issues here? The indictment fully states the crime to which the defendant has entered a plea of guilty. The counsel for the defense claims, and would have this Court believe, that the mere act of entering a plea of guilty to this indictment should be accepted as evidence mitigating punishment.

"Speaking for the grief-stricken families of Mary Dalton and Bessie Mears, and for the People of the State of Illinois, thousands of whom are massed out beyond that window waiting for the law to take its course, I say that no such quibbling, no such trickery shall pervert this Court and cheat the law!

"A man commits two of the most horrible murders in the history of American civilization; he confesses; and his counsel would have us believe that because he pleads guilty after dodging the law, after attempting to murder the officers of the law, that his plea should be looked upon as evidence mitigating his punishment!

"I say, Your Honor, this is an insult to the Court and to the intelligent people of this state! If such crimes admit of such defense, if this fiend's life is spared because of such a defense, I shall resign my office and tell those people out there in the streets that I can no longer protect their lives and property! I shall tell them that our courts, swamped with mawkish sentimentality, are no longer fit instruments to safeguard the public peace! I shall tell them that we have abandoned the fight for civilization!

"After entering such a plea, the counsel for the defense indicates that he shall ask this Court to believe that the mental and emotional life of the defendant are such that he does not bear full responsibility for these cowardly rapes and murders. He asks this Court to imagine a legendary No Man's Land of human thought and feeling. He tells us that a man is sane enough to commit a crime, but is not sane enough to be tried for it! Never in my life have I heard such sheer legal cynicism, such a cold-blooded and calculated attempt to bedevil and evade the law in my life! I say that this shall *not* be!

"The State shall insist that this man be tried by jury, if the defense continues to say that he is insane. If his plea is simply guilty, then the State demands the death penalty for these black crimes.

"At such time as the Court may indicate, I shall offer evidence and put witnesses upon the stand to testify that this defendant is sane and is responsible for these bloody crimes. . . ."

"Your Honor!" Max called.

"You shall have time to plead for your client!" Buckley shouted. "Let me finish!"

"Do you have an objection?" the judge asked, turning to Max.

"I do!" Max said. "I hesitate to interrupt the State's Attorney, but the impression he is trying to make is that I claim that this boy is insane. That is *not* true. Your Honor, let me state once again that this poor boy, Bigger, enters a plea of guilty. . . ."

"I object!" Buckley shouted. "I object to the counsel for the defendant speaking of this defendant before this Court by any name other than that written in the indictment. Such names as 'Bigger' and 'this poor boy' are used to arouse sympathy. . . ."

"Sustained," the judge said. "In the future, the defendant should be designated by the name under which the indictment was drawn. Mr. Max, I think you should allow the State's Attorney to continue."

"There's nothing further I have to say, Your Honor," Buckley said. "If it pleases the Court, I am ready to call my witnesses."

"How many witnesses have you?" Max asked.

"Sixty," Buckley said.

"Your Honor," Max said. "Bigger Thomas has entered a plea of guilty. It seems to me that sixty witnesses are not needed."

"I intend to prove that this defendant is sane, that he was and is responsible for these frightful crimes," Buckley said.

"The Court will hear them," the judge said.

"Your Honor," Max said. "Let me clear this thing up. As you know, the time granted me to prepare a defense for Bigger Thomas is pitifully brief, so brief as to be without example. This hearing was rushed to the top of the calendar so that this boy might be tried while the temper of the people is white-hot.

"A change of venue is of no value now. The same condition of hysteria exists all over this state. These circumstances have placed me in a position of not doing what I think wisest, but of doing what I must. If anybody but a Negro boy were charged with murder, the State's Attorney would not have rushed this case to trial and demanded the death penalty.

"The State has sought to create the impression that I am going to say that this boy is insane. That is *not* true. I shall put no witnesses upon the stand. *I* shall witness for Bigger Thomas. I shall present argument to show that his extreme youth, his mental and emotional life, and the reason why he has pleaded guilty, should and must mitigate his punishment.

"The State's Attorney has sought to create the belief that I'm trying to spring some surprise upon this Court by having my client enter a plea of guilty; he has sought to foster the notion that some legal trick is involved in the offering of evidence to mitigate this boy's punishment. But we have had many, many such cases to come before the courts of Illinois. The Loeb and Leopold case, for example. This is a regular procedure provided for by the enlightened and progressive laws of our state. Shall we deny this boy, because he is poor and black, the same protection, the same chance to be heard and understood that we have so readily granted to others?

"Your Honor, I am not a coward, but I could not ask that this boy be freed and given a chance at life while that mob howls beyond that window. I ask what I *must*. I ask, over the shrill cries of the mob, that you spare his life!

"The law of Illinois, regarding a plea of guilty to murder before a court, is as follows: the Court may impose the death penalty, imprison the defendant for life, or for a term of not less than fourteen years. Under this law the Court is able to hear evidence as to the aggravation or mitigation of the offense. The object of this law is to caution the Court to seek to find out *why* a man killed and to allow that *why* to be the measure of the mitigation of the punishment.

"I noticed that the State's Attorney did not dwell upon why Bigger Thomas killed those two women. There is a mob waiting, he says, so let us kill. His only plea is that if we do not kill, then the mob will kill.

"He did not discuss the motive for Bigger Thomas' crime because he *could* not. It is to his advantage to act quickly, before men have had time to think, before the full facts are known. For he knows that if the full facts were known, if men had time to reflect, he could not stand there and shout for death!

"What motive actuated Bigger Thomas? There was no motive as motive is understood under our laws today, Your Honor. I shall go deeper into this when I sum up. It is because of the almost instinctive nature of these crimes that I say that the mental and emotional life of this boy is important in deciding his punishment. But, as the State whets the appetite of the mob by needlessly parading witness after witness before this Court, as the State inflames the public mind further with the ghastly details of this boy's crimes, I shall listen for the State's Attorney to tell this Court *why* Bigger Thomas killed.

"This boy is young, not only in years, but in his attitude toward life. He is not old enough to vote. Living in a Black Belt district, he is younger than most boys of his age, for he has not come in contact with the wide variety and depths of life. He has had but two outlets for his emotions: work and sex—and he knew these in their most vicious and degrading forms.

"I shall ask this Court to spare this boy's life and I have faith enough in this Court to believe that it will consent."

Max sat down. The court room was filled with murmurs.

"The Court will adjourn for one hour and reconvene at one o'clock," the judge said.

Flanked by policemen, Bigger was led back into the crowded hall. Again he passed a window and he saw a sprawling mob held at bay by troops. He was taken to a room where a tray of food rested on a table. Max was there, waiting for him.

"Come on and sit down, Bigger. Eat something."

"I don't want nothing."

"Come on. You've got to hold up."

"I ain't hungry."

"Here; take a smoke."

"Naw."

"You want a drink of water?"

"Naw."

Bigger sat in a chair, leaned forward, rested his arms on the table and buried his face in the crooks of his elbows. He was tired. Now that he was out of the court room, he felt the awful strain under which he had been while the men had argued about his life. All of the vague thoughts and excitement about finding a way to live and die were far from him now. Fear and dread were the only possible feelings he could have in that court room. When the hour was up, he was led back into court. He rose with the rest when the judge came, and then sat again.

"The State may call its witnesses," the judge said.

"Yes, Your Honor," Buckley said.

The first witness was an old woman whom Bigger had not seen before. During the questioning, he heard Buckley call her Mrs. Rawlson. Then he heard the old woman say that she was the mother of Mrs. Dalton. Bigger saw Buckley give her the earring he had seen at the inquest, and the old woman told of how the pair of earrings had been handed down through the years from mother to daughter. When Mrs. Rawlson was through, Max said that he had no desire to examine her or any of the State's witnesses. Mrs. Dalton was led to the stand and she told the same story she had told at the inquest. Mr. Dalton told again why he had hired Bigger and pointed him out as "the Negro boy who came to my home to work." Peggy also pointed him out, saying through her sobs, "Yes; he's the boy." All of them said that he had acted like a very quiet and sane boy.

Britten told how he had suspected that Bigger knew something of the disappearance of Mary; and said that "that black boy is as sane as I am." A newspaperman told of how the smoke in the furnace had caused the discovery of Mary's bones. Bigger heard Max rise when the newspaperman had finished.

"Your Honor," Max said. "I'd like to know how many more newspapermen are to testify?"

"I have just fourteen more," Buckley said.

"Your Honor," Max said. "This is totally unnecessary. There is a plea of guilty here. . . ."

"I'm going to prove that that killer is sane!" Buckley shouted.

"The Court will hear them," the judge said. "Proceed, Mr. Buckley."

Fourteen more newspapermen told about the smoke and the bones and said that Bigger acted "just like all other colored boys." At five o'clock the court recessed and a tray of food was placed before Bigger in a small room, with six policemen standing guard. The nerves of his stomach were so taut that he could only drink the coffee. Six o'clock found him back in court. The room grew dark and the lights were turned on. The parade of witnesses ceased to be real to Bigger. Five white men came to the stand and said that the handwriting on the kidnap note was his; that it was the same writing which they had found on his "homework papers taken from the files of the school he used to attend." Another white man said that the fingerprints of Bigger Thomas were found on the door of "Miss Dalton's room." Then six doctors said Bessie had been raped. Four colored waitresses from Ernie's Kitchen Shack pointed him out as the "colored boy who was at the table that night with the white man and the white woman." And they said he had acted "quiet and sane." Next came two white women, school teachers, who said that Bigger was "a dull boy, but thoroughly sane." One witness melted into another. Bigger ceased to care. He stared listlessly. At times he could hear the faint sound of the winter wind blowing outdoors. He was too tired to be glad when the session ended. Before they took him back to his cell, he asked Max,

"How long will it last?"

"I don't know, Bigger. You'll have to be brave and hold up."

"I wish it was over."

"This is your life, Bigger. You got to fight."

"I don't care what they do to me. I wish it was over."

The next morning they woke him, fed him, and took him back to court. Jan came to the stand and said what he had said at the inquest. Buckley made no attempt to link Jan with the murder of Mary. G.H. and Gus and Jack told of how they used to steal from stores and newsstands, of the fight they had had the morning they planned to rob Blum's. Doc told of how Bigger had cut the cloth of his pool table and said that Bigger was "mean and bad, but sane." Sixteen policemen pointed him out as "the man we captured, Bigger Thomas." They said that a man who could elude the law as skilfully as Bigger had was "sane and responsible." A man whom Bigger recognized as the manager of the Regal Theatre told how Bigger and boys like him masturbated in the theatre, and of how he had been afraid to speak to them about it, for fear that they might start a fight and cut him. A man from the juvenile court said that Bigger had served three months in a reform school for stealing auto tires.

There was a recess and in the afternoon five doctors said that they thought Bigger was "sane, but sullen and contrary." Buckley brought forth the knife and purse Bigger had hidden in the garbage pail and informed the Court that the city's dump had been combed for four days to find them. The brick he had used to strike Bessie with was shown; then came the flashlight, the Communist pamphlets, the gun, the blackened earring, the hatchet blade, the signed confession, the kidnap note, Bessie's bloody clothes, the stained pillows and quilts, the trunk, and the empty rum bottle which had been found in the snow near a curb. Mary's bones were brought in and women in the court room began to sob. Then a group of twelve workmen brought in the furnace, piece by piece, from the Dalton basement and mounted it upon a giant wooden platform. People in the room stood to look and the judge ordered them to sit down.

Buckley had a white girl, the size of Mary, crawl inside of the furnace "to prove beyond doubt that it could and did hold and burn the ravished body of innocent Mary Dalton; and to show that the poor girl's head could not go in and the sadistic Negro cut it off." Using an iron shovel from the Dalton basement, Buckley showed how the bones had been raked out; explained how Bigger had "craftily crept up the stairs during the excitement and taken flight." Mopping sweat from his face, Buckley said,

"The State rests, Your Honor!"

"Mr. Max," the judge said. "You may proceed to call your witnesses."

"The defense does not contest the evidence introduced here," Max said. "I therefore waive the right to call witnesses. As I stated before, at the proper time I shall present a plea in Bigger Thomas' behalf."

The judge informed Buckley that he could sum up. For an hour Buckley commented upon the testimony of the State's witnesses and interpreted the evidence, concluding with the words,

"The intellectual and moral faculties of mankind may as well be declared impotent, if the evidence and testimony submitted by the State are not enough to compel this Court to impose the death sentence upon Bigger Thomas, this despoiler of women!"

"Mr. Max, will you be prepared to present your plea tomorrow?" the judge asked.

"I will, Your Honor."

Back in his cell, Bigger tumbled lifelessly onto his cot. Soon it'll all be over, he thought. Tomorrow might be the last day; he hoped so. His sense of time was gone; night and day were merged now.

The next morning he was awake in his cell when Max came. On his way to court he wondered what Max would say about him. Could Max really save his life? In the act of thinking the thought, he thrust it from him. If he kept hope from his mind, then whatever happened would seem natural. As he was led down the hall, past windows, he saw that the mob and the troops still surrounded the court house. The building was still jammed with muttering people. Policemen had to make an aisle for him in the crowd.

A pang of fear shot through him when he saw that he had been the first to get to the table. Max was somewhere behind him, lost in the crowd. It was then that he felt more deeply than ever what Max had grown to mean to him. He was defenseless now. What was there to prevent those people from coming across those railings and dragging him into the street, now that Max was not here? He sat, not daring to look round, conscious that every eye was upon him. Max's presence during the trial had made him feel that somewhere in that crowd that stared at him so steadily and resentfully was something he could cling to, if only he could get at it. There smoldered in him the hope that Max had made him feel in the first long talk they had had. But he did not want to risk trying to make it flare into flame now, not with this trial and the words of hate from Buckley. But neither did he snuff it out; he nursed it, kept it as his last refuge.

When Max came Bigger saw that his face was pale and drawn. There were dark rings beneath the eyes. Max laid a hand on Bigger's knee and whispered,

"I'm going to do all I can, son."

Court opened and the judge said,

"Are you ready to proceed, Mr. Max?"

"Yes, Your Honor."

Max rose, ran his hand through his white hair and went to the front of the room. He turned and half-faced the judge and Buckley, looking out over Bigger's head to the crowd. He cleared his throat.

"Your Honor, never in my life have I risen in court to make a plea with a firmer conviction in my heart. I know that what I have to say here today touches the destiny of an entire nation. My plea is for more than one man and one people. Perhaps it is in a manner fortunate that the defendant has committed one of the darkest crimes in our memory; for if we can encompass the life of this man and find out what has happened to him, if we can understand how subtly and yet strongly his life and fate are linked to ours—if we can do this, perhaps we shall find the key to our future, that rare vantage point upon which every man and woman in this nation can stand and view how inextricably our hopes and fears of today create the exultation and doom of tomorrow.

"Your Honor, I have no desire to be disrespectful to this Court, but I must be honest. A man's life is at stake. And not only is this man a criminal, but he is a black criminal. And as such, he comes into this court under a handicap, notwithstanding our pretensions that all are equal before the law.

"This man is *different*, even though his crime differs from similar crimes only in degree. The complex forces of society have isolated here for us a symbol, a test symbol. The prejudices of men have stained this symbol, like a germ stained for examination under the microscope. The unremitting hate of men has given us a psychological distance that will enable us to see this tiny social symbol in relation to our whole sick social organism.

"I say, Your Honor, that the mere act of understanding Bigger Thomas will be a thawing out of icebound impulses, a dragging of the sprawling forms of dread out of the night of fear into the light of reason, an unveiling of the unconscious ritual of death in which we, like sleep-walkers, have participated so dreamlike and thoughtlessly.

"But I make no excessive claims, Your Honor. I do not deal in magic. I do not say that if we understand this man's life we shall solve all our problems, or that when we have all the facts at our disposal we shall automatically know how to act. Life is not that simple. But I do say that, if, after I have finished, you feel that death is necessary, then you are making an open choice. What I want to do is inject into the consciousness of this Court, through the discussion of evidence, the two possible courses of action open to us and the inevitable consequences flowing from each. And then, if we say death, let us mean it; and if we say life, let us mean that too; but whatever we say, let us know upon what ground we are putting our feet, what the consequences are for us and those whom we judge.

"Your Honor, I would have you believe that I am not insensible to the deep burden of responsibility I am throwing upon your shoulders by the manner in which I have insisted upon conducting the defense of this boy's life, and in my resolve to place before you the entire degree of his guilt for judgment. But, under the circumstances, what else could I have done? Night after night, I have lain without sleep, trying to think of a way to picture to you and to the world the causes and reasons why this Negro boy sits here a self-confessed murderer. But every time I thought I had discovered a vital piece of evidence bearing upon his fate, I could hear in my mind's ear the low, angry muttering of that mob which the state troops are holding at bay beyond that window.

"How can I, I asked myself, make my voice heard with effect above the hungry yelping of hounds on the hunt? How can I, I asked myself, make the picture of what has happened to this boy show plain and powerful upon a screen of sober reason, when a thousand newspaper and magazine artists have already drawn it in lurid ink upon a million sheets of public print? Dare I, deeply mindful of this boy's background and race, put his fate in the hands of a jury (not of his peers, but of an alien and hostile race!) whose minds are already conditioned by the press of the nation; a press which has already reached a decision as to his guilt, and in countless editorials suggested the measure of his punishment?

"No! I could not! It would be better if we had no courts of law, than that justice should be administered under such conditions! An outright lynching would be more honest than a "mock trial"! Rather that courts be abolished and each man buy arms and proceed to protect himself or make war for what he thinks is rightfully his own, than that a man should be tried by men who have already made up their minds that he is guilty. I could not have placed at the disposal of a jury the evidence, so general and yet so confoundingly specific, so impalpable and yet so disastrous in its terrible consequences—consequences which have affected my client and account for his being here today before the bar of judgment with his life at stake—I could not have done that and have been honest with myself or with this boy.

"So today I come to face this Court, rejecting a trial by jury, willingly entering a plea of guilty, asking in the light of the laws of this state that this boy's life be spared for reasons which I believe affect the foundations of our civilization.

"The most habitual thing for this Court to do is to take the

line of least resistance and follow the suggestion of the State's
Attorney and say, 'Death!' And that would be the end of this
case. But that would not be the end of this crime! That is why
this Court must do otherwise.

"There are times, Your Honor, when reality bears features
of such an impellingly moral complexion that it is impossible
to follow the hewn path of expediency. There are times when
life's ends are so raveled that reason and sense cry out that we
stop and gather them together again before we can proceed.

"What atmosphere surrounds this trial? Are the citizens
soberly intent upon seeing that the law is executed? That ret-
ribution is dealt out in measure with the offense? That the
guilty and only the guilty is caught and punished?

"No! Every conceivable prejudice has been dragged into
this case. The authorities of the city and state deliberately inflamed the public mind to the point where they could not
keep the peace without martial law. Responsible to nothing
but their own corrupt conscience, the newspapers and the
prosecution launched the ridiculous claim that the Communist Party was in some way linked to these two murders. Only
here in court yesterday morning did the State's Attorney cease
implying that Bigger Thomas was guilty of other crimes,
crimes which he could not prove. And, because I, a Jew,
dared defend this Negro boy, for days my mail has been
flooded with threats against my life. The manner in which
Bigger Thomas was captured, the hundreds of innocent
Negro homes invaded, the scores of Negroes assaulted upon
the streets, the dozens who were thrown out of their jobs,
the barrage of lies poured out from every source against a
defenseless people—all of this was something unheard of in
democratic lands.

"The hunt for Bigger Thomas served as an excuse to ter-
rorize the entire Negro population, to arrest hundreds of
Communists, to raid labor union headquarters and workers'
organizations. Indeed, the tone of the press, the silence of the
church, the attitude of the prosecution and the stimulated
temper of the people are of such a nature as to indicate that
more than revenge is being sought upon a man who has
committed a crime.

"What is the cause of all this high feeling and excitement?

Is it the crime of Bigger Thomas? Were Negroes liked yesterday and hated today because of what he has done? Were labor unions and workers' halls raided solely because a Negro committed a crime? Did those white bones lying on that table evoke the gasp of horror that went up from the nation? Did the feeling against the Jews in the city rise only because a Jewish lawyer is defending a black boy?

"Your Honor, you know that that is *not* the case! All of the factors in the present hysteria existed before Bigger Thomas was ever heard of. Negroes, workers, and labor unions were hated as much yesterday as they are today.

"Crimes of even greater brutality and horror have been committed in this city. Gangsters have killed and have gone free to kill again. But none of that brought forth an indignation to equal this.

"Your Honor, that mob did not come here of its own accord! It was *incited*! Until a week ago those people lived their lives as quietly as always.

"Who, then, fanned this latent hate into fury? Whose interest is that thoughtless and misguided mob serving? Why did every agency of communication in the city suddenly spew forth lies, telling our citizens that they had to protect what they owned against Bigger Thomas and men like him? Who provoked this hysteria so that they might profit by it?

"The State's Attorney knows, for he promised the Loop bankers that if he were re-elected demonstrations for relief would be stopped! The Governor of the state knows, for he has pledged the Manufacturers' Association that he would use troops against workers who went out on strike! The Mayor knows, for he told the merchants of the city that the budget would be cut down, that no new taxes would be imposed to satisfy the clamor of the masses of the needy!

"There is guilt in the rage that demands that this man's life be snuffed out quickly! There is fear in the hate and impatience which impels the action of the mob congregated upon the streets beyond that window! Each of them—the mob and the mob-masters; the wire-pullers and the frightened; the leaders and their pet vassals—know and feel that their lives are built upon a historical deed of wrong against many people, people from whose lives they have bled their leisure and their luxury! Their feeling of guilt is as deep as that of the boy who sits here on trial today. Fear and hate and guilt are the keynotes of this drama!

"Your Honor, for the sake of this boy and myself, I wish I could bring to this Court evidence of a morally worthier nature. I wish I could say that love, ambition, jealousy, the quest for adventure, or any of the more romantic feelings were back of these two murders. If I could honestly invest the hapless actor in this fateful drama with feelings of a loftier cast, my task would be easier and I would feel confident of the outcome. The odds would be with me, for I would be appealing to men bound by common ideals to judge with pity and understanding one of their brothers who erred and fell in struggle. But I have no choice in this matter. Life has cut this cloth; not I.

"We must deal here with the raw stuff of life, emotions and impulses and attitudes as yet unconditioned by the strivings of science and civilization. We must deal here with a first wrong which, when committed by us, was understandable and inevitable; and then we must deal with the long trailing black sense of guilt stemming from that wrong, a sense of guilt which self-interest and fear would not let us atone. And we must deal here with the hot blasts of hate engendered in others by that first wrong, and then the monstrous and horrible crimes flowing from that hate, a hate which has seeped down into the hearts and molded the deepest and most delicate sensibilities of multitudes.

"We must deal here with a dislocation of life involving millions of people, a dislocation so vast as to stagger the imagination; so fraught with tragic consequences as to make us rather not want to look at it or think of it; so old that we would rather try to view it as an order of nature and strive with uneasy conscience and false moral fervor to keep it so.

"We must deal here, on both sides of the fence, among whites as well as blacks, among workers as well as employers, with men and women in whose minds there loom good and bad of such height and weight that they assume proportions of abnormal aspect and construction. When situations like this arise, instead of men feeling that they are facing other men, they feel that they are facing mountains, floods, seas:

forces of nature whose size and strength focus the minds and emotions to a degree of tension unusual in the quiet routine of urban life. Yet this tension exists within the limits of urban life, undermining it and supporting it in the same gesture of being.

"Allow me, Your Honor, before I proceed to cast blame and ask for mercy, to state emphatically that I do *not* claim that this boy is a victim of injustice, nor do I ask that this Court be sympathetic with him. That is not my object in embracing his character and his cause. It is not to tell you only of suffering that I stand here today, even though there are frequent lynchings and floggings of Negroes throughout the country. If you react only to that part of what I say, then you, too, are caught as much as he in the mire of blind emotion, and this vicious game will roll on, like a bloody river to a bloodier sea. Let us banish from our minds the thought that this is an unfortunate victim of injustice. The very concept of injustice rests upon a premise of equal claims, and this boy here today makes no claim upon you. If you think or feel that he does, then you, too, are blinded by a feeling as terrible as that which you condemn in him, and without as much justification. The feeling of guilt which has caused all of the mob-fear and mob-hysteria is the counterpart of his own hate.

"Rather, I plead with you to see a mode of *life* in our midst, a mode of life stunted and distorted, but possessing its own laws and claims, an existence of men growing out of the soil prepared by the collective but blind will of a hundred million people. I beg you to recognize human life draped in a form and guise alien to ours, but springing from a soil plowed and sown by all our hands. I ask you to recognize the laws and processes flowing from such a condition, understand them, seek to change them. If we do none of these, then we should not pretend horror or surprise when thwarted life expresses itself in fear and hate and crime.

"This is life, new and strange; strange, because we fear it; new, because we have kept our eyes turned from it. This is life lived in cramped limits and expressing itself not in terms of our good and bad, but in terms of its own fulfilment. Men are men and life is life, and we must deal with them as they are; and if we want to change them, we must deal with them in the form in which they exist and have their being.

"Your Honor, I must still speak in general terms, for the background of this boy must be shown, a background which has acted powerfully and importantly upon his conduct. Our forefathers came to these shores and faced a harsh and wild country. They came here with a stifled dream in their hearts, from lands where their personalities had been denied, as even we have denied the personality of this boy. They came from cities of the old world where the means to sustain life were hard to get or own. They were colonists and they were faced with a difficult choice: they had either to subdue this wild land or be subdued by it. We need but turn our eyes upon the imposing sweep of streets and factories and buildings to see how completely they have conquered. But in conquering they *used* others, used their lives. Like a miner using a pick or a carpenter using a saw, they bent the will of others to their own. Lives to them were tools and weapons to be wielded against a hostile land and climate.

"I do not say this in terms of moral condemnation. I do not say it to rouse pity in you for the black men who were slaves for two and one-half centuries. It would be foolish now to look back upon that in the light of injustice. Let us not be naïve: men do what they must, even when they feel that they are being driven by God, even when they feel they are fulfilling the will of God. Those men were engaged in a struggle for life and their choice in the matter was small indeed. It was the imperial dream of a feudal age that made men enslave others. Exalted by the will to rule, they could not have built nations on so vast a scale had they not shut their eyes to the humanity of other men, men whose lives were necessary for their building. But the invention and widespread use of machines made the further direct enslavement of men economically impossible, and so slavery ended.

"Let me, Your Honor, dwell a moment longer upon the danger of looking upon this boy in the light of injustice. If I should say that he is a victim of injustice, then I would be asking by implication for sympathy; and if one insists upon looking at this boy as a victim of injustice, he will be swamped by a feeling of guilt so strong as to be indistinguish-able from hate.

"Of all things, men do not like to feel that they are guilty of wrong, and if you make them feel guilt, they will try desper-ately to justify it on any grounds; but, failing that, and seeing no immediate solution that will set things right without too much cost to their lives and property, they will kill that which evoked in them the condemning sense of guilt.

"And this is true of all men, whether they be white or black; it is a peculiar and powerful, but common, need. Your Honor, let me give you an example. When this poor black boy, Bigger Thomas, was trying to cast the blame for his crime upon one of the witnesses, Jan Erlone, a Communist, who faced this Court yesterday—and this boy thought he would be able to blame his crime upon the Communists with impunity, because the newspapers had convinced him that Communists were criminals—an example of such fear-guilt occurred. Jan Erlone confronted Bigger Thomas upon a street corner and sought to have it out with him, demanding to know why Bigger was trying to blame the crime upon him. Jan Erlone told me that Bigger Thomas acted as hysterically as those people are acting at this moment in that mob outdoors. Bigger Thomas drew a gun and commanded Jan Erlone to leave him. Bigger Thomas was almost a stranger to Jan Erlone and Jan Erlone was almost a stranger to him; yet they hated each other.

"Today Bigger Thomas and that mob are strangers, yet they hate. They hate because they fear, and they fear because they feel that the deepest feelings of their lives are being as-saulted and outraged. And they do not know why; they are powerless pawns in a blind play of social forces.

"This guilt-fear is the basic tone of the prosecution and of the people in this case. In their hearts they feel that a wrong has been done and when a Negro commits a crime against them, they fancy they see the ghastly evidence of that wrong. So the men of wealth and property, the victims of attack who are eager to protect their profits, say to their guilty hirelings, 'Stamp out this ghost!' Or, like Mr. Dalton, they say, 'Let's do something for this man so he won't feel that way.' But then it is too late.

"Do I say this to make you believe that this boy is blameless? No. Bigger Thomas' own feeling of hate feeds the feeling of guilt in others. Hemmed in, limited, circumscribed, he sees and feels no way of acting except to hate and kill that which he thinks is crushing him.

"Your Honor, I'm trying to wipe out this circle of blood, trying to cut down into this matter, beneath hate and fear and guilt and revenge and show what impulses are twisted.

"If only ten or twenty Negroes had been put into slavery, we could call it injustice, but there were hundreds of thousands of them throughout the country. If this state of affairs had lasted for two or three years, we could say that it was unjust; but it lasted for more than two hundred years. Injustice which lasts for three long centuries and which exists among millions of people over thousands of square miles of territory, is injustice no longer; it is an accomplished fact of life. Men adjust themselves to their land; they create their own laws of being; their notions of right and wrong. A common way of earning a living gives them a common attitude toward life. Even their speech is colored and shaped by what they must undergo. Your Honor, injustice blots out one form of life, but another grows up in its place with its own rights, needs, and aspirations. What is happening here today is not injustice, but *oppression*, an attempt to throttle or stamp out a new form of life. And it is this new form of life that has grown up here in our midst that puzzles us, that expresses itself, like a weed growing from under a stone, in terms we call crime. Unless we grasp this problem in the light of this new reality, we cannot do more than salve our feelings of guilt and rage with more murder when a man, living under such conditions, commits an act which we call a crime.

"This boy represents but a tiny aspect of a problem whose reality sprawls over a third of this nation. Kill him! Burn the life out of him! And still when the delicate and unconscious machinery of race relations slips, there will be murder again. How can law contradict the lives of millions of people and hope to be administered successfully? Do we believe in magic? Do you believe that by burning a cross you can frighten a multitude, paralyze their will and impulses? Do you think that the white daughters in the homes of America will be any safer if you kill this boy? No! I tell you in all solemnity that they won't! The surest way to make certain that there will be more such murders is to kill this boy. In your rage and guilt, make thousands of other black men and women feel that the barriers are tighter and higher! Kill him and swell the tide of pent-up lava that will some day break loose, not in a single, blundering, accidental, individual crime, but in a wild cataract of emotion that will brook no control. The all-important thing for this Court to remember in deciding this boy's fate is that, though his crime was accidental, the emotions that broke loose were *already* there; the thing to remember is that this boy's way of life was a way of guilt; that his crime existed long before the murder of Mary Dalton; that the accidental nature of his crime took the guise of a sudden and violent rent in the veil behind which he lived, a rent which allowed his feelings of resentment and estrangement to leap forth and find objective and concrete form.

"Obsessed with guilt, we have sought to thrust a corpse from before our eyes. We have marked off a little plot of ground and buried it. We tell our souls in the deep of the black night that it is dead and that we have no reason for fear or uneasiness.

"But the corpse returns and raids our homes! We find our daughters murdered and burnt! And we say, 'Kill! Kill!'

"But, Your Honor, I say: 'Stop! Let us look at what we are doing!' For the corpse is not dead! It still lives! It has made itself a home in the wild forest of our great cities, amid the rank and choking vegetation of slums! It has forgotten our language! In order to live it has sharpened its claws! It has grown hard and calloused! It has developed a capacity for hate and fury which we cannot understand! Its movements are unpredictable! By night it creeps from its lair and steals toward the settlements of civilization! And at the sight of a kind face it does not lie down upon its back and kick up its heels playfully to be tickled and stroked. No; it leaps to kill!

"Yes, Mary Dalton, a well-intentioned white girl with a smile upon her face, came to Bigger Thomas to help him. Mr. Dalton, feeling vaguely that a social wrong existed, wanted to give him a job so that his family could eat and his sister and brother could go to school. Mrs. Dalton, trying to grope her way toward a sense of decency, wanted him to go to school and learn a trade. But when they stretched forth their helping hands, death struck! Today they mourn and wait for revenge. The wheel of blood continues to turn!

"I have only sympathy for those kind-hearted, white-haired parents. But to Mr. Dalton, who is a real estate operator, I say now: 'You rent houses to Negroes in the Black Belt and you refuse to rent to them elsewhere. You kept Bigger Thomas in that forest. You kept the man who murdered your daughter a stranger to her and you kept your daughter a stranger to him.'

"The relationship between the Thomas family and the Dalton family was that of renter to landlord, customer to merchant, employee to employer. The Thomas family got poor and the Dalton family got rich. And Mr. Dalton, a decent man, tried to salve his feelings by giving money. But, my friend, gold was not enough! Corpses cannot be bribed! Say to yourself, Mr. Dalton, 'I offered my daughter as a burnt sacrifice and it was not enough to push back into its grave this thing that haunts me.'

"And to Mrs. Dalton, I say: 'Your philanthropy was as tragically blind as your sightless eyes!'

"And to Mary Dalton, if she can hear me, I say: 'I stand here today trying to make your death *mean* something!'

"Let me, Your Honor, explain further the meaning of Bigger Thomas' life. In him and men like him is what was in our forefathers when they first came to these strange shores hundreds of years ago. We were lucky. They are not. We found a land whose tasks called forth the deepest and best we had; and we built a nation, mighty and feared. We poured and are still pouring our soul into it. But we have told them: 'This is a white man's country!' They are yet looking for a land whose tasks can call forth their deepest and best.

"This is not something that we have to be told. We know this. And, in some of us, as in Mr. Dalton, the feeling of guilt, stemming from our moral past, is so strong that we try to undo this thing in a manner as naïve as dropping a penny in a blind man's cup! But, Your Honor, life will not be dealt with in such a fashion. It rushes on its fateful course, mocking our delicate feelings. Let us hope that this Court at least will indicate a line of action that is not childish!

"Consider, Your Honor, the peculiar position of this boy. He comes of a people who have lived under queer conditions of life, conditions thrust outside the normal circle of our civilization. But even in living outside of our lives, he has not had a full life of his own. We have seen to that. It was convenient to keep him close to us; it was nice and cheap. We told him what to do; where to live; how much schooling he could get; where he could eat; where and what kind of work he could do. We marked up the earth and said, 'Stay there!' But life is not stationary.

"He attended school, where he was taught what every white child was taught; but the moment he went through the door of the school into life he knew that the white boy went one way and he went another. School stimulated and developed in him those impulses which all of us have, and then he was made to realize that he could not act upon them. Can the human mind devise a trap more skilful? This Court should not sit to fix punishment for this boy; it should sit to ponder why there are not more like him! And there are, Your Honor. If it were not for the backwaters of religion, gambling and sex draining off their energies into channels harmful to them and profitable to us, more of them would be here today. Be assured!

"Your Honor, consider the mere physical aspect of our civilization. How alluring, how dazzling it is! How it excites the senses! How it seems to dangle within easy reach of everyone the fulfilment of happiness! How constantly and overwhelmingly the advertisements, radios, newspapers and movies play upon us! But in thinking of them remember that to many they are tokens of mockery. These bright colors may fill our hearts with elation, but to many they are daily taunts. Imagine a man walking amid such a scene, a part of it, and yet knowing that it is *not* for him!

"We planned the murder of Mary Dalton, and today we come to court and say: 'We had nothing to do with it!' But every school teacher knows that this is not so, for every school teacher knows the restrictions which have been placed upon Negro education. The authorities know that it is not so, for they have made it plain in their every act that they mean to keep Bigger Thomas and his kind within rigid limits. All real estate operators know that it is not so, for they have agreed among themselves to keep Negroes within the ghetto-areas of cities. Your Honor, we who sit here today in this court room are witnesses. We know this evidence, for we helped to create it.

"It is not my duty here, today, to say how this great problem can be solved. My job is to show how nonsensical it is to seek revenge on this boy under the pretense that we are making a great fight for justice. If we do that, we shall be merely hypnotizing ourselves, and to our own ultimate disadvantage.

"But the question may be asked, 'If this boy thought that he was somehow wronged, why did he not go into a court of law and seek a redress of his grievances? Why should he take the law into his own hands?' Your Honor, this boy had no notion before he murdered, and he has none now, of having been wronged by any specific individuals. And, to be honest with you, the very life he has led has created in him a frame of mind which makes him expect much less of this Court than you will ever know.

"It is indeed unfortunate that Mary Dalton should have been the woman who approached him that night; and it is unfortunate that Jan Erlone should have been the man who sought to help him. He murdered one and tried to lay the blame for that murder on the other. But Jan and Mary were not human beings to Bigger Thomas. Social custom had shoved him so far away from them that they were not real to him.

"What would a boy, free from the warping influences which have played so hard upon Bigger Thomas, have done that night when he found himself alone with that drunk girl? He would have gone to Mr. or Mrs. Dalton and told them that their daughter was drunk. And the thing would have been over. There would have been no murder. But the way we have treated this boy made him do the *very* thing we did not want.

"Or, am I wrong? Maybe we *wanted* him to do it! Maybe we would have had no chance or justification to stage attacks against hundreds of thousands of people if he had acted sanely and normally! Maybe we would have had to go to the expensive length of inventing theories to justify our attacks if we had treated him fairly!

"This boy's crime was not an act of retaliation by an injured man against a person who he thought had injured him. If it were, then this case would be simple indeed. This is the case of a man's mistaking a whole race of men as a part of the natural structure of the universe and of his acting toward them accordingly. He murdered Mary Dalton accidentally, without thinking, without plan, without conscious motive. But, after he murdered, he accepted the crime. And that's the important thing. It was the first full act of his life; it was the most meaningful, exciting and stirring thing that had ever happened to him. He accepted it because it made him free, gave him the possibility of choice, of action, the opportunity to act and to feel that his actions carried weight.

"We are dealing here with an impulse stemming from deep down. We are dealing here not with how man acts toward man, but with how a man acts when he feels that he must defend himself against, or adapt himself to, the total natural world in which he lives. The central fact to be understood here is not who wronged this boy, but what kind of a vision of the world did he have before his eyes, and where did he get such a vision as to make him, without premeditation, snatch the life of another person so quickly and instinctively that even though there was an element of accident in it, he was willing after the crime to say: 'Yes; I did it. I had to.'

"I know that it is the fashion these days for a defendant to say: 'Everything went blank to me.' But this boy does not say that. He says the opposite. He says he knew what he was doing and felt he *had* to do it. And he says he feels no sorrow for having done it.

"Do men regret when they kill in war? Does the personality of a soldier coming at you over the top of a trench matter?

"No! You kill to keep from being killed! And after a victorious war you return to a free country, just as this boy, with his hands stained with the blood of Mary Dalton, felt that he was free for the first time in his life.

"Your Honor, the most pathetic aspect of this case is that a young white woman, a student at a university, ignorant and thoughtless, though educated, tried to undo as an individual a gigantic wrong accomplished by a nation through three hundred long years, and was misunderstood and is now dead because of that misunderstanding. It has been said that the proof of the corrupt and vile heart of this boy is that he slew a woman who was trying to be kind to him. In the face of that assertion, I ask the question: Is there any greater proof that his heart is not corrupt and vile than that he slew a woman who was trying to be kind? Oh, yes; he hated the girl. And why not? She was acting toward him in such a way as no white face usually acts toward a Negro, and as a white face acts only when it is about to fleece a Negro of something. He did not understand her. She confounded him. Her actions made him feel that the entire universe was tumbling about his head. What would any man in this court room do if the sun should suddenly turn green?

"Look, Your Honor, with great and elaborate care we conditioned Mary Dalton so that she would regard Bigger Thomas as a kind of beast. And, under the penalty of death, we commanded Bigger Thomas to avoid Mary Dalton. Fateful circumstances threw them together. Is it surprising that one of them is dead and the other is on trial for his life?

"Look, Your Honor. Even in this court room, even here today, Negro and white are separated. See those Negroes sitting together, behind that railing? No one told them to sit there. They sat there because they knew that we did not want them on the same bench with us.

"Multiply Bigger Thomas twelve million times, allowing for environmental and temperamental variations, and for those Negroes who are completely under the influence of the church, and you have the psychology of the Negro people. But once you see them as a whole, once your eyes leave the individual and encompass the mass, a new quality comes into the picture. Taken collectively, they are not simply twelve million people; in reality they constitute a separate nation, stunted, stripped, and held captive *within* this nation, devoid of political, social, economic, and property rights.

"Do you think that you can kill one of them—even if you killed one every day in the year—and make the others so full of fear that they would not kill? No! Such a foolish policy has never worked and never will. The more you kill, the more you deny and separate, the more will they seek another form and way of life, however blindly and unconsciously. And out of what can they weave a different life, out of what can they mold a new existence, living organically in the same towns and cities, the same neighborhoods with us? I ask, out of what—but what we *are* and *own*? We allow them nothing. We allowed Bigger Thomas nothing. He sought another life and accidentally found one, found it at the expense of all that we cherish and hold dear. Men once oppressed our forefathers to the extent that they viewed other men as material out of which to build a nation; we in turn have oppressed others to such a degree that they, fumblingly as yet, try to construct meaningful lives out of *us*! Cannibalism still lives!

"Your Honor, there are four times as many Negroes in America today as there were people in the original Thirteen Colonies when they struck for their freedom. These twelve million Negroes, conditioned broadly by our own notions as we were by European ones when we first came here, are struggling within unbelievably narrow limits to achieve that feeling of at-home-ness for which we once strove so ardently. And, compared with our own struggle, they are striving under conditions far more difficult. If anybody can, surely we ought to be able to understand what these people are after. This vast stream of life, dammed and muddied, is trying to sweep toward that fulfilment which all of us seek so fondly, but find so impossible to put into words. When we said that men are 'endowed with certain inalienable rights, among these are life, liberty, and the pursuit of happiness,' we did not pause to define 'happiness.' That is the unexpressed quality in our quest, and we have never tried to put it into words. That is why we say, 'Let each man serve God in his own fashion.'

"But there are some broad features of the kind of happiness we are seeking which are known. We know that happiness comes to men when they are caught up, absorbed in a meaningful task or duty to be done, a task or duty which in turn sheds justification and sanction back down upon their humble labors. We know that this may take many forms: in religion it is the story of the creation of man, of his fall, and of his redemption; compelling men to order their lives in certain ways, all cast in terms of cosmic images and symbols which swallow the soul in fulness and wholeness. In art, science, industry, politics, and social action it may take other forms. But these twelve million Negroes have access to none of these highly crystallized modes of expression, save that of religion. And many of them know religion only in its most primitive form. The environment of tense urban centers has all but paralyzed the impulse for religion as a way of life for them today, just as it has for us.

"Feeling the capacity to be, to live, to act, to pour out the spirit of their souls into concrete and objective form with a high fervor born of their racial characteristics, they glide through our complex civilization like wailing ghosts; they spin like fiery planets lost from their orbits; they wither and die like trees ripped from native soil.

"Your Honor, remember that men can starve from a lack of self-realization as much as they can from a lack of bread! And they can *murder* for it, too! Did we not build a nation, did we not wage war and conquer in the name of a dream to realize our personalities and to make those realized personalities secure!

"Do we think that the laws of human nature stopped operating after we had got our feet upon our road? Have we had to struggle so hard for our right to happiness that we have all but destroyed the conditions under which we and others can still be happy? This Negro boy, Bigger Thomas, is a part of a furious blaze of liquid life-energy which once blazed and is still blazing in our land. He is a hot jet of life that spattered itself in futility against a cold wall.

"But did Bigger Thomas really *murder*? At the risk of offending the sensibilities of this Court, I ask the question in the light of the ideals by which *we* live! Looked at from the outside, maybe it was murder; yes. But to him it was *not* murder. If it was murder, then what was the motive? The prosecution has shouted, stormed and threatened, but he has not said *why* Bigger Thomas killed! He has not said why because he does not know. The truth is, Your Honor, there was no motive as you and I understand motives within the scope of our laws today. The truth is, this boy did *not* kill! Oh, yes; Mary Dalton is dead. Bigger Thomas smothered her to death.

Bessie Mears is dead. Bigger Thomas battered her with a brick in an abandoned building. But did he murder? Did he kill? Listen: what Bigger Thomas did early that Sunday morning in the Dalton home and what he did that Sunday night in that empty building was but a tiny aspect of what he had been doing all his life long! He was *living*, only as he knew how, and as we have forced him to live. The actions that resulted in the death of those two women were as instinctive and inevitable as breathing or blinking one's eyes. It was an act of *creation*!

"Let me tell you more. Before this trial the newspapers and the prosecution said that this boy had committed other crimes. It is true. He is guilty of numerous crimes. But search until the day of judgment, and you will find not one shred of evidence of them. He has murdered many times, but there are no corpses. Let me explain. This Negro boy's entire attitude toward life is a *crime*! The hate and fear which we have inspired in him, woven by our civilization into the very structure of his consciousness, into his blood and bones, into the hourly functioning of his personality, have become the justification of his existence.

"Every time he comes in contact with us, he kills! It is a physiological and psychological reaction, embedded in his being. Every thought he thinks is potential murder. Excluded from, and unassimilated in our society, yet longing to gratify impulses akin to our own but denied the objects and channels evolved through long centuries for their socialized expression, every sunrise and sunset makes him guilty of subversive actions. Every movement of his body is an unconscious protest. Every desire, every dream, no matter how intimate or personal, is a plot or a conspiracy. Every hope is a plan for insurrection. Every glance of the eye is a threat. *His very existence is a crime against the state!*

"It so happened that that night a white girl was present in a bed and a Negro boy was standing over her, fascinated with fear, hating her; a blind woman walked into the room and that Negro boy killed that girl to keep from being discovered in a position which he knew *we* claimed warrants the death penalty. But that is only *one* side of it! He was impelled toward murder as much through the thirst for excitement, exultation, and elation as he was through fear! It was his way of *living*!

"Your Honor, in our blindness we have so contrived and ordered the lives of men that the moths in their hearts flutter toward ghoulish and incomprehensible flames!

"I have not explained the relationship of Bessie Mears to this boy. I have not forgotten her. I omitted to mention her until now because she was largely omitted from the consciousness of Bigger Thomas. His relationship to this poor black girl also reveals his relationship to the world. But Bigger Thomas is not here on trial for having murdered Bessie Mears. And he knows that. What does this mean? Does not the life of a Negro girl mean as much in the eyes of the law as the life of a white girl? Yes; perhaps, in the abstract. But under the stress of fear and flight, Bigger Thomas did not think of Bessie. He could not. The attitude of America toward this boy regulated his most intimate dealings with his own kind. After he had killed Mary Dalton he killed Bessie Mears to silence her, to save himself. After he had killed Mary Dalton the fear of having killed a white woman filled him to the exclusion of everything else. He could not react to Bessie's death; his consciousness was determined by the fear that hung above him.

"But, one might ask, did he not love Bessie? Was she not his girl? Yes; she was his girl. He had to have a girl, so he had Bessie. But he did not love her. Is love possible to the life of a man I've described to this Court? Let us see. Love is not based upon sex alone, and that is all he had with Bessie. He wanted more, but the circumstances of his life and her life would not allow it. And the temperament of both Bigger and Bessie kept it out. Love grows from stable relationships, shared experience, loyalty, devotion, trust. Neither Bigger nor Bessie had any of these. What was there they could hope for? There was no common vision binding their hearts together; there was no common hope steering their feet in a common path. Even though they were intimately together, they were confoundingly alone. They were physically dependent upon each other and they hated that dependence. Their brief moments together were for purposes of sex. They loved each other as much as they hated each other; perhaps they hated each other more than they loved. Sex warms the deep roots of life; it is the soil out of which the tree of love grows. But these were trees without roots, trees that lived by the light of the sun and what chance rain that fell upon stony ground. Can disembodied spirits love? There existed between them fitful splurges of physical elation; that's all.

"With cunning calculated to outrage the moral sense, the prosecution brought into this court room a man, a manager from a theatre, who told us that Bigger Thomas and boys like him frequented his theatre and committed acts of masturbation in the darkened seats. A gasp of horror went through the court room. But what is so strange about that? Was not Bigger Thomas' relationship to his girl a masturbatory one? Was not his relationship to the whole world on the same plane?

"His entire existence was one long craving for satisfaction, with the objects of satisfaction denied; and we regulated every part of the world he touched. Through the instrument of fear, we determined the mode and the quality of his consciousness.

"Your Honor, is this boy alone in feeling deprived and baffled? Is he an exception? Or are there others? There are others, Your Honor, millions of others, Negro and white, and that is what makes our future seem a looming image of violence. The feeling of resentment and the balked longing for some kind of fulfilment and exultation—in degrees more or less intense and in actions more or less conscious—stalk day by day through this land. The consciousness of Bigger Thomas, and millions of others more or less like him, white and black, according to the weight of the pressure we have put upon them, form the quicksands upon which the foundations of our civilization rest. Who knows when some slight shock, disturbing the delicate balance between social order and thirsty aspiration, shall send the skyscrapers in our cities toppling? Does that sound fantastic? I assure you that it is no more fantastic than those troops and that waiting mob whose presence and guilty anger portend something which we dare not even *think*!

"Your Honor, Bigger Thomas was willing to vote for and follow any man who would have led him out of his morass of pain and hate and fear. If that mob outdoors is afraid of *one* man, what will it feel if *millions* rise? How soon will someone speak the word the resentful millions will understand: the word to be, to act, to live? Is this Court so naïve as to think that they will not take a chance that is even less risky than that Bigger Thomas took? Let us not concern ourselves with that part of Bigger Thomas' confession that says he murdered accidentally, that he did not rape the girl. It really does not matter. What does matter is that he was guilty *before* he killed! That was why his whole life became so quickly and naturally organized, pointed, charged with a new meaning when this thing occurred. Who knows when another 'accident' involving millions of men will happen, an 'accident' that will be the dreadful day of our doom?

"Lodged in the heart of this moment is the question of power which time will unfold!

"Your Honor, another civil war in these states is not impossible; and if the misunderstanding of what this boy's life means is an indication of how men of wealth and property are misreading the consciousness of the submerged millions today, one may truly come.

"Listen, I've talked with this boy. He has no education. He is poor. He is black. And you know what we have made those things mean in our country. He is young and not yet thoroughly experienced in the ways of life. He is unmarried and does not know the steadying influence of a woman's love, or what such a love can mean to him. I say I talked with him. Did I find ambition there? Yes. But it was blurred and hazy; with no notion of where it was to find an outlet. He knew he did not have a chance; he *believed* it. His ambition was chained, held back; a pool of stagnant water. I say I talked with him. Did he have the hope of a better life? Yes. But he kept it down, under rigid control. He moved through our crowded streets, drove our cars for us, waited upon our tables, ran our elevators, holding this thing tightly down in him. In every town and city you see him, laughing because we pay and expect him to laugh. What would happen if he wanted to get what the very atmosphere of our times has taught him as well as us that every man should have if he is able-bodied, of average intelligence, and sane? You know as well as I. There would be riots.

"Your Honor, if ever there was the unpredictable in our midst, this is it!

"I do not propose that we try to solve this entire problem here in this court room today. That is not within the province of our duty, nor even, I think, within the scope of our ability. But our decision as to whether this black boy is to live or die can be made in accordance with what actually exists. It will at least indicate that we *see* and *know!* And our seeing and knowing will comprise a consciousness of how inescapably this one man's life will confront us ten million fold in the days to come.

"I ask that you spare this boy, send him to prison for life. I ask this, not because I want to, but because I feel I must. I speak under the threat of mob-rule and have no desire to intensify the already existing hate.

"What would prison mean to Bigger Thomas? It holds advantages for him that a life of freedom never had. To send him to prison would be more than an act of mercy. You would be for the first time conferring *life* upon him. He would be brought for the first time within the orbit of our civilization. He would have an identity, even though it be but a number. He would have for the first time an openly designated relationship with the world. The very building in which he would spend the rest of his natural life would be the best he has ever known. Sending him to prison would be the first recognition of his personality he has ever had. The long black empty years ahead would constitute for his mind and feelings the only certain and durable object around which he could build a meaning for his life. The other inmates would be the first men with whom he could associate on a basis of equality. Steel bars between him and the society he offended would provide a refuge from hate and fear.

"You cannot kill this man, Your Honor, for we have made it plain that we do not recognize that he lives! So I say, 'Give him life!'

"This will not solve the problem which this crime exemplifies. That remains, perhaps, for the future. But if we say that we must kill him, then let us have the courage and honesty to say: 'Let us kill them all. They are not human. There's no room for them.' Then let us do it.

"We cannot, by giving him life in prison, help the others. We do not ask that this Court even try. But we can remember that whether this boy lives or dies, the marked-off ghettoes where this boy lived will remain. The mounting tide of hate on the one hand, and guilt on the other, one engendering fear and hate and the other engendering guilt and rage, will continue to grow. But at least this ruling, the sending of this boy to jail, out of the considerations I have named, will be the first recognition of what is involved here.

"I say, Your Honor, give this boy his life. And in making this concession we uphold those two fundamental concepts of our civilization, those two basic concepts upon which we have built the mightiest nation in history—personality and security—the conviction that the person is inviolate and that which sustains him is equally so.

"Let us not forget that the magnitude of our modern life, our railroads, power plants, ocean liners, airplanes, and steel mills flowered from these two concepts, grew from our dream of creating an invulnerable base upon which man and his soul can stand secure.

"Your Honor, this Court and those troops are not the real agencies that keep the public peace. Their mere presence is proof that we are letting peace slip through our fingers. Public peace is the act of public trust; it is the faith that *all* are secure and will *remain* secure.

"When men of wealth urge the use and show of force, quick death, swift revenge, then it is to protect a little spot of private security against the resentful millions from whom they have filched it, the resentful millions in whose militant hearts the dream and hope of security still lives.

"Your Honor, I ask in the name of all we are and believe, that you spare this boy's life! With every atom of my being, I beg this in order that not only may this black boy live, but that we ourselves may not die!"

Bigger heard Max's last words ring out in the court room. When Max sat down he saw that he saw that his eyes were tired and sunken. He could hear his breath coming and going heavily. He had not understood the speech, but he had felt the meaning of some of it from the tone of Max's voice. Suddenly he felt that his life was not worth the effort that Max

had made to save it. The judge rapped with the gavel, calling
a recess. The court was full of noise as Bigger rose. The policemen marched him to a small room and stood waiting, on
guard. Max came and sat beside him, silent, his head bowed.
A policeman brought a tray of food and set it on the table.

"Eat, son," Max said.

"I ain't hungry."

"I did the best I could," Max said.

"I'm all right," Bigger said.

Bigger was not at that moment really bothered about
whether Max's speech had saved his life or not. He was hugging the proud thought that Max had made the speech all for
him, to save his life. It was not the meaning of the speech that
gave him pride, but the mere act of it. That in itself was
something. The food on the tray grew cold. Through a partly
opened window Bigger heard the rumbling voice of the mob.
Soon he would go back and hear what Buckley would say.
Then it would all be over, save for what the judge would say.
And when the judge spoke he would know if he was to live or
die. He leaned his head on his hands and closed his eyes. He
heard Max stand up, strike a match and light a cigarette.

"Here; take a smoke, Bigger."

He took one and Max held the flame; he sucked the smoke
deep into his lungs and discovered that he did not want it. He
held the cigarette in his fingers and the smoke curled up past
his blood-shot eyes. He jerked his head when the door
opened; a policeman looked in.

"Court's opening in two minutes!"

"All right," Max said.

Flanked again by policemen, Bigger went back to court. He
rose when the judge came and then sat again.

"The Court will hear the State," the judge said.

Bigger turned his head and saw Buckley rise. He was
dressed in a black suit and there was a tiny pink flower in the
lapel of his coat. The man's very look and bearing, so grimly
assured, made Bigger feel that he was already lost. What
chance had he against a man like that? Buckley licked his lips
and looked out over the crowd; then he turned to the judge.

"Your Honor, we all dwell in a land of living law. Law
embodies the will of the people. As an agent and servant of

the law, as a representative of the organized will of the people, I am here to see that the will of the people is executed firmly and without delay. I intend to stand here and see that that is done, and if it is not done, then it will be only over my most solemn and emphatic protest.

"As a prosecuting officer of the State of Illinois, I come before this honorable Court to urge that the full extent of the law, the death penalty—the only penalty of the law that is feared by murderers!—be allowed to take its course in this most important case.

"I urge this for the protection of our society, our homes and our loved ones. I urge this in the performance of my sworn duty to see, in so far as I am humanly capable, that the administration of law is just, that the safety and sacredness of human life are maintained, that the social order is kept intact, and that crime is prevented and punished. I have no interest or feeling in this case beyond the performance of this sworn duty.

"I represent the families of Mary Dalton and Bessie Mears and a hundred million law-abiding men and women of this nation who are laboring in duty or industry. I represent the forces which allow the arts and sciences to flourish in freedom and peace, thereby enriching the lives of us all.

"I shall not lower the dignity of this Court, nor the righteousness of the People's cause, by attempting to answer the silly, alien, communistic and dangerous ideas advanced by the defense. And I know of no better way to discourage such thinking than the imposition of the death penalty upon this miserable human fiend, Bigger Thomas!

"My voice may sound harsh when I say: *Impose the death penalty and let the law take its course in spite of the specious call for sympathy!* But I am really merciful and sympathetic, because the enforcement of this law in its most drastic form will enable millions of honest men and women to sleep in peace tonight, to know that tomorrow will not bring the black shadow of death over their homes and lives!

"My voice may sound vindictive when I say: *Make the defendant pay the highest penalty for his crimes!* But what I am really saying is that the law is sweet when it is enforced and protects a million worthy careers, when it shields the infant, the aged, the helpless, the blind and the sensitive from the ravishing of men who know no law, no self-control, and no sense of reason.

"My voice may sound cruel when I say: *The defendant merits the death penalty for his self-confessed crimes!* But what I am really saying is that the law is strong and gracious enough to allow all of us to sit here in this court room today and try this case with dispassionate interest, and not tremble with fear that at this very moment some half-human black ape may be climbing through the windows of our homes to rape, murder, and burn our daughters!

"Your Honor, I say that the law is holy; that it is the foundation of all our cherished values. It permits us to take for granted the sense of the worth of our persons and turn our energies to higher and nobler ends.

"Man stepped forward from the kingdom of the beast the moment he felt that he could think and feel in security, knowing that sacred law had taken the place of his gun and knife.

"I say that the law is holy because it makes us human! And woe to the men—and the civilization of those men!—who, in misguided sympathy or fear, weaken the stout structure of the law which insures the harmonious working of our lives on this earth.

"Your Honor, I regret that the defense has raised the viperous issue of race and class hate in this trial. I sympathize with those whose hearts were pained, as mine was pained, when Mr. Max so cynically assailed our sacred customs. I pity this man's deluded and diseased mind. It is a sad day for American civilization when a white man will try to stay the hand of justice from a bestial monstrosity who has ravished and struck down one of the finest and most delicate flowers of our womanhood.

"Every decent white man in America ought to swoon with joy for the opportunity to crush with his heel the woolly head of this black lizard, to keep him from scuttling on his belly farther over the earth and spitting forth his venom of death!

"Your Honor, literally I shrink from the mere recital of this dastardly crime. I cannot speak of it without feeling somehow contaminated by the mere telling of it. A bloody crime has that power! It is that steeped and dyed with repellent contagion!

"A wealthy, kindly disposed white man, a resident of Chicago for more than forty years, sends to the relief agency for a Negro boy to act as chauffeur to his family. The man specifies in his request that he wants a boy who is handicapped either by race, poverty, or family responsibility. The relief authorities search through their records and select the Negro family which they think merits such aid: that family was the Thomas family, living then as now at 3721 Indiana Avenue. A social worker visits the family and informs the mother that the family is to be taken off the relief rolls and her son placed in private employment. The mother, a hard-working Christian woman, consents. In due time the relief authorities send a notification to the oldest son of the family, Bigger Thomas, this black mad dog who sits here today, telling him that he must report for work.

"What was the reaction of this sly thug when he learned that he had an opportunity to support himself, his mother, his little sister and his little brother? Was he grateful? Was he glad that he was having something offered to him that ten million men in America would have fallen on their knees and thanked God for?

"No! He cursed his mother! He said that he did not want to work! He wanted to loaf about the streets, steal from newsstands, rob stores, meddle with women, frequent dives, attend cheap movies, and chase prostitutes! That was the reaction of this sub-human killer when he was confronted with the Christian kindness of a man he had never seen!

"His mother prevailed upon him, pled with him; but the plight of his mother, worn out from a life of toil, had no effect upon this hardened black thing. The future of his sister, an adolescent school girl, meant nothing to him. The fact that the job would have enabled his brother to return to school was not enticing to Bigger Thomas.

"But, suddenly, after three days of persuasion by his mother, he consented. Had any of her arguments reached him at long last? Had he begun to feel his duty toward himself and his family? No! Those were not the considerations that drove this rapacious beast from his den into the open! He consented only when his mother informed him that the relief would cut off their supply of food if he did not accept. He agreed to go to work, but forbade his mother to speak to him within the confines of the home, so outraged was he that he had to earn his bread by the sweat of his brow. It was hunger that drove him out, sullen, angry, still longing to stay upon the streets and steal as he had done before, and for which he had once landed in a reform school.

"The counsel for the defendant, with characteristic Communistic cunning, boasted that I could not supply a motive for the crimes of this beast. Well, Your Honor, I shall disappoint him, for I shall divulge the motive.

"On the very day that Bigger Thomas was to report to the Dalton home for work, he saw a newsreel in a movie. This newsreel showed Mary Dalton in a bathing suit upon a Florida beach. Jack Harding, a friend of Bigger Thomas, under persistent questioning, admitted that Bigger Thomas was enthralled by the idea of driving such a girl around the city. Let us be frank and not gloss over words. This Court has already heard of the obnoxious sexual perversions practiced by these boys in darkened theatres. Though Jack Harding would not admit it outright, we got enough information out of him to know that when the shadow of Mary Dalton was moving upon that screen those boys indulged in such an act! It was *then* that the idea of rape, murder, and ransom entered the mind of this moron! There is your motive and the vile circumstances under which it was conceived!

"After seeing that movie, he went to the Dalton home. He was welcomed there with lavish kindness. He was given a room; he was told that he would receive extra money for himself, over and above his weekly wages. He was fed. He was asked if he wanted to go back to school and learn a trade. But he refused. His mind and heart—if this beast can be said to have a mind and a heart!—were not set upon any such goals.

"Less than an hour after he had been in that house, he met Mary Dalton, who asked him if he wanted to join a union. Mr. Max, whose heart bleeds for labor, did not tell us why his client should have resented that.

"What black thoughts passed through that Negro's scheming brain the first few moments after he saw that trusting white girl standing before him? We have no way of knowing, and perhaps this piece of human scum, who sits here today begging for mercy, is wise in not telling us. But we can use our imagination; we can look upon what he subsequently did and surmise.

"Two hours later he was driving Miss Dalton to the Loop. Here occurs the first misunderstanding in this case. The general notion is that Miss Dalton, by having this Negro drive her to the Loop instead of to school, was committing an act of disobedience against her family. But that is not for us to judge. That is for Mary Dalton and her God to settle. It was admitted by her family that she went contrary to a wish of theirs; but Mary Dalton was of age and went where she pleased.

"This Negro drove Miss Dalton to the Loop where she was joined by a young white man, a friend of hers. From there they went to a South Side café and ate and drank. Being in a Negro neighborhood, they invited this Negro to eat with them. When they talked, they included him in their conversation. When liquor was ordered, enough was bought so that he, too, could drink.

"Afterwards he drove the couple through Washington Park for some two hours. Around two o'clock in the morning this friend of Miss Dalton's left the car and went to visit some friends of his. Mary Dalton was left alone in that car with this Negro, who had received nothing from her but kindness. From that point onward, we have no exact knowledge of what really happened, for we have only this black cur's bare word for it, and I am convinced that he is not telling us all.

"We don't know just when Mary Dalton was killed. But we do know this: her head was completely severed from her body! We know that both the head and the body were stuffed into the furnace and burned!

"My God, what bloody scenes must have taken place! How swift and unexpected must have been that lustful and murderous attack! How that poor child must have struggled to escape that maddened ape! How she must have pled on bended knee, with tears in her eyes, to be spared the vile touch of his horrible person! Your Honor, must not this infernal monster have burned her body to destroy evidence of offenses *worse* than rape? That treacherous beast must have known that if the marks of his teeth were ever seen on the innocent white flesh of her breasts, he would not have been accorded the high honor of sitting here in this court of law! O suffering Christ, there are no words to tell of a deed so black and awful!

"And the defense would have us believe that this was an act of *creation*! It is a wonder that God in heaven did not drown out his lying voice with a thunderous 'NO!' It is enough to make the blood stop flowing in one's veins to hear a man excuse this cowardly and beastly crime on the ground that it was 'instinctive'!

"The next morning Bigger Thomas took Miss Dalton's trunk, half-packed, to the La Salle Street Station and prepared to send it off as though nothing had happened, as though Miss Dalton were still alive. But the bones of Miss Dalton's body were found in the furnace that evening.

"The burning of the body and the taking of the half-packed trunk to the station mean just one thing, Your Honor. It shows that the rape and murder were *planned*, that an attempt was made to destroy evidence so that the crime could be carried on to the point of ransom. If Miss Dalton were accidentally killed, as this Negro so pathetically tried to make us believe when he first 'confessed,' then why did he burn her body? Why did he take her trunk to the station when he knew that she was dead?

"There is but one answer! He planned to rape, to kill, to collect! He burned the body to get rid of evidences of *rape*! He took the trunk to the station to gain time in which to burn the body and prepare the kidnap note. He killed her because he *raped* her! Mind you, Your Honor, the central crime here is *rape*! Every action points toward that!

"Knowing that the family had called in private investigators, the Negro tried to throw the suspicion elsewhere. In other words, he was not above seeing an innocent man die for his crime. When he could not kill any more, he did the next best thing. He lied! He sought to blame the crime upon one of Miss Dalton's friends, whose political beliefs, he thought, would damn him. He told wild lies of taking the two of them, Miss Dalton and her friend, to her room. He said that he had been told to go home and leave the car ut in the snow in the driveway all night. Knowing that his lies were being found out, he tried yet another scheme. He tried to collect money!

"Did he flee the scene when the investigators were at work? No! Coldly, without feeling, he stayed on in the Dalton home, ate, slept, basking in the misguided kindness of Mr. Dalton, who refused to allow him to be questioned upon the theory that he was a poor boy who needed *protection*!

"He needed as much protection as you would give a coiled rattler!

"While the family was searching heaven and earth for their daughter, this ghoul writes a kidnap note demanding ten thousand dollars for the *safe return* of Miss Dalton! But the discovery of the bones in the furnace put that foul dream to an end!

"And the defense would have us believe that this man acted in fear! Has fear, since the beginning of time, driven men to such lengths of calculation?

"Again, we have but the bare word of this worthless ape to go on. He fled the scene and went to the home of a girl, Bessie Mears, with whom he had long been intimate. There something occurred that only a cunning beast could have done. This girl had been frightened into helping him collect the ransom money, and he had placed in her keeping the money he had stolen from the corpse of Mary Dalton. He killed that poor girl, and even yet it staggers my mind to think that such a plan for murder could have been hatched in a human brain. He persuaded this girl, who loved him deeply—despite the assertions of Mr. Max, that Godless Communist who tried to make you believe otherwise!—as I said, he persuaded this girl who loved him deeply to run away with him. They hid in an abandoned building. And there, with a blizzard raging outside, in the sub-zero cold and darkness, he committed rape and murder again, *twice* in twenty-four hours!

"I repeat, Your Honor, I cannot understand it! I have dealt with many a murderer in my long service to the state, but never have I encountered the equal of this. So eager was this demented savage to rape and kill that he forgot the only thing that might have helped him to escape; that is, the money he had stolen from the dead body of Mary Dalton, which was in the pocket of Bessie Mears' dress. He took the ravished body of that poor working girl—the money was in her dress, I say—and dumped it four floors down an air-shaft. The doctors told us that that girl was not dead when she hit the bottom of that shaft; she froze to death later, trying to climb out!

"Your Honor, I spare you the ghastly details of these murders. The witnesses have told all.

"But I demand, in the name of the people of this state, that this man die for these crimes!

"I demand this so that others may be deterred from similar crimes, so that peaceful and industrious people may be safe. Your Honor, millions are waiting for your word! They are waiting for you to tell them that jungle law does not prevail in this city! They want you to tell them that they need not sharpen their knives and load their guns to protect themselves. They are waiting, Your Honor, beyond that window! Give them your word so that they can, with calm hearts, plan for the future! Slay the dragon of doubt that causes a million hearts to pause tonight, a million hands to tremble as they lock their doors!

"When men are pursuing their normal rounds of duty and a crime as black and bloody as this is committed, they become paralyzed. The more horrible the crime, the more stunned, shocked, and dismayed is the tranquil city in which it happens; the more helpless are the citizens before it.

"Restore confidence to those of us who still survive, so that we may go on and reap the rich harvests of life. Your Honor, in the name of Almighty God, I plead with you to be merciful to us!"

Buckley's voice boomed in Bigger's ears and he knew what the loud commotion meant when the speech had ended. In the back of the room several newspapermen were scrambling for the door. Buckley wiped his red face and sat down. The judge rapped for order, and said:

"Court will adjourn for one hour."

Max was on his feet.

"Your Honor, you cannot do this . . . . Is it your intention . . . . More time is needed . . . . You. . . ."

"The Court will give its decision then," the judge said.

There were shouts. Bigger saw Max's lips moving, but he could not make out what he was saying. Slowly, the room quieted. Bigger saw that the expressions on the faces of the men and women were different now. He felt that the thing had been decided. He knew that he was to die.

"Your Honor," Max said, his voice breaking from an intensity of emotion. "It seems that for careful consideration of the evidence and discussion submitted, more time is. . . ."

"The Court reserves the right to determine how much time is needed, Mr. Max," the judge said.

Bigger knew that he was lost. It was but a matter of time, of formality.

He did not know how he got back into the little room; but when he was brought in he saw the tray of food still there, uneaten. He sat down and looked at the six policemen who stood silently by. Guns hung from their hips. Ought he to try to snatch one and shoot himself? But he did not have enough spirit to respond positively to the idea of self-destruction. He was paralyzed with dread.

Max came in, sat, and lit a cigarette.

"Well, son. We'll have to wait. We've got an hour."

There was a banging on the door.

"Don't let any of those reporters in here," Max told a policeman.

"O.K."

Minutes passed. Bigger's head began to ache with the suspense of it. He knew that Max had nothing to say to him and he had nothing to say to Max. He had to wait; that was all; wait for something he knew was coming. His throat tightened. He felt cheated. Why did they have to have a trial if it had to end this way?

"Well, I reckon it's all over for me now," Bigger sighed, speaking as much for himself as for Max.

"I don't know," Max said.

"I know," Bigger said.

"Well, let's wait."

"He's making up his mind too quick. I know I'm going to die."

"I'm sorry, Bigger. Listen, why don't you eat?"

"I ain't hungry."

"This thing isn't over yet. I can ask the Governor. . . ."

"It ain't no use. They got me."

"You don't know."

"I know."

Max said nothing. Bigger leaned his head upon the table and closed his eyes. He wished Max would leave him now. Max had done all he could. He should go home and forget him.

The door opened.

"The judge'll be ready in five minutes!"

Max stood up. Bigger looked at his tired face.

"All right, son. Come on."

Walking between policemen, Bigger followed Max back into the court room. He did not have time to sit down before the judge came. He remained standing until the judge was seated, then he slid weakly into his chair. Max rose to speak, but the judge lifted his hand for silence.

"Will Bigger Thomas rise and face the Court?"

The room was full of noise and the judged rapped for quiet. With trembling legs, Bigger rose, feeling in the grip of a nightmare.

"Is there any statement you wish to make before sentence is passed upon you?"

He tried to open his mouth to answer, but could not. Even if he had had the power of speech, he did not know what he could have said. He shook his head, his eyes blurring. The court room was profoundly quiet now. The judge wet his lips with his tongue and lifted a piece of paper that crackled loudly in the silence.

"In view of the unprecedented disturbance of the public mind, the duty of this Court is clear," the judge said and paused.

Bigger groped for the edge of the table with his hand and clung to it.

"In Number 666-983, indictment for murder, the sentence of the Court is that you, Bigger Thomas, shall die on or before midnight of Friday, March third, in a manner prescribed by the laws of this State.

"This Court finds your age to be twenty.

"The Sheriff may retire with the prisoner."

Bigger understood every word; and he seemed not to react to the words, but to the judge's face. He did not move; he stood looking up into the judge's white face, his eyes not blinking. Then he felt a hand upon his sleeve; Max was pulling him back into his seat. The room was in an uproar. The judge rapped with his gavel. Max was on his feet, trying to say something; there was too much noise and Bigger could not tell what it was. The handcuffs were clicked upon him and he was led through the underground passage back to his cell. He lay on the cot and something deep down in him said, It's over now. . . . It's all over. . . .

Later on the door opened and Max came in and sat softly beside him on the cot. Bigger turned his face to the wall.

"I'll see the Governor, Bigger. It's not over yet. . . ."

"Go 'way," Bigger whispered.

"You've got to. . . ."

"Naw. Go 'way. . . ."

He felt Max's hand on his arm; then it left. He heard the steel door clang shut and he knew that he was alone. He did not stir; he lay still, feeling that by being still he would stave off feeling and thinking, and that was what he wanted above all right now. Slowly, his body relaxed. In the darkness and silence he turned over on his back and crossed his hands upon his chest. His lips moved in a whimper of despair.

.   .   .   .

In self-defense he shut out the night and day from his mind, for if he had thought of the sun's rising and setting, of the moon or the stars, of clouds or rain, he would have died a thousand deaths before they took him to the chair. To accustom his mind to death as much as possible, he made all the world beyond his cell a vast grey land where neither night nor day was, peopled by strange men and women whom he could not understand, but with those lives he longed to mingle once before he went.

He did not eat now; he simply forced food down his throat without tasting it, to keep the gnawing pain of hunger away, to keep from feeling dizzy. And he did not sleep; at intervals he closed his eyes for a while, no matter what the hour, then opened them at some later time to resume his brooding. He wanted to be free of everything that stood between him and his end, him and the full and terrible realization that life was over without meaning, without anything being settled, without conflicting impulses being resolved.

His mother and brother and sister had come to see him and he had told them to stay home, not to come again, to forget him. The Negro preacher who had given him the cross had come and he had driven him away. A white priest had tried to persuade him to pray and he had thrown a cup of hot coffee into his face. The priest had come to see other prisoners since then, but had not stopped to talk with him. That had evoked in Bigger a sense of his worth almost as keen as that which Max had roused in him during the long talk that night. He felt that his making the priest stand away from him and wonder about his motives for refusing to accept the consolations of religion was a sort of recognition of his personality on a plane other than that which the priest was ordinarily willing to make.

Max had told him that he was going to see the Governor, but he had heard no more from him. He did not hope that anything would come of it; he referred to it in his thoughts and feelings as something happening outside of his life, which could not in any way alter or influence the course of it.

But he did want to see Max and talk with him again. He recalled the speech Max had made in court and remembered with gratitude the kind, impassioned tone. But the meaning of the words escaped him. He believed that Max knew how he felt, and once more before he died he wanted to talk with him and feel with as much keenness as possible what his living and dying meant. That was all the hope he had now. If there were any sure and firm knowledge for him, it would have to come from himself.

He was allowed to write three letters a week, but he had written to no one. There was no one to whom he had anything to say, for he had never given himself whole-heartedly to anyone or anything, except murder. What could he say to his mother and brother and sister? Of the old gang, only Jack had been his friend, and he had never been so close to Jack as he would have liked. And Bessie was dead; he had killed her.

When tired of mulling over his feelings, he would say to himself that it was he who was wrong, that he was no good. If he could have really made himself believe that, it would have been a solution. But he could not convince himself. His feelings clamored for an answer his mind could not give.

All his life he had been most alive, most himself when he had felt things hard enough to fight for them; and now here in this cell he felt more than ever the hard central core of what he had lived. As the white mountain had once loomed over him, so now the black wall of death loomed closer with each fleeting hour. But he could not strike out blindly now; death was a different and bigger adversary.

Though he lay on his cot, his hands were groping fumblingly through the city of men for something to match the feelings smoldering in him; his groping was a yearning to know. Frantically, his mind sought to fuse his feelings with the world about him, but he was no nearer to knowing than ever. Only his black body lay here on the cot, wet with the sweat of agony.

If he were nothing, if this were all, then why could not he die without hesitancy? Who and what was he to feel the agony of a wonder so intensely that it amounted to fear? Why was this strange impulse always throbbing in him when there was nothing outside of him to meet it and explain it? Who or what had traced this restless design in him? Why was this eternal reaching for something that was not there? Why this black gulf between him and the world: warm red blood here and cold blue sky there, and never a wholeness, a oneness, a meeting of the two?

Was *that* it? Was it simply fever, feeling without knowing, seeking without finding? Was this the all, the meaning, the end? With these feelings and questions the minutes passed. He grew thin and his eyes held the red blood of his body.

The eve of his last day came. He longed to talk to Max more than ever. But what could he say to him? Yes; that was the joke of it. He could not talk about this thing, so elusive it was; and yet he acted upon it every living second.

The next day at noon a guard came to his cell and poked a telegram through the bars. He sat up and opened it.

BE BRAVE GOVERNOR FAILED DONE ALL
POSSIBLE SEE YOU SOON
                                                MAX

He balled the telegram into a tight knot and threw it into a
corner.

He had from now until midnight. He had heard that six
hours before his time came they would give him some more
clothes, take him to the barber shop, and then take him to the
death cell. He had been told by one of the guards not to
worry, that "eight seconds after they take you out of your cell
and put that black cap over your eyes, you'll be dead, boy."
Well, he could stand that. He had in his mind a plan: he
would flex his muscles and shut his eyes and hold his breath
and think of absolutely nothing while they were handling
him. And when the current struck him, it would all be over.

He lay down again on the cot, on his back, and stared at
the tiny bright-yellow electric bulb glowing on the ceiling
above his head. It contained the fire of death. If only those
tiny spirals of heat inside of that glass globe would wrap
round him now—if only someone would attach the wires to
his iron cot while he dozed off—if only when he was in a
deep dream they would kill him. . . .

He was in an uneasy sleep when he heard the voice of a
guard.

"Thomas! Here's your lawyer!"

He swung his feet to the floor and sat up. Max was standing at the bars. The guard unlocked the door and Max walked
in. Bigger had an impulse to rise, but he remained seated.
Max came to the center of the floor and stopped. They looked
at each other for a moment.

"Hello, Bigger."

Silently, Bigger shook hands with him. Max was before
him, quiet, white, solid, real. His tangible presence seemed to
belie all the vague thoughts and hopes that Bigger had woven
round him in his broodings. He was glad that Max had come,
but he was bewildered.

"How're you feeling?"

For an answer, Bigger sighed heavily.

"You get my wire?" Max asked, sitting on the cot.

Bigger nodded.

"I'm sorry, son."

There was silence. Max was at his side. The man who had lured him on a quest toward a dim hope was there. Well, why didn't he speak now? Here was his chance, his last chance. He lifted his eyes shyly to Max's; Max was looking at him. Bigger looked off. What he wanted to say was stronger in him when he was alone; and though he imputed to Max the feelings he wanted to grasp, he could not talk of them to Max until he had forgotten Max's presence. Then fear that he would not be able to talk about this consuming fever made him panicky. He struggled for self-control; he did not want to lose this driving impulse; it was all he had. And in the next second he felt that it was all foolish, useless, vain. He stopped trying, and in the very moment he stopped, he heard himself talking with tight throat, in tense, involuntary whispers; he was trusting the sound of his voice rather than the sense of his words to carry his meaning.

"I'm all right, Mr. Max. You ain't to blame for what's happening to me . . . . I know you did all you could . . . ." Under the pressure of a feeling of futility his voice trailed off. After a short silence he blurted, "I just r-r-reckon I h-had it coming. . . ." He stood up, full now, wanting to talk. His lips moved, but no words came.

"Is there anything I can do for you, Bigger?" Max asked softly.

Bigger looked at Max's grey eyes. How could he get into that man a sense of what he wanted? If he could only tell him! Before he was aware of what he was doing, he ran to the door and clutched the cold steel bars in his hands.

"I—I. . . ."

"Yes, Bigger?"

Slowly, Bigger turned and came back to the cot. He stood before Max again, about to speak, his right hand raised. Then he sat down and bowed his head.

"What is it, Bigger? Is there anything you want me to do on the outside? Any message you want to send?"

"Naw," he breathed.

"What's on your mind?"

"I don't know."

He could not talk. Max reached over and placed a hand on his shoulder, and Bigger could tell by its touch that Max did not know, had no suspicion of what he wanted, of what he was trying to say. Max was upon another planet, far off in space. Was there any way to break down this wall of isolation? Distractedly, he gazed about the cell, trying to remember where he had heard words that would help him. He could recall none. He had lived outside of the lives of men. Their modes of communication, their symbols and images, had been denied him. Yet Max had given him the faith that at bottom all men lived as he lived and felt as he felt. And of all the men he had met, surely Max knew what he was trying to say. Had Max left him? Had Max, knowing that he was to die, thrust him from his thoughts and feelings, assigned him to the grave? Was he already numbered among the dead? His lips quivered and his eyes grew misty. Yes; Max had left him. Max was not a friend. Anger welled in him. But he knew that anger was useless.

Max rose and went to a small window; a pale bar of sunshine fell across his white head. And Bigger, looking at him, saw that sunshine for the first time in many days; and as he saw it, the entire cell, with its four close walls, became crushingly real. He glanced down at himself; the shaft of yellow sun cut across his chest with as much weight as a beam forged of lead. With a convulsive gasp, he bent forward and shut his eyes. It was not a white mountain looming over him now; Gus was not whistling "The Merry-Go-Round Broke Down" as he came into Doc's poolroom to make him go and rob Blum's; he was not standing over Mary's bed with the white blur hovering near;—this new adversary did not make him taut; it sapped strength and left him weak. He summoned his energies and lifted his head and struck out desperately, determined to rise from the grave, resolved to force upon Max the reality of his living.

"I'm glad I got to know you before I go!" he said with almost a shout; then was silent, for that was not what he had wanted to say.

Max turned and looked at him; it was a casual look, devoid of the deeper awareness that Bigger sought so hungrily.

"I'm glad I got to know you, too, Bigger. I'm sorry we

have to part this way. But I'm old, son. I'll be going soon myself. . . ."

"I remembered all them questions you asked me. . . ."

"What questions?" Max asked, coming and sitting again on the cot.

"That night. . . ."

"What night, son?"

Max did not even *know*! Bigger felt that he had been slapped. Oh, what a fool he had been to build hope upon such shifting sand! But he had to *make* him know!

"That night you asked me to tell all about myself," he whimpered despairingly.

"Oh."

He saw Max look at the floor and frown. He knew that Max was puzzled.

"You asked me questions nobody ever asked me before. You knew that I was a murderer two times over, but you treated me like a man. . . ."

Max looked at him sharply and rose from his cot. He stood in front of Bigger for a moment and Bigger was on the verge of believing that Max knew, understood; but Max's next words showed him that the white man was still trying to comfort him in the face of death.

"You're human, Bigger," Max said wearily. "It's hell to talk about things like this to one about to die. . . ." Max paused; Bigger knew that he was searching for words that would soothe him, and he did not want them. "Bigger," Max said, "in the work I'm doing, I look at the world in a way that shows no whites and no blacks, no civilized and no savages. . . . When men are trying to change human life on earth, those little things don't matter. You don't notice 'em. They're just not there. You forget them. The reason I spoke to you as I did, Bigger, is because you made me feel how badly men want to live. . . ."

"But sometimes I wish you hadn't asked me them questions," Bigger said in a voice that had as much reproach in it for Max as it had for himself.

"What do you mean, Bigger?"

"They made me think and thinking's made me scared a little. . . ."

Max caught Bigger's shoulders in a tight grip; then his fingers loosened and he sank back to the cot; but his eyes were still fastened upon Bigger's face. Yes; Max knew now. Under the shadow of death, he wanted Max to tell him about life.

"Mr. Max, how can I die!" Bigger asked; knowing as the words boomed from his lips that a knowledge of how to live was a knowledge of how to die.

Max turned his face from him, and mumbled,

"Men die alone, Bigger."

But Bigger had not heard him. In him again, imperiously, was the desire to talk, to tell; his hands were lifted in mid-air and when he spoke he tried to charge into the tone of his words what he *himself* wanted to hear, what *he* needed.

"Mr. Max, I sort of saw myself after that night. And I sort of saw other people, too." Bigger's voice died; he was listening to the echoes of his words in his own mind. He saw amazement and horror on Max's face. Bigger knew that Max would rather not have him talk like this; but he could not help it. He had to die and he had to talk. "Well, it's sort of funny, Mr. Max. I ain't trying to dodge what's coming to me." Bigger was growing hysterical. "I know I'm going to get it. I'm going to die. Well, that's all right now. But really I never wanted to hurt nobody. That's the truth, Mr. Max. I hurt folks 'cause I felt I had to; that's all. They was crowding me too close; they wouldn't give me no room. Lots of times I tried to forget 'em, but I couldn't. They wouldn't let me. . . ." Bigger's eyes were wide and unseeing; his voice rushed on: "Mr. Max, I didn't mean to do what I did. I was trying to do something else. But it seems like I never could. I was always wanting something and I was feeling that nobody would let me have it. So I fought 'em. I thought they was hard and I acted hard." He paused, then whimpered in confession, "But I ain't hard, Mr. Max. I ain't hard even a little bit. . . ." He rose to his feet. "But. . . . I—I won't be crying none when they take me to that chair. But I'll b-b-be feeling inside of me like I was crying. . . . I'll be feeling and thinking that they didn't see me and I didn't see them. . . ." He ran to the steel door and caught the bars in his hands and shook them, as though trying to tear the steel from its concrete moorings. Max went to him and grabbed his shoulders.

"Bigger," Max said helplessly.

Bigger grew still and leaned weakly against the door.

"Mr. Max, I know the folks who sent me here to die hated me; I know that. B-b-but you reckon th-they was like m-me, trying to g-get something like I was, and when I'm dead and gone they'll be saying like I'm saying now that they didn't mean to hurt nobody . . . th-that they was t-trying to get something, too. . . . ?"

Max did not answer. Bigger saw a look of indecision and wonder come into the old man's eyes.

"Tell me, Mr. Max. You think they was?"

"Bigger," Max pleaded.

"*Tell* me, Mr. Max!"

Max shook his head and mumbled,

"You're asking me to say things I don't want to say. . . ."

"But I want to *know*!"

"You're going to die, Bigger. . . ."

Max's voice faded. Bigger knew that the old man had not wanted to say that; he had said it because he had pushed him, had made him say it. They were silent for a moment longer, then Bigger whispered,

"That's why I want to know. . . . I reckon it's 'cause I know I'm going to die that makes me want to know. . . ."

Max's face was ashy. Bigger feared that he was going to leave. Across a gulf of silence, they looked at each other. Max sighed.

"Come here, Bigger," he said.

He followed Max to the window and saw in the distance the tips of sun-drenched buildings in the Loop.

"See all those buildings, Bigger?" Max asked, placing an arm about Bigger's shoulders. He spoke hurriedly, as though trying to mold a substance which was warm and pliable, but which might soon cool.

"Yeah. I see 'em. . . ."

"You lived in one of them once, Bigger. They're made out of steel and stone. But the steel and stone don't hold 'em together. You know what holds those buildings up, Bigger? You know what keeps them in their place, keeps them from tumbling down?"

Bigger looked at him, bewildered.

"It's the belief of men. If men stopped believing, stopped having faith, they'd come tumbling down. Those buildings sprang up out of the hearts of men, Bigger. Men like you. Men kept hungry, kept needing, and those buildings kept growing and unfolding. You once told me you wanted to do a lot of things. Well, that's the feeling that keeps those buildings in their places. . . ."

"You mean. . . . You talking about what I said that night, when I said I wanted to do a lot of things?" Bigger's voice came quiet, childlike in its tone of hungry wonder.

"Yes. What you felt, what you wanted, is what keeps those buildings standing there. When millions of men are desiring and longing, those buildings grow and unfold. But, Bigger, those buildings aren't growing any more. A few men are squeezing those buildings tightly in their hands. The buildings can't unfold, can't feed the dreams men have, men like you. . . . The men on the inside of those buildings have begun to doubt, just as you did. They don't believe any more. They don't feel it's their world. They're restless, like you, Bigger. They have nothing. There's nothing through which they can grow and unfold. They go in the streets and they stand outside of those buildings and look and wonder. . . ."

"B-b-but what they hate me for?" Bigger asked.

"The men who own those buildings are afraid. They want to keep what they own, even if it makes others suffer. In order to keep it, they push men down in the mud and tell them that they are beasts. But men, men like you, get angry and fight to re-enter those buildings, to live again. Bigger, you killed. That was wrong. That was not the way to do it. It's too late now for you to . . . work with . . . others who are t-trying to . . . believe and make the world live again. . . . But it's not too late to believe what you felt, to understand what you felt. . . ."

Bigger was gazing in the direction of the buildings; but he did not see them. He was trying to react to the picture Max was drawing, trying to compare that picture with what he had felt all his life.

"I always wanted to do something," he mumbled.

They were silent and Max did not speak again until Bigger looked at him. Max closed his eyes.

"Bigger, you're going to die. And if you die, die free. You're trying to believe in yourself. And every time you try to find a way to live, your own mind stands in the way. You know why that is? It's because others have said you were bad and they made you live in bad conditions. When a man hears that over and over and looks about him and sees that his life *is* bad, he begins to doubt his own mind. His feelings drag him forward and his mind, full of what others say about him, tells him to go back. The job in getting people to fight and have faith is in making them believe in what life has made them feel, making them feel that their feelings are as good as those of others.

"Bigger, the people who hate you feel just as you feel, only they're on the other side of the fence. You're black, but that's only a part of it. Your being black, as I told you before, makes it easy for them to single you out. Why do they do that? They want the things of life, just as you did, and they're not particular about how they get them. They hire people and they don't pay them enough; they take what people own and build up power. They rule and regulate life. They have things arranged so that they can do those things and the people can't fight back. They do that to black people more than others because they say that black people are inferior. But, Bigger, they say that *all* people who work are inferior. And the rich people don't want to change things; they'll lose too much. But deep down in them they feel like you feel, Bigger, and in order to keep what they've got, they make themselves believe that men who work are not quite human. They do like you did, Bigger, when you refused to feel sorry for Mary. But on both sides men want to live; men are fighting for life. Who will win? Well, the side that feels life most, the side with the most humanity and the most men. That's why . . . y-you've got to b-believe in yourself, Bigger. . . ."

Max's head jerked up in surprise when Bigger laughed.

"Aw, I reckon I believe in myself. . . . I ain't got nothing else. . . . I got to die. . . ."

He stepped over to Max. Max was leaning against the window.

"Mr. Max, you go home. I'm all right. . . . Sounds funny, Mr. Max, but when I think about what you say I kind of feel

what I wanted. It makes me feel I was kind of right. . . ."
Max opened his mouth to say something and Bigger drowned
out his voice. "I ain't trying to forgive nobody and I ain't
asking for nobody to forgive me. I ain't going to cry. They
wouldn't let me live and I killed. Maybe it ain't fair to kill,
and I reckon I really didn't want to kill. But when I think of
why all the killing was, I begin to feel what I wanted, what I
am. . . ."

Bigger saw Max back away from him with compressed lips.
But he felt he had to make Max understand how he saw
things now.

"I didn't want to kill!" Bigger shouted. "But what I killed
for, I *am*! It must've been pretty deep in me to make me kill!
I must have felt it awful hard to murder. . . ."

Max lifted his hand to touch Bigger, but did not.

"No; no; no. . . . Bigger, not that. . . ." Max pleaded
despairingly.

"What I killed for must've been good!" Bigger's voice was
full of frenzied anguish. "It must have been good! When a
man kills, it's for something. . . . I didn't know I was really
alive in this world until I felt things hard enough to kill for
'em. . . . It's the truth, Mr. Max. I can say it now, 'cause I'm
going to die. I know what I'm saying real good and I know
how it sounds. But I'm all right. I feel all right when I look at
it that way. . . ."

Max's eyes were full of terror. Several times his body
moved nervously, as though he were about to go to Bigger;
but he stood still.

"I'm all right, Mr. Max. Just go and tell Ma I was all right
and not to worry none, see? Tell her I was all right and wasn't
crying none. . . ."

Max's eyes were wet. Slowly, he extended his hand. Bigger
shook it.

"Good-bye, Bigger," he said quietly.

"Good-bye, Mr. Max."

Max groped for his hat like a blind man; he found it and
jammed it on his head. He felt for the door, keeping his face
averted. He poked his arm through and signaled for the
guard. When he was let out he stood for a moment, his back
to the steel door. Bigger grasped the bars with both hands.

"Mr. Max. . . ."

"Yes, Bigger." He did not turn around.

"I'm all right. For real, I am."

"Good-bye, Bigger."

"Good-bye, Mr. Max."

Max walked down the corridor.

"Mr. Max!"

Max paused, but did not look.

"Tell. . . . Tell Mister. . . . Tell Jan hello. . . ."

"All right, Bigger."

"Good-bye!"

"Good-bye!"

He still held on to the bars. Then he smiled a faint, wry, bitter smile. He heard the ring of steel against steel as a far door clanged shut.

HOW "BIGGER" WAS BORN

To

Abe, Belle, Mannie and Lora

How "Bigger" Was Born

I AM NOT so pretentious as to imagine that it is possible for
me to account completely for my own book, *Native Son*.
But I am going to try to account for as much of it as I can,
the sources of it, the material that went into it, and my own
years' long changing attitude toward that material.

In a fundamental sense, an imaginative novel represents the
merging of two extremes; it is an intensely intimate expression on the part of a consciousness couched in terms of the
most objective and commonly known events. It is at once
something private and public by its very nature and texture.
Confounding the author who is trying to lay his cards on the
table is the dogging knowledge that his imagination is a kind
of community medium of exchange: what he has read, felt,
thought, seen, and remembered is translated into extensions
as impersonal as a worn dollar bill.

The more closely the author thinks of why he wrote, the
more he comes to regard his imagination as a kind of self-
generating cement which glued his facts together, and his
emotions as a kind of dark and obscure designer of those
facts. Always there is something that is just beyond the tip of
the tongue that could explain it all. Usually, he ends up by
discussing something far afield, an act which incites skep-
ticism and suspicion in those anxious for a straight-out
explanation.

Yet the author is eager to explain. But the moment he
makes the attempt his words falter, for he is confronted and
defied by the inexplicable array of his own emotions. Emotions are subjective and he can communicate them only when
he clothes them in objective guise; and how can he ever be so
arrogant as to know when he is dressing up the right emotion
in the right Sunday suit? He is always left with the uneasy
notion that maybe *any* objective drapery is as good as *any*
other for any emotion.

And the moment he does dress up an emotion, his mind is
confronted with the riddle of that "dressed up" emotion, and
he is left peering with eager dismay back into the dim reaches
of his own incommunicable life. Reluctantly, he comes to the

conclusion that to account for his book is to account for his life, and he knows that that is impossible. Yet, some curious, wayward motive urges him to supply the answer, for there is the feeling that his dignity as a living being is challenged by something within him that is not understood.

So, at the outset, I say frankly that there are phases of *Native Son* which I shall make no attempt to account for. There are meanings in my book of which I was not aware until they literally spilled out upon the paper. I shall sketch the outline of how I *consciously* came into possession of the materials that went into *Native Son*, but there will be many things I shall omit, not because I want to, but simply because I don't know them.

The birth of Bigger Thomas goes back to my childhood, and there was not just one Bigger, but many of them, more than I could count and more than you suspect. But let me start with the first Bigger, whom I shall call Bigger No. 1.

When I was a bareheaded, barefoot kid in Jackson, Mississippi, there was a boy who terrorized me and all of the boys I played with. If we were playing games, he would saunter up and snatch from us our balls, bats, spinning tops, and marbles. We would stand around pouting, sniffling, trying to keep back our tears, begging for our playthings. But Bigger would refuse. We never demanded that he give them back; we were afraid, and Bigger was bad. We had seen him clout boys when he was angry and we did not want to run that risk. We never recovered our toys unless we flattered him and made him feel that he was superior to us. Then, perhaps, if he felt like it, he condescended, threw them at us and then gave each of us a swift kick in the bargain, just to make us feel his utter contempt.

That was the way Bigger No. 1 lived. His life was a continuous challenge to others. At all times he *took* his way, right or wrong, and those who contradicted him had him to fight. And never was he happier than when he had someone cornered and at his mercy; it seemed that the deepest meaning of his squalid life was in him at such times.

I don't know what the fate of Bigger No. 1 was. His swaggering personality is swallowed up somewhere in the amnesia of my childhood. But I suspect that his end was violent.

Anyway, he left a marked impression upon me; maybe it was because I longed secretly to be like him and was afraid. I don't know.

If I had known only one Bigger I would not have written *Native Son*. Let me call the next one Bigger No. 2; he was about seventeen and tougher than the first Bigger. Since I, too, had grown older, I was a little less afraid of him. And the hardness of this Bigger No. 2 was not directed toward me or the other Negroes, but toward the whites who ruled the South. He bought clothes and food on credit and would not pay for them. He lived in the dingy shacks of the white land-lords and refused to pay rent. Of course, he had no money, but neither did we. We did without the necessities of life and starved ourselves, but he never would. When we asked him why he acted as he did, he would tell us (as though we were little children in a kindergarten) that the white folks had everything and he had nothing. Further, he would tell us that we were fools not to get what we wanted while we were alive in this world. We would listen and silently agree. We longed to believe and act as he did, but we were afraid. We were Southern Negroes and we were hungry and we wanted to live, but we were more willing to tighten our belts than risk conflict. Bigger No. 2 wanted to live and he did; he was in prison the last time I heard from him.

There was Bigger No. 3, whom the white folks called a "bad nigger." He carried his life in his hands in a literal fash-ion. I once worked as a ticket-taker in a Negro movie house (all movie houses in Dixie are Jim Crow; there are movies for whites and movies for blacks), and many times Bigger No. 3 came to the door and gave my arm a hard pinch and walked into the theater. Resentfully and silently, I'd nurse my bruised arm. Presently, the proprietor would come over and ask how things were going. I'd point into the darkened theater and say: "Bigger's in there." "Did he pay?" the proprietor would ask. "No, sir," I'd answer. The proprietor would pull down the corners of his lips and speak through his teeth: "We'll kill that goddamn nigger one of these days." And the episode would end right there. But later on Bigger No. 3 was killed during the days of Prohibition: while delivering liquor to a customer he was shot through the back by a white cop.

And then there was Bigger No. 4, whose only law was death. The Jim Crow laws of the South were not for him. But as he laughed and cursed and broke them, he knew that some day he'd have to pay for his freedom. His rebellious spirit made him violate all the taboos and consequently he always oscillated between moods of intense elation and depression. He was never happier than when he had outwitted some foolish custom, and he was never more melancholy than when brooding over the impossibility of his ever being free. He had no job, for he regarded digging ditches for fifty cents a day as slavery. "I can't live on that," he would say. Ofttimes I'd find him reading a book; he would stop and in a joking, wistful, and cynical manner ape the antics of the white folks. Generally, he'd end his mimicry in a depressed state and say: "The white folks won't let us do nothing." Bigger No. 4 was sent to the asylum for the insane.

Then there was Bigger No. 5, who always rode the Jim Crow streetcars without paying and sat wherever he pleased. I remember one morning his getting into a streetcar (all streetcars in Dixie are divided into two sections: one section is for whites and is labeled—FOR WHITES; the other section is for Negroes and is labeled—FOR COLORED) and sitting in the white section. The conductor went to him and said: "Come on, nigger. Move over where you belong. Can't you read?" Bigger answered: "Naw, I can't read." The conductor flared up: "Get out of that seat!" Bigger took out his knife, opened it, held it nonchalantly in his hand, and replied: "Make me." The conductor turned red, blinked, clenched his fists, and walked away, stammering: "The goddamn scum of the earth!" A small angry conference of white men took place in the front of the car and the Negroes sitting in the Jim Crow section overheard: "That's that Bigger Thomas nigger and you'd better leave 'im alone." The Negroes experienced an intense flash of pride and the streetcar moved on its journey without incident. I don't know what happened to Bigger No. 5. But I can guess.

The Bigger Thomases were the only Negroes I know of who consistently violated the Jim Crow laws of the South and got away with it, at least for a sweet brief spell. Eventually, the whites who restricted their lives made them pay a terrible price. They were shot, hanged, maimed, lynched, and generally hounded until they were either dead or their spirits broken.

There were many variations to this behavioristic pattern. Later on I encountered other Bigger Thomases who did not react to the locked-in Black Belts with this same extremity and violence. But before I use Bigger Thomas as a springboard for the examination of milder types, I'd better indicate more precisely the nature of the environment that produced these men, or the reader will be left with the impression that they were essentially and organically bad.

In Dixie there are two worlds, the white world and the black world, and they are physically separated. There are white schools and black schools, white churches and black churches, white businesses and black businesses, white graveyards and black graveyards, and, for all I know, a white God and a black God. . . .

This separation was accomplished after the Civil War by the terror of the Klu Klux Klan, which swept the newly freed Negro through arson, pillage, and death out of the United States Senate, the House of Representatives, the many state legislatures, and out of the public, social, and economic life of the South. The motive for this assault was simple and urgent. The imperialistic tug of history had torn the Negro from his African home and had placed him ironically upon the most fertile plantation areas of the South; and, when the Negro was freed, he outnumbered the whites in many of these fertile areas. Hence, a fierce and bitter struggle took place to keep the ballot from the Negro, for had he had a chance to vote, he would have automatically controlled the richest lands of the South and with them the social, political, and economic destiny of a third of the Republic. Though the South is politically a part of America, the problem that faced her was peculiar and the struggle between the whites and the blacks after the Civil War was in essence a struggle for power, ranging over thirteen states and involving the lives of tens of millions of people.

But keeping the ballot from the Negro was not enough to hold him in check; disfranchisement had to be supplemented by a whole panoply of rules, taboos, and penalties designed not only to insure peace (complete submission), but to guarantee that no real threat would ever arise. Had the Negro lived upon a common territory, separate from the bulk of the white population, this program of oppression might not have assumed such a brutal and violent form. But this war took place between people who were neighbors, whose homes adjoined, whose farms had common boundaries. Guns and disfranchisement, therefore, were not enough to make the black neighbor keep his distance. The white neighbor decided to limit the amount of education his black neighbor could receive; decided to keep him off the police force and out of the local national guards; to segregate him residentially; to Jim Crow him in public places; to restrict his participation in the professions and jobs; and to build up a vast, dense ideology of racial superiority that would justify any act of violence taken against him to defend white dominance; and further, to condition him to hope for little and to receive that little without rebelling.

But, because the blacks were so *close* to the very civilization which sought to keep them out, because they could not *help* but react in some way to its incentives and prizes, and because the very tissue of their consciousness received its tone and timbre from the strivings of that dominant civilization, oppression spawned among them a myriad variety of reactions, reaching from outright blind rebellion to a sweet, other-worldly submissiveness.

In the main, this delicately balanced state of affairs has not greatly altered since the Civil War, save in those parts of the South which have been industrialized or urbanized. So volatile and tense are these relations that if a Negro rebels against rule and taboo, he is lynched and the reason for the lynching is usually called "rape," that catchword which has garnered such vile connotations that it can raise a mob anywhere in the South pretty quickly, even today.

Now for the variations in the Bigger Thomas pattern. Some of the Negroes living under these conditions got religion, felt that Jesus would redeem the void of living, felt that the more bitter life was in the present the happier it would be in the hereafter. Others, clinging still to that brief glimpse of post–Civil War freedom, employed a thousand ruses and stratagems of struggle to win their rights. Still others projected their hurts and longings into more naïve and mundane forms—blues, jazz, swing—and, without intellectual guidance, tried to build up a compensatory nourishment for themselves. Many labored under hot suns and then killed the restless ache with alcohol. Then there were those who strove for an education, and when they got it, enjoyed the financial fruits of it in the style of their bourgeois oppressors. Usually they went hand in hand with the powerful whites and helped to keep their groaning brothers in line, for that was the safest course of action. Those who did this called themselves "leaders." To give you an idea of how completely these "leaders" worked with those who oppressed, I can tell you that I lived the first seventeen years of my life in the South without so much as hearing of or seeing one act of rebellion from *any* Negro, save the Bigger Thomases.

But why did Bigger revolt? No explanation based upon a hard and fast rule of conduct can be given. But there were always two factors psychologically dominant in his personality. First, through some quirk of circumstance, he had become estranged from the religion and the folk culture of his race. Second, he was trying to react to and answer the call of the dominant civilization whose glitter came to him through the newspapers, magazines, radios, movies, and the mere imposing sight and sound of daily American life. In many respects his emergence as a distinct type was inevitable.

As I grew older, I became familiar with the Bigger Thomas conditioning and its numerous shadings no matter where I saw it in Negro life. It was not, as I have already said, as blatant or extreme as in the originals; but it was there, nevertheless, like an undeveloped negative.

Sometimes, in areas far removed from Mississippi, I'd hear a Negro say: "I wish I didn't have to live this way. I feel like I want to burst." Then the anger would pass; he would go back to his job and try to eke out a few pennies to support his wife and children.

Sometimes I'd hear a Negro say: "God, I wish I had a flag and a country of my own." But that mood would soon vanish and he would go his way placidly enough.

Sometimes I'd hear a Negro ex-soldier say: "What in hell

did I fight in the war for? They segregated me even when I was offering my life for my country." But he, too, like the others, would soon forget, would become caught up in the tense grind of struggling for bread.

I've even heard Negroes, in moments of anger and bitterness, praise what Japan is doing in China, not because they believed in oppression (being objects of oppression themselves), but because they would suddenly sense how empty their lives were when looking at the dark faces of Japanese generals in the rotogravure supplements of the Sunday newspapers. They would dream of what it would be like to live in a country where they could forget their color and play a responsible role in the vital processes of the nation's life.

I've even heard Negroes say that maybe Hitler and Mussolini are all right; that maybe Stalin is all right. They did not say this out of any intellectual comprehension of the forces at work in the world, but because they felt that these men "did things," a phrase which is charged with more meaning than the mere words imply. There was in the back of their minds, when they said this, a wild and intense longing (wild and intense because it was suppressed!) to belong, to be identified, to feel that they were alive as other people were, to be caught up forgetfully and exultingly in the swing of events, to feel the clean, deep, organic satisfaction of doing a job in common with others.

It was not until I went to live in Chicago that I first thought seriously of writing of Bigger Thomas. Two items of my experience combined to make me aware of Bigger as a meaningful and prophetic symbol. First, being free of the daily pressure of the Dixie environment, I was able to come into possession of my own feelings. Second, my contact with the labor movement and its ideology made me see Bigger clearly and feel what he meant.

I made the discovery that Bigger Thomas was not black all the time; he was white, too, and there were literally millions of him, everywhere. The extension of my sense of the personality of Bigger was the pivot of my life; it altered the complexion of my existence. I became conscious, at first dimly, and then later on with increasing clarity and conviction, of a vast, muddied pool of human life in America. It was as though I had put on a pair of spectacles whose power was that of an x-ray enabling me to see deeper into the lives of men. Whenever I picked up a newspaper, I'd no longer feel that I was reading of the doings of whites alone (Negroes are rarely mentioned in the press unless they've committed some crime!), but of a complex struggle for life going on in my country, a struggle in which I was involved. I sensed, too, that the Southern scheme of oppression was but an appendage of a far vaster and in many respects more ruthless and impersonal commodity-profit machine.

Trade-union struggles and issues began to grow meaningful to me. The flow of goods across the seas, buoying and depressing the wages of men, held a fascination. The pronouncements of foreign governments, their policies, plans, and acts were calculated and weighed in relation to the lives of people about me. I was literally overwhelmed when, in reading the works of Russian revolutionists, I came across descriptions of the "holiday energies of the masses," "the locomotives of history," "the conditions prerequisite for revolution," and so forth. I approached all of these new revelations in the light of Bigger Thomas, his hopes, fears, and despairs; and I began to feel far-flung kinships, and sense, with fright and abashment, the possibilities of *alliances* between the American Negro and other people possessing a kindred consciousness.

As my mind extended in this general and abstract manner, it was fed with even more vivid and concrete examples of the lives of Bigger Thomas. The urban environment of Chicago, affording a more stimulating life, made the Negro Bigger Thomases react more violently than even in the South. More than ever I began to see and understand the environmental factors which made for this extreme conduct. It was not that Chicago segregated Negroes more than the South, but that Chicago had more to offer, that Chicago's physical aspect— noisy, crowded, filled with the sense of power and fulfillment—did so much more to dazzle the mind with a taunting sense of possible achievement that the segregation it did impose brought forth from Bigger a reaction more obstreperous than in the South.

So the concrete picture and the abstract linkages of rela-

tionships fed each other, each making the other more meaningful and affording my emotions an opportunity to react to
them with success and understanding. The process was like a
swinging pendulum, each to and fro motion throwing up its
tiny bit of meaning and significance, each stroke helping to
develop the dim negative which had been implanted in my
mind in the South.

During this period the shadings and nuances which were
filling in Bigger's picture came, not so much from Negro life,
as from the lives of whites I met and grew to know. I began
to sense that they had their own kind of Bigger Thomas
behavioristic pattern which grew out of a more subtle and
broader frustration. The waves of recurring crime, the silly
fads and crazes, the quicksilver changes in public taste, the
hysteria and fears—all of these had long been mysteries to
me. But now I looked back of them and felt the pinch and
pressure of the environment that gave them their pitch and
peculiar kind of being. I began to feel with my mind the inner
tensions of the people I met. I don't mean to say that I think
that environment *makes* consciousness (I suppose God makes
that, if there is a God), but I do say that I felt and still feel
that the environment supplies the instrumentalities through
which the organism expresses itself, and if that environment is
warped or tranquil, the mode and manner of behavior will be
affected toward deadlocking tensions or orderly fulfillment
and satisfaction.

Let me give examples of how I began to develop the dim
negative of Bigger. I met white writers who talked of their
responses, who told me how whites reacted to this lurid
American scene. And, as they talked, I'd translate what they
said in terms of Bigger's life. But what was more important
still, I read their novels. Here, for the first time, I found ways
and techniques of gauging meaningfully the effects of American civilization upon the personalities of people. I took these
techniques, these ways of seeing and feeling, and twisted
them, bent them, adapted them, until they became *my* ways of
apprehending the locked-in life of the Black Belt areas. This
association with white writers was the life preserver of my
hope to depict Negro life in fiction, for my race possessed no
fictional works dealing with such problems, had no back-

ground in such sharp and critical testing of experience, no novels that went with a deep and fearless will down to the dark roots of life.

Here are examples of how I culled information relating to Bigger from my reading:

There is in me a memory of reading an interesting pamphlet telling of the friendship of Gorky and Lenin in exile. The booklet told of how Lenin and Gorky were walking down a London street. Lenin turned to Gorky and, pointing, said: "Here is *their* Big Ben." "There is *their* Westminster Abbey." "There is *their* library." And at once, while reading that passage, my mind stopped, teased, challenged with the effort to remember, to associate widely disparate but meaningful experiences in my life. For a moment nothing would come, but I remained convinced that I had heard the meaning of those words sometime, somewhere before. Then, with a sudden glow of satisfaction of having gained a little more knowledge about the world in which I lived, I'd end up by saying: "That's Bigger. That's the Bigger Thomas reaction."

In both instances the deep sense of exclusion was identical. The feeling of looking at things with a painful and unwarrantable nakedness was an experience, I learned, that transcended national and racial boundaries. It was this intolerable sense of feeling and understanding so much, and yet living on a plane of social reality where the look of a world which one did not make or own struck one with a blinding objectivity and tangibility, that made me grasp the revolutionary impulse in my life and the lives of those about me and far away.

I remember reading a passage in a book dealing with old Russia which said: "We must be ready to make endless sacrifices if we are to be able to overthrow the Czar." And again I'd say to myself: "I've heard that somewhere, sometime before." And again I'd hear Bigger Thomas, far away and long ago, telling some white man who was trying to impose upon him: "I'll kill you and go to hell and pay for it." While living in America I heard from far away Russia the bitter accents of tragic calculation of how much human life and suffering it would cost a man to live as a man in a world that denied him the right to live with dignity. Actions and feelings of men ten thousand miles from home helped me to understand the moods and impulses of those walking the streets of Chicago and Dixie.

I am not saying that I heard any talk of revolution in the South when I was a kid there. But I did hear the lispings, the whispers, the mutters which some day, under one stimulus or another, will surely grow into open revolt unless the conditions which produce Bigger Thomases are changed.

In 1932 another source of information was dramatically opened up to me and I saw data of a surprising nature that helped to clarify the personality of Bigger. From the moment that Hitler took power in Germany and began to oppress the Jews, I tried to keep track of what was happening. And on innumerable occasions I was startled to detect, either from the side of the Fascists or from the side of the oppressed, reactions, moods, phrases, attitudes that reminded me strongly of Bigger, that helped to bring out more clearly the shadowy outlines of the negative that lay in the back of my mind.

I read every account of the Fascist movement in Germany I could lay my hands on, and from page to page I encountered and recognized familiar emotional patterns. What struck me with particular force was the Nazi preoccupation with the construction of a society in which there would exist among all people (*German* people, of course!) *one* solidarity of ideals, *one* continuous circulation of fundamental beliefs, notions, and assumptions. I am not now speaking of the popular idea of regimenting people's thought; I'm speaking of the implicit, almost unconscious, or pre-conscious, assumptions and ideals upon which whole nations and races act and live. And while reading these Nazi pages I'd be reminded of the Negro preacher in the South telling of a life beyond this world, a life in which the color of men's skins would not matter, a life in which each man would know what was deep down in the hearts of his fellow man. And I could hear Bigger Thomas standing on a street corner in America expressing his agonizing doubts and chronic suspicions, thus: "I ain't going to trust nobody. Everything is a racket and everybody is out to get what he can for himself. Maybe if we had a true leader, we could do something." And I'd know that I was still on the track of learning about Bigger, still in the midst of the modern struggle for solidarity among men.

When the Nazis spoke of the necessity of a highly ritualized and symbolized life, I could hear Bigger Thomas on Chicago's South Side saying: "Man, what we need is a leader like Marcus Garvey. We need a nation, a flag, an army of our own. We colored folks ought to organize into groups and have generals, captains, lieutenants, and so forth. We ought to take Africa and have a national home." I'd know, while listening to these childish words, that a white man would smile derisively at them. But I could not smile, for I knew the truth of those simple words from the facts of my own life. The deep hunger in those childish ideas was like a flash of lightning illuminating the whole dark inner landscape of Bigger's mind. Those words told me that the civilization which had given birth to Bigger contained no spiritual sustenance, had created no culture which could hold and claim his allegiance and faith, had sensitized him and had left him stranded, a free agent to roam the streets of our cities, a hot and whirling vortex of undisciplined and unchannelized impulses. The results of these observations made me feel more than ever estranged from the civilization in which I lived, and more than ever resolved toward the task of creating with words a scheme of images and symbols whose direction could enlist the sympathies, loyalties, and yearnings of the millions of Bigger Thomases in every land and race. . . .

But more than anything else, as a writer, I was fascinated by the similarity of the emotional tensions of Bigger in America and Bigger in Nazi Germany and Bigger in old Russia. All Bigger Thomases, white and black, felt tense, afraid, nervous, hysterical, and restless. From far away Nazi Germany and old Russia had come to me items of knowledge that told me that certain modern experiences were creating types of personalities whose existence ignored racial and national lines of demarcation, that these personalities carried with them a more universal drama-element than anything I'd ever encountered before; that these personalities were mainly imposed upon men and women living in a world whose fundamental assumptions could no longer be taken for granted: a world ridden with national and class strife; a world whose metaphysical meanings had vanished; a world in which God no longer existed as a daily focal point of men's lives; a world in which men could no longer retain their faith in an ultimate here-after. It was a highly geared world whose nature was conflict and action, a world whose limited area and vision imperiously urged men to satisfy their organisms, a world that existed on a plane of animal sensation alone.

It was a world in which millions of men lived and behaved like drunkards, taking a stiff drink of hard life to lift them up for a thrilling moment, to give them a quivering sense of wild exultation and fulfillment that soon faded and let them down. Eagerly they took another drink, wanting to avoid the dull, flat look of things, then still another, this time stronger, and then they felt that their lives had meaning. Speaking figura-tively, they were soon chronic alcoholics, men who lived by violence, through extreme action and sensation, through drowning daily in a perpetual nervous agitation.

From these items I drew my first political conclusions about Bigger: I felt that Bigger, an American product, a na-tive son of this land, carried within him the potentialities of either Communism or Fascism. I don't mean to say that the Negro boy I depicted in *Native Son* is either a Communist or a Fascist. He is not either. But he is product of a dislocated society; he is a dispossessed and disinherited man; he is all of this, and he lives amid the greatest possible plenty on earth and he is looking and feeling for a way out. Whether he'll follow some gaudy, hysterical leader who'll promise rashly to fill the void in him, or whether he'll come to an understand-ing with the millions of his kindred fellow workers under trade-union or revolutionary guidance depends upon the fu-ture drift of events in America. But, granting the emotional state, the tensity, the fear, the hate, the impatience, the sense of exclusion, the ache for violent action, the emotional and cultural hunger, Bigger Thomas, conditioned as his organism is, will not become an ardent, or even a lukewarm, supporter of the *status quo*.

The difference between Bigger's tensity and the German variety is that Bigger's, due to America's educational restric-tions on the bulk of her Negro population, is in a nascent state, not yet articulate. And the difference between Bigger's longing for self-identification and the Russian principle of self-determination is that Bigger's, due to the effects of

American oppression, which has not allowed for the forming of deep ideas of solidarity among Negroes, is still in a state of individual anger and hatred. Here, I felt, was *drama*! Who will be the first to touch off these Bigger Thomases in America, white and black?

For a long time I toyed with the idea of writing a novel in which a Negro Bigger Thomas would loom as a symbolic figure of American life, a figure who would hold within him the prophecy of our future. I felt strongly that he held within him, in a measure which perhaps no other contemporary type did, the outlines of action and feeling which we would encounter on a vast scale in the days to come. Just as one sees when one walks into a medical research laboratory jars of alcohol containing abnormally large or distorted portions of the human body, just so did I see and feel that the conditions of life under which Negroes are forced to live in America contain the embryonic emotional prefigurations of how a large part of the body politic would react under stress.

So, with this much knowledge of myself and the world gained and known, why should I not try to work out on paper the problem of what will happen to Bigger? Why should I not, like a scientist in a laboratory, use my imagination and invent test-tube situations, place Bigger in them, and, following the guidance of my own hopes and fears, what I had learned and remembered, work out in fictional form an emotional statement and resolution of this problem?

But several things militated against my starting to work. Like Bigger himself, I felt a mental censor—product of the fears which a Negro feels from living in America—standing over me, draped in white, warning me not to write. This censor's warnings were translated into my own thought processes thus: "What will white people think if I draw the picture of such a Negro boy? Will they not at once say: 'See, didn't we tell you all along that niggers are like that? Now, look, one of their own kind has come along and drawn the picture for us!' " I felt that if I drew the picture of Bigger truthfully, there would be many reactionary whites who would try to make of him something I did not intend. And yet, and this was what made it difficult, I knew that I could not write of Bigger convincingly if I did not depict him as he *was*: that is, resentful toward whites, sullen, angry, ignorant, emotionally unstable, depressed and unaccountably elated at times, and unable even, because of his own lack of inner organization which American oppression has fostered in him, to unite with the members of his own race. And would not whites misread Bigger and, doubting his authenticity, say: "This man is preaching hate against the whole white race"?

The more I thought of it the more I became convinced that if I did not write of Bigger as I saw and felt him, if I did not try to make him a living personality and at the same time a symbol of all the larger things I felt and saw in him, I'd be reacting as Bigger himself reacted: that is, I'd be acting out of *fear* if I let what I thought whites would say constrict and paralyze me.

As I contemplated Bigger and what he meant, I said to myself: "I must write this novel, not only for others to read, but to free *myself* of this sense of shame and fear." In fact, the novel, as time passed, grew upon me to the extent that it became a necessity to write it; the writing of it turned into a way of living for me.

Another thought kept me from writing. What would my own white and black comrades in the Communist party say? This thought was the most bewildering of all. Politics is a hard and narrow game; its policies represent the aggregate desires and aspirations of millions of people. Its goals are rigid and simply drawn, and the minds of the majority of politicians are set, congealed in terms of daily tactical maneuvers. How could I create such complex and wide schemes of associational thought and feeling, such filigreed webs of dreams and politics, without being mistaken for a "smuggler of reaction," "an ideological confusionist," or "an individualistic and dangerous element"? Though my heart is with the collectivist and proletarian ideal, I solved this problem by assuring myself that honest politics and honest feeling in imaginative representation ought to be able to meet on common healthy ground without fear, suspicion, and quarreling. Further, and more importantly, I steeled myself by coming to the conclusion that whether politicians accepted or rejected Bigger did not really matter; my task, as I felt it, was to free myself of this burden of impressions and feelings, recast them into the image of Bigger and make him *true*. Lastly, I felt that a right more immediately deeper than that of politics or race was at stake; that is, a *human* right, the right of a man to think and feel honestly. And especially did this personal and human right bear hard upon me, for temperamentally I am inclined to satisfy the claims of my own ideals rather than the expectations of others. It was this obscure need that had pulled me into the labor movement in the beginning and by exercising it I was but fulfilling what I felt to be the laws of my own growth.

There was another constricting thought that kept me from work. It deals with my own race. I asked myself: "What will Negro doctors, lawyers, dentists, bankers, school teachers, social workers and business men, think of me if I draw such a picture of Bigger?" I knew from long and painful experience that the Negro middle and professional classes were the people of my own race who were more than others ashamed of Bigger and what he meant. Having narrowly escaped the Bigger Thomas reaction pattern themselves—indeed, still retaining traces of it within the confines of their own timid personalities—they would not relish being publicly reminded of the lowly, shameful depths of life above which they enjoyed their bourgeois lives. Never did they want people, especially *white* people, to think that their lives were so much touched by anything so dark and brutal as Bigger.

Their attitude toward life and art can be summed up in a single paragraph: "But, Mr. Wright, there are so many of us who are *not* like Bigger! Why don't you portray in your fiction the *best* traits of our race, something that will show the white people what we have done in *spite* of oppression? Don't represent anger and bitterness. Smile when a white person comes to you. Never let him feel that you are so small that what he has done to crush you has made you hate him! Oh, above all, save your *pride*!"

But Bigger won over all these claims; he won because I felt that I was hunting on the trail of more exciting and thrilling game. What Bigger meant had claimed me because I felt with all of my being that he was more important than what any person, white or black, would say or try to make of him, more important than any political analysis designed to explain or deny him, more important, even, than my own sense of fear, shame, and diffidence.

But Bigger was still not down upon paper. For a long time I had been writing of him in my mind, but I had yet to put him into an image, a breathing symbol draped out in the guise of the only form of life my native land had allowed me to know intimately, that is, the ghetto life of the American Negro. But the basic reason for my hesitancy was that another and far more complex problem had risen to plague me. Bigger, as I saw and felt him, was a snarl of many realities; he had in him many levels of life.

First, there was his personal and private life, that intimate existence that is so difficult to snare and nail down in fiction, that elusive core of being, that individual data of consciousness which in every man and woman is like that in no other. I had to deal with Bigger's dreams, his fleeting, momentary sensations, his yearning, visions, his deep emotional responses.

Then I was confronted with that part of him that was dual in aspect, dim, wavering, that part of him which is so much a part of *all* Negroes and *all* whites that I realized that I could put it down upon paper only by feeling out its meaning first within the confines of my own life. Bigger was attracted and repelled by the American scene. He was an American, because he was a native son; but he was also a Negro nationalist in a vague sense because he was not allowed to live as an American. Such was his way of life and mine; neither Bigger nor I resided fully in either camp.

Of this dual aspect of Bigger's social consciousness, I placed the nationalistic side first, not because I agreed with Bigger's wild and intense hatred of white people, but because his hate had placed him, like a wild animal at bay, in a position where he was most symbolic and explainable. In other words, his nationalist complex was for me a concept through which I could grasp more of the total meaning of his life than I could in any other way. I tried to approach Bigger's *snarled* and *confused* nationalist feelings with *conscious* and *informed* ones of my own. Yet, Bigger was not nationalist enough to feel the need of religion or the folk culture of his own people. What made Bigger's social consciousness most complex was

the fact that he was hovering unwanted between two worlds
—between powerful America and his own stunted place
in life—and I took upon myself the task of trying to make
the reader feel this No Man's Land. The most that I could
say of Bigger was that he felt the *need* for a whole life and
acted out of that need; that was all.

Above and beyond all this, there was that American part of
Bigger which is the heritage of us all, that part of him which
we get from our seeing and hearing, from school, from the
hopes and dreams of our friends; that part of him which the
common people of America never talk of but take for granted.
Among millions of people the deepest convictions of life are
never discussed openly; they are felt, implied, hinted at tacitly
and obliquely in their hopes and fears. We live by an idealism
that makes us believe that the Constitution is a good docu-
ment of government, that the Bill of Rights is a good legal
and humane principle to safeguard our civil liberties, that
every man and woman should have the opportunity to realize
himself, to seek his own individual fate and goal, his own
peculiar and untranslatable destiny. I don't say that Bigger
knew this in the terms in which I'm speaking of it; I don't say
that any such thought ever entered his head. His emotional
and intellectual life was never that articulate. But he knew it
emotionally, intuitively, for his emotions and his desires were
developed, and he caught it, as most of us do, from the mental and emotional climate of our time. Bigger had all of this in
him, dammed up, buried, implied, and I had to develop it in
fictional form.

There was still another level of Bigger's life that I felt
bound to account for and render, a level as elusive to discuss
as it was to grasp in writing. Here again, I had to fall back
upon my own feelings as a guide, for Bigger did not offer in
his life any articulate verbal explanations. There seems to
hover somewhere in that dark part of all our lives, in some
more than in others, an objectless, timeless, spaceless element
of primal fear and dread, stemming, perhaps, from our birth
(depending upon whether one's outlook upon personality is
Freudian or non-Freudian!), a fear and dread which exercises
an impelling influence upon our lives all out of proportion to
its obscurity. And, accompanying this *first fear*, is, for the

want of a better name, a reflex urge toward ecstasy, complete submission, and trust. The springs of religion are here, and also the origins of rebellion. And in a boy like Bigger, young, unschooled, whose subjective life was clothed in the tattered rags of American "culture," this primitive fear and ecstasy were naked, exposed, unprotected by religion or a framework of government or a scheme of society whose final faiths would gain his love and trust; unprotected by trade or profession, faith or belief; opened to every trivial blast of daily or hourly circumstance.

There was yet another level of reality in Bigger's life: the impliedly political. I've already mentioned that Bigger had in him impulses which I had felt were present in the vast upheavals of Russia and Germany. Well, somehow, I had to make these political impulses felt by the reader in terms of Bigger's daily actions, keeping in mind as I did so the probable danger of my being branded as a propagandist by those who would not like the subject matter.

Then there was Bigger's relationship with white America, both North and South, which I had to depict, which I had to make known once again, alas; a relationship whose effects are carried by every Negro, like scars, somewhere in his body and mind.

I had also to show what oppression had done to Bigger's relationships with his own people, how it had split him off from them, how it had baffled him; how oppression seems to hinder and stifle in the victim those very qualities of character which are so essential for an effective struggle against the oppressor.

Then there was the fabulous city in which Bigger lived, an indescribable city, huge, roaring, dirty, noisy, raw, stark, brutal; a city of extremes: torrid summers and sub-zero winters, white people and black people, the English language and strange tongues, foreign born and native born, scabby poverty and gaudy luxury, high idealism and hard cynicism! A city so young that, in thinking of its short history, one's mind, as it travels backward in time, is stopped abruptly by the barren stretches of wind-swept prairie! But a city old enough to have caught within the homes of its long, straight streets the symbols and images of man's age-old destiny, of truths as old as the mountains and seas, of dramas as abiding as the soul of man itself! A city which has become the pivot of the Eastern, Western, Northern, and Southern poles of the nation. But a city whose black smoke clouds shut out the sunshine for seven months of the year; a city in which, on a fine balmy May morning, one can sniff the stench of the stockyards; a city where people have grown so used to gangs and murders and graft that they have honestly forgotten that government can have a pretense of decency!

With all of this thought out, Bigger was still unwritten. Two events, however, came into my life and accelerated the process, made me sit down and actually start work on the typewriter, and just stop the writing of Bigger in my mind as I walked the streets.

The first event was my getting a job in the South Side Boys' Club, an institution which tried to reclaim the thousands of Negro Bigger Thomases from the dives and the alleys of the Black Belt. Here, on a vast scale, I had an opportunity to observe Bigger in all of his moods, actions, haunts. Here I felt for the first time that the rich folk who were paying my wages did not really give a good goddamn about Bigger, that their kindness was prompted at bottom by a selfish motive. They were paying me to distract Bigger with ping-pong, checkers, swimming, marbles, and baseball in order that he might not roam the streets and harm the valuable white property which adjoined the Black Belt. I am not condemning boys' clubs and ping-pong as such; but these little stopgaps were utterly inadequate to fill up the centuries-long chasm of emptiness which American civilization had created in these Biggers. I felt that I was doing a kind of dressed-up police work, and I hated it.

I would work hard with these Biggers, and when it would come time for me to go home I'd say to myself, under my breath so that no one could hear: "Go to it, boys! Prove to the bastards that gave you these games that life is stronger than ping-pong. . . . Show them that full-blooded life is harder and hotter than they suspect, even though that life is draped in a black skin which at heart they despise. . . ."

They did. The police blotters of Chicago are testimony to how *much* they did. That was the only way I could contain myself for doing a job I hated; for a moment I'd allow myself, vicariously, to feel as Bigger felt—not much, just a little, just a *little*—but, still, there it was.

The second event that spurred me to write of Bigger was more personal and subtle. I had written a book of short stories which was published under the title of *Uncle Tom's Children*. When the reviews of that book began to appear, I realized that I had made an awfully naïve mistake. I found that I had written a book which even bankers' daughters could read and weep over and feel good about. I swore to myself that if I ever wrote another book, no one would weep over it; that it would be so hard and deep that they would have to face it without the consolation of tears. It was this that made me get to work in dead earnest.

Now, until this moment I did not stop to think very much about the plot of *Native Son*. The reason I did not is because I was not for one moment ever worried about it. I had spent years learning about Bigger, what had made him, what he meant; so, when the time came for writing, *what had made him and what he meant* constituted my plot. But the far-flung items of his life had to be couched in imaginative terms, terms known and acceptable to a common body of readers, terms which would, in the course of the story, manipulate the deepest held notions and convictions of their lives. That came easy. The moment I began to write, the plot fell out, so to speak. I'm not trying to oversimplify or make the process seem oversubtle. At bottom, what happened is very easy to explain.

Any Negro who has lived in the North or the South knows that times without number he has heard of some Negro boy being picked up on the streets and carted off to jail and charged with "rape." This thing happens so often that to my mind it had become a representative symbol of the Negro's uncertain position in America. Never for a second was I in doubt as to what kind of social reality or dramatic situation I'd put Bigger in, what kind of test-tube life I'd set up to evoke his deepest reactions. Life had made the plot over and over again, to the extent that I knew it by heart. So frequently do these acts recur that when I was halfway through the first draft of *Native Son* a case paralleling Bigger's flared forth in the newspapers of Chicago. (Many of the newspaper items and some of the incidents in *Native Son* are but fictionalized versions of the Robert Nixon case and rewrites of news stories from the *Chicago Tribune*.) Indeed, scarcely was *Native Son* off the press before Supreme Court Justice Hugo L. Black gave the nation a long and vivid account of the American police methods of handling Negro boys.

Let me describe this stereotyped situation: A crime wave is sweeping a city and citizens are clamoring for police action. Squad cars cruise the Black Belt and grab the first Negro boy who seems to be unattached and homeless. He is held for perhaps a week without charge or bail, without the privilege of communicating with anyone, including his own relatives. After a few days this boy "confesses" anything that he is asked to confess, any crime that handily happens to be unsolved and on the calendar. Why does he confess? After the boy has been grilled night and day, hanged up by his thumbs, dangled by his feet out of twenty-story windows, and beaten (in places that leave no scars—cops have found a way to do that), he signs the papers before him, papers which are usually accompanied by a verbal promise to the boy that he will not go to the electric chair. Of course, he ends up by being executed or sentenced for life. If you think I'm telling tall tales, get chummy with some white cop who works in a Black Belt district and ask him for the lowdown.

When a black boy is carted off to jail in such a fashion, it is almost impossible to do anything for him. Even well-disposed Negro lawyers find it difficult to defend him, for the boy will plead guilty one day and then not guilty the next, according to the degree of pressure and persuasion that is brought to bear upon his frightened personality from one side or the other. Even the boy's own family is scared to death; sometimes fear of police intimidation makes them hesitate to acknowledge that the boy is a blood relation of theirs.

Such has been America's attitude toward these boys that if one is picked up and confronted in a police cell with ten white cops, he is intimidated almost to the point of confessing anything. So far removed are these practices from what the average American citizen encounters in his daily life that it takes a huge act of his imagination to believe that it is true;

yet, this same average citizen, with his kindness, his American sportsmanship and good will, would probably act with the mob if a self-respecting Negro family moved into his apartment building to escape the Black Belt and its terrors and limitations. . . .

Now, after all of this, when I sat down to the typewriter, I could not work; I could not think of a good opening scene for the book. I had definitely in mind the kind of emotion I wanted to evoke in the reader in that first scene, but I could not think of the type of concrete event that would convey the motif of the entire scheme of the book, that would sound, in varied form, the note that was to be resounded throughout its length, that would introduce to the reader just what kind of an organism Bigger's was and the environment that was bearing hourly upon it. Twenty or thirty times I tried and failed; then I argued that if I could not write the opening scene, I'd start with the scene that followed. I did. The actual writing of the book began with the scene in the pool room.

Now, for the writing. During the years in which I had met all of those Bigger Thomases, those varieties of Bigger Thomases, I had not consciously gathered material to write of them; I had not kept a notebook record of their sayings and doings. Their actions had simply made impressions upon my sensibilities as I lived from day to day, impressions which crystallized and coagulated into clusters and configurations of memory, attitudes, moods, ideas. And these subjective states, in turn, were automatically stored away somewhere in me. I was not even aware of the process. But, excited over the book which I had set myself to write, under the stress of emotion, these things came surging up, tangled, fused, knotted, entertaining me by the sheer variety and potency of their meaning and suggestiveness.

With the whole theme in mind, in an attitude almost akin to prayer, I gave myself up to the story. In an effort to capture some phase of Bigger's life that would not come to me readily, I'd jot down as much of it as I could. Then I'd read it over and over, adding each time a word, a phrase, a sentence until I felt that I had caught all the shadings of reality I felt dimly were there. With each of these rereadings and rewritings it seemed that I'd gather in facts and facets that tried to run away. It was an act of concentration, of trying to hold within one's center of attention all of that bewildering array of facts which science, politics, experience, memory, and imagination were urging upon me. And then, while writing, a new and thrilling relationship would spring up under the drive of emotion, coalescing and telescoping alien facts into a known and felt truth. That was the deep fun of the job: to feel within my body that I was pushing out to new areas of feeling, strange landmarks of emotion, tramping upon foreign soil, compounding new relationships of perceptions, making new and—until that very split second of time!—unheard-of and unfelt effects with words. It had a buoying and tonic impact upon me; my senses would strain and seek for more and more of such relationships; my temperature would rise as I worked. That is writing as I feel it, a kind of significant living.

The first draft of the novel was written in four months, straight through, and ran to some 576 pages. Just as a man rises in the mornings to dig ditches for his bread, so I'd work daily. I'd think of some abstract principle of Bigger's conduct and at once my mind would turn it into some act I'd seen Bigger perform, some act which I hoped would be familiar enough to the American reader to gain his credence. But in the writing of scene after scene I was guided by but one criterion: to tell the truth as I saw it and felt it. That is, to objectify in words some insight derived from my living in the form of action, scene, and dialogue. If a scene seemed improbable to me, I'd not tear it up, but ask myself: "Does it reveal enough of what I feel to stand in spite of its unreality?" If I felt it did, it stood. If I felt that it did not, I ripped it out. The degree of morality in my writing depended upon the degree of felt life and truth I could put down upon the printed page. For example, there is a scene in *Native Son* where Bigger stands in a cell with a Negro preacher, Jan, Max, the State's Attorney, Mr. Dalton, Mrs. Dalton, Bigger's mother, his brother, his sister, Al, Gus, and Jack. While writing that scene, I knew that it was unlikely that so many people would ever be allowed to come into a murderer's cell. But I wanted those people in that cell to elicit a certain important emotional response from Bigger. And so the scene stood. I felt that what I wanted that scene to say to the reader was *more important than its surface reality or plausibility.*

Always, as I wrote, I was both reader and writer, both the conceiver of the action and the appreciator of it. I tried to write so that, in the same instant of time, the objective and subjective aspects of Bigger's life would be caught in a focus of prose. And always I tried to *render, depict,* not merely to tell the story. If a thing was cold, I tried to make the reader *feel* cold, and not just tell about it. In writing in this fashion, sometimes I'd find it necessary to use a stream of consciousness technique, then rise to an interior monologue, descend to a direct rendering of a dream state, then to a matter-of-fact depiction of what Bigger was saying, doing, and feeling. Then I'd find it impossible to say what I wanted to say without stepping in and speaking outright on my own; but when doing this I always made an effort to retain the mood of the story, explaining everything only in terms of Bigger's life and, if possible, in the rhythms of Bigger's thought (even though the words would be mine). Again, at other times, in the guise of the lawyer's speech and the newspaper items, or in terms of what Bigger would overhear or see from afar, I'd give what others were saying and thinking of him. But always, from the start to the finish, it was Bigger's story, Bigger's fear, Bigger's flight, and Bigger's fate that I tried to depict. I wrote with the conviction in mind (I don't know if this is right or wrong; I only know that I'm temperamentally inclined to feel this way) that the main burden of all serious fiction consists almost wholly of character-destiny and the items, social, political, and personal, of that character-destiny.

As I wrote I followed, almost unconsciously, many principles of the novel which my reading of the novels of other writers had made me feel were necessary for the building of a well-constructed book. For the most part the novel is rendered in the present; I wanted the reader to feel that Bigger's story was happening *now*, like a play upon the stage or a movie unfolding upon the screen. Action follows action, as in a prize fight. Wherever possible, I told of Bigger's life in close-up, slow-motion, giving the feel of the grain in the passing of time. I had long had the feeling that this was the best way to "enclose" the reader's mind in a new world, to blot out all reality except that which I was giving him.

Then again, as much as I could, I restricted the novel to what Bigger saw and felt, to the limits of his feeling and thoughts, even when I was conveying *more* than that to the reader. I had the notion that such a manner of rendering made for a sharper effect, a more pointed sense of the character, his peculiar type of being and consciousness. Throughout there is but one point of view: Bigger's. This, too, I felt, made for a richer illusion of reality.

I kept out of the story as much as possible, for I wanted the reader to feel that there was nothing between him and Bigger; that the story was a special *première* given in his own private theater.

I kept the scenes long, made as much happen within a short space of time as possible; all of which, I felt, made for greater density and richness of effect.

In a like manner I tried to keep a unified sense of background throughout the story; the background would change, of course, but I tried to keep before the eyes of the reader at all times the forces and elements against which Bigger was striving.

And, because I had limited myself to rendering only what Bigger saw and felt, I gave no more reality to the other characters than that which Bigger himself saw.

This, honestly, is all I can account for in the book. If I attempted to account for scenes and characters, to tell why certain scenes were written in certain ways, I'd be stretching facts in order to be pleasantly intelligible. All else in the book came from my feelings reacting upon the material, and any honest reader knows as much about the rest of what is in the book as I do; that is, if, as he reads, he is willing to let his emotions and imagination become as influenced by the materials as I did. As I wrote, for some reason or other, one image, symbol, character, scene, mood, feeling evoked its opposite, its parallel, its complementary, and its ironic counterpart. Why? I don't know. My emotions and imagination just like to work that way. One can account for just so much of life, and then no more. At least, not yet.

With the first draft down, I found that I could not end the

book satisfactorily. In the first draft I had Bigger going smack to the electric chair; but I felt that two murders were enough for one novel. I cut the final scene and went back to worry about the beginning. I had no luck. The book was one-half finished, with the opening and closing scenes unwritten. Then, one night, in desperation—I hope that I'm not disclosing the hidden secrets of my craft!—I sneaked out and got a bottle. With the help of it, I began to remember many things which I could not remember before. One of them was that Chicago was overrun with rats. I recalled that I'd seen many rats on the streets, that I'd heard and read of Negro children being bitten by rats in their beds. At first I rejected the idea of Bigger battling a rat in his room; I was afraid that the rat would "hog" the scene. But the rat would not leave me; he presented himself in many attractive guises. So, cautioning myself to allow the rat scene to disclose *only* Bigger, his family, their little room, and their relationships, I let the rat walk in, and he did his stuff.

Many of the scenes were torn out as I reworked the book. The mere rereading of what I'd written made me think of the possibility of developing themes which had been only hinted at in the first draft. For example, the entire guilt theme that runs through *Native Son* was woven in *after* the first draft was written.

At last I found out how to end the book; I ended it just as I had begun it, showing Bigger living dangerously, taking his life into his hands, accepting what life had made him. The lawyer, Max, was placed in Bigger's cell at the end of the novel to register the moral—or what *I* felt was the moral— horror of Negro life in the United States.

The writing of *Native Son* was to me an exciting, enthralling, and even a romantic experience. With what I've learned in the writing of this book, with all of its blemishes, imperfections, with all of its unrealized potentialities, I am launching out upon another novel, this time about the status of women in modern American society. This book, too, goes back to my childhood just as Bigger went, for, while I was storing away impressions of Bigger, I was storing away impressions of many other things that made me think and wonder. Some experience will ignite somewhere deep down in me the smoldering embers of new fires and I'll be off again to write yet another novel. It is good to live when one feels that such as that will happen to one. Life becomes sufficient unto life; the rewards of living are found in living.

I don't know if *Native Son* is a good book or a bad book. And I don't know if the book I'm working on now will be a good book or a bad book. And I really don't care. The mere writing of it will be more fun and a deeper satisfaction than any praise or blame from anybody.

I feel that I'm lucky to be alive to write novels today, when the whole world is caught in the pangs of war and change. Early American writers, Henry James and Nathaniel Hawthorne, complained bitterly about the bleakness and flatness of the American scene. But I think that if they were alive, they'd feel at home in modern America. True, we have no great church in America; our national traditions are still of such a sort that we are not wont to brag of them; and we have no army that's above the level of mercenary fighters; we have no group acceptable to the whole of our country upholding certain humane values; we have no rich symbols, no colorful rituals. We have only a money-grubbing, industrial civilization. But we do have in the Negro the embodiment of a past tragic enough to appease the spiritual hunger of even a James; and we have in the oppression of the Negro a shadow athwart our national life dense and heavy enough to satisfy even the gloomy broodings of a Hawthorne. And if Poe were alive, he would not have to invent horror; horror would invent him.

RICHARD WRIGHT.
New York, March 7, 1940.

Chronology

1908 Born Richard Nathaniel Wright, September 4, on Ruck-
er's Plantation, a farm near Roxie, Mississippi, 22 miles
east of Natchez, first child of Nathan Wright, an illiterate
sharecropper, and Ella Wilson Wright, a schoolteacher.
(All four grandparents had been born in slavery. Father
was born shortly before 1880, the son of Nathaniel
Wright, a freed slave who farmed a plot of land he had
been given at the end of the Civil War. Maternal grandfather, Richard Wilson, born March 21, 1847, served in the
United States Navy in 1865, then became disillusioned because of a bureaucratic error that deprived him of his pen-
sion. Maternal grandmother, Margaret Bolton Wilson, of
Irish, Scottish, American Indian, and African descent, was
virtually white in appearance. A house slave before the
Emancipation, she later became a midwife nurse, a devoted Seventh-day Adventist, and the strict head of her
Natchez household, which included eight surviving children. Mother, born 1883, married Nathan Wright in 1907
despite her parents' disapproval, and then gave up school
teaching to work on the farm.)

1910 Brother Leon Alan, called Alan, born September 24.

1911–12 Unable to care for her children while working on the
farm, mother takes Wright and his brother to live with
Wilson family in Natchez. Father rejoins family and finds
work in a sawmill. Wright accidentally sets fire to grandparents' house.

1913–14 Family moves to Memphis, Tennessee, by steamboat. Father deserts family to live with another woman, leaving
them impoverished. Mother finds work as a cook.

1915–16 Wright enters school at Howe Institute, Memphis, in September 1915. Mother falls seriously ill in early 1916. Grandmother comes to care for family. After grandmother
returns home, mother puts Wright and his brother in the
Settlement House, Methodist orphanage in Memphis,
where they stay for over a month. Spends relatively pleas-
ant summer at 1107 Lynch Street in Jackson, Mississippi,

where maternal grandparents now live, before going with mother and brother to Elaine, Arkansas, to live with his favorite aunt, Maggie (his mother's younger sister), and her husband, Silas Hoskins, a saloon-keeper.

1917–18   After Hoskins is murdered by whites who want his prosperous liquor business, terrified family flees to West Helena, Arkansas, then returns to Jackson with Aunt Maggie to live with the Wilsons. After several months they go back to West Helena, where mother and aunt find work cooking and cleaning for whites. Aunt Maggie leaves with her lover, "Professor" Matthews, a fugitive from the law (they eventually settle in Detroit).

1918–19   Wright enters local school in fall 1918. Mother's health deteriorates early in 1919 and Wright is forced to leave school to earn money. Delivers wood and laundry and carries lunches to railroad workers. Family moves frequently because of lack of rent money; Wright gathers stray pieces of coal along railroad tracks to heat their home. Mother suffers paralyzing stroke, and grandmother comes to bring the family back to Jackson. Aunt Maggie helps care for mother, then takes Leon Alan back to Detriot with her; other aunts and uncles help pay for mother's treatment.

1919–20   Wright moves into home of aunt and uncle, Clark and Jody Wilson, in nearby Greenwood, Mississippi, where he is able to attend school. Finds household calm and orderly but his aunt and uncle cold and unsympathetic, and is terrified by episodes of sleepwalking. Returns to grandparents' home in Jackson. Mother begins to show signs of recovery from paralysis, then has relapse caused by a cerebral blood clot that leaves her virtually crippled. Her illness impoverishes the family, already hurt by the rheumatism that makes Grandfather Wilson unable to work.

1920–21   Enters Seventh-day Adventist school taught by his youngest aunt, Addie. Only nine years older than Wright, she is a rigid disciplinarian often at odds with him. Wright rebels against the rules and practices of the religion, including its diet, which forbids eating pork. Finds himself opposed to his family in general, except for his mother, who is too sick to help him.

1921–22   Enters the fifth grade of the Jim Hill School in Jackson,
           two years behind his age group. Does well, quickly gains
           in confidence, and is soon promoted to the sixth grade.
           Begins friendships, some of them lasting into his adult-
           hood, with a number of other students, including Dick
           Jordan, Joe Brown, Perry Booker, D. C. Blackburn, Lewis
           Anderson, Sarah McNeamer, and Essie Lee Ward. Takes
           job as a newsboy, which gives him the chance to read ma-
           terial forbidden at home because of religious prohibitions.
           Family life continues to be difficult, although his mother's
           health improves slightly. Travels briefly during summer in
           the Mississippi Delta region as "secretary-accountant" to
           an insurance agent, W. Mance. The trip allows him to
           know better the rural South, but he is dismayed by the
           illiteracy and lack of education he encounters among
           blacks.

1922–23   Enters the seventh grade. Grandfather Wilson dies No-
           vember 8. After many arguments, grandmother reluctantly
           lets Wright take jobs after school and on Saturday (the
           Seventh-day Adventist sabbath). Runs errands and per-
           forms small chores, mainly for whites. For the first time
           has enough money to buy school books, food to combat
           his chronic hunger, and clothing. Baptized in the Method-
           ist Church, mainly to please his mother. Avidly reads pulp
           magazines, dime novels, and books and magazines dis-
           carded by others. Uncle Thomas Wilson, his wife, and
           their two daughters come to live with the family in spring
           1923. Mother's health worsens. Wright works during the
           summer at a brickyard and as a caddy at a golf course.

1923–24   Enters eighth grade at the Smith Robertson Junior High
           School, Jackson (a former slave, Smith Robertson had be-
           come a successful local barber and a community leader;
           the school, built in 1894, was the first black institution of
           its kind in Jackson). Until he can afford a bicycle, Wright
           walks several miles daily to and from the school. Makes
           new friends at school, including Wade Griffin, Varnie
           Reed, Arthur Leaner, and Minnie Farish. Begins working
           for the Walls, a white family he finds kindly (will serve
           them for two years). Later remembers writing his first
           short story, "The Voodoo of Hell's Half-Acre," in late
           winter (story is reported to have been published in the

spring as "Hell's Half-Acre" in the Jackson *Southern Regis-ter*, a black weekly newspaper; no copies are known to be extant). Brother Leon Alan returns from Detroit. Wright is initially pleased, but their relationship soon disappoints him. Works for the American Optical Company, cleaning workshop and making deliveries.

1924–25   Enters ninth grade at Smith Robertson Junior High School, and graduates on May 29, 1925, as valedictorian. Rejects graduation speech prepared for him by the principal and instead delivers his own, "The Attributes of Life." Works as a delivery boy, sales clerk, hotel hallboy and bellboy, and in a movie theater. Begins classes in fall at newly founded Lanier High School, but quits a few weeks later to earn money. Leaves Jackson for Memphis, Tennessee, where he boards with a family at 570 Beale Street.

1926   Works for low pay as a dishwasher and delivery boy and at the Merry Optical Company. Reads widely in *Harper's*, *Atlantic Monthly*, *The American Mercury*, and other magazines. Moves to 875 Griffith Place.

1927   Joined by mother, who is still in poor health, and brother; they take an apartment together at 370 Washington Street. After reading an editorial highly critical of H. L. Mencken, long noted as a critic of the white South, Wright seeks out Mencken's *Prejudices* and *A Book of Prefaces* and is particularly impressed by Mencken's iconoclasm and use of "words as weapons." These books serve as guides to further reading, including works by Theodore Dreiser, Sinclair Lewis, Sherwood Anderson, the elder Alexandre Dumas, Frank Harris, and O. Henry. Aunt Maggie, who has been deserted by "Professor" Matthews, joins family in the fall. In December, Wright and Maggie, who hopes to open a beauty salon, move to the South Side of Chicago, while mother and Leon Alan return to Jackson. Sees his aunt Cleopatra ("Sissy"), but is disappointed to find that she lives in a rooming house, not an apartment, and moves into a rooming house with Aunt Maggie.

1928   Works as delivery boy in a delicatessen, then as a dishwasher. Wright finds Chicago stimulating and less racially oppressive than the South, but is often dismayed by the pace and disarray of urban life. Passes written examination for the postal service in the spring, then begins work in the summer as a temporary employee at 65 cents an hour. Rents an apartment with Aunt Maggie and is joined by mother and brother. In the fall Wright fails the postal service medical examination required for a permanent position because of chronic undernourishment and returns to dishwashing. Disputes over money and his reading cause tension with Aunt Maggie. Wright takes another apartment for family and invites his aunt Cleopatra to move in with them.

1929   After undertaking a crash diet to increase his weight, Wright passes the physical examination and is hired by the central post office at Clark Street and Jackson Boulevard as a substitute clerk and mail sorter. Moves with family to four rooms at 4831 Vincennes Avenue, which allows him to read and write in relative comfort. Dislikes the post office bureaucracy, but becomes friendly with many fellow workers, both black and white. Among his friends are schoolmates from the South, including Essie Lee Ward, Arthur Leaner, and Joe Brown. Writes steadily and attends meetings of a local black literary group, but feels distant from its middle-class members. Attracted by the Universal Negro Improvement Association, a group inspired by Marcus Garvey, but does not join it.

1930   Volume of mail drops in decline following the 1929 Wall Street crash; Wright has his working hours cut back before losing his job altogether. South Side sinks into economic depression. Works temporarily for post office in the summer. Mother suffers a relapse, aunt Cleopatra has a heart attack, and brother develops stomach ulcers. Begins work on "Cesspool," novel about black life in Chicago. Enrolls in tenth grade at Hyde Park Public School, but soon drops out.

1931   Reads books recommended by friend William Harper (who will later own a bookstore on the South Side). Wright is particularly impressed by Dreiser and Joseph Conrad, and continues to write. Short story "Superstition" is published in April *Abbott's Monthly Magazine*, a black journal (magazine fails before Wright is paid). Through a distant relative, finds job as a funeral insurance agent for several burial societies. Also works as an assistant to a black Republican precinct captain during the mayoral campaign, and at the post office in December. Becomes interested in views of Communist orators and organizers, especially those in the League of Struggle for Negro Rights.

1932   Sells insurance policies door-to-door and works briefly as an assistant to a Democratic precinct captain. Family moves to slum apartment as Wright is increasingly unable to sell policies to blacks impoverished by the Depression. Asks for and receives relief assistance from the Cook County Bureau of Public Welfare, which finds him a temporary job as a street cleaner. Works at the post office during the Christmas season.

1933   Digs ditches in the Cook County Forest Preserves, then works at Michael Reese Hospital, caring for animals used in medical research. Recruited by fellow post office worker Abraham Aaron to join the newly formed Chicago branch of the John Reed Club, a national literary organization sponsored by the Communist party. Welcomed and encouraged by the almost entirely white membership of the club, Wright begins to read and study *New Masses* and *International Literature*, the organ of the International League of Revolutionary Writers. Writes and submits revolutionary poems ("I Have Seen Black Hands," "A Red Love Note") to *Left Front*, the magazine of the midwestern John Reed Clubs. Elected executive secretary of the Chicago John Reed Club and organizes a successful lecture series which allows him to meet a variety of intellectuals. Gives lecture at open forum on "The Literature of the Negro."

1934   Hoping to consolidate his position in the John Reed Club, Wright joins the Communist party; is also impressed by the party's opposition to racial discrimination. Publishes poetry in *Left Front*, *Anvil*, and *New Masses*. Becomes a member of the editorial board of *Left Front*. Enjoys literary and social friendships with Bill Jordan, Abraham Chapman, Howard Nutt, Laurence Lipton, Nelson Algren, Joyce Gourfain, and Jane Newton. Grandmother Wilson comes to Chicago to join the family; they move to apartment at 4804 St. Lawrence Avenue, near the railroad tracks. Mother's paralysis returns after attack of encephalitis. Wright is laid off by the hospital in the summer, and again works as a street sweeper and ditch digger before being hired to supervise a youth club organized to counter juvenile delinquency among blacks on the South Side. Attends Middle West Writers' Congress in August and the national congress of John Reed Clubs in September. Dismayed by party decision to cease publication of *Left Front* and to dissolve the John Reed Clubs in 1935 as part of its Popular Front strategy. Meets Jack Conroy, editor of *Anvil*. Reading in Chicago by this time includes Henry James (especially the Prefaces to the New York Edition), Gertrude Stein (notably her *Three Lives*, with its portrait of a black character, Melanctha Herbert), Faulkner, T. S. Eliot, Sherwood Anderson, Dos Passos, O'Neill, Stephen Crane, Dreiser, Whitman, Poe, D. H. Lawrence, Conrad, Galsworthy, Hardy, Dickens, George Moore, Carlyle, Swift, Shakespeare, Tolstoy, Dostoevsky, Turgenev, Chekhov, Proust, Dumas, and Balzac. Lectures on the career of Langston Hughes to the Indianapolis John Reed Club in November and contributes fee to new publication *Midland Left*.

1935   Publishes leftist poetry in *Midland Left*, a short-lived journal, *New Masses* ("Red Leaves of Red Books" and "Spread Your Sunshine"), and *International Literature* ("A Red Slogan"). Family moves to 2636 Grove Avenue. Begins submitting novel "Cesspool" to publishers (later retitled *Lawd Today!* by Wright; it is rejected repeatedly over the next two years, then published posthumously as *Lawd Today* in 1963 by Walker and Company). Wright attends the first American Writers' Congress, held in New York in April. Speaks on "The Isolation of the Negro Writer," meets Chicago novelist James T. Farrell, and becomes one of fifty members of the national council of the newly formed League of American Writers. Works on story "Big Boy Leaves Home." Publishes "Between the World and Me," poem about lynching, in July–August *Partisan Review*. Falls seriously ill with attack of pneumonia during the summer. Article "Avant-Garde Writing" wins second prize in contest sponsored by two literary magazines but is never published. First piece of journalism, "Joe Louis

Uncovers Dynamite," describing the reaction of Chicago blacks to the Louis–Max Baer fight, published in *New Masses*. Grandmother Wilson dies. Family, with Wright still virtually its sole support, moves to 3743 Indiana Avenue. Wright is hired by the Federal Writers' Project (part of the Works Progress Administration) to help research the history of Illinois and of the Negro in Chicago for the Illinois volume in the American Guide Series. Discusses influence of Hemingway with fellow writers in federal project.

1936   Publishes "Transcontinental," a six-page radical poem influenced by Whitman and Louis Aragon, in January *International Literature*. Becomes a principal organizer of the Communist party–sponsored National Negro Congress (successor to the League of Struggle for Negro Rights), held in Chicago in February, and reports on it for *New Masses*. Transferred in spring to the Federal Theatre Project, where he serves as literary adviser and press agent for the Negro Federal Theatre of Chicago and becomes involved in dramatic productions. Finishes two one-act plays based in part on a section of his unpublished novel. In April, Wright takes a leading role in the new South Side Writers' Group (members will include Arna Bontemps, Frank Marshall Davis, Theodore Ward, Fenton Johnson, Horace Cayton, and Margaret Walker). Takes an active role in the Middle West Writers' Congress, held in Chicago June 14–15. Because of what he later describes as a Communist plot against him on the Federal Theatre Project assignment, Wright returns to the Writers' Project, where he becomes a group coordinator. Story "Big Boy Leaves Home" appears in anthology *The New Caravan* in November and receives critical attention and praise in mainstream newspapers and journals.

1937   Publishes poem "We of the Streets" in April *New Masses* and story "Silt" in the August number. Breaks with the Communist party in Chicago, basically over the question of his freedom as a writer. Brother finds job with the Works Progress Administration and assumes some responsibility for support of the family. Wright ranks first in postal service examination in Chicago, but turns down offer in May of permanent position at approximately $2,000 a year in order to move to New York City to pursue career as a writer. Stays briefly with artist acquaintances in Greenwich Village, then moves to Harlem; by mid-June he has a furnished room in the Douglass Hotel at 809 St. Nicholas Avenue. Attends Second American Writers' Congress as a delegate and serves as a session president; stresses the need for writers to think of themselves as writers first and not as laborers. Becomes Harlem editor of the Communist newspaper *Daily Worker* and writes over 200 articles for it during the year, including pieces on blues singer Leadbelly and the continuing Scottsboro Boys controversy. With Dorothy West and Marian Minus, helps launch magazine *New Challenge*, designed to present black life "in relationship to the struggle against war and Fascism." Wright publishes "The Ethics of Living Jim Crow—An Autobiographical Sketch" in *American Stuff: WPA Writers' Anthology* (essay is later included in the second edition of *Uncle Tom's Children* and incorporated into *Black Boy*). In November, publishes influential essay "Blueprint for Negro Writing" in *New Challenge*, criticizing past black literature and urging a Marxist-influenced approach that would transcend nationalism. Lacking party support, *New Challenge* fails after one number. Befriends 23-year-old Ralph Ellison. Wright's second novel, "Tarbaby's Dawn," about a black adolescent in the South, is rejected by publishers (it remains unpublished). Learns that story "Fire and Cloud" has won first prize ($500) among 600 entries in *Story Magazine* contest. Wright joins the New York Federal Writers' Project (will write the Harlem section for *New York Panorama* and work on "The Harlems" in *The New York City Guide*).

1938   Rents furnished room at 139 West 143rd Street. Engages Paul Reynolds, Jr., as literary agent. Reynolds makes arrangements to place *Uncle Tom's Children: Four Novellas* ("Big Boy Leaves Home," "Down by the Riverside," "Long Black Song," and "Fire and Cloud") with editor Edward Aswell at Harper and Brothers, beginning Wright's long association with Aswell and Harper; book is published in March and is widely praised. Sends Aswell outline of novel about a black youth in Chicago. Announces plans to marry daughter of his Harlem landlady in May, but then cancels wedding, telling friends that a medical examination had revealed that the young woman has congenital syphilis. Moves into home of friends from

Chicago, Jane and Herbert Newton, at 175 Carleton Avenue in Brooklyn. Story "Bright and Morning Star" appears in May *New Masses*. Writes about the second Joe Louis–Max Schmeling fight in the June *Daily Worker* and July *New Masses*. In June, replaces Horace Gregory on the editorial board of the literature section of *New Masses*. Works steadily on new novel; often writes in Fort Greene Park in the mornings, and discusses his progress with Jane Newton. Asks Margaret Walker to send him newspaper accounts of the case of Robert Nixon, a young Chicago black man accused of murder (executed in August 1939). Moves in the fall with the Newtons to 522 Gates Avenue. Congressman Martin Dies, chairman of the House Special Committee on Un-American Activities, denounces "The Ethics of Living Jim Crow" during an investigation of the Federal Writers' Project. Finishes first draft of novel, now titled *Native Son*, in October and receives $400 advance from Harper in November. "Fire and Cloud" wins the O. Henry Memorial Award ($200). Travels to Chicago in November to research settings and events used in *Native Son*. Moves with Newtons to 87 Lefferts Place.

1939   Meets Ellen Poplar (b. 1912), daughter of Polish Jewish immigrants and a Communist party organizer in Brooklyn. Completes revised version of novel in February and shows it to Reynolds. Awarded Guggenheim Fellowship ($2,500) in March and resigns from the Federal Writers' Project in May. Discusses black American writing with Langston Hughes, Alain Locke, Countee Cullen, and Warren Cochrane during meeting of Harlem Cultural Congress. After Newtons' landlord evicts them, Wright moves to Douglass Hotel at 809 St. Nicholas Avenue in May, renting room next to Theodore Ward, a friend from Chicago. Becomes close to Ellen Poplar and considers marrying her, but also sees Dhima Rose Meadman, a modern-dance teacher of Russian Jewish ancestry. Plays active role at Third American Writers' Congress. Finishes *Native Son* on June 10. Ward dramatizes "Bright and Morning Star." The story is included in Edward O'Brien's *Best American Short Stories, 1939* and *Fifty Best American Short Stories (1914–1939)*. Begins work on new novel, "Little Sister." Marries Dhima Rose Meadman in August in Episcopal church on Convent Avenue, with Ralph Ellison serving as best man. Lives with his wife, her two-year-old son by an earlier marriage, and his mother-in-law in large apartment on fashionable Hamilton Terrace in Harlem. Attends Festival of Negro Culture held in Chicago in September. Moves to Crompond, New York, to work on "Little Sister" (it is never completed).

1940 Visits Chicago in February and buys house for his family on Vincennes Avenue. Has lunch in Chicago with W.E.B. Du Bois, Langston Hughes, and Arna Bontemps. *Native Son* published by Harper and Brothers March 1 and is offered by the Book-of-the-Month Club as one of its two main selections. In three weeks it sells 215,000 copies. Wright delivers talk "How 'Bigger' Was Born" at Columbia University on March 12 (later published as a pamphlet by Harper, then added to future printings of *Native Son*). *Native Son* is banned in Birmingham, Alabama, libraries. Takes his first airplane flight when he accompanies *Life* magazine photographers to Chicago for an article on the South Side; tours the area with sociologist Horace Cayton, beginning long friendship (article is later canceled). Sails in April for Veracruz, Mexico, with wife, her son, mother-in-law, and wife's pianist. Rents ten-room villa in the Miraval Colony in Cuernevaca. Takes lessons in Spanish and studies the guitar. Reunited with Herbert Kline, friend from the Chicago John Reed Club, who is filming documentary *The Forgotten Village* with John Steinbeck; Wright travels with them through the countryside and takes an interest in the filming. Signs contract with John Houseman and Orson Welles for stage production of *Native Son*. Marriage becomes strained. Wright leaves Mexico in June and travels through the South alone. Visits his father, a poor and broken farm laborer, in Natchez, but is unable to make anything other than a token reconciliation with him. Goes to Chapel Hill, North Carolina, to begin collaboration with Paul Green on stage adaptation of *Native Son*. Meets producer John Houseman and drives to New York with him. Travels to Chicago to do research for book on black American life featuring photographs selected by Edwin Rosskam. Wright and Langston Hughes are guests of honor at reception given by Jack Conroy and Nelson Algren to launch magazine *New Anvil*. Returns to Chapel Hill in July to continue work with Paul Green. Elected vice-president of the League of American Writers. Harper reissues story collection as *Uncle Tom's Children:*

Five Long Stories with "Bright and Morning Star" added
and "The Ethics of Living Jim Crow" as an introduction.
Starts divorce proceedings. Moves in with the Newtons,
now at 343 Grand Avenue in Brooklyn; in the autumn
Ellen Poplar moves into the Newton house. In September
Wright is elected a vice-president of American Peace Mobilization, a Communist-sponsored group opposed to
American involvement in World War II. Works with Houseman on revising stage version of *Native Son* (both Wright
and Houseman think that Green has diverged too much
from the novel); Houseman agrees that Orson Welles, who
is finishing *Citizen Kane*, should direct. Story "Almos' a
Man" appears in *O. Henry Award Prize Stories of 1940*.

1941   In January the National Association for the Advancement
of Colored People awards Wright the Spingarn Medal,
given annually to the black American judged to have made
the most notable achievement in the preceding year. Re-
hearsals for *Native Son* begin in February. Marries Ellen
Poplar in Coytesville, New Jersey, on March 12. They
move to 473 West 140th Street. *Native Son*, starring Canada Lee, opens at St. James Theatre on March 24 after a
benefit performance for the NAACP. Reviews are generally favorable, though the play is attacked in the Hearst
papers, which are hostile to Welles following *Citizen
Kane*. Production runs in New York until June 15. Welles'
striking but costly staging causes production to lose some
money, but it recovers during successful tour of Pitts-
burgh, Boston, Chicago, Milwaukee, Detroit, St. Louis,
and Baltimore. Wright asks the governor of New Jersey to
parole Clinton Brewer, a black man imprisoned since 1923
for murdering a young woman, arguing that Brewer, who
had taught himself music composition, has rehabilitated
himself (Brewer is released July 8; Wright had previously
sent one of his pieces to his friend, record producer and
talent scout John Hammond, who arranged for Count
Basie to record it). Begins novel "Black Hope" (never
completed). Introduces Ellen to his family in Chicago during visit in April. Signs appeal of forty members of the
League of American Writers against American intervention in the war that appears in *New Masses* May 27, and
publishes "Not My People's War" in *New Masses* June 17.
After Germany invades the Soviet Union, June 22, American Peace Mobilization changes its name to American

People's Mobilization. Wright travels to Houston with Horace Cayton and John Hammond to accept Spingarn award from NAACP convention on June 27. Delivers enthusiastically received speech, in which his criticism of Roosevelt administration racial policies is muted in response to Communist party pressure. Lectures at Writers' Schools sponsored by the League of American Writers. Wrights move to 11 Revere Place, Brooklyn, in July. At John Hammond's request, Wright writes "Note on Jim Crow Blues" as a preface to the blues singer Josh White's *Southern Exposure,* an album of three recordings attacking segregation. Hammond then produces recording of Paul Robeson singing Wright's blues song "King Joe," accompanied by the Count Basie orchestra. *12 Million Black Voices: A Folk History of the Negro in the United States,* with photographs selected by Edwin Rosskam (one taken by Wright), published by Viking Press in October to enthusiastic reviews. Wright reads *Dark Legend,* a psychoanalytic study of matricide by psychiatrist Frederic Wertham, then writes to Wertham about Clinton Brewer, who had murdered another young woman within months of his release. Wertham intervenes in the case and helps save Brewer from execution (Wright and Wertham begin close friendship, and Wright becomes increasingly interested in psychoanalysis). Finishes draft of novel "The Man Who Lived Underground." Signs petition "Communication to All American Writers" in December 16 *New Masses,* supporting America's entry into the war after the December 7 Japanese attack on Pearl Harbor.

1942   Mother and Aunt Maggie rejoin Addie in Jackson, Mississippi (brother remains in Chicago, though house on Vincennes Avenue is sold two years later). Daughter Julia, Wright's first child, born April 15. Wrights move in summer to 7 Middagh Street, a 19th-century house near the Brooklyn Bridge shared by George Davis, Carson McCullers, and other writers and artists. Excerpts from "The Man Who Lived Underground" appear in *Accent.* As the sole support of his family, Wright is classified 3-A and not drafted. Unsuccessfully tries to secure a special commission in the psychological warfare or propaganda services of the army. *Native Son* returns to Broadway in October (runs until January 1943). Publishes "What You Don't Know Won't Hurt You," article describing some of his

experiences as a hospital janitor in Chicago, in December
Harper's Magazine. Breaks quietly with the Communist
party over its unwillingness to confront wartime racial discrimination and its continuing attempts to control his
writing.

1943   Accompanied by Horace Cayton, Wright goes to Fisk
University, Nashville, in April to deliver talk on his experiences with racism. Strong reaction from the audience
leads Wright to begin autobiography *American Hunger*.
Neighbors and associates are interviewed by the Federal
Bureau of Investigation. (Files obtained under the Freedom of Information Act in the 1970s show that the FBI
began an investigation in December 1942 to determine if
12 Million Black Voices was prosecutable under the sedition
statutes. Although the sedition investigation is concluded
in 1943, the FBI will continue to monitor Wright's activities, chiefly through the use of informers, for the remain-
der of his life.) Wrights move in August to 89 Lefferts
Place in Brooklyn Heights. Helps organize the Citizens'
Emergency Conference for Interracial Unity in response to
widespread riots in Harlem following the wounding of a
black soldier by white police in August. Finishes *American
Hunger* in December.

1944   Writes film scenario "Melody Limited," about group of
black singers during Reconstruction (scenario is never
produced). Becomes friends with C.L.R. James, a
Trinidad-born historian and Trotskyist, with whom he
plans a book, "The Negro Speaks," and a journal, "American Pages" (neither of these projects appear), and his
wife, Constance Webb. Writes series of radio programs on
the life of a black family for producer Leston Huntley and
is frustrated when Huntley is unable to place the series, in
part because of criticism by middle-class blacks. Attends
party held in honor of Theodore Dreiser on June 2, where
Wright and Dreiser discuss the influence of life in Chicago
on their attitudes. Deepens friendship with Dorothy Norman, New York *Post* editorial writer and editor of *Twice a
Year*, who introduces him to existentialist philosophy and
literature. Book-of-the-Month Club tells Harper that it
will accept only the first section of *American Hunger*, describing Wright's experiences in the South; Wright agrees
to this arrangement. Changes title to *Black Boy*. (Second

section, telling of Wright's life in Chicago, is published as *American Hunger* by Harper & Row in 1977.) Wrights vacation in August outside Ottawa and in the nearby Gatineau country in Quebec. Excerpts from second section of autobiography appear as "I Tried to Be a Communist" in *Atlantic Monthly*, August–September, making public Wright's break with the Communist party. He is denounced by various party organs, including *New Masses* and the *Daily Worker*. Helps the Chicago poet Gwendolyn Brooks to place her first book, *A Street in Bronzeville*. Expanded version of "The Man Who Lived Underground" is published as a novella in *Cross Section*.

1945   To circumvent racial discrimination, Wrights form the "Richelieu Realty Co." and use their lawyer as an intermediary in buying a house at 13 Charles Street in Greenwich Village. (Residence is delayed by their waiting for a Communist tenant hostile to Wright to leave and by redecorating.) Reviews books for *P.M.* newspaper; his highly favorable review of Gertrude Stein's *Wars I Have Seen* leads to correspondence with her. *Black Boy: A Record of Childhood and Youth* published by Harper and Brothers in March to enthusiastic reviews. The book is number one on the bestseller list from April 29 to June 6 and stirs controversy when it is denounced as obscene in the U.S. Senate by Democrat Theodore Bilbo of Mississippi. Takes part in several radio programs, including the nationally influential "Town Meeting," where he argues the negative on the question "Are We Solving America's Race Problem?" In the summer, Wrights vacation on island off Quebec City, and Wright lectures at the Bread Loaf writers' school in Middlebury, Vermont. Writes long introduction to *Black Metropolis*, a sociological study of black Chicago by Horace Cayton and St. Clair Drake. Befriending a number of younger writers, white and black, Wright helps the 20-year-old James Baldwin win a Eugene F. Saxton Foundation Fellowship. Publishes a favorable review of Chester Himes's first novel, *If He Hollers Let Him Go*, and lends Himes $1,000. In the fall, Wrights move to an apartment at 82 Washington Place in Greenwich Village to be closer to a school for Julia. Wright undertakes four-month lecture tour but stops after six weeks because of exhaustion.

1946   Serves as honorary pallbearer at funeral on January 12 of poet Countee Cullen, attending service at Salem Methodist Church in Harlem and burial at Woodlawn Cemetery in the Bronx. By January 19, *Black Boy* has sold 195,000 copies in the Harper trade edition and 351,000 through the Book-of-the-Month Club, making it the fourth best-selling non-fiction title of 1945. Wright, his psychiatrist friend Dr. Frederic Wertham, and others found the Lafargue Clinic, a free psychiatric clinic in Harlem. Meets Jean-Paul Sartre in New York. Receives invitation to visit France, but requests for a passport meet with opposition. Wright goes to Washington for an interview and enlists the aid of Dorothy Norman (who appoints him co-editor of *Twice a Year*), Gertrude Stein, and French cultural attaché, anthropologist Claude Lévi-Strauss, who sends him an official invitation from the French government to visit Paris for a month. Wright leaves New York on May 1. In Paris, welcomed by Gertrude Stein and by almost all the important French literary societies and circles. (Stein dies on July 27 after operation for cancer.) Meets Simone de Beauvoir and André Gide, whose *Travels in the Congo* has impressed Wright, as well as Léopold Sédar Senghor of Senegal, Aimé Césaire of Martinique, and others in the *Négritude* movement. Assists Senghor, Césaire, and Alioune Diop of Senegal in founding the magazine *Présence Africaine* and attends its first board meeting at the Brasserie Lipp. Donates a manuscript to an auction for benefit of experimental dramatist Antonin Artaud. "The Man Who Killed a Shadow" published in French in *Les Lettres Françaises* (first appears in English in 1949 in magazine *Zero*). Leaves Paris in late December and travels to London.

1947   Meets the Trinidad-born intellectual George Padmore and dines with members of the Coloured Writers' Association, including its president, Cedric Dover, author of *Half Caste*, and the colored South African journalist and novelist Peter Abrahams. Returns to New York in January. Moves with family into their Charles Street house in Greenwich Village. Helps to welcome Simone de Beauvoir to New York in the spring. Refuses offer from Hollywood producer to film *Native Son* with character Bigger Thomas changed to a white man. Wright's works are being translated into French, Italian, German, Dutch, and Czech. Decides to return to Europe permanently with his family, partially in response to the racial hostility they are encountering in New York. Sells Greenwich Village house in June. Vacations at a cottage at Wading River, Long Island, owned by a friend. Buys an Oldsmobile sedan to take to Europe. Wright, his wife, and daughter reach Paris in August. They rent rooms from a friend, Odette Lieutier, in her apartment on the rue de Lille, then move into an apartment at 166 Avenue de Neuilly. Albin Michel publishes French translation of *Native Son* in autumn.

1948   Begins to read more deeply in existentialism, including Heidegger and Husserl. Sees much of Sartre and Simone de Beauvoir. Wright is particularly impressed by Camus' *The Stranger*, and begins work on an existentialist novel, eventually titled *The Outsider*. Gallimard translation of *Black Boy* wins French Critics' Award. Wright establishes friendships with the Reverend Clayton Williams, pastor of the American Church, and with Harry Goldberg of the American Library. Becomes unofficial spokesman for African-American colony in Paris, which includes James Baldwin. Visits Italy for the publication there of *Native Son*. Meets with Carlo Levi and Ignazio Silone, who later introduces him to Arthur Koestler in Paris. Interviewed by his Italian translator, Fernanda Pivano, Wright says he likes to read *Metamorphosis*, *Moby-Dick*, *Ulysses*, and *The Sound and the Fury*. Travels through Belgium to London, where he sees a performance of *Native Son* and renews friendship with George Padmore, who stirs Wright's interest in the question of colonialism in Africa. Moves with family to 14 rue Monsieur le Prince in the Latin Quarter in May. Ellen returns to New York in June to select furniture and other possessions for their new life in France. Wright is beset by recurring sinus problems and influenza. His tonsils are removed. Aids Sartre and Camus in the leadership of the Rassemblement Démocratique Révolutionnaire (RDR), an organization of intellectuals critical of both the Soviet Union and the United States. Wright plays prominent role in its writers' congress, held in Paris on December 13, delivering lengthy speech (translated by Simone de Beauvoir). Spends $6,000 to buy Paul Green's share of film rights to *Native Son* in hopes of making screen version with French director Pierre Chenal.

1949   Daughter Rachel born January 17 at the American Hospi-
        tal. Wright travels again to Rome and to Switzerland, for
        the publication of *Black Boy*. In April, James T. Farrell and
        Nelson Algren visit him in Paris. Suspects socialist David
        Rousset of trying to shift the RDR toward a more pro-
        American, anti-Soviet stance. Refuses to attend large
        RDR rally held on April 30 (organization soon splits and
        dissolves). In May, visits London to consult with Richard
        Crossman, who is including "I Tried to Be a Communist"
        with similar essays by Koestler, Gide, Silone, Stephen
        Spender, and Louis Fischer in collection *The God That
        Failed* (published later in year, book is widely reviewed).
        Continues work on his existentialist novel. Assists George
        Plimpton and others in launching of *Paris Review*. James
        Baldwin's essay "Everybody's Protest Novel," attacking
        Stowe's *Uncle Tom's Cabin* but including criticism of *Na-
        tive Son*, sours relationship between Wright and Baldwin.
        Wright writes screenplay for *Native Son*, adding several
        dream sequences to the story, then revises it with Chenal.
        After Canada Lee withdraws from project because of new
        commitments and worsening health, Wright undertakes to
        play the main role of Bigger Thomas. Sails for the United
        States in August, briefly visiting New York before going
        to Chicago for filming of exteriors for *Native Son*. Sees
        old friends Horace Cayton, St. Clair Drake, and others.
        Leaves New York in September for Argentina, where film
        is being made (Chenal had worked there during World
        War II, and political pressure had blocked access to French
        studios). Makes brief stops in Trinidad, Brazil, and Uru-
        guay before arriving in Buenos Aires in October. Loses 35
        pounds in preparation for the role by following strict diet
        and exercise program. Continues working on screenplay
        with Chenal.

1950   Production is delayed by financial problems. Wright finds
        atmosphere of Argentine life under the Perón dictatorship
        oppressive. Filming ends in June. Wright leaves Buenos
        Aires in July. Stops briefly in Brazil and Trinidad, spends
        two weeks in Haiti, then returns to Paris by way of New
        York, where he visits Frederic Wertham and the Lafargue
        Clinic. In Paris, begins work on screenplay about Tous-
        saint L'Ouverture of Haiti. Works with Aimé Césaire on
        "Revelation of Negro Art," an exhibition that includes
        works from the Musée de l'Homme and song and dance

performances at the Cité Universitaire. Vacations in the fall in the Swiss and French Alps, visiting Basel, Zurich, and the Aoste Valley, where he is a jury member with Paul Eluard, Louis Bromfield, and others for international San Vicente literary prize. Founds and becomes president of the Franco-American Fellowship, intended to protest official American policies and oppose racial discrimination by American companies and organizations active in France. Fellowship members take precautions when meeting in anticipation of surveillance by the American government (files released in the 1970s show that the Fellowship was monitored by informers employed by the Central Intelligence Agency and the FBI).

1951   Lectures in Turin, Genoa, and Rome in January. *Sangre Negra* (the film version of *Native Son*) opens to acclaim in Buenos Aires on March 30. American distributor cuts almost 30 minutes from film under pressure from New York state censors (original length was approximately 105 minutes); shortened version opens in New York on June 16 to unfavorable reviews. (Several states ban the film, but it is shown in Beverly Hills and, in spring 1952, in Mississippi, where members of Wright's family see it.) A partially restored print is warmly received at the Venice Film Festival in August. The Milan press praises Wright's acting; in general, his performance is deemed sincere but awkward, especially by American critics who compare it with Canada Lee's stage version. Wright visits the sociologist Gunnar Myrdal in Geneva, beginning a long friendship. With Jean Cocteau, inaugurates the Cercle International du Théâtre et du Cinéma. *New Story Magazine* accepts excerpts from Jean Genet's *Our Lady of the Flowers* on Wright's recommendation. Baldwin's essay "Many Thousands Gone," an explicit attack on Wright in *Partisan Review* (November–December), leads to painful break between the writers. Submits screenplay about refugees forced to choose between sides in the Cold War to the French Association of Film Writers.

1952   Travels to England in February. Spends several months in London and Catford, Surrey, completing the first full version of *The Outsider*. Vacations with his family in Corrèze at the end of August and continues to revise and cut novel. Refuses suggestion by John Fischer, his new Harper editor, that he come to the United States for the publication of his book, citing the risk that he would be subpoenaed by an anti-Communist congressional investigating committee. Begins work in December on a novel about a white psychopathic murderer, based in part on his experience with Clinton Brewer.

1953   Begins correspondence with Frantz Fanon. *The Outsider* published by Harper and Brothers in March. Reviews are mixed; sales are initially brisk but eventually disappointing in comparison to *Native Son* and *Black Boy.* Wright composes an introduction to *In the Castle of My Skin*, first novel by the young Barbados writer George Lamming. Friendship with Sartre cools as Sartre moves closer to Communism. Wright's circle of friends remains wide, including Americans such as Chester Himes and William Gardner Smith, but he begins to withdraw from official organizations and to avoid formal gatherings. He is a regular at favorite cafés such as the Monaco and Tournon, where he entertains a steady stream of visitors from America, including Elmer Carter, Dorothy Norman, Nelson Algren, E. Franklin Frazier, and Louis Wirth. Discusses treatment of Algerians in France with Ben Burns, editor of *Ebony* magazine, during his visit. Wright tells Burns that he avoids criticizing French policies for fear of being deported. Ellen Wright begins work as a literary agent with Hélène Bokanowski, a prolific translator of Wright's work. From June to August, Wright travels in the Gold Coast (then a British colony with limited self-government, after 1957 the independent country of Ghana) to collect material for a book on Africa. Boat stops briefly in Freetown, Sierra Leone, en route to Takoradi; from there travels by road 170 miles to Accra, his main stop. Meets Prime Minister Kwame Nkrumah and other members of the pro-independence Convention People's Party, as well as Osei Agyeman Prempeh II, king of the Ashanti, and other traditional leaders. Excursions take him from Accra to Cape Coast, Christianborg, and Prampram; visits slave-trading fortresses and dungeons. Travels almost 3,000 miles in a chauffeur-driven car, touring the interior through Koforidua to Mampong, and the Secondi-Takoradi to Kumasi regions. In general, Wright is fascinated by Africans but is reinforced in his sense of self as a

Western intellectual. Visits England to discuss his impressions with George and Dorothy Padmore before returning to Paris in September to begin work on book about his trip. Undergoes surgery for hernia.

1954   Revises book on Africa. Decides to write an account of Spanish life and culture. Drives his Citroen almost 4,000 miles between August 15 and September 9 on a route that includes Barcelona, Valencia, Saragossa, Guadalajara, Madrid, Córdoba, Seville, Granada, and Málaga. On September 16 State Department and FBI officials interview Wright in Paris about his relationship to the Communist party when he goes to renew his passport. *Black Power: A Record of Reactions in a Land of Pathos*, about his African trip, published by Harper and Brothers September 22. Receives mixed reviews in America, but is widely praised in France. *Savage Holiday*, novel about psychopathic murderer, is published as a paperback original by Avon after having been rejected by Harper. Book attracts little attention in the United States but is well received as *Le Dieu de Mascarade* in France. Visits Geneva with Gunnar Myrdal for further research on Spain at the United Nations library. Lectures on Africa in Amsterdam in October, where he meets Margrit de Sablonière, his Dutch translator, and begins an important friendship with her. Returns to Spain on November 8. Hires a driver and travels through Irun and on to Madrid, where he stays before returning to Paris in mid-December.

1955   An old Chicago friend, the cartoonist Ollie "Bootsie" Harrington, arrives to live in France. Wright secures funding for his attendance at forthcoming conference of non-aligned nations in Bandung, Indonesia, from the Paris office of the Congress for Cultural Freedom, an international alliance of anti-Communist intellectuals. Returns to Spain February 20, and spends several weeks there, including Holy Week in Granada and Seville. Leaves Spain on April 10 for Indonesia. At Bandung, Wright shares room with missionary Winburn T. Thomas. Leaders attending conference include Nehru (with whom Wright speaks), Sukarno, Sihanouk, Nasser, and Zhou Enlai. Remains in Indonesia at home of Thomas until May 5, working on notes of his impressions, then returns to Europe via

Ceylon and Kenya. Begins writing an account of the conference. Spends July to October with family at their new country home, a small farm in village of Ailly in eastern Normandy. Plans series of novels dealing with the conflicts between individuals and society (including one set in Aztec Mexico), but abandons the project on the advice of Reynolds and Aswell (now with McGraw-Hill). Returns to Paris when daughter Rachel falls ill with scarlet fever, then goes back to Ailly when her continued quarantine makes work at home difficult. *Bandoeng: 1.500.000.000 hommes*, French translation of book on non-aligned conference, published in December.

1956   Prepares manuscript of book on Spain in February and March, often living alone at Ailly, where he enjoys hours of gardening. Fearing deportation, remains silent on Algerian war of independence while in France (will offer guarded criticism of war when in other European countries). *The Color Curtain: A Report on the Bandung Conference*, with an introduction by Gunnar Myrdal, published March 19 by World Publishers in America and receives favorable reviews. Revises and cuts book on Spain. Adapts Louis Sapin's play *Papa Bon Dieu* as *Daddy Goodness* but is unable to have it produced. First Congress of Negro Artists and Writers, sponsored by *Présence Africaine* and which Wright had helped plan, meets in Paris in September, attended by delegates from Africa, the United States, and the Caribbean. Wright speaks on "Tradition and Industrialization: The Tragic Plight of the African Elites" and participates in several sessions. Suspects that *Présence Africaine* is being secretly taken over by the French government through anti-nationalist Africans and considers withdrawing from its activities. Lectures in Hamburg on "The Psychological Reactions of Oppressed Peoples" and tours the city with Ellen. Attends a meeting in London of the Congress for Cultural Freedom, organized by Arthur Koestler. Travels alone to Stockholm in late November for the Swedish publication of *The Outsider*; it sells 35,000 copies in four days (*Native Son* had sold 75,000 copies and *Black Boy* 65,000). Lectures in Sweden, Norway, and Denmark before returning to Paris in early December. Agrees to help found the American Society for African Culture, inspired by the French Société Africaine de Culture.

Returning to native material, Wright begins work on novel set in Mississippi.

1957   Aunt Maggie dies January 20 in Jackson, Mississippi, where she had been taking care of Wright's mother (Wright has continued to help support them through the years). Mother moves in with a niece, then goes to Chicago at the end of June to live with Leon Alan. *Pagan Spain* published by Harper in February to good reviews but weak sales. Works at Ailly on new novel. Travels throughout Italy with Ellen during the spring. Visits West Germany in July to interview black American servicemen stationed there. *White Man, Listen!*, a collection of essays drawn from Wright's lectures, published October 15 by Doubleday (where Edward Aswell is now an editor). The book is especially well-received by the black press in the United States.

1958   Finishes *The Long Dream*, Mississippi novel, and begins "Island of Hallucinations," sequel set in France. Seeking to renew his passport, he is again compelled to report to the American embassy in February and sign a statement admitting his past membership in the Communist party. Becomes increasingly alienated from the black community in Paris, which is torn by suspicion and dissension; finds himself the object of resentment, including rumors that he is an agent of the FBI or the CIA. Depressed and isolated from other blacks, Wright suspects that he is being persecuted by agents of the U.S. government. Takes part in a session of the Congress for Cultural Freedom, and in seminars on American literature sponsored by the American Cultural Center in Paris. Supports Sartre and Simone de Beauvoir in their opposition to the new regime of General de Gaulle. Works on new novel at Ailly during summer. *The Long Dream* published by Doubleday in October to often hostile reviews and flat sales. When Leon Alan telegraphs that their mother is seriously ill, Wright is forced to borrow extra money from Reynolds to send to his brother. Edward Aswell, his long-time editor, dies November 5. Considers moving to England and enlists aid of Labour member of Parliament John Strachey, who obtains assurances from the Home Secretary that Wright's application for residence will be fairly considered. Wright distances himself from various organizations he had previously supported, including *Présence Africaine* and the Société Africaine de Culture.

1959   Mother dies January 14. Wright sends the manuscript of "Island of Hallucinations" to Reynolds in February. Later in the month, he spends a day with Martin Luther King, Jr., who is passing through Paris en route to India. Timothy Seldes (Aswell's successor at Doubleday) asks for major revisions in "Island of Hallucinations"; Wright puts book aside (it is never completed). Discouraged by financial worries, weak reviews, poor health, and frustrating state of his novel, Wright continues to curtail his public activities. Declines to attend the second Congress of Black Writers and Artists in Rome. Plans a study of French Africa. After Doubleday promises a $2,500 advance, Wright asks the American Society for African Culture for an additional $7,500, but is turned down; believes CIA infiltration of the organization is responsible for his rejection. Tired of what he considers to be growing American political and cultural influence in French life and in the wake of increased attacks by other expatriate black writers, Wright prepares to leave France and live in England. Sells farm at Ailly. His play *Daddy Goodness* is produced in Paris in the spring. Wright falls ill in June with attack of amoebic dysentery, probably picked up in Africa. Illness persists despite treatment at American Hospital. Vacations at the Moulin d'Andé near Saint-Pierre du Vauvray in Normandy. With daughter Julia now at the University of Cambridge, his wife Ellen and daughter Rachel establish themselves in London. Ellen works there as a literary agent and looks for a permanent home for the family. Wright begins writing haiku (eventually completes some 4,000 pieces). Harassed by British passport officials during visit to England in September. Sees George Padmore, who dies not long after Wright's visit. Wright returns to England for the funeral. Tries to obtain resident visa from the Home Office, but is denied one without explanation. Alone in Paris, he sells home on rue Monsieur le Prince and moves to a two-room apartment on rue Régis. Recovers from dysentery but continues to have intestinal problems. Among his close friends at this time are Michel and Hélène Bokanowski, Colette and Rémi Dreyfus, Simone de Beauvoir, Ollie Harrington, and the Reverend Clayton Williams. "Big Black Good Man" is included in *Best American Stories of 1958.*

1960   *The Long Dream*, adapted by Ketti Frings, opens on Broadway February 17 to poor reviews and closes within a week. Translation of *The Long Dream* well-received in France, but earnings are not enough to quell Wright's deepening anxiety about money. In April, driving his own Peugeot, Wright accompanies his gastroenterologist, Victor Schwartzmann, and Dr. Schwartzmann's father to medical conference in Leiden, Holland, where he visits Magrit de Sablonière. Selects and arranges 811 haiku for possible publication. Declines offers from Congress for Cultural Freedom to attend conferences on Tolstoy in Venice and New Delhi, believing that the organization is controlled by the American government (the Congress is later shown to have received substantial covert funding from the CIA). Records series of interviews concerning his work in June for French radio. Spends much of summer at Moulin d'Andé, where he begins new novel, "A Father's Law." Falls ill on return to Paris in September. Julia Wright decides to study at the Sorbonne and visits her father before returning to England to pack her belongings. In September, Dorothy Padmore comes to visit. Later, old Chicago friend Arna Bontemps makes his first visit to Paris. Wright delivers lecture on November 8 at the American Church on the situation of black artists and intellectuals. Accuses the American government of creating and manipulating dissension among them through spies and provocateurs. Continues to suffer from intestinal difficulties and dizzy spells. Finishes complete proofreading of collection of stories, *Eight Men* (published by World Publishers in 1961). Welcomes Langston Hughes to his home for a brief but enjoyable visit on the morning of November 26, then enters the Eugene Gibez Clinic for diagnostic examinations and convalescence. Dies there of a heart attack shortly before 11:00 P.M., November 28. Cremated, along with a copy of *Black Boy*, at the Père Lachaise cemetery December 3, where his ashes are interred.

Note on the Texts

This volume presents four works by Richard Wright: two novels (one of which was not published until after his death), a collection of stories, and an essay on the writing of *Native Son*. All were completed between 1936 and 1940. The text of *Lawd Today!* printed here is from the finished typescript, the texts of the five stories and one essay in *Uncle Tom's Children* are from their first collected appearance, the text of *Native Son* is from the completed page proofs, and the text of the essay "How 'Bigger' Was Born" is from its first pamphlet publication. This text of *Native Son* is the last version of the text that Wright prepared without external intervention, and in all the other cases these texts are the last, or last-known, versions that Wright approved. A great deal of material pertaining to the publication of these works, including typescripts, page proofs, and correspondence between Wright and his publishers, is contained in the James Weldon Johnson Collection of the Beinecke Library at Yale University. Other significant materials are held in the Fales Collection of the New York University Library and the Firestone Library at Princeton University.

Lawd Today! was the first novel Wright completed. Originally titled "Cesspool," it has its source in Wright's experiences as a clerk at Chicago's Central Post Office in the late twenties and early thirties. Between 1935 and 1937, various versions of the novel were submitted to and rejected by Alfred A. Knopf, Charles Scribner's Sons, Vanguard Press, Norton, Simon and Schuster, Reynal and Hitchcock, Random House, and Stackpole Sons. By 1937, Wright had retitled the novel *Lawd Today!*, but after *Uncle Tom's Children* was accepted for publication in 1938, he laid the novel aside permanently. *Lawd Today!* was published posthumously in 1963 by Walker and Company, using a surviving typescript. Walker and Company's edition emended Wright's experimental punctuation, capitalization, and usage, and it also introduced a number of verbal changes, particularly to eliminate words considered obscene and to regularize colloquialisms.

Two typescripts of *Lawd Today!* prepared by Wright are

now in the James Weldon Johnson Collection of the Beinecke Library at Yale University. The earlier typescript of the two is a combination of previous drafts prepared on several different typewriters, containing handwritten revisions that appear in type in the body of the second typescript. The later typescript was prepared during 1937–38 and was then revised with the typed interlinear corrections and heavily blocked-out deletions that Wright normally used. This typescript is complete, and it represents the latest version of the work known to be extant. Therefore, the text of *Lawd Today!* presented in this volume is that of the revised typescript prepared by Wright in 1937–38 (Beinecke Library, JWJ Wright 180).

Uncle Tom's Children was Wright's first book to be published. Issued by Harper and Brothers in 1938 as a Story Press Book, it contained four stories, two of which had been published previously: "Big Boy Leaves Home" in *The New Caravan* in 1936; and "Fire and Cloud" in the March 1938 *Story Magazine*. The other two stories—"Long Black Song" and "Down by the Riverside"—appeared for the first time in the Harper collection in 1938. Wright had entered the stories in a contest for members of the Federal Writers' Project sponsored by *Story Magazine*, and "Fire and Cloud" won the first prize of $500. Collation of the periodical texts of the two previously published stories with the book publication reveals a number of differences, and the extant typescripts and proofs for *Story Magazine* reveal that the book publication of "Fire and Cloud" follows the typescript rather than the periodical version. In addition, the correspondence between Wright and Edward Aswell, his editor at Harper and Brothers, shows that Wright oversaw the production of the book collection in each of its stages—from assembling the manuscript to reading proofs. Therefore the text of these four stories presented in this volume is that of the first book printing, published by Harper and Brothers in 1938.

Wright sent a fifth story, "Bright and Morning Star," in January 1938 for inclusion in the first edition of *Uncle Tom's Children*, but Harper and Brothers rejected it. The story was first published in a literary supplement to the May 10, 1938, issue of *New Masses* and was later collected in Edward O'Brien's *Best Short Stories of 1939* and in *The Fifty Best American Short Stories 1914–1939*. In 1940 Wright arranged for a second printing of *Uncle Tom's Children* and offered to pay the costs of including "Bright and Morning Star" and his essay "The Ethics of Living Jim Crow," which had first appeared in *American Stuff: WPA Writers' Anthology*, published by Viking in 1937. Harper and Brothers absorbed the costs of including the new pieces, and correspondence between Wright and Aswell shows that Wright read and corrected proofs for the two additions. The second printing of *Uncle Tom's Children* in 1940 used the 1938 plates for the first four stories and new plates for the additional two parts. The texts of "Bright and Morning Star" and "The Ethics of Living Jim Crow" presented in this volume are those published in the expanded second printing of *Uncle Tom's Children*, published by Harper and Brothers in 1940.

Wright sent an outline for *Native Son* to Harper and Brothers in February 1938, and delivered the final typescript to Aswell at Harper in June 1939. This copy was prepared by a typist working with Wright from a corrected second draft that included typed changes inserted with paste. This typescript, showing a copy-editor's markings, is now at the Beinecke Library. The markings generally have to do with capitalization, hyphenation, typographical errors, and changing numerals to words. There are also a few cases where conjunctions have been added or deleted.

Two sets of page proofs for *Native Son* are known to exist. The first set, in the Fales Collection at New York University, contains markings in various hands, including Wright's. Apparently this set was corrected by the Harper and Brothers editors and reviewed and approved by Wright. The second, and later, set (Beinecke Library, Zan W936 94C na) shows the earlier corrections now set in type. It is a bound set of page proofs that Harper and Brothers sent to the Book-of-the-Month Club in August 1939. The bound set was originally intended as a reviewer's copy for the previously announced fall publication, but the interest expressed by the Book-of-the-Month Club caused the publication date to be delayed from month to month while the book club deliberated.

On August 22, 1939, Aswell wrote to Wright: "And incidentally the Book Club wants to know whether, if they do choose *Native Son*, you would be willing to make some changes in that scene early in the book where Bigger and his friends are sitting in the moving picture theatre. I think you will recognize the scene I mean and will understand why the Book Club finds it objectionable. They are not a particularly squeamish crowd, but that scene, after all, is a bit on the raw side. I daresay you could revise it in a way to suggest what happens rather than to tell it explicitly."

This scene, as contained in the typescripts, the Fales Collection proofs, and the bound set of proofs, was drastically altered for the published text. Wright rewrote the entire scene, making only passing reference to a newsreel and describing at length a feature film, *The Gay Woman*. In so doing, he eliminated all mention of Mary Dalton (who is featured in the newsreel in the original scene) and all references to masturbation. This change also required him to revise other passages further on, including the prosecutor's speech at Bigger's trial. Other changes were also requested: toning down explicit sexual language, altering details of plot, and shortening the speeches of Bigger's lawyer and the district attorney. A few paragraphs were added, and some changes may have been made to avoid resetting long stretches of type. On September 28, 1939, Aswell wrote to Wright: "I have looked over your revisions, and they seem to me to take care of everything essential. I want, however, to look them over once more just to make sure that we haven't missed anything. As for the question of Bigger's articulateness at the end, it is my recollection that only one person questioned this, and that most of them had not noticed it in reading the book and did not attach great importance to it when it was pointed out. My hunch is to let it stand as you have it. There is no news as yet, but there may be shortly." Later, on January 11, 1940, Aswell wrote in a letter to Wright, "We've had a cable from London that Gollancz will bring out an English edition. In this connection, you will be interested to know that Gollancz turned it down flatly when they reviewed the first uncorrected proofs. After you made the changes for the Book Club, we sent Gollancz a revised set, and this apparently made them change their minds and they accepted it."

By January 1940, the Book-of-the-Month Club had decided to accept the novel. The changes requested by the book club had previously been incorporated into a new set of proofs, which Wright reviewed in November 1939. *Native Son*, with an introduction by Dorothy Canfield Fisher, was published on March 1, 1940, by Harper and Brothers and was a dual-selection of the Book-of-the-Month Club. All subsequent editions used this revised text. In July 1940, Wright sent Aswell a list of three corrections to be made in later printings. These were not incorporated into the plates until late 1941 or early 1942. All have to do with Chicago geography: "Adams Street" becomes "Seventh Street" at 505.38 in this volume; "northward" becomes "westward" at 606.15; and "HAL-STEAD" (a street name) becomes "HALSTED" at 685.2.

Because major alterations were made in *Native Son* as a consequence of the book club's intervention in the publication process, the text of *Native Son* presented in this volume is that of the bound page proofs, which were sent to Book-of-the-Month Club in August 1939, and which are now held at the Beinecke Library (Zan W936 94C na) at Yale University. The three corrections Wright sent to Aswell in 1940 have been incorporated into the text. All changes in wording that Wright made between August 1939 and the publication of the first edition in 1940 are presented in the notes to pages 443–830 of this volume.

"How 'Bigger' Was Born" was delivered as a lecture on March 12, 1940, at Columbia University and was delivered again a few weeks later at the Schomberg Library in Harlem. Most of the text appeared in the *Saturday Review of Literature* for June 1, 1940, and a more condensed version was published in *Negro Digest* in the fall of 1940. The first complete printed text was published by Harper and Brothers as a separate 39-page pamphlet in August 1940. Harper and Brothers had intended to use the essay as an introduction to a special "Author's Edition" of *Native Son*, but when sales slowed, they put off the special edition and issued the essay in pamphlet form. Harper and Brothers added the essay to later printings of *Native Son* in early 1942, using the same plates as the pamphlet. This volume prints the text of "How 'Bigger' Was Born" from the 1940 pamphlet published by Harper and Brothers.

This volume presents the texts of the original editions or typescripts chosen for inclusion; it does not attempt to reproduce features of the typographic design, such as the display capitalization of chapter openings. The texts are reproduced without change, except for the correction of typographical errors (and the inclusion of the three corrections requested by Wright in *Native Son*). Spelling, punctuation, and capitalization often are expressive features and they are not altered, even when inconsistent or irregular. The following is a list of the typographical errors corrected, cited by page and line number: 12.23, cause; 13.8, every; 19.33, *is one*; 33.40, *Red?*; 56.27, Schmelling; 61.40, it'; 76.21, guy!; 78.4, He's; 82.33, slim; 82.40, it"; 83.35, You; 96.8, 'n; 96.35, may; 98.21, men; 98.23, 't; 100.34, That; 101.22, operation.; 103.31, "gimme"; 106.23, smugly; 110.26, "L"; 116.27, Jones?; 117.8, mens'; 137.5–6, honeyconelike; 140.17–18, was section; 148.17, not; 148.26, a a; 153.22, let's; 166.4, let's; 167.7, he; 167.19, he; 168.22, penantwinning; 170.8 Schmelling; 171.20, "Say; 171.22, Jefferies."; 176.16, cause; 182.8, it's; 198.18, girl's; 200.36, barbacue; 206.22, Bob; 208.5, mean?; 209.37, her,; 211.33, up; 213.34, potatoe; 215.35, it; 265.35, trou; 300.7, says; 300.7, boys; 315.22, Ahll; 340.36, mantle; 342.27, mantle; 344.11, mantle; 344.28, Eh; 348.5, cried; 374.16, "There; 382.18, gonan; 393.12, days; 404.13, though; 411.24, chile; 415.16, mucha like; 422.38, Gut; 430.15, on way; 439.2, sheriffs; 462.26, note. . . . ; 492.9, drive car; 506.16, by and by; 530.8, mucles; 578.14, is?; 620.34, W—what's; 634.18, anounce; 657.17, oughn't've; 787.6, capitol; 819.24, damned; 856.11, saw; 869.28, Bigger?; 879.36, complimentary.

Notes

In the notes below, the reference numbers denote page and line of this volume (the line count includes chapter headings). No note is made for information available in standard desk-reference books such as *Webster's Collegiate* and *Webster's Biographical* dictionaries. Footnotes in the text are Wright's own. For more biographical background than is included in the Chronology, see: Michel Fabre, *The Unfinished Quest of Richard Wright*, translated from the French by Isabel Barzun (New York: William Morrow & Company, Inc., 1973); Addison Gayle, *Richard Wright: Ordeal of a Native Son* (Garden City, New York: Anchor Books/Doubleday, 1980); Constance Webb, *Richard Wright: A Biography* (New York: G. P. Putnam's Sons, 1968). For references to works by Wright and to other studies, see: Charles T. Davis and Michael Fabre, *Richard Wright: a primary bibliography* (Boston: G. K. Hall & Co., 1982); Keneth Kinnamon, *A Richard Wright Bibliography: Fifty Years of Criticism and Commentary, 1933–1982* (Westport, Connecticut: Greenwood Press, 1988); and "Introduction" to *New Essays on Native Son*, edited by Keneth Kinnamon (Cambridge and New York: Cambridge University Press, 1990).

LAWD TODAY!

4.2   STATION . . . SQUARE,] Tribune Square, the location of the studios and offices of WGN, a radio station owned by the parent company of the Chicago *Tribune* newspaper.

6.32–34   . . . I AM . . . HEARD . . .] William Lloyd Garrison's proclamation appeared in the first issue (January 1, 1831) of *The Liberator*, an abolitionist journal he founded and published until the Thirteenth Amendment, prohibiting slavery, was ratified in 1865.

23.4–12   *"I woke . . . mine . . ."*] "I Woke Up Too Soon" (1935), by Dave Franklin.

23.14–21   *"You took . . . blue . . ."*] Popular song, "I'm Just Little Boy Blue."

23.25–28   *"Got me . . . adore-o-o . . ."*] "Got Me Doin' Things" (1935), composed by Harry Revel, lyrics by Mack Gordon.

26.28–31   *"I think . . . for you . . ."*] "With Every Breath I Take" (1935), music by Ralph Rainger, lyrics by Leo Robin.

28.32   *ROOSEVELT . . . CHANGERS*] Franklin Delano Roosevelt's inauguration as president of the United States on March 4, 1933, followed by three days the declaration of banking holidays in six states as the national banking system veered close to collapse. Although the passage by Congress in June of the Banking Act of 1933, establishing the Federal Deposit Insurance Corporation, was welcomed by bankers, the relationship between the president and leaders of the banking industry was characterized for much of the Depression by mutual distrust and resentment.

29.37–38   *GERMANY . . . DENIED*]   As early as January 1931, German officials threatened to leave the League of Nations if the restrictions on rearmament set in 1919 in the Versailles Treaty were not rescinded. Hitler announced Germany's withdrawal from the League on October 14, 1933.

56.23–24   old Mussellinni . . . Ethiopia]   On the order of Benito Mussolini, the Fascist leader of Italy since 1922, Italian armed forces invaded Ethiopia on October 3, 1935. Adjoined by the Italian colonies of Eritrea and Italian Somalia, Ethiopia was the only African country, besides Liberia, not under European domination at the time. The immediate pretext for the attack was a December 1934 border clash near Italian Somalia, although Italy had longstanding expansionist ambitions in the region. Following the invasion of 1935, the League of Nations branded the Italians aggressors but proposed only ineffective economic sanctions that did not include a ban on oil exports to Italy. Using modern weapons, air power, and poison gas, the Italian forces defeated the Ethiopians and completed their conquest on May 5, 1936, by seizing Addis Ababa, the capital. Emperor Haile Selassie (1892–1975) went into exile under British protection. The Italian action and the tepid response by the other European powers and the United States was bitterly resented by many black Americans, especially those on the left.

56.27   Joe . . . Schmeling.]   At Yankee Stadium in New York on June 19, 1936, Joe Louis—"the Brown Bomber"—lost by a knockout in the 12th round to the German prizefighter Max Schmeling. Because of Louis's popularity and his apparent invincibility (since turning professional in 1934 he had won 26 fights, 22 by knockouts), his defeat was greeted with shock and dismay by blacks. The following year, when he defeated James A. Braddock, he became heavyweight champion of the world, and the second black to hold the crown (Jack Johnson held it from 1908 to 1915). On June 22, 1938, he knocked Schmeling out in the first round in a rematch in New York City, a win that was hailed as "a victory for democracy."

59.36   Loop]   Chicago's downtown section. It took its name from the elevated railways that meet there, forming a huge rectangle that allows passengers convenient transfer from one line to another.

64.34–39   . . . THE MYSTIC . . . NATURE . . .]   Cf. Abraham Lincoln's first inaugural address, March 4, 1861. In the address, "as they surely will be" reads "as surely they will be . . ."

66.23–27   . . . PRESIDENT . . . ARMIES . . . .]   Lincoln issued a proclamation calling forth 75,000 militia on April 15, 1861, three days after the

Confederate attack on Fort Sumter in Charleston, South Carolina. The flood of volunteers (more than 200,000 by July 4, 1861) in response to it and a subsequent proclamation of May 3 became known as "the uprising of the North."

67.4–6   . . . JOHN . . . ON . . .]   See *John Brown's Body*, stanza 1. The original words were written by Union soldiers in 1861, and the eponymous hero was Sergeant John Brown of the 2nd Battalion, Boston Light Infantry, a member of the battalion choral society that first performed the song, setting it to the tune of a familiar hymn, "Say, Brothers, Will You Meet Us" ("Battle Hymn of the Republic" by Julia Ward Howe, published in 1862, was set to the same music). It became a popular Union marching tune, quickly evolving into a song about the abolitionist John Brown (1800–59).

78.26–28   Bible . . . against . . ."]   Cf. Matthew 16:18.

90.12   dozens]   A ritualized game in which the players attempt to outdo one another in swapping insults about the opponents' relatives, usually the mother.

93.14   John Gilbert]   Gilbert (1897–1936), a romantic film actor, was one of the most popular stars of the silent film era.

103.15–17   . . . IN THE LATTER . . . BLOW . . .]   After the Army of the Potomac under George G. Meade repulsed the Confederate Army of Northern Virginia under Robert E. Lee at Gettysburg (July 1–3, 1863), Lee retreated into Virginia. Meade did not press his advantage, and although the armies maneuvered and fought several limited engagements before going into winter quarters in December, they engaged in no full-scale battles that pitted their main strengths against each other.

103.22   "Somebody . . . hell."]   William Tecumseh Sherman (1820–91), in a speech at a veteran's reunion in Columbus, Ohio, August 11, 1880, said: "There is many a boy here today who looks on war as all glory, but, boys, it is all hell."

105.8–11   . . . AND THE WHOLE . . . COME? . . .]   John G. Nicolay and John Hay, Lincoln's private secretaries, described Lincoln as anxiously waiting on the afternoon of April 23, 1861, for Union troops to reach Washington, D.C. The capital had been cut off from the rest of the North since April 19, 1861, when railroad bridges in Baltimore were burned following a day of pro-secessionist rioting. The first reinforcements reached Washington on April 25, 1861.

106.12–14   . . . WE . . . SHORE . . .]   "We Are Coming, Father Abraham, 300,000 More," a poem by the Quaker abolitionist James Sloan Gibbons, appeared anonymously in the *New York Evening Post* July 16, 1862. Lincoln had called for 300,000 additional volunteers on July 2, following Major General George B. McClellan's defeat in the Seven Days' Battles outside of Richmond. The poem was set to music by Luther Emerson and Stephen

Foster, among others; with Emerson's setting it became one of the most popular Civil War songs.

106.15–16   *Onward Christian Soldiers*]   Hymn (1864) by the English author Sabine Baring-Gould.

106.30   Balled the Jack]   Like the better-known Charleston, Black Bottom, and Lindy, "Balling the Jack" was a popular dance among blacks in the 1920s and later.

107.8   a fat, black man]   This portrait is drawn from accounts and images of Marcus Garvey (1887–1940), the charismatic Jamaican-born leader whose Universal Negro Improvement Association attracted unprecedented support from the black masses around 1920. Wright never met Garvey, who was deported in 1927 after serving more than two years in federal prison in Atlanta after being convicted on charges of mail fraud. The appeal of the UNIA had much to do with its Back-to-Africa program, which advocated the resettlement of American blacks in Africa. This resettlement was to be facilitated by the UNIA's Black Star Line, a steamship company. Uniforms, titles, medals, flags, and parades also played a crucial role in the recruiting effort of Garvey and the Association.

114.2–10   GENERAL LEE . . . FIELD.]   The events referred to are the Seven Days' Battles, June 25– July 1, 1862, in which General Robert E. Lee's Army of Northern Virginia drove the Army of the Potomac under Major General George B. McClellan away from the outskirts of Richmond; the movements of Union forces under Major General Don C. Buell and Confederate troops under General Braxton Bragg through Tennessee and Kentucky in late August and September 1862, culminating in the Union victory at Perryville, Kentucky, on October 8, 1862; and Major General Ulysses S. Grant's first attempt to capture Vicksburg, Mississippi, in December 1862, which ended in the repulse of the Union attack at Chickasaw Bluffs on December 29, 1862.

136.21   Loeb and Leopold]   In Chicago on May 21, 1924, Richard Loeb (1906?–36) and Nathan Leopold, Jr., (1905?–71) kidnapped and murdered 14-year-old Robert Franks, a victim chosen at random, in an attempt to commit a "perfect crime." They were sentenced to life imprisonment after a sensational trial in which they were defended by Clarence Darrow. (See also note 571.20–26.)

165.7–8   old song's . . . bye and bye.]   For example, "Farther Along," a gospel song by W. P. Joy.

169.18   old Joe socked Baer."]   Joe Louis knocked out former world heavyweight champion Max Baer in New York, September 24, 1935.

170.11–12   Jack Johnson]   The black boxer John Arthur "Jack" Johnson (1878–1946) was heavyweight champion of the world from 1908 until 1915, when he was defeated by Jess Willard in Havana, Cuba, in the 26th round of their match. Born in Galveston, Texas, Johnson worked as a longshoreman before turning to boxing. He was known both for his defensive and offensive skills in the ring and has been called by at least one expert the greatest heavyweight boxer of all time. He was also famous for his personal flamboyance. Johnson antagonized many whites by his bravado and also because three of his four marriages were to white women. During his reign, a search was mounted for a "great white hope" to regain the crown. One of Johnson's great passions was the motorcar. Eventually he died from injuries suffered in a high-speed crash not far from Raleigh, North Carolina.

171.17   Jack . . . Jeffries]   The white fighter James J. Jeffries, heavyweight champion of the world from 1899 to 1905, refused to fight Jack Johnson because of his race. In 1905, after he retired, he declared the white boxer Tommy Burns the new champion after Burns defeated Marvin Hart. Burns eventually agreed to fight Johnson, who defeated him soundly on December 26, 1908, in Australia. Responding to persistent calls for a white champion, an overweight, rusty Jeffries came out of a five-year retirement to fight Johnson at Reno, Nevada, in one of the most celebrated boxing matches of all time. Jeffries was knocked out in the 15th round. The result sparked fatal clashes between blacks and whites in several parts of the country.

172.2   big riot]   The Chicago race riot of 1919 started on July 27 over racial segregation at adjoining local beaches. One beach was traditionally reserved for whites, the other for blacks. When four blacks tried to enter the water from the white beach, they were routed by whites throwing stones. Other blacks joined the fray. Subsequent events leading to the riot are a matter of controversy. A 17-year-old black, Eugene Williams, clinging to a makeshift raft, then either drifted or propelled himself across an imaginary line in the water off the two beaches. Stoned by whites, Williams was either struck and lost consciousness, as some blacks claimed, or grew tired but was afraid to come ashore at the "white" beach, as an official inquest later decided. In any event, he drowned. Police refused to arrest a white man accused by black observers of throwing the stone that struck Williams, and instead arrested a black man for creating a disturbance. They were soon involved in a melee with blacks. Violence spread to other parts of the city. That night, more than three dozen blacks were beaten, stabbed, or shot in predominantly white neighborhoods, and their houses attacked and in some cases looted and burned. Acts of violence continued over the next few days, until 6,000 National Guardsmen, requested by the mayor, began to restore order. In the end, 15 whites and 23 blacks died, and more than 500 persons were injured.

174.9–10   white woman . . . rose]   Gertrude Stein (1874–1946) in "Sacred Emily" (written 1913).

174.14   sounds . . . . Calloway]   Cab Calloway (b. 1907), a singer, composer, and leader of one of the most successful bands in the United States in the 1930s and '40s, was famed as a scat singer. His works included "The Scat Song," "Hi-De-Ho," "Zaz Zuh Zaz," and "Minnie the Moocher."

174.16–17   Big Bill Thompson] William Hale "Big Bill" Thompson (1869–1944), a Republican, was mayor of Chicago from 1915 to 1923 and again from 1927 to 1931. Widely seen as a friend of the black migrants to Chicago, his policies toward them were blamed by some whites for the bloody riot in the summer of 1919. The Chicago *Tribune* endorsed him for mayor in 1915, but soon opposed him strongly because of his isolationist and anti-British opposition to American entry into World War I. Accusations of fiscal irresponsibility and corruption in his political machine soon followed. In September 1917, Thompson filed a personal libel suit against the newspaper, asking for $500,000 in damages. He later filed at least four additional suits against the *Tribune*, including one for ten million dollars in December 1920. His popularity eventually waned, and he was defeated when he ran for the governorship of the state in 1936.

174.30–31   Teddy . . . soft] In a speech at the Minnesota State Fair, September 2, 1901, Roosevelt said: "There is a homely adage which runs, 'Speak softly and carry a big stick; you will go far.' If the American nation will speak softly and yet build and keep at a pitch of the highest training a thoroughly efficient navy, the Monroe Doctrine will go far."

174.40   Red's international] The Third International, also known as the Communist International (Comintern), was founded by Lenin in 1919 to provide revolutionary Communist leadership to the worldwide socialist movement. It was dissolved in 1943.

175.28–36   Tricksky . . . always . . ."] Russian revolutionary leader Leon Trotsky (1879–1940) developed his theory of "permanent revolution" in 1904–6. Trotsky argued that because Russia was a backward country where the great majority of the population were peasants, a Russian workers' revolution would inevitably be crushed by counter-revolution unless it inspired a socialist revolution in the more advanced European countries. However, Trotsky believed that a successful revolution in Europe would allow a Russian socialist regime to be established "in permanence." In the mid-1920s Trotsky modified his views, writing that the new Soviet state would be able to move toward socialism without further revolutions in Europe, but that a completely achieved socialist society was impossible within the borders of only one country. His position was attacked by Joseph Stalin, who argued that the "complete building" of socialism was possible within the Soviet Union alone.

176.3–4   Reds . . . Scottsboro boys] On March 25, 1931, nine black youths, aged 13 to 20, were accused of having raped two young white women onboard a freight train in northern Alabama. They were tried in Scottsboro, Alabama, beginning on April 6, 1931, and on April 9 eight of the defendants were sentenced to death (the case of the 13-year-old resulted in a mistrial when a jury deadlocked over whether to impose the death penalty). The

Communist party of the United States immediately denounced the outcome as a legal lynching and made the case the focus of a nationwide propaganda campaign, while engaging in a fierce and eventually successful struggle with the National Association for the Advancement of Colored People over which organization would represent the defendants on appeal. In 1932 the U.S. Supreme Court overturned the verdicts on the grounds that the inadequate counsel provided to the accused at their trial violated their right to due process under the Fourteenth Amendment. Attorneys engaged by International Labor Defense, a Communist legal group, represented the two defendants who were retried and again sentenced to death in 1933, despite the recantation by one of the alleged victims of her previous testimony (the trials of the remaining defendants were postponed pending the appeal of the new conviction). The U.S. Supreme Court overturned one of the new convictions in 1935, ruling that the systematic exclusion of blacks from grand and trial jury duty violated the right to equal protection of the law under the Fourteenth Amendment. All of the defendants were then reindicted by Alabama authorities. In accordance with the new Popular Front strategy of the Communist party, the ILD agreed in December 1935 to join with the NAACP (which had been contributing money to the ILD legal effort since the summer of 1933), the American Civil Liberties Union, the League for Industrial Democracy, and other non-Communist groups in forming a new Scottsboro Defense Committee. Four of the defendants were retried and convicted between January 1936 and July 1937; one was sentenced to death (commuted in 1938 to life imprisonment), one to 99 years in prison, and two to 75-year terms. A fifth defendant received 20 years for assaulting a deputy while in custody, and charges against the remaining four were dropped in July 1937. Four of the imprisoned men were paroled between 1943 and 1950; a fifth escaped in 1948 to Michigan, where the governor refused to have him extradited back to Alabama.

179.6–9   *Shake . . . best*]   From "Shake That Thing," a blues standard. Originally a folk song, it was used and featured by jazz singer Ethel Waters in 1921 and recorded by her and Charlie Jackson in 1925.

181.34–35   Bible . . . day."]   Cf. Psalm 68:31: "Princes shall come out of Egypt; Ethiopia shall soon stretch out her hands unto God."

182.15–20   Pumpkin . . . man]   Russian poet Alexander Sergeyevich Pushkin (1799–1837) was born to a noble Moscow family. According to family tradition, his maternal great-grandfather, Abram Hannibal, was an Abyssinian prince who was brought to Russia as a slave, then adopted by Peter the Great and made a general. Pushkin was killed in a duel fought to defend his wife's honor.

182.28–29   "A colored . . . was black!"]   Perhaps J. A. (Joel Augustus) Rogers (1883–1965), author of *From Superman to Man* (1917), *100 Amazing Facts About the Negro, with Complete Proof; a Short Cut to the World History of the Negro* (c. 1934), *World's Greatest Men of African Descent* (1936), and several other pioneering works on the neglected history of blacks from the days of antiquity to the present. Jamaican-born and self-educated for the most part, Rogers emigrated to the United States in 1906 and became a citizen in 1917. Rogers' books, published and distributed usually at his own expense, were immensely popular in the black community, although more formally trained historians and other scholars sometimes questioned his scholarly methods and aims.

189.1   RATS' ALLEY]   From *The Waste Land* (1922), line 115: "I think we are in rats' alley / Where the dead men lost their bones." The epigraph is lines 185–86.

194.17   Aggravating Papas!]   A reference to "Aggravatin' Papa (Don't You Try to Two Time Me)" (1922), by Roy Turk, J. Russel, and Addy Britt.

197.13   *St. Louis Blues*]   Written by W. C. Handy in 1914.

201.29–31   . . . WITH . . . IN . . .]   Cf. Lincoln's second inaugural address (March 4, 1865). In the address, "let us finish the work" reads "let us strive on to finish the work".

203.1   *Tiger Rag*]   A popular dance tune in New Orleans at the turn of the century, "Tiger Rag" was also known as "Number Two Rag," and was based on an old French quadrille, "La Marseillaise."

203.13–14   *Is it . . . Dixie?*]   Song (1936) composed by Gerald Marks, lyrics by Irving Caesar and Sammy Lerner.

204.24   *Sister Kate*]   Blues composition by Clarence Williams.

204.30–36   *Handy Man . . . around . . . "*]   Written by the blues singer Victoria Spivey and introduced by her on October 19, 1928.

205.10–11   '*Yes, . . . tonight*']   A play on lines from the popular song "Yes, We Have No Bananas" (1923) by Frank Silver and Irving Cohn.

205.15–16   '*Darling . . . gold*']   A play on lines from "Silver Threads Among The Gold" (1873), a song by Eben Eugene Rexford.

UNCLE TOM'S CHILDREN

236.13   13th . . . Constitution]   The Thirteenth Amendment, proposed to the states by Congress and ratified in 1865, prohibited slavery throughout the United States. The Fourteenth Amendment, proposed to the states in 1866 and ratified in 1868, granted national and state citizenship to all persons born or naturalized in the United States. It prohibited states from making or enforcing laws that abridged "the privileges or immunities of citizens of the United States," deprived "any person of life, liberty, or property, without due process of law," or denied "any person . . . the equal protection of the laws." Further clauses made denial of the right to vote grounds for reapportioning the House of Representatives, specified the classes of former Confederates disqualified from holding government office, and protected the validity of the public debt while repudiating all debts incurred by the Confederacy and all claims for the loss or emancipation of slaves. Although the citizenship, due process, and equal protection clauses had been intended to protect newly freed blacks against discriminatory state legislation, a series of Supreme Court decisions culminating in *Plessy* v. *Ferguson* in 1896, which declared "separate but equal" segregation constitutional, made it increasingly difficult to argue civil rights cases on Fourteenth Amendment grounds.

238.1–9   *Is it true . . . Song.*] See note 203.13–14.

240.33–241.10   *Dis train . . . train . . .*] "This Train," an African-American spiritual.

269.22   *"We'll . . . tree . . ."*] A parody of "They will hang Jeff Davis from a sour apple tree," a line from "John Brown's Body." See note 67.4–6.

277.2   *Down . . . Riverside*] In this story, Wright perhaps draws on accounts of the great Mississippi River flood of 1927, when the Mississippi overflowed its banks from Arkansas in the north to the Gulf of Mexico. In spite of often heroic efforts by local authorities, the flood devastated the region and left thousands homeless.

285.38–286.11   *Ahm gonna . . . no mo . . .*] From the popular hymn "Down by the Riverside."

335.3–18   *When . . . be there . . .*] From the hymn "When the Roll Is Called Up Yonder," by J. M. Black.

404.38–405.2   *"So . . . way . . ."*] From an old hymn. Cf. Exodus 40:38.

408.5–6   *Hes . . . soul*] From "The Lily of the Valley," a Protestant hymn. See Song of Solomon 2:1 and 5:10, and Revelation 22:16.

409.23–24   *He walks . . . own . . . .*] From the hymn "In the Garden," by C. Austin Miles.

NATIVE SON

443.2–4   *Even . . . —Job*] Job 23:2. In the King James Bible, "rebellious" reads "bitter." "Rebellious" is used in some other translations, but in those the rest of the verse reads differently from the version in Wright's text.

454.8–11   *Life . . . grave. . . .*] "Life Is Like a Mountain Railroad," a gospel song, stanza 1.

472.18   *"Trader . . . again*] Filmed primarily in Kenya, then a British colony, *Trader Horn* opened in February 1931. A popular success, it was nominated for an Acadamy Award for Best Picture. It is about a woman who is kidnapped by an African "tribe" who worship her as a white goddess. She is found by Trader Horn and another white man, both of whom fall in love with her. Their guide, played by Mutia Omooloo, is killed helping them escape. The film was especially famous for scenes of wildlife (35 species appear in the film). Directed by W. S. Van Dyke, it starred Harry Carey, Edwina Booth, and Duncan Renaldo. Van Dyke said that the film company in Africa included 35 whites and 180 blacks, and used many Africans as extras.

472.23–475.38   They walked . . . me know."]   This section was omitted from the 1940 and all later editions. It was replaced by the following:

Bigger strode silently beside Jack for six blocks. It was noon when they reached Forty-seventh Street and South Parkway. The Regal was just opening. Bigger lingered in the lobby and looked at the colored posters while Jack bought the tickets. Two features were advertised: one, *The Gay Woman,* was pictured on the posters in images of white men and white women lolling on beaches, swimming, and dancing in night clubs; the other, *Trader Horn,* was shown on the posters in terms of black men and black women dancing against a wild background of barbaric jungle. Bigger looked up and saw Jack standing at his side.

"Come on. Let's go in," Jack said.

"O.K."

He followed Jack into the darkened movie. The shadows were soothing to his eyes after the glare of the sun. The picture had not started and he slouched far down in a seat and listened to a pipe organ shudder in waves of nostalgic tone, like a voice humming hauntingly within him. He moved restlessly, looking round as though expecting to see someone sneaking upon him. The organ sang forth full, then dropped almost to silence.

"You reckon we'll do all right at Blum's?" he asked in a drawling voice tinged with uneasiness.

"Aw, sure," Jack said; but his voice, too, was uneasy.

"You know, I'd just as soon go to jail as take that damn relief job," Bigger said.

"Don't say that. Everything'll be all right."

"You reckon it will?"

"Sure."

"I don't give a damn."

"Let's think about how we'll do it, not about how we'll get caught."

"Scared?"

"Naw. You?"

"Hell, naw!"

They were silent, listening to the organ. It sounded for a long moment on a trembling note, then died away. Then it stole forth again in whispering tones that could scarcely be heard.

"We better take our guns along this time," Bigger said.

"O.K. But we gotta be careful. We don't wanna kill nobody."

"Yeah. But I'll feel safer with a gun this time."

"Gee, I wished it was three o'clock now. I wished it was over."

"Me too."

The organ sighed into silence and the screen flashed with the rhythm of moving shadows. There was a short newsreel which Bigger watched without much interest. Then came *The Gay Woman* in which, amid scenes of cocktail drinking, dancing, golfing, swimming, and spinning roulette wheels, a rich young white woman kept clandestine appointments with her lover while her millionaire husband was busy in the offices of a vast paper mill. Several times Bigger nudged Jack in the ribs with his elbow as the giddy young woman duped her husband and kept from him the knowledge of what she was doing.

"She sure got her old man fooled," Bigger said.

"Looks like it. He's so busy making money he don't know what's going on," Jack said. "Them rich chicks'll do anything."

"Yeah. And she's a hot looking number, all right," Bigger said. "Say, maybe I'll be working for folks like that if I take that relief job. Maybe I'll be driving 'em around . . ."

"Sure," Jack said. "Man, you ought to take that job. You don't know what you might run into. My ma used to work for rich white folks and you ought to hear the tales she used to tell . . ."

"What she say?" Bigger asked eagerly.

"Ah, man, them rich white women'll go to bed with anybody, from a poodle on up. Shucks, they even have their chauffeurs. Say, if you run into anything on that new job that's too much for you to handle, let me know . . ."

They laughed. The play ran on and Bigger saw a night club floor thronged with whirling couples and heard a swing band playing music. The rich young woman was dancing and laughing with her lover.

"I'd like to be invited to a place like that just to find out what it feels like," Bigger mused.

"Man, if them folks saw you they'd run," Jack said. "They'd think a gorilla broke loose from the zoo and put on a tuxedo."

They bent over low in their seats and giggled without restraint. When Bigger sat up again he saw the picture flashing on. A tall waiter was serving two slender glasses of drinks to the rich young woman and her lover.

"I bet their mattresses is stuffed with paper dollars," Bigger said.

"Man, them folks don't even have to turn over in their sleep," Jack said. "A butler stands by their beds at night, and when he hears 'em sigh, he gently rolls 'em over . . ."

They laughed again, then fell silent abruptly. The music accompanying the picture dropped to a low, rumbling note and the rich

young woman turned and looked toward the front door of the night
club from which a chorus of shouts and screams was heard.

"I bet it's her husband," Jack said.

"Yeah," Bigger said.

Bigger saw a sweating, wild-eyed young man fight his way past a
group of waiters and whirling dancers.

"He looks like a crazy man," Jack said.

"What you reckon he wants?" Bigger asked, as though he himself
was outraged at the sight of the frenzied intruder.

"Damn if I know," Jack muttered preoccupiedly.

Bigger watched the wild young man elude the waiters and run in
the direction of the rich woman's table. The music of the swing band
stopped and men and women scurried frantically into corners and
doorways. There were shouts: *Stop 'im! Grab 'im!* The wild man
halted a few feet from the rich woman and reached inside of his coat
and drew forth a black object. There were more screams: *He's got a
bomb! Stop 'im!* Bigger saw the woman's lover leap to the center of
the floor, fling his hands high into the air and catch the bomb just as
the wild man threw it. As the rich woman fainted, her lover hurled
the bomb out of a window, shattering a pane. Bigger saw a white
flash light up the night outside as the bomb exploded deafeningly.
Then he was looking at the wild man who was now pinned to the
floor by a dozen hands. He heard a woman scream: *He's a Communist!*

"Say, Jack?"

"Hunh?"

"What's a Communist?"

"A Communist is a red, ain't he?"

"Yeah; but what's a red?"

"Damn if I know. It's a race of folks who live in Russia, ain't it?"

"They must be wild."

"Looks like it. That guy was trying to kill somebody."

The scenes showed the wild man weeping on his knees and cursing through his tears. *I wanted to kill 'im,* he sobbed. Bigger now understood that the wild bomb-thrower was a Communist who had
mistaken the rich woman's lover for her husband and had tried to
kill him.

"Reds must don't like rich folks," Jack said.

"They sure must don't," Bigger said. "Every time you hear about
one, he's trying to kill somebody or tear things up."

The picture continued and showed the rich young woman in a fit
of remorse, telling her lover that she thanked him for saving her life,
but that what had happened had taught her that her husband needed
her. *Suppose it had been he?* she whimpered.

"She's going back to her old man," Bigger said.

"Oh, yeah," Jack said. "They got to kiss in the end."

Bigger saw the rich young woman rush home to her millionaire

husband. There were long embraces and kisses as the rich woman
and the rich man vowed never to leave each other and to forgive
each other.

"You reckon folks really act like that?" Bigger asked, full of the
sense of a life he had never seen.

"Sure, man. They rich," Jack said.

"I wonder if this guy I'm going to work for is a rich man like
that?" Bigger asked.

"Maybe so," Jack said.

"Shucks. I got a great mind to take that job," Bigger said.

"Sure. You don't know what you might see."

476.28–29   Mr. . . . girl;]   In the 1940 and all later editions, this was
revised to read:

Maybe Mr. Dalton was a millionaire. Maybe he had a daughter who
was a hot kind of girl;

477.26–29   Lord . . . heart . . . .]   "I Want To Be a Christian," an
African-American spiritual.

479.26–27   "The Merry-Go-Round Broke Down . . . ."]   Popular song
(1937) by Dave Franklin.

488.29–30   Henry." / The man]   In the 1940 and all later editions, the
following was inserted:

"You shouldn't be alone this way. When is Mrs. Patterson coming
back?" the man asked.

"She'll be back Monday. But Mary's here. I'm all right; don't
worry about me. Is someone with you?"

"Oh, yes. This is the boy the relief sent."

"The relief people were very anxious for you to work for us," the
woman said; she did not move her body or face as she talked, but
she spoke in a tone of voice that indicated that she was speaking to
Bigger. "I hope you'll like it here."

"Yessum," Bigger whispered faintly, wondering as he did so if he
ought to say anything at all.

"How far did you go in school?"

"To the eighth grade, mam."

"Don't you think it would be a wise procedure to inject him into
his new environment at once, so he could get the feel of things?" the
woman asked, addressing herself by the tone of her voice to the man
now.

"Well, tomorrow'll be time enough," the man said hesitantly.

"I think it's important emotionally that he feels free to trust his
environment," the woman said. "Using the analysis contained in the
case record the relief sent us, I think we should evoke an immediate
feeling of confidence . . ."

"But that's too abrupt," the man said.

Bigger listened, blinking and bewildered. The long strange words they used made no sense to him; it was another language. He felt from the tone of their voices that they were having a difference of opinion about him, but he could not determine what it was about. It made him uneasy, tense, as though there were influences and presences about him which he could feel but not see. He felt strangely blind.

"Well, let's try it," the woman said.

"Oh, all right. We'll see. We'll see," the man said.

493.7–8   Yes; . . . movie.]   Omitted in the 1940 and all later editions.

494.28–29   No . . . right.]   Omitted in the 1940 and all later editions.

496.22–25   the girl . . . way.]   In the 1940 and all later editions, revised to read:

> . . . this rich girl was from the one he had seen in the movies. The woman he had watched on the screen had not seemed dangerous and his mind had been able to do with her as it liked, but this rich girl walked over everything, put herself in the way and, what was strange beyond understanding, talked and acted so simply and directly that she confounded him.

498.23–28   "She's . . . the girl,]   In the 1940 and all later editions, revised to read:

> "She's a sweet thing, she is," she said. "I've known her since she was two years old. To me she's still a baby and will always be one. But she's kind of wild, she is. Always in hot water. Keeps her folks worried to death, she does. She runs around with a wild and crazy bunch of reds . . ."
>
> "*Reds!*" Bigger exclaimed.
>
> "Yes. But she don't mean nothing by it," Peggy said. "Like her mother and father, she feels sorry for people and she thinks the reds'll do something for 'em. The Lord only knows where she got her wild ways, but she's got 'em. If you stay around here, you'll get to know her. But don't you pay no attention to her red friends. They just keep up a lot of fuss."
>
> Bigger wanted to ask her to tell him more about the girl,

506.14–16   a song . . . bye and bye?"]   For example, "Farther Along," a gospel song by W. P. Joy.

507.3–5   At once . . . movie.]   Omitted in the 1940 and all later editions.

515.30–33   Scottsboro . . . those boys?"]   See note 176.3–4.

516.27   Y. C. L.-er]   The Young Communist League was founded by U.S. Communists in April 1922 at a clandestine convention, following the call by the Comintern in 1921 for the establishment around the world of Communist youth movements. The Y.C.L. played an important role in recruiting and then training young Communists for leadership roles in the party. The organization dissolved itself at a special convention on October 17, 1943, and reconstituted as American Youth for Democracy. Unlike the Y.C.L., the new body allowed non-Communists as members.

517.31–32   "*Swing . . . home. . . .*"]   Refrain from the spiritual "Swing Low, Sweet Chariot."

518.31–33   He looked . . . thigh.]   In the 1940 and all later editions, revised to read:

He looked in the mirror. They were drinking again.

518.37–39   Filled . . . again.]   Omitted in the 1940 and all later editions.

519.2   spooning]   Omitted in the 1940 and all later editions.

519.3   Jan . . . with him.]   Omitted in the 1940 and all later editions.

519.21–23   He swung . . . Bigger!"]   In the 1940 and all later editions, revised and enlarged to read:

Bigger drove out of the park onto Cottage Grove Avenue and headed north. The city streets were empty and quiet and dark and the tires of the car hummed over the asphalt. When he reached Forty-sixth Street, a block from the Dalton home, he heard a street car rumbling faintly behind him, far down the avenue.

"Here comes my car," Jan said, turning to peer through the rear window.

"Oh, gee, honey!" Mary said. "You've got such a long way to go. If I had the time, I'd ride you home. But I've been out so late as it is that Mama's going to be suspicious."

"Don't worry. I'll be all right."

"Oh, say! Let Bigger drive you home."

"Nonsense! Why should he drive me all that distance this time of morning?"

"Then you'd better take this car, honey."

"No. I'll see you home first."

"But, honey, the cars run only every half hour when it's late like this," Mary said. "You'll get ill, waiting out here in the cold. Look, you take this car. I'll get home all right. It's only a block. . . ."

"Are you sure you'll be all right?"

"Of course. I'm in sight of home now. There; see. . . ."

Through the rear mirror Bigger saw her pointing to the Dalton home.

"O.K.," Jan said. "You'd better stop here and let me off, Bigger."

520.21   Loop-bound] The Loop, a huge rectangle formed by elevated railway lines in Chicago's downtown section, allowed passengers easy transfer from one line to another; the name also refers to that section of the city.

520.22   far . . . avenue.] In the 1940 and all later editions, revised to read: "forward."

524.23–28   He tightened . . . deep.] Omitted in the 1940 and all later editions.

532.29–30   Now! / He shut] In the 1940 and all later editions, the following paragraph was inserted:

> Then, abruptly, he stepped back from the furnace and looked at it, his mouth open. Hell! Folks'd *smell* it! There would be an odor and someone would look in the furnace. Aimlessly, his eyes searched the basement. There! That ought to do it! He saw the smutty blades of an electric exhaust fan high up in the wall of the basement, back of the furnace. He found the switch and threw it. There was a quick whir, then a hum. Things would be all right now; the exhaust fan would suck the air out of the basement and there would be no scent.

547.37–548.3   "How you . . . we like that,"] In the 1940 and all later editions, revised to read:

> "How you like it?"
> "Aw, swell,"

551.16   Japan . . . China] Japanese troops seized control of Manchuria in the autumn of 1931, and in 1932 Japan established and recognized a puppet Manchurian state, Manchukuo, under the leadership of the former Manchu emperor Puyi. In 1933 the Japanese army advanced into northeast China as far as Tianjin and forced the Chinese to establish a demilitarized zone on the southern side of the Great Wall and acknowledge Japanese control of the territory on the northern side. An accidental clash in July 1937 between Chinese troops and the Japanese Peking garrison force (established by treaty in the aftermath of the 1900 Boxer Rebellion to guard foreign legations) led to renewed fighting in northeast China. Chinese Nationalist leader Chiang Kai-shek responded by launching a major offensive against the Japanese concession in Shanghai, resulting in a full-scale, though undeclared, war between the two countries. By October 1938 Japan occupied almost all of eastern China and began establishing a series of puppet regimes in the area under its control. Fighting among Nationalist, Communist, and Japanese forces in China continued until the Japanese surrender to the Allies in August 1945.

551.17   Mussolini . . . Spain.] Benito Mussolini began aiding the right-wing forces rebelling against the recently elected Popular Front government of the Spanish Republic within two weeks of the military uprising of July 17–18, 1936. Italy sent aircraft and arms to the insurgents and Italian ships helped move rebel troops from Spanish Morocco to the mainland. Although both Italy and Germany participated in the nonintervention committee established in September 1936 by France and Britain, their support of the insurrection became more open as the civil war progressed, as did Soviet assistance to the Loyalists defending the Republic. Italy and Germany recognized the Nationalist regime of General Francisco Franco as the legitimate government of Spain on November 18, 1936, and by mid-1937 Italian forces in Spain numbered approximately 50,000, the largest foreign contingent on either side of the war. Italian ground, naval, and air forces continued to fight in support of Franco until the final defeat of the Loyalists in March 1939.

554.36   blaze, then vanish.]   In the 1940 and all later editions, an added sentence completed the paragraph:

He shut off the fan; there was no danger of scent now.

555.13–14   He went . . . door,]   In the 1940 and all later editions this was enlarged to read:

He went back to the basement and stood uncertainly in front of the furnace. He felt that he had left something undone, something that would betray him. Maybe he ought to shake the ashes down? Yes. The fire must not become so clogged with cinders that it would not burn. At the moment he stooped to grasp the protruding handle of the lower bin to shake it to and fro, a vivid image of Mary's face as he had seen it upon the bed in the blue light of the room gleamed at him from the smoldering embers and he rose abruptly, giddy and hysterical with guilt and fear. His hands twitched; he could not shake the ashes now. He had to get out into the air, away from this basement whose very walls seemed to loom closer about him each second, making it difficult to breathe.

He went to the trunk, grasped its handle and dragged it to the door,

567.12–14   To let . . . mouth.]   In the 1940 and all later editions, revised to read:

To let her know that he loved her he circled her waist with his arm and squeezed her tightly.

569.22–25   He placed . . . say:]   In the 1940 and all later editions, revised to read:

He leaned over her, full of desire, and lowered his head to hers and kissed her. When he took his lips away for breath he heard her say:

570.8   and he . . . her body,]   In the 1940 and all later editions, revised
to read: "and he floated on a wild tide, . . . "

570.30–31   and he lay . . . Bessie's body,]   In the 1940 and all later editions, revised to read:

> . . . and he lay in the darkness, gazing with vacant eyes at the
> shadowy ceiling, . . .

571.20–26   Loeb . . . Leopold.]   On May 21, 1924, Richard Loeb, an 18-
year-old graduate of the University of Michigan, and Nathan Leopold, Jr., a
19-year-old graduate of the University of Chicago, both sons of wealthy busi-
nessmen, lured 14-year-old Robert Franks into their car, where Loeb murdered him with a chisel. After hiding the boy's naked body in a railway
culvert, Loeb and Leopold sent Mr. Franks a ransom note demanding
$10,000 for his son's safe return. Mr. Franks withdrew the money from his
bank, but learned that his son's body had been found before the time ap-
pointed to drop the ransom from a railroad car. Investigators found a pair of
spectacles with unusual horn rims near the body and traced them to Leopold.
Under questioning both men confessed to the murder, which they said had
been motivated by a desire to commit a perfect crime. They were defended by
Clarence Darrow, who changed their plea from not guilty to guilty on July 21,
1924, and argued that their disturbed mental condition be accepted as a mitigating factor in determining their punishment. The state's attorney asked for
the death penalty for both defendants, but on September 10 Judge John
Caverly sentenced them to life imprisonment for the murder, plus 99 years
for the kidnapping. Loeb was killed by a fellow inmate in 1936; Leopold was
paroled in 1958 and died in 1971.

594.25   Daily]   The Daily Worker, newspaper of the American Communist
party, founded in 1924.

604.11–12   red . . . driveway,]   In the 1940 and all later editions, enlarged
and revised to read:

> . . . red now. But how long would it keep that way, if he did not
> shake the ashes down? He remembered the last time he had tried and
> how hysterical he had felt. He must do better than this. He stooped
> and touched the handle of the ash bin with the fingers of his right
> hand, keeping his eyes averted as he did so. He imagined that if he
> shook it he would see pieces of bone falling into the bin and he
> knew that he would not be able to endure it. He jerked upright and,
> lashed by fiery whips of fear and guilt, backed hurriedly to the door.
> For the life of him, he could not bring himself to shake those ashes.
> But did it really matter? No. He tried to console himself with the
> thought that he was safe. No one would look into the bin. Why
> should they? No one suspected him; things were going along
> smoothly; he would be able to send the kidnap note and get the

money without bothering about the ashes and before anyone discovered that Mary was dead and in the fire. Then he went into the driveway, . . .

625.7 Bruno Hauptmann] Hauptmann (1899–1936), a German emigrant, was executed for the 1932 abduction and murder of Charles and Anne Morrow Lindbergh's 13-month-old son. Hauptmann always maintained his innocence. He was arrested in 1934 after a portion of the $50,000 ransom money, which had been paid in marked bills, was found in his garage.

650.5 sheet of fear.] In the 1940 and all later editions, the paragraph continues:

Yes; he should have cleaned those ashes out; but he had been too excited and scared; he had trapped himself. Now, he must leave; they must not catch him. . . . With the rush of lightning, these thoughts flashed through his mind, leaving him weak and helpless.

653.16 he saw that it was] In the 1940 and all later editions, this reads: "he saw it was . . ."

664.3–7 His cold . . . horror accepted.] In the 1940 and all later editions, revised to read:

He was swept by a sudden gust of passion and his arms tightened about her. Bessie was still, inert, unresisting, without response. He kissed her again and at once she spoke, not a word, but a resigned and prolonged sound that gave forth a meaning of horror accepted.

664.24–33 Yes. Bessie. His . . . All. *Bigger*. . . .] In the 1940 and all later editions, revised to read:

Imperiously driven, he rode roughshod over her whimpering protests, feeling acutely sorry for her as he galloped a frenzied horse down a steep hill in the face of a resisting wind. *don't don't don't Bigger* And then the wind became so strong that it lifted him high into the dark air, turning him, twisting him, hurling him; faintly, over the wind's howl, he heard: *don't Bigger don't don't* At a moment he could not remember, he had fallen; and now he lay, spent, his lips parted.

683.5–8 *Steal away, . . . stay here*] From "Steal Away, Steal Away," an African-American spiritual.

797.34 Loeb . . . case] Illinois law required that a plea of not guilty by reason of insanity be tried before a jury, which in the case of a conviction on a capital charge would then determine whether the defendant would receive the death penalty. If the defendant entered a guilty plea, however, punishment was set by the trial judge, who was required to weigh both aggravating and mitigating circumstances before passing sentence. In the Loeb and Leopold case, Clarence Darrow changed the defense plea to guilty because he thought a jury of twelve, with shared responsiblity, would find it easier to impose the death penalty than a single judge would. He then presented extensive testimony by medical experts regarding Loeb and Leopold's mental and physical condition, arguing that a combination of hereditary and environmental factors had disturbed their minds to the point where they bore diminished responsibility for their crimes. See also note 571.20–26.

801.20–24   A man . . . cut him.]   Omitted in the 1940 and all later editions.

805.6–11   But every . . . hunt?]   Omitted in the 1940 and all later editions.

805.22–35   It would be better . . . this boy.]   Omitted in the 1940 and all later editions.

806.23–31   And, because I . . . lands.]   Omitted in the 1940 and all later editions.

807.5–7   Did the feeling . . . boy?]   Omitted in the 1940 and all later editions.

807.20–24   Why did . . . by it?]   Omitted in the 1940 and all later editions.

810.40   looking at . . . injustice,]   In the 1940 and all later editions, revised to read: "looking at this boy in the light of sympathy, . . . "

811.10–31   Your Honor, . . . social forces.]   Omitted in the 1940 and all later editions.

812.1–8   "Do I say . . . twisted.]   Omitted in the 1940 and all later editions.

814.33–815.23   "This is not . . . assured!"]   Omitted in the 1940 and all later editions.

816.6–11   "It is not . . . disadvantage.]   Omitted in the 1940 and all later editions.

816.21–817.2   "It is indeed . . . fairly!"]   Omitted in the 1940 and all later editions.

817.38–818.26   "Your Honor, . . . with us.]   Omitted in the 1940 and all later editions.

819.6–13   We allow . . . lives!]   Omitted in the 1940 and all later editions.

820.22–29   "Do we . . . cold wall.]   Omitted in the 1940 and all later editions.

823.7–19   "With . . . cunning . . . consciousness.]   Omitted in the 1940 and all later editions.

824.21–825.2   "Listen, . . . this is it!]   Omitted in the 1940 and all later editions.

825.12–15   I ask this, . . . hate.]   Omitted in the 1940 and all later editions.

825.33–826.9   "You cannot . . . involved here.]   Omitted in the 1940 and all later editions.

831.7–25   "The counsel . . . conceived!]   Omitted in the 1940 and all later editions.

831.26   "After seeing that movie,]   In the 1940 and all later editions, revised to read: "After seeing a movie that Saturday morning, . . ."

HOW "BIGGER" WAS BORN

865.4   Marcus Garvey]   See note 107.8.

872.36   city so young]   Chicago was gradually settled from 1830 and received a city charter in 1837.

875.3   Robert Nixon case]   In May 1938, police in Chicago arrested Robert Nixon and an accomplice; both were described as "Negro vagrants." They were accused of the murder of a woman beaten to death with a brick earlier that week when she was awakened by robbers in her apartment. Under questioning, Nixon confessed to another murder, committed two years before, in which another woman had been killed with a brick. He was further implicated in the killings, also carried out with a brick, of a woman and her 12-year-old daughter in Los Angeles, California. The subsequent trial of Nixon in Chicago was reported in sensational and frankly racist detail by local newspapers, notably the *Tribune*. Wright arranged to have clippings from the newspaper accounts methodically saved for him by his young friend Margaret Walker, then an aspiring poet. Nixon was executed in August 1939.

875.5–7   Black . . . methods]   In 1940 Justice Black (1886–1940) wrote the opinion for the unanimous court in the case of *Chambers* v. *Florida*. Four black tenant farmers had appealed their convictions for the robbery and murder of a white man on the grounds that their confessions had been coerced after six days of constant and grueling cross-examination by the police. Black described how the defendants had undergone "protracted interrogation by state officers and other white citizens in a fourth-floor jail room, where as prisoners they were without friends, advisors, or counselors," circumstances he said were calculated "to break the strongest nerves and the stoutest resistance." The court ruled that their treatment had violated their right to due process of law under the Fourteenth Amendment and reversed the convictions.

880.34–36   I am . . . society.]   Probably "Little Sister," a novel Wright never completed.

CATALOGING INFORMATION

Wright, Richard, 1908–1960.
    Early Works: Lawd Today!, Uncle Tom's Children, Native Son.
    Edited by Arnold Rampersad.

    (The Library of America ; 55)
    I. Afro-Americans—Literary Collections. I. Title: Lawd today! II. Title:
Uncle Tom's children. III. Title: Native son. IV. Series: The Library of
America.
PS3545.R815   1991   813'.52—dc20   91-60540
ISBN 0-940450-66-6 (alk. paper)

This book is set in 10 point Linotron Galliard,
a face designed for photocomposition by Matthew Carter
and based on the sixteenth-century face Granjon. The paper
is acid-free Ecusta Nyalite and meets the requirements for perma-
nence of the American National Standards Institute. The binding
material is Brillianta, a 100% woven rayon cloth made by
Van Heek-Scholco Textielfabrieken, Holland. The com-
position is by Haddon Craftsmen, Inc., and The
Clarinda Company. Printing and binding
by R. R. Donnelley & Sons Company.
Designed by Bruce Campbell.

THE LIBRARY OF AMERICA SERIES

1. Herman Melville, *Typee, Omoo, Mardi* (1982)
2. Nathaniel Hawthorne, *Tales and Sketches* (1982)
3. Walt Whitman, *Poetry and Prose* (1982)
4. Harriet Beecher Stowe, *Three Novels* (1982)
5. Mark Twain, *Mississippi Writings* (1982)
6. Jack London, *Novels and Stories* (1982)
7. Jack London, *Novels and Social Writings* (1982)
8. William Dean Howells, *Novels 1875–1886* (1982)
9. Herman Melville, *Redburn, White-Jacket, Moby-Dick* (1983)
10. Nathaniel Hawthorne, *Novels* (1983)
11. Francis Parkman, *France and England in North America* vol. I, (1983)
12. Francis Parkman, *France and England in North America* vol. II, (1983)
13. Henry James, *Novels 1871–1880* (1983)
14. Henry Adams, *Novels, Mont Saint Michel, The Education* (1983)
15. Ralph Waldo Emerson, *Essays and Lectures* (1983)
16. Washington Irving, *History, Tales and Sketches* (1983)
17. Thomas Jefferson, *Writings* (1984)
18. Stephen Crane, *Prose and Poetry* (1984)
19. Edgar Allan Poe, *Poetry and Tales* (1984)
20. Edgar Allan Poe, *Essays and Reviews* (1984)
21. Mark Twain, *The Innocents Abroad, Roughing It* (1984)
22. Henry James, *Essays, American & English Writers* (1984)
23. Henry James, *European Writers & The Prefaces* (1984)
24. Herman Melville, *Pierre, Israel Potter, The Confidence-Man, Tales & Billy Budd* (1985)
25. William Faulkner, *Novels 1930–1935* (1985)
26. James Fenimore Cooper, *The Leatherstocking Tales* vol. I, (1985)
27. James Fenimore Cooper, *The Leatherstocking Tales* vol. II, (1985)
28. Henry David Thoreau, *A Week, Walden, The Maine Woods, Cape Cod* (1985)
29. Henry James, *Novels 1881–1886* (1985)
30. Edith Wharton, *Novels* (1986)
31. Henry Adams, *History of the United States during the Administrations of Jefferson* (1986)
32. Henry Adams, *History of the United States during the Administrations of Madison* (1986)
33. Frank Norris, *Novels and Essays* (1986)
34. W. E. B. Du Bois, *Writings* (1986)
35. Willa Cather, *Early Novels and Stories* (1987)
36. Theodore Dreiser, *Sister Carrie, Jennie Gerhardt, Twelve Men* (1987)
37. Benjamin Franklin, *Writings* (1987)
38. William James, *Writings 1902–1910* (1987)
39. Flannery O'Connor, *Collected Works* (1988)
40. Eugene O'Neill, *Complete Plays 1913–1920* (1988)
41. Eugene O'Neill, *Complete Plays 1920–1931* (1988)
42. Eugene O'Neill, *Complete Plays 1932–1943* (1988)
43. Henry James, *Novels 1886–1890* (1989)
44. William Dean Howells, *Novels 1886–1888* (1989)
45. Abraham Lincoln, *Speeches and Writings 1832–1858* (1989)
46. Abraham Lincoln, *Speeches and Writings 1859–1865* (1989)
47. Edith Wharton, *Novellas and Other Writings* (1990)
48. William Faulkner, *Novels 1936–1940* (1990)
49. Willa Cather, *Later Novels* (1990)
50. Ulysses S. Grant, *Personal Memoirs and Selected Letters* (1990)
51. William Tecumseh Sherman, *Memoirs* (1990)
52. Washington Irving, *Bracebridge Hall, Tales of a Traveller, The Alhambra* (1991)
53. Francis Parkman, *The Oregon Trail, The Conspiracy of Pontiac* (1991)
54. James Fenimore Cooper, *Sea Tales: The Pilot, The Red Rover* (1991)
55. Richard Wright, *Early Works* (1991)
56. Richard Wright, *Later Works* (1991)